Who's Who
IN WORLD WAR ONE

THE ROUTLEDGE WHO'S WHO SERIES

Accessible, authoritative and enlightening, these are the definitive
biographical guides to a diverse range of subjects drawn from literature
and the arts, history and politics, religion and mythology.

Who's Who in Ancient Egypt
Michael Rice

Who's Who in the Ancient Near East
Gwendolyn Leick

Who's Who in Christianity
Lavinia Cohn-Sherbok

Who's Who in Classical Mythology
Michael Grant and John Hazel

*Who's Who in Contemporary
Gay and Lesbian History*
Edited by Robert Aldrich and
Garry Wotherspoon

*Who's Who in Contemporary Women's
Writing*
Edited by Jane Eldridge Miller

*Who's Who in Contemporary World
Theatre*
Edited by Daniel Meyer-Dinkgräfe

Who's Who in Dickens
Donald Hawes

Who's Who in Europe 1450–1750
Henry Kamen

Who's Who in Gay and Lesbian History
Edited by Robert Aldrich and Garry
Wotherspoon

Who's Who in the Greek World
John Hazel

Who's Who in Jewish History
Joan Comay, new edition revised by
Lavinia Cohn-Sherbok

Who's Who in Military History
John Keegan and Andrew Wheatcroft

Who's Who in Nazi Germany
Robert S. Wistrich

Who's Who in the New Testament
Ronald Brownrigg

Who's Who in the Old Testament
Joan Comay

Who's Who in the Roman World
John Hazel

Who's Who in Russia since 1900
Martin McCauley

Who's Who in Shakespeare
Peter Quennell and Hamish Johnson

*Who's Who of Twentieth-Century
Novelists*
Tim Woods

Who's Who in Twentieth-Century Warfare
Spencer Tucker

*Who's Who in Twentieth-Century World
Poetry*
Edited by Mark Willhardt and
Alan Michael Parker

Who's Who in World Mythology
Egerton Sykes, new edition revised by
Alan Kendall

Who's Who in World War One
J.M. Bourne

Who's Who in World War Two
Edited by John Keegan

Who's Who
IN WORLD
WAR ONE

J.M. Bourne

London and New York

First published 2001
by Routledge
11 New Fetter Lane, London EC4P 4EE

Simultaneously published in the USA and Canada
by Routledge
29 West 35th Street, New York, NY 10001

Routledge is an imprint of the Taylor & Francis Group

© 2001 J.M. Bourne

Typeset in Sabon by Taylor & Francis Books Ltd
Printed and bound in Great Britain by TJ International Ltd,
Padstow, Cornwall

British Library Cataloguing in Publication Data
A catalogue record for this book is available from the British Library

Library of Congress Cataloging in Publication Data
Bourne, J.M.
Who's who in World War One / John Bourne.
p. cm. – (The Routledge who's who series)
Includes bibliographical references and index.
1. World War, 1914–1918 – Biography. 2. Heads of state – Biography.
3. Generals – Biography. 4. Admirals – Biography. I. Title: Who's who in
World War One. II. Title. III. Who's who series.

D507 .B67 2001
940.3′092′52–dc21   2001019942

ISBN 0–415–14179–6

FOR
BOB BUSHAWAY

Contents

Preface

The First World War was one of the seminal events of the twentieth century. It was global in scale. Major land fighting took place in France and Belgium, eastern Europe, Italy, the Balkans, the Caucasus, Egypt, Palestine, Mesopotamia (modern Iraq), East and South West Africa and on the Gallipoli peninsula. Surface fleets and submarines contested naval supremacy in the North Sea, the Pacific and Atlantic oceans, the Mediterranean, the Baltic Sea and the Black Sea. In all theatres air power became an increasing factor in the successful conduct of military operations. Armies were counted in millions and so were their losses. Nearly 8M service men were killed and more than 21M wounded. The war cast a shadow of grief, bereavement and pain that still darkens many lives. The insatiable demands of war extended far beyond the battlefields, not only to the factories and farms of the belligerents but also to those of neutral countries and colonies. Great Britain and France were imperial powers with access to global resources of manpower, raw materials and food. The 'British' army eventually recruited 1.6M Indians, 630,000 Canadians, 412,000 Australians, 136,000 South Africans, 130,000 New Zealanders and around 50,000 Africans, as well as several hundred thousand Chinese 'coolies'. The 'French' army recruited 600,000 North and West Africans as combat troops and a further 200,000 as labourers. The political and economic impact of this global mobilisation was immense. The map of the world, and especially of Europe, was redrawn. Monarchical authoritarianism suffered an historic and irreversible defeat. 'Third World' nationalism began to stir, encouraged by the emergence of the first workers' state in the Soviet Union. Few who lived through the era doubted that the world had changed for ever.

This *Who's Who* contains almost a thousand biographies. The leading political and military figures of the major belligerent powers are naturally represented: heads of state; commanders-in-chief; senior army and navy commanders. But a biographical dictionary restricted to them would do scant justice to the individual human impact of the war and to the importance of individual human agency. A conscious attempt has been made to include 'lesser' figures who nevertheless made important contributions to the prosecution of the war, not only as soldiers, sailors and airmen but also as scientists, engineers and designers. Some of these have been included in a work of this kind for the first time. In choosing subjects for entry I was aware that others might have been chosen as well or instead of those included. There is undoubtedly an element of the 'representative' in some choices, particularly lower-level military commanders. I have also tried to strike a balance between subjects who were thought to have been important at the time but are now largely forgotten and those who were unknown at the time (such as Wilfred Owen) but who became of major importance later. No attempt has been made to include every known fact or date about each subject or to give systematic consideration to subjects' post-war careers. The entries are essentially vignettes, designed to introduce the subject, to explain his or her importance in relation to the war and to give some idea of their current place in history.

An undertaking of this kind would have been much more difficult and far less enjoyable but for the willingness of many friends and colleagues to share their expertise. I should particularly like to thank the following: Professor Margaret Atack; Dr Stephen Badsey; Mike Bullock; Colonel Terry Cave; Mark Derez; Dr Stephen Gower; Dr Jeffrey Grey; Dr Paddy Griffith; Dr Paul Harris; Dr Donald Huffer; John Hussey; Dr David Jordan; the late Peter Lawrence; Dr Sanders Marble, Dr Helen McCartney; Dr Geoffrey Noon; Andy Rawson; Trevor Richards; Professor Peter Simkins; the late Professor Jack Simmons; Dr Michael Snape; William Spencer; Paul Spencer-Longhurst; David Thistlethwaite; Alun Thomas; Major-General Julian Thompson; Rob Thompson; Dr Ian Whitehead; Robert Williams; Dr Graham Winton. My greatest debt is acknowledged in the dedication to the book. Responsibility for factual errors and for the opinions expressed in the book remains mine alone.

J.M. Bourne
The University of Birmingham
25 April 2001

A guide to further reading

The literature of the Great War is immense. For a sparkling introduction, see Ian F.W. Beckett, 'Facing Armageddon: A Select Bibliography', in Hugh Cecil and Peter H. Liddle (eds) *Facing Armageddon. The First World War Experienced* (Barnsley: Leo Cooper Pen & Sword, 1996), pp. 891–95.

For general histories, see Sir Martin Gilbert *The First World War* (London: HarperCollins, 1995), Trevor Wilson *The Myriad Faces of War: Britain and the Great War 1914–1918* (Cambridge: Polity, 1986) and Niall Fergusson *The Pity of War* (London: Allen Lane, 1998). Hugh Cecil and Peter H. Liddle (eds) *Facing Armageddon. The First World War Experienced* (Barnsley: Leo Cooper Pen & Sword, 1996) is a superb collection of essays by leading authorities on many aspects of the war. See also J.M. Winter *The Experience of World War I* (London: Macmillan, 1988) and Hew Strachan (ed.) *The Oxford Illustrated History of the First World War* (Oxford: Oxford University Press, 1998).

Allan Millet and Williamson Murray (eds) *Military Effectiveness* (London: Unwin Hyman, 1988) provides an overview of military operations for all the major powers. For the Eastern Front, see Norman Stone *The Eastern Front 1914–1917* (London: Penguin, 1998). For Gallipoli, see Michael Hickey *Gallipoli* (London: John Murray, 1995). There are no good modern English language operational studies of the war in Macedonia (Salonika), Palestine, Mesopotamia or the Balkans. For the British army, see Paddy Griffith *Battle Tactics of the Western Front. The British Army's Art of Battle 1916–1918* (London: Yale University Press, 1994) and Robin Prior and Trevor Wilson *Command on the Western Front. The Military Career of Sir Henry Rawlinson* (Oxford: Blackwell, 1992). For the German army, see Robert B. Asprey *The German High Command at War: Hindenburg and Ludendorff Conduct World War I* (London: Warner, 1994), Rod Paschall *The Defeat of Imperial Germany* (Chapel Hill, N.C.: Algonquin Books, 1989) and Bruce I. Gudmundsson *Stormtroop Tactics: Innovation in the German Army 1914–1918* (London: Praeger, 1989). For the Russian army, see Ward Rutherford *The Russian Army in World War I* (London: Gordon Cremonesi, 1975) and A.K. Wildman *The End of the Russian Imperial Army* (Princeton: Princeton University Press, 1980). For the

Italian army, see John Whittam *The Politics of the Italian Army* (London: Croom Helm, 1977). For the United States Army, see Edward M. Coffman *The War to End All Wars: The American Military Experience in World War I* (Oxford: Oxford University Press, 1968).

On the naval war, see Paul G. Halpern *A Naval History of World War I* (London: UCL Press, 1995) and Richard Hough *The Great War at Sea 1914–1918* (Oxford: Oxford University Press, 1983). For the Royal Navy, see A.J. Marder's classic *From the Dreadnought to Scapa Flow: The Royal Navy in the Fisher Era* (5 vols, London: Oxford University Press, 1961–70). For the German navy, see Holger Herwig *"Luxury Fleet": The Imperial German Navy* (London: Allen & Unwin, 1987). For the Austrian, French, Italian and Ottoman navies, see Paul G. Halpern *The Naval War in the Mediterranean 1914–1918* (London: Allen & Unwin, 1987). There is no authoritative study of the war in the air.

For the British home front, see Arthur Marwick *The Deluge. British Society in the the First World War* (1965; Basingstoke: Macmillan, 1991), J.M. Winter *The Great War and the British People* (London: Macmillan, 1986) and John Turner *British Politics and the Great War: Coalition and Conflict 1915–1918* (London: Yale University Press, 1992). For France, see Jean-Jacques Becker *The Great War and the French People* (Leamington Spa: Berg, 1985). Russian history during the Great War has been overshadowed by the focus on the Bolshevik revolution, but see W. Bruce Lincoln *Passage Through Armageddon: The Russians at War and in Revolution, 1914–1918* (New York: Simon & Schuster, 1986) and Orlando Figes *A People's Tragedy: The Russian Revolution, 1891–1924* (London: Jonathan Cape, 1996). There is no modern account in English of Italy at war, but see Martin Clark *Modern Italy 1871–1995* (London: Longman, 1999), Chapter Nine. For the United States, see David M. Kennedy *Over Here: The First World War and American Society* (Oxford: Oxford University Press, 1980). For Germany, see Roger Chickering *Imperial Germany and the Great War, 1914–1918* (Cambridge: Cambridge University Press, 1998). For Austria-Hungary, see Holger Herwig *The First World War. Germany and Austria-Hungary 1914–1918* (London: Arnold, 1997). For the Ottoman Empire, see Elie Kedourie *The Destruction of the Old Ottoman Empire 1914–1921* (Hassocks: Harvester, 1978).

For war literature and art, see Paul Fussell's influential *The Great War and Modern Memory* (Oxford: Clarendon Press, 1975). The theme of the war's impact on 'modernism' is taken up in Modris Eksteins *Rites of Spring: The Great War and the Birth of the Modern Age* (London: Bantam Press, 1989). For art, see Richard Cork *A Bitter Truth: Avant Garde Art and the Great War* (London: Yale University Press, 1994). For British fiction, see Hugh Cecil *The Flower of Battle: How Britain Wrote the Great War* (London: Secker & Warburg, 1996). For British poetry, see Dominic Hibberd and John Onions *Poetry of the Great War: An Anthology* (Basingstoke: Macmillan, 1986) and Martin Stephen's determinedly revisionist *The Price of Pity. Poetry, History and Myth in the Great War* (London: Leo Cooper, 1996). Cyril Falls' classic *War Books. An Annotated Bibliography of Books About the Great War* (1930; London: Greenhill Books,

1989) is still of great value. Tim Cross *The Lost Voices of World War I: An International Anthology of Writers, Poets and Playwrights* (London: Blooms-bury, 1988) deals with the work of those who died during the war.

For remembrance, see Adrian Gregory *The Silence of Memory* (Oxford: Berg, 1994), Robert Wheldon Whalen *Bitter Wounds: German Victims of the Great War* (Ithaca and London: Cornell University Press, 1984), George Mosse *Fallen Soldiers: Shaping the Memory of the World Wars* (New York: Oxford University Press, 1990) and J.M. Winter *Sites of Memory, Sites of Mourning: The Great War in European Cultural History* (Cambridge: Cambridge University Press, 1995).

Works of reference: Philip J. Haythornthwaite *The World War One Source Book* (London: Arms & Armour Press, 1992), Stephen Pope and Elizabeth-Anne Wheal *The Macmillan Dictionary of the First World War* (London: Macmillan, 1995), Spencer C. Tucker (ed.) *The European Powers in the First World War. An Encylopaedia* (New York and London: Garland, 1996) and Anne Cipriano Venzon (ed.) *The United States in the First World War. An Encyclopaedia* (New York and London: Garland, 1995), all of which have excellent biographical entries.

There is an enormous amount of material available on the Web, but try starting with The Great War Society (http://www.worldwar1.comt//gws); Trenches on the Web (http://www.worldwar1.com); and The Western Front Association (http://www.westernfront.co.uk).

For a detailed chronology, see Randal Gray (with Christopher Carlyle) *Chronicle of the First World War* (2 vols, London: Facts on File, 1990, 1991).

Abbreviations

ADC	Aide-de-Camp
AEF	American Expeditionary Force
AIF	Australian Imperial Force
ANZAC	Australian and New Zealand Army Corps
BEF	British Expeditionary Force
BGGS	Brigadier-General General Staff
BGRA	Brigadier-General Royal Artillery
CBSO	Counter Battery Staff Officer
CGS	Chief of the General Staff
CIGS	Chief of the Imperial General Staff
C-in-C	Commander-in-Chief
CO	Commanding Officer
CRA	Commanding Royal Artillery
DCM	Distinguished Conduct Medal
DGMS	Director-General of Medical Services
DSC	Distinguished Service Cross
DSO	Distinguished Service Order
EEF	Egyptian Expeditionary Force
GHQ	General Headquarters
GOC	General Officer Commanding
GOC-in-C	General Officer Commanding in Chief
GOCRA	General Officer Commanding Royal Artillery
GQG	*Grand Quartier Général* [French GHQ]
GQGA	*Grand Quartier Général des armées Alliées* [GHQ Allied forces in France]
GSO1	General Staff Officer (1st Grade)
HQ	Headquarters
IWGC	Imperial War Graves Commission
MC	Military Cross
MEF	Mediterranean Expeditionary Force
MGGS	Major-General General Staff

MGRA	Major-General Royal Artillery
MM	Military Medal
NCO	Non Commissioned Officer
OHL	*Oberste Heeresleitung* [German GHQ]
RAF	Royal Air Force
RFA	Royal Field Artillery
RFC	Royal Flying Corps
USN	United States Navy
VAD	Voluntary Aid Detachment [British volunteer nurses]
VC	Victoria Cross
WPB	War Propaganda Bureau
WRAF	Women's Royal Air Force
WRNS	Women's Royal Naval Service

A

Abdullah ibn Hussein (1882–1951) Leader of the Arab Revolt and founder of the Hashemite Kingdom of Jordan. Abdullah was the son of the Sherif of Mecca, ibn Ali ibn Mohammed HUSSEIN. His meeting in 1914 with KITCHENER, then British High Commissioner in Egypt, inaugurated the secret MCMAHON–Hussein correspondence that led directly to British sponsorship of the Arab Revolt in June 1916, during which Abdullah showed himself to be a shrewd diplomat.

Abruzzi, Amedeo di Savoia-Aosta, Duke of the (1873–1933) Commander-in-Chief of the Italian navy, 1915–17. He shared the frustrations felt by the naval commanders of other countries in finding an effective role for his fleet. The disinclination of the Austrians to risk their navy in a major engagement and the unwillingness of the Italian army to support amphibious operations meant that his ships were limited to sporadic raiding of the Austrian coast. This was too little for many critics and he resigned in February 1917.

Addison, Christopher (1869–1951) British politician, an East End doctor, professor of anatomy and Liberal MP whose assiduous canvassing of the Liberal back benches in the House of Commons during the political crisis of December 1916 was instrumental in the overthrow of ASQUITH and the formation of the LLOYD GEORGE coalition government. Acting on his own initiative, Addison found forty-nine Liberal MPs who were willing to support Lloyd George unconditionally and a further 126 who would support Lloyd George if he succeeded in forming a government. 'By this canvass,' wrote A.J.P. Taylor, 'Addison became the real maker of the Lloyd George government.' His reward was to be made Minister of Munitions. Later, as Minister of Reconstruction, he provided Lloyd George, never a man to dwell on gratitude, with a convenient scapegoat when the post-war 'homes fit for heroes' failed to materialise.

Adler, Viktor (1852–1918) Austro-Hungarian politician, a Social Democrat and reformist who viewed the war with grave misgivings but who supported close ties with Germany. His death, on 11 November 1918, while working towards the union of a republican Austria with a republican Germany, is symbolic of the end of an era in Central Europe. His son, Friedrich, assassinated the Austrian Prime Minister, Count Karl von STÜRGKH, on 21 October 1916.

Aitken, Arthur Edward (1861–1924) British military commander. In November 1914 Aitken, an Indian army officer, was given command of Indian Expeditionary Force 'B', a motley collection of 8,000 untrained Indian reserves, for an amphibious assault on Tanga, principal port of the German East African colony of Tanganika. He was complacently self-confident, commenting to the staff officer Richard MEINERTZHAGEN that: 'The Indian army will make short work of a lot of niggers'. He was sadly mistaken. Aitken's leadership did nothing to compensate for the inadequacy of his resources. Disregarding some of the fundamental principles of war, such as deception and reconnaissance, he then failed to secure his defensive positions, suffering a rout so ignominious that it was kept secret for months. The battle made the reputation of the German commander, Paul von LETTOW-VORBECK.

Aitken, William Maxwell, Lord Beaverbrook (1879–1964) British and Canadian politician and newspaper proprietor. Accounts of Max Aitken's wartime career have tended to focus on his role in the political intrigues that brought LLOYD GEORGE to power in December 1916 and on his subsequent role as Britain's first Minister of Information (February–October 1918). But his role as propagandist for the Canadian Expeditionary Force is equally important. As 'Canadian Eye Witness' at the front, he deployed a very modern range of public relations skills that were almost entirely lacking in the British army as a whole. His three-volume *Canada in Flanders* (1916) was an enormous best-seller. He showed a particular grasp of photo-journalism and the newly emerging medium of film. As a result, the Canadian Corps generated a disproportionate number of the 'British' images of the Western Front. The establishment of what eventually became known as the Canadian War Records Office in London also ensured that the Canadians' achievements would not be lost to posterity. It was Aitken's success in this role, rather than his ownership of the *Daily Express*, that recommended his appointment as Britain's chief propagandist. His partisan but immensely vivid and readable post-war memoirs, *Politicians and the War* (1928) and *Men and Power* (1956), have exercised enormous influence on subsequent perceptions of wartime politics.

Albert I (1875–1934) King of the Belgians. His decision to resist by force of arms German violation of his country's neutrality was of immense significance not only for his own country but also for France, Great Britain and Germany. Albert's decision was determined by fears for his country's survival in a continent dominated by Germany. Maintaining the sovereignty of Belgium was his guiding principle throughout the war. The withdrawal of the remnants of the Belgian army to Flanders was influenced not only by considerations of military prudence but also by a wish to preserve a degree of detachment and independence from the French and British. This often made him a difficult and uncomfortable 'ally'. Until the defeat of Germany became certain he was prepared to consider a negotiated peace. Only in the final autumn of the war, when he took personal command of the Flanders Army Group, did he throw his full political and military weight behind an Allied offensive, entering Brussels in triumph on 22 November 1918.

Albrecht von Württemberg, Duke (1865–1939) German military commander, who led the Fourth Army in the opening battles of the war, advancing through Luxemburg as far south as the Marne. The 'race to the sea' took his army, heavily reinforced with young German volunteers, to the Flanders front. Here, the Fourth Army was thrown against the desperate Allied defences in front of Ypres, its poorly trained and ill-equipped troops suffering huge casualties as a result of advancing in dense masses against the accurate rifle of the British Regulars. Albrecht remained in command of the Flanders sector, taking part in the first gas attack in April 1915, until February 1917, when he was transferred to the southernmost part of the Western Front, where he sat out the rest of the war in comparative tranquillity.

Alderson, Edwin Alfred Harvey (1859–1927) British military commander. Although he served in the infantry, Alderson was a master of everything connected with horses. He was an enthusiastic huntsman who believed strongly in hunting as a school for young officers, even publishing a book on the subject, *Pink and Scarlet, or Hunting as a School for Soldiering* (1900). In September 1914 he was given command of the 1st Canadian Division, which he led during the first German gas attack, and in September 1915 was promoted to command the new Canadian Corps. The Canadian debacle at St Eloi in March 1916 led to his being kicked upstairs as Inspector-General of Canadian Forces. Alderson's replacement, however, owed at least as much to Canadian politics, particularly his conflict with the Minister of Militia, Sam HUGHES, over the Ross rifle, as it did to his own limitations. He was succeeded by Julian BYNG.

Aldington, Edward Godfree 'Richard' (1892–1962) British poet, novelist, biographer and soldier. Together with his future wife, Hilda Doolittle, and Ezra Pound, Aldington was one of the original 'Imagist' poets, who favoured clarity of expression through the use of precise images. Aldington volunteered for military service on the outbreak of war, but was prevented by medical problems from being accepted until 1916. He joined the Royal Sussex Regiment as a private soldier and was later commissioned. He served on the Western Front, where he was gassed and suffered from shell shock. His enduring literary reputation is based on his anti-war novel *Death of a Hero* (1929). The book caught the flood tide of post-war disillusionment that set in with the Great Depression, bringing him instant recognition and international fame. Much of his work in the 1920s and 1930s was characterised by bitterness towards the British literary establishment, not least T.S. Eliot, and he spent most of his time abroad. In 1955 he published a sensational and controversial debunking biography of T.E. LAWRENCE.

Aleksandra Feodorovna (1872–1918) Empress of Russia, grand-daughter of Queen Victoria and wife of Tsar NICHOLAS II. Aleksandra is undoubtedly a tragic figure, orphaned at 6, dispatched as a young bride to endure loneliness and isolation in a country she detested, mother of a beloved but cruelly ill son, brutally murdered together with her husband and family. Contemplation of her life ought to evoke pity yet it does not. The Tsar's fateful decision to assume command of the Russian army in September 1915 and go to the front left his government in the hands of a superstitious, jealous, intriguing, vindictive woman with no political judgement, whose unyielding support for authoritarianism and repression, dismissal of loyal and competent ministers, and unsurpassed stupidity helped destroy what slim hope there was for the survival of her husband's throne.

Alekseev, Mikhail Vasilevich (1857–1918) Russian staff officer. Alekseev, the son of a private soldier, replaced the spectacularly incompetent YANUSHKEVICH as Russian chief of staff in September 1915, following the Tsar's decision to assume direct command of the army himself. Alekseev was a much more substantial and able soldier than his predecessor. He had planned the Galician offensive that came close to knocking Austria out of the war and had retrieved what credit there was from General IVANOV's crushing defeat by the Germans at Gorlice-Tarnów. With the Tsar little more than a nominal commander-in-chief, Alekseev found himself in a position of unusual influence. He did much to restore the fighting capacity of the Russian army, particularly its logistics. He must share some credit for the spectacular success of the BRUSILOV offensive in the summer of 1916. But with only a small staff, and handicapped by an inability to delegate, a wretchedly unreliable communications system and the ineffable intrigues of the Russian court, he found it difficult to impose real authority and direction on Russian strategy. The heart attack that he suffered in November 1916, and his subsequent six-week recuperation, further undermined his effectiveness. Within a few weeks of his return the tsarist regime collapsed. Alekseev was appointed Commander-in-Chief by the Provisional Government, but resigned in protest against the KERENSKY offensive. After the October Revolution he joined with General KORNILOV in forming the anti-Bolshevik Volunteer Army but died after a second heart attack on 8 October 1918.

Alexander, Ernest Wright (1870–1934) British artillery commander. Alexander was the son of a Liverpool shipowner. He was commissioned in the Royal Artillery in 1889; by the outbreak of war he had advanced, unspectacularly, to the rank of major in command of a battery of field artillery. He was 43. The war, however, was to prove a great professional opportunity and a personal triumph. Alexander won one of the first Victoria Crosses of the war, at Elouges on 24 August 1914. Within a year, he was a brigadier-general; in the spring of 1916 he was promoted BGRA XV Corps, with a key role to play in the forthcoming Somme offensive. The success of XV Corps' initial attacks at Mametz and Fricourt on 1 July 1916 was due in large part to the effectiveness of Alexander's barrage. The British official historian, Sir James EDMONDS, was so impressed that he reproduced the barrage plans in full in the official history as an example of 'good practice'. This first attempt at a 'creeping barrage' was

greatly improved upon within a fortnight, proving instrumental in the spectacular success of XV Corps' 'dawn assault' on 14 July 1916. These early successes on the Somme were also instrumental in advancing the career of XV Corps' commander, Henry HORNE, who was promoted GOC First Army in September. He was aware of his debt to Alexander. They renewed their partnership in the spring of 1918 when Alexander became First Army's artillery commander (with the rank of major-general), a post he held for the remainder of the war, playing a central part in the success of First Army's operations, both in defence and attack.

Alexander Karadjordjevic (1888–1934) Crown Prince, Regent and Commander-in-Chief of Serbia. Alexander became Regent in June 1914 owing to the ill health of his father, King Peter I. Within six weeks his country was at war. Serbia's resistance to successive Austrian invasions, skilfully organised by General PUTNIK, was epic, but her small, ill-equipped army proved no match for the joint Austro-German-Bulgarian attack which followed Bulgaria's decision to join the Central Powers in October 1915. By 23 November Alexander was forced to join his army in the great retreat through the freezing mountains of Albania. Shattered remnants of the Serb army, less than 90,000 strong, were evacuated to Corfu at the end of the year. A government in exile was established, the Serb army, under General PAŠIĆ, reformed and redeployed to Salonika, where it played an important part in the successful Allied offensive of October–November 1918. Alexander was active in lobbying Allied and other governments for the creation of a 'greater Serbia', including Croatia and Slovenia, after the war. He proclaimed such a state in Belgrade on 31 October 1918. As King Alexander I of Yugoslavia, he suffered the occupational hazard of Balkan monarchs, being assassinated by

Croat separatists in Marseilles on 9 October 1934.

Alexander-Sinclair, Edwyn Sinclair (1865–1945) British naval commander. After early war service as Captain of the battleship HMS *Temeraire*, Alexander-Sinclair was promoted Commodore in 1915 and given command of the 1st Light Cruiser Squadron. At 2.28 p.m. on 31 May 1916, while scouting ahead of Admiral BEATTY's battle cruisers, Alexander-Sinclair's flagship, HMS *Galatea*, fired the first salvoes of what became the battle of Jutland, attacking the German light cruiser *Elbing* while both were engaged in checking the credentials of an innocent Danish steamer. He also alerted Beatty with the famous 'enemy in sight' signal. Alexander-Sinclair was promoted Rear-Admiral in 1917 and given command of the 6th Light Cruiser Squadron, flying his flag in HMS *Cardiff*. He had the honour of leading the surrendered German fleet into Rosyth in November 1918.

Allen, James (1855–1942) New Zealand politician, an ardent imperialist and navalist, he did much to strengthen New Zealand's pre-war defence arrangements, including the creation of New Zealand's naval forces. As Minister of Defence in the coalition government formed in August 1915 much of the domestic management of New Zealand's war effort fell on Allen in the absence at the Imperial War Cabinet in London of the Prime Minister, W.F. MASSEY, and the leader of the Liberal Party, Sir Joseph WARD. Allen took the important decision to introduce conscription in August 1916, which ensured that the New Zealand division on the Western Front was always maintained at full strength.

Allen, (Reginald) Clifford (1889–1939) British pacifist. Allen converted to socialism at Peterhouse, Cambridge (probably a unique event in the history of that college), and later moved in Fabian circles. In 1911 he was appointed general manager of the *Daily Citizen*, Labour's first daily newspaper. He was strongly opposed to Britain entering the war, a view he shared with his friend Ramsay MACDONALD. When this view did not prevail, Allen and Fenner BROCKWAY co-founded the No-Conscription Fellowship, an organisation devoted to persuading men not to volunteer for military service. When conscription was introduced in 1916, Allen refused to undertake military service. He was imprisoned three times, for a total of sixteen months. His incarceration badly affected his health and certainly shortened his life. After the war he chaired the Independent Labour Party (1922–26) and was closely involved with the *Daily Herald*. He risked accusations of socialist betrayal by supporting MacDonald's National Government and became Baron Allen of Hurtwood in 1932.

Allenby, Edmund Henry Hynman (1861–1936) British military commander, who began the war as GOC Cavalry Division in the original British Expeditionary Force, being rapidly promoted GOC Cavalry Corps, V Corps and (from 23 October 1915) Third Army. He commanded Third Army at the Battle of Arras (April–May 1917), which began extremely well, especially to the north of the river Scarpe, but south of the river the advance halted in the face of stiffening German resistance in the fortified village of Monchy-le-Preux and casualties began to mount. The battle was eventually broken off in May after protests by some of Allenby's subordinate commanders to Field-Marshal HAIG. In terms of *per diem* casualties, Arras was one of the costliest British battles of the war. In June Allenby was relieved of his command and 'promoted' GOC-in-C Egyptian Expeditionary Force, in succession to General A.J. MURRAY. Allenby himself regarded his supercession as a demotion and a badge of failure, but it was to be the start of a dramatic revival in his personal fortunes and those of the army he commanded. LLOYD GEORGE was desperate for a mor-ale-boosting victory in Palestine after two years of unparalleled yet barren effort on the Western Front. Allenby was ordered to take Jerusalem by Christmas. He did even better, entering the city on 9 Decem-ber, after breaking through the Turkish lines between Beersheba and Gaza. Allen-by's entry into Jerusalem was on foot, deliberately understated to contrast with that of the Kaiser during his visit before the war, and showed a fine understanding of politics that was badly needed in Middle East operations. In 1918, despite losing much of his British infantry to the effort to counter the German spring offensive in France, Allenby sat down to plan the annihilation of Turkish forces in Palestine. He had both numerical and qualitative superiority, especially in artil-lery, and almost complete control of the air, but he made superbly intelligent use of his excellent resources, displaying a capa-city to mislead and surprise his enemy that contrasted markedly with his opera-tions in France. In September 1918 he inflicted a shattering defeat on the Otto-man army at Megiddo, rapidly followed by the capture of Damascus and the capitulation of Turkey. Allenby was a large, irascible man with a ferocious temper, known as 'The Bull'. Unfortu-nately, his towering rages were too often directed at subordinates on quite incon-sequential matters and so indiscriminate as to provoke resentment among fighting soldiers. This ferocity was rarely directed towards his superiors and he had particu-lar difficulty in standing up to Haig. As a commander, however, he was undoubt-edly well known to his troops and his striking personality contributed much to the cohesion of his polyglot army in Palestine. In private he was an intelligent, well-read man with a love of nature. He was devastated by the death in action of his only son in July 1917, but he showed no public emotion on learning of his son's death, neatly folding the telegram that brought the news, putting it in his pocket and carrying on with his work.

Altvater, Vasilij Michaijıovic (1883–1919) Russian naval commander, who rose through the ranks to the position of rear-admiral. In 1917 he sided with the revo-lutionaries and in 1918 became first Commander-in-Chief of the Soviet navy.

Amery, Leopold Charles Maurice Stennett (1873–1955) British politician. After a brilliant academic career that culminated in his election as a Fellow of All Souls, Leo Amery joined the editorial staff of *The Times*. He was responsible for orga-nising the paper's war correspondents in South Africa and later wrote *The Times History of the South African War* (7 vols). In 1911 he was elected to parliament as the Unionist member for Birmingham South (later Sparkbrook), where his views on tariff reform were sure of a favourable reception in the heartland of Chamber-lainism. After the outbreak of war he played a leading part in the Parliamentary Recruiting Committee (PRC) that rescued the War Office Recruiting Department from the welter of muddle and confusion into which it had fallen by September 1914. The PRC did much to co-ordinate the local recruiting initiatives that sprang up across the country. Amery, like other leading figures in the PRC, was an advo-cate of conscription and other forms of 'total' mobilisation. These views pros-pered during the LLOYD GEORGE coalition government, when Amery became Assis-tant Secretary of the War Cabinet, later serving on the staff of the Allied Supreme War Council at Versailles and on the personal staff of the Secretary of State for War, Lord MILNER, his fellow 'English Prussian'.

Amey, William (1881–1940) British sol-dier. Lance Corporal Amey was a small, frail-looking man who served in the Ter-ritorial 8th Battalion Royal Warwickshire Regiment (the 'Aston Pals'). His military record before 4 November 1918 appears to have been as blameless as it was ordinary, leaving no trace in the records of the battalion. But on that day, a week before the Armistice, near Landrecies he suddenly turned into a warrior, three times leading assaults against German machine-gun nests that had been missed by the leading attackers owing to fog, capturing seventy prisoners and several machine guns and killing two Germans. He was subsequently awarded the Victoria Cross. Amey's story provides little evidence to support the view that the British army was 'taking it easy' with 'victory in sight'. The nature of his exploits also shows how far the war had moved away from the classic image of 'trench warfare', being by this stage much closer in spirit to 1944 than to 1914.

Anderson, (Warren) Hastings (1872–1930) British staff officer. Anderson was a staff officer at the Staff College when the war broke out, but he soon found himself at the front as chief of staff (GSO1) to the newly formed 8th Division. He became chief of staff of XI Corps, with the rank of brigadier-general, in October 1915, transferring to XV Corps in September 1916. Anderson overlapped with XV Corps' commander, Henry HORNE, for only a week before Horne was promoted to command First Army, but Anderson eventually followed him there in February 1917. Horne was characteristically honest in admitting to Anderson that he had not been his first choice as chief of staff (Horne wanted Louis VAUGHAN). His brief acquaintance with Anderson on the Somme, however, had convinced him of Anderson's acceptability. This was, in fact, quite a compliment. Anderson was temperamentally fair-minded. He gave different sides of the question appropriate consideration, but then expressed himself with clarity and conviction. These were qualities designed to endear him to Horne, who could not abide anyone who was not

'straight'. Anderson remained Horne's chief of staff for the rest of the war. Together they formed an effective combination that resulted in the capture of Vimy Ridge (April 1917) and a resolute defence against the German spring offensive (March–April 1918).

Andrássy von Csik-Szent Király und Kraszna-Horka, Count Julius the Younger (1860–1929) Austro-Hungarian politician. On 24 October 1918 Andrássy succeeded Count Istvan BURIAN as the last Foreign Minister of Imperial Austria, charged by Emperor KARL I with ending the German alliance, which – ironically – his father had originally helped negotiate. Ending Austria's relationship with her oldest ally proved easier than arranging a new one with her enemies. Andrássy's offer of a separate peace to the Allies, made through President WILSON, was predictably fruitless and he resigned on 1 November.

Angell, Norman (1872–1967) Pen name of Ralph Norman Angell-Lane, British writer and pacifist, author of the much read and highly influential *The Great Illusion* (1910). The great illusion was that war could be rational and profitable. Angell restated, in a popular and accessible way, the classic liberal free-trade argument that, in a world of increasingly integrated economic systems, going to war was suicidal. The intellectual and emotional appeal of free trade remained immensely powerful in Edwardian Britain. The Conservative Party's flirtation with protection had resulted in division and electoral disaster. Many Liberals took Angell's views for granted and believed that free trade had made war a thing of the past. Lord Cunliffe, Governor of the Bank of England, famously announced to a party of house guests during the first weekend of August 1914 that war was 'unthinkable' because the Kaiser did not have sufficient 'credits'. Militarists were not alone in suffering from delusion.

Anthoine, François Paul (1860–1944) French military commander and staff officer, who began the war as CASTELNAU's chief of staff before receiving field command, first as a divisional, then as a corps and finally as an army commander. As GOC First Army he supported the northern flank of the British attacks at Ypres in the summer and autumn of 1917, his demand for more time for artillery preparation contributing to the last-minute delays to the opening of the offensive. In November 1917 he became chief of staff to the French Commander-in-Chief, Philippe PÉTAIN, a fellow gunner, but was replaced in July 1918 as scapegoat for the dramatic German successes on the Aisne and Matz.

Aosta, Duke Emmanuel Philibert (1869–1931) Italian military commander, whose Third Army was responsible for the one significant success during CADORNA's repeated attacks on the Isonzo, the capture of Gorizia in August 1916, though much of the popular credit went to the self-promoting CAPELLO. When Capello's characteristic overconfidence brought about the disaster of Caporetto (October–November 1917), Aosta retrieved what little credit there was by organising the safe and orderly retreat of his army beyond the Tagliamento.

Apollinaire, Guillaume (1880–1918) Pen name of Wilhelm de Kostrowitzky, French poet, playwright, art critic and soldier. Apollinaire was born in Rome, the illegitimate son of a Polish woman and an Italian army officer. His upbringing was rootless and Bohemian, but he finally settled in Paris in 1900. His assimilation of French language and culture was total and by the outbreak of war he was a leader of the modernist *avant garde*, a close friend of Picasso and a supporter of his painting. A major collection of poetry, *Alcools*, was published in 1913. Apollinaire was still not a French citizen. He had been briefly imprisoned in 1911 on a false charge of stealing the 'Mona Lisa' and threatened with deportation as an undesirable alien. In August 1914, however, he did not hesitate to volunteer for military service. He served in the artillery until November 1915, when he was commissioned as an infantry officer. He was wounded in the head and permanently scarred by a piece of shrapnel on 17 March 1916. The wound necessitated long periods of hospitalisation and his eventual invaliding from the army. His final two years were, however, astonishingly productive. He wrote poetry, art criticism, plays, short stories and journalism. His play *Les Mamelles de Tirésias* had a great influence on surrealism, a word Apollinaire himself coined. He died two days before the Armistice during the great influenza pandemic, his lungs having been ruined by gas.

Arbuthnot, Robert Keith (1864–1916) British naval commander, a courageous but unpopular officer renowned as a fierce disciplinarian. He began the war as second in command of the 2nd Battle Squadron, flying his flag in HMS *Orion*, but in January 1915 he was given an independent command, the 1st Cruiser Squadron, composed of obsolete ships. This was an unfortunate inheritance for such an ambitious and aggressive commander. Arbuthnot's squadron was totally unfit to take part in a fleet action, but this did not prevent Arbuthnot throwing it against overwhelmingly superior German forces at the battle of Jutland (31 May–1 June 1916). The 1st Cruiser Squadron's job was to protect JELLICOE's battleships. Arbuthnot was willing to take virtually any risk to do this but he and his men paid a high price for their commander's reckless courage. He lost three of his four ships, with 1,800 men. His flagship, HMS *Defence*, blew up and sank with all hands. In launching his attack Arbuthnot not only suffered grievous loss but also severely impeded the fire of more powerful British ships.

Arnauld de la Perière, Lothar von (1886–1941) German naval officer, the most successful U-boat commander of both world wars. He sank 189 merchant ships, totalling 453,718 tons, mostly as Captain of *U-35* operating in the Mediterranean.

Arz von Straussenberg, Artur (1857–1935) Austro-Hungarian military commander and chief of staff. Arz began the war as a divisional commander but first came to notice through his able handling of a corps at Gorlice-Tarnów (May–June 1915). This promise was confirmed the following year in Romania, where he commanded the Austrian First Army. Such an unbroken record of success was uncommon in the Austro-Hungarian armies and in February 1917 he was chosen to replace CONRAD as Chief of the Imperial General Staff. He was not without achievements in this much more difficult post. He repelled the Russian KERENSKY offensive in the summer of 1917 and played a key part in securing the German reinforcements that routed the Italian army at Caporetto in the autumn. But, in 1918, the political disintegration of the empire gathered pace, undermining Arz's control of military events. His reluctant support for a foolish two-pronged offensive on the Piave in June 1918 destroyed what slim hope there was of holding the army together. Arz was an able, level-headed professional soldier, devoid of political ambition (and, to a great extent, also of political understanding). His appreciation of the fighting capacity of the Austrian army was more realistic than that of Conrad. By the time he was appointed chief of staff much of the damage had already been done.

Ashmead-Bartlett, Ellis (1881–1931) British journalist. By 1914 Ashmead-Bartlett was already a veteran war correspondent, having covered the Graeco-Turkish War (1897), the Russo-Japanese War (1904–05), and the first and second Balkan Wars (1912–13) for the *Daily Telegraph*. But it was his reporting of the Gallipoli disaster of 1915 that made him famous. It also helped make him solvent. His lucrative appointment as the Newspaper Proprietors' Association (NPA) special correspondent with the Royal Navy at the Dardanelles was of considerable help in paying off his large debts and in allowing him to maintain a characteristically sumptuous encampment close to British GHQ on the island of Imbros. He was warmly welcomed by the British Commander-in-Chief, Sir Ian HAMILTON, who had a more progressive attitude to journalists than his old mentor KITCHENER. Ashmead-Bartlett agreed to abide by the wartime censorship and began his coverage of the campaign in patriotic mode. His dramatic account of the landing at Anzac Cove first brought the courage of Australian and New Zealand soldiers to the attention of the world and led to a recruitment surge in Australia. As the campaign floundered in bloody stalemate, however, Ashmead-Bartlett became increasingly contemptuous of British generalship, staff work and medical arrangements and frustrated by the censorship. He returned to London and began to abuse the British High Command to anyone who would listen. This naturally got back to Hamilton, who requested that Ashmead-Bartlett not be allowed to return. The NPA's insistence that Ashmead-Bartlett should return persuaded Hamilton to enlarge the press corps in the hope of obtaining less hostile coverage. Despite giving his word that he would keep to the regulations, Ashmead-Bartlett continued to write severely critical dispatches, which were suppressed by the censor. The Australian journalist Keith MURDOCH eventually came to his rescue, agreeing to carry an uncensored dispatch to England and hand it to Prime Minister ASQUITH. The military authorities were alerted by another war correspondent, an old friend of Hamilton's, H.W. NEVINSON, who was appalled by Ashmead-Bartlett's betrayal of trust. Murdoch's ship was boarded in Marseilles and the dispatch confiscated.

Ashmead-Bartlett was expelled from the peninsula, but when he got back to London he published his *Despatches from the Dardanelles*. Only the ANZACs escaped Ashmead-Bartlett's strictures, and he must take pride of place as the founder of the ANZAC legend. Later he was called as the first witness before the Dardanelles committee of inquiry that eventually concluded that the whole enterprise had been mistaken. His even more critical and controversial account *The Uncensored Dardanelles* appeared in 1928.

Ashmore, Edward Bailey (1872–1953) British air defence pioneer, who began the war as a major in the Royal Field Artillery and ended it as commander of the London Air Defence Area (LADA) with the rank of major-general. On 25 May 1917 the German air raid on the coastal town of Folkestone (not the intended target) inaugurated a new era in the history of war, mass attacks by heavy bombers against urban centres. London (the intended target in May) was bombed on 13 June and again on 7 July. On 3 September 1917 the Germans turned to night attacks, the last and biggest of which took place on 19–20 May 1918. During this period 434 people were killed and another 989 injured. The psychological effect on the civilian population was considerable. Munitions production on the night shift at the great Woolwich Arsenal slumped: 300,000 Londoners took shelter in the Underground system. The explosion of popular fear and anger led to demands for retaliatory action against Germany and played a significant role in the formation of the world's first independent, strategic air force, the Royal Air Force, on 1 April 1918. It also forced the government to do something about defending the capital. Ashmore was brought back from France to organise London's defences. He responded brilliantly, despite being hampered by a shortage of anti-aircraft guns and the lack of effective air to air and air to ground

communications. He quickly identified the key elements of air defence: early warning; interception; and air raid precautions. A chain of observer posts between the Channel coast and London provided early warning. Interception was achieved through an integrated system of anti-aircraft guns, searchlights, barrage balloons and fighter aircraft based at airfields in Kent and Essex. Air raid precautions led to a blackout of London. By September 1918 two-way radio eventually made it possible for the LADA headquarters to control gun batteries, searchlights, barrage balloons, air fields and observer posts in a system which was remarkably similar to that used in the Second World War.

Asquith, Arthur Melland (1883–1939) British military commander, third son of the Prime Minister. 'Oc' Asquith was destined forever to live in the shadow of his supposedly brilliant elder brother, Raymond, who was killed on the Somme in September 1916, an event that some scholars believe undermined his father's will to govern. Oc's war, however, was remarkable. After an interesting and productive career in the Egyptian Civil Service (1906–11), he joined the firm of Franklin & Herrera, which had extensive business interests in South America, especially Argentina. He was still working for them when the war broke out. He was the first of Asquith's sons to volunteer, declaring in his letter of resignation to his employers that he could not 'sit quietly by reading the papers'. On 23 September 1914 he was commissioned a temporary second lieutenant in that exotic hybrid the Royal Naval Division, brainchild of Winston CHURCHILL. His fellow officers included Rupert BROOKE, Bernard FREYBERG and A.P. HERBERT. He fought with the division at Antwerp, on Gallipoli and on the Western Front, succeeding Freyberg as CO of the Hood Battalion in April 1917 and winning three DSOs. On 16 December 1917 he was promoted to command the Royal Naval Division's 189th Brigade, completing a remarkable rise from civilian to general in just over three years. He was 34. His career as a general, however, was short lived. He received his fourth wound of the war on 20 December and his leg was amputated three weeks later. He ended the war in the Ministry of Munitions.

Asquith, Herbert Henry (1852–1928) British Prime Minister 1908–16. Asquith's reputation as a wartime leader has been eclipsed by that of his erstwhile colleague and successor David LLOYD GEORGE. His government is commonly portrayed as directionless, staggering from one inadequate and shoddy compromise to another, perpetrated by a man desperate to hang on to power, his judgement increasingly weakened by drink, disappointment and grief. This portrait is the merest caricature. Asquith was a formidably intelligent, experienced politician endowed with infinite cunning. His will to govern never diminished. Above all, he knew what he wanted. This was to win the war without destroying the delicate national consensus that he himself had been instrumental in retrieving from the destructive bitterness of pre-war politics and upon which, he believed, future social and political progress depended. It was this that made him reluctant to embrace the win-at-all-costs policies of the 'English Prussians' – military conscription, the direction of labour, a war economy, a streamlined war cabinet with enhanced executive powers. His ambition was far from contemptible. But it became increasingly difficult to achieve. Asquith's ultimate failure owed little to his supposed personal flaws and much more to the intractable nature of events, especially the inability of the French and British armies to defeat the German army in the field. His governments took the most important decisions of the war: the dispatch of the British Expeditionary Force to France (August 1914); the raising of a mass army (August 1914); the

launching and termination of the Gallipoli campaign (April/December 1915); the formation of a coalition government (May 1915); the establishment of the Ministry of Munitions (May 1915); the introduction of conscription (January–May 1916). Lloyd George was unable to find an alternative to Asquith's Western Front strategy and the changes he introduced to central administration were often cosmetic. What he did change, however, was the image of government. 'Wait and see' was not an effective rallying cry during a great war. No one asked Lloyd George, as they did Asquith, whether he 'took an interest in the war'. Other than adultery, winning the war was his only interest. Asquith paid a high price for his failure to realise that, in war, the appearance of dynamism was important, a weakness that his long-term enemies in the Tory press exploited to the full. His eldest son, Raymond, was killed on the Somme in September 1916; his third son, Arthur, joined the Royal Naval Volunteer Reserve on the outbreak of war and rose from civilian to brigadier-general in three years.

Auffenberg-Komarów, Moritz von (1852–1928) Austro-Hungarian military commander. As Minister of War, 1911–12, Auffenberg had attempted the (perhaps impossible) task of modernising the Austro-Hungarian army, predictably making many enemies, especially in Hungary, though he did succeed in increasing military expenditure and in enlarging the army. In 1914 he commanded the Austrian Fourth Army, advancing 100 miles into Galicia, capturing Komarów and threatening to outflank the Russian Fifth Army, but CONRAD, the Austrian Commander-in-Chief, ordered Auffenberg to disengage, turn south and go to the aid of the Austrian Third Army. This caused a gap to open between the Austrian First and Fourth Armies that was immediately exploited by the Russian Fifth Army. Auffenberg was almost surrounded at Rawa Ruska early in September, escaping only through a long and humiliating retreat and suffering heavy losses of men and equipment. Although the disaster was principally Conrad's responsibility, Auffenberg was scapegoated and never held another military command.

Augagneur, Jean Victor (1855–1931) French politician. A moderate socialist whose principal interest was in public health reform, he was surprisingly propelled into office as Minister of Marine in VIVIANI's new government during the July Crisis of 1914, when his predecessor had a nervous breakdown. Augagneur's tenure at the Ministry of Marine was dominated by his limited support for the British-led attempt to force the Dardanelles (February–March 1915), an attempt to which professional French naval opinion was hostile. The predicted failure of the naval attack, in which the French lost two battleships (*Bouvet* and *Gaulois*), and the subsequent calamity that befell the Anglo-French assault on Gallipoli brought odium upon Augagneur. He did not survive the fall of the Viviani government in October 1915 and spent the rest of the war in political obscurity. In retrospect, whatever the operational dangers, French involvement in the Dardanelles seems both prudent and inevitable. The dangers of associating France with a British disaster in the eastern Mediterranean were outweighed by the possibility of failing to associate her with a British triumph.

Averescu, Aleksandr (1859–1938) Romanian military commander and Prime Minister. Averescu is generally regarded as Romania's best military leader during the Great War, though the competition was not particularly strong. His performance was more impressive in defence than attack. His attempt to outflank Bulgarian-Ottoman forces occupying the Dobrudja in September 1916 was imaginatively designed but beyond the power of his troops, who were subsequently routed. His defence of the Foscani line in August 1917 restored his reputation, however, and in January 1918 he was made Prime Minister. The collapse of Russia had made Romania's military position untenable. Averescu was handed the unenviable task of negotiating favourable terms from the truculent Central Powers, a task in which he failed. He resigned rather than become party to the humiliating Treaty of Bucharest (7 May 1918), which treated Romania as little more than an agricultural and industrial milch cow for the German war effort.

B

Babtie, William (1859–1920) British medical officer, a courageous man who won the Victoria Cross during the South African War (1899–1902) for treating wounded under enemy fire. When the war broke out he was Director Medical Service, India, a post in which he was responsible for providing medical support for military operations in the demanding Mesopotamia theatre. In the early days of the campaign medical arrangements left much to be desired. The Mesopotamia commission of inquiry set up after General TOWNSHEND's humiliating surrender at Kut-al-Amara, in April 1916, laid some of the blame at Babtie's door. From June 1915 to 1916 Babtie was Principal Director of Medical Services, Mediterranean, with responsibility for medical arrangements on Gallipoli and in Egypt and Salonika, which again attracted censure. This did not prevent his promotion to Director of Medical Services at the War Office and a knighthood. After the war he chaired the Babtie Committee on Reorganisation of the Army Medical Service.

Bachmann, Gustav (1860–1943) German naval staff officer, closely associated with Admiral TIRPITZ, whose aggressive strategy he strongly supported. He was promoted Chief of the Admiralty Staff in February 1915, in succession to Hugo von POHL, but resigned the following September in protest against government restrictions on submarine warfare following the international outcry in the aftermath of the sinking of the *Lusitania* and the *Arabic*. He resumed command of the Baltic Station. He was also a strenuous advocate of the aerial bombing of civilian targets.

Bacon, Reginald Hugh Spencer (1863–1952) British naval commander. Bacon resigned as Director of Naval Ordnance in 1909 to become managing director of the Coventry Ordnance Works. But he returned to the Royal Navy on the outbreak of war, briefly commanding a battery of 15-inch howitzers manufactured by his own firm before being given command of the Dover Patrol in January 1915. He retained this post until December 1917, when he became controller of the munitions inventions department of the Admiralty. Bacon was one of the pre-war navy's ablest officers. A close friend and ally of J.A. FISHER, he played a leading part in the establishment of the British submarine service. There was a certain irony, therefore, in his dismissal because of the Dover Patrol's perceived failure to prevent German U-boats passing through the Channel. Despite this, the Dover Patrol under Bacon's command did largely ensure the uninterrupted passage of men, munitions, supplies and equipment to the huge British armies in

France and Belgium. Few Allied vessels were lost in the Channel.

Bacon, Robert (1860–1919) US philanthropist, who organised the privately funded volunteer hospital the American Ambulance of Paris, which became the focus of American humanitarian relief in France. After US entry into the war, Bacon was appointed chief liaison officer of the American Expeditionary Force at British GHQ.

Baden, Max, Prince von *see* MAX, PRINCE VON BADEN.

Badoglio, Pietro (1871–1956) Italian military commander, who escaped censure for the disastrous performance of his XXVII Corps at Caporetto in November 1917 largely owing to the suppression of evidence by Prime Minister ORLANDO, an intervention that saved his career and allowed him to perpetuate further military disasters as the Italian army's chief of staff under MUSSOLINI.

Bairnsfather, (Charles) Bruce (1888–1959) British cartoonist, inventor of the immortal character 'Old Bill', whose phlegmatic demeanour and practical philosophy ('If you knows of a better 'ole, go to it') seemed to capture the essential spirit of the British army. Bairnsfather was a pre-war Regular. Bored by military service, he left the army and trained as an artist, securing employment in advertising. He was recalled in September 1914 and soon found himself on the Western Front with the 1st Battalion Royal Warwickshire Regiment. In 1915 the *Bystander* magazine launched Bairnsfather's career by publishing some of his trench drawings. Later, when Bairnsfather was recovering from shell shock in hospital, the *Bystander* commissioned him to produce a weekly drawing. These were eventually published in the six-volume *Fragments from France* (1917). He also published two books on his war experi-

ences, *Bullets and Billets* (1916) and *From Mud to Mufti* (1919). The government quickly caught on to Bairnsfather's popularity with the troops and the public, and he was sent on drawing missions to cover the American and Italian forces. He never returned to combat.

Baker, Newton Diehl (1871–1937) US politician. Baker established his Progressive credentials as the reforming Democrat Mayor of Cleveland between 1911 and 1915. He was not, however, a man ambitious for Federal office and had already spurned one invitation to join the WILSON government when the President persuaded him to become Secretary for War in March 1916. The appointment was forced on Wilson by the resignation of Lindley M. Garrison in protest against the President's failure to support his scheme to create a Federal-controlled military reserve. Wilson was attracted to Baker by his pacifist beliefs. It is somewhat ironic, therefore, that one of Baker's first tasks was to order the punitive expedition against Mexico. And even more ironic that, following US entry into the war in April 1917, this most unbellicose of men should be called upon to act as a war leader. Baker, unlike his chief of staff General Peyton MARCH, had no vision of what the US army should be and how it should be organised. Fundamental issues of command and control were temporarily shelved rather than solved. Baker approached problems in the calm and conciliatory manner of the corporate lawyer he was. He and his President performed an immediate *volte face* over conscription. Baker presided over the introduction of the Selective Service system, receiving much criticism from his political friends for his failure to defend civil liberties. He supported General PERSHING, Commander-in-Chief of the American Expeditionary Force, in his attempts to preserve the independence of his command in the face of the British and French desire to employ US forces piecemeal.

Although Baker's administration attracted vehement criticism from the right, notably from Henry Cabot LODGE, for its apparent failure to expand US military force with sufficient dispatch, this very hesitation and reluctance to embrace 'militarism' was deeply reassuring to the administration's strongest supporters on the left. Baker was a humane and decent man, well aware that under the harsh discipline of events his record as Secretary of War left much to be desired, but equally clear that his role in avoiding difficult issues, rather than confronting them, was of real value to the US war effort.

Baker-Carr, Christopher D'Arcy Bloomfield Saltern (1878–1949) British staff officer and military commander. Baker-Carr left the army before the war with the rank of captain but returned to the colours when the war broke out. His first post was driver at GHQ, his last was GOC 1st Tank Brigade. This remarkable change of fortunes gave him the felicitous title of his irreverent memoir, *From Chauffeur to Brigadier* (1930). In between, Baker-Carr played a leading part in the development of British machine gun tactics and organisation, establishing the BEF Machine Gun School at Camiers, an endeavour in which he had the vital support of Lord KITCHENER, and later of the Machine Gun Corps. Like many of those most closely associated with the wartime history of the machine gun, Baker-Carr was no respecter of persons, as his memoir humorously confirms.

Balfour, Arthur James (1848–1930) British politician, leader of the Conservative Party 1902–11; Prime Minister 1902–05; First Lord of the Admiralty 1915–16; Foreign Secretary 1916–19. Balfour was an influential man, in and out of office. Even in opposition, at the invitation of his friend ASQUITH, he regularly attended meetings of the Committee of Imperial Defence, which he had founded in 1902, and was a prominent Tory addition to the coalition government formed by Asquith in May 1915. Balfour's appointment as First Lord of the Admiralty seemed almost to be an antidote to that of his predecessor, Winston CHURCHILL. His somnolent stewardship of the Royal Navy made no impact on naval strategy. The official dispatch that he wrote after the battle of Jutland in 1916 was a propaganda and public relations disaster, seeming to confirm German claims of a British defeat. His defection from the Asquith coalition camp during the political crisis of December 1916, following the offer of the foreign secretaryship, astonished many observers and played a significant part in LLOYD GEORGE's rise to power. Balfour's tenure of the Foreign Office was marked principally by the Balfour Declaration of 2 November 1917, announcing British support for the establishment of a 'national home' for the Jewish people in Palestine. Devious and cynical, Balfour's languid manner bordered at times on lethargy, but at his best – during the Paris Peace Conference, for example – his pragmatic cast of mind and high intelligence could be fruitful in results.

Ball, Albert (1896–1917) British fighter ace. The British, unlike the French and Germans, did not really operate a proper 'ace' system, essentially a form of propaganda. Many of the British pilots whose names are now most celebrated were little known to the public during the war. Ball's name was an exception. Together with William LEEFE-ROBINSON, he was the first pilot to become a national hero. Ball scored forty-four victories before his death on 7 May 1917, a month short of his twenty-first birthday, preferring always to fly alone so that he could attack and escape quickly. This meant that he had little influence on unit tactics, but he always sought to improve his own combat effectiveness and that of his aircraft, usually a French Nieuport. He modified his controls and experimented with the configuration of his machine guns, including a fixed, upward firing MG that allowed him to attack enemy aircraft from below, normally a dangerous tactic. He was awarded the DSO and two bars, the MC and a posthumous VC.

Baracca, Francesco (1888–1918) Italian fighter ace, who destroyed thirty-four enemy aircraft. He was shot down and killed during a ground attack mission on 19 July 1918 while commanding 91 Squadron of the Italian Air Service. After reaching ace status, Baracca painted a prancing horse on his aircraft. His widow gave permission for Enzo Ferrari to use it on his racing cars, where it has remained ever since.

Barbusse, Henri (1874–1935) French writer and soldier, whose novel *Le Feu* (1916) (published in English as *Under Fire* in 1918) was the first literary exposé of the war to emerge from the conflict, focusing on the suffering of ordinary soldiers. It pre-dated the success of Remarque's *All Quiet on the Western Front*, enjoying a huge international readership. *Le Feu* was a self-conscious exercise in anti-war propaganda, and Barbusse's portrayal of war is even more harrowing than that of Remarque. The only positive feature to emerge from the enveloping destructive brutality was the experience of comradeship. Barbusse later embraced the political creed that seemed most to offer the prospect of fraternity in the post-war world, communism. He eventually settled in the Soviet Union.

Baring, Maurice (1874–1945) British Royal Flying Corps staff officer, poet and man of letters, allegedly David HENDERSON's intelligence officer but in reality an emollient PA. TRENCHARD kept him on after discovering he would be useful when Baring brought him some Oxford marmalade for breakfast. Baring spent a lot of time making notes for Trenchard, retiring to clubland after the war.

Barker, William George (1894–1930) Canadian fighter ace, whose outstanding record of fifty enemy aircraft/balloons shot down is often overlooked because most of his victories were achieved on the Italian front. Barker's VC, DSO and bar, MC and two bars made him Canada's most decorated war hero. In the dogfight that resulted in the award of the Victoria Cross, his Sopwith Snipe was attacked by fifteen Fokker D VIIs. He shot down three and drove off the rest, despite being wounded three times, before crash landing in his own lines.

Barnes, George Nicoll (1859–1940) British labour leader and politician, general secretary of the Amalgamated Society of Engineers 1896–1908, and MP for Gorbals 1906–22. Barnes was a strong supporter of British involvement in the war. He was active in the voluntary recruiting movement but later became a convert to conscription. LLOYD GEORGE, ever sensitive to the importance of organised labour, brought Barnes into his coalition government as Minister of Pensions, and later (in 1917) into the War Cabinet. He put Barnes in charge of the Commission of Inquiry into Industrial Unrest following the wave of strikes that broke out in the spring of 1917. Barnes dismissed feelings of a 'revolutionary nature' as a significant cause of the unrest and highlighted specific grievances to do with food prices, rent and the operation of the Military Service Acts. He broke with Labour in 1918. In 1919 he was one of the principal founders of the International Labour Organisation. His youngest son was killed at Loos in September 1915.

Bartholomew, Harry Guy (1878–1965) British journalist. 'Bart' Bartholomew was one of the pioneers of British photojournalism. He became art director of the photography conscious *Daily Mirror* in 1913 at the age of 28. In November 1917 he was the controversial and belligerent choice of Lord Beaverbrook (*see* AITKEN,

WILLIAM MAXWELL) to co-ordinate official photography on the Western Front, a position that brought him into frequent conflict not only with the military authorities but also with the Ministry of Information, which did not assume responsibility for official photography until April 1918.

Battenberg, Prince Louis Alexander of
see LOUIS ALEXANDER, PRINCE OF BATTENBERG.

Bauer, Hermann (1875–1956) German submariner. As *Führer* of the High Seas Fleet U-boat flotillas from 1914 until June 1917, Bauer was the first man to command a submarine fleet in war. He recognised the strategic possibilities of the submarine in a naval war against Britain but was continually frustrated by the lack of resources provided. A fellow officer had calculated before the war that it would take 222 submarines to achieve an effective blockade of Britain. By the end of 1914 Germany had only twenty-eight U-boats, only twenty-one of which were in the North Sea and only three or four of which could be maintained on patrol at any one time. Later in the war, Bauer advocated the 'wolf pack' tactics used by the German navy in the Second World War as well as the adoption of 'milch cow' supply ships that would enable U-boats to operate as far away as the east coast of the United States.

Bauer, Max Hermann (1875–1956) German staff officer, who established a pre-war reputation as the German army's leading artillery expert. This was confirmed by his starring role in the destruction of the Liège forts during the opening offensive of the war. Promotion duly followed. In July 1915 he was appointed Chief of Section I of the German General Staff with responsibility for artillery. His importance, however, was much greater than either his post or his rank implies. Bauer was a man of decided views. These included violent anti-Semitism and con-

tempt for parliamentary government. He favoured a ruthless prosecution of the war. This led him to conspire against FALKENHAYN, whose attrition strategy at Verdun he opposed. Bauer played a leading part in the appointment of HINDENBURG and LUDENDORFF to the Supreme Command at the end of August 1916. In the summer of 1917 Bauer conspired again to remove the Chancellor, BETHMANN-HOLLWEG, his ally in replacing Falkenhayn. He gave great support to the ambitious Hindenburg programme of military and economic mobilisation, favouring the establishment of a military dictatorship. He also played a leading part in the development of German stormtroop tactics. By the end of the war not even the Kaiser or Ludendorff lived up to Bauer's exacting standards and he conspired to get rid of both, succeeding in the case of Ludendorff. After the war Bauer took part in the KAPP putsch and was forced into a long exile, culminating in his death from smallpox in Shanghai, where he was acting as military adviser to Chiang Kai-shek.

Bauer, Otto (1882–1938) Austrian politician. Bauer was the leading 'left' socialist in pre-war Austria, but his Marxism was heavily seasoned with nationalism and pan-Germanism. He fought on the Eastern Front, where he was captured in the autumn of 1914. He was released from captivity after the Bolshevik Revolution and returned to Austria, where he became Foreign Secretary in November 1918. He resigned in July 1919 after the Treaty of Versailles eclipsed his hope of achieving the union of Austria and Germany.

Bayly, Lewis (1857–1938) British naval commander. As C-in-C Western Approaches 1915–19, Bayly had a key role in the war against German submarines. He favoured the stern, unbending style of command that earned him the soubriquet 'Old Frozen Face'. He had a reputation for being difficult and a little mad. But he was also able and energetic. His difficulties were considerably lessened by the United States' entry into the war, which also produced a remarkable change in Bayly's personality. He liked the Americans and they liked him. American sailors called him 'Uncle Lewis'. His relationship with the Anglophile Admiral SIMS, the US Navy's liaison officer with the British, was close and resulted in a remarkable degree of operational integration. The introduction of the convoy system certainly reduced shipping losses to a sustainable level but it did not entirely solve the problem. In the last few months of the war, however, Bayly began to enjoy greater success in destroying German submarines as the naval war swung decisively in favour of the Allies.

Bean, Charles Edwin Woodrow (1879–1968) Australian war correspondent and official historian, a careful and accurate observer of the war, often viewed from a front-line trench. Australian-born of British parents, Bean was educated at an English public school (Clifton College) and Oxford University. Travel through the outback of New South Wales, after his return to Australia in 1904, transformed his life. He discovered his Australian identity, becoming fiercely proud of the continent's frontier society that had produced a race of hardy, independent, generous men. Bean believed that these qualities had been stifled in the urban society of the mother country, populated by the stunted detritus of the Industrial Revolution, physically weak, socially deferential and without initiative. It was the democratic spirit of the Australian soldier that accounted for his military and moral superiority and that Bean chose to celebrate in his self-consciously epic and elegiac official history, 'a monument to great-hearted men'. It is difficult to overstate Bean's influence on Australian views of the Great War and of themselves.

Beatty, David (1871–1936) British naval commander. As C-in-C Battle Cruiser Fleet, Beatty led the successful raid into the Heligoland Bight (28 August 1914), during which his ships sank three German cruisers and a destroyer, intercepted HIPPER's battle cruisers at the Dogger Bank (24 January 1915) on their way back from bombarding the British coast, sinking the *Blücher*, and succeeded in luring SCHEER's High Seas Fleet on to the guns of JELLICOE's Grand Fleet at Jutland (31 May 1916), despite suffering serious losses in his encounter with Hipper's squadron. Handsome, debonair, fearless and resourceful, Beatty fitted the image of a British naval hero much more than his rather colourless predecessor, Jellicoe. To his admirers, not least Winston CHURCHILL, Beatty's leadership of the Grand Fleet at Jutland would have ensured a much more satisfactory outcome. To his detractors, he was a brainless commander whose impetuosity might well have lost the war in an afternoon. As Jellicoe's successor, however, Beatty showed that he could be an equally calculating, far-sighted commander, who was not prepared to risk all on headline-grabbing operations. He encouraged initiative, made important technical improvements in the fleet and strongly supported the convoy system. He also did much, through his personal visits to ships, to maintain the Grand Fleet's morale in the remaining years of the war. He took the surrender of the German fleet at Scapa Flow in November 1918.

Beauchamp-Proctor, Andrew Frederick Weatherby (1894–1921) South African fighter ace, who won the VC, DSO, MC and DFC. Beauchamp-Proctor was a quiet, amiable, modest man, qualities not always associated with fighter aces. He did not become a pilot until 1917, joining 84 Squadron, commanded by Sholto Douglas. Beauchamp-Proctor was so small (five feet one inch) that wooden blocks had to be fitted to his rudder pedals to enable him to reach them. He was not a great pilot. He crashed three times before he made his first 'kill'. But like most aces he was an excellent shot. The death of his parents in quick succession in December 1917 seemed to change his personality. He became much more aggressive and began to attack any enemy aircraft, seemingly oblivious of danger. He became an ace in March 1918. On 9 August he helped to destroy nine balloons in a single day, a record. During the 'Great Advance' he also did outstanding ground attack and reconnaissance work. He was wounded on 8 October after attacking eight enemy fighters single-handed and was sent home. 'For all his size,' remarked Sholto Douglas, 'that little man had the guts of a lion.' His final score was 54 'kills'.

Beaverbrook, Lord *see* AITKEN, WILLIAM MAXWELL.

Bell, Gertrude Margaret Lothian (1868–1926) British Arabist, archaeologist, explorer and intelligence officer. Gertrude Bell was the grand-daughter of the great Teesside iron smelter Sir Isaac Bell. After becoming the first female student to take a First in Modern History at Oxford, she travelled widely in the Middle East, becoming fluent in Arabic and Persian and establishing a reputation as an archaeologist. During her travels she met the British army officer and consul 'Dick' DOUGHTY-WYLIE, a married man, with whom she eventually became romantically involved. When the war broke out, Bell ran the Red Cross missing persons bureau in Boulogne, before returning home to reorganise, in trenchant fashion, the London headquarters. Her language skills and her network of contacts in the Arab world were, however, at a premium. On 30 November 1915 she was appointed to the Arab Bureau in Cairo and was later seconded to the Mesopotamian Expeditionary Force, first in Basra, then in Baghdad, where she worked closely with

Sir Percy COX. After the war she was a powerful, though unavailing, advocate of the Arab nationalist cause and one of the leading figures in establishing the kingdom of Iraq.

Below, Fritz Wilhelm Theodor Karl von (1853–1918) German military commander, who first came to prominence as GOC XXI Corps during the second battle of the Masurian Lakes (February 1915). Later the same year he was promoted to command Second Army on the Western Front, replacing the worn out General Karl von BÜLOW. Below found himself occupying the front between Noyon (on the river Oise) and Gommecourt with only three corps. The German Commander-in-Chief, General FALKENHAYN, warned his army commanders, after the launching of the German offensive at Verdun in February 1916, that a 'relief' attack further north was inevitable. During the spring Below became increasingly convinced, mainly from aerial observation, that the attack would be made against his army. Falkenhayn, however, was certain that the attack would be made against the sector opposite Arras and, despite accumulating evidence to the contrary, he made little effort to reinforce Below other than to send him extra labour and a few heavy guns captured from the Russians. The C-in-C did make it abundantly clear, however, that he expected every foot of ground to be contested in the event of any attack. This meant that the front line would have to be held in strength. Below responded to being forced to place the bulk of his infantry within range of the enemy's divisional artillery by providing it with the maximum of protection in the form of deep dugouts and interconnected galleries. This decision rendered even more ineffective the wholly inadequate British artillery bombardment and helped inflict the disaster that befell the British infantry on 1 July 1916. German success on the first day of the Somme was, however, far from apparent at the time. Below was more concerned by the incursions made into his second line by the French near Péronne. And so was Falkenhayn, who blamed Below's chief of staff, General Grünert, for sanctioning a retirement and replaced him two days later with Fritz von LOSSBERG. Grünert's dismissal was undoubtedly a warning to Below (and to other German commanders) of the consequences of further failure to carry out Falkenhayn's orders to recapture lost ground immediately. The message was clearly understood. Repeated German counter-attacks gave the Somme campaign what John Terraine called its 'texture' and were enormously costly to the German army. Falkenhayn never really forgave Below for the events of 1 July and in the middle of the month he transferred him to command of the newly created First Army, south of the Somme. As GOC First Army, in April 1917, Below conducted a capable defence against the ill-fated NIVELLE offensive. He spent the latter part of the war directing the writing of a new German army infantry manual, incorporating the lessons of the war. Below was a capable soldier whose reputation has been rather overshadowed by that of his younger brother, Otto.

Below, Otto Ernst Vinzent Leo von (1857–1944) German military commander. Below was one of the most able German field commanders of the war, serving on the Eastern Front, in the Balkans and Italy, and on the Western Front. Below established his reputation in East Prussia, where he commanded I Reserve Corps at Gumbinnen and the first battle of the Masurian Lakes (September 1914) and Eighth Army at the second battle of the Masurian Lakes (February 1915). This led to further army commands in Courland, Salonika and (briefly) on the Western Front between 1915 and 1917. Below's fame, however, rests principally on his command of the newly created Austro-German Fourteenth Army,

which played the leading part in the crushing defeat of the Italians at Caporetto (October–November 1917). Below's success in executing 'infiltration' tactics earned him no promotion but led to another key command, that of Seventeenth Army, where he was expected to repeat the victory of Caporetto but this time against the British on the Western Front in the great spring offensive of March 1918. Unfortunately for Below, his fame preceded him. His appearance in the line became known to British Third Army intelligence and was interpreted by them as a firm indication that they were about to be attacked. Unfortunately also for Below, his attack would be made against a much stronger position than those faced by the German Eighteenth Army to the south. Below's inability to capture Arras, one of his principal objectives, was ultimately instrumental in the failure of the German attack on the Somme. He ended the war in command of First Army, charged with conducting the retreat from Reims. He was the younger brother of General Fritz von BELOW.

Benedict XV (1854–1922) Roman Catholic pontiff 1914–22, who succeeded Pius X on 3 September 1914. He was dismayed by the war and was especially fearful of its effects on Austria-Hungary. His dismay was deepened by Italian belligerency in May 1915, which brought two of Europe's great Catholic powers into conflict. His regular denunciations of the war, which he characterised as 'useless carnage' and 'the suicide of Europe', were resented by Italian interventionists who believed that papal pronouncements undermined national and army morale. Pope Benedict made repeated unsuccessful attempts at mediation, most notably in his seven-point peace plan sent to the Great Powers on 1 August 1917 but treated seriously only by Austria. He was also active in organising humanitarian relief and supported a peace of reconciliation.

Beneš, Eduard (1884–1948) Czech nationalist. Despite his peasant birth, Beneš was an educated man with a doctorate in the emerging discipline of sociology. During the war he attached himself to the exiled Czech nationalist leader Tomáš MASARYK, acting as Masaryk's liaison officer with nationalist leaders in Prague. But in 1915 he fled to France, where he established himself as chief Czech representative in Paris, tirelessly lobbying leading French political figures on behalf of the Czech cause and becoming Masaryk's closest and most trusted lieutenant. He was Czech Foreign Minister from 1918 to 1935, and President from 1935 to 1938 and from 1945 to 1948.

Bennett, (Enoch) Arnold (1867–1931) British novelist and wartime propagandist. Bennett was among the leading figures of the literary establishment invited by Charles MASTERMAN, head of the secret War Propaganda Bureau, to a meeting at Wellington House, London, on 2 September 1914, to discuss how writers might best aid the war effort. Bennett was not an automatic jingo. He had not anticipated the outbreak of war. Like many Liberals, he viewed Russia as the real enemy, not Germany. But he was also a Francophile, married to a Frenchwoman. He gave thought to the nature of the war before concluding that it was just. He was aware that as a public figure his pronouncements might have some small influence. He decided to place them at the service of the state. One of his first contributions was 'Liberty: A Statement of the British Case', which appeared first in the *Daily News* and was reprinted in the American *Saturday Evening Post*. It sold 4,600 copies in Britain when published as a pamphlet. Bennett continued to defend the British cause in the American press, especially after the damage inflicted by the suppression of the Irish Easter Rising in April 1916. He also contributed numerous articles to the British press. Later, in 1918, he accepted the invitation of Britain's first Minister of Information, Lord Beaverbrook (*see* AITKEN, WILLIAM MAXWELL), to join the British War Memorial Committee, charged with selecting artists to support the war effort. Bennett got on well with Beaverbrook, who invited him to become director of propaganda in France, a position that he accepted. It is difficult to know what Bennett's real views of the war were. His public writing, such as that found in the pamphlet *Over There: War Scenes on the Western Front* (1915), was deliberately cheerful and in marked contrast to the flat, phlegmatic account of his visit to the front found in his *Journals*. The war featured very little in his subsequent writing. He believed in the justice of the cause and did his best to sustain it. After the war, like the majority of his fellow countrymen, he did his best to carry on where he left off only to find the world much changed.

Bennett, Henry Gordon (1887–1962) Australian military commander. At the time of his appointment to command 3rd (Australian) Brigade in December 1916, Bennett was the youngest general in the British army. As a brigade commander he retained the instincts of a front-line soldier, paying little regard to his own safety and constantly associating himself with the welfare and interests of his men. As a subordinate he was vain, arrogant, quarrelsome and difficult. These characteristics resurfaced in the Second World War, when his role in the surrender of Singapore made him one of the most controversial figures in Australian military history.

Benson, William Shepherd (1855–1920) US naval staff officer, who became the US Navy's first Chief of Naval Operations in May 1915 and succeeded in bringing a calm, apolitical professionalism to his task. By the time the United States entered the war in April 1917, Benson had established good relations with the suspicious political head of the US Navy (USN), Josephus DANIELS, had centralised naval administration under the control of his own office and had played a leading part in obtaining Congressional sanction for the wholesale expansion of the American fleet. The USN, unlike the US army, was in a position to influence the conduct of the war from day one. This influence, in the view of the USN's liaison officer with the Royal Navy, Admiral SIMS, ought to be directed against the German submarine campaign, with immediate priority being given to the construction of anti-submarine vessels rather than capital ships. Benson disagreed with this, taking a longer-term view of the USN's role in the post-war world, in which he believed a 'balanced fleet' would be the most appropriate 'force projector' for a nation with aspirations to global influence. Like many American admirals, except perhaps the Anglophile Sims, he was also aware that the principal obstacle to US dominion of the seas was not the German High Seas Fleet but the Royal Navy. In the end, US resources proved sufficient for the navy to have its cake and eat it. Although priority was eventually given to the anti-submarine campaign, to which the USN made a major contribution, there was no sacrifice of Benson's ambition to build a fleet 'second to none'.

Berchtold von und zu Ungarschitz, Fratting und Pullitz, Leopold Anthony Johann, Count von (1863–1942) Austro-Hungarian politician. After service in the diplomatic corps, culminating in the ambassadorship to St Petersburg, Berchtold became Austrian Foreign Minister in 1912. His was a disastrous appointment. He is commonly portrayed as a vacillating man, whose policy lacked clear purpose as he gravitated towards whichever powerful personality came within his orbit. This was often the belligerent chief of staff CONRAD. Under his influence Berchtold is supposed to have become bellicose but incapable of pursuing a

hardline policy consistently. This pattern of behaviour is thought to be apparent during the July Crisis of 1914 that followed the assassination of the Archduke FRANZ FERDINAND. Initially, Berchtold is believed to have favoured Conrad's idea of a pre-emptive strike against Serbia, but allowed himself to be talked out of this by the Hungarian Prime Minister, TISZA, who advocated a diplomatic strategy that would humiliate Serbia and provoke her into striking the first blow. Serbia's acceptance of all but one of Austria's demands effectively undermined this strategy and necessitated Austria's striking the first blow, but now without the advantage of surprise. More recent research, however, attributes to Berchtold a more central and consistent role in the decisions that led to a European war. He was, in fact, resolute in his view that the fate of the Habsburg Empire depended upon a successful final reckoning with Serbia and that this could only be achieved by war. He was also clear sighted in accepting the probability that this reckoning would involve war with Russia. His principal fear during the July Crisis was not that a European conflagration would ensue but that the Great Powers would, at the last moment, opt for peace. To this end he kept Austrian diplomacy under a tight personal rein that allowed little initiative either to Austria's ambassadors in France and Russia or to her allies in Berlin. Berchtold's fall in January 1915, however, was of a piece with traditional interpretations of his character. He initially resisted Italy's demands to be compensated with Austrian territory in the Trentino and the southern Tyrol as a reward for her (belated) adherence to the Triple Alliance with Austria and Germany, but then climbed down under German pressure only to be ignominiously forced to resign when Conrad and Tisza learned of his willingness to make concessions.

Bergson, Henri (1859–1941) French philosopher, whose theory of *Creative Evolution*

(1907), at the heart of which was the *élan vital* that placed action, instinct and will above reason, appealed enormously to the '1914 generation' of French intellectuals and patriots, especially their iconic figure Charles PÉGUY. It also provided powerful intellectual support for the dominant French military doctrine of the 'offensive spirit', developed by FOCH and GRAND-MAISON.

Berlin, Irving (1888–1989) US songwriter. Israel Baline was born in Russia. He emigrated with his large family to the United States in 1893, where he grew up in poverty on New York's Lower East Side. Although he could neither read nor write music he had an excellent ear for a tune and a remarkable facility with words. Irving Berlin's genius was first declared to the world in 1911, four years after he changed his name, with the worldwide smash hit 'Alexander's Rag-time Band'. He followed this three years later with a major Broadway musical success, 'Watch Your Step'. After the United States entered the war, Berlin was drafted, but someone in the War Department was shrewd enough to realise that his talents were not best used for soldiering. He was invited to write a recruiting song, producing 'For Your Country and My Country' and the amusing 'They Were All Out of Step but Jim', which captured the tribulations of conscripts adjusting to army life. He saw out the war at Camp Upton on Long Island. Berlin's fame grew after the war, when he wrote some of the most famous songs of the twentieth century, including 'Blue Skies', 'God Bless America', 'White Christmas', 'Cheek to Cheek' and 'Puttin' on the Ritz'. During the Second World War his travelling show 'This is the Army' entertained US troops across the world.

Bernhardi, Friedrich von (1849–1930) German soldier and writer, whose book *Germany and the Next War* (1911), written in the wake of his country's diplomatic humiliation during the Second Moroccan Crisis, caused an international sensation. The book deploys two principal ideas. The first was that the struggle for survival, identified by Darwin in the natural world, was equally applicable to international relations. Germany's choice was to expand or die. The second was that the needs of the state transcended those of the individual and of conventional morality. War was not only a policy option but also a moral requirement. Bernhardi's views did not represent those of Wilhelmine government, of which his book is explicitly and repeatedly critical. But, for Germany's enemies and critics, the outbreak of war seemed merely to confirm the pervasive nature of Bernhardi's views in German culture. One of the most savage critics of German policy, the Dutch cartoonist Louis RAEMAKERS, often used quotations from Bernhardi as captions to his portraits of German barbarism.

Bernstorff, Johnann Heinrich, Count von (1862–1939) German diplomat, Ambassador to the United States 1908–17. Count Johann von Bernstorff was a political moderate with an American wife. His personal charm and lavish party-giving made him popular in Washington political and social circles. He immediately recognised the battle of the Marne in 1914 as a disaster for Germany and advocated a negotiated peace, a position that found favour with President WILSON. But Bernstorff's hopes of maintaining friendly relations between Germany and the USA were constantly undermined by his government's policy of submarine warfare (which he opposed) and by the reckless activities of his subordinates, Franz von PAPEN and Karl BOY-ED, which were an affront to American sovereignty. Political moderation rarely found favour in Wilhelmine Germany. Bernstorff was treated as a pariah after his recall. The Kaiser refused to receive him and Ludendorff denounced him as a 'democrat'. He ended the war as German Ambassador in Constantinople.

Berthelot, Henri Mathias (1863–1931) French staff officer and military commander. Berthelot was a protégé of JOFFRE, whose chief of staff he became on the outbreak of war. During the climactic events of August and September 1914 Berthelot's chief role was to act as Joffre's 'flak catcher', allowing his chief the space and calm in which to make the vital decisions that resulted in the 'miracle of the Marne'. In 1915 he transferred to field command, as GOC 53rd Division and then XXXIII Corps. After the fall of Joffre, in December 1916, Berthelot was sent to Romania as head of the French military mission, in which capacity he struggled to reorganise the remnants of the shattered Romanian army. He did not return to the Western Front until 1918, when he was given command of the French Fifth Army. His absence had not improved his operational skill. Prior to the last German offensive of the war, on 15 July, he refused to implement PÉTAIN's prudent instruction to carry out 'elastic defence in depth', reluctantly adhered to by GOURAUD's Fourth Army on his flank. As a result, Fifth Army suffered a palpable defeat, from which Berthelot was rescued principally by the resistance of fresh American troops at Château-Thierry. In October 1918 he returned to the Balkans to assist Romania's opportunistic and providential return to the war. Berthelot was a notorious Anglophobe.

Bertie, Francis Leveson, Viscount Bertie of Thame (1844–1919) British diplomat. As Ambassador to Paris 1905–18, Bertie was the still centre of the turning world of Anglo-French relations. These often suffered from the friction of misunderstanding, rivalry, jealousy and contrary interests. His was a stressful task; ambassadors are an easy target for abuse. But he brought great experience, honesty and integrity to his important and sensitive

post. CLEMENCEAU, with whom he forged close links during the last tumultuous year of the war, particularly admired him and appreciated his contribution to maintaining the Entente.

Beseler, Hans Hartwig von (1850–1921) German military commander. After being recalled from retirement in August 1914, Beseler had an eventful war. He took part in the invasion of France, during which he commanded a corps in Alexander von KLUCK's First Army, the spearhead of the German advance. In October he was given responsibility for the capture of Antwerp. In 1915 he transferred to the Eastern Front and, in August, was appointed Military Governor of Warsaw, with responsibility for the whole of Russian Poland, captured as a result of the Gorlice-Tarnów offensive. He established a semi-independent Polish state, 'Congress Poland', in November 1916. This was ruled by an aristocratic puppet government, the Council of State, but the arrangement contained hints that real independence might be granted after the war. Predictably, it fell foul of the determination of HINDENBURG and LUDEN-DORFF to extort the maximum economic resources from subjugated territories, including the deportation of workers to Germany. PIŁSUDSKI's refusal to co-operate with the Germans in July 1917 effectively terminated Beseler's attempt to mediate with the Polish nationalists, an attempt that made him suspect in the eyes of the German High Command, for whom he was dangerously 'pro-Polish'. Beseler more or less abandoned his command after the Armistice and returned to Germany, where he became the object of right-wing nationalist animosity.

Bethell, (Hugh) Keppel (1882–1947) British military commander, who assumed command of the shattered 66th (2/East Lancashire) Division in March 1918 at the age of 35, making him the youngest British divisional commander of both world wars. Bethell, universally known as 'The Beetle', began the war as a captain in the 7th Hussars, but he had also served in the Royal Artillery and Indian army, an indication of his restless character that abhorred inaction. Neither superiors nor subordinates were exempt from his towering rages and impossible, often contradictory, demands. His career on the Western Front as staff captain, brigade major, infantry battalion, brigade and divisional commander was marked by complete contempt for all rules, regulations and procedures. One of his staff officers, Walter Guinness, described him as 'the most insubordinate person that I have ever come across'. He was notorious for poaching officers and stealing equipment from other units. In March 1918 he sought to reinforce the firepower of his new command by commandeering all the weapons from the British army's Machine-Gun School at Camiers, reassuring his (totally unauthorised) staff that he would soon square things with his friend 'Duggie'. (In fact, Field-Marshal HAIG was not amused; 66th Division was pulled out of the line and sent to train American drafts.) In the 'Hundred Days', however, Bethell got his chance. His division, supported by two squadrons of the Royal Air Force, a brigade of cavalry and other units, operated as the all-arms spearhead of the Fourth Army in the advance to the Rhine.

Bethmann-Hollweg, Theobald von (1856–1921) German politician. As German Chancellor from 1909 until 1917, Bethmann-Hollweg spent much of his career trying to reconcile the irreconcilable. His recognition of the need for Germany to evolve politically and constitutionally, if social peace was to be maintained, inclined him to moderate reform at home. This was too moderate for the Social Democrats who dominated the Reichstag after the 1912 election. His inability to command a parliamentary majority drew him back into the suffocating embrace of the crown and army, whose more extreme members regarded his commitment to reform as little more than treason. He found it increasingly difficult to moderate the ambition of Germany's military leaders, especially Admiral TIRPITZ, whose policies were so damaging to Anglo-German relations. Bethmann's dismay at the seeming impasse of German politics did much to inform his actions in 1914. During the July Crisis he was at the forefront of those who wished to encourage Austrian action against Serbia. At the very least, this presented the opportunity of smashing the Anglo-French-Russian Entente and winning a diplomatic triumph that would redeem the loss to German prestige suffered during the first (1905–06) and second (1911) Moroccan crises. A successful short war would be instrumental in delivering him and his country from its internal and external dilemmas. He was intelligent enough shortly to realise that the guarantee of German support to Austria he had authorised on 6 July was more likely to bring about a general war than a limited one. But he remained willing to take the risk in the belief that a military defeat of Russia and France would restore German security. His defence of the German violation of Belgian neutrality, during which he denounced the international treaty guaranteeing Belgian sovereignty as 'a scrap of paper', became infamous. It seemed to associate him with the more rabid supporters of German expansionism and was a godsend to British propaganda. And it is true that in the heady days of August and early September 1914, when a crushing German victory seemed imminent, he did support an expansionist programme that would have left Germany the hegemonic power of Europe. In reality, once the 'miracle of the Marne' had punctured the short war illusion, Bethmann spent the remainder of his chancellorship ineffectually trying to moderate the increasing influence of the military on all aspects of German life and policy. This became especially difficult after HINDENBURG and LUDENDORFF assumed control of the German war effort in late August 1916. His unsuccessful opposition to the resumption of unrestricted submarine warfare in February 1917 further weakened his position. By the time he resigned in July 1917, after right-wing criticism of his handling of the Reichstag peace resolution, the ruthless militarisation of the German economy under the Hindenburg programme was wrecking what was left of the social peace he had been so determined to uphold.

Bettignies, Louise de (1880–1918) French war heroine. The highly intelligent, well-travelled daughter of a Lille manufacturing family, Louise de Bettignies was contemplating entering a Carmelite convent when the war broke out. Instead, she escaped to England, where she was recruited by British intelligence and sent back to German-occupied France, with the brief to establish a network of observers. Operating under the name 'Alice Dubois', she proved remarkably adept at her work, making some 15–20 clandestine crossings into neutral Holland to report to her British controller, based in Flushing. Although de Bettignies and her network were captured in September 1915, the work of observation continued, providing the Allies with important information on German troop movements during the spring offensive of 1918. Louise de Bettignies was sentenced to death but this was later commuted to life imprisonment. She died in Siegburg women's prison in September 1918, probably from pneumonia but possibly from cancer. In either case the harsh conditions of her captivity and the lack of medical care certainly contributed to her death.

Bigge, Arthur John, Baron Stamfordham (1849–1931) British courtier, Private Secretary to King George V. Bigge was the son of a clergyman and, like many other sons of the manse, chose a military career, being commissioned into the Royal Artil-

lery in 1869. He came to royal notice for his part in returning to Britain the body of the Prince Imperial (son of Emperor Napoleon III) after his death in the Zulu War of 1879. He cemented the royal connection in 1895, when he succeeded Sir Henry Ponsonby as Queen Victoria's Private Secretary. His star was partially eclipsed by the accession to the throne of Edward VII, who had his own Private Secretary, Sir Francis Knollys. Bigge then began his long attachment to the Duke of York. When the Duke succeeded to the throne as King George V in 1910, Bigge became his Private Secretary, at first sharing the position until Knollys' retirement in 1913. George V succeeded to the throne at a time of grave political and civil unrest, but Bigge was determined to maintain the tradition of strict political impartiality established by Ponsonby. This brought him close in spirit to his sovereign. Bigge was a man of great industry and rectitude. Throughout the war he was the main channel through which the king corresponded with his generals and with political figures. He was much respected by successive prime ministers and party leaders. To him is due the credit for the choice of 'Windsor' as the royal family's new name in 1917. He was elevated to the peerage as Lord Stamfordham in 1911. His only son, Captain Hon. John Neville Bigge, 1st Battalion King's Royal Rifle Corps, was killed in action on the Western Front on 15 May 1915 and has no known grave.

Billing, N(oel) Pemberton (1880–1948) British politician. Billing was the son of a Birmingham iron founder and served in the Royal Naval Air Service from 1914 until 1916, when he resigned to become a political agitator. In March 1916 he became the first person successfully to challenge the electoral truce between the main parties when he won the seat of East Hertfordshire at a by-election. He owed his success to his populist agitation for improved air defence, something of particular concern to his constituents, who lived in fear of Zeppelin raids, and he styled himself the 'Member for Air'. Billing was among the first public figures to advocate the indiscriminate bombing of civilian targets and he must be counted among the unlikely founders of the independent Royal Air Force, which was created for this purpose. Billing was, together with the ineffable Horatio BOTTOMLEY, the leading demagogue of wartime Britain. In 1918 he was involved in a spectacular libel case, during which he proclaimed that the Germans had in their possession a 'Black Book' containing the names of 47,000 British perverts in high places. The names included not only those of Mr ASQUITH and his wife but also that of the judge trying the case, Mr Justice Darling! Mr LLOYD GEORGE was, unaccountably, missing from the list.

Binding, Rudolf Georg (1867–1938) German cavalry officer, who spent most of the war on the Western Front, serving from October 1914 with one of the *Jungdeutschland* divisions until he became ADC on a divisional staff in August 1916. His contemporary diaries and letters were published in German in 1927 and in English in 1929 under the title *A Fatalist at War*. The account is full of interesting detail and observations, pervaded by a sense of the ultimate futility of trying to communicate the reality of life in the front line to those who did not experience it themselves.

Binyon, (Robert) Laurence (1869–1943) British poet, fated to be remembered only for the fifth stanza of one poem, 'For the Fallen', which adorns countless war memorials throughout the Commonwealth and is regularly intoned at Remembrance Day ceremonies and meetings of the Western Front Association.

Birch, (James Frederick) Noel (1865–1939) British artilleryman. 'Curly' Birch was HAIG's chief artillery adviser from May 1916 until the end of the war, by which time his responsibilities also included Tank Corps gunnery and chemical warfare. Birch enjoyed Haig's complete confidence. Haig slipped him into the first CRA post that became available after his elevation to Commander-in-Chief and carefully supervised Birch's progress through corps and army to GHQ. An enormously tall man, reputedly 'two metres', Birch was an international authority on horses, though this did not prevent him from taking a thoroughly modern, scientific approach to his job. He saw this divided into three parts: tactical, technical and intelligence. These were beyond the ability of any one man to deal with alone and he built round himself an able staff that he worked hard. He did much to give gunners their proper status and authority in the conduct of the war, though his innovative approach often fell foul of more conservative gunners and commanders. He did not believe that artillery could win the war alone and was anxious to encourage infantry commanders to realise the importance of fighting their own way forward using their own firepower and flexible tactics.

Birdwood, William Riddell (1865–1951) British military commander. An Indian army officer and protégé of KITCHENER, he was chosen to command the Australian and New Zealand Army Corps (ANZAC) on Gallipoli in 1915, despite never having commanded a division. He remained in command of the Australians when they moved to France in 1916 until his promotion to GOC Fifth Army in the summer of 1918. From May 1915 he was given administrative control of the whole Australian Imperial Force, a position he retained even after his elevation to army command and one which gave him considerable influence over appointments. Birdwood left most of the day-to-day running of the Australian and New Zealand Army Corps and Fifth Army to his Australian chief of staff, Brudenell WHITE.

A handsome, affable man, and a shameless self-publicist, he liked to 'get around the troops'. He was popular with the Australian soldiers, who called him 'Birdy'. 'Pompey' ELLIOTT, who blamed Birdwood's indulgent style of command for the Australians' setbacks in 1916 and 1917, especially Bullecourt, thought his professed liking of Australians was put on for effect and that deep down he distrusted the Australians' independent spirit and democratic instincts. Birdwood was also much distrusted by HAIG, who thought he sacrificed discipline to popularity.

Bishop, William Avery (1884–1956) Canadian fighter ace, generally credited with seventy-two victories. Billy Bishop was the top-scoring Canadian pilot and the second top-scoring ace in the Royal Flying Corps, after Mick MANNOCK. Bishop was a rather poor pilot with an unenviable record of crash landings. He was due to be sent back to England for remedial flying training when he shot down his first aircraft. After that there was no stopping him. Unlike some other high-scoring RFC aces, he became a celebrity during the war, not least in Canada where he was greeted as a national hero when he returned on leave to get married in October 1917. Like Albert BALL, whom he revered, Bishop preferred to fly alone. And it was while flying alone that he won the Victoria Cross for a raid on Estmourmel airfield on 2 June 1917. After the war considerable doubts arose about the authenticity of this attack, which became the subject of a Canadian Senate inquiry. Bishop ended the war as CO 88 Squadron. A decision was taken at quite a high level to take him out of combat in June 1918, lest his loss damage morale. He published an account of his wartime service, *Winged Warfare*, in 1918. He was awarded the VC, DSO and bar, MC and DFC.

Bissolati, Leonida (1857–1920) Italian politician. After an unpromising start to life as the illegitimate son of a man in holy orders, Bissolati forged a successful career in journalism, during which his experience of rural poverty converted him to socialism. In the last years of peace, however, he became increasingly sceptical about the ability of international socialism to prevent war, his advocacy of military preparedness earning him expulsion from the Italian Socialist Party. He welcomed Italian belligerency as an opportunity to guarantee Italian democracy and to advance the cause of a free Europe, the greatest obstacle to which he saw as German militarism. There can be no doubting Bissolati's patriotism. In 1915, at the age of 58, he joined the army and served as a sergeant in a combat unit. Rather like LLOYD GEORGE in Britain, Bissolati began to develop grave doubts about the quality of Italian military leadership, especially that of CADORNA, but remained committed to a full mobilisation of Italian strength. If necessary, he was prepared to execute socialists opposing the war effort. Bissolati's instinctive liberalism and aspirations for the post-war world, however, met a ready response in the idealism of Woodrow WILSON, to whose ideas Bissolati gave unstinting support. This brought him into ever sharper conflict with the annexationist ambitions of Foreign Minister SONNINO and Prime Minister ORLANDO. Bissolati's advocacy of a policy of co-operation, however, appears – in retrospect – to show a much more realistic appreciation of Italy's post-war interests than the ideas of the Fascists who came to power after his death.

Blamey, Thomas Albert (1884–1951) Australian staff officer. He began his working life as a schoolteacher before abandoning the classroom for a commission in Australia's small regular military forces, in which he excelled. As a trained staff officer, Blamey's skills were at a premium in the Australian Imperial Force and he could not be spared for command positions. He spent most of the war in staff appointments, principally with the 1st Australian Division, first on Gallipoli (1915), then on the Western Front. He served as Major-General H.B. WALKER's chief of staff from July 1916 until May 1918, when he succeeded Brudenell WHITE as chief of staff of the Australian Corps, where he formed an effective partnership with Lieutenant-General Sir John MONASH. His post-war career was filled with controversy, fuelled by his belligerent personality and reputation for loose living. He was appointed Commander-in-Chief of Australian Military Forces in March 1942, a position he retained until the end of the war. He was promoted Field-Marshal in 1950, making him the highest-ranking soldier in Australian history.

Bliss, Tasker Howard (1853–1930) US staff officer. After a distinguished career, mostly spent in staff positions, Bliss rose to Assistant Chief of Staff of the United States Army in February 1915. In May 1917, shortly after the United States entered the war, he became Acting Chief of Staff and, from September to December 1917, Chief of Staff. On 31 December 1917 he reached his 64th birthday. This was the mandatory retirement age. Although he was compelled to retire as Chief of Staff, he continued in the important role of US military representative to the Supreme War Council at Versailles. The United States' involvement in this body was somewhat arm's length politically, reflecting the nation's status as an associated power rather than an ally. Bliss therefore often found himself as the most senior US representative, which gave him greater importance than many of his military colleagues from other countries. He also served on the Supreme War Council during its most important phase, before the impact of the German spring offensive in 1918 brought about a greater degree of Allied unity under the command of Ferdinand FOCH. Bliss supported, in principle, PERSHING's refusal to allow US troops to be used piecemeal but was rather more pragmatic and flexible in his attitude during the height of the spring fighting, not that this had much effect on Pershing. After the Armistice he was appointed as one of the five US commissioners to the Paris Peace Conference, where he advocated – without success – a policy of disarmament. An able and thoughtful man, his integrity and humanity, rooted in wide reading of the classics, impressed all those who came into contact with him.

Bloch, Marc Leopold Benjamin (1886–1944) French historian and soldier. Bloch is principally – and rightly – remembered as co-founder, with Lucien Fèvre, of the influential 'Annales' school of history. During the First World War, however, he served as a front-line infantryman with a group of tough miners from the Pas-de-Calais, from whose courage and patriotism he took inspiration. Bloch left a short, but valuable, addition to the literature of war experience, *Memoirs of War 1914–15*, notable for its severe realism but lack of morbidity or 'disillusionment'. He made no attempt to hide the institutional weaknesses of the French army or the individual failings of some of its members (he despised cowards and never hid his scorn for them). His descriptions of the violence of war are chilling. But there is no attempt, common in many accounts written by 'Anglo-Saxon' intellectuals, to deny the war meaning. His memoir is suffused with a sense of the justice of France's cause, and there can be no doubt of Bloch's willingness to defend it even at the cost of his own life. He possessed in full measure the virtues of the republican patriot that he so admired. His last words, when facing a German firing squad in 1944, were 'Vive la France'.

Blomfield, Reginald Theodore (1856–1942) British architect, whose work included important commissions for the

Imperial War Graves Commission. He designed the 'Cross of Sacrifice', found in many Commonwealth war cemeteries, and the Menin Gate at Ypres.

Blunden, Edmund Charles (1896–1974) British soldier and poet. Like Edward THOMAS, Blunden was essentially a poet of nature rather than a poet of war. He described himself as 'a harmless young shepherd in a soldier's coat', regarding the battlefield always with a countryman's eye but also with an imagination steeped from an early age in English literature. He volunteered for military service, enlisting in the Royal Sussex Regiment. As a front-line infantryman he served in some inhospitable parts of the Western Front, winning the Military Cross in 1917. His autobiographical *Undertones of War* (1929) remains one of the finest and most vivid prose accounts of trench warfare. Blunden never entirely shook off the effects of military service, retaining throughout his long life deep feelings of attachment to his wartime comrades. After the war, he became one of the greatest champions of Wilfred OWEN and, as a tutor at Oxford, taught one of the Second World War's finest poets, Keith Douglas.

Boelcke, Oswald (1891–1916) German air ace, considered by many to be the father of air combat. Boelcke, together with Max IMMELMANN, was one of the leading German aces of the first half of the war with forty 'kills'. But he was much more than a skilful pilot and crack shot. He was among the first to think seriously about air combat and to devise operational tactics. Significantly, these were based not on individual machines but on formations of aircraft, *Jagdstaffel* (hunting squadrons). Boelcke's prowess and modest, engaging personality made him a national hero. His death, in a mid-air collision with another German aircraft on 28 October 1916, was the occasion for widespread mourning in Germany, one of the disadvantages of the 'ace' system.

Böhm-Ermolli, Baron Eduard von (1856–1941) Austro-Hungarian military commander, who led Second Army in 1914 and 1915 and Army Group Böhm-Ermolli in 1916. As a military commander his operations were often characterised by weak planning and the fatal mixture of ambition and uncertainty. His greatest achievement was the capture of Lvov (Lemberg) in June 1915, but in 1916 his line was shattered by the power and speed of the BRUSILOV offensive. This led to his temporary supercession but he was later reinstated, finally being relieved of command in May 1918 under German pressure.

Bolfras, Arthur, Baron von (1838–1922) Austro-Hungarian military administrator. Bolfras was old enough to have fought in the campaigns of 1859 (against France) and 1866 (against Prussia), both defeats. In 1889 he took up his long tenure as Emperor FRANZ JOSEF I's Adjutant-General and head of the military chancery, posts he held until 1916. During the war he witnessed, with increasing alarm, the power and ambition of the imperial chief of staff, CONRAD, but was able to do nothing about it.

Bols, Louis Jean (1867–1930) British staff officer, the son of a Belgian diplomat. As CO of the 1st Battalion Dorsetshire Regiment, in November 1914 Bols was wounded and briefly made a prisoner of war but managed to escape. In October 1915 he became ALLENBY's chief of staff at Third Army, a post from which he was removed in May 1917 at the end of the Arras offensive and given command of 24th Division. Whether this was a demotion is a moot point, but he did not let it distract him. 24th Division played a leading part in the capture of Messines Ridge in June, and in September he renewed his partnership with Allenby, by now

Commander-in-Chief Egypt. This was at Allenby's insistence. He greatly valued Bols' cheerful disposition, which did much to soothe feelings often ruffled by the Commander-in-Chief's abrasive personality. They were an effective combination.

Bonar Law, Andrew *see* LAW, ANDREW BONAR.

Bone, Muirhead (1876–1953) British war artist. Bone was recruited in May 1916 by Charles MASTERMAN, head of the War Propaganda Bureau, to become Britain's first official war artist. He made two visits to France, producing a prolific number of drawings, notable for their clear draughtsmanship and intricate detail. His work was in great demand, not only for its quality but also because it reproduced well in black and white.

Borden, Robert Laird (1854–1937) Canadian Prime Minister 1911–20. Throughout the war Borden pursued a policy of maximum Canadian support for the British war effort. He single-mindedly forced conscription through parliament, provoking riots in French-speaking Quebec, formed a Union government and won the general election of 1917. He was equally determined that Canada's role in the war should be recognised by Dominion representation on the Imperial War Cabinet and at the Paris Peace Conference. His signature on the Treaty of Versailles is often held to mark Canada's emergence as an autonomous state. Despite this his reputation in Canada is currently low, damaged by his willingness to cut constitutional and liberal corners in the ruthless pursuit of victory.

Boroević von Bojna, Svetozar (1856–1920) Austro-Hungarian military commander. Boroević was an able commander whose realism was often mistaken for defeatism and lack of nerve by his superiors, especially CONRAD. Boroević's temperament, however, made him the ideal man for defensive operations. He distinguished himself in 1914 against overwhelmingly superior Russian forces in the Carpathians. Defensive fighting in mountainous terrain became the hallmark of his generalship and he took part in all eleven battles of the Isonzo on the Italian front from 1915 onwards. His conduct of offensive operations, however, was less impressive, and he incurred heavy losses in uncharacteristically over-ambitious attacks. He played only a small and ineffective part in the crushing German–Austrian victory at Caporetto (October–November 1917), signally failing to destroy the retreating Italian army. His realism reasserted itself in 1918 and led him to oppose the Austrian offensive on the Piave. His defeat after crossing the river came as no surprise, and as summer turned to autumn not even the exemplary discipline that he imposed on his army could prevent its eventual disintegration.

Boselli, Paolo (1838–1932) Italian politician. Even in an age notable for elderly political leaders, the elevation of the 78-year-old Boselli to the prime ministership of Italy after the fall of the SALANDRA government in June 1916 was remarkable. His government was a 'national coalition', including men from a broad spectrum of Italian political life, united by their support for the war. But they were no more successful than their predecessors in rescuing control of the war from the autocratic Commander-in-Chief, Luigi CADORNA, or in ending the bloody stalemate battles of attrition on the Isonzo River. It is surprising perhaps that the government lasted as long as it did, aided in a curious way by the lethargy of its leader. But the Austrian breakthrough at Caporetto finally dispatched it on 25 October 1917. Boselli was replaced as Prime Minister by ORLANDO.

Botchkareva, Maria Leontievna ('Yashka') (1889–19??) Russian soldier, the daughter of a peasant family, who escaped from a violent, alcoholic father at the age of 15 by marrying a violent, alcoholic husband, with whom she worked as a labourer on a construction site, wearing men's clothes. After attempting suicide and to murder her husband, she took up with another man, who also treated her badly, and with whom she was exiled to Siberia. In August 1914 she volunteered for military service, in which she distinguished herself after overcoming intense male hostility, being three times decorated for bravery. In May 1917 she persuaded Alexander KER-ENSKY to allow her to form a Women's Battalion, which she commanded. The remnants of the 'Battalion of Death', originally 2,000 strong, defended the Winter Palace from the Bolsheviks in October 1917. Botchkareva avoided the brutal fate of her comrades by escaping to the United States, where the publication in 1919 of her fanciful and ghosted memoirs, *Yashka, My Life*, made her a temporary celebrity before she disappeared into the obscurity from which she came.

Botha, Louis (1862–1919) South African politician and military commander. Although a leading Boer general during the South African War (1899–1902), as Prime Minister of the Union of South Africa (1910–19) Botha offered immediate military aid to Britain in August 1914. This declaration provoked a rebellion among sections of the Afrikaner population, which he subsequently crushed. In his treatment of the rebels he was careful not to make any martyrs, a shrewd and humane tactic from which the British failed to learn in their treatment of the Irish Easter Rising in 1916. In February 1915 Botha invaded the German colony of South West Africa (Namibia), completing its occupation by July. He remained Prime Minister throughout the war, striving always to maintain political unity but also continuing to support the British war effort. At the end of the war he attended the Paris peace negotiations, arguing for

lenient treatment of Germany, in which he was disappointed.

Bothmer, Felix, Count von (1852–1937) German military commander. Bothmer was a skilful professional who successfully led numerically inferior German forces on the southern part of the Eastern Front for much of the war after succeeding LINSINGEN in command of the *Südarmee* in the summer of 1915. He was sent to the Western Front in 1918 but his command was uneventful. Shortly before the Armistice he returned to his native Bavaria to prepare its defences against Allied invasion. He retired soon afterwards.

Bottomley, Horatio William (1860–1933) British journalist, politician and crook. A self-made and self-broken man who started life in an orphanage, Bottomley was a brilliant journalist and orator, who founded the populist and rabble-rousing *John Bull* in 1906. Bottomley's weakness was his overwhelming desire for a life of luxury. This took him away from what he was good at into the shady world of the company promoter, where he made and lost millions before going spectacularly bankrupt in 1911, an event that cost him his seat in parliament as Liberal member for South Hackney. The coming of war allowed him to demonstrate conclusively that patriotism is the last refuge of the scoundrel. He rehabilitated himself as a patriotic speaker and fund-raiser, raising subscriptions of almost £1M and styling himself 'the soldier's friend'. He was discharged from bankruptcy in 1918, winning back his parliamentary seat as an Independent. He was convicted of fraud in 1922 and spent five years in prison. During his time in gaol he was visited by Lord Birkenhead, who found him stitching mailbags. 'Sewing, Bottomley?' his Lordship enquired. 'No, reaping,' Bottomley replied. It is possible to forgive him many things for this remark. He died in the poverty and obscurity from which he came.

Boué de Lapeyrère, Auguste Emmanuel Hubert Gaston Marie (1852–1924) French naval commander, the most dynamic and charismatic figure in the pre-war French navy, a sort of French Jacky FISHER. As Minister of Marine from 1909 until 1911, he devoted his considerable energies to building a great battleship fleet. By arrangement with the British, in the event of a war with Germany the French fleet would be confined to the Mediterranean, leaving the Royal Navy to protect France's Atlantic coast. Boué de Lapeyrère was C-in-C of the fleet he had done most to create from August 1911 until his sudden resignation in October 1915. A man of his self-confidence and aggressive spirit wished for nothing more than to engage the battlefleets of Austria and Italy in a great battle of annihilation, but in this he was doomed to frustration. The Austrians were simply not interested in being annihilated. Their strategy was to maintain a 'fleet in being'. They pursued a policy of naval guerrilla war, with coastal raids by light vessels and, increasingly, submarine attacks against merchant shipping. And the Italians remained neutral. Boué de Lapeyrère had the mortifying experience that the fleet he had built was totally unsuitable for the kind of warfare it actually faced. He struggled to impose any kind of control over the thousands of miles of trade routes and to support military campaigns in the Dardanelles and Salonika, woefully short of escort vessels. The entry of the Italians into the war on the Allied side in May 1915 further complicated his task, intruding another difficult ally reluctant to accept his authority, and in October he gave up the attempt, pleading ill health.

Bourgeois, Léon Victor Auguste (1881–1925) French politician and diplomat. He spent the first three years of the war holding only minor office before emerging in 1917 as the leading French advocate of the League of Nations, in which he later sat as French representative. He won the Nobel Prize for Peace in 1920.

Bourne, Francis Alphonsus (1861–1935) British spiritual leader. As Archbishop of Westminster from 1903 to 1935, Cardinal Bourne was the leader and public face of English Roman Catholicism throughout the Great War. During the previous generation English Catholicism had made considerable progress towards integration and acceptance in a society with a long history of anti-Catholic feeling that its leaders desired. The outbreak of war provided a golden opportunity to advance this progress further. The Catholic Church's official position was that the war represented a divine punishment for the sins of man, especially for the apostasy of the modern world. Germany was, therefore, a convenient enemy, an arch-apostate, cradle of the Reformation and of godless philosophers, which had within recent times waged a concerted campaign of oppression against its own Catholic population. Cardinal Bourne was in no doubt that the war was just, declaring that: 'In this war every reasonable man who had tried to understand the real issues at stake ... can only give one answer.' That answer was to join the army. He encouraged Catholic recruiting and took particular pride in associating the Catholic Church with the bravery of its soldiers, especially those who won the Victoria Cross. (The first VC of the war was awarded to a Roman Catholic, Lieutenant Maurice DEASE.) The bravery of Roman Catholic chaplains was also a source of pride and a source of superiority in view of the criticism often made of the performance of Anglican chaplains. Bourne succeeded to a remarkable degree in securing public recognition of the loyalty and devotion of English Catholicism. This did something to counteract increasing British resentment towards Catholic Ireland in the aftermath of the Easter

Rising and towards the role of Pope BENEDICT XV, whose peace initiatives met with little response from Bourne and the English Catholic hierarchy.

Bowlby, Anthony Alfred (1855–1929) British surgeon. As 'Advising Consultant Surgeon, British Armies in France' from early 1916 Bowlby was responsible for co-ordinating surgery in the British Expeditionary Force on the Western Front. He was instrumental in making Casualty Clearing Stations, rather than Field Ambulances, the focal point for surgical operations and in locating Casualty Clearing Stations much closer to the front line. This enabled surgery on wounded soldiers to be carried out much more quickly, a reform of vital importance in a war fought without antibiotics.

Boy-Ed, Karl (1872–1943) German spymaster, naval attaché in Washington DC 1911–17, who ran an organisation of spies and saboteurs in the USA. His activities became so blatant that not even President Woodrow WILSON could ignore them and was forced to demand Boy-Ed's recall shortly before the United States entered the war.

Bradbury, Edward Kinder (1881–1914) British soldier. On 1 September 1914 'L' Battery Royal Horse Artillery, part of the 1st (Cavalry) Brigade, was surprised by units of the German 4th (Cavalry) Division advancing out of the fog on the far right of the German line at Néry. Two of the battery's 13-pounder guns were speedily overrun, but the third – commanded by Bradbury – fought on. Bradbury continued to direct the fire despite losing his leg, a wound that was to prove mortal. He and two of his team, Battery Sergeant-Major DORRELL and Sergeant NELSON, were subsequently awarded the Victoria Cross. The German division was scattered by Bradbury's actions and effectively rendered *hors de combat* for some time. The story of 'L' Battery, memorably depicted

by Fortunino MATANIA, captured the British public imagination and became one of the most celebrated incidents of the early part of the war. The gun is now in the Royal Artillery Museum at Woolwich.

Bradford, (Roland) Boys (1892–1917) British military commander. Bradford was the youngest British general of the twentieth century. He joined the Regular Army from the Territorials in 1912 and began the war as a Second Lieutenant in the Durham Light Infantry. On 1 October 1916 he won the Victoria Cross on the Somme while commanding 9th Durham Light Infantry. He was promoted Brigadier-General, commanding 186th Brigade, on 10 November 1917 at the age of 25 and was killed twenty days later during the battle of Cambrai. Two of his brothers were also killed during the war, George winning a posthumous Victoria Cross at Zeebrugge in April 1918.

Bragg, (William) Lawrence (1890–1971) British scientist, who won the Nobel Prize for Physics in 1915 (at the age of 25) for work done with his father on X-ray crystallography. During the war he became a key figure in the development of sound ranging, an important technique for locating and identifying enemy gun batteries. Peter Chasseaud has described sound ranging as the 'Manhattan Project of the 1914–18 war'. Besides Bragg, it employed some 200 leading British scientists and engineers, including many members of Ernest Rutherford's research team from Manchester University. Bragg was director of the Cavendish Laboratory at Cambridge after the war.

Braithwaite, Walter Pipon (1865–1945) British staff officer and military commander, the youngest son and twelfth child of a Yorkshire parson, who became one of the most controversial British soldiers of the first part of the war. After twelve years of regimental soldiering with the Somerset Light Infantry, Braithwaite entered the Staff College in 1898 and spent the rest of his career, until 1916, in staff positions. When war broke out he was commandant of the Indian Staff College at Quetta. When this was closed, he returned to England and, in March 1915, was appointed chief of staff of the Mediterranean Expeditionary Force, under the command of Sir Ian HAMILTON. During the fateful Gallipoli campaign of 1915, Braithwaite and his staff achieved an unenviable reputation for arrogance and incompetence. This opinion was not shared by General Hamilton, who referred to Braithwaite as a 'rock'. Both Hamilton and Braithwaite were recalled in October 1915. Braithwaite was given command of a second-line Territorial division, the 62nd (2/West Yorkshire), which languished in England until January 1917. After a difficult baptism at Bullecourt in May 1917, the division performed well at Cambrai in checking the German spring offensive and in the 'Great Advance'. After a brief period as temporary GOC XXII Corps, Braithwaite was promoted GOC IX Corps on 13 September 1918. Sixteen days later this corps spearheaded Fourth Army's breaking of the Hindenburg Line and continued to lead the advance on the extreme right of the British line. In the immediate aftermath of the Armistice, Braithwaite was commissioned by Field-Marshal HAIG, an old friend and admirer, to report on staff work during the war, producing conclusions that were generally favourable.

Brancker, William Sefton (1877–1930) British air force commander. Brancker was an artilleryman whose career took a staff path before the war. His interest in aviation dates from 1910, when he was charged with welcoming the group that first demonstrated aircraft in India, where he was stationed. In 1911 he was air observer during the Indian army military manoeuvres that witnessed the first use of aircraft for military purposes on the subcontinent. His report was enthusiastic

about the military possibilities of aircraft. One of its readers was Sir Douglas HAIG. In 1913 Brancker qualified as a pilot (though he remained a pretty average one) and joined the staff of Sir David HENDERSON, Director of Military Aeronautics. When Henderson took the Royal Flying Corps to France in August 1914, Brancker remained at the War Office as Deputy Director of Military Aeronautics, presiding over the early expansion of British air power in the face of considerable scepticism and competition for scarce resources. Brancker later commanded III Wing RFC on the Western Front and was GOC RFC Middle East, based in Cairo. In January 1918, however, he was brought home to join the new Air Council as Controller-General of Equipment. After the war he was a pioneer of civil aviation, serving as Director of Civil Aviation at the Air Ministry from 1922 until his death in the crash of the airship R101 in 1930. Brancker was among the first to appreciate the military and civilian possibilities of powered flight. He brought great vision and administrative abilities to the nurturing of British military and civil aviation.

Bratianu, Ion (1864–1927) Romanian politician. Bratianu was Romanian Prime Minister for much of the war. As a liberal, he was by instinct pro-Allies. His instincts, however, were tempered by calculation and caution. Calculation favoured an Austro-Hungarian defeat that would allow Romanian expansion into Transylvania, where a large Romanian-speaking population lived under Hungarian control. Caution favoured waiting on events for the right moment to enter the war. This came in August 1916, by which time the BRUSILOV offensive appeared to have brought Austria to the brink of defeat. But, in the event, neither calculation nor caution was enough. Bratianu was to learn the price of pursuing a policy of territorial aggrandisement without the military power to back it up. Romania was invaded by two German armies.

Bucharest fell on 6 December. Instead of finding himself Prime Minister of a triumphantly expanded state, Bratianu found himself confined to a rump of independent territory in the north-east of the country. Bratianu's career, however, is a testimony to the power of endurance and of luck. Although he resigned in December 1917 following the signing of an armistice with the Central Powers, Bratianu never lost the confidence of King FERDINAND I. He continued to exercise much backstairs control and on 10 November 1918, a day before the end of the war, he and the king engineered Romania's re-entry into the war. This *was* a triumph of timing. Romania ended the war on the winning side. At the Paris Peace Conference Bratianu was in a powerful position to extract territorial concessions not only from a defeated enemy, Austria-Hungary, but also from a defeated ally, Russia, so that both Transylvania and Bessarabia became part of Romania.

Brett, Reginald Baliol, Viscount Esher (1852–1930) The ubiquitous *éminence grise* of British public life in the Edwardian period who moved effortlessly in royal, ministerial and journalistic circles, exercising a degree of power and influence most politicians can only dream of. Despite having sat briefly in the House of Commons as a Liberal in the 1880s, he was close to the Unionist leader, Arthur BALFOUR. Esher was an important influence on Balfour's establishment of the Committee of Imperial Defence (CID), which was intended to co-ordinate British strategy and defence planning. Esher was a permanent member of the CID from its foundation in 1902 right through to the end of the Great War, despite his occupying no official position or public office. He used his membership of the War Office Reconstruction Committee, established in the wake of the South African War (1899–1902), to advance his views on military preparedness. (That the com-

mittee was invariably referred to as the Esher Committee is indicative of his key role.) The establishment of the Army Council and of the General Staff was a direct result of the committee's report. Esher favoured conscription but recognised that its introduction was politically impossible. Instead, he gave his support to R.B. HALDANE's scheme for a Territorial Army. His opinions on appointments and promotions were often sought and often acted upon. Esher was never a professional soldier. His views were derived from history. These made him a strong advocate of what would later be called 'deterrence' but an opponent of war, and he supported a compromise peace in 1917. He always preferred to exercise power without responsibility, and occasionally uncomfortable questions were asked about his role. He was a promiscuous and predatory homosexual.

Briand, Aristide (1862–1932) French politician. Briand was France's longest-serving wartime Prime Minister (October 1915–March 1917), an office he held jointly with that of Foreign Minister. His principal aim was to maintain Allied unity, to which end he advocated frequent political and diplomatic meetings, though his attempts to establish an international council of war met without success. He was also France's leading 'Easterner'. He favoured Allied military action in the Balkans, and the dispatch of the Salonika expedition owed most to his support. The aim of this expedition was not only to open another flank against the Central Powers but also to provide the basis for post-war French hegemony in the Eastern Mediterranean. Briand's political position was a difficult one. A powerful Radical bloc dominated the French parliament; the autocratic Commander-in-Chief, General JOFFRE, dominated conduct of the war. This left Briand with very little room for manoeuvre and he found it hard to drag Joffre's attention away from the Western Front, despite giving the C-in-C control of all fronts in the hope that this would lead him to take Salonika more seriously. The German offensive at Verdun, launched in February 1916, began to loosen Briand's grip on power. The parliamentary Radicals became more and more restive following revelations about the poor state of French defences and demanded that the military be brought under political control. By the end of the year Briand was only able to preserve his position by jettisoning Joffre. France was increasingly suffering from war weariness. Briand's reluctance to suppress pacifist dissent alienated the Right, for whom he became a symbol of defeatism. He desperately needed a victory and threw himself wholeheartedly behind the offensive strategy of Joffre's successor, Robert NIVELLE. Other members of the government, however, began to harbour grave misgivings about Nivelle's plans, notably the Minister of War, General LYAUTEY, whose resignation brought down the administration on 16 March 1917 but did not prevent the Nivelle offensive from proceeding to its disastrous conclusion. After the war Briand served three more terms as Prime Minister. He became a leading supporter of the League of Nations and of international pacifism and was awarded the Nobel Prize for Peace in 1926.

Bridges, (George) Tom (Molesworth) (1871–1939) British military commander. Bridges began the war as a somewhat elderly major in the 4th Dragoon Guards but achieved rapid promotion as a youthful major-general in command of the 19th (Western) Division. He led 19th Division from 13 December 1915 until 20 September 1917 when his right leg was shattered by a shell during a visit to one of his front-line brigades. He amazed the hospital staff by ordering them to feed his amputated leg to 19th Division's mascot, a lion that a friend had won in a Red Cross raffle in Paris. Bridges' most distinctive contribution came, however, during the BEF's retreat from Mons, when he

rallied exhausted British troops at St Quentin with a tin whistle and a drum, an episode recalled in Sir Henry NEWBOLT's poem 'The Toy Band – A Song for the Retreat'. Later, and more forcefully, he placed two battalion commanders under arrest, assembled their men in the town square of St Quentin and threatened to shoot them if they did not resume the march. His book *Alarms and Excursions* (1940) is an entertaining account of his unusual military career.

Bridges, Robert Seymour (1844–1930) British Poet Laureate, whose contribution to the war effort was the splendidly idiosyncratic *The Spirit of Man*, 'an anthology in English and French from the Philosophers and Poets'. First published in January 1916, it was an instant success, being reprinted three times in 1916, once in 1917 and once in 1918. The poet Ivor GURNEY described *The Spirit of Man* as 'a good book, though very far below what it might be ... about one third of the book is worth having, some of it foolish merely.' Many British soldiers in both world wars carried the volume in their packs. It was, perhaps, the most influential anthology in twentieth-century English literature. Robert Bridges was the uncle of Major-General Tom BRIDGES, who in 1940 himself produced an anthology specially for use by the forces, *Word from England*.

Bridges, William Throsby (1861–1915) Australian military commander. Bridges' military career was a series of 'firsts': first Commandant of the Royal Military College, Duntroon, first Australian representative on the Imperial General Staff, first Australian to reach general officer rank. He was also the first Australian general to be killed in action, mortally wounded by a Turkish sniper on 15 May 1915 while GOC 1st Australian Division on Gallipoli. Bridges took an 'imperial' view of Australia's military organisation and obligations that was similar to that of his mentor, Sir E.T.H. Hutton (GOC Australian Military Forces 1901–4). An austere, aloof man in the pre-war British Regular Army image, he never sought popularity. His troops found him hard and alien, but they respected his courage. Bridges was a dedicated professional soldier, committed to the highest standards of discipline and military efficiency, values that left their mark on the college he founded at Duntroon.

Briggs, Charles James (1865–1941) British military commander. Briggs was one of the most talented cavalry officers of his generation. He served with distinction as GOC 1st (Cavalry) Brigade in the original BEF, later commanding the 3rd (Cavalry) Division. His claims to command the Cavalry Corps were substantial, but he was overlooked in favour of the amiable Hon. C.E. 'Cis' Bingham. Instead, in October 1915, he found himself commanding an infantry division in the malarial backwater of Salonika, later (in May 1916) succeeding Sir George MILNE as GOC XVI Corps, a post he retained for the rest of the war. At Doiran, in September 1918, XVI Corps played an important part in the offensive that knocked Bulgaria out of the war.

Brittain, Vera Mary (1896–1970) British writer and wartime nurse. A spirited and independent young woman from a provincial industrial family, she overcame considerable parental disapproval to win a place at Somerville College, Oxford, determined to become a writer. During the last summer of peace she fell in love with her brother's best friend, Roland Leighton, and they became engaged in August 1915. Leighton died of wounds four months later. Vera heard the news of his death while waiting at the Grand Hotel, Brighton, for him to come home on leave. In June 1915 she had abandoned her studies and joined the Voluntary Aid Detachment as a nurse, first in London, then in Malta and finally (from August

1917) in France. She was compelled to break her VAD contract at the end of April 1918, returning home to look after her parents. In 1933 she published a celebrated memoir of her experiences, *Testament of Youth*. A selection of her correspondence (published in 1998) with Leighton, her brother Edward and their friends Victor Richardson and Geoffrey Thurlow, all of whom were killed in the war, is almost unbearably poignant. After the war Vera Brittain became a pacifist and socialist, but during it she remained committed to an Allied victory, which alone could justify the losses she had suffered.

Brock, Frank Arthur (1884–1918) British naval officer. Brock belonged to the celebrated family of fireworks manufacturers. As a schoolboy, he announced his intention to maintain the pyrotechnic tradition by blowing up a stove in his form room at Dulwich College. After leaving school he joined the family firm, where he became a director. When the war broke out, he obtained a commission in the Royal Artillery but within a month was 'loaned' to the Royal Naval Air Service, to which he shortly transferred. He soon obtained his wings and was rapidly promoted. His innovative and imaginative mind was apparent to all and it was allowed full scope. He served on the Board of Invention and Research as well as founding and commanding the Royal Navy Experimental Station at Stratford. He was responsible for developing the Dover flare, used in anti-submarine warfare, the Brock colour filter, and the Brock incendiary bullet for use against airships. The Brock bullet was particularly sensitive, flaming on impact and blowing a hole large enough to allow the rapid escape of gas. The first German airship to be shot down was destroyed by a Brock bullet. Its importance was recognised by a grant of £12,000. Brock also devised and executed the smoke screen used in the Royal Navy's attack on Zeebrugge on 23 April 1918. He brought on board with him a box marked 'Highly Explosive. Do Not Open'. It contained bottles of vintage port. These were drunk before the assault, which Brock joined. He was killed on the Mole while examining a German range-finder. He has no known grave.

Brock, Osmond de Beauvoir (1869–1947) British naval commander, who led the 1st Battle Cruiser Squadron at the battles of Heligoland (28 August 1914), Dogger Bank (24 January 1915) and Jutland (31 May–1 June 1916) in his flagship HMS *Princess Royal*. Brock's career was thus closely associated with that of David BEATTY, whose chief of staff he became in December 1916 when Beatty succeeded JELLICOE as C-in-C Grand Fleet. Brock was one of the cleverest men in the Royal Navy, and he also had nerve, a quality that doubtless did much to purge the sin of intelligence among his contemporaries in a service that often seemed to despise brains.

Brockdorff-Rantzau, Ulrich, Count von (1869–1928) German diplomat, who spent the war as German minister in Copenhagen, maintaining good relations with Denmark, a useful source of food for the hard-pressed German economy, and supporting sedition in Russia. After the Armistice he became German Foreign Minister in the hope that his reputation as 'the acceptable face of German diplomacy' would secure favourable terms from the Allies. In this he was disappointed. He resigned in protest at the harshness of the Treaty of Versailles but later became the Weimar Republic's first Ambassador to the Soviet Union.

Brockway, (Archibald) Fenner (1888–1988) British pacifist. As a young journalist Brockway was converted to socialism during an interview with Keir Hardie. He was soon moving in Fabian circles and later joined the Independent Labour Party. In 1913, at the age of 25, he was

appointed editor of the *Labour Elector*. He was strongly opposed to British entry into the war and used the pages of his newspaper to campaign against it, incurring a failed charge of sedition. Together with Clifford ALLEN, he founded the No-Conscription Fellowship, an organisation devoted to persuading men not to volunteer for military service. In 1916 he was arrested for campaigning against the introduction of conscription. He served two months in prison and was immediately re-arrested under the provisions of the Military Service Act. He remained in gaol until six months after the end of hostilities. His wartime experiences did nothing to diminish his support for peace and for other progressive causes, including Indian independence. He was one of the founders of the Campaign for Nuclear Disarmament and a passionate opponent of apartheid in South Africa.

Brodie, John L. (18??–19??) British inventor. A feature of the early months of the Great War was the large number of soldiers suffering from head and facial wounds caused by shrapnel. The French responded to this by introducing the Adrian steel helmet in mid-1915. The British soon followed. The 'Inventions Committee' at the War Office investigated the problem, eventually favouring the anti-shrapnel helmet patented by Brodie in August 1915. Brodie's design, stronger and easier to manufacture than the French model, was further improved by the decision to use 'Hadfield' hardened manganese steel in the production. A few of the 'Type A' helmets entered service as early as the autumn of 1915, but they did not become widely available until 1916. Experience of the helmet under combat conditions led to criticisms and suggestions for improvement, not least by General PLUMER. The familiar Mark I version, with its matt khaki finish, entered production in May 1916 and became the standard British army helmet for the remainder of the war.

Brooke, Rupert Chawner (1887–1915) British poet and soldier. Just as Wilfred OWEN is now firmly established as the iconographic symbol of 'disillusionment', so Brooke has become embalmed as the symbol of naive idealism. Brooke was certainly an idealist, as was Owen in 1914, but it is more difficult to categorise him as 'naive'. By the time war broke out Brooke was a mature poet whose superficial celebration of 'Englishness' in poems such as 'The Old Vicarage, Grantchester' disguised a subtle, ironic and complicated poetic imagination that dazzled his own generation. He was also, it is often forgotten, a socialist. As a volunteer for the Royal Naval Division he very quickly saw action in the abortive expedition to Antwerp. His letters to friends leave no doubts that he had witnessed and understood the destructive power of modern war. It was *after* this experience that he wrote the five sonnets that were to make him famous ('Peace', 'Safety', two called 'The Dead', and 'The Soldier'). These were published in *1914 and Other Poems* in May 1915, shortly after his death from blood poisoning on 23 April (St George's Day) while on his way to the Dardanelles. The volume sold in huge numbers throughout the war (my own copy is the 25th impression, published in October 1918). Brooke did not only speak to the '1914 generation' or to the generation that fought the First World War. His poetry, especially perhaps 'The Soldier', also stirred the feelings of many British soldiers during the Second World War. Rupert Brooke is buried on the Greek island of Skyros.

Brooking, Harry Triscott (1854–1944) British military commander. By 1914, during a thirty-year career spent almost entirely in the Indian army, Brooking had acquired an impressive combat pedigree in the small colonial wars of the North-West Frontier and Burma. The qualities of self-reliance, initiative and independence of judgement which he developed in counter-insurgency warfare stood him in good stead during the Great War, which – from July 1915 – he spent entirely in the demanding environment of Mesopotamia, finally (and most importantly) as GOC 15th Indian Division. A small, slight man, he was nevertheless an implacable and enterprising commander. His operational method was to 'mystify, mislead and surprise'. He displayed something of a genius for subterfuge and preferred night-time deployments. His victories at Ramadi (28–29 September 1917) and Khan Baghdadi (26–27 March 1918) have been described as 'among the most perfectly conceived and conducted minor battles of the whole war'.

Brooks, Ernest (18??–19??) British war photographer. The military authorities on the Western Front were suspicious of photography, and it was not until March 1916 that the first official photographer was appointed. Brooks was a natural choice. He had learned his trade on the pre-war *Daily Mirror*, the leading pictorial newspaper of the period, before establishing a reputation as a 'war photographer' in the Gallipoli campaign (1915). Photographs of the fighting there increased public and press demand for 'news' images of the bigger war on the Western Front. Brooks, like the other official photographers, a small group numbering no more than a dozen, was given military rank and uniform and subject to military censorship. As the longest-serving war photographer, Brooks took about a fifth of the British photographs of the Western Front (some 4,400), despite spending much of 1918 in Italy.

Broqueville, Charles Marie Pierre Albert, Baron de (1860–1940) Belgian politician. Broqueville was leader of the Catholic Party, the majority party in the Belgian parliament, and Prime Minister from 1911 until May 1918. Both before and during the war, he clashed frequently with King ALBERT I. He opposed the King's attempts to deploy the army along the border with Germany in the last days of peace, preferring instead to leave it scattered around the country as a clear statement of Belgian neutrality. During the war (when he was also Foreign Minister), however, he opposed the king's refusal to abandon Belgian neutrality and his leaving open the possibility of negotiating a separate peace with Germany, only to make peace approaches himself to the Central Powers in October 1917. News of this fundamentally damaged his political authority. He was compelled to yield the foreign ministry to Paul HYMANS in January 1918 and to resign as Prime Minister in May after losing the support of his coalition cabinet.

Brown, (Arthur) Roy(al) (1893–1944) Canadian fighter ace, whose fame is accounted for not by his modest score (eleven victories) but by his claim to have shot down Manfred von RICHTHOFEN. Whether he did, or whether Richthofen succumbed to Australian ground fire, remains much debated.

Browning, John Moses (1855–1926) US weapons designer, responsible for three of the most successful and enduring small arms in twentieth century military history, the Colt 45 M1911 semi-automatic pistol, the Browning automatic rifle and the Browning machine gun, all characterised by their simplicity of design, ease of manufacture and effectiveness under combat conditions. Gavrilo PRINCIP used a 7.65mm 'Old Model' Browning 1900, manufactured – somewhat ironically – in Belgium, to murder the Archduke FRANZ FERDINAND and his wife in Sarajevo on 28 June 1914.

Brownrigg, Douglas (1867–1939) British naval officer. Brownrigg was brought out of retirement in 1914 to act as Naval Censor. A cultivated and polite man with a mischievous sense of humour, he interpreted his role more widely than was

perhaps intended by those who appointed him. He recognised the importance of public opinion in modern war and did more than anyone to persuade the Royal Navy that it had to be taken seriously, without compromising operational secrecy. His commissioning of Rudyard KIPLING to write about the navy's war was something of a coup. In 1916 Brownrigg staunchly defended BALFOUR and JACKSON's post-Jutland communiqué that admitted to heavy British losses. He believed it undercut German attempts to maximise the propaganda value of the battle and established the veracity of British naval reporting for the rest of the war. After the war he wrote an amusing memoir of his work, *Indiscretions of the Naval Censor* (1920).

Bruce, Henry Harvey (1862–1948) British sailor. Harvey began the war as Captain of the battleship HMS *Hercules*, a post he had held since June 1913. But in June 1915 he was brought ashore as first Commodore Superintendent of the new Rosyth dockyard, on the Firth of Forth near Edinburgh, which he commanded for the rest of the war, presiding over its expansion and increasing efficiency. In 1918 Admiral BEATTY felt able to move the Grand Fleet's base from Scapa Flow to Rosyth.

Bruchmüller, Georg (1853–1928) German artillery commander, who retired in 1913 after an undistinguished career that the war was destined to resurrect. He was recalled in 1914 and sent to command an artillery regiment on the Eastern Front. It was here that he became an advocate of short, intense artillery bombardments that retained the element of surprise when planning and executing offensives. He also favoured the neutralisation of the enemy's command and control systems rather than the physical destruction of his defences, targeting command posts, telephone exchanges, forming-up areas and crossroads, and making sophisticated use of smoke and gas shells. His method was triumphantly demonstrated in the crushing defeat of General EVERT's Russian army at Lake Naroch in March 1916. After this, Bruchmüller planned the artillery bombardments for all subsequent German offensives on the Eastern Front until his transfer to the west in December 1917 to plan the preparatory bombardments for the great German spring offensive that inflicted a heavy defeat on GOUGH's British Fifth Army. Bruchmüller's success earned him the nickname 'Durchbruch-müller' ('Break-though Müller'). He was one of the most outstanding German soldiers of the war.

Brumowski, Godwin (1889–1936) Austro-Hungarian fighter ace. Brumowski transfered from the artillery to the Austro-Hungarian air service in 1916, first as an observer before qualifying as a pilot. Within two months of obtaining his wings he achieved ace status. As a squadron commander he modelled himself on Manfred von RICHTHOFEN, even painting his aircraft red. In 1918 he was given command of all Austro-Hungarian air forces involved in the Isonzo offensive. He is generally recognised as Austria-Hungary's leading ace, with thirty-five victories.

Brusilov, Aleksei Alekseevich (1853–1926) Russian military commander. Brusilov's war almost came to a premature conclusion. He was on holiday in Germany in July 1914 but managed to leave the country before hostilities broke out. A few days later he found himself GOC Eighth Army in Galicia. Brusilov was a cavalryman from an aristocratic background, but he had an open mind and was quick to realise the importance of artillery and machine guns on a modern battlefield. His careful planning, attention to detail and tactical flexibility that emphasised all-arms co-operation made Eighth Army the most consistently successful in the Russian order of battle. It

enjoyed some early successes and was one of the few formations to emerge with credit from the Russian disasters of 1915. In March 1916 Brusilov was chosen to replace the incompetent IVANOV in command of the south-west army group. During the spring of 1916 Russia came under intense pressure from Italy to launch an offensive on the Eastern Front. This gave Brusilov the opportunity to put into practice the operational principles he had distilled from the Russian failures of 1914 and 1915. Many of his fellow commanders attributed these failures to inadequate resources, and EVERT, in particular, chose to sit behind a mountain of shells and wait for something to happen. Brusilov's analysis was different. He believed that the failures had been operational. His campaign would be built on the principles of deception, surprise and momentum, designed to throw the enemy off balance, disrupt his reserves and puncture his front, prefiguring later Red Army theory. He used careful concealment of his attack formations and deployed a formidable artillery bombardment controlled from the air by radio. The blow fell on 4 June and inflicted stunning losses on the Austrian Fourth and Seventh Armies. The Austro-Hungarian armies lost 1.5M men, including 400,000 prisoners and 25,000 square kilometres of territory. The 'Brusilov offensive' terminated what hopes remained of an Austrian victory in the East, halted Austrian attacks in Italy and brought Romania into the war on the Allied side (a mixed blessing). The attack might have reaped an even richer reward had the pusillanimous EVERT, with far more men and guns than Brusilov, not failed to attack the Germans in the north, as agreed. Brusilov's advance was disrupted by the need to rescue Romania from German invasion and gradually petered out. Brusilov was among the officers who favoured the Tsar's abdication. The Provisional Government made him Commander-in-Chief in 1917. He led the Seventh and Eleventh Armies in the KER-

ENSKY offensive (July 1917) before he was replaced by KORNILOV on 1 August. Brusilov later offered his services to the Bolsheviks and took the army to the gates of Warsaw in 1920. He was one of the greatest and most innovative commanders to emerge from the war.

Bryan, William Jennings (1860–1925) US politician. After three times failing to win the presidency of the United States as the Democratic nominee, Bryan served as Woodrow WILSON's Secretary of State from 1913 until 1915, when he resigned in the aftermath of the sinking of the *Lusitania*, having become convinced that Wilson would eventually abandon the policy of neutrality and become involved in a war that Bryan regarded as entirely avoidable and wholly unnecessary. His resignation freed him to oppose 'preparedness' and to advocate the virtues of 'absolute neutrality' and impartial treatment of the belligerents that would have prevented US economic aid to the Allies. Wilson's re-election in November 1916, ironically on a peace platform, marginalised Bryan's influence, while US entry into the war five months later virtually extinguished it.

Bryce, James, Viscount Bryce (1838–1922) British jurist, historian and diplomat. His *Report of the Committee on Alleged German Outrages*, which appeared in May 1915, struck a damaging propaganda blow against Germany, especially in the United States, where Bryce had achieved a high reputation as a scholar and admirer of American institutions during his period as British Ambassador (1907–13). Although German behaviour in the invasion of Belgium had deliberately broken the laws of war in an attempt to intimidate the civilian population and prevent them from sabotaging the German lines of communication, Bryce's account of the violations was extreme and based on unreliable evidence. The eventual discrediting of the Bryce report

provided ammunition for those, such as Arthur PONSONBY, who argued that the war was the result of sinister manipulation by undemocratic forces. More seriously, it also led to a cynical attitude that all accounts of atrocities must be exaggerated or even completely fraudulent, which undoubtedly played a part in British and American reluctance to accept accounts of the fate of the Jews in Nazi-occupied Europe.

Buchan, John (1875–1940) British author and propagandist. Buchan was the son of a Scottish Free Church minister. After a successful academic career at Glasgow and Oxford universities, he served as Private Secretary to Lord MILNER in South Africa, before turning to publishing and writing. His spy story, *The Thirty-Nine Steps*, began its serialisation on the eve of war and was a phenomenal success. This brought Buchan to the attention of Charles MASTERMAN, head of the government's secret War Propaganda Bureau, who recruited him to write an account of the war. Buchan agreed to do this, but under his own auspices. The first of twenty-four volumes appeared in February 1915 as *Nelson's History of the War*, with the profits distributed to war charities. Later the same year he was appointed one of the five official war correspondents on the Western Front, where his openly propagandist approach to reporting endeared him to high military authority. In June 1916 he joined the British Expeditionary Force's GHQ to write its official communiqués. (He was later to be responsible for the supreme clarity of Field-Marshal HAIG's Final Dispatch of April 1919.) From February 1917 Buchan became Director of the new Department of Information, which greatly increased the scale of Britain's propaganda effort. The appointment of Lord Beaverbrook (*see* AITKEN, WILLIAM MAXWELL) as Britain's first Minister of Information in February 1918 somewhat reduced Buchan's role, but he worked well with Beaverbrook, whose ministerial clout did much to protect Buchan from his enemies in the liberal press.

Buchanan, George William (1854–1924) British diplomat, Ambassador to St Petersburg 1910–18. Buchanan was an experienced, cultivated, plain-dealing, plain-spoken, far-sighted man. He immediately recognised that war was likely to bring revolution to Russia in its wake. But he carried out his duty to try to maximise the Russian war effort. He admired Tsar NICHOLAS II as a man and could even find virtue in the Tsarina ALEKSANDRA FEODOROVNA, but his admiration never blinded him to their complete lack of political imagination and understanding, which he felt duty bound to bring to their attention in uncompromising fashion. Although he deployed all his influence and energy to prevent Russia making a separate peace after the fall of the tsar, he was pessimistic about the possibilities of democracy and doubted Russia's ability to contribute more to the Allied war effort. He left Russia in January 1918 but retained an influence on British policy. He regarded Bolshevism as potentially disastrous for Russia and for Europe and advocated intervention in the civil war. His memoir *My Mission to Russia*, published in 1923, and his daughter Meriel's *The Dissolution of an Empire*, published in 1932, provide valuable accounts of Russia's slide into disintegration and revolution.

Budworth, Charles Edward Dutton (1869–1921) British soldier, RAWLINSON's chief gunner in Fourth Army from May 1916 until the end of the war. He is credited by the British official history with being the first to advocate use of the creeping barrage.

Bulfin, Edward Stanislaus (1862–1939) British military commmander. Bulfin began the war as GOC 2nd Brigade in the original British Expeditionary Force. He

established a reputation as a cool, courageous and inspirational leader, principally as organiser of the makeshift 'Bulfin's force', which he led in an important attack near Gheluvelt at the height of the fighting at First Ypres on 31 October 1914, driving back the German line half a mile. HAIG described Bulfin at this time as a 'tower of strength'. But from the autumn of 1915 his career stalled. He was sent home sick on 11 October and did not return to action until June 1916. His new command, the 60th Division, a second-line Territorial unit, played no significant part in the historic fighting of 1916 and in December was transferred to the malarial backwater of Salonika. Bulfin's career was rescued in June 1917 from possible oblivion by the division's transfer to Egypt, where the new Commander-in-Chief, Sir Edmund ALLENBY, recognised the qualities of its commander and promptly made him GOC XXI Corps. Bulfin proved to be a very dependable subordinate, playing the bludgeon to Sir Philip CHETWODE's rapier (GOC XX Corps) during Allenby's campaigns in 1917 (which led to the capture of Jerusalem) and 1918 (which brought about the destruction of Turkish military power in Palestine). Bulfin was a man of considerable moral as well as physical courage, perfectly prepared to tell his superiors uncomfortable truths. Although an exacting commander, he retained the regimental officer's concern for the welfare of his men. In his professional competence and humane paternalism he represented the best qualities of the British Edwardian officer corps.

Bull, Lucien (1876–1972) Anglo-French inventor. Bull's expertise in the design of graphical recording devices for use in cardiovascular diagnosis at the Institut Marey in Paris, where he was Deputy Director, made him a central figure in the history of 'sound ranging', a technology that emerged during the war to identify enemy gun positions instrumentally. Bull was particularly supportive of the pioneering work of Charles NORDMANN. The work of Bull's team also stimulated the British into action and a committee under Major Harold WINTERBOTHAM, Royal Engineers, was sent to report on the apparatus developed by Bull. The outcome of Winterbotham's report was the dispatch to France in August 1915 of the leading British physicist, Lawrence BRAGG, who established the first British sound-ranging unit (section 'W') in October.

Bullard, Eugene Jacques (1894–1961) US-French airman. Gene Bullard was the United States' first black pilot. He was born in Georgia, the son of a former slave, and left for Europe after the lynching of his brother, arriving first in Britain then moving to France. He joined the French Foreign Legion in October 1914 and was later wounded. He obtained his wings in 1917 and flew combat missions later in the year, scoring two 'kills'.

Bullard, Robert Lee (1861–1947) US military commander. A southerner from Alabama, he showed remarkable precociousness at the age of 6 by persuading his parents to change his name from William Robert Bullard to Robert Lee Bullard in honour of the Confederate leader in the American Civil War. During a varied pre-war career, he became close to General John J. PERSHING. When the United States entered the war in April 1917, Bullard was well placed to rise. And this he duly did, from GOC US 2nd Brigade in June 1917 to GOC US Second Army by the end of the war. His US 1st Infantry Division ('The Big Red One') distinguished itself in carrying out the American Expeditionary Force's first major offensive of the war, at Cantigny in April 1918. In July, as GOC III Corps, he took part in the sanguinary Aisne-Marne and Meuse-Argonne offensives. He allowed a surprising degree of latitude to his chief of staff at III Corps, the brilliant Brigadier-General A.W. Bjornstad, a state of affairs that was speedily terminated

by Bullard's successor, Major-General J.L. Hines. Bullard often served in mixed Franco-American operations, during which he showed a commendable awareness of French sensibilities, helped by his fluency in the French language. Like the army in which he served, Bullard came a long way in a short time during the war.

Bülow, Karl Wilhelm Paul von (1846–1921) German military commander, who led the Second Army in the invasion of Belgium and France, capturing Namur and defeating LANREZAC's French Fifth Army at Charleroi (22–23 August 1914). He inflicted a second defeat on Lanrezac at Guise (29–30 August) but at the cost of opening a worrying gap between his army and that of General Alexander von KLUCK to his right. In order to close the gap, he requested Kluck to alter his axis of advance towards the south-east. This opened Kluck's right flank to the possibility of an attack from the French Sixth Army, garrisoning Paris, and created the conditions for the Allied counter-attack, known as the battle of the Marne. The attack against Kluck dismayed Bülow, who sensed disaster. The retreat of Second Army threatened First Army with encirclement and brought about the retreat of the whole German right-wing. Bülow's caution and pessimism has often been held responsible for the failure of the SCHLIEFFEN Plan, though this view seems rather simplistic. Surprisingly, perhaps, he was not relieved of command. He was promoted Field-Marshal in January 1915 but suffered a heart attack in March and never returned to active duty.

Burian von Rajecz, Istvan, Count (1851–1922) Austro-Hungarian politician. Burian succeeded BERCHTOLD as Foreign Minister in January 1915. The principal test of his diplomatic skill was presented by Austria's ally rather than her enemies. He successfully resisted German pressure to make territorial concessions to Italy, demanded recognition of Austrian equality in the conduct of the war on the Eastern Front and showed himself determined to obtain German acceptance of Austrian interests in Poland. He also opposed German threats to launch a campaign of unrestricted submarine warfare. He was instrumental in bringing Bulgaria into the war on the side of the Central Powers and strengthened Austrian ties with the Ottoman Empire. But, in the end, he was undone by the reality of the German–Austrian relationship and the conflict between German and Austrian interests. His advocacy of a compromise peace that would restore Allied territory in the West in return for Allied acceptance of the Central Powers' gains in the East was anathema to Germany. Burian was forced to resign in December 1916. He returned to office only in April 1918 with a brief to end the war. When it became apparent that the Allies would never accept a negotiated settlement he resigned for the final time in October 1918.

Burney, Cecil (1858–1929) British naval commander. Burney was JELLICOE's second in command at the battle of Jutland (31 May–1 June 1916), during which he led the 1st Battle Squadron in his flagship, HMS *Marlborough*. He was yet another of Jellicoe's 'autocue admirals', competent and reliable as long as they did not have to depart from the script. In Burney's case orthodoxy and lack of imagination were reinforced by ill health (rheumatism), whose depressing effect tended to make him even more cautious and pessimistic.

Burrowes, Arnold Robinson (1869–1949) British soldier. As a major in the Royal Irish Fusiliers before the war, Burrowes designed the service web equipment adopted as standard throughout the army after 1908. Practical and ergonomic, especially after modifications in the light of trench warfare and combat conditions, it served the British soldier well throughout the war.

Burstall, Henry Edward (1870–1945) Canadian military commander. Burstall was that rare bird, a Canadian Regular. After graduating from the Royal Military College of Canada, at Kingston, Ontario, he joined the Royal Canadian Artillery. He served in the South African War (1899–1902). He was CO of the Royal Canadian Horse Artillery from 1907 to 1911, when he became Inspector of Canadian Artillery, a post he still held when war broke out. His expertise as a gunner initially confined him to artillery appointments in the Canadian Corps on the Western Front, first as BGRA 1st (Canadian) Division and then as MGRA Canadian Corps. But at the end of the Somme fighting in 1916 he was given his chance as a field commander, as GOC 2nd (Canadian) Division. He commanded the division for the rest of the war, and his achievements included the capture of Vimy Ridge and Passchendaele in 1917 and the breaking of the Hindenburg Line in 1918.

Butler, Richard Harte Keating (1870–1935) British staff officer and military commander. Butler was an able and ambitious officer, with a fine reputation as a trainer of troops and leader of men, who was fated to spend most of the war as a staff officer. This was due almost entirely to Douglas HAIG, who developed a high regard for Butler's administrative abilities while he was GOC Aldershot. Haig was equally impressed by Butler's loyalty. His trust became almost total. On two occasions, in December 1915 and again in January 1918, the Commander-in-Chief tried unsuccessfully to get Butler as his Chief of the General Staff. Butler did, however, serve on Haig's staff for three years, first as BGGS I Corps, then as MGGS First Army and, finally, as Deputy Chief of the General Staff. In the latter post, he displayed a genius for giving offence, and his relations with the BEF's army commanders were poor. GOUGH and RAWLINSON, in particular, were critical of Butler's control of access to Haig. Butler, although fiercely loyal to Haig, was resentful at being kept in a 'staff ghetto' where the chances of promotion, honour and fame available to field commanders were denied him. However, when he did get command of III Corps, as a result of the sweeping changes to Haig's GHQ in February 1918, his performance was notably indifferent.

Butterworth, George Sainton Kaye (1885–1916) British composer, critic and collector of folk songs, killed in action on 5 August 1916 at Pozières while serving as a subaltern with the 13th Battalion Durham Light Infantry. His body was never recovered and his name is commemorated on the Memorial to the Missing of the Somme at Thiepval. Butterworth's setting of Housman's 'A Shropshire Lad' and his rhapsody 'The Banks of Green Willow' had established him as a composer of exceptional promise. He won the Military Cross.

Byng, Julian Hedworth George (1862–1935) British military commander. Byng was a cavalryman whose service on the Western Front began with command of the 3rd Cavalry Division at Ypres in 1914. After a brief period in command of the Cavalry Corps in 1915 he was transfered to Gallipoli, where he succeeded the inadequate STOPFORD in command of IX Corps too late to make any difference to the campaign's outcome. Byng's rise to eminence began with his appointment as GOC Canadian Corps in May 1916 in succession to Sir Edwin ALDERSON. Byng commanded the corps during its famous capture of Vimy Ridge in April 1917, an achievement that did much to secure his command of Third Army in June in succession to Sir Edmund ALLENBY. In November 1917 Third Army launched a surprise attack against the German line at Cambrai. Tanks were used *en masse* for the first time in the history of war, preceded by dummy smokescreens designed to confuse the defenders as to the actual point of assault and a sophisticated artillery bombardment made without pre-registering the guns. The initial attack was so successful that church bells were rung in Britain to proclaim the 'victory', but the British line crumpled in the face of a concerted German counter-attack using 'infiltration' tactics. Byng, however, deflected criticism of his actions by removing three corps commanders and casting shameful aspersions on the courage and competence of junior officers and men. Neither he nor his chief of staff gave evidence to the Cambrai commission of inquiry. During the German spring offensive Byng again scapegoated subordinate commanders after his somewhat tardy evacuation of the Flesquières salient. The otherwise resolute defence of Arras against the German *Mars* attack, however, did much to restore Byng's reputation. During the 'Great Advance' in the second half of 1918 Third Army was the largest of the five armies in the BEF. It played a vital role in the German defeat and one that has – as yet – to receive the recognition it deserves. After the war Byng served as Governor-General of Canada (1921–26) and Chief Commissioner of the Metropolitan Police (1928–31).

C

Cabrinovic, Nedjelko (1895–1916) Failed assassin. Cabrinovic was one of the seven assassins assembled by the Serb 'Black Hand' terror group to murder the Archduke FRANZ FERDINAND during his visit to Sarajevo in June 1914. He and the eventual assassin, Gavrilo PRINCIP, were the only two to act. Cabrinovic threw a bomb at the Archduke's car but it failed to explode. One failure, however, was not enough. He next failed to kill himself with the poison thoughtfully provided by his controllers and then failed to escape. Like Princip, Cabrinovic was a combustible mixture of half-educated, unfocused political idealism, poverty and ambition. Unlike Princip, he showed remorse for his actions. He died in prison from tuberculosis in January 1916.

Cadorna, Luigi (1850–1928) Italian Commander-in-Chief 1915–17. Cadorna commanded the Italian army, which he had done his utmost to prepare for war, from May 1915 until he was replaced after the humiliating defeat at Caporetto in November 1917. Italy's strategic position was a difficult one, with the Austrians strongly entrenched on the high ground. This left little room for the war of manoeuvre and 'shock' that Cadorna favoured, and he was reduced to launching a series of 'breakthrough' offensives along the Isonzo river that consisted of little more than infantry frontal assaults with inadequate artillery support. He did, however, succeed in stopping the Austrian Trentino offensive (May–June 1916) and captured Gorizia in August 1916. Cadorna's command style was autocratic. He treated politicians and the press with contempt. He regularly castigated public opinion for apathy and defeatism, a condition that he did nothing to repair. He ruthlessly dismissed senior commanders (217 in all) and sought to maintain military morale through a series of brutal, summary executions (of which there were some 750) more appropriate to a barbarian horde than the army of a constitutional monarchy. Even though he succeeded in halting the Austro-German advance on the Piave after Caporetto, Cadorna's position had become untenable, and he was replaced by General DIAZ. He was heavily criticised by an official inquiry into the Caporetto defeat in 1919, though the blame did not entirely belong with him.

Caillaux, Joseph Marie Auguste (1863–1944) French politician. During his brief prime ministership, during the Agadir Crisis, Caillaux made concessions to Germany of French territory in Cameroon in order to avoid war over Morocco. This policy was entirely sensible. France was not well placed to fight a war with Germany in 1911. His actions were characterised by his enemies as those of a

Germanophile and pacifist, however, a view that was reinforced by his later opposition to the extension of conscription through the Three-Year Service Law. He was subjected to a virulent press campaign of abuse that culminated in Mme Caillaux's sensational murder of the editor of *Le Figaro*. During the war Caillaux came to symbolise defeatism for many ultra-patriots. In January 1918 CLEMENCEAU had him arrested and imprisoned. He was not brought to trial until 1920, when he was acquitted. Although increasing French disillusionment with the war that followed the Calvary of Verdun encouraged Caillaux to entertain thoughts of becoming a 'peace prime minister', it is clear that he was not prepared to contemplate any settlement that did not include the return of Alsace-Lorraine.

Callaghan, George Astley (1852–1920) British naval commander. Callaghan was C-in-C Home Fleet when the war broke out. His appointment, which had already been extended for a year, was due to expire on 1 October. The First Sea Lord, Winston CHURCHILL, however, lost no time in expediting Callaghan's retirement and replacing him immediately with his designated successor Admiral JELLICOE, eight years his junior. Jellicoe was embarrassed by the whole proceeding and did his best to prevent it, displaying a degree of sensitivity to the feelings of others that doubtless did him credit but was interpreted by some as a worrying lack of ruthlessness and a subconscious indication of self-doubt.

Calthorpe, Somerset Arthur Gough (1864–1937) British naval commander, who was appointed C-in-C Mediterranean with a brief to wrest control over the anti-submarine campaign from the French. This was predictably difficult, and he enjoyed only partial success. He did succeed, however, in concluding an armistice with the Turks at Mudros in October 1918 that excluded the French.

The honour of leading the Allied fleet through the Dardanelles on 12 November also fell to him, three years after the British and French navies had failed to achieve this by force of arms.

Cambon, Paul (1843–1924) French diplomat, Ambassador to Great Britain 1898–1920. Cambon took up his appointment during the Fashoda Crisis of 1898 and devoted the rest of his long embassy to improving Anglo-French relations. He was one of the principal architects of the Anglo-French Entente (the 'Entente Cordiale') of 1904 and of the eventual Franco-British alliance that fought and won the First World War. His skilful diplomacy during the Moroccan Crisis of 1905 greatly strengthened France's diplomatic position, and he was a chief sponsor of the Anglo-French military staff talks that followed from it.

Campbell, David Graham Muschet (1869–1936) British military commander. Campbell's pre-war reputation was based on his fame as a horseman. In 1896 he won the Grand National, the Irish National Hunt Cup and the Grand Military Steeplechase, a unique record. Campbell began the war as CO of the 9th Lancers, a regiment with a reputation for 'smartness' (in the military rather than the social sense). In many respects, Campbell's war career reflects that of the British Expeditionary Force (BEF) as a whole. In August and September 1914 he led some of the last cavalry charges made by the British army. (Significantly, perhaps, Campbell was obeying orders and would have preferred to fight dismounted.) On 7 September he became one of the last men in military history to be wounded by a lance. His promotion to GOC 6th (Cavalry) Brigade in November 1914 did not diminish his front line instincts. He was again wounded, this time by a shell, on 13 May 1915 in the same incident that resulted in the death of the poet Julian GRENFELL. On 22 May 1916 Campbell was promoted again, this time to command the 21st Division, which had been so cruelly used at the battle of Loos the previous September. He commanded 21st Division for the rest of the war, during which it saw much combat, not least in the German spring offensive of 1918, when it fought three major actions at Epéhy and Chapel Hill, Messines Ridge and the Aisne. Campbell was among the British officers who protested fiercely but ineffectually to the commander of the French Sixth Army, General DUCHÊNE, about his disastrous deployment on the Aisne. Campbell described 27 May 1918 as 'the worst day I have spent in this war, which is saying a lot'. By the Armistice he was the fifth longest serving divisional commander in the BEF. Campbell was a pukka Regular. He did not compromise the military standards with which he was inculcated as a regimental officer. He did not suffer fools gladly, and he was quite prepared to protest to his seniors when he thought that their orders were unreasonable, which was quite often. But he was also prepared to listen. He had a penetrating mind and would spare no effort to find solutions to tactical problems. He regarded visits to the front line as a duty and carried out his own aerial reconnaissance. He was also an excellent trainer of troops. His man-management skills were also exceptional, and he enjoyed the support and confidence of some remarkable subordinates, including Cecil RAWLING, George GATER and Hanway CUMMING.

Campbell, Ronald Bruce (1878–1963) British army officer, whose blood-curdling lecture on bayonet fighting, delivered in the notorious Bull Ring training camp at Étaples, made lasting impressions (of varied kinds) on many who heard it. Few men were killed by bayonets during the Great War, and the majority of them probably had their hands in the air at the time, but troop trainers, then and since, valued the 'spirit of the bayonet' for the

aggression and willingness to kill that it imparted to often deeply civilian recruits.

Campbell, Walter (1864–1936) British staff officer. A Cambridge and Staff College graduate, Campbell spent most of his military career as an administrative staff officer, a role in which he performed with outstanding success. He began the war as Assistant Adjutant and Quartermaster-General in 6th Division, part of the British Expeditionary Force on the Western Front, but was rapidly promoted Deputy Adjutant and Quartermaster-General (DAQMG) III Corps and then Third Army. In October 1915, however, he left the Western Front for the post of Deputy Quartermaster-General of the Egyptian Expeditionary Force, a post he retained for the rest of the war. For the first month, until succeeded by Brigadier-General G.F. MACMUNN, he supervised the logistical arrangements at the Dardanelles, where he did much to overcome administrative confusion and set an inspiring example of high-minded duty. MacMunn's appointment allowed him to concentrate on Egypt, where he transformed the EEF's logistical infrastructure, building railways and pipelines across the Sinai and rapidly reorganising captured ports, such as Haifa and Beirut, immediately after their capture. His work in supplying the EEF did much to sustain morale and was fundamental to the strategic and operational successes achieved by ALLENBY in 1917 and 1918. 'I wish I could feel that I had done half as much for the world as Walter Campbell,' his former commander at Third Army, Sir Charles MONRO, later declared.

Cannan, May Wedderburn (1893–1973) British poet. Cannan was the daughter of an Oxford don. She joined the Voluntary Aid Detachment before the war, at the outbreak of which she was sent to France to organise a sixty-bed hospital in Rouen (the subject of one of her best-known poems), but she was soon compelled to yield its management to a senior RAMC officer. After a few weeks as a nurse, she returned to England, where she worked at the Oxford University Press, at that time considerably involved in publishing the propaganda output of the secret War Propaganda Bureau. She later worked for British intelligence in Paris. She published three volumes of poetry, *In War Time* (1917), *The Splendid House* (1919) and *The House of Hope* (1920). Cannan was a convinced believer in the rightness of the British cause. Her failure to embrace the literature of disillusionment means that her work is now little read, but it stands as a timely reminder of contemporary attitudes. In 1976 her very fine posthumous autobiography, *Grey Ghosts and Voices*, was published. Her correspondence with her fiancé, Bevil Quiller-Couch, who died during the great influenza pandemic in 1919, was published in 2000.

Capelle, Eduard von (1855–1931) German sailor and politician. An early associate and supporter of TIRPITZ, for whom he drafted the expansionist Navy Laws of 1898 and 1900, Capelle eventually developed a more realistic appreciation of the surface fleet's capabilities. This distanced him from his former mentor and hastened his retirement in 1915. Following Tirpitz's dismissal in March 1916, however, Capelle replaced him as State Secretary of the Navy Office, a post he held with diminishing effectiveness until October 1918. Throughout his career Capelle disappointed his superiors, not because he was strong and independent minded but because he was weak and independent minded. Appointed in March 1916 to add support to BETHMANN-HOLLWEG's opposition to submarine warfare, Capelle gradually came to advocate it but in such a way that he retained the respect of neither side in the argument. Only the Kaiser's fear of Tirpitz's return kept Capelle in office during the last year of the war.

Capello, Luigi Atillio (1859–1941) Italian military commander. An ambitious self-publicist who knew how to use the press, he rose swiftly during the war from GOC 25th Division in 1915 to GOC Second Army in 1917. He was distrusted by the Italian Commander-in-Chief, CADORNA, who transferred him to the relative backwater of the Trentino sector. He returned to the Isonzo for the Eleventh Battle in the late summer and autumn of 1917, playing a decisive role in the capture of Bainsizza. Ironically, this was to prove Capello's undoing. Their reverse persuaded the Austrians to seek German support for the counter-attack that became the battle of Caporetto. Capello, with characteristic self-confidence and bombast, ignored signs of the impending Austro-German attack, refused Cadorna's order to withdraw his artillery to safety and – in a FOCH-like gesture – prepared his own troops to attack. The result was a virtual rout that threatened to knock Italy out of the war and ruined Capello's reputation.

Capper, John Edward (1861–1955) British armoured warfare pioneer. Capper was an adventurous officer who spent much of his career on the experimental edge of emerging military technologies. He was Commandant of the Balloon School 1903–10, during which time he was co-pilot on a record-breaking non-rigid airship flight (1907). During the war, after spells as a chief engineer and divisional commander, he became first Director-General of the Tank Corps (1917). He was the brother of Major-General Thompson CAPPER.

Capper, Thompson (1863–1915) British military commander, who died of wounds received during the battle of Loos while GOC 7th Division. Tommy Capper was a man who divided opinion. Some considered him to be touched by genius, a soldier whose mastery of the unpredictable was often favourably compared with the stolidity of his contemporary Douglas HAIG. As an instructor at the Staff College before the war Capper won golden opinions as an inspirational teacher, credited with introducing a range of practical innovations. His critics, including Haig, thought him an unbalanced crank, whose unyielding sense of duty resulted in a fixation with the 'offensive spirit' and a morbid fascination with death. He was the brother of Major-General J.E. CAPPER.

Carden, Sackville Hamilton (1857–1930) British naval commander. Carden began the war as superintendent of the naval dockyard at Malta, a post from which he was somewhat surprisingly promoted to replace Admiral MILNE as C-in-C Eastern Mediterranean Squadron in the wake of the *Goeben* fiasco. It was Carden who received Winston CHURCHILL's fateful telegram, in January 1915, enquiring whether he thought it was 'a practicable operation to force the Dardanelles by the use of ships alone'. Carden replied that he did not think it was practicable to 'rush' the Dardanelles but believed that they 'might be forced by extended operations with a large number of ships'. He then submitted a detailed three-phase plan. The systematic reduction of the Turkish forts guarding the entrance to the Dardanelles by naval gunfire would be followed by destruction of the defences on the Gallipoli peninsula along the Narrows. Minesweeping operations could then take place in safety, allowing the British fleet to sail into the Sea of Marmora, where its appearance was expected to compel a Turkish surrender. Armed with these plans, Churchill convinced the War Committee to support the operation. This began on 19 February. Hampered by poor visibility, inadequate ammunition and the constant threat of Turkish mines and torpedoes, naval gunfire proved disappointing. The attack was renewed on 25 February and did sufficient damage to the Turkish forts to convince Carden to begin minesweeping operations the following day. These were a disaster. Batteries of mobile KRUPP howitzers, untouched by

the bombardment, wreaked havoc on the morale of the civilian minesweeping crews on their converted North Sea trawlers. Carden's plan began to unravel ominously. The refusal of the minesweepers to renew the attack until the guns were silenced forced him, on 13 March, to reverse his plan and send ships to demolish the Turkish defences before the minesweeping was completed. Already ill with an ulcer, he broke down under the strain four days later and was replaced by Admiral Sir John DE ROBECK.

Carline, Sydney (1888–1929) British war artist, best known for his paintings of the war in the Middle East, especially *The Destruction of the Turkish Transport*. After the war he illustrated T.E. LAWRENCE's *Revolt in the Desert*.

Carol I (1839–1914) King of Romania. A Prussian prince by birth, he was pro-German by inclination, but lacked the power to bring Romania into the war on the side of the Central Powers. Humiliated by Romanian neutrality, he was contemplating abdication when he died in October 1914.

Carpenter, Alfred Francis Blakeney (1881–1955) British naval hero. As Captain of HMS *Vindictive* Carpenter was given a leading part in the British attempt to block the exits to Zeebrugge and Ostend harbours in April 1918, penning the German submarines and patrol boats based there. *Vindictive* was charged with landing troops to destroy the German shore batteries but (in complete darkness) managed to moor in the wrong place and came under heavy fire. Carpenter, in a display of great courage and calmness, walked the decks, supervising the landing. Without support from *Vindictive*'s guns, however, the troops failed in their objective, suffering heavy casualties. Although blockships were sunk, little disruption of German operations was actually achieved. British propaganda, however, turned the raid (which took place on St George's Day) into a major success, in the tradition of Drake's attack on Cadiz. Carpenter was subsequently awarded the Victoria Cross on the ballot of those involved in the operation.

Carrel, Alexis (1873–1944) French doctor, an authority on the treatment of infected wounds. Carrel and the British-born Dr Henry DAKIN, both of whom were based in New York, developed a method of treatment that involved cleaning wounds with a solution of sodium hypochlorite administered through a system of tubes. Its widespread adoption in 1917 produced a significant reduction in casualties suffered from gas gangrene. In March 2000 two of the world's first batch of cloned pigs were named 'Alexis' and 'Carrel' in his honour. His pioneering work on suturing blood vessels, for which he was awarded the Nobel Prize for Medicine in 1912, later became essential to the technique of organ transplant surgery.

Carrington, Charles Edmund (1897–1990) British soldier and memoirist. Carrington enlisted as a 17-year-old in 1914 and the following year was commissioned in a Territorial battalion of the Royal Warwickshire Regiment (1/5th), serving in France and Italy and winning the Military Cross. He went to Oxford after the war and spent most of his working life as a teacher, publisher and author, becoming an authority on KIPLING. He was Professor of British Commonwealth Relations at the Royal Institute of International Affairs from 1954 until 1962. In 1964 he published *Soldier from the Wars Returning*, an expanded account of his wartime experiences that first appeared as *A Subaltern's War* (written under the pseudonym 'Charles Edmonds' in 1929). Carrington's memoir voices the thoughts and feelings of the '1914 generation', many of whom were appalled by the pitying condescension of posterity that had come to regard the men who fought

the war as 'victims' without the capacity for moral choice. The book has even less patience with those who would condemn British commanders as 'donkeys'.

Carson, Edward Henry (1854–1935) British politician. Carson was a formidable advocate, one of the greatest of his generation. As the leader of Ulster Unionism, however, he showed himself more than willing to tread the path of violence as well as that of reason. In 1912 he organised the 80,000-strong paramilitary Ulster Volunteer Force (UVF) to resist, if necessary by force, the imposition of Irish Home Rule. On the outbreak of war, many members of the UVF, with Carson's encouragement, volunteered for military service with the 36th (Ulster) Division. Carson himself embraced the spirit of national unity by joining ASQUITH's coalition government in May 1915 as Attorney-General, but he soon became disillusioned, and his resignation in October 1916 was consciously designed to undermine Asquith's leadership. In December 1916 he joined LLOYD GEORGE's government as First Lord of the Admiralty. His judgement in naval matters, especially with regard to convoy, was sound but – for such a forceful personality – he was curiously reluctant to impose his will on naval professionals. In July 1917 he was replaced by Eric GEDDES, a man with no such inhibitions, but remained in government as a minister without portfolio. Carson was temperamentally better suited to opposition than to government, but Lloyd George was shrewd enough to recognise that it was much better to have him 'inside the tent pissing out' than 'outside the tent pissing in'.

Carter, Evan Eyare (1866–1933) British staff officer. Carter was commissioned in the Leicestershire Regiment in 1889 but transferred to the Army Service Corps (ASC) the following year. The ASC was one of the least glamorous formations in the British army, but during the Great

War its essential role was reflected in its tremendous growth. In August 1914 the ASC had 819 officers and 13,672 other ranks; by September 1918 it had 11,840 and 316,123 men, larger than the entire British army at the outbreak of war. Carter was not only a trained staff officer who had passed Staff College but he had also attended special courses in the financial management of large institutions run by the London School of Economics. This unusual combination of skills was recognised by Sir William ROBERTSON. On 27 September 1915, two days after Robertson became Chief of the General Staff of the British Expeditionary Force (BEF), Carter was appointed Director of Supplies. This anodyne sounding post, which he retained until the end of the war, gave him responsibility for the supply services of the largest army Britain has ever put into the field, with an annual turnover of more than £80M. This was quite a transformation in the career of a man who began the war as i/c Records, Woolwich Dockyard. Carter's contribution to the successful feeding of the BEF was instrumental in the maintenance of morale and fighting efficiency. He was a high-ranking Freemason.

Carter, William Henry 'Harry' (1879–1951) British army officer. He was a native of Wolverhampton who joined the 2nd Battalion South Staffordshire Regiment as a private soldier in 1899, serving in the South African War and in India. By August 1914 he had reached the dizzy heights of battalion signals sergeant. The British Expeditionary Force's heavy losses in officers, however, quickly opened up unimagined opportunities of promotion. Carter was commissioned in the field in January 1915 and soon became battalion adjutant. Between August 1916 and July 1917 he was placed successively in temporary command of the 17th Battalion Middlesex Regiment and the 13th Battalion Essex Regiment. On 22 July 1917 he became Commanding Officer of the 7th

Battalion South Staffordshire Regiment (33rd Brigade, 11th (Northern) Division) and commanded it with gallantry and distinction for the rest of the war. He was awarded the DSO and bar and MC and bar. After demobilisation he invested his gratuity of £1,500 in a poultry farm near Kidderminster, which failed. He then tried the taxi business, but this also failed. He worked for five years as a mechanic at AJS motorcycles in Wolverhampton; when interviewed by the *Birmingham Post* in 1934, he was a steel erector at James Gibbons & Co. Ltd. A fellow townsman recalled him as a 'common, rough Black Country working man', but on his wartime photographs he looks every inch the colonel. His career is a useful antidote to the stereotype of the public school Great War officer.

Casement, Roger David (1864–1916) British traitor and Irish nationalist hero. Casement was born in Dublin, the son of a Protestant father and a Roman Catholic mother. He spent most of his working life in the British consular service, first in Africa, then in Brazil. His reports strongly criticised the treatment of native workers in the Congo and the Amazon and created a public demand for reform. Casement was knighted for his work in 1911 and retired to Ireland. There his instinctive anti-imperialism began to take on an Irish nationalist perspective, and in 1913 he joined the Irish Volunteers. When war broke out he travelled from the United States, where he had been fund raising, to Berlin, hoping to secure German support for an Irish national uprising. In this he was disappointed. But in April 1916, on the eve of the Easter Rising, he was landed from a German submarine on a beach in County Kerry, intending to counsel against a rebellion. He was soon arrested, tried and hanged. The British establishment began a posthumous campaign against his reputation, leaking details of homosexual activities with native boys revealed in his so-called 'Black

Diary', the authenticity of which remains disputed.

Castelnau, Noel Joseph Edouard de Curières de (1851–1944) French military commander. Castelnau, although an able soldier, was a devout Roman Catholic and a lay member of the Capuchin order, nicknamed *Le Capuchin Botte* (the 'Fighting Friar'). This did nothing to recommend him to France's anti-clerical republican establishment and permanently blighted his career. As GOC Second Army his offensive in Lorraine, in August 1914, suffered a shattering defeat, but – like his former chief JOFFRE – Castlenau kept his nerve and eventually stabilised the front before being transferred to the French left during the so-called Race to the Sea. In 1915 Joffre chose him to command the Army Group Centre, responsible for conducting the costly and indecisive offensive in the Champagne. At Verdun Castelnau was Joffre's chief of staff. It was on his recommendation that PÉTAIN was placed in charge of Verdun's defence, a decision with far-reaching consequences, not least for Castelnau and his chief. Joffre's dismissal in December 1916 brought Castelnau's career to a shuddering halt. He remained unemployed until the autumn of 1918, when he was appointed to the command of Army Group East in Lorraine, thus ending the war where he began. Castelnau was an intelligent soldier, with a capacity for decision. His tactics in 1914 and 1915 were characterised by the optimism of the era, but his absence from the battlefield for almost two years of the war, during which many things changed, makes it difficult to form a fair judgement of him as a field commander.

Cavan, Earl of *see* LAMBART, FREDERICK RUDOLF.

Cavell, Edith (1865–1915) British nurse and war heroine. Her execution by a German firing squad in Brussels on 12 October 1915 for 'conducting soldiers to the enemy' confirmed, for many, Allied claims about German 'barbarism' and provided powerful propaganda at home and abroad. Cavell was not running an escape network but providing humanitarian relief for Allied soldiers separated from their units. Her execution was therefore contrary to German military law. Her treatment in captivity was harsh and her 'trial' a travesty. Cavell was a humane and decent woman who had done much to modernise Belgian nursing. Her famous declaration that 'patriotism is not enough' is indicative of her real motives. The values she truly represented have too often been traduced by the use made of her memory by British propagandists, for whom patriotism was more than enough.

Cavid Bey, Mehmet *see* DJAVED BEY, MEHMET.

Cemal Pasa, Ahmed *see* DJEMAL PASHA, AHMED.

Chamberlain, (Arthur) Neville (1869–1940) British politician, appointed by LLOYD GEORGE as the first Director-General of National Service in December 1916. Lloyd George's determination to win the war told him to extend compulsion to civilian life, but his political instincts told him that this was impossible. This ambiguity was implicit in the legislation that established the Ministry of National Service in March 1917. Chamberlain was given responsibilities that only the power of compulsion could fulfil while being hamstrung by retention of the voluntary principle. Any prospect of his being able to establish a rational manpower plan was further undermined by his complete lack of authority over military recruiting. Realising that his position was impossible, Chamberlain resigned in August 1917. His experience left him with a lifelong distrust of Lloyd George.

Chamberlain, (Joseph) Austen (1863–1937) British politician, who became Secretary of State for India in the ASQUITH coalition government, retaining the post under LLOYD GEORGE. F.E. Smith famously said of Chamberlain that 'Austen always played the game and always lost'. During the First World War he got to play the 'Great Game' of Indian imperial power. He lost that, too. Both Chamberlain and his predecessor, the Marquis of Crewe, failed to act on their doubts about military operations in Mesopotamia and blithely accepted the facile assurances of the Indian authorities that important victories could be achieved at little risk or cost. This proved not to be the case and resulted, in April 1916, in the humiliating surrender of General TOWNSHEND's army at Kut. Chamberlain resigned in 1917 after being criticised in the report of the Mesopotamia Commission of Inquiry. He joined Lloyd George's War Cabinet in 1918.

Chapman, Guy (1889–1972) British soldier. Chapman volunteered for military service on the outbreak of war and served in the 13th Battalion Royal Fusiliers on the Western Front. After the war he abandoned law for an academic career and became Professor of Modern History at Leeds University. In 1933 he published *A Passionate Prodigality*, an account of his wartime experiences. He was also responsible for an influential collection of prose accounts of the war, *Vain Glory* (1937).

Charlton, (Arthur) Humphrey (1892–1982) British soldier. Charlton was the son of a Staffordshire clergyman and a farmer by occupation. He volunteered in December 1914, joining the Army Veterinary Corps as a private soldier, with special responsibility for horses. He was not commissioned until November 1915. He served on the Western Front before and after his commissioning and was gassed in March 1917. On 29 September 1918 the 46th (North Midland) Division,

spearheaded by the 137th (Staffordshire) Brigade, broke the Hindenburg Line at Bellenglise. Charlton's battalion, 1/6th North Staffordshire, was on the left of the 46th Division's front. 'B' company was tasked with capture of the key Riqueval bridge spanning the St Quentin canal. Charlton, together with nine men, eight from his own battalion and a sapper from the 466th (1/2nd North Midland) Field Company, R.E., stormed the machine gun defending the bridge. It was the sapper, Lance-Corporal F. Openshaw, who bayoneted two members of the German demolition party trying to detonate the charges that had been laid, before assisting Charlton to defuse them. They were protected from enemy interference by the actions of Lance-Corporal J. Smith, who had earlier killed the German machine-gun team guarding the bridge. 'B' company then crossed the canal, capturing 130 prisoners and a battalion staff. Charlton was later awarded the DSO for his exploit, to which he added a Military Cross on 3 October after capturing two German field guns and a machine-gun nest. (Openshaw was awarded the DCM and Smith a bar to his DCM.) The Allied Commander-in-Chief, FOCH, described the breaking of the Hindenburg Line as 'the blow from which there could be no [German] recovery'. As a decisive actor at a vital point of a vital attack, Charlton therefore has a modest claim to be 'the man who won the war'. The bridge was subsequently renamed 'Charlton Bridge' in his honour.

Charteris, John (1877–1946) British staff officer. Charteris was Chief Intelligence Officer at GHQ from December 1915 until January 1918. As a day-to-day intelligence officer, providing accurate and up-to-date information about the German order of battle, he was conscientious, methodical and efficient. He built well on the foundations that he inherited, and left to his successors a smoothly functioning organisation. His assessments of wider intelligence matters, especially those relating to German morale and manpower were less impressive, however, bordering at times on wishful thinking. This has often led to his depiction as HAIG's 'evil counsellor', deliberately telling the 'Chief' what he most wanted to hear and encouraging the 'disastrous grandiosity' of his strategy, especially at 'Passchendaele'. There is no substance to this charge. Charteris' contemporary papers show that he shared Haig's optimism about the course of the war rather than being the cause of it. Charteris was never popular – even with Lady Haig. His rapid promotion – in 1915 he made brigadier-general at the then early age of 38 – led to his being stigmatised as 'the Principal Boy'. By the winter of 1917–18 he had many enemies, not least the Secretary of State for War, Lord DERBY, 'the genial Judas', who never forgave him for his embarrassing failure to censor an unfortunate interview which Haig gave to French journalists in 1917. The Cambrai debacle in November 1917 gave Derby his chance and Charteris paid the price for the successful German counter-attack, which he was accused of having failed to predict.

Chauvel, Henry 'Harry' George (1865–1945) Australian military commander. After serving on Gallipoli, latterly as GOC 1st Australian Division during the successful evacuation, 'Light Horse Harry' spent the remainder of the war in the Egyptian Expeditionary Force, first as GOC ANZAC Mounted Division, then as second in command and GOC Desert Column and, finally, as GOC Desert Mounted Corps. Chauvel played a leading part in stopping the Turkish advance at Romani (4–5 August 1916), a contribution for which he received little contemporary recognition. He enjoyed further success, as second in command to Sir Philip CHETWODE, at Magdhaba (23 December 1916) and Rafa (9 January 1917). At the first battle of Gaza (26–27 March) Chauvel's cavalry was ordered to with-

draw in the face of an expected Turkish counter-attack after confusion and indecision in the British High Command. Chauvel's fame, however, rests principally on the role played by the Desert Mounted Corps in Allenby's autumn offensive of 1917, during which it captured Beersheba in the last great (successful) cavalry charge in military history. The attack, made by horsemen using bayonets as swords against entrenched defenders armed with machine guns and artillery, greatly demoralised the Turks but so exhausted the attackers that they were unable to execute a truly decisive blow against the retreating forces. This mistake was not repeated the following year when Chauvel's cavalry completed the overwhelming nature of ALLENBY's victory at Megiddo (19–25 September 1918) before going on to capture Damascus and Aleppo. Chauvel was the first Australian to command a corps and the first to reach the rank of lieutenant-general. He was a man of great courage and calm, always well forward in battle. Although some found him aloof he always made a point of visiting troops who had been in action. Many Great War commanders understood the importance of criticism; Chauvel also understood the importance of praise.

Chavasse, Noel Godfrey (1884–1917) British war hero, one of only three men to win the Victoria Cross twice and the only man to win it twice during the Great War. Chavasse was the son of the Bishop of Liverpool. An Oxford Blue and Olympic athlete, he was the epitome of 'muscular Christianity'. He qualified as a doctor and joined the Territorial Army, serving with the socially elite 1/10th King's (Liverpool) Regiment, the Liverpool Scottish. His first VC was awarded for saving twenty badly wounded men at Guillemont, on the Somme, in August 1916, during which he was himself wounded. His second VC was awarded posthumously for his repeated attempts to rescue men under heavy fire at Wieltje, despite being badly wounded himself. He was also awarded the Military Cross.

Chetwode, Philip Walhouse (1869–1950) British military commander. A dapper Etonian cavalryman, known throughout the army as 'the Bart', Chetwode's aristocratic drawl and perennial cigarette holder gave him a raffish and frivolous air that disguised an energetic, imperturbable and professional soldier. After commanding 5th Cavalry Brigade and 2nd Cavalry Division on the Western Front, he was sent to Egypt, a more promising theatre for cavalry. Although his own performance as GOC Desert Mounted Column at the first and second battles of Gaza (March–April 1917) was flawed, he survived the purge of the Egyptian Expeditionary Force's high command that accounted for Generals A.J. MURRAY and DOBELL. In August 1917 Murray's successor, ALLENBY, a fellow cavalryman, appointed Chetwode GOC XX Corps, a post in which he performed with admirable skill, breaking the Beersheba line (October–November 1917) and capturing Jerusalem (December 1917). During the opening of Allenby's autumn offensive of 1918, XX Corps was allotted a secondary role but played a key part in exploiting the breakthrough at Megiddo, one of the last great cavalry pursuits in military history. Chetwode ended his career as Commander-in-Chief, India, and a field-marshal. His daughter, Penelope, married the poet John Betjeman.

Chicherin, Georgy Vasilevich (1872–1936) Bolshevik diplomat, who succeeded TROTSKY as Commissar for Foreign Affairs in May 1918 and played a leading part in establishing Soviet foreign policy and diplomacy on a proper administrative basis. He remained, however, essentially a mouth-piece of LENIN rather than an independent force.

Childers, (Robert) Erskine (1870–1922) British writer and pilot and Irish nationalist. Childers sprang to fame in 1903 with the publication of a popular spy novel about a planned German invasion of Britain, *The Riddle of the Sands*. The book captured the contemporary mood of public anxiety about national security and may even have influenced official naval concern about the possibility of a surprise German invasion, 'the bolt from the blue'. From 1910 Childers became increasingly committed to the cause of Irish Home Rule and in July 1912 used his yacht, the *Asgard*, to run guns into southern Ireland to support the nationalist cause. Despite this, he served as a pilot in the Royal Naval Air Service during the war, winning the DSC. When the war ended, however, he took up Irish citizenship and became an active republican. His opposition to the treaty establishing the Irish Free State and his membership of the Irish Republican Army led to his arrest by the Irish Free State authorities. He was executed by firing squad in Dublin on 24 November 1922.

Chkeidze, Nikolai Semenovich (1864–1926) Leader of the Russian Social Democrat Party (the Mensheviks) in the Fourth State Duma (1912–17), first President of the Petrograd Soviet and President of the Constituent Assembly of Georgia (1918), a relatively moderate man of very moderate abilities.

Churchill, Winston Leonard Spencer (1874–1965) British politician. Churchill began the war as First Lord of the Admiralty (1911–15), political head of the Royal Navy, the most awesome instrument of international relations since the Roman army. Even before war broke out Churchill demonstrated his self-confidence by ordering the fleet to its battle stations without first obtaining Cabinet agreement. This was an early indication of the restlessness and aggression that led to his involvement in the expedition to Antwerp and the loss of Admiral CRADOCK's squadron at Coronel.

These misadventures sowed the first poisonous seeds of doubt about Churchill's judgement. Worse was to come. It was not enough for Churchill simply to maintain naval supremacy. The point was to use naval power to bring the war to a swift and successful conclusion. This, in his judgement, could best be done by using the navy to knock the Ottoman Empire out of the war. Such an eventuality would guarantee the security of the Suez Canal and of Egypt, stifle the threat of disaffection from Britain's Muslim subjects, demonstrate the omnipotence of British power to friend and foe alike, bring Italy, Greece, Bulgaria and Romania into the war on the Allied side, effect the salvation of Serbia and provide a year-round, warm water supply route to Russia. Churchill's advocacy and confident belief that the Dardanelles could be forced using 'surplus' naval forces only was instrumental in securing British government approval for the ultimately disastrous Gallipoli campaign. Churchill's admirers have often claimed his plan as the work of a 'strategic genius', but in truth it was a half-baked endeavour rooted in complacency and racial arrogance that never had sufficient resources made available for it to succeed. Churchill's increasing use of precious naval assets brought him into conflict with the navy's professional head, the formidable Admiral J.A. FISHER, whose resignation in May 1915 brought Churchill's glittering career to a shuddering halt and helped instigate the formation of the ASQUITH coalition government. After a brief period as Chancellor of the Duchy of Lancaster, Churchill resigned and joined a battalion of the Royal Scots Fusiliers on the Western Front. His political rehabilitation was begun in 1917 by his old friend LLOYD GEORGE, who appointed him Minister of Munitions. This began one of the least known but most impressive periods of Churchill's long and extraordinary career, more important than his role as one of the many fathers of the tank. Under Churchill's guidance British munitions production was transformed in quantity and quality, allowing the British army in 1918, perhaps for the only time in its history, to fight a rich man's war.

Clam-Martinic, Heinrich, Count von (1853–1932) Prime Minister of Austria-Hungary 1916–17. Clam-Martinic's credentials as a German-speaking Czech with close links to the Czech nationalists and a record as a conservative constitutional reformer sympathetic to the ideas of Archduke FRANZ FERDINAND won him first place in the multiracial cabinet established in December 1916, but they availed him nothing in the face of nationalist opposition, and he resigned in June 1917.

Clarke, Travers Edwards (1871–1962) British staff officer, who succeeded R.C. MAXWELL as Quartermaster-General of the British Expeditionary Force (BEF) on 23 December 1917. Clarke was a brilliant administrator, undaunted by the scale and complexity of his task: to keep supplied with arms, ammunition, food, clothing, medicine and other equipment one of the largest organisations in the world in constant contact with the main forces of a powerful enemy. He not only successfully sustained the BEF during the March Retreat but also adapted its logistical arrangements to the mobile warfare of the 'Hundred Days'. Major-General Hubert Essame called him the 'Carnot of Haig's armies'.

Clausen, George (1852–1927) Dutch-born British painter, whose best-known wartime works are *Youth Mourning* and the specially commissioned *In the Gun Factory at Woolwich Arsenal*.

Clayton, Philip Thomas Byard 'Tubby' (1885–1972) British priest. Clayton volunteered for service with the army on the outbreak of war and was invited by the senior chaplain of the 6th Division, Neville Talbot, to set up a rest house for soldiers near Ypres. A suitable property was found at Poperinghe. It was named Talbot House in memory of Neville Talbot's brother but soon became known in signallers' parlance as 'Toc H'. Clayton's energy and humanity made him a well-known figure to the countless British troops who passed through the Salient. He was awarded the Military Cross in 1917. In 1920 he re-established Talbot House in London, where it eventually became the centre of the worldwide 'Toc H' movement.

Clemenceau, Georges (1841–1929) French Prime Minister 1906–9, 1917–20. Clemenceau was 73 when the war broke out and 76 when he became Prime Minister, but age did nothing to diminish his belligerence and energy. A veteran radical, anti-clerical and Dreyfusard who took great pride in the nickname 'Tiger', he spent the first three years of the war vehemently criticising successive governments from the pages of his newspaper, *L'Homme libre*, which he renamed *L'Homme enchaîné* as a protest against government censorship. His appointment as Prime Minister, on 16 November 1917, at the end of a traumatic year for France during which the nation's ability and willingness to continue the war was called into question, represented a conscious decision by President POINCARÉ that the war would be fought to a finish. Clemenceau was certainly the man for the job. He galvanised the home front, waging war on political defeatism, arresting leading 'pacifists', simultaneously coercing and conciliating the forces of industrial unrest. In Ferdinand FOCH, whose appointment as Allied Supreme Commander he did much to effect, he found a military commander who shared his patriotism and remorseless aggression. Clemenceau's indomitable courage during the difficult weeks of the German spring offensive did much to sustain French and Allied morale. After the Armistice he found it more difficult to wage peace than war. His

attempts to secure France's long-term security against her powerful neighbour foundered on American idealism and British pragmatism. Despite France's sacrifices he feared for her future and even foresaw 1940 as the year of danger from a revanchist Germany. He was a great man.

Clynes, J[oseph] R[obert] (1869–1949) British labour leader and politician, whose credentials as a supporter of the war and an influential trade unionist endeared him to LLOYD GEORGE. Clynes was appointed Parliamentary Secretary to the Food Controller in July 1917, becoming Food Controller himself in 1918.

Cochin, Denys Marie Pierre Augustin (1851–1922) French chemist and politician, who played an important part in the expansion of munitions production and the development of chemical weapons before entering BRIAND's government in October 1915. As Undersecretary of State in the foreign ministry he was given special responsibility for the economic blockade of the Central Powers. His powers were extended in March 1916 and again in August. The appointment of a right-wing Catholic deputy to such a sensitive and important ministerial post is an interesting comment on contemporary French politics.

Cohan, George M[ichael] (1878–1942) US musical entertainer and songwriter. Cohan was the son of travelling vaudeville artists, and his childhood was essentially an apprenticeship for the musical stage. He formed an act, known as 'The Four Cohans', with his parents and sister and at 16 wrote his first song, 'Why Did Nellie Leave Home?', before establishing himself as one of America's leading song and dance men. In 1904 he wrote his first major Broadway musical success, 'Little Johnny Jones', a show that included the songs 'The Yankee Doodle Boy' ('I'm a Yankee Doodle Dandy') and 'Give My

Regards to Broadway'. Cohan's patrio-tism was never far from the surface. One of his trademarks, first seen in the 1906 musical 'George Washington Jr', was to march up and down the stage carrying a huge American flag while singing a pa-triotic song. It was, therefore, hardly surprising that Cohan became caught up in the explosion of popular jingoism that accompanied US entry into the war. In 1917, while commuting into New York by train, he wrote the song that is associated more than any other with the United States in the First World War, 'Over There'. It was a huge hit that captured American optimism and deter-mination ('We're going over, We're going over, And we won't be back, Till it's over over there'). The song's importance was recognised in 1942, when it was awarded the Congressional Medal of Honor.

Collins, Michael (1890–1922) Irish na-tionalist. 'The Big Fellow' helped organise the Easter Rising against British rule in April 1916 and was interned. After his release in December 1916, he organised a clandestine military network that suc-ceeded in penetrating British intelligence. Informers were speedily identified and ruthlessly executed by a gang known as the Twelve Apostles. Collins proved him-self a brave and ruthless commander of the Irish Republican Army during the Anglo-Irish war (1919–21) and signed the treaty that ended it, becoming the first prime minister of the Irish Free State. Rejection of the treaty by Eamon DE VALERA and others provoked a civil war in which Collins was ambushed and murdered on 12 August 1922.

Collishaw, Raymond (1893–1976) Cana-dian fighter ace, whose sixty victories flying with the Royal Naval Air Service placed him second only to Billy BISHOP among Canadian aces. Collishaw re-mained in the Royal Air Force after the war and rose to high rank in the Second World War, where he played a leading

part in the air war over the Western Desert.

Coltman, William Harold (1891–1974) British soldier. Bill Coltman was a gar-dener from Burton-on-Trent. He volun-teered in January 1915 and the following June was sent to France, where he joined the 1/6th Battalion North Staffordshire Regiment, part of 137th (Staffordshire) Brigade, 46th (North Midland) Division, the first Territorial Army division to arrive complete in France. Coltman be-longed to a non-conformist sect, the Brethren, for whom he taught Sunday School. After telling his commanding officer that to take life was against his religious convictions, he was allowed to become a stretcher-bearer in 'A' Company. In this capacity he displayed extraordin-ary valour, winning the Victoria Cross, Distinguished Conduct Medal and bar, and Military Medal and bar, all awarded for attending the wounded under fire. The bar to his DCM and his VC were awarded for actions within a week of one another in September–October 1918. Coltman was the most decorated British 'Other Rank' of the war, but even the remarkable degree of official recognition that his courage received was only the tip of the iceberg in a military career where heroism was standard. He returned to Burton-on-Trent after the war, working as a gardener and groundsman until his retirement. During the Second World War he reached the rank of captain in the Army Cadet Force.

Colville, Stanley Cecil James (1861–1939) British naval commander. The war came a little too late for Colville, who completed his tour of duty as Rear-Admiral 1st Battle Squadron in June 1914 and was placed on half pay. His attempts to obtain employment met with deaf ears until the C-in-C Grand Fleet, Admiral JELLICOE, rescued him in September. One of Jelli-coe's most urgent concerns was the secur-ity of the Grand Fleet's anchorage at

Scapa Flow. Jellicoe's well-documented fear of German underwater weapons, mines and submarines, was intensified by the loss of three British cruisers to a German submarine, U-9, on 22 September. He asked for a senior officer to be appointed to take charge of the defences of Scapa Flow. Colville was steady and competent, rather than brilliant, but undertook the task with energy, thoroughness and common sense. No German submarine succeeded in penetrating the defences he set up. In February 1916 he was appointed C-in-C Portsmouth, a post he retained until the end of the war.

Congreve, Walter Norris (1862–1927) British military commander, GOC XIII Corps 1915–17, VII Corps 1918. Congreve was a contemporary of HAIG at Oxford but left without taking his degree after shooting a senior member of Pembroke College with an air rifle, an early indication of his commitment to musketry skills. He won the Victoria Cross in the South African War, an achievement posthumously matched by his son, Billy, on the Somme in 1916, making them one of only three father and son VCs. Congreve never lost the instincts of a front-line soldier, even as a corps commander. He was indefatigable in going to see for himself, even making personal aerial reconnaissance. He was the only corps commander to be wounded during the war, losing his left hand at Arras, an affliction that he bore with his customary nonchalance. He was an outstanding trainer of troops, insisting on the high standard of musketry that he himself had done so much to inculcate while Commandant of the School of Musketry at Hythe before the war. His corps achieved the only real success on 1 July 1916, capturing Montauban. He took a leading part in the decision to undertake a night advance and make the highly successful dawn assault of 14 July 1916, restoring a valuable element of surprise to the operational and tactical agenda. A spare, frail-looking man, he was afflicted throughout the war by poor health, including bronchitis, asthma and cholera. By the end of 1917 he was very tired and ought probably to have been replaced. His determination to maintain a rigid linear defence against the German attack on 21 March 1918 contributed significantly to the scale of the defeat of VII Corps and Fifth Army.

Conner, Fox (1874–1951) US staff officer. Conner was, perhaps, better prepared for the war than any other US army officer, having spent time attached to a French artillery regiment in 1913 and a period as an observer on the Western Front in 1916. He also spoke fluent French. He was hand picked by General PERSHING as a member of the American Expeditionary Force's advanced staff. Later, as Pershing's G-3 (chief of operations), much responsibility was delegated to him, and he played a leading part in planning the major American offensives of 1918, especially that at St Mihiel. As a brigade commander in Panama after the war, Conner was the first to recognise the abilities of Dwight D. Eisenhower, whose military education he did much to shape.

Connolly, James (1868–1916) Irish socialist and leader of the Citizen's Army, whose execution in the wake of the Easter Rising (April 1916) against British rule in Ireland helped turn a military defeat into a propaganda and moral triumph.

Conrad von Hötzendorf, Count Franz (1852–1925) Austro-Hungarian chief of staff and Commander-in-Chief 1906–17. Conrad was an energetic and far-sighted military reformer who worked hard to modernise the Austrian army, pioneering signals intelligence and aerial reconnaissance. His political judgement was, however, suspect. Confidence in his own ability and that of his army led him to advocate 'preventive' wars against the empire's enemies, seemingly blind to the destructive forces that war would release.

A cooler head than his might have done something to reduce the explosive temperature of pre-war Balkan politics. His contemporary reputation as a brilliant strategist is also difficult to understand. He muddled Austria's initial mobilisation, so that neither the Russian nor the Serbian fronts deployed their full strength, a factor in the army's dismal early defeats. He also greatly underestimated the likely strength of Serbian resistance and the difficulties of fighting in mountainous terrain. His fixation with the Italian front undermined Austrian resistance to the formidable Russian BRUSILOV offensive of June 1916, which came perilously close to knocking Austria out of the war. Conrad's strategic vision may have been Napoleonic but he had neither Napoleon's resources nor his luck. His inability to tailor military operations to the limited capabilities of the armies he commanded was instrumental in bringing ruin to the empire to which he had dedicated his life.

Constantine I (1868–1923) King of Greece 1913–17, 1920–22, whose pro-German sympathies (he was the brother-in-law of Kaiser WILHELM II) conflicted with the realities of his political and diplomatic situation, dominated by British and French naval power, and were at odds with the pro-Entente policies of his pan-Greek nationalist Prime Minister, Eleutherios VENIZELOS. Venizelos's decision to allow a Franco-British army to land at Salonika in October 1915 was made without consulting the King. Constantine's attempts to rule autocratically foundered on the ineffectiveness of German support. In June 1917 Britain and France threatened to invade Greece unless he abdicated. He spent the rest of the war in Switzerland, briefly returning to the throne after the war.

Coppard, George (1898–1984) British soldier. Coppard illegally volunteered for military service in August 1914, aged only 16. He served in the 6th Battalion Royal West Surrey Regiment and then the Machine Gun Corps on the Western Front, taking part in the battles of Loos and the Somme before suffering a serious thigh wound during the battle of Cambrai. He kept a diary throughout the war. This formed the basis of his account of his wartime experiences, *With a Machine Gun to Cambrai*, published in 1969. The book's success stimulated the publication of similar accounts by other old soldiers, often displaying a phlegmatic wartime resilience and a sense of post-war betrayal and disillusionment.

Coppens, Willy Omer François Jean (1892–1986) Belgian fighter ace. Coppens did not become an operational pilot until April 1917 and did not join a fighter squadron until July. He specialised in shooting down German observation balloons. Only two of his thirty-seven 'kills' were aircraft. Balloons were essential to the effectiveness of German artillery fire and were heavily defended by anti-aircraft batteries. Shooting them down was a particularly hazardous activity. His comment that 'being under fire is bad for the nerves' was undoubtedly authoritative. He was hit by flak on 14 October 1918, while trying to down his second balloon of the day. His left leg was smashed and had to be amputated.

Cornwell, John Travers (1900–1916) British war hero, posthumously awarded the Victoria Cross for remaining alone at his exposed post on HMS *Chester* during the battle of Jutland, despite a serious chest wound from which he later died. His sacrifice became the subject of considerable propaganda at the time, but he is now almost forgotten, as neglected in death as he was in life.

Cowans, John Steven (1862–1921) British staff officer, Quartermaster-General of the British army throughout the war (1912–19). Jack Cowans was an urbane and exceptionally able administrator with a penchant for other men's wives that un-doubtedly endeared him to LLOYD GEORGE, a great admirer. In an army that was historically small-scale, Cowans proved he had the flair and imagination to 'think big'. Completely unfazed by the task confronting him, he carried out with the minimum of dislocation a massive and rapid expansion of army services, includ-ing barrack accommodation, training fa-cilities, hospitals, food, transport, horses and personnel, a triumph of administra-tive improvisation.

Cowdray, Viscount *see* PEARSON, WEETMAN DICKINSON.

Cox, Edgar William (1882–1918) British staff officer, who succeeded John CHAR-TERIS as HAIG's chief of intelligence in January 1918. Cox is invariably described as 'brilliant'. He was an outstanding scholar, captain of his school (Christ's Hospital), head of his intake at the Royal Military Academy, recipient of the Queen Victoria, Pollock and Haynes medals, which placed him at the forefront of his generation of sapper officers. Cox's earlier career in intelligence was closely asso-ciated with that of Sir George MACDO-NOGH. His abilities were demonstrated in the handbook *The German Army in the Field* (first produced in 1915), which Macdonogh described as 'the bible of all intelligence officers', 'the first and most essential step towards placing the British Intelligence Service on a scientific foot-ing'. This work had seen Cox 'saturated with detail', but in 1917 he was given responsibility for analysing political con-ditions in Germany and Austria, an ap-pointment which allowed him to demonstrate that he also had breadth of view. Cox was drowned while swimming off Berck Plage on 26 August 1918.

Cox, Percy Zachariah (1864–1937) Brit-ish soldier, administrator and diplomat. Cox's career began as an infantry officer in the Cameronians, but he soon dis-played the linguistic ability and political astuteness that distinguished his career. By the time war broke out he had established a formidable reputation for his knowledge of the Persian Gulf, whose oil resources made it of prime strategic importance to Britain, following the Royal Navy's con-version to oil-fired ships in 1912. He accompanied Indian Expeditionary Force 'D' to the Gulf in 1914, taking charge of its political relationships in Mesopotamia. At first he worked alone but later sur-rounded himself with a number of able subordinates, including his oriental secre-tary, the Arabist Gertrude BELL. He was the first to recognise the importance of the ambitious Arab leader IBN SAUD and to advocate a British alliance with him. The appointment of Sir Stanley MAUDE as GOC-in-C Mesopotamia curbed Cox's influence, and it took a very high-level intervention by Lord CURZON to restore it. After the war Cox played a leading part in establishing the kingdom of Iraq.

Cradock, Christopher George Francis Maurice (1862–1914) British naval com-mander, whose defeat on 1 November 1914 at Coronel, off the coast of Chile, fed the suspicion that something was 'not quite right with the Royal Navy' and sowed the first poisonous seeds of doubt about the judgement of the navy's politi-cal head, Winston CHURCHILL. Since Oc-tober Cradock's small, obsolescent 4th Cruiser Squadron had been pursuing, on Admiralty orders, Admiral Graf von SPEE's larger, faster, more modern force of commerce raiders. It is difficult to know what Cradock was expected to do when he found them. His squadron was too weak to fight and too slow to run. He chose to fight and was annihilated within two hours, losing his own life, his two main ships, the *Good Hope* and the *Monmouth*, and 1,600 men.

Creel, George (1876–1953) US journalist and propagandist, a prominent pre-war 'muckraker' journalist and passionate advocate of Wilsonian progressivism. President WILSON's choice of Creel as chairman of the Committee on Public Information (CPI), following the United States' declaration of war, was controversial but inspired. Creel exceeded his brief to operate a government news agency. He rapidly turned the CPI into a very modern-looking propaganda organisation that made full and effective use of the emerging techniques of advertising and embraced the whole range of media, including film, music, posters, cartoons and paintings. (Creel's account of his wartime exploits, published in 1920, were significantly entitled *How We Advertised America*.) He masterminded Wilson's two triumphant visits to Europe after the Armistice and did more than anyone to popularise the Fourteen Points. His contempt for Wilson's critics, however, alienated powerful forces in the Congress that later did much to undermine political support for the Treaty of Versailles.

Crooks, William (1852–1921) British Labour leader. An implacable opponent of 'German militarism', Will Crooks enthusiastically supported British entry into the war, lending his services as a recruiting agent and morale booster.

Crozier, Frank Percy (1879–1937) British military commander. Crozier was forced to resign from the army in 1908, on pain of dismissal, after failing to honour cheques, a lifelong habit. When war broke out he was employed as a mercenary involved in training Sir Edward CARSON's Ulster Volunteer Force. In August 1914 he was recalled, eventually finding a berth as second in command 9th Battalion Royal Irish Rifles, part of the 36th (Ulster) Division. Crozier succeeded to the command in November 1915 and led the battalion during its costly baptism of fire at Thiepval on 1 July 1916. On 20 November 1916 he was promoted Brigadier-General and given command of 119th [Welsh Bantam] Brigade, 40th Di-

vision, a post he retained until the end of the war. Crozier was a warrior. Later a critic described his wartime record as 'not a very distinguished one except in the matter of gallantry. He is, in fact, that well known type, a regular swashbuckler'. Like many of his kind, Crozier found the post-war adjustment painful. In 1920 he resigned his command of an auxiliary division of the Royal Ulster Constabulary ('the Black and Tans') in controversial circumstances that earned him the undying enmity of official opinion, not least that of MI5. He found it impossible to secure official employment and turned to writing to earn a living. In a series of remarkable books, especially *A Brass Hat in No Man's Land* (1930) and the controversial *The Men I Killed* (1937), he portrayed war in an uncompromising fashion intended to reinforce the pacifist position that he had adopted in the 1920s.

Cumming, Hanway Robert (1867–1921) British military commander. Cumming spent the first half of the war as a staff officer in India and on the Western Front. On 27 August 1916, however, he was given command of 2nd Battalion Durham Light Infantry. Promotion to brigade command soon followed. From November 1916 to May 1917 he was GOC 91st Brigade, 7th Division. During the battle of Arras he found himself increasingly at odds with his divisional commander, Major-General Herbert Shoubridge. Cumming believed that Shoubridge never allowed sufficient time to organise attacks and always asked too much of his subordinate formations. He eventually put his criticisms in writing and was sent home. Cumming was, however, indefatigable. As Commandant of the Machine Gun Training School at Grantham, from August 1917 to February 1918, he played a leading part in the reorganisation of the Machine Gun Corps that saw the introduction of machine gun battalions attached to each division. On 16 March 1918 he returned to the Western Front as

GOC 110th Brigade in David CAMPBELL's 21st Division, a command he retained until the end of the war. He proved himself to be an outstanding brigade commander, not only energetic and determined but also prudent and humane. His incisive and outspoken account *A Brigadier in France 1917–1918* was published posthumously in 1922.

Currie, Arthur William (1875–1933) Canadian military commander. Currie was an insurance broker, estate agent and militia officer in British Columbia before the war. His business activities were somewhat dubious and only the timely financial intervention of friends in 1914 prevented him facing a charge of embezzlement that would have destroyed his military career before it began. Currie made his name as GOC 2nd (Canadian) Brigade (1914–15) during the first German gas attack at Ypres in April 1915. His command of 1st (Canadian) Division (1915–16) was equally impressive. When Sir Julian BYNG was promoted to command Third Army in June 1917, Currie was the natural choice to succeed him as GOC Canadian Corps, the largest homogeneous unit in the British army, more a 'mini-army' than a corps. Currie's command enjoyed unbroken success at Third Ypres (1917) and in the Hundred Days (1918) and came to be seen increasingly as the spearhead of the BEF. Currie had a 'managerial' view of war and rarely went near the front line. Thorough preparation and planning were his watchwords. He recognised the vital importance of firepower and his use of artillery was devastating. Large, self-confident and foulmouthed, he was the only senior officer in the BEF who did not wear a moustache. HAIG was one of his greatest admirers.

Curtiss, Glenn Hammond (1878–1930) US aircraft designer. Curtiss is widely regarded as the father of US naval aviation, pioneering both the flying boat and the concept of the aircraft carrier. By 1917 his Curtiss Aeroplane Company was the United States' leading producer. Many of his aircraft had already seen service with the British, proving particularly useful in early anti-Zeppelin operations. During the war Curtiss applied the mass-production techniques developed in the motor industry by Henry FORD, manufacturing large numbers of aircraft (notably the JN 'Jennie' series) and aircraft engines (notably the OX-5) for British and US service.

Curzon, George Nathaniel (1859–1925) British politician and imperial proconsul, who spent much of the war in rather lowly positions for a former viceroy of India until called upon by LLOYD GEORGE in December 1916 to lend aristocratic tone to his War Cabinet. Here he exercised important influence on British foreign policy in the Middle East.

Cushing, Harvey Williams (1869–1939) US doctor, one of the great neurosurgeons of the twentieth century, an innovative and original thinker who pioneered the use of X-rays and sphygmomanometers and did formative research on blood flow to the brain. As Moseley Professor of Surgery at Harvard he organised the Harvard medical unit and served with it for two months as part of the volunteer American Ambulance in France. When the United States entered the war, he returned to France to organise Base Hospital No. 5. Extracts from his voluminous wartime diaries were published in *From a Surgeon's Journal* in 1936.

Czernin und zu Chudenitz, Ottokar, Count von (1872–1932) Austro-Hungarian politician, who succeeded Count BURIAN as Austrian Foreign Minister in December 1916. CLEMENCEAU's revelation of Czernin's role in Emperor KARL I's attempts to instigate peace negotiations with the Entente in March 1917, made at the height of the German spring offensive in 1918, fatally compromised him with his German allies and he resigned on 14 April 1918.

D

Dadeshkeliani, Kati (1891–1934) Russian nurse, the daughter of a Georgian prince, whose account of her wartime service, during which she was wounded, was published in 1934 under the title *Princess in Uniform*.

Dakin, Henry Drysdale (1880–1952) British biochemist. As Professor at the Rockefeller Institute in New York, Dakin established a reputation as an authority on antisepsis. He co-developed the CARREL–Dakin method for treating wounds. This involved cleaning wounds by a solution of sodium hypochlorite administered through an arrangement of tubes. Although a time-consuming and labour-intensive system that posed difficulties for front-line surgeons in the casualty clearing stations, it was widely adopted in 1917, helping significantly to reduce the incidence of gas gangrene, which otherwise frequently resulted in amputation or death or both.

Dallolio, Alfredo (1853–1952) Italian soldier and politician, an artillery officer and logistics expert who in July 1915 became Undersecretary (from June 1917 Minister) of Arms and Munitions, responsible for mobilising the Italian economy for war and for supplying the Italian army, handicapped by desperate shortages. He was not afraid to use the stick provided by the government's emergency powers, but he recognised also the importance of the financial carrot in securing the collaboration of key industrialists. Dallolio was a master of expedients, uninterested in administrative and financial niceties so long as the desired outcome of increased production was achieved. Unfortunately, this left many opportunities for corruption and a financial scandal forced his resignation in May 1918.

Daniels, Josephus (1862–1948) US Secretary of the Navy 1912–20. Daniels was a competent administrator of somewhat autocratic temper who was determined to keep the US Navy (USN) firmly under (his own) political control, a policy that brought him into frequent conflict with his professional advisers, especially Admiral FISKE. Daniels' leadership of the USN conformed closely to the convolutions of President WILSON's foreign policy as it moved reluctantly and uncertainly from neutrality, through armed neutrality to war. Daniels' political instincts were those of a liberal pacifist. He was happy to demonstrate the United States' commitment to neutrality by halving the shipbuilding programme and by curbing the militarist instincts of the naval staff, whose formation he had opposed. Under the discipline of events, however, he drew up mobilisation plans, inaugurated US naval aviation and instituted serious planning to deal with the U-boat menace. Once the USA joined the war he threw his energy behind a naval expansion programme that gave priority to anti-submarine warfare. His appointment of Admiral SIMS to liaise with the British was a happy one, though Sims later became a stern critic of the Navy Department's performance during the war, especially during the first key months (April–December 1917).

Danilov, Yury Nikiforovich (1866–1937) Russian military commander, generally regarded as one of the Russian army's ablest staff officers. Danilov played an important part in pre-war discussions about the appropriate deployment strategy for the Russian army in the event of war. He favoured concentrating against Germany, which he saw as Russia's principal enemy, advocating an invasion of East Prussia in order to threaten Berlin. Unfortunately, he was unsuccessful in carrying his point, and the eventual Russian deployment plan (Plan XIX) was an unhappy compromise between those who wished to concentrate against Germany and those who wished to concentrate against Austria. In the event, the actual Russian invasion of East Prussia, made under intense French pressure in August 1914, was an inadequate, poorly co-ordinated, rushed affair that culminated in the disaster of Tannenberg, a defeat for which Danilov must share some of the responsibility. Despite his energy and intelligence the Russian army's hopeless communications system meant that he struggled to have any effect on military operations in 1915, and he was replaced in the wake of further Russian defeats when the Tsar assumed personal command of his armies in September 1915.

Dankl von Krasnik, Viktor, Count (1854–1941) Austro-Hungarian military commander, whose First Army suffered a heavy defeat by the Russians at Rava Russka in Galicia in the opening campaign of the war. He transferred to the Italian front in April 1915, enjoying no

greater success. The Austrian Commander-in-Chief, CONRAD, blamed Dankl for the failure of the Trentino offensive (May–June 1916), whereupon Dankl asked to be relieved of his command.

D'Annunzio, Gabriele (1863–1938) Italian writer and political agitator, who strongly supported Italian entry into the First World War. Despite his age (52), he joined the Italian air service, losing an eye in an accident and ending the war as a popular hero. Like many Italians he was dismayed by delays in deciding the future of the disputed city of Fiume, so in September 1919 he led a band of mutineers in its capture, remaining in control for over a year. This enhanced his stature as a national hero but did great damage to Italy's reputation in the world, not that this would have bothered him. In 1922 he gave support to MUSSOLINI's Fascists, who were much influenced by his theatrical politics, and retired to a dissolute life of cocaine-fuelled self-indulgence. D'Annunzio was a 'goggle-eyed dwarf' whose numerous amatory conquests were a triumph of personality over physique. A fantasist, narcissist, libertine and self-proclaimed poetic genius, his life would have been a comic opera but for the streak of racism, cruelty and violence at its core. His influence was almost entirely corrupting.

Dartige du Fournet, Louis René Charles Marie (1856–1940) French naval commander, whose first task following his appointment as C-in-C Mediterranean in October 1915 was to organise the successful evacuation of the Serbian army from Albania to Corfu. During 1916 he struggled ineffectually to defeat the German submarine threat, hampered by inadequate resources (especially escort vessels) and Allied squabbling. He was dismissed in December 1916 after the French forces landed in Athens to apply pressure on the neutralist King CONSTANTINE I suffered heavy losses in an attack by pro-monarchy Greek forces that he was accused of having failed to anticipate or prepare for.

Daszynski, Ignacy (1866–1936) Polish socialist leader. For much of the war he supported the 'Triple' Monarchy solution to the question of Polish independence, but in 1918, with Russia already defeated and Austria on the brink of defeat, he became an out-and-out Polish nationalist. He formed a Polish government in Lublin on 7 November but resigned a week later when Jósef PIŁSUDSKI became head of the new Polish state.

David, (Tannatt William) Edgeworth (1858–1934) British geologist. In 1891, at the age of 33, David became Professor of Geology at the University of Sydney. He was, however, far from being a desk-bound academic. He led an expedition to the Ellice Islands in 1897 and served as Scientific Officer with Ernest Shackleton's Antarctic Expedition (1907–09), leading the party that reached the South Magnetic Pole in January 1909. When war broke out he raised the Australian Mining Corps and then enlisted himself. David did geological work on Gallipoli and, following the British withdrawal, took the expertise of his mining engineers and geologists to France, where they played a leading part in the success of British mining operations, culminating in the Battle of Messines (June 1917). David was Geologist to the British Expeditionary Force from 1918 to 1919.

Davidson, John Humphrey (1876–1954) British staff officer. 'Tavish' Davidson's close association with Douglas HAIG began in 1915 when he became GSO1 at First Army. He followed Haig to GHQ in December 1915 as BGGS (later MGGS) in the operations section. Davidson was an advocate of the 'set-piece battle' and the strategy of 'limited objectives' that formed the basis of British success in the autumn of 1918, but his quietly reasoned objec-

tions to the grandiosity of Haig's schemes in 1916 and 1917 usually had little effect. He also opposed the Cambrai attack. Like BUTLER, he chafed somewhat at his retention by Haig at GHQ when field command seemed to offer greater opportunities for professional advancement but, unlike Butler, Davidson never effected his escape. Towards the end of his life, he wrote a restrained study of Haig's generalship, *Haig: Master of the Field* (1953).

Davidson, Randall Thomas (1848–1930) British cleric, Archbishop of Canterbury 1903–28. Davidson had close links with German theologians. Before the war he made the promotion of Anglo-German friendship a major part of his ministry. He was not alone in believing that war was impossible between two such civilised Christian countries with so much in common. Nor was he alone in being shocked and dismayed by the war when it came. Nevertheless, he accepted the official reasons for British belligerency, the sanctity of international treaties and the rights of small nations, and sent a measured defence of Britain's actions to German theological critics. During the war, however, he remained an opponent of extremism, never succumbing to the pervasive anti-German rhetoric of the press and many other public figures (including some churchmen). He protested against ill treatment of interned enemy aliens. His opposition to British use of poison gas (in 1915) and to the popular demand for reprisal air raids against German cities (1917) made him unusually controversial and the object of odium. But this did not prevent him from supporting a peace of reconciliation and being an early advocate of the League of Nations. During the 1920s, as post-war disillusionment set in and the nation collectively recoiled from the excesses of wartime feeling, Davidson's stature rose. By the time of his retirement he was in some danger of being popular.

Davies, Richard Hutton (1861–1918) New Zealand military commander. Davies emigrated to New Zealand after leaving school in England. He qualified as a surveyor and engineer, opening up the rugged hinterland of the North Island. He had no military experience until he was 31, when he joined the Hawera Mounted Rifles, becoming their commanding officer within six weeks. During the South African War his surveying skills made him an outstanding scout and brought him to the attention of Sir John FRENCH. Davies ended the war as CO of the Eighth New Zealand Contingent, the first New Zealander to command an independent force overseas. He was also the only colonial officer to be given command of a composite mobile force during the South African War. From 1902 to 1909 he played a leading part in the reform of the New Zealand military forces, before being sent to England to prepare him for promotion. He so impressed the British military authorities that he was given command of 6th Brigade, based at Aldershot. He took this unit to war in 1914 as part of the British Expeditionary Force. His insistence on marching to the front with his men, however, proved to be a serious error of judgement. He became exhausted even before the retreat from Mons began, and in September he was relieved of command and sent home to raise and train the 20th (Light) Division, a New Army formation. He was the first New Zealander to command a division. He led 20th Division in only one minor action on the Western Front before ill health compelled his return to England in March 1916. In April 1916 he was appointed GOC Reserve Centre Cannock Chase (in Staffordshire), one of the British army's major wartime training grounds, until he was relieved again in the spring of 1918. He committed suicide on 9 May 1918 by slashing his throat in a London nursing home that specialised in the treatment of army officers suffering from mental disorders.

Dease, Maurice James (1889–1914) British soldier, who won the first Victoria Cross of the Great War while serving as a subaltern in the 4th Battalion Royal Fusiliers. On 23 August 1914 Dease's machine-gun section, together with a company of Fusiliers, found itself defending the bridge across the Mons–Condé canal at Nimy during the battle of Mons. Dease kept firing the machine gun until he was wounded for the fifth time and carried to a place of shelter, where he died. The machine gun was taken over by Private S.F. GODLEY, who held out for a further two hours, covering the company's retreat.

Debs, Eugene Victor (1855–1926) US socialist. As titular head of the perennially fissiparous Socialist Party and its candidate in presidential elections, Debs was the public face of American socialism. The Socialist Party was the only significant political organisation to oppose the apparent preparation of the American people for war by the WILSON government. Debs continued to speak against the war even after the United States entered it. Following an impassioned speech at Canton, Ohio, in June 1918, he was arrested, charged under the Espionage Act and sentenced to ten years in prison. He ran for president from his prison cell in 1920, receiving one million votes.

Deguise, Victor (1855–1922) Belgian military commander, who directed the defence of Antwerp, of which he was Military Governor, until its surrender to the Germans on 9 October 1914, managing to escape to Holland where he was interned for the rest of the war.

De Havilland, Geoffrey (1882–1965) British aircraft designer, whose achievements during the Great War were considerably handicapped by the Royal Aircraft Factory for which he worked, an organisation whose record for making wrong decisions has rarely been bettered. De Havilland's DH4 and DH9, however, were notable bomber aircraft.

Delbrück, Clemens von (1856–1921) German politician. As Minister of the Interior from 1909 Delbrück had attempted to attach workers, especially miners, to the Wilhelmine regime through a programme of social welfare reform. But he was fated to watch the war undo his work. After the outbreak of hostilities Delbrück assumed responsibility for economic mobilisation, but he was already a sick man and the strain proved too much for him. Food supply became an increasing problem: the commitment to maintaining meat supplies (rather than grain) was a serious misjudgement, and it proved impossible to institute a fair system of rationing. Delbrück resigned on 23 May 1916 in the face of increasing working-class unrest, including strikes and food protests.

Delcassé, Théophile (1852–1923) French politician. As Minister of Foreign Affairs from 1898 until his forced resignation during the Moroccan Crisis of 1905, Delcassé was one of the principal architects of the Anglo-French Entente. As Navy Minister from 1911 until 1913 he also greatly increased French naval power and formalised naval co-operation with Great Britain. The agreement that in the event of war the French fleet would be concentrated in the Mediterranean, leaving the French Atlantic coast to be defended by the Royal Navy, added considerably to Britain's 'moral obligations' to France in August 1914. As Minister of Foreign Affairs in the VIVIANI government Delcassé played a leading part in bringing Italy into the war. However, his pro-Russian views, and willingness to encourage Russian annexationist ambitions towards Constantinople and the Straits, seriously compromised his Balkan policy. Allied influence in Greece and Romania

was weakened and Bulgaria joined the Central Powers in October 1915, a decision that sealed the fate of the Serbian army. He resigned immediately and did not hold office again.

De Lisle, (Henry de) Beauvoir (1864–1955) British military commander. De Lisle's pre-war reputation was based to a great extent on his skill at polo and prowess as an athlete. He captained the Durham Light Infantry polo team for ten years, famously leading it to victory in the Championship of India in 1898, an unprecedented achievement for an infantry team. De Lisle transferred to the cavalry in 1902, first the 5th Dragoon Guards and then the 1st Dragoons, which he later commanded. He also enjoyed the patronage of Field-Marshal Lord Roberts and was an able self-publicist. During the war he commanded 5th (Cavalry) Brigade, 1st (Cavalry) Division, 29th Division (on Gallipoli and the Western Front) and XIII Corps and XV Corps. De Lisle was a hard man. BIRDWOOD described him as a 'real thruster' and a 'brute'. He was invariably unpopular with those he commanded, but he also had the moral courage to stand up to his superiors. He was one of the officers who complained to HAIG over ALLENBY's head about the latter's conduct of the later stages of the battle of Arras. De Lisle was an excellent trainer of troops and a fierce disciplinarian, but he was also a fighter who kept a cool head in a crisis and retained the power of decision. As a corps commander he left much operational detail to subordinate formations, a style that fitted well the fighting conditions of 1918.

Denikin, Anton Ivanovich (1872–1947) Russian military commander. Denikin came to prominence after the February Revolution of 1917 that overthrew the Tsar, emerging as chief of staff to successive commanders-in-chief, ALEKSEEV, BRUSILOV and KORNILOV. He supported the coup led by Kornilov and was imprisoned in September 1917. He escaped at the end of the year to play a leading role in the formation of a Volunteer Army (the 'Whites'). He became commander of the Whites after Kornilov's death and enjoyed considerable success in South Russia, but in 1919 he over-reached himself in an attempt to capture Moscow and was routed at Orel. He was forced into exile in 1920, later writing his memoirs and an account of the revolution and civil war.

Derby, Earl of *see* STANLEY, EDWARD GEORGE VILLIERS.

De Robeck, John Michael (1862–1928) British naval commander. De Robeck succeeded the ailing Admiral CARDEN as commander of the Royal Navy's East Mediterranean Squadron on 16 March 1915, two days before its fateful attempt to renew the attack at the Dardanelles begun in February. The attack was an unmitigated disaster. Three British warships (*Irresistible, Inflexible* and *Ocean*) and two French (*Bouvet* and *Gaulois*) were sunk or disabled by mines. De Robeck resisted fierce pressure from his belligerent chief of staff, Commodore Roger KEYES, and from the First Lord of the Admiralty, Winston CHURCHILL, to renew the attack. De Robeck believed there was no prospect of passing the fleet through the Dardanelles at acceptable cost unless an invasion of the Gallipoli peninsula first secured the high ground and destroyed the Turkish guns and fortifications. General Sir Ian HAMILTON, recently appointed GOC Mediterranean Expeditionary Force, agreed to undertake this enterprise at a meeting with De Robeck on 22 March. This probably saved De Robeck from dismissal. De Robeck has been fiercely criticised for his failure to renew the attack and for failing to recognise that the fruits of victory justified what Churchill called 'severe loss'. In retrospect, his judgement appears prudent, though – in the end – it succeeded only in creating the circumstances

for a worse disaster that began with the amphibious assault on the Gallipoli peninsula on 25 April 1915.

de Valera, Eamon (1882–1975) Irish nationalist leader, born in New York. The son of a Spanish father and Irish mother, his American connections saved him from execution for his part in the Easter Rising against British rule in April 1916. He was absent in the United States for most of the Anglo-Irish war (1919–21), but on his return he repudiated the Anglo-Irish Treaty, which established the Irish Free State, helping to provoke a civil war in which he was defeated. As Prime Minister and, later, President of Ireland for much of the 1930s, 1940s and 1950s, his narrow-minded, sectarian version of Irish nationalism ensured that his country remained the most backward in western Europe.

Dewar, Kenneth Gilbert Balmain (1879–1964) British naval officer, one of the Royal Navy's Young Turks, who came increasingly to the fore from 1917 onwards. He was a supporter of BEATTY and a formidable critic of JELLICOE, whose failure to deliver the expected victory of annihilation at Jutland (31 May–1 June 1916) he attributed to the 'tactical arthritis' brought about by over-centralisation and lack of initiative. His views have exercised great influence on subsequent perceptions of the Royal Navy during the Great War.

Diaz, Armando (1861–1928) Italian military commander. Diaz replaced the discredited CADORNA as chief of staff in the wake of the Italian defeat at Caporetto in November 1917 even though he was only a corps commander. He held the Austro-German attack on the line of the Piave before turning his attention to very necessary improvements in the living conditions of ordinary soldiers in an effort to improve their morale and give them a reason for continuing the war. In the autumn of 1918, later than his critics would have liked, he planned and executed the decisive battle of Vittorio Veneto, which destroyed the Austro-Hungarian army on the Italian front and restored Italian national pride so badly damaged at Caporetto.

Dimitrijević, Dragutin (1877–1917) Serbian terrorist, founding member and leader of the Black Hand secret society, who organised the murder of Archduke FRANZ FERDINAND in Sarajevo on 28 June 1914. Dimitrijević was an ardent nationalist and pan-Serb. His reputation was established by his part in the assassination of King Alexander on 10 June 1903, an act that restored the grateful Karadjordjevic family to the throne. He became a professional conspiracist and terrorist, though many of his plans failed. Even the successful attempt on the life of Franz Ferdinand was notable for the bungling incompetence and cowardice of the assassins. Even so, the shadowy nature of the organisation Dimitrijević led magnified his power and he was much feared. In 1917, for reasons never quite satisfactorily explained, the Serb government decided to crack down on the Black Hand's activities. Dimitrijević was arrested, tried before a kangaroo court and executed on 24 June 1917.

Dix, Otto (1891–1969) German soldier and realist painter, best known for his vivid, savage and shocking portrayal of military casualties, notably in his book of etchings *The War* (1924) and the painting *Flanders* (1934) in which soldiers are shown as rotting tree stumps. Dix hated soldiering, which he characterised as: 'Lice, rats, barbed wire, fleas, shells, bombs, underground caves, corpses, blood, liquor, mice, cats, artillery, filth, bullets, mortars, fire, steel ... the work of the devil'. He also developed a fierce hatred for civilians and profiteers who pontificated about the glories of war. Dix's post-war portraits of Berlin prosti-

tutes led the Nazis to brand him 'degenerate' and to dismiss him from his post at the Dresden Academy. As a soldier he carried copies of the Bible and Nietzsche in his pack. In later life he chose God, painting religious subjects in virtual seclusion.

Djaved Bey, Mehmet (1875–1926) Ottoman Finance Minister, whose financial expertise made him virtually indispensable to government. He proved remarkably adept at securing loans from Germany without surrendering to German economic pressure. He went into exile after the Turkish defeat but returned in 1922 only to be executed for subversion.

Djemal Pasha, Ahmed (1872–1922) Ottoman politician and military commander, one of the few pro-Entente leaders among the Young Turks, whose attempts to broker an alliance with Britain and France during the July Crisis of 1914 foundered on Entente determination not to alienate Russia. Djemal's diplomatic preferences did not imply liberal sensibilities. As Military Governor of the province of Syria from 1915, he subjected what was in effect a vast personal fiefdom, covering Palestine and most of Arabia, to ruthless control. He did not exercise personal field command after the defeat of his attack on the Suez Canal in 1915. He fled into exile in October 1918 and was assassinated by Armenian nationalists on 21 July 1922.

Dmitriev, Radko R. (1859–1918) Bulgarian general, an ardent Russophile who resigned as Bulgarian Ambassador to St Petersburg in August 1914 in order to serve as a general in the Russian army. Zeal, however, was not accompanied by any special ability. Although Dmitriev's Third Army enjoyed some success in the opening campaign in Galicia, it was virtually annihilated in the German counterattack at Gorlice in May 1915. He later commanded the Twelfth Army before falling victim to Communist forces in the Russian civil war.

Dmowski, Roman (1864–1939) Polish nationalist, who formed the Polish National Committee and a Polish army in France in 1917, gaining diplomatic acceptance as Poland's official representative. He represented Poland at the Paris Peace Conference and was one of the signatories of the Treaty of Versailles.

Dobell, Charles Macpherson (1869–1954) British military commander. Dobell was appointed Inspector-General of the West African Frontier Force (WAFF) in 1913 but was on leave in London when war broke out. In September 1914 he returned to take command of an Anglo-French force charged with invading the German colony of Kamerun (Cameroon). The initial operation went well. Douala and its important radio station were swiftly captured. But conquest of the whole colony was a much more hazardous undertaking. The WAFF was not equipped, organised or trained for large-scale operations. Fighting in the vast and hostile interior of Cameroon against a resolute and skilful enemy absorbed almost 20,000 British and French troops, a fifth of whom became casualties, mostly from disease. The German capital, Yaounda, did not fall until 1 January 1916, and the Allies partitioned the colony in March. Dobell was rewarded with a knighthood, promotion to Lieutenant-General and a new command in the Egyptian Expeditionary Force. As GOC Eastern Force, under General Archibald MURRAY, Dobell played a leading part in the British defeats at the first and second battles of Gaza (March–April 1917). Shoddy staff work, poor communications, inadequate supplies of water, and inept and indecisive leadership by Dobell resulted in heavy British losses, double those of the Turks. Dobell was replaced by Sir Philip CHETWODE and sent to command a division in India, the 'sin bin of the First World War'.

Donop, Stanley Brenton von (1860–1941) British soldier, principally famous for being the butt of David LLOYD GEORGE's considerable scorn. As Master-General of the Ordnance (1913–16) von Donop was responsible for the provision of munitions to the British army. Pre-war arrangements were small scale and dependent on the output of a limited number of War Office approved manufacturers. The British Expeditionary Force's consumption of munitions quickly outstripped all predictions and the capacity of the traditional manufacturers to meet demand. A 'shells crisis' ensued, much encouraged by Field-Marshal Sir John FRENCH in order to obscure his own inadequacies as Commander-in-Chief. In May 1915 Lloyd George was made Minister of Munitions with a brief that amounted to the full mobilisation of British industry for war. Lloyd George was savagely critical of von Donop, seeing in him an example of the military apathy and inflexibility that he came increasingly to distrust. He was, as usual, unjust. Von Donop could be held responsible neither for the pre-war scale of British munitions production nor for the failure to remedy it, which was far beyond the power of a middle-ranking soldier. Nor was lethargy a charge that could be fairly laid at von Donop's door. During the first six months of the war, the Ordnance Department presided over a nineteen-fold increase in munitions production. Orders placed by the Department were principally responsible for supplying the army in the field well into 1916. The increase in the scale of provision brought about by the Ministry of Munitions was achieved, in the short term, by a noticeable decline in quality, as von Donop predicted and as the British soldiers who attacked on 1 July 1916 discovered to their cost. Von Donop's survival in post until 1916, despite his powerful and well-placed enemy and his German-sounding name, is a mystery. The fact that he spent the remainder of the war as GOC Humber Garrison is not.

Dorrell, George Thomas (1880–1971) British soldier. Battery Sergeant-Major Dorrell took over command of 'L' Battery, Royal Horse Artillery, during its gallant stand at Néry on 1 September 1914, after the death of Captain BRADBURY, continuing to fire the gun until its ammunition was expended. Dorrell was subsequently awarded the Victoria Cross. He was commissioned in October 1914, continuing to serve on the Western Front. He was mentioned in dispatches in 1917. Dorrell retired from the Regular Army in 1921 but served with the Territorials. He retired with the rank of lieutenant-colonel.

Doughty-Wylie, Charles Hotham Montagu (1868–1915) British soldier and war hero. 'Dick' Doughty-Wylie sprang to international prominence in 1909 for his heroic part, as British military consul in the Turkish province of Konia, in saving the Christian community of Adana from an attempted massacre. Later, during the Balkan War of 1912, he was a key figure in organising Turkish medical relief. When war broke out he was British Consul in Addis Ababa, but the entry of Turkey into the war in October 1914 placed his extensive knowledge of the Ottoman Empire at a premium and won him a place on Sir Ian HAMILTON's staff for the Gallipoli expedition. On 25 April 1915 he was on board the SS *River Clyde* off 'V' beach at Cape Helles. Troops landed from the *River Clyde* suffered heavy losses and became pinned down on the beach. Doughty-Wylie made a reconnaissance at nightfall to assess the situation. He returned to the beach the following day, rallied the men and led them in the capture of Sedd-el-Bahr. He then turned his attention to the commanding position of Hill 141. After arranging for a naval bombardment of the Turkish positions, he led the charge armed only with a cane out of respect for his connections with the Turks, being killed almost at the moment of victory, shot through the head. He was buried where he fell and the Turks respected his grave throughout the war. He was posthumously awarded the Victoria Cross, the first of the campaign. Doughty-Wylie's fame and the heroic nature of his death caught the public imagination and helped distract attention from what was a disastrous passage of British arms.

Douglas-Pennant, Violet Blanche (1869–1945) British public servant, sixth daughter of Lord Penrhyn, who – as National Health Insurance Commissioner for Wales from 1911 – was reputed to be the highest paid woman in Britain. She played a leading part in volunteer and official women's organisations during the war, including the Scottish Women's Hospital, the Women's Army Auxiliary Corps (WAAC), the Women's Royal Naval Service (WRNS) and the Women's Royal Air Force (WRAF). She resigned as commander of the WRAF in 1918 in protest against what she regarded as the Royal Air Force's patronising indifference. She was persuaded into returning on the promise of reform but was swiftly dismissed after a hostile report on the operation of the WRAF by Margaret Haig THOMAS (Lady Rhondda). She was replaced by the formidable Helen GWYNNE-VAUGHAN.

Douhet, Giulio (1869–1930) Italian air force commander and air war theorist, who commanded the first aerial bombing operation in history, against Libya during the Italo-Turkish war (1911–12). Douhet became head of the Italian army's aviation section in 1915 but was court-martialed and imprisoned later in the year for criticising the army high command in a cabinet memorandum. It took the disaster of Caporetto (November 1917) to restore his fortunes. He was rehabilitated and made head of the Central Aeronautical Bureau. However, his fame chiefly rests on his book *Command of the Air*, published in 1921, in which he visualised aircraft as the most potent offensive weapon of future war, advocating independent air forces and strategic bombing directed at enemy industrial, transport and social infrastructure. His views had enormous influence on inter-war military theory and public and political fears about the nature of future wars in which 'the bomber would always get through'.

Dowbor-Muśnicki, Józef (1867–1937) Polish general, who commanded I Polish Corps in the Russian army from the summer of 1917 until its disarmament by the Germans in July 1918. I Polish Corps later provided a core of trained officers and NCOs for the new Polish national army.

Doyle, Arthur Conan (1859–1930) British writer and wartime propagandist. Doyle was among the group of leading writers invited to a secret meeting on 2 September 1914 by Charles MASTERMAN, head of the equally secret War Propaganda Bureau (WPB). Doyle agreed to write for the cause. The work was not new to him. He had served as a doctor in the South African War and in 1902 published a vindication of Britain's role, *The War in South Africa. Its Cause and Conduct*. He quickly contributed a recruiting pamphlet, *To Arms!* (1914), and later wrote *A Visit to the Three Fronts* (1916). The death of Doyle's son in 1917, partly resulting from war service, intensified his father's post-war absorption in spiritualism.

Doyle, William Joseph Gabriel (1873–1917) British army chaplain. Willie Doyle was the youngest of seven children of a devout Irish Catholic family, four of whom entered holy orders. Doyle became a novitiate in the Society of Jesus in 1891 and was ordained a priest in 1907. He offered his services as an army chaplain to the order in November 1914 and was appointed to the 16th (Irish) Division a year later. Doyle saw the war as an opportunity for martyrdom and for proselytisation. He earned an enviable repu-

tation as a front-line chaplain, being attached successively to the 8th Royal Irish Fusiliers and the 8th Royal Dublin Fusiliers. Between arriving in France in February 1916 and his death on Frezenberg Ridge on 16 August 1917, Doyle was awarded the MC and was recommended for the DSO. His work at Frezenberg elicited a further recommendation for a posthumous VC from Major-General Sir William Hickie and other officers of the 16th Division. Doyle's biographer later ascribed the recommendation's rejection to his 'triple disqualification of being an Irishman, a Catholic and a Jesuit'. Although the case of Doyle's VC may have been an illustration of the often injudicious handling of the largely nationalist 16th Division by the military authorities, Doyle was nevertheless the subject of a glowing and unusual obituary by a Belfast Orangeman in the *Glasgow Weekly News* in September 1917. In the post-war years, the cause for Doyle's canonisation was promoted by a major biography by Professor Alfred O'Rahilly of University College, Cork, which ran to seven editions between February 1920 and April 1932.

Dreyer, Frederic Charles (1878–1956) British naval officer. Dreyer's pre-war reputation was based upon his achievements as a gunnery officer. His expertise first came to prominence in 1903, when his ship HMS *Exmouth* excelled in gunnery during naval trials. This led to his prestigious appointment as gunnery officer on the revolutionary HMS *Dreadnought* in 1907. He worked closely with the inventor Arthur POLLEN to produce an aim corrector for naval gunfire. Later, in competition with Pollen, he developed improved range finding and gun control systems that earned him a reward of £5,000. Dreyer's technical expertise naturally endeared him to Admiral JELLICOE, another gunnery expert, and the two became close friends. Dreyer served as Jellicoe's Flag Captain on board HMS

Iron Duke during the battle of Jutland. He was later a key member of the committee of inquiry into British material inadequacies during the battle, especially the ineffectiveness of British shells. As Director of Naval Ordnance and later Director of Naval Artillery and Torpedoes at the Admiralty, Dreyer was able to implement the committee's findings, which resulted in the manufacture and introduction of greatly superior ammunition for the fleet.

Driant, Emile (1855–1916) French army officer, whose inspirational defence of the Bois des Caures during the initial German assault on Verdun helped dislocate German plans and gave an indication of the grim and resolute French defence to come. Driant's pre-war career had been notably unsuccessful. His right-wing, clerical sympathies and his relationship to the disgraced advocate of a war of revenge against Germany, General Boulanger (who was his father-in-law), ruined any prospect of military preferment. He left the army to write futuristic anti-British works under the pen name of Captain Danrit. But he was also elected to the Chamber of Deputies. When in 1915 he found himself, as a reserve officer, commanding two battalions of Chasseurs on the Meuse, he was easily able to draw to the attention of powerful allies his concerns about the weakness of French defences. A letter he wrote in August 1915 to the President of the Chamber of Deputies found its way to the Minister of War, GALLIÉNI, who sent a delegation to investigate. The French Commander-in-Chief, JOFFRE, was furious when he found out. Never a man to suffer contradiction by subordinates and even less by politicians, Joffre dismissed Driant's claims and nothing was done to reinforce the French position. A luckier man than Driant would have been dismissed from his post, but instead he was left to defend a position which he knew was indefensible and which he increasingly feared the Germans would be unable to resist attacking. His gloomy forebodings were realised on 21 February 1916, when a massive German artillery bombardment signalled the start of the battle of Verdun. Driant's men conducted an heroic defence against overwhelming odds for twenty-four hours before Driant was killed as he withdrew from the remnants of his position under German flame-thrower attack.

Drum, Hugh Aloysius (1879–1951) US staff officer, who had acquired considerable pre-war experience in the Philippines and at Veracruz that brought him to the attention of senior officers, including General PERSHING. Drum joined the American Expeditionary Force (AEF) staff in 1917. He was one of the principal architects of the 'double-size' American infantry divisions, with more than twice as many men as their British and French equivalents. In July 1918 he became Chief of Staff US First Army. Pershing was, for some time, commander of First Army as well as Commander-in-Chief of the AEF and he allowed considerable latitude to Drum, who played a key role in planning the St Mihiel and Meuse–Argonne offensives. Drum ended the war as a brigadier-general.

Dubail, Auguste Yvon Edmond (1851–1934) French military commander, whose First Army spearheaded the French attack in Lorraine in the opening campaign of the war. His successful defence of the heights of the Meuse against German counter-attack anchored the whole of the French line, preventing a rout. In 1915 he was promoted to command Army Group East, whose share of the front included Verdun. Unfortunate public statements about the military obsolescence of fortresses and the unlikelihood of a German attack (about which he changed his mind) allowed JOFFRE to deflect much of the blame on to Dubail when the German attack duly came in February 1916. He was the highest-ranking officer to be dismissed as a result of the Verdun debacle and spent the remainder of the war as military governor of Paris.

Duchêne, Denis Auguste (1862–1950) French military commander. Duchêne began the war as a brigade commander, rising steadily through division and corps to army command. In December 1917 he was made GOC Sixth Army, charged with defence of the Aisne front. He was determined to hold the high ground along the Chemin des Dames and refused to employ 'elastic defence-in-depth'. Instead, the bulk of his infantry was committed to holding forward trench lines, many of them north of the Aisne. Three of Duchêne's divisions were British, sent to this 'quiet sector' to recuperate after twice being involved in the desperate fighting on the Somme and in Flanders. The commanding officers of the British divisions, Major-General W.C.G. HENEKER (8th Division), Major-General D.G.M. CAMPBELL (21st Division) and Major-General H.C. Jackson (50th Division), had painful experience of the dangers of linear defence against the German tactics. They were appalled by Duchêne's dispositions and went personally to protest to him, explaining that he was inviting disaster. Duchêne was unmoved, dismissing them with the curt phrase 'J'ai dit'. Disaster duly arrived on 27 May. LUDENDORFF launched three armies across the Aisne, achieving one of the greatest strategic surprises of the war. Duchêne's army was overwhelmed, its British divisions suffering especially badly. German troops advanced twelve miles in three days, once more reaching the fateful Marne and threatening Paris. Duchêne was dismissed on 9 June.

Duff, Alexander Ludovic (1862–1933) British naval staff officer. Duff began the war as director of the mobilisation division of the naval war staff, but in October 1914 he was promoted Rear-Admiral, 4th Battle Squadron. The C-in-C Grand Fleet,

Sir John JELLICOE, had great admiration for Duff's technical abilities and placed him in charge of finding counter-measures against German mines. Duff fought at Jutland, flying his flag in the battleship HMS *Superb*, but in December 1916 he followed Jellicoe ashore as Director of the Anti-Submarine Division at the Admiralty. The war against the U-boats was taking on ever greater importance and Duff's was a key role. His appointment ensured that the search for effective countermeasures would be pursued on rational, staff lines. This did not guarantee success but it was a positive sign. In June 1917 Duff was promoted Assistant Chief of the Naval Staff and given responsibility for co-ordinating all branches of the navy involved in the anti-submarine war. Duff was as slow as Jellicoe to be convinced of the efficacy of convoy, but he later initiated a steady flow of new weapons and dedicated anti-submarine warfare vessels that began to turn the tide of the naval war in 1918.

Duff, Beauchamp (1855–1918) British military commander. Duff succeeded Sir O'Moore Creagh as Commander-in-Chief, India, in March 1914. He was also Military Member of the Council of India. The Indian army was the principal strategic reserve of the British Empire and, although it was only trained and equipped for frontier warfare, Duff was called upon to send substantial expeditionary forces abroad, to the Western Front and to East Africa, within weeks of the outbreak of war. These losses depleted India of military stores and equipment and especially medical supplies. This situation was aggravated by Turkey's entry into the war in October 1914. Another expeditionary force was required for service in Mesopotamia, initially to defend the important oil installations at the port of Basra. Duff was opposed to an advance into the interior of Mesopotamia. He was concerned that the lack of suitable river transport would make it impossible to keep open sufficient supply lines or allow the effective evacuation of casualties. He communicated these fears to the Viceroy of India, Lord HARDINGE, but Hardinge did not pass them on to the Secretary of State for India in London. Instead, both the British and Indian governments were seduced by the optimism and ambition of the field commander in Mesopotamia, Sir John NIXON. Subsequent events entirely justified Duff's warnings. After initial successes, Major-General TOWNSHEND's army was defeated outside Baghdad in November 1915 and compelled to retreat to Kut-al-Amara, where it was besieged. Townshend's surrender in April 1916 and the sufferings experienced by his troops, especially the wounded, shocked public and official opinion in Britain. A Royal Commission of Inquiry was set up in August 1916, and Duff was recalled to give evidence. The Inquiry's report was critical. Only Nixon and Hardinge were more severely censured. Duff was a man of sound judgement and energy. The double burden of being Commander-in-Chief and Military Member of Council was too much for one man in time of war. Duff was trapped at his desk, leaving him with responsibility but no power. Ultimately, however, he paid the price for lacking the courage of his convictions.

Dukhonin, Nikolai Nikolaevich (1876–1917) Russian military commander, whose dramatic rise from regimental commander in 1914 to chief of staff and *de facto* commander-in-chief by the autumn of 1917 was ended by the Bolshevik Revolution.

Duncan, George Simpson (1884–1965) British army chaplain. After a glittering academic career at Edinburgh and Cambridge and periods of study at several German universities, Duncan was ordained into the Church of Scotland in 1915. The same year he went to France as Presbyterian Chaplain at GHQ, a post he retained until 1919. Field-Marshal HAIG,

a fellow Scot, took great comfort and inspiration from Duncan's preaching. Haig rarely missed Duncan's Sunday sermons and invariably invited him for lunch afterwards. Duncan's interesting account of his time at GHQ, *Douglas Haig as I Knew Him* (1968), was published after his death; an edited version of his contemporary diary was published by the Army Records Society in 1996.

Dunn, James Churchill (1871–1955) British medical officer and memoirist, responsible for compiling the hugely influential *The War the Infantry Knew 1914–1919* (1938; reprinted 1989), based on the experiences of the Royal Welsh Fusiliers, a regiment which included Siegfried SASSOON, Robert GRAVES and Vivian de Solo Pinto among its officers and Frank RICHARDS and David JONES among its Other Ranks. Dunn was a great admirer of Regular officers provided they were not above the rank of lieutenant-colonel. His attitude to generals and staff officers is eloquent of front-line prejudices.

Dunning, Edwin Harris (1888–1917) British naval aviator. Dunning was one of a small number of officers who recognised the importance of aircraft carriers and who campaigned against official hostility and indifference to develop the naval air arm. On 2 August 1917 he became the first pilot to land a plane on the deck of an aircraft carrier, HMS *Furious*. He was killed five days later, attempting to make his third landing.

Dunsterville, Lionel Charles (1865–1946) British military commander. Dunsterville, a Russian-speaking Indian army officer, was appointed at the end of 1917 to lead a composite force of Australian, British, Canadian and New Zealand troops charged with preventing a Germano-Turkish invasion of India and establishing an independent Trans-Caucasia. Supported by a detachment of armoured cars, 'Dunsterforce' marched 700 miles across Persia

[Iran] before being turned back by Russian revolutionary forces at Enzeli. A later attempt to occupy the important oil port of Baku had to be abandoned in the face of a superior Turkish force in September 1918, though the port was reoccupied at the Armistice. 'Dunsterforce's' achievements were a logistic miracle, but the force was too small (no more than 1,000 men) to have any real or lasting effect, amounting to little more than an exciting adventure. Dunsterville was at school with Rudyard KIPLING, for whom he provided the model of 'Stalky'.

Dyson, William Henry (1880–1938) Australian cartoonist. Will Dyson came to England in 1909 and was soon drawing cartoons for the *New Age*, whose publisher A.R. Orage introduced him to the social credit theories of Major Clifford Hugh Douglas. In 1912 he became the first cartoonist to draw for the socialist newspaper the *Daily Herald*, soon establishing himself as a major talent and doing much to establish the title. Despite his radical socialist credentials and contempt for the propertied classes, Dyson volunteered for military service and was twice wounded. His drawings of Australian soldiers did much to establish the image of the 'Digger' in the mind of posterity.

E

Eberhardt, Andrei Augustovich (1856–1919) Russian naval commander, who became Chief of the Russian Naval General Staff in 1908, in the aftermath of his country's crushing naval defeat in the Russo-Japanese war. In 1911 he was appointed Commander-in-Chief of the Black Sea fleet. The outbreak of war found him with a command largely composed of obsolete ships and new ones not scheduled for delivery until 1915. This seemed to him to dictate a defensive strategy, an argument which was certainly correct but which did not endear him to high authority in St Petersburg. Nevertheless, he made impressive use of his resources, skilfully employing mines to defend Russia's Black Sea ports and carrying the war to the Turks by bombarding strategically important parts of the Anatolian coast. These achievements availed him nothing, however, when in 1916 his failure to counter German submarines and to prevent the bombardment of the Russian coast led to his replacement.

Ebert, Friedrich (1871–1925) German politician. The son of a Heidelberg tailor, he began his working life as a saddler, the sort of artisan occupation which so often proved a fertile breeding ground for socialist ideas in nineteenth-century Europe. Ebert later became a journalist and in 1912 was elected to the Reichstag as a member of the Social Democratic Party (SPD). In 1913 he succeeded to the party leadership. Ebert's fate was to be a moderate man in an immoderate age. Within the SPD he was a revisionist, favouring the parliamentary road to socialism. He had a fear and loathing of revolution as deep as that of any conservative. He originally opposed German entry to the war but once it had begun consistently opposed an offensive war of expansion and called for a negotiated peace. With Germany on the brink of defeat in October 1918, he was invited to join the government by Prince MAX von Baden. Two days before the Armistice, Prince Max handed over the chancellorship to Ebert, confident that he would fight the coming revolution 'tooth and nail'. Ebert vacillated over the fate of the Kaiser, but his hopes of establishing a constitutional monarchy were immediately dashed by his colleague Philipp SCHEIDEMANN's unauthorised declaration of a German republic from the balcony of the Reichstag on 9 November. Nevertheless, Ebert valiantly attempted to establish the infant and unloved regime on a firm constitutional foundation. In 1919 he accepted assistance from the army and the paramilitary Free Corps (*Freikorps*) in order to suppress the Spartacist rising in Berlin led by Rosa LUXEMBURG and the break-away Bavarian Republic led by Kurt EISNER. In 1923 he put down Hitler's Munich beerhall putsch. The price of military support was his agreement not to reform the army. The deal ensured the short-term establishment of order but at the cost of perpetuating a military caste inherently hostile to the republican government. In his love of order and respect for authority, Ebert reflected the true temper of the German people, especially the middle class, but his chance of becoming the 'Adenauer of the 1920s' foundered amid the poisonous animosities of post-war Germany. To the left he was a traitor to the revolution, to the right one of the 'November criminals' who had stabbed the army in the back and signed the hated Treaty of Versailles.

Edmonds, James Edward (1861–1956) British official historian. Edmonds has been accused of deliberately falsifying the official record in order to protect the reputations of senior commanders. His account certainly eschewed sensationalism and was intended principally as a staff document for the education of future Regular soldiers. During the 1930s he undoubtedly began to take a more pro-high command and pro-HAIG line, goaded by the self-serving and vitriolic attack on the integrity, intelligence and professional competence of British generalship found in LLOYD GEORGE's *War Memoirs*. The official history, however, is not uncritical. Many writers of the popular 'mud and blood school' often simply take Edmonds' account and give it a debunking spin. Without Edmonds' devotion, the official history would never have been completed. It remains an essential text for anyone wishing to understand the British army during the Great War. In private Edmonds was a gossip and his correspondence was often sly, malicious and misleading.

Eichorn, Hermann von (1848–1918) German military commander, who spent the whole of the war on the Eastern Front. Eichorn was a veteran of the Prussian service, already 66 when the war broke out. But his years did not seem to inhibit him. He was given command of the newly formed Tenth Army in January 1915. In August 1916 his troops captured Kovno and in September Vilna. He was promoted Field-Marshal in December 1917. After Russia's defeat he was made Military Governor of the Ukraine, charged with its economic exploitation under the terms of the punitive Treaty of Brest-Litovsk (March 1918). His oppressive regime was unpopular and ineffective, leading to his murder by a Ukrainian socialist on 30 July 1918.

Einem, Karl von (1853–1934) German military commander. As Prussian Minister of War from 1903 to 1909, Einem pursued a policy of modernisation. When war came he commanded VII Corps, part of BÜLOW's Second Army, in the invasion of France. During the battle of the Marne he succeeded the exhausted HAUSEN as commander of Third Army, a post he retained for the rest of the war. He opposed the German first use of chlorine gas as morally repugnant and likely to be counter-productive. Third Army was eventually located in Champagne, a front that Einem successfully defended against a series of (mostly) French attacks in 1915 and 1917. His own unsuccessful attack against the French and Americans near Rheims in July 1918 was the last German offensive of the war and was followed by a heavy defeat in the Meuse–Argonne at the hands of the United States army. On 12 November 1918 Einem took command of the former Crown Prince WILHELM's Army Group, supervising its return to Germany, whereupon he retired.

Eisner, Kurt (1867–1919) German socialist and revolutionary, who took advantage of the political and social dislocation following Germany's defeat in 1918 to proclaim a short-lived Bavarian Soviet Republic. This was crushed by the army and paramilitary *Freikorps* on the orders of the German Republic's first Chancellor, Frierich EBERT. Eisner was assassinated in Munich in 1919.

Elles, Hugh Jamieson (1880–1945) British military commander, tank pioneer and first commander of the Tank Corps. Elles (pronounced 'Ellis') owed his advancement to the influence of Sir William ROBERTSON. When he became Chief of the General Staff in January 1915, Robertson gathered around him a group of able young officers known as 'the Creche'. These were to act as his 'eyes and ears', to go round the army and report back on what they saw. After Robertson went home as Chief of the Imperial General Staff in December 1915 Elles remained in France as a staff officer in the Operations Section at GHQ. Early in 1916 HAIG selected him to return to England and report on the progress of the tank. Haig was so impressed by Elles's initial report on the new weapon and his performance at interview that in September 1916 he put him in command of tanks, a position he held until the end of the war. He was 36. Despite enjoying the patronage of senior officers, Elles was the least pliant of men in public or private. Outspoken and stubborn, he spared no one's feelings, including those of his superiors, but his energy, determination and organisational ability helped to establish the Tank Corps as an integral part of the British order of battle and, at Cambrai in November 1917, to foreshadow the future of armoured warfare.

Elliott, Harold Edward (1878–1931) Australian military commander. A Melbourne lawyer who had served briefly in the South African War as a British Regular, 'Pompey' Elliott commanded 15th (Australian) Brigade from April 1916 until the end of the war. He was a big man with a bigger ego, fiercely independent and very self-consciously 'Australian'. A profound student of military history, he had nothing but contempt for the British Regular Army and for the fighting spirit of the British soldier. He refused to have British officers in his brigade, described one British regiment as the 'Scarlet Runners'

and ordered British stragglers during the retreat in March 1918 to be shot, an order that had to be countermanded by his long-suffering divisional commander, Talbot HOBBS. He was an impossible subordinate, constantly at odds with Australian High Command, especially BIRDWOOD and WHITE, denouncing them in the Australian federal parliament after the war for their part in the disastrous battle of Bullecourt in 1917. Elliott believed that White's appointments were governed by snobbery. He never forgave him for promoting the British-trained Staff College graduate and public schoolboy John GELLIBRAND to the command of 3rd (Australian) Division, an appointment for which Elliott believed himself far more fitted. As a commander Elliott was heroworshipped by his men. He was remorselessly aggressive but capable of displaying real tactical flair and flexibility in the heat of battle. The performance of his brigade at Polygon Wood (25 September 1917) and in the celebrated night attack that recaptured the important village of Villers-Bretonneux (24–25 April 1918) was outstanding. After the war Elliott's sense of thwarted ambition corroded his soul and unbalanced his judgement, and he committed suicide by slashing his throat on 23 March 1931. In another time and another place he may well have been Alexander the Great or Napoleon.

Elstob, Wilfrith (1888–1918) British soldier. Elstob, a schoolmaster with the build of a rugby forward, volunteered for military service in 1914, joining the 16th Battalion Manchester Regiment as a private. By 21 March 1918 he was the battalion's commanding officer, with the rank of lieutenant-colonel. 16th Manchesters, part of 42nd Brigade, 14th (Light) Division, were serving with Fifth Army on the Somme, a position that would see them bear the full force of the German spring offensive. Elstob was aware of the impending storm. A few days before, he had pointed out the position of his battalion headquarters on the map and declared: 'Here we fight, and here we die'. In the event, the Manchesters did not become seriously engaged with the enemy until the fog lifted in the middle of the afternoon. Elstob, despite being wounded twice, moved about his men constantly encouraging them. He repelled one attack single-handedly and made several journeys to the rear under heavy fire to bring forward fresh supplies of grenades. It was on one of these journeys that he was killed. In one of his last messages to brigade headquarters, made by means of a buried cable, he stated that: 'The Manchester Regiment will hold Manchester Hill to the last'. This later fuelled the legend that the position had been held to the last man, though large numbers were captured, more indeed than were killed. Elstob was awarded a posthumous Victoria Cross in 1919. He also won the DSO and MC.

Enver Pasha (1881–1922) Ottoman politician and military commander, one of the leaders of the Young Turk revolution of 1908. His later prominent role in the coup that brought the Young Turks to full power (1912) and in the capture of Adrianople (1913) won him national fame. He replaced IZZET PASHA as Minister of War in February 1914, immediately instigating a purge of senior officers. During his posting as military attaché to Berlin (1909–11), Enver formed a favourable and lasting impression of the power of Germany and saw a German alliance as Turkey's best road to modernisation, though his wartime attempts to 'Germanise' Turkish government and administration produced much debilitating confusion. Germanophilia also led him to favour a military solution to Turkey's problems. It was Enver who granted the German ships *Goeben* and *Breslau* sanctuary from the guns of the British fleet in Turkish territorial waters, a decision that was instrumental in Turkey's entering the war on the side of the Central Powers in October 1914. Enver assumed command of the Third Army, which occupied a key position opposite Russian forces in the Caucasus. Expansion in the Caucasus and among the Turkic peoples of Russian Central Asia was at the heart of Enver's strategy. Unfortunately, he was a contemptible general, barren in operational judgement and tactical flexibility, seemingly incapable of learning from his mistakes. Third Army suffered a major defeat at Sarakamish on 29 December 1914. Throughout 1915 Russian forces, for once capably commanded by General YUDENICH, inflicted repeated dispiriting reverses on Enver's forces. Enver's fixation with the Caucasus also weakened the Turkish position in Palestine, which came under increasing pressure from the British General ALLENBY from the summer of 1917. Enver was a man whose ambition outstripped his ability and the resources of his country. He fled after the fall of the Young Turks in October 1918 and died fighting the Red Army in Uzbekistan on 4 August 1922.

Erzberger, Matthias (1875–1921) German politician. Erzberger was a leading figure on the left wing of the German Catholic Centre Party, a patriot and nationalist. During 1914 and 1915 he was entrusted with the thankless task of organising German overseas propaganda, but in 1916 he became increasingly concerned about the course of the war and was converted to the idea of a negotiated peace. In July 1917 he introduced a Peace Resolution into the Reichstag. His influence, however, like that of all German moderates, remained marginal until it was too late. In November 1918 he was fated to be a member of the German Armistice delegation, an act of betrayal for which he was never forgiven by the German right and which led to his assassination by nationalist fanatics on 26 August 1921.

Esher, Viscount *see* BRETT, REGINALD BALIOL.

Essen, Nikolai Ottovich von (1860–1915) Russian naval commander. Nikolai von Essen was an able, energetic sailor who played a leading part in the reform of the Russian navy after its disastrous experience in the Russo-Japanese war (1904–5). By 1914 he had brought the Baltic Fleet to a state of war readiness that was unusual, if not unique, among the Russian armed forces. Like able and energetic commanders in other navies, he was frustrated by the reluctance of his superiors to allow him to engage in offensive action, though he did succeed in disrupting German Baltic commerce through aggressive mining operations before his sudden death in May 1915.

Estienne, Jean Baptiste Eugene (1860–1936) French soldier and armoured warfare pioneer. During 1915 Estienne turned his mind, as did many on the Allied side, to the problem of breaking the deadlock of trench warfare. After rejecting the idea of wire-crushing tractors, he devised a plan for a mobile, armour-protected gun that could be brought up close to the enemy's lines. The French and British worked quite separately and in secrecy. Although the first order for 400 French 'tanks' was placed with the Schneider company in February 1916, the French, to their surprise, were beaten into the field by the British. The first British use of tanks was at Flers-Courcelette on the Somme on 15 September 1916; the first French use of tanks was not until 16 April 1917 on the Chemin des Dames. Although himself a gunner, Estienne's thoughts soon began to turn away from the idea of tanks as 'artillery carriers'. These were difficult to manufacture and subject to constant mechanical failure that compromised their ability to obtain funding and generate support among more conservative-minded military leaders. Instead, he came to advocate tanks as armoured 'machine gun carriers', much smaller and easier to produce in large numbers. A contract for their manufac-ture was signed with the car-maker Renault. The greater availability of this type of 'light tank' led Estienne to advocate the concept of a mass, surprise armoured attack, and he may have had some influence on the British preparations for the battle of Cambrai. Although Estienne himself always understood the need for heavy tank development, the production of large numbers of small, light tanks with poor cross-country performance became a hallmark of French armoured policy between the wars, with disastrous consequences in 1940.

Eugen, Archduke (1863–1954) Austro-Hungarian Commander-in-Chief on the Italian front, 1915–18. Eugen was no mere courtier and chocolate-box soldier but a staff-trained professional devoted to the welfare of his troops. After doing what he could to retrieve some credit from General POTIOREK's disastrous winter offensive against Serbia, in May 1915 Eugen was appointed Commander-in-Chief in Italy, following Italy's entry into the war on the Allied side. He remained in command, at least nominally, for the rest of the war, suffering constant interference from the Austrian chief of staff, CONRAD, and the truculent arrogance of his German allies. As a field commander he lacked the strategic and operational ability to overcome these considerable burdens, exhibiting the common Habsburg failure of mixing rashness with caution, which resulted in a dispersion of effort in both attack and defence. Eugen was a decent, competent and well-meaning man within the considerable confines of his caste, whose fate was to be promoted above his level of ability in a war where all the cards were stacked heavily against him.

Evans, Edward Ratcliffe (1881–1957) British naval commander, immortalised in Royal Navy history as 'Evans of the *Broke*'. An enterprising and adventurous man, Evans was second-in-command to

Captain R.F. Scott's Antarctic Expedition of 1909, bringing the survivors home after Scott's death. On 20 April 1917, while in command of the destroyer HMS *Broke*, he engaged six German destroyers off the coast of Holland. The *Broke* sank one and rammed another. This episode, which took place in the dark and involved hand-to-hand fighting on the *Broke*'s deck, appealed hugely to a British public brought up on stories of naval derring-do and provided a propaganda godsend at a low point in the naval war.

Evan-Thomas, Hugh (1862–1928) British naval commander. In 1915 Evan-Thomas was given command of the Royal Navy's 5th Battle Squadron, consisting of four super-dreadnought battleships, *Barham*, *Malaya*, *Valiant* and *Warspite*, one of the most powerful naval forces ever assembled. During the clash between the British and German battle-cruiser squadrons which constituted the first part of the battle of Jutland (31 May 1916), Evan-Thomas's ships were sailing five miles behind Admiral BEATTY's. His flagship, HMS *Barham*, crucially took six minutes to detect Beatty's visual signal to turn towards the enemy. This failure left Evan-Thomas ten miles behind Beatty, unable to bring his massive firepower to bear against HIPPER's battle cruisers. Evan-Thomas was equally slow to react when Beatty turned away from the oncoming German High Seas Fleet, leaving his own ships vulnerable to annihilation. Posterity has generally acquitted Evan-Thomas of blame, but his leadership seems remarkably lacking in initiative and decision, characteristics that were unhappily commonplace in the British fleet at Jutland.

Evert, Aleksei Ermolaevich (1857–1918?) Russian military commander, who led the Fourth Army in Galicia during the Polish campaign of 1914. The stalemate into which this campaign descended was violently broken by the Austro-German at-

tack of May 1916. Evert's army was separated from the rest of the Russian forces and compelled into a 300-mile long fighting retreat, one of the most difficult operations in war. In September 1915, when the Tsar took personal control of the Russian armies, Evert was given command of the Western Army Group, which comprised the bulk of the Russian army. He spent the next eighteen months painstakingly augmenting his strength, which he then dissipated in a spectacularly ill conceived and costly attack at Lake Naroch in March 1916. This reverse strengthened his innate caution, and during the following summer he gave very inadequate support to General BRUSILOV's offensive. His indecision was final in the significant failure to capture the rail junction at Kovel, which he then proceeded to invest ineffectually for three months. He was dismissed in March 1917 by the Provisional Government and disappeared. The manner and date of his death have never been properly established. Evert had military ability, especially in defence, but in the circumstances in which he was called on to command, his pusillanimous hoarding of men and equipment proved disastrous.

Ewing, (James) Alfred (1855–1935) British engineer and physicist, naval administrator and cryptanalyst. A Scot, educated at Edinburgh University, Ewing later occupied university chairs at Tokyo (1878–83), Dundee (1883–90) and Cambridge (1890–1903). From 1903 to 1916 he was Director of Naval Education, instituting major reforms of naval engineering training, vital in a service where technology was becoming increasingly paramount. From 1914 to 1917 he was head of the celebrated 'Room 40' at the Admiralty, providing inspired leadership to a brilliant, if motley, collection of dons, naval officers and civilian professionals charged with the decryption of intercepted German wireless messages. Room 40's success earned Ewing the nickname of 'the Whitehall Sherlock Holmes'. He left Room 40 in May 1917 to become Principal of Edinburgh University, a post in which he acquitted himself with equal distinction and success, and was replaced by 'Blinker' HALL.

F

Faisal ibn Hussein, Prince (1885–1933)
Arab leader, third son of ibn Ali HUSSEIN,
Sherif of Mecca, who joined his father in
raising the Arab Revolt against Turkish
rule in June 1916. Faisal's role as the
Arabs' leading military commander has
been overshadowed by the legend of his
British liaison officer, Colonel T.E. LAWR-
ENCE, but he was an extremely competent
guerrilla leader and an even more astute
diplomat who succeeded in holding together the naturally fissiparous Arab
tribes. His army constantly harassed Ottoman forces from its strongholds in the
Hejaz, helping to secure the right flank of
the British army in Palestine and offering
a permanent threat to the Turks' lines of
communications and retreat. He captured
Aqaba in 1917 and liberated Damascus in
October 1918. British and French dupli-
city denied him the post-war Arab state
he coveted. He was deposed as King of
Syria and Palestine by the French in June
1920 but – with British support – became
King of Iraq in 1921.

**Falkenhayn, Erich Georg Anton Sebastian
von** (1861–1922) German Chief of the
General Staff and military commander.
Falkenhayn succeeded the broken MOLTKE
as German chief of staff in September
1914 after the disaster of the Marne. His
attempt to bring the war to a successful
conclusion in 1914, by repeated attempts
to outflank the British and French line in

the so-called 'Race to the Sea', was halted
in desperate fighting around Ypres in
November. In 1915 he stood on the
defensive in the west, reluctantly sending
reinforcements to the east, where they
won stunning victories over the Russian
army. In February 1916 he turned his
attention again to the west, seeking to
'bleed the French Army white' in a battle
of attrition at Verdun. The German army's failure to break the French resulted
in Falkenhayn's dismissal on 29 August
1916. He accepted a humiliating demotion to command of Ninth Army with
remarkable equanimity, taking a leading
part in the conquest of Romania, including the capture of Bucharest on 6 December. In 1917 he was transferred to
Palestine, where the small and poorly
equipped German *Yilderim* forces were
no match for General ALLENBY's well-led
and powerful British army. He ended the
war as commander of the Tenth Army in
Lithuania.

Falkenhayn's generalship was a combination of strategic caution and operational ruthlessness. In a multi-front war
he was unwilling to risk concentrating his
forces in order to win a decisive victory in
one theatre. He was unusual, perhaps
unique, among German commanders in
being sceptical about the possibility of
winning shattering victories of total annihilation. Nor did he think such victories
were essential in achieving an outcome to

the war satisfactory to German national interests. These could be achieved by 'attrition'. He was also unusual in identifying Britain, rather than Russia, as Germany's principal enemy, though his decision in 1916 to target the French Army, 'the sword in Britain's hand', seems a remarkably convoluted piece of thinking. This relative restraint, however, was entirely absent from his conduct of battlefield operations, which was marked by a disregard for casualties that was impressive even by Great War standards. His willingness to expend human life in the pursuit of military objectives became apparent at First Ypres. At Verdun 'strategic' attrition was not matched by 'operational' or 'tactical' attrition. He seemed quite willing to allow his subordinate commanders and their troops to believe they were fighting a breakthrough battle on the psychological grounds that they would try harder, a decision that undoubtedly contributed to the increasing scale of German losses. On the Somme his determination to contest every foot of ground, if necessary by launching immediate and costly counter-attacks, turned the battle into the 'muddy field grave of the German army'.

Farquhar, Francis Douglas (1874–1915) British soldier. 'Fanny' Farquhar was a Coldstream Guards officer who found himself, on the outbreak of war, as Military Secretary to the Governor-General of Canada, the Duke of Connaught. Farquhar was a very competent professional soldier, with a charming manner and an adroit way of handling difficult people. He needed all these talents when he was appointed first commanding officer of a new regiment, Princess Patricia's Canadian Light Infantry, raised by a Montreal millionaire, Hamilton Gault, and named after the Duke of Connaught's glamorous younger daughter, who became its colonel-in-chief. The Princess's glamour rubbed off on the regiment, which attracted recruits from some of the most famous and influential families in Canada, men with views of their own and political connections. Farquhar nevertheless established the regiment as a serious military unit and presided over its first actions on the Western Front, where it won Canada's first decorations for gallantry in the war. He was killed by a German sniper on 20 March 1915, near St Eloi.

Fawcett, Millicent Garrett (1847–1929) British feminist and suffragist. Mrs Fawcett founded the National Union of Women's Suffrage Societies (NUWSS) in 1897. Although the NUWSS's constitutional and rational approach to the campaign for female suffrage was too timid for some, it was by far the most important suffrage organisation, with more than 50,000 members by 1914. Mrs Fawcett's leadership was impressive and achieved much, but the realisation of the NUWSS's final objective foundered on the considerable obstacle of Prime Minister ASQUITH. As the diplomatic crisis of July and August 1914 deepened, Mrs Fawcett addressed a women's protest against war. Within days of the war's outbreak, however, she firmly allied the NUWSS with the national struggle, calling on its members to put themselves at the disposal of the war effort, a call that was echoed by her militant opponents in the suffrage movement.

Fay, Sam[uel] (1856–1953) British railway manager and wartime administrator. Fay joined the London & South Western Railway (LSWR) in 1872, rapidly establishing a reputation for efficiency and for reviving lame ducks. He first became involved with the army in 1888, when serious rioting in Trafalgar Square by the unemployed resulted in the military being called out to assist the civil power. As the LSWR controlled the lines from Aldershot to London, Fay – as Superintendent of the Line – was brought in to find a regiment that the military authorities had managed to lose in transit! Fay left the War Office in no doubt that he was unimpressed with their attitudes and methods. During the South African War, however, Fay's responsibility for troop movements brought him into contact with an impressive soldier, the then Lieutenant-Colonel J.S. COWANS, with whom he developed a close friendship. In 1911 Fay was invited by the Secretary of State for War, Richard HALDANE, to join a new committee of Britain's six main railway managers set up to examine the problem of feeding London in the event of the east and south coast ports being closed by enemy action. This led to the creation of an executive committee whose function would be to control the railways in the event of a national emergency. Fay remained on this committee until December 1916, when he joined the War Office, forming a powerful civilian railway triumvirate with Sir Guy GRANET and Sir Eric GEDDES at the heart of Britain's wartime logistics.

Fayolle, Marie-Émile (1852–1928) French military commander. Fayolle was 'dug out' of retirement in 1914 to command a division. His rapid promotion, to corps and then army command, owed much to the swathe cut through senior ranks of the French army by General JOFFRE in the aftermath of the early French defeats. Fayolle was a gunner in a war that came to be dominated by artillery. He shared PÉTAIN's belief that 'artillery conquers, infantry occupies'. He was predictably horrified by British infantry tactics at the opening of the Somme campaign, in which he commanded the French Sixth Army on the British right. Skilfully using his much greater artillery resources, especially heavy artillery, and employing much more sophisticated infantry tactics, Fayolle inflicted a substantial defeat on the Germans on 1 July 1916, even penetrating their second line near Péronne, an achievement that caused consternation in German ranks and cost General Grünert, the chief of staff of German Second Army his job. The elevation of PÉTAIN to Commander-in-Chief in May 1917 saw Fayolle succeed him in command of Army Group Centre, covering the Champagne and Verdun. He was one of the Allied commanders transferred to Italy in November 1917 after the Caporetto disaster, briefly commanding the Italian Tenth Army. Fayolle's was a career that flourished in the adversity of others. At the end of March 1918, with the German spring offensive threatening to drive a wedge between the British and French armies on the Somme and with the Allies staring at the possibility of defeat, he was given command of the Army Group Reserve, blocking the axis of any German advance. During the Allied counter-offensive that began in July Fayolle commanded a group of armies almost as large as the entire British Expeditionary Force. But he did so under a new Allied Commander-in-Chief, Ferdinand FOCH, to whose belligerent approach and offensive predilections even this most cautious of generals eventually succumbed.

Ferdinand I (1861–1948) Tsar of Bulgaria. Born in Austria, the youngest son of a Saxon prince and a French princess, Ferdinand exchanged the life of a junior officer in the Austro-Hungarian army for the throne of Bulgaria in 1887 at the age of 26. He took surprisingly well to the job, eventually establishing almost complete authority over his government. Ferdinand could not have flourished in Bulgarian politics without a refined sense of danger. The outbreak of war in August 1914 set off many warning signals. But it also presented possibly unique opportunities for Bulgarian aggrandisement and a chance to reverse the shattering Bulgarian defeat in the Second Balkan War (1913). He decided to wait upon events. By the autumn of 1915 these seemed to favour the Central Powers. Successive French offensives on the Western Front had succeeded only in achieving massive losses for negligible gains. The Italians were faring little better against Austria. The

Anglo-French attack on Gallipoli had reached a humiliating stalemate. The determination of the Allies, especially French Foreign Minister DELCASSÉ, to maintain good relations with Russia offered no prospect of a sympathetic response to Bulgarian aspirations. On the Eastern Front German arms were everywhere triumphant. Warsaw, Ivangorod, Kovno, Novo-Georgiesk and Brest-Litovsk had all been occupied. It was time to choose. Ferdinand chose Germany. It was a fatal mistake. Short-term military successes against Serbia proved difficult to repeat. The Germans were a demanding ally, ruthlessly exploiting Bulgarian economic and military resources for their own ends. That Ferdinand was able to hang on to his throne in the face of internal unrest and military defeat until forced to abdicate by Allied pressure in October 1918 is a testimony to his feral political instincts. Balkan monarchs often lost their thrones. There was triumph of a kind in keeping his head.

Ferdinand I (1865–1927) King of Romania. Much courted by the belligerent powers throughout 1915, Ferdinand bided his time, but under the influence of his pro-Allied Prime Minister Ion BRATIANU and impressed by the success of the Russian BRUSILOV offensive, he declared war on the Central Powers in August 1916. His reward was to be invaded by two German armies. Bucharest fell on 6 December, and the remnants of the Romanian army were pinned in the northeast of the country. With three-quarters of the country occupied and the army virtually destroyed, Romania was able to make little contribution to the Allied cause. Indeed, the contrary was probably the case. Ruthless exploitation of Romanian natural resources made a significant contribution to Germany's ability to continue the war for a further two years. The collapse of Russia at the end of 1917 persuaded Ferdinand to seek an armistice with the Central Powers on 9 December.

German exasperation at Romania's failure to come to terms finally resulted in their overrunning the country in March 1918. Romania was compelled to accept a humiliating peace. Ferdinand, however, refused to sign the Treaty of Bucharest. On 10 November 1918 he re-entered the war on the Allied side, a shrewd and cynical move for which Romania was handsomely rewarded with territorial gains at the Paris Peace Conference in 1919.

Fisher, Andrew (1862–1928) Australian Prime Minister 1908–9 and 1910–15. Fisher's reputation has, to an extent, been blighted by the statement he made during an election campaign at the height of the July Crisis in Europe: that Australia would stand by Britain to its 'last man and last shilling'. This apparent belligerency and acceptance of Australia's subordinate status did not, in fact, truly reflect Fisher's ambivalent and unenthusiastic attitude to the war though it proved a considerable embarrassment to him and his party during the later agonised Australian debates about conscription for overseas military service. Fisher resigned in October 1915 and was appointed Australian High Commissioner in London. He was a decent, honourable man, overshadowed by his more martial successor, Billy HUGHES.

Fisher, Herbert Albert Laurens (1865–1940) British historian, university administrator and educational reformer, who was President of the Board of Education in LLOYD GEORGE's coalition government. Fisher was responsible for the Education Act of 1918 that raised the school leaving age to 15, established medical inspection of school children and introduced nursery schools. The more radical proposal to make part-time education compulsory for children aged 14 to 18 fell victim to postwar national expenditure cuts (the 'GEDDES axe').

Fisher, John Arbuthnot (1841–1920) British naval administrator, who – as First Sea Lord from 1904 to 1910 – devoted his colossal energies to the reform and modernisation of the Royal Navy, effecting a revolution in warship design, introducing the *Dreadnought* class of battleships and the battle cruiser, and provoking an international arms race. Fisher was convinced that war with Germany was inevitable and that the Royal Navy would play a key role. He would let nothing stand in the way of his creating an efficient, modern, fast, all big-gun fleet capable of destroying the German High Seas Fleet in a battle of annihilation, a new Trafalgar, which would decide the outcome of the war and the fate of the world. He ruthlessly manipulated naval patronage, making some careers and breaking others. He showed a keen appreciation of the power of the press and public opinion which remains impressive even in a much more media-conscious age. He was master of the 'leak'. His ability to sell naval reform to Liberal governments as an economy measure showed a fine political understanding as well. His achievements, however, were flawed. His haste and willingness to cut corners in a climate of financial stringency produced a fleet with some inadequate types of ship and an inferior fire-control system. Fisher's belief in the battle cruiser proved especially fallacious. In battle their speed did not compensate for inadequate armour and, in retrospect, they look like an expensive error of judgement. Fisher also believed in 'the man'. The great commander was everything in war. This led him to despise staff work. He vehemently opposed the creation of a naval staff. As a result the Royal Navy was hopelessly deficient in staff training, incapable of effective war planning and hostile to inter-service co-operation. It was also riven with favouritism and cliques. Many of these inadequacies were violently exposed at the battle of Jutland in 1916.

Fisher returned from retirement to the Admiralty in October 1914 at Winston CHURCHILL's invitation. The two men had much in common, but their relationship soon began to deteriorate as a result of Churchill's determination to use 'spare' naval capacity to force the Dardanelles. Fisher was dubious about the enterprise from the start, believing in the Nelsonian dictum that 'a ship cannot defeat a fort', but he kept uncharacteristically quiet in the face of Churchill's aggressive optimism. Fisher's policy was one of 'steady pressure'. Naval blockade of Germany would force her either to collapse economically or – more likely – to seek a naval decision against the British in the North Sea. This would constitute the decisive moment of the war. The Royal Navy had to be ready. This meant preserving its numerical advantage and its best ships in home waters. Churchill's willingness to risk them recklessly against Turkish mines in a minor theatre of operations eventually wore Fisher down and in the end he cracked. His dramatic resignation in May 1915 precipitated a political crisis that ended the life of Britain's last Liberal government and catapulted Churchill into the political wilderness.

Fiske, Bradley Allen (1854–1942) US naval officer. Fiske became professional head of the US Navy (USN) in February 1913 after an outstanding career notable for innovation and technical inventiveness. Fiske envisaged the USN as a major instrument of national policy and wished to see its preparedness for war enhanced by the creation of a naval war staff with responsibility for strategic and operational planning. The advent of war in Europe gave greater urgency to these ambitions but brought him into increasing conflict with the liberal, pacifist sensibilities of the USN's political head, Josephus DANIELS. Daniels was hostile to a naval war staff, fearing that it would endanger the administration's neutrality policy, which he strongly supported. He halved the USN's shipbuilding programme after the outbreak of war in Europe and refused to allow the staff to organise war games or undertake contingency planning. Fiske's position eventually became untenable and he resigned with effect from May 1916. Nevertheless, he succeeded in establishing the USN's importance and in laying the foundations of its operational effectiveness. He also has strong claims to be the father of US naval aviation.

Fitzclarence, Charles (1865–1914) British military commander, who ordered the attack of 2nd Battalion Worcestershire Regiment at Gheluvelt on 31 October 1914, restoring the broken British line before the vital town of Ypres. A tall, athletic officer, Fitzclarence was described in his pre-war annual confidential reports as 'very cool headed and fearless of responsibility', 'full of energy and self-reliance'. His actions at Gheluvelt, while GOC 1st (Guards) Brigade, demonstrate his decision and resource as a field commander. They also display his courage and willingness to lead from the front, characteristics which led to his death in action on 12 November 1914.

Foch, Ferdinand (1851–1929) French and Allied military commander, a military intellectual whose pre-war lectures as Professor at the École Supérieure de la Guerre had an electrifying effect on the French army still traumatised by its defeat in the Franco-Prussian War (1870–71). Foch's military views have often been caricatured as little more than a mindless belief in the superiority of the offensive and the importance of the 'will', but this is far from the truth. He also understood firepower. His actions as a field commander in 1914 confirm that he was no ideologue but a flexible and resourceful general who could respond swiftly to the challenge of events. He also demonstrated at this early stage of the war his indefatigable spirit. His famous signal to JOFFRE as GOC Ninth Army during the battle of the

Marne – 'My centre is giving way, my right is falling back, situation excellent, I attack' – has become the stuff of legend. During the savage and chaotic fighting round Ypres in October and November 1914 Foch's seemingly bottomless well of courage did much to sustain the faltering spirits of the British Commander-in-Chief, Sir John FRENCH. Foch's leading role at First Ypres is rarely acknowledged in British popular accounts, which continue to portray the battle, quite erroneously, as a largely British affair. During 1915 and 1916 Foch co-ordinated French forces in the north and on the Somme, but his star was extinguished with that of Joffre in December 1916. He was sidelined for six months until recalled as French chief of staff, in succession to PÉTAIN, in the aftermath of the Nivelle offensive (April–May 1917). On 26 March 1918, with the German spring offensive threatening to drive a wedge between the British and French armies, Foch was appointed *de facto* Allied Commander-in-Chief, an appointment suggested by HAIG and confirmed by CLEMENCEAU, both of whom wanted a general who would fight. Foch was certainly that. His calm and courage, rather than any great act of generalship, were instrumental in stabilising the Allied line. He overcame the defeatism of Pétain and established excellent relations with the British Commander-in-Chief, Douglas Haig, a kindred spirit. Even during the worst moments of defeat and retreat Foch was thinking about a counter-attack and began to put together a reserve. A limited attack in July signalled his intentions and a general advance (*tout le monde á la battaille*) began on 8 August. On 11 November, at a railway carriage in the forest of Compiègne, he dictated surrender terms to the German Armistice delegation. Foch did not enjoy the kind of authority that General Eisenhower had as Allied Commander-in-Chief in 1944–45, especially in the early months of his appointment, but he soon established his practical authority over the conduct of strategy. He was not afraid to defer to his subordinate commanders, especially Haig, in operational matters. His role in the Allied victory was vital and indispensable. He was a great soldier and one of the greatest Frenchmen of the twentieth century.

Fokker, Anton Herman Gerard (1890–1939) Dutch/German aircraft designer and manufacturer, who built his first aircraft at the age of 20 and taught himself to fly. In 1912, at the age of 22, he opened a small aircraft factory near Berlin. On the outbreak of war he offered his designs to both sides but the Allies declined them. Fokker, instead, became one of the leading manufacturers in Germany and was forced to take German citizenship. He designed many leading German aircraft of the war, including – finally – the impressive D-VII, and invented the interrupter gear which allowed a machine gun to fire straight ahead through the propellers, revolutionising air combat and placing the German airforce temporarily in a position of air superiority.

Fonck, (Paul) René (1894–1953) French fighter ace, who took up flying in 1912 and flew with a French air force reconnaissance unit in the early part of the war before transferring to the fighter service, shooting down his first aircraft on 6 August 1916. Fonck looked more like an accountant than a fighter pilot and his approach to air combat was suitably meticulous and cold-blooded. Like many of the leading aces his prowess was based on shooting rather than flying skill. His shooting *was* incredible. On 9 May 1918 he downed six German aircraft in a single dogfight using only fifty-six bullets. He ended the war as the top scoring French and Allied ace and was the only top-scoring ace among the leading belligerents on the Western Front to survive the war. He is generally credited with seventy-five 'kills' but personally estimated that he

had shot down at least 127 aircraft, a statistic he was not afraid to advertise. During the Second World War he was tainted with the stigma of collaboration and died in obscurity.

Ford, Henry (1863–1947) US industrialist. Ford founded his famous car company in 1903. His successful six-year legal battle to break the monopoly of the Association of Licensed Automobile Manufacturers and the introduction of the Model T car in 1908 had a dramatic effect not only on the American car industry but also on American society. The Model T was a cheap, robust product, manufactured using the assembly line techniques advocated by theorists of 'scientific management' such as F.W. Taylor. Ford aimed from the start at a mass market and was responsible for putting America 'on wheels'. His decision to pay his workers $5 a day, twice the normal rate, also ensured that he had an equally dramatic effect on the US labour market and labour relations. Ford was a vehement opponent of US entry into the war and went to some lengths to prevent his company's cars from being sold to any of the belligerents. In November 1915 he attracted widespread publicity (and ridicule) by sponsoring the Ford Peace Ship, which took Ford and fellow pacifists to Europe, where they attempted (and predictably failed) to end the war by means of 'continuous mediation'. After the United States entered the war, however, Ford dedicated his company wholeheartedly to war production, including tractors, aero engines, ships (especially anti-submarine boats) and tanks, though the war ended before many of Ford's products could see action. Nearly 40,000 Model Ts did see service on the Western Front, however.

Foulkes, Charles Howard (1875–1969) British soldier and gas warfare pioneer. Foulkes was born in India, the son of an Indian government chaplain. His upbringing seems to have been more successful in inculcating muscularity than Christianity, however. His temperament was severely practical and impatient of anything that could not be demonstrated experimentally. He was an outstanding athlete, representing Heart of Midlothian at football and Scotland at hockey, for which he won an Olympic medal in 1908. The Royal Engineers, with its immense variety of demanding tasks often given to young officers, suited him perfectly. As a junior officer he showed himself to be energetic, ambitious and independent-minded, but when the war broke out he was 39 and still only a major; when it ended he was a 43-year-old brigadier-general in command of the British Expeditionary Force's Gas Services. Foulkes, like the rest of the BEF, was appalled by the German gas attack at Ypres on 22 April 1915, but outrage soon convinced him of the need for retaliation. When Sir William ROBERTSON recommended Foulkes to Sir John FRENCH as the best man to organise the retaliation, he therefore welcomed his appointment. He set about the task with characteristic determination, undeterred by his complete ignorance of chemical warfare. Foulkes' unit was known as the Special Brigade. From the start Foulkes envisaged its role as waging offensive war, a view that surprised and dismayed some of the professional chemists who were recruited. Foulkes was very ambitious for the Special Brigade, wasting no opportunity to press the belief that gas, in sufficient quantities and properly delivered, could have a decisive outcome on the battlefield. The 'proper delivery', for Foulkes, was always by release from cylinders. This was the method first used by the British at Loos in September 1915, when the gas release caused as much consternation to the British as it did to the Germans. Front-line troops and commanders never really recovered from the suspicion and distrust provoked by gas at Loos. Foulkes ignored their concerns but later in the war was forced to go on a 'charm offensive' to persuade the BEF of the efficacy of gas.

Cylinder release had the important advantage, for Foulkes, of remaining under the control of the Special Brigade, unlike gas delivered in shells, which was controlled by the artillery. Foulkes opposed but did not prevent development of the LIVENS gas projector, a sort of mortar, very inaccurate but cheap to produce and effective. The cost effectiveness of the Livens projector was uncharacteristic of British gas warfare as a whole, however. Despite Foulkes' energy, the ingenuity of his men and the consumption of expensive resources, gas was ultimately disappointing as a weapon, despite its terrifying reputation. Foulkes' account of his war, *Gas! The Story of the Special Brigade*, was published in 1934.

Fournier, Henri Alban ('Alain-Fournier') (1886–1914) French writer and soldier, author of the romantic novel *Le Grand Meaulnes* (1913), killed in action on the Marne on 22 September 1914. He has no known grave.

Fowke, George Henry (1864–1936) Engineer-in-Chief and then Adjutant-General [chief personnel officer] of the British Expeditionary Force. Fowke was a big man in all senses of the term, a talented linguist and raconteur, armed with a formidable memory. His facile and indolent manner disguised a serious professional. His influence grew with that of the importance of engineering, but his dominating personality came to antagonise many at GHQ, where the appointment of his more emollient (though less able) successor, Robert RICE, was greeted with relief. Fowke found his new job, although a promotion, something of a disappointment and a doddle compared with the huge challenges he faced as Engineer-in-Chief. As Adjutant-General he took no interest in office routine but was always ready with advice for those who needed it. His forte was problem solving and he had an enviable capacity for decision. His knowledge of the officers of the Corps of

Royal Engineers was unrivalled. His knowledge of the officers of the army as a whole was rivalled only by that of HAIG. His role in appointments was great but remains as yet undocumented.

Fowler, John Sharman (1864–1939) British staff officer, an Irishman who – as Director of Army Signals – commanded the British Expeditionary Force's electronic communications system throughout the war. He made excellent use of civilian expert staff to assist in perfecting and standardising equipment and presided over a massive increase in the scale, complexity and efficiency of a British army communications system that in 1914 was based largely on visual signalling. These achievements were essential to the increasing power of British artillery in locating and destroying enemy targets, including pioneering improvements in air to ground communications. But the failure to develop a man-portable wireless meant that ground to ground communications often failed once the forward trench system was left behind, imposing fundamental problems of command and control which were never really solved.

Franchet d'Esperey, Louis Felix Marie François (1856–1942) French and Allied military commander, whose reputation in the English-speaking world has suffered from his well-known British soubriquet 'Desperate Frankie', evoking a manic and somewhat comic image. This is unfair. Franchet d'Esperey's energy was immense and his confidence infectious. POINCARÉ called him 'a stranger to depression'. 'He moved quickly, almost fiercely, bent arms keeping time like those of a runner with the movement of his legs,' recalled Sir Edward SPEARS. 'His dark eyes were piercing, his voice sharp, his diction precise … . He kept all in place by his manner. Never did he solicit or permit advice or suggestions, which indeed no one would have dared to offer. He was a genuine commander.' This spirit first manifested itself in 1914. His important victory at Guise on 29 August, while commanding I Corps, played a significant role in the disruption of the SCHLIEFFEN Plan. It also won him command of Fifth Army five days later, replacing the beaten and defeatist LANREZAC. His impact on Fifth Army was immediate and Napoleonic. He made it clear that there would be no more withdrawal and that any man who failed in his duty would be shot. Thus galvanised, Fifth Army resumed its place in the French line as an effective fighting force, an achievement which had considerable impact also on the neighbouring BEF, which felt itself badly let down by Lanrezac. In 1916 and 1917 Franchet d'Esperey commanded Army Group East, then Army Group North. Like FOCH, he remained throughout an advocate of offensive operations. In May 1918 his refusal to contemplate the doctrine of 'defence in depth' led to serious reverses in the face of a surprise German attack on the Aisne. He was replaced and sent as Allied Commander-in-Chief to the malarial backwater of Salonika. Like ALLENBY, however, he rescued fame and honour from the jaws of failure. Franchet d'Esperey had long advocated a strong Allied offensive in the Balkans, an area he knew well, and he brought a renewed sense of purpose to military operations there. His Vardar offensive, launched in September 1918, achieved dramatic success, forcing Bulgaria to accept an armistice at the end of the month, an event that finally convinced LUDENDORFF that the war was lost and that Germany, too, must seek terms. Franchet d'Esperey was a staunch Roman Catholic and his career was undoubtedly harmed by the suspicion of the Third Republic's anti-clerical political establishment.

François, Hermann von (1856–1933) German military commander. As commander of I Corps in East Prussia in August 1914, François' refusal to accept a defensive brief and subsequent insubordination, twice disobeying direct orders, contributed – somewhat fortuitously perhaps – to the crushing German victory at Tannenberg. François' role did not sit comfortably with the emerging HINDENBURG–LUDENDORFF legend. Ludendorff, in particular, was especially distrustful, regarding François as a loose cannon, and his career did not flourish. Except for a brief spell in command of Eighth Army in the autumn of 1918, he spent the war in corps commands, mostly on the Eastern Front.

Frankau, Gilbert (1884–1953) British poet, novelist and soldier. Frankau worked in the family cigar business before the war. He took the many opportunities that this offered for travel and displayed a remarkable facility for acquiring foreign languages, including German, Italian and Turkish. He volunteered for military service on the outbreak of war and was commissioned in the 9th Battalion East Surrey Regiment. He later transferred to the Royal Field Artillery and served on the Western Front. In October 1916 his linguistic and literary skills resulted in his being put in charge of a unit designed to counter German propaganda in Italy. He was invalided out of the army in February 1918. His novel *Peter Jackson, Cigar Merchant* (1920) was a huge success, bringing him wealth and fame and allowing him to ape the aristocratic lifestyle. His war poetry is now little regarded and even less read. It is, however, an interesting body of work that never avoided the realities of war, which he characterised in 'The Other Side' (1918) as 'This loathliest task of murderous servitude', but cannot in any conventional sense be described as 'anti-war'.

Franks, George Mckenzie (1868–1958) British artillery expert and military commander. Franks was PLUMER's chief artillery adviser in Second Army from December 1915 until July 1917. He planned the eleven-day preliminary artillery bombardment for the battle of Messines (7–15 June 1917), perhaps the first really striking British success of trench warfare. Plumer had so much confidence in Franks' arrangements that he allowed him to go on leave just before the battle. Franks enjoyed less success as a field commander. He was sacked as GOC 35th Division during the German spring offensive, accused of making an unsanctioned retirement.

Franz Ferdinand, Archduke (1863–1914) Heir apparent to the Austro-Hungarian throne, whose assassination in Sarajevo on 28 June 1914 ignited a diplomatic crisis that resulted six weeks later in the outbreak of a European war. The publicity given to his visit and the appallingly lax security arrangements were such that even the cowardly and incompetent group of assassins assembled to kill him could hardly fail, though they did their best. Franz Ferdinand was targeted mainly because of who he was, but his ideas for reform of the Habsburg Empire, which included a move from a 'Dual' to a 'Triple' monarchy that would give greater representation to the Slavs, were also anathema to his Serb murderers.

Franz Josef I (1830–1916) Emperor of Austria-Hungary. Franz Josef came to the throne amid the revolutionary ferment of 1848 at the age of 18. He died at the age of 86, after the longest reign of any European monarch, in the middle of a ruinous war that had already inflicted mortal damage on the Habsburg monarchy. This was in keeping with the rest of a life that had witnessed the death of his first-born child, the execution of his brother Maximilian, Emperor of Mexico, the suicide of his son, the murder of his wife and the assassination of his nephew and designated successor, FRANZ FERDINAND. His trials, however, were not only private. His reign was also marked by a procession of humiliating military defeats, by France at Magenta and Solferino

(1859) and by Prussia at Sadowa (1866). Austria was removed from Italy and Germany and forced to accept a 'Dual' monarchy which gave equal status to Hungary (the *Ausgleich* of 1867). After the defeat by Prussia, until the fateful decision to chastise Serbia in 1914, Franz Josef chose the path of peace. The Dual Alliance with Germany (1879) seemed to offer the Empire the protection it needed in a hostile world and became the bedrock of his foreign policy throughout the rest of his reign. Franz Josef was narrow-minded and illiberal, isolated from normal human intercourse by rigid court protocol, completely incapable of understanding the forces that were excavating the foundations of his Empire. He had a high sense of duty and was true to the values he inherited at great cost to himself. His was a tragic life.

French, John Denton Pinkstone (1852–1925) Commander-in-Chief of the British Expeditionary Force (BEF). 'Johnny' French was 62 when appointed to command Britain's expeditionary force of six infantry divisions and a cavalry division in August 1914. A *bon viveur* with an eye for the ladies, he had made his reputation as a cavalry commander in the South African War. He exuded charm and confidence. He was comfortable in the company of politicians, especially Liberals, and was a close friend of Winston CHURCHILL. He was popular with ordinary soldiers and treated them with a tolerant and humane affection. There were few to query and none to dispute his selection as Commander-in-Chief. But doubts soon surfaced. French's task was a difficult one. His orders emphasised that he was an independent commander, responsible for the safety of Britain's limited and precious trained military manpower, but he was also enjoined to co-operate wholeheartedly with the French. It quickly became apparent that these two things might be contradictory, especially when the BEF's position on the extreme

left of the French line placed it in the direct path of the main German advance, spearheaded by First Army. The unannounced withdrawal of General LANREZAC's French Fifth Army on his right flank left him with a distrust of his ally that he never entirely lost, though his inability to stand up to JOFFRE had important consequences in 1915. During the retreat from Mons and in the battles of the Marne and the Aisne it is difficult to detect French in the act of generalship. The most important decision was taken by a subordinate, Sir Horace SMITH-DORRIEN, against French's wishes. French's relations with Smith-Dorrien were notoriously poor, and he was furious when 'S-D' was foisted on him after the sudden death of General GRIERSON. Although French was publicly supportive of Smith-Dorrien's decision to make a stand at Le Cateau on 26 August 1914, he was privately dismayed, believing that 'S-D' had recklessly jeopardised the safety of the whole BEF. When Smith-Dorrien was temporarily embarrassed by the German gas attack at Ypres in April 1915, French took the opportunity to get rid of him. He was not a man to be crossed. During the vicious fighting around Ypres that ended the 'Race to the Sea' in October and November 1914, French's character showed alarming mood swings between aggressive optimism and black despair. On one occasion he declared that there was nothing left to do but ride up to the front and die at the head of his men. 1915 brought little respite. The obligations of the French alliance compelled the BEF to take part in the wearing down process of the German army in trench warfare for which it was singularly ill-equipped. French proved himself a good ally, but the cost to the BEF of the battles at Neuve Chapelle (March), Aubers Ridge and Festubert (May), and especially Loos (September) was severe. An acrimonious dispute about the deployment of reserves with his First Army commander, Douglas HAIG, an erstwhile friend who had long harboured doubts about French's capacity for command that he was quite willing to voice to both the King and the Prime Minister, resulted in French's dismissal. He became Commander-in-Chief Home Forces and, from May 1918, Lord Lieutenant of Ireland during a difficult period.

French's current reputation is low. The historian David French – no relation – described him rather cruelly as an 'over-promoted Victorian cavalry colonel'. He was undoubtedly impetuous and brittle and lacked the true self-confidence of great commanders, especially in crises, of which he had to face many. Although French may not have played his hand very well, there can be no doubt that he was dealt a bad one. He was compelled to fight a major war against the main forces of the world's greatest military power in a difficult coalition war on the national territory of Britain's main ally, and with a small army that was hopelessly ill-equipped for its task. The decision to transfer the BEF to the left flank of the Allied line during the 'Race to the Sea', made on his own initiative and at first resisted by the formidable Joffre, had important consequences. It secured a limited degree of operational independence and placed the BEF close to its line of supply (and retreat) through the Channel ports. ASQUITH believed that the decision alone justified French's appointment. His self-interested publicising of a 'shell scandal' in May 1915 contributed to the political crisis that resulted in the formation of the Asquith coalition and the Ministry of Munitions and the eventual mobilisation of British industry, one of the principal foundations of Allied victory.

Freyberg, Bernard Cyril (1889–1963) British military commander. Freyberg was born in England but brought up in New Zealand, where his family emigrated in 1891. He qualified as a dentist in 1911 and was commissioned in the New Zealand Territorials a year later. But in 1913 he abandoned dentistry for a job as a ship's stoker. It was in this capacity that he found himself in London on the outbreak of war. Somehow he managed to obtain an interview with Winston CHURCHILL, who gave him a commission in the Hood Battalion of the infant Royal Naval Division. Freyberg's brother officers included Arthur 'Oc' ASQUITH (son of the Prime Minister), Rupert BROOKE and the satirist A.P. HERBERT. Freyberg's extraordinary courage and physical toughness first announced themselves to the world during the Gallipoli landings (25 April 1915), when he swam two miles from ship to shore in order to light flares as part of a deception operation, for which he was awarded the first of his four DSOs. In November 1916, as CO of the Hood Battalion, he won the Victoria Cross for his leading part in the capture of the German fortified village of Beaucourt-sur-Ancre, during which he was wounded four times and his battalion captured 500 prisoners. On 21 April 1917 he was promoted GOC 173rd Brigade, 58th Division. He was 27, the youngest general in the British army. He was again wounded on 19 September 1917, but on 22 January 1918 returned to command 88th Brigade, in the elite 29th Division. Freyberg was one of the greatest British soldiers of the war, a fearless front-line leader who inspired all around him. He remained in the army after the war, rising to the rank of lieutenant-general. He had less success in higher command, presiding ineffectually over the humiliating British defeat on Crete in 1941.

Freytag-Loringhoven, Alexander von (1849–1926) German staff officer. Quartermaster-General on Falkenhayn's staff in 1915, he became Deputy Chief of the General Staff in the autumn of 1918, a position he retained for the rest of the war.

Friedrich, Archduke (1856–1936) Austro-Hungarian Commander-in-Chief 1914–16.

Friedrich was little more than a figure-head behind whom lurked the substantive power and ambition of his chief of staff, CONRAD. Although Friedrich was a typical reactionary, unable to rise above the limitations of his caste, he was intelligent enough to foresee the disastrous consequences of Austria's multi-front war but had no solution save pessimism.

Frunze, Mikhail Vasilevich (1885–1925) Russian revolutionary. Frunze joined the Bolsheviks in 1904, when he went to study in St Petersburg. He took a prominent part in the uprising of December 1905 and was sentenced to ten years' hard labour in Siberia. But he escaped from exile in 1914 and by 1916 was established as head of the Bolshevik underground in Minsk. In May 1917 he was elected a delegate to the First Congress of the Soviet of Peasant Deputies, where he met LENIN. He was chosen as Chairman of the Soviet of Workers', Peasants', and Soldiers' Deputies in Shuya and led the Ivanovo-Voznesensk and Shuya Red Guards in the Moscow Uprising on 30 October 1917. Frunze showed an immediate aptitude for war. He quickly rose to command the Bolshevik Fourth Army in the civil war, during which he defeated the forces of both KOLCHAK and WRANGEL. As a member of the Central Committee and the Politburo and as Commissar for Military and Naval Affairs (in which post he succeeded TROTSKY), Frunze laid the administrative and doctrinal foundations of the Red Army.

Fullard, Philip Fletcher (1897–1984) British fighter ace. Fullard is now virtually forgotten, but he shot down a remarkable forty-two enemy aircraft in five months, flying Nieuports with 1 Squadron Royal Flying Corps. His flying career was terminated in November 1917 when he broke his leg playing football (he had played centre-half for Norwich City reserves before the war). The leg was badly set and required extensive treatment. As soon as he was rested, Fullard succumbed to shell shock and could not be returned to duty until September 1918. He eventually rose to Air Commodore.

Fuller, John Frederick Charles (1878–1966) British staff officer and armoured warfare pioneer. Fuller was one of nature's heretics. Clever and imaginative, he was completely unable to suffer fools gladly. He was known to his contemporaries as 'Boney' (after Napoleon). Although he was blessed with Napoleonic energy and curiosity, he lacked Bonaparte's practicality. Given Fuller's personality, it is difficult to see why he joined such a conservative and hierarchical institution as the army, with which he was always at odds throughout his career. Regimental soldiering especially bored him. He found solace in books, especially those on military history and religion, including eastern mysticism and the occult, a lifelong interest. He entered the Staff College in 1913 at his second attempt. His staff training put him at a premium during the war, and in 1915 he was given responsibility by the chief of staff Third Army, Major-General A.L. LYNDEN-BELL, for organising training programmes for senior officers. But his real career breakthrough came in December 1916 when he was appointed chief of staff to what later became the Tank Corps. Fuller was entirely ignorant of tanks, but he had already developed a weapons-centred view of tactics which emphasised the importance of firepower and the new weapon captured his imagination. He quickly emerged as one of the tank's principal advocates, fertile in schemes for its use. He played a key role in planning the tank assault at Cambrai (November 1917) and later drew up a fanciful scheme ('Plan 1919') for an armour-air offensive using massed tanks attacking in depth. After the war, as a journalist and military historian, his fertile pen did much to influence British perceptions of the war. He portrayed British armoured development as a struggle between prophetic innovators and a reactionary establishment. The view has had a profound, but malign, effect on British understanding of the war and the role of the tank within it. It is well to remember when reading Fuller that his views on the tank during the Great War are almost entirely partial, self-interested and wrong.

Furse, Katharine (1875–1952) British nursing organiser and founder of the Women's Royal Naval Service. Katharine Furse joined the volunteer nursing organisation the Voluntary Aid Detachment (VAD) in 1909, five years after the death from tuberculosis of her husband, the painter Charles Furse. In October 1914 she took the first VAD Corps to France, where she established a Rest Station at Boulogne. She returned to England in January 1915 to become head of the British Red Cross Women's VAD department. She resigned from this post in 1917 owing to opposition to her support for a greater role for women in the organisation. Despite this, under her leadership the number of female VADs greatly increased. There were some 90,000 serving when the war ended. She was not unemployed for long. The Admiralty snapped up her services, asking her to establish a naval organisation for women that eventually became the Women's Royal Naval Service (WRNS). After the war Dame Katharine Furse became a leading figure in the Girl Guides movement.

Fyfe, Henry Hamilton (1869–1951) British journalist, whose service as a war correspondent made an important contribution to the leftward drift of his views that had been apparent even before the war began. Fyfe made an outstanding contribution to the development of popular journalism in Britain as editor of Alfred Harmsworth's *Daily Mirror*, where he pioneered 'photo-journalism' and the 'scoop' and discovered the popular appeal of 'Royal' stories, especially illustrated ones, and 'stunts'. His appointment in 1907 as 'special correspondent' for the *Daily Mail* took him all round the world and began the transformation of his political views, originally those of an unreconstructed Tory. By 1914 he had joined the Fabian Society and was a supporter of the progressive Liberal policies associated with David LLOYD GEORGE. When war broke out he immediately went to report the war on the Western Front, a decision that did not endear him to military authority, which regarded journalists as more dangerous than the enemy. KITCHENER was especially hostile and threatened to have him arrested, a fate that Fyfe avoided for several weeks by joining the French Red Cross as a stretcher bearer. In the face of continued official hostility, he left for the Eastern Front, where the restrictions on journalists were less severe. He did not return to the Western Front, this time with official accreditation, until 1917. He turned down the offer of a knighthood for his services after the war, when he became a fierce critic of the Versailles settlement and a supporter of the Union of Democratic Control. He was editor of the socialist *Daily Herald* from 1922 to 1926 and twice failed to enter parliament as a Labour candidate. Fyfe was one of the great journalists of his generation, a man of firm convictions, unwilling to accept limitations to his freedom of speech from whatever the source.

G

Galliéni, Joseph Simon (1849–1916) French military commander and Minister of War. Galliéni received his real military education not at St Cyr but in the hard school of colonial warfare, particularly in Indo-China. It was here that he developed the theories of pacification he was to implement as Governor of Mauritius (1896–1905). In 1911 he was considered for the post of French chief of staff, but his age (62) was held against him and the appointment went to JOFFRE. On the outbreak of war in August 1914 Galliéni was made Military Governor of Paris. He immediately set about remedying the poor state of the capital's defences. The decision of General Alexander von KLUCK, commander of the German First Army, to alter his line of advance to the south-east of Paris alerted Galliéni to the possibility of attacking the Germans' right flank. He urged this strategy upon Joffre, readied General MAUNOURY's Sixth Army, which was under his command, for the attack, and – in a brilliant gesture that became the stuff of legend – rushed reinforcements to Maunoury in a fleet of taxis. Galliéni's actions made him the 'Saviour of Paris' and allowed him to contest with Joffre the honour of 'Saviour of France'. He became Minister of War in October 1915 but found it impossible to influence strategy and military planning, which were entirely dominated by Joffre. He resigned in poor health in March 1916 and died soon afterwards.

Gallwitz, Max von (1852–1937) German military commander, who served on the Western, Eastern and Balkan fronts, always displaying a cool and capable professionalism in both attack and defence. His Eleventh Army captured Belgrade on 9 October 1915. During the autumn of 1918 he conducted a resolute and skilful defence against greatly superior numbers of US troops at St Mihiel and the Meuse-Argonne. A devout Roman Catholic, Gallwitz lacked the fanaticism of some of his contemporaries.

Garros, Roland (1888–1918) French fighter ace, a well-known stunt pilot who immediately joined the famous Storks squadron (*Les Cicognes*) when war broke out. Garros helped revolutionise aerial combat by developing the forward-firing machine gun, using steel deflector plates on his propeller blades to prevent the propeller from being shot off. Unfortunately, this device came to the attention of the Germans after Garros crash-landed behind enemy lines in April 1915. Anton FOKKER, the German aircraft designer, took up the concept and developed the much more efficient and safer interrupter gear that gave German aircraft immediate air superiority. Garros escaped from captivity in February 1918, returned to France and rejoined the air service. He was shot down and killed on 5 October 1918.

Gater, George Henry (1886–1963) British military commander. In August 1914 Gater was Assistant Director of Education for Nottinghamshire, with no previous military experience beyond the school cadet corps at Winchester. He was commissioned in the 9th Battalion Sherwood Foresters in September 1914 and fought with the battalion on Gallipoli. He later commanded 9th Sherwoods and subsequently the 6th Battalion Lincolnshire Regiment on the Somme and at Third Ypres. He was twice wounded, winning the DSO and bar. On 1 November 1917 he was promoted GOC 62nd Brigade, in David CAMPBELL's 21st Division. This completed a remarkable rise from civilian to brigadier-general in just over three years. He was not quite 31. Gater commanded 62nd Brigade for the rest of the war in heavy fighting. After the war he returned to educational administration, later becoming a senior civil servant. He was knighted in 1936. His *Who's Who* entry is remarkably restrained about his remarkable war.

Gauchet, Dominique-Marie (1853–1931) French naval commander, who succeeded DARTIGE DU FOURNET as French Commander-in-Chief in the Mediterranean in December 1916, retaining the post for the remainder of the war. Gauchet was the worst type of prickly Frenchman, sensitive to perceived slights, temperamental and vain. His appointment was regarded with some trepidation by his Italian and British allies, who had not been impressed with his collegiality at the Dardanelles and Salonika. As Commander-in-Chief, however, he did not so much mellow as become irrelevant, spending most of his time at Corfu polishing his battleships in preparation for a great, classical fleet engagement with the Austrian navy that

never transpired, leaving the British to assume control of the messy and intractable anti-submarine campaign.

Gaudier, Henri (1891–1915) French sculptor. In 1911 Gaudier moved to London with his lover, Sophie Brzeska, quickly establishing himself as a member of the artistic avant garde. He was a founder member of the London Group and a signatory of the Vorticist Manifesto. He volunteered for military service on the outbreak of war and was killed in action on 5 June 1915 at Neuville St Vaast. The importance of his work was recognised only after his death.

Geddes, Auckland Campbell (1879–1954) British politician, brother of Sir Eric GEDDES. A surgeon by profession, he became a leading wartime administrator, first as Director of Recruiting (1916) and then as Minister of National Service (1917). As Minister of National Service, he enjoyed greater power and authority than his predecessor, Neville CHAMBERLAIN. He acquired control of military recruiting and clarified important issues of labour supply with the equally new Ministry of Labour, becoming – in effect – Britain's 'manpower supremo', a position that came rather too late in the day to have the beneficial effect on manpower planning that it might have done. By the end of 1917 Geddes could do little more than point out the dire state of Britain's manpower situation. The expedients adopted in 1918 of extending conscription to all males aged 18–51 and of cancelling exemptions from military service disturbed trade union opinion and resulted in a rash of strikes. The attempt to impose conscription on Ireland also had to be abandoned.

Geddes, Eric Campbell (1875–1937) British businessman, wartime administrator and politician. Geddes joined the North Eastern Railway in 1904, becoming its General Manager in 1914 at the age of

39. He specialised in 'scientific management' and statistical analysis, neither technique being prominent in much contemporary British business practice. These talents were, however, at a premium during the war, especially in the field of what subsequently became known as 'logistics'. He was co-opted to the Ministry of Munitions in 1915 by LLOYD GEORGE, who admired him as a 'man of push and go'. The following year Geddes was sent to France, becoming Inspector-General of Transportation, in which post he achieved something of a revolution in the British Expeditionary Force's transport and supply systems. He split the BEF's transport arrangements into four areas: docks, railways, light railways, and roads. He brought in other civilian experts and introduced business techniques such as prioritisation and statistical prediction, which brought about great improvements in efficiency and capacity. In May 1917 he was invited to perform the same trick as Controller of the Navy, before succeeding CARSON as First Lord of the Admiralty in July. As political head of the Royal Navy, Geddes came into increasing conflict with his First Sea Lord, JELLICOE, over the issue of convoys, eventually dismissing him in a curt interview at Christmas 1917. During his short military career (1916–17) Geddes held only two ranks, major-general and vice-admiral. His post-war career has been somewhat overshadowed by his association with national expenditure cuts (the 'Geddes Axe' of 1922) and his infamous declaration during the general election of 1918 that Germany would be squeezed 'until the pips squeak'. He was the brother of Sir Auckland GEDDES.

Gellibrand, John (1872–1945) Australian military commander. Gellibrand was an ex-British Regular and Staff College graduate, who served in South Africa with the 1st Battalion South Lancashire Regiment. He left the army after being placed on half pay as a result of army reductions

and returned to his birthplace, Tasmania, in June 1912. It was somewhat surprising that the British army let go a man of Gellibrand's abilities (he had passed out top at Sandhurst), but he was notoriously outspoken and unconventional, which doubtless did not endear him to his superiors. On the outbreak of war his staff training was at a premium, and he was made Deputy Adjutant and Quartermaster-General of the 1st Australian Division by Sir William BRIDGES. Gellibrand did very well on Gallipoli, where he was wounded twice, and rose rapidly, first to CO of the 12th Battalion, Australian Imperial Force (AIF), then to GOC 6th Australian Brigade on the Western Front. He asked to be relieved of his command in May 1917 after the Australian debacle at Bullecourt. He was unhappy with the conduct of the 2nd Australian Division, which had a British GOC, Major-General N.M. SMYTHE, as well as other British officers, many of whom he regarded as incompetent. He was sent back to England, where he reorganised the training regime of the AIF depots. He returned to the Western Front in November 1917 as GOC 12th Australian Brigade. He succeeded Sir John MONASH as GOC 3rd Australian Division in May 1918 and commanded it for the rest of the war. Gellibrand was a sensitive man with a wonderful understanding of human nature. He did not have the same hold over his men as ELLIOTT or JACKA, but he was an inspiring leader and trainer of officers. His habit of wearing the same uniform as private soldiers appalled the British (especially General BIRDWOOD) but endeared him to the Australian official historian, Charles BEAN, who saw it as a manifestation of the democratic spirit that made the AIF so formidable. Gellibrand devoted much of his time after the war to the care of veterans and their dependants.

George V (1865–1936) King of Great Britain and Emperor of India. King George was endowed with the Hanoverian virtues of conscientiousness, orderliness, attention to detail and common sense. He had fewer of the Hanoverian vices, except perhaps philistinism. Both his virtues and his vices brought him close to the temper of the British people, for whom he provided an admirable wartime symbol of national unity and determination. He was much more accessible to his subjects than many of his predecessors. He regularly and willingly carried out the boring but useful round of visits to military units, hospitals and factories, including five visits to the Western Front. He also set an example of sobriety and modest living that was not always adhered to by either his subjects or his ministers. The decision to renounce his German titles and change the name of the royal family from Saxe-Coburg-Gotha to Windsor, made in 1917, shows fine political judgement and an awareness of the extent to which the future of the monarchy depended upon popular opinion. He was one of the few monarchs to end the war more secure than before. At his death he was genuinely mourned.

Gerard, James Watson (1867–1951) US diplomat, Ambassador to Germany 1913–17. A New York lawyer with little diplomatic experience and no German, Gerard presided somewhat ineffectually over the progressive decline in US–German relations in the face of US arms sales to Britain and France and the German sinking of American ships. He himself believed that his meeting with the Kaiser was instrumental in getting Germany to abandon unrestricted submarine warfare in April 1916, though there is little evidence for this. After the United States entered the war, Gerard returned home, where he made a considerable impact as a propagandist for the American war effort, particularly through his skill as a public speaker. He was also a regular campaigner for the Liberty Loan, a role in which he was not outshone by a galaxy of Hollywood stars.

Gertler, Mark (1881–1939) British artist and pacifist, the son of Polish Jewish immigrants, whose wartime paintings, especially *The Creation of Eve* and *Merry-Go-Round*, caused a furore among supporters of the war, who regarded his work as subversive.

Geyr, Hermann (1882–1946) German staff officer. Geyr was one of the small group of officers at German GHQ [OHL] on the Western Front responsible for 'doctrine'. He was the principal author of *The Attack in Position Warfare*, the German stormtroopers' bible, and played a leading role in the preparation of the German army for the spring offensive of 1918.

Gibbs, Philip Armand Hamilton (1877–1962) British war correspondent. Gibbs was one of five men to be selected as official war correspondents with the army in 1915. His dispatches, which appeared in the *Daily Telegraph* and *Daily Chronicle*, were subject to censorship. Some of the frustrations of this are apparent in his book *The Realities of War* (1920), an unflattering account of HAIG and his GHQ. Gibbs' discontent with the conduct of the war and his part in it did not prevent him from accepting a knighthood as a reward for his services.

Gibson, Wilfrid Wilson (1878–1962) British soldier-poet. W.W. Gibson was the son of a pharmacist from Hexham in Northumberland. He published his first volume of poems in 1902, establishing himself as the poet of the dispossessed, and soon began to move in the highest London literary circles, becoming close friends with Rupert BROOKE and one of the original 'Georgian poets', presided over by Eddie Marsh. In 1913, following his marriage, Gibson settled at Dymock in Gloucestershire, where – along with Robert Frost and Lascelles Abercrombie – he became one of the 'Dymock Poets'. At 36, and with poor eyesight, he was declared unfit for military service despite four attempts to enlist. He spent the war entirely at home as a driver and clerk in the Army Service Corps. Despite this, in 1914 he produced a fine collection of poems, *Before Action*, including the celebrated and much anthologised 'Breakfast'. This was followed by *Battle* in 1916, although he had never been anywhere near a battlefield. His 'war poetry' was a triumph of imagination over experience.

Gillain, Cyriaque Cyprien (1857–1931) Belgian military commander, who rose from cavalry regiment commander in 1914 to chief of staff by April 1918. He planned the attack at Thourout in October 1918 that cleared the Belgian coast of all German forces.

Gillies, Harold Delf (1882–1960) New Zealand plastic surgeon. While working as an ear, nose and throat surgeon during the early part of the war, Gillies was not only appalled but also fascinated by the increasing numbers of severe, often disfiguring, facial wounds that he saw. He became convinced that specialist treatment must be provided and began a successful campaign to obtain official sanction. He worked originally at the Cambridge Military Hospital at Aldershot and, from early 1918, at an extensive new hospital, St Mary's, Sidcup, specifically for facial injuries. Gillies pioneered many new techniques, most famously perhaps the 'tube pedicle' method of skin grafting that established him as one of the century's great plastic surgeons. His work gave hope and self-respect to some of the war's most traumatised victims.

Giolitti, Giovanni (1842–1928) Italian politician, the dominant figure in Italian politics in the years before the outbreak of war, during which he was four times Prime Minister, establishing a parliamentary dominance through the shrewd and ruthless use of patronage and corruption. He maintained the Triple Alliance with Austria and Germany but sought to im-

prove relations with France and was a powerful advocate of neutrality during the July Crisis of 1914. He vehemently opposed Italian entry into the war in 1915. Appalled by popular militarism, he retired to his tent for the duration, emerging in 1919 for a fifth term as Prime Minister, in the course of which he ejected the odious D'ANNUNZIO from Fiume, ended the workers' occupation of factories and unwittingly paved the way for the seizure of power by Mussolini's Fascists, whom he mistakenly thought he could 'tame'.

Glasgow, (Thomas) William (1876–1955) Australian military commander. Bill Glasgow was a former bank clerk who had served in the South African War, where he won the DSO. On 7 August 1915 he led the assault of the 2nd Australian Light Horse on Dead Man's Ridge during the Gallipoli campaign and was one of only forty-six (out of 200) men to survive unscathed. As GOC 13th Australian Brigade he fought on the Somme, at Messines and at Third Ypres. On 25 April 1918, together with 'Pompey' ELLIOTT, he played a leading part in the important counter-attack at Villers-Bretonneux that helped to turn the tide of the German spring offensive. From June 1918 until the end of the war he commanded 1st Australian Division. Glasgow was a formidable commander, clear-sighted, energetic and determined, but seemingly without vanity or personal ambition. He was also generous and co-operative without being in any way pliant or weak. He favoured the introduction of the death penalty in the Australian Corps. After the war he shared GELLIBRAND's concern for the welfare of veterans and their families.

Glidden, Joseph Farwell (1813–1906) US inventor, who – in 1873 – devised improvements to barbed wire, for which he later secured the patent. Together with his partner Isaac L. Ellwood in the Barb Fence Company of De Kalb, Illinois,

Glidden produced the first commercially successful barbed wire, a simple device that transformed the American west and had an enormous impact on the conduct of war.

Godley, Alexander 'Alick' John (1867–1957) British military commander. Godley commanded the New Zealand and Australian Division on Gallipoli and II Australian and New Zealand Army Corps (later XXII Corps) on the Western Front. His close association with New Zealand troops began with his appointment as GOC New Zealand Military Forces in 1910. His task of establishing a territorial force capable of being integrated into the British army was interrupted by the outbreak of the war, but in the time available to him he displayed considerable energy and organisational ability, succeeding in laying the foundations of a disciplined, well trained force. As a field commander, at divisional and corps level, Godley was less impressive. Chris Pugsley's verdict that he was a bad commander of good troops is difficult to refute. His tactical method on Gallipoli was to 'hammer away', and he seems never to have changed it. He was often out of touch with front-line realities, and his corps' staff were notorious for their inability to co-ordinate operations. An aloof, tactless disciplinarian, Godley was deeply unpopular among the New Zealanders, who told many tales against him and his formidable wife, Louisa.

Godley, Sidney Frank (1889–1957) British soldier. Sid Godley was the first private soldier to win the Victoria Cross during the Great War. The son of a painter and decorator from East Grinstead in Sussex, he joined the army at the age of 20. In 1914 he went to war with his battalion, the 4th Royal Fusiliers. On 23 August, during the battle of Mons, he took over a machine gun after the battalion machine-gun officer, Lieutenant Maurice DEASE, had been mortally wounded and used it single-handedly to defend the bridge over the Mons–Condé canal at Nimy for more than two hours under heavy fire and against overwhelming odds. He was wounded twice. Just before being captured, he destroyed the gun and threw the parts into the canal. He spent the rest of the war in a German prison camp. Godley has been claimed as the inspiration for Bruce BAIRNSFATHER's 'Old Bill'. He often played the role after the war in order to raise money for service charities.

Gold, Ernest (1881–1976) British meteorologist. A grammar school meritocrat, Gold graduated Third Wrangler at Cambridge in 1903. By the outbreak of war he had established himself as one of Britain's leading meteorologists. In 1915 he joined the intelligence staff of First Army, initially to provide meteorological information for gas warfare, then dependent upon wind conditions, but he soon expanded his operations to include data for the artillery. Gold's research into the effects of wind on projectiles at different altitudes proved conclusively that accurate artillery fire would have to allow for these effects. On 12 April 1916 GHQ issued a directive that in future, at 0900 and 1500 hours, a meteorological report would be issued to each battery giving the wind speed and direction at 2,000 and 4,000 feet. This was the beginning of the increasingly sophisticated contribution of meteorology to 'scientific' gunnery, on which much of the British Expeditionary Force's success in 1917 and 1918 came to depend. During the course of the war Gold's staff rose from three to 120.

Goltz, Colmar von der (1843–1916) German military commander, whose close association with the Ottoman Empire began in 1883 when he took up a training post with the Turkish army, in which he was destined to become a field-marshal. Goltz was a thoughtful well-read man with a sceptical intelligence that made him an ideal teacher but a somewhat insipid commander. He spent the first few months of the war as Military Governor of Belgium, a post in which his distaste for oppressing the civilian population was only too apparent. He greeted his transfer to Constantinople with relief and as an opportunity to get back to real soldiering among people he knew and admired. But he was again to find disappointment. His ill-defined role as 'military adviser to the Sultan' brought him into conflict with the German commander on Gallipoli, LIMAN VON SANDERS, and with the Young Turk leader, ENVER PASHA. In October 1915 he at last secured the field command he coveted, that of the Ottoman Sixth Army in Mesopotamia. He halted the advance of British forces under General TOWN-SHEND amid the ancient ruins of Ctesiphon in November, forcing Townshend's army to retreat to Kut, where it was besieged. Goltz died a few days before Kut surrendered, giving rise to persistent but unproved rumours that he was poisoned.

Goltz, Rüdiger, Count von der (1865–1946) German military commander, who led the German forces dispatched to Finland to assist General MANNERHEIM and the Finnish nationalists establish their independence from Russia in February 1918. He captured Helsinki in April and helped to secure the surrender of Bolshevik forces in May.

Gompers, Samuel (1850–1924) US labour leader. As President of the American Federation of Labor (AFL) from its foundation in 1886, Gompers promoted co-operation between business and labour, firmly establishing the AFL as a nationalist, anti-socialist and politically non-partisan organisation. He was a declared pacifist until 1914 but quickly realised the advantages to the AFL's members, mostly skilled white males, of the 'war boom' produced by Allied demands for American products, especially munitions. By 1916 he openly supported war 'prepared-

ness', though he retained a concern that US entry into the war might prejudice the workers' rights for which he had long campaigned. Before war was declared, he tried hard to extract as many concessions as possible from the WILSON administration, which had been disappointingly slow in responding to the AFL's demands. When the US entered the war, Gompers worked closely with George CREEL, America's chief propagandist, and was active in lobbying Allied labour leaders, not least those in his native Britain, to support Wilson's Fourteen Points. As Gompers feared, however, the war resulted in a sharp move to the right in American public opinion. This, together with the Congress's repudiation of the Treaty of Versailles, which Gompers supported, and President Wilson's incapacitating stroke, greatly undermined Gompers' influence and ability to deal with rejuvenated big business on an equal footing.

Goodenough, William Edmund 'Barge' (1867–1945) British naval commander. Goodenough was an outstanding commander of light cruisers, the 'eyes' of the fleet. He led the 2nd Light Cruiser Squadron in his flagship HMS *Southampton* from 1913 until 1916. He took part in the battles of the Heligoland Bight and Dogger Bank and was one of the few subordinate commanders to distinguish himself at Jutland (31 May–1 June 1916). JELLICOE's anguished complaint 'Why doesn't anyone tell me anything?' could not be addressed to Goodenough, whose scouting performance was exemplary. A courageous and intelligent officer, Goodenough trained his captains to know his mind, so that they could act appropriately without orders in the confusion of battle. He was promoted Rear-Admiral in 1916 and given command of the 2nd Battle Squadron, a post he retained until the end of the war.

Goremykin, Ivan Longinovich (1839–1917) Russian Prime Minister 1914–16, whose contempt for public opinion and subservient bureaucratic conservatism naturally endeared him to the Tsar, who – alone except for his wife – seemed incapable of comprehending the damage being done to the regime and to Russia's war effort by the corruption and inefficiency of his administration. Goremykin was the only minister to support the Tsar's disastrous decision to go to the front and assume personal command of his armies in September 1915, leaving government in the hands of the Tsarina, for whom even Goremykin was too moderate an absolutist. He was replaced in January 1916 by the odious Boris STÜRMER.

Göring, Hermann Wilhelm (1893–1946) German fighter ace. Those brought up on newsreel images of the Nazi Reichsmarschall Göring find it hard to believe that he could even fit into a First World War fighter, much less become an ace. But his twenty-two victories are a reminder that behind the public façade of the jolly, fun-loving Nazi with a taste for Ruritanian uniforms and Old Masters there was a brutal and cold-blooded killer.

Gorringe, George Frederick (1868–1945) British military commander. In 1911, at the age of 43, Gorringe became one of the youngest major-generals in the British army. Seven years later, at the time of the Armistice, he was still a major-general, commanding the 47th (2nd London) Territorial division. He spent the first two years of the war with the Indian army. From March 1916, as GOC Tigris Corps, he was given the thankless task of trying to relieve General TOWNSHEND's besieged army at Kut. Gorringe's tactics, based on contempt for the fighting capacity of the Turkish army and reckless optimism, were as unsuccessful as they were crude. His nickname, 'Blood Orange', was not complimentary. After the fall of Kut, Gorringe was sent to the Western Front. In October 1916 he succeeded Sir Charles Barter as GOC 47th Division and commanded it for the rest of the war. As a man, Gorringe was a brutal, arrogant, tactless bully; as a commander, he was relentless and cool-headed. His chief of staff from July 1918, Lieutenant-Colonel B.L. MONTGOMERY, always spoke well of him, attributing the success of his own 'chief of staff system' in Eighth Army during the Second World War to lessons taught by Gorringe at 47th Division.

Gotō, Simpei (1857–1929) Japanese politician. After an early career in medicine Gotō had emerged as a major figure in Japanese politics by 1914. In April 1918 he was appointed Foreign Minister. The last few months of the war were a time of opportunity and danger for Japan. The nation's immediate war aims, the occupation of Germany's Pacific island colonies and her concession in China (Tsingtao), had been speedily achieved. Japanese control over Manchuria had been extended and, with Russia defeated and wracked by civil war, prospects for further expansion in Siberia loomed. The British were keen for the Japanese to land military forces at Vladivostock and to intervene in the Russian civil war in support of the Whites. The Americans were not. Gotō was wary of the United States. In the long term the USA would probably be Japan's greatest rival for Pacific and Chinese hegemony, but during the war trade with America had grown enormously, to the advantage of the Japanese economy. Gotō steered a careful course, doing nothing to alarm US opinion but steadily advancing the Japanese position in eastern Siberia.

Gough, Hubert de la Poer (1870–1963) British military commander. Gough's career was perhaps fortunate to survive his involvement in the so-called Curragh Mutiny of March 1914, when fifty-seven officers of the 3rd Cavalry Brigade, commanded by Gough, announced that they would prefer to accept dismissal from the army if ordered to impose Irish Home

Rule on Ulster. The outbreak of war five months later proved doubly fortunate. It temporarily shelved the 'Irish problem' and it offered unprecedented opportunities for professional advancement. Gough's rise was swift. This owed much to Douglas HAIG, the British Commander-in-Chief, who admired Gough's aggression and saw him as the man to exploit any breakthrough achieved by the great Somme offensive in July 1916. Gough was appointed GOC Reserve (later Fifth) Army in May 1916 at the age of 45, younger than most divisional commanders at that time. Although no breakthrough appeared for him to exploit, Gough added to his reputation on the Somme. Fifth Army achieved the greatest gains for the least cost, but his bungled diversionary attack at Bullecourt in the spring of 1917 revealed weaknesses of planning and control. Fifth Army became increasingly unpopular with subordinate commanders and troops, especially the Australians. Nevertheless, Haig chose Gough to spearhead the attack at Ypres on 31 July 1917, a choice for which he has received much criticism. Gough was a stranger to the Ypres salient and Haig had, in General PLUMER, a proved commander with two years' experience of the sector and its particular difficulties. Gough's attack on 31 July went much better than his critics are often prepared to admit, but in failing to take the Gheluvelt plateau he compromised a further successful advance. This, and the rapidly deteriorating weather, destroyed any immediate hopes of a breakthrough. At the end of August Gough's role was marginalised. Haig handed offensive operations back to Plumer's Second Army. Gough's performance is often unfavourably compared with Plumer's, but Plumer's carefully planned set-piece assaults were never cheap, often succeeding only in driving troops forward into narrow salients where they were subjected to German flanking fire. On 21 March 1918 Gough's Fifth Army, strung out along a massive forty-two mile front with only eleven divisions in line and four in reserve (three of which were cavalry), felt the full force of LUDENDORFF's first spring offensive. Fifth Army was driven back more than forty miles, suffering the worst British defeat of the war on the Western Front. Gough had been placed in an impossible position. During the battle he received exiguous help from his Commander-in-Chief and none at all from his French ally. Public opinion, nevertheless, demanded a scapegoat and Gough was sacrificed on 28 March.

Gouraud, Henri Joseph Eugène (1867–1946) French military commander, to whom real distinction came late in the war. In July 1918 his Fourth Army, forewarned by German prisoners and somewhat reluctantly employing 'elastic defence in depth', inflicted a substantial defeat on the last German offensive of the war at the Second Battle of the Marne, a victory that earned Gouraud the nickname 'Lion of Champagne'. Fourth Army, reinforced by strong American divisions, spent the autumn pursuing the retreating Germans beyond the Meuse. Shortly before the Armistice, Gouraud effected the symbolic capture of Sedan, scene of the French army's catastrophe in 1870. On 30 June 1915, while commanding the French Expeditionary Force to the Dardanelles, he became one of the most senior officers of the war to be wounded, breaking both legs and losing his right arm after being hit by shell fragments.

Grandmaison, Louis Loyzeau de (1861–1915) French soldier and military theorist. As director of military operations on the French General Staff (1908–14), Grandmaison developed the theory of offensive warfare first enunciated by FOCH. He was, however, far more doctrinaire than Foch. He was little interested in tactics, giving primacy to the 'will' and 'offensive spirit' in battle, which it was the function of training to inculcate. He was aware of the effects of firepower on the modern battlefield, but this merely reinforced his belief in psychological factors. His work had intellectual connections with the contemporary philosophy of BERGSON but was ultimately rooted in French belief that only the offensive could capture the initiative in war and prevent another Sedan. Fittingly, Major-General Grandmaison died of wounds received in combat on 19 February 1915.

Granet, (William) Guy (1867–1943) British wartime administrator. Granet was unusual among leading contemporaries in British railway management in having come to his pre-war position of prominence from a background in the law. As a barrister, he was appointed Secretary to the Railway Companies Association in 1900. He was so successful in expanding its influence that he was head-hunted as Assistant General Manager of the Midland Railway in 1905, rising to Manager a year later at the age of 39. During the war he served in the War Office, playing a leading part with Sam FAY and Eric GEDDES in running Britain's wartime logistics.

Grant-Duff, Adrian (1869–1914) British soldier and staff officer. As Assistant Secretary (Military) of the Committee of Imperial Defence from 1910 to 1913, Grant-Duff was responsible for introducing the invaluable 'War Book', which laid down the administrative measures to be taken by all departments of central government in the event of war. Despite being one of the British army's precious pool of trained staff officers, Grant-Duff was allowed to go to war with his regiment, the Black Watch, and was killed in action on 21 September 1914.

Graves, Robert von Ranke (1895–1985) British soldier, poet, novelist, essayist and critic. Although Graves was a wartime volunteer, he served in the 2nd Battalion Royal Welsh Fusiliers, a tough Regular battalion that took pride in its martial tradition, where he became friends with a

fellow officer, the poet Siegfried SASSOON. In 1917 Graves was instrumental in helping prevent Sassoon's court martial after the publication of his celebrated declaration against the war. Graves himself published two volumes of poetry during the war, *Over the Brazier* (1916) and the wonderfully named *Fairies and Fusiliers* (1917). But it was the appearance of his supposedly autobiographical *Goodbye to All That* in 1929 that established him as an iconographic figure in the cultural history of the war. *Goodbye to All That* is a book which must be treated with caution. It was more fictional than it appears, and also more ambivalent about the war than its superficial reputation as an anti-war book would suggest. Unlike his friend Sassoon, Graves did eventually succeed in saying goodbye to the war, establishing a major literary reputation on the basis of his historical novels and, ironically for someone still commonly regarded as a 'war poet', his love poems.

Graves, William Sidney (1865–1940) US military commander. Graves was a Texan veteran of the Philippine Insurrection (1899–1902) who spent most of the war on the Army General Staff in Washington DC. But in July 1918 Secretary of War Newton D. BAKER gave him command of the American intervention force in Siberia, a sensitive post in which he performed with admirable skill, mostly in fending off the machinations of his allies but also successfully helping to prevent Japanese aggrandisement in the region, the principal reason for the presence of the US force.

Gray, Joseph Alexander (1884–1966) Canadian physicist. Joe Gray was already eminent in his field by the time he joined Lawrence BRAGG's experimental 'W' section, working on the problem of 'sound ranging' enemy guns, in the autumn of 1916. He played a leading part in developing sound ranging into an effective weapon in the artillery war through his advocacy of a regular base (eventually established as an arc) from which to make calculations. This made it much easier to distinguish individual German guns. He also did valuable work on establishing wind and temperature corrections that added a new dimension of accuracy to enemy gun location.

Grenfell, Julian Henry Francis (1888–1915) British soldier-poet. Grenfell came from a wealthy family. His father was a renowned sportsman and Conservative MP, his mother a society beauty and one of the 'Souls'. He grew up amid the magnificent splendour of the family home at Taplow, before going to Eton and Balliol College, Oxford. In 1910 he was commissioned in the socially elite cavalry regiment the 1st (Royal) Dragoons. He went to war with his regiment in 1914, immediately took to fighting (and killing) and won the DSO. On 13 May 1915 he was hit in the head by a shell splinter. Grenfell prided himself on what he called his ''ard 'ead' and at first the wound was not thought to be serious. It took an X-ray to reveal the true extent of the damage. He underwent brain surgery but died on 26 May, Ascension Day. Two weeks before he was wounded Grenfell wrote the poem by which he is principally remembered, the serene 'Into Battle'. Its publication in *The Times*, in the wake of Grenfell's death, immediately established him as the romantic symbol of golden youth cut down before its prime. The reality, as with Rupert BROOKE, was more complicated and ambiguous. Grenfell, like all poets, possessed the gift of detachment. He had the ability to stand back from the glittering world in which he grew up and to see its imperfections. He was less clear about what to do about them. He greeted the war almost with relief as a necessary simplification of a contradictory life.

Grey, Edward (1862–1933) British politician. Grey is now principally remembered for his gloomy declaration of foreboding on the outbreak of war: 'The lamps are going out all over Europe; we shall not see them lit again in our lifetime.' Few men did more than Grey to keep them lit. As Foreign Secretary 1905–16, he constantly sought to bring sanity and reason to the conduct of international relations, carefully securing Britain's imperial interests by continuing the policy of détente with France and initiating détente with Russia. He also sought good relations with the United States and Japan. He did not share the anti-German sentiments of some of his officials and did not see Germany as an 'inevitable enemy' that would one day have to be crushed. During the July Crisis of 1914 Grey did more than anyone to try to preserve peace, repeatedly urging restraint and compromise. His masterly speech to the House of Commons on 3 August 1914 was instrumental in rallying British opinion behind the guarantee of Belgian neutrality, placing British belligerency firmly on the moral high ground on which it camped throughout the war.

Criticisms of Grey's policy are legion and contradictory. He is accused of following a secret diplomacy, beyond public or even parliamentary scrutiny. To some, he is a Machiavellian Germanophobe, deliberately seeking to isolate and destroy Germany behind a mask of friendship. To others, he is the weak and inadequate dupe of French intrigue, an idle, aristocratic Edwardian 'appeaser', allowing British policy to become so compromised by sanctioning Anglo-French military and naval staff talks that Britain had no choice but to go to war in 1914. Almost uniquely among contemporary diplomats, he is also charged with a lack of bellicosity, sending contradictory signals to the German government that left them in doubt about the nature of British policy and the inevitable consequences of German violation of Belgian neutrality. As the Foreign Secretary of a 'satiated' power, he was aware that Britain's best interests lay in peace. However, there was little, in practice, that he could do to satisfy the desires and ambitions, or to quell the fears, of those powers for which war was a policy option. He continued in government, increasingly marginalised by failing eyesight, until the formation of the LLOYD GEORGE coalition government in December 1916, when he was replaced by BALFOUR. Grey was Foreign Secretary for the longest continuous period in British political history and the first to write an account of his ministry.

Grierson, James Moncrieff (1859–1914) British military commander. Jimmy Grierson established a dazzling pre-war reputation as a staff officer. A talented linguist, with an intelligence background, he was the British army's leading authority on the armies of Germany, Russia and Japan, on all of which he had published books. As Director of Military Operations at the War Office 1904–06, in the wake of the Anglo-French Entente, he helped lay the foundations of military co-operation between Great Britain and France. In the British army manoeuvres of 1912 he famously bested his rival Douglas HAIG. Grierson was a convivial man, fond of travel, music, good company and good food. He once claimed that he had fought his best battles with a knife and fork. On the outbreak of war he was appointed to command II Corps of the British Expeditionary Force but died of a heart attack in the train taking him to the front on 17 August 1914.

Griffith, Arthur (1872–1922) Irish nationalist. Griffith belonged to that most radical of nineteenth-century professions, printing, and as a young man became a convert to the cause of Irish nationalism, which he propagandised in his weekly newspaper, the *United Irishman*. He was initially contemptuous both of the parliamentary road to independence advocated by the Irish National Party and of the use of violence. He supported passive resis-

tance, non-co-operation with British institutions and the establishment of an Irish parliament in Dublin. In 1905 he was one of the founders of Sinn Fein, a movement committed to the doctrine of Irish self-help and self-reliance. His involvement with Sinn Fein changed his attitude to the use of political violence. He supported the creation of the Irish National Volunteers in 1913 and took part in gun running. He opposed any Irish participation in the Great War, during which his newspapers were suppressed. He was imprisoned from May to December 1916, even though he took no part in the Easter Rising. After the 1918 general election he was one of the Sinn Fein MPs who refused to sit in the British parliament and declared an Irish Republic, of which he became Vice-President. In the Anglo-Irish war he acted as the Irish head of state during the absence in the United States of Eamon DE VALERA. Griffith led the delegation to London that ended the war and established the Irish Free State, of which he became the first President. He died of a cerebral haemorrhage before the resulting Irish civil war, provoked by de Valera's repudiation of the Anglo-Irish Treaty, was resolved.

Grigorovich, Ivan Konstantinovich (1853–1930) Russian Minister of the Navy 1911–17. Grigorovich established a reputation for courage and competence during the defence of Port Arthur in the Russo-Japanese war. As Navy Minister he laid down long-term plans for naval expansion and modernisation that were interrupted by the outbreak of war. He concentrated the Russian navy in the Baltic, protected by huge minefields and ready to strike. The subordination of Russian naval forces to the army General Staff, however, limited his influence and ensured that the navy played virtually no role as an offensive force. His warnings of growing unrest in the fleet during 1916 were ignored by the Tsar. After the February Revolution the navy became increasingly combustible and ultimately beyond the ability even of an able man like Grigorovich to control.

Groener, Wilhelm (1867–1939) German Commander-in-Chief on the Western Front 1918. Fate decreed that Groener would be responsible for sending the German army to war and for bringing it home again. The son of an NCO, throughout his life he retained much of the NCO's bluntness. He was equally methodical, and these two qualities were the foundation of his career, which was spent largely as a staff officer and railway expert. In 1914 he masterminded the transport and supply arrangements of the German deployment. From the autumn of 1916 he became increasingly associated with the Third Supreme Command of HINDENBURG and LUDENDORFF. As head of the Supreme War Bureau he was charged with implementing the huge production targets of the Hindenburg programme. His recognition of the need to involve workers in decision-making did not endear him to employers and others in the high command, however, and in August 1917 he was rewarded for his views by being sent to the Western Front to command a division. In 1918, following the Treaty of Brest-Litovsk, he became chief of staff to Field-Marshal Hermann von EICHORN, with responsibility for economic exploitation of the Ukraine. On 29 October 1918, without being consulted, he was brought back to Berlin and appointed to replace Ludendorff. He assessed the situation in the west within days. On 6 November he told Prince MAX von Baden, the Chancellor, that an armistice was essential. On 9 November, in an even more spectacular display of bluntness, Groener told the Kaiser that he must abdicate, later the same day doing a deal with Friedrich EBERT that guaranteed the role of an unreformed officer corps in the new republic. After the war Groener became one of the leading advocates of the SCHLIEFFEN Plan's genius and one of MOLTKE's severest critics.

Grosz, George (1893–1959) German artist and pacifist. A savage satirist with a dark view of urban life, his sinister Expressionist paintings are stalked by violence, alcoholism, disease and death. His experiences in the army and in a military asylum were searing. He turned his formidable anger against German militarism and the supine materialism of middle-class profiteers and warmongers.

Guchkov, Aleksandr Ivanovich (1862–1936) Russian industrialist and politician, founder of the Octobrist Party and speaker of the Third Duma (1907–12), who shared STOLYPIN's vision of a Russia modernised and transformed by economic and political liberalism, though he was no democrat. He was an early opponent of RASPUTIN. Guchkov's clandestine circulation of correspondence between ALEKSANDRA FEODOROVNA and Rasputin enraged the Tsarina, who demanded that the Tsar have Guchkov hanged. But he survived to become an important member of the Progressive Bloc in the Duma. As Chairman of the War Industries Committee he attempted to co-ordinate Russian war production. His determination to reform Russia had extended also to her defences. He found himself briefly Minister of War after the February Revolution, but was soon replaced by Aleksandr KERENSKY. The Bolshevik Revolution terminated his hopes for a liberal future. He went into exile and died in Paris.

Guépratte, Émile Paul Aimable (1856–1939) French naval commander at the Dardanelles, who shared Commodore Roger KEYES' offensive instincts, despite the vulnerability of his obsolete ships. He was equally suspect in the eyes of his superiors, who sought to control and eventually replace him. Unlike Keyes, he never again held an active command.

Guillaumat, Marie Louis Adolphe (1863–1940) French military commander, with a merited reputation as a safe pair of hands.

A courteous, level-headed commander, his Second Army was trusted with the first serious attack made by the French army after the mutinies of May–June 1917. In December 1917 he replaced General SARRAIL as Commander-in-Chief at Salonika, where he did much to repair inter-allied relations strained by months of intrigue and military stalemate and to improve the military efficiency of the Greek army. He planned the Allied offensive that was to knock Bulgaria out of the war but was recalled to the Western Front in July 1918 before he could carry it out, leaving the honours to his successor, General FRANCHET D'ESPEREY.

Gurko, Vasily Iosiforich (1864–1937) Russian military commander. Gurko was one of the Russian army's leading advocates of reform before the war, when he became closely associated with the Octobrist leader GUCHKOV. During the early months of the war Gurko commanded the 1st Cavalry Division, before becoming chief of staff to General ALEKSEEV. He later received a corps command and was then chosen to rehabilitate the Guards Army, one of the Russian army's elite units, which had been shattered in the disastrous campaigns of 1915. He was briefly Russian Commander-in-Chief while Alekseev recovered from a heart attack in the winter of 1916–17. His attempts to improve the fighting capacity of the Russian army by reducing its size and improving its quality, especially its artillery, were imaginative but foundered on the conservative opposition of the Tsar. After the February Revolution Gurko succeeded EVERT as Commander-in-Chief but found his new masters no wiser than the old. His opposition to the KERENSKY offensive led to his dismissal in June 1918. After the Bolshevik Revolution he went into exile.

Gurney, Ivor (1890–1937) British composer, poet and soldier. Gurney served in the Territorial 2/5th Battalion Gloucestershire Regiment and the Machine Gun Corps on the Western Front, where he was wounded and gassed. He was best known in his lifetime for his music, especially his settings of contemporary poems, notably those of W.W. GIBSON, A.E. Housman, Walter de la Mare and Edward THOMAS. The war seems to have stimulated his poetry principally by separating him from his piano. His individual and unique voice was little appreciated until after his death (none of his poems appears in W.B. Yeats' *Oxford Book of Modern Verse*, published in 1935), but – like Owen – he found a doughty champion in his fellow countryman Edmund BLUNDEN. Gurney's death in a lunatic asylum led to the conceit that he was driven mad by war, but he had a pre-war history of mental illness which makes this seem improbable. His war poems are remarkably lacking in morbidity, and it is difficult to categorise him in any straightforward way as an 'anti-war' poet. He saw neither himself nor his fellow soldiers as victims, portraying them in his poems and letters as phlegmatic and resilient.

Guynemer, Georges (1894–1917) French fighter ace. Guynemer is probably the most famous and revered French ace of the war. A member of the elite Storks squadron (*Les Cicognes*), he achieved fifty-four victories before his death on 11 September 1917. He had the hunter's instinct, describing himself as a 'Boche hunter'. Guynemer's short life was characterised by his devotion to duty, but this ultimately undermined his frail constitution and sapped his combat skills. The strain of combat is readily apparent in his photograph. He should have been relieved of flying duties well before his death.

Gwynne-Vaughan, Helen (1879–1967) British scientist and public servant. Gwynne-Vaughan established a pre-war reputation as a botanist and authority on fungi and became head of the Botany Department at Birkbeck College, London, in 1909. In January 1917 she accepted the appointment of Chief Controller (Overseas) of the new Women's Auxiliary Army Corps (WAAC), whose female clerks, telephonists and catering staff were intended to release more men for the firing line. In 1918 she succeeded Violet DOU-GLAS-PENNANT as commander of the Women's Royal Air Force (WRAF). She was Chief Controller of the Women's Auxiliary Territorial Service from 1939 to 1941. Helen Gwynne-Vaughan was an outstanding administrator who did much to establish female military service in Britain.

H

Haase, Hugo (1863–1919) German politician, a leading figure on the left wing of the Social Democratic Party (SPD), who opposed his party's support for war in 1914. The progress of the war dismayed him, and in April 1917 he left the SPD to lead the pacifist Independent Social Democratic Party (USPD). A decent man, with no appetite for violence, he collaborated with EBERT in November 1918 but was alienated by the army's suppression of unrest in Berlin. A right-wing fanatic assassinated him in November 1919.

Haber, Fritz (1868–1934) German chemist. An ardent patriot, Haber placed himself and the Kaiser Wilhelm Institute for Physical Chemistry, of which he was Director, at the service of government when the war began. He played a leading part in the development of Germany's chemical warfare capability, personally directing the first use of chlorine gas on the Western Front at Ypres on 22 April 1915. His wife was appalled by what she saw as a prostitution of science. When her appeals to him to desist were rejected, she killed herself. Poison gas caused moral outrage in much greater measure than the casualties it inflicted, and Haber was regarded by some as a war criminal. The award of the Nobel Prize for Chemistry in 1919, for his pre-war work on the synthesisation of ammonia, led to protests. Haber was a Jew. His war record counted

for nothing in Nazi Germany. He fled the country in 1933 and died in exile.

Hadik, Count János (1863–1933) Hungarian politician, appointed Prime Minister of Hungary on 28 October 1918, in one of the last acts of Emperor KARL I, in order to forestall a KÁROLYI government. Hadik's ministry lasted three days before succumbing to popular unrest.

Haig, Douglas (1861–1928) British Commander-in-Chief. After a glittering pre-war career, during which he was one of R.B. HALDANE's most valued military supporters, Haig spent the whole of the war in senior command positions on the Western Front. As GOC I Corps (5 August–26 December 1914), he was little involved in the retreat from Mons but played a leading role in the savage fighting around Ypres in October and November. As GOC First Army (26 December 1914–22 December 1915) he exercised operational control over the first battles of trench warfare at Neuve Chapelle (10–12 March), Aubers Ridge (9 May), Festubert (15–25 May) and Loos (25 September–8 October). An unseemly dispute with his superior and erstwhile friend, Field-Marshal Sir John FRENCH, over the release of reserves at Loos led to French's dismissal. As Commander-in-Chief of the British Expeditionary Force (19 December 1915–April 1919), it fell to Haig to lead the largest ever British armies in the most costly and controversial battles in the nation's history, including the Somme (1 July–18 November 1916) and Third Ypres ('Passchendaele') (31 July–10 November 1917).

Haig ended the war as a national hero: vast reverential crowds witnessed the passing of his funeral cortège in 1928. But his reputation did not long survive the onset of post-war disillusionment, revulsion against the human costs of victory and the poisonous assault on his humanity and professional competence spearheaded by LLOYD GEORGE's *War Memoirs*. Haig has become one of the most reviled men in modern British history, vilified as a bone-headed butcher with no more idea of how to win the war than by piling corpse upon corpse. Responsibility for the unprecedented number of British casualties has been attributed to Haig's 'unimaginative' strategy, his operational obsession with achieving a 'breakthrough' and continuation of offensives long past their point of usefulness, his tactical rigidity, fixation with cavalry and contempt for technology. He is accused of surrounding himself with a young, mediocre staff who owed their positions to him and were unable or unwilling to curb his delusions. He has also been accused by some, notably Denis Winter, of seeking to avoid responsibility for these failings by falsifying his wartime diary and corrupting the public record.

These grave charges are difficult to reconcile with the actual fate of the British Expeditionary Force under Haig's command. The inept and costly performance of the inexperienced and poorly equipped BEF between 1915 and the end of 1917, and the British public's understandable fascination with the fate of the Pals' battalions on 1 July 1916, have disguised the extent to which the BEF improved as a fighting force between the summer of 1917 and the end of the war. During this period it discovered an effective operational method, based on all-

arms co-operation within the context of the 'set piece battle', an attack with limited objectives and time scale under the cover of an intense rolling artillery barrage. By the end of the war the BEF had become the most mechanised army in the world, utilising sophisticated artillery and infantry tactics, incorporating chemical and armoured warfare and ground attack aircraft. Between 8 August and 11 November 1918 the BEF inflicted an unbroken series of heavy defeats on the German army that finally destroyed its will to resist. Haig began the war as a corps commander in an army of six infantry divisions. He ended it as Commander-in-Chief of an army of sixty infantry divisions. The BEF's expansion was rapid and haphazard. Its re-equipment, the transformation of its transport, supply and medical arrangements, and the evolution of its training, tactical doctrine and command and control systems, were achieved while in constant contact with the main forces of a powerful enemy in the demanding environment of a coalition war fought principally on the national territory of Britain's main ally. Haig was not the sole cause of these achievements. In some respects his contribution to them was tardy and inadequate. But much of the credit was undoubtedly his. He was much more open to new ideas than he is given credit for by his opponents. He quickly realised the value of tanks and was a firm supporter of air power. He calmly bore a crushing burden of responsibility that would have broken a lesser man. He never lost his nerve or the confidence of his subordinates, his allies and his political masters, with the exception of LLOYD GEORGE. It remains difficult to see how British casualties could have been significantly reduced other than by ending the war earlier through negotiations. The continued scapegoating of Haig serves only to obscure more important issues and to confine discussion of the Great War to what Robin Prior and

Trevor Wilson have called its 'absurdly prolonged adolescence'.

Haking, Richard Cyril Byrne (1862–1945) British military commander. After a successful pre-war career in which he was Professor at the Staff College, Haking commanded 5th Brigade in the original British Expeditionary Force. Although he was kept out of action for three months following a head wound suffered on 14 September 1914, he achieved rapid promotion, first to GOC 1st Division (19 December 1914–11 September 1915) and then to GOC XI Corps, a post he retained until the end of the war. Haking was very much a HAIG man. Like Haig, he corresponded with the King and had no compunction in complaining about Sir John FRENCH's unfitness as Commander-in-Chief. XI Corps was the unit principally involved in the acrimonious dispute about GHQ's release of the reserves at Loos, a dispute in which Haking took Haig's side. As a corps commander Haking quickly established an unenviable reputation as a 'butcher' and an organiser of pointless 'stunts', notably the attack at Fromelles in July 1916 which earned him the undying contempt of the Australian general 'Pompey' ELLIOTT. XI Corps spent most of 1916 and 1917 in quiet sectors and, in November 1917, was selected to go to Italy to shore up the Italian line after the Caporetto debacle. But in March 1918 it returned to the Western Front, holding its old part of the front near Béthune. Three weeks later it was violently attacked by the German Sixth Army, which broke through the Portuguese Corps on XI Corps' left. XI Corps' dogged defence, in which Major-General JEUDWINE's 55th Division played a leading part, helped to hold the line and protect the Channel ports. Haig's attempts to promote Haking to army command were vetoed by the War Office.

Haldane, James Aylmer Lowthorp (1862–1950) British military commander. Haldane became well known for his exploits during the South African War, where he was captured on the same armoured train as Winston CHURCHILL and later escaped with him. He was one of the British military attachés sent to observe the Russo-Japanese war. As GOC 10th Brigade from 1912 he established an excellent reputation as a trainer of troops, basing his methods on those of his Peninsular War hero Sir John Moore. His command of 10th Brigade in 1914 won glowing opinions from his superiors, though these were not always reciprocated. Haldane was intensely ambitious. He was concerned that the reverses he suffered at St Eloi in March 1916, while GOC 3rd Division, would result in his being 'degummed' and sent home, but he survived and prospered. His army nickname was 'Foxy'. He knew his way around and was not above scapegoating subordinates to protect his own position. 3rd Division did well in the early Somme fighting and Haldane was promoted GOC VI Corps on 8 August 1916, retaining the post for the remainder of the war. Haldane was independent minded and often severely critical of higher authority. As a commander he was methodical, efficient and energetic. He lived austerely and attracted some notoriety for banning the rum ration in units under his command. The performance of VI Corps in the initial stages of the battle of Arras in April 1917 and throughout 1918 was impressive.

Haldane, Richard Burdon (1856–1928) British politician, Secretary of State for War 1905–12, Lord Chancellor 1912–15. Haldane was one of the greatest war ministers in British history, a garland for which he has few rivals. He brought to army reform the analytical intelligence of a philosopher and the forensic skills of a lawyer. During his period as Secretary of State for War, despite vehement and often petty opposition from the right and indifference from the left, he succeeded in carrying through sweeping changes that included the creation of the Territorial Force, the British Expeditionary Force, the Officers Training Corps and the Special Reserve as well as effecting a tremendous improvement in medical and nursing facilities. It was due in no small part to him that Britain was able to go to war in August 1914. This did not prevent his being scandalously hounded from office by the NORTHCLIFFE press, especially the *Daily Mail*, for his supposed 'German sympathies' in 1915.

Hall, (William) Reginald (1871–1943) British naval cryptographer. 'Blinker' Hall was appointed Director of Naval Intelligence in October 1914. He established wireless direction finding stations along the east and south-east coasts of Britain that provided the foundation of Britain's naval signals intelligence system. He also founded 'Room 40', the hugely successful cryptanalysis organisation that cracked the German naval codes, decrypted the ZIMMERMAN telegram and was instrumental in the capture of Sir Roger CASEMENT. Hall took over as head of Room 40 in May 1917, after EWING left to become Principal of Edinburgh University. Dismayed by the failures of the Royal Navy's Operations Division to make effective use of Room 40 decrypts at the time of Jutland, Hall – despite opposition from Admiral OLIVER – converted Room 40 into a section of the Intelligence Division. From July 1917 Room 40 sent intelligence reports, rather than raw decrypts, to the Operations Division. This had important consequences for the future conduct of anti-submarine warfare. Hall was an outstanding officer, one of the Royal Navy's greatest successes in what was a disappointing war for the navy.

Haller, Józef (1873–1960) Polish soldier and nationalist. Haller was a former officer of the Austro-Hungarian army who came out of retirement to fight on the Austrian side as a regimental commander in the Polish Legion. But the victory of the Central Powers on the Eastern Front brought him no satisfaction. Dismayed by the Treaty of Brest-Litovsk (3 March 1918), which paid no regard to Polish interests, freeing Poland from Russian domination only to impose a German hegemony, Haller switched sides. He survived the defeat in May 1918 of the Russian-sponsored Polish II Corps by the Germans and escaped to France, where he became Commander-in-Chief of Polish forces. He played a leading part in the defence of Warsaw during the Russo-Polish war.

Halsey, Lionel (1872–1949) British naval commander and staff officer. Halsey's career was closely connected with the British Dominions. During the South African War he found himself involved in the defence of Ladysmith. This turned out to be a piece of good fortune that earned him accelerated promotion. Later he became Flag Captain to the C-in-C Australia, Sir Wilmot Fawkes. And in 1912 he was given command of the battle cruiser *New Zealand*, funds for whose construction had been largely raised by the people of that Dominion. Professor Marder tells the story that during the ship's goodwill trip to New Zealand shortly before the outbreak of war, a Maori chief presented Halsey with a traditional grass skirt said to possess magical powers of protection in battle. Halsey's successor as captain of the *New Zealand*, Captain J.F.E. Green, always wore the skirt over his uniform when the ship was in action and the charm prevailed despite the grievous fate of some of her sister ships. Halsey himself commanded the *New Zealand* at the Dogger Bank (January 1915), before being summoned by Jellicoe in June 1915 to be his Captain of the Fleet. In this capacity he served on HMS *Iron Duke* during the battle of Jutland (31 May–1 June 1916). Halsey followed Jellicoe to the Admiralty in December 1916 as Fourth Sea Lord. When Eric GEDDES succeeded CARSON as First Lord of the

Admiralty in July 1917, he gave Halsey special responsibility for naval design. In 1918 Halsey resumed his links with the Dominions by assuming command of the 2nd Battle Cruiser Squadron, flying his flag in HMS *Australia*. He witnessed the German surrender at Scapa Flow.

Hamilton, Ian Standish Monteith (1853–1947) British military commander. Hamilton was the fateful choice of his old patron Lord KITCHENER to command the Mediterranean Expeditionary Force in March 1915. The choice seemed an excellent one. Hamilton was intelligent, literate and courageous. He had extensive combat experience and knew the eastern Mediterranean well. But in the event this was not enough. Hamilton's task was difficult. The Gallipoli campaign was an afterthought, conceived in haste after the failure of the navy to force a passage through the Dardanelles. Kitchener's instructions were vague and contradictory. The manpower and logistical resources placed at Hamilton's disposal were hopelessly inadequate. He had no control over the appointment of his subordinate commanders, many of whom were old and incompetent. The only intelligence information he received consisted of a 1912 handbook of the Turkish army, a pre-war report on the Dardanelles defences and an out-of-date map. It would have taken a man with remarkable qualities to overcome these obstacles. Unfortunately, Hamilton did not possess them. The slow assembly of the attacking force – six weeks – allowed Turkish forces to recover from the naval bombardment and to repair their defences. When the original landings, made on 25 April 1915, succeeded only in establishing beachheads, Hamilton failed to control, inspire, drive or replace his subordinate commanders. He remained remote both physically and mentally from the combat zone and his continued optimism flew in the face of reality. A fresh landing at Suvla Bay on 7 August, together with attacks from the beachheads at Cape Helles and Anzac Cove, also failed. Stalemate ensued. The living and fighting conditions of Allied troops continued to deteriorate. Battle and medical casualties rose and with no prospect of victory in sight Hamilton was replaced on 15 October. He never again held an active command.

Hamilton Gordon, Alexander (1859–1939) British military commander. Hamilton Gordon was a gunner, but his pre-war career was spent mainly in administrative posts. From 1904 until 1908 he was a staff officer at the War Office. This was the period when Douglas HAIG was Director of Military Operations. Haig formed a high opinion of Hamilton Gordon's abilities that was not shared by other senior officers. BULFIN described Hamilton Gordon's appointment as GOC IX Corps in June 1916 as 'Haig's idea of a joke'. RAWLINSON was another who harboured grave doubts about Hamilton Gordon's fitness for a command. Hamilton Gordon had a melancholy disposition and was known throughout the army as 'Sunny Jim' or 'Merry and Bright'. IX Corps enjoyed its one real moment of success at Messines in June 1917. Ironically, it lost this position during the German offensive of April 1918. In May Hamilton Gordon's inability to recognise German offensive preparations on the Aisne, despite visits to the front line and the urgent representations of his divisional commanders, and his inability and unwillingness to stand up to the French commander, General DUCHÊNE, were instrumental in the subsequent defeat. Unlike Duchêne, however, Hamilton Gordon survived in command until September, when Rawlinson got rid of him shortly before the attack on the Hindenburg line, completing the remarkable rehabilitation of Hamilton Gordon's successor, Walter BRAITHWAITE, another great friend of Haig.

Hankey, Donald William Alers (1885–1916) British writer and soldier. Hankey volunteered for military service and was commissioned, appropriately for an old Rugbeian, in the Royal Warwickshire Regiment. He served on the Western Front with the 1st Battalion and wrote a series of articles, mostly for *The Spectator*, chronicling his observation of military life. These were collected together in a celebrated book, *A Student in Arms*, first published in 1916. Hankey appears very much as a 'Happy Warrior', for whom the war was a mixture of the 'Great Game', the 'Great Adventure' and the 'Great Sacrifice'. His brand of public school piety and belief in the redemptive power of war are now very difficult to appreciate without either pity or scorn. 'If wounded, Blighty,' he is said to have shouted to his men as they went over the top, 'if killed, the Resurrection.' He himself was killed in action on 12 October 1916 on the Somme. He was the younger brother of Maurice HANKEY, who treated news of Donald's death in his customary understated fashion.

Hankey, Edward Barnard (1875–1959) British soldier. Hankey's wartime career was, in many ways, a microcosm of the British army's experience, beginning with an act of traditional valour on a battlefield little changed from Napoleonic times and ending with a command at the leading edge of military technology on a modern, technological battlefield. On 31 October 1914 he led the famous charge of the 2nd Battalion Worcestershire Regiment at Gheluvelt that stopped the threatened German breakthrough and saved Ypres. He commanded 2nd Worcesters in 1915, before transferring to the newly formed Machine Gun Corps, and then in 1917 to the Tank Corps, becoming one of the world's first 'tank generals' in April 1918 as GOC 4th Tank Brigade.

Hankey, Maurice Pascal Alers (1877–1963) British soldier and civil servant. In 1908 Hankey moved from that backwater of British military life, the Royal Marines,

to the obscure post of Assistant Secretary to the Committee of Imperial Defence (CID), a body established in 1902 by A.J. BALFOUR to co-ordinate British strategy and defence planning, a task which it largely failed to fulfil. It was the unpromising beginning to an extraordinary and unparalleled rise to a permanent place at the centre of British government that lasted for a generation. In 1912 Hankey became Secretary of the CID, a post he retained until 1938. Hankey's principal genius was to make himself indispensable. The CID was chaired by the Prime Minister and successive PMs came to appreciate his organisational ability, his willingness to undertake the boring but vital jobs that no one else wanted and, not least, his tact and discretion. No committee seemed complete without his presence. Even though the CID was in effect abandoned on the outbreak of war, Hankey continued to serve on the ad hoc committees, the War Council and the Dardanelles Committee, which succeeded it. He survived the fall of ASQUITH in December 1916 to become Secretary of LLOYD GEORGE's War Cabinet, a post he held until 1919. From 1919 to 1938 he was Secretary of the Cabinet. Hankey was, however, more than a clerk with a good memory and a tidy mind. He was a man of systems. The principal system he invented was modern British cabinet government. Until his advent that institution had no agenda, proper record keeping or minutes. Hankey introduced them all from December 1916, giving continuity and authority to cabinet decisions. He also had views on the conduct of the war. These were always lucid, occasionally far-sighted, but too little acted upon. Hankey came to appreciate the better qualities of all the prime ministers he served, but his preferences were best expressed in the names he gave his eldest son, Henry (after Asquith) and Arthur (after Balfour). The appreciation was reciprocated. 'Without Hankey', declared Balfour, 'we should have lost the war.'

Harbord, James Guthrie (1866–1947) US staff officer and military commander, whose career was closely associated with that of General John J. PERSHING, who was an unequivocal admirer. Harbord served as Pershing's chief of staff from May 1917 until May 1918, when he was given field command. As GOC 4th US Marine Brigade he halted the German attack in Belleau Wood (6–25 June 1918). Promoted GOC 2nd US Infantry Division, he participated in the Second Battle of the Marne in July at one day's notice, struggling to bring together his scattered units in pouring rain and dense woodland in the face of exiguous French assistance. It is no wonder that the division suffered heavy casualties; more surprising, perhaps, that they took most of their objectives. Within a few days, on 28 July, Harbord was placed in command of the American Expeditionary Force's troubled Services of Supply, transforming its logistics arrangements into a miracle of efficiency.

Hardinge, Charles, Baron Hardinge of Penshurst (1858–1944) British imperial pro-consul, Viceroy of India 1910–1916. Hardinge was a career diplomat with a wide variety of experience in key foreign capitals, including Berlin, Constantinople, Paris, St Petersburg and Washington DC. He developed a reputation for success in delicate negotiations and played a leading part in the ententes with France (1904) and Russia (1907). He was a close confidant of King Edward VII, whom he accompanied on his European tour of 1908. As Viceroy of India, Hardinge sought to quell rising discontent with British rule through a policy of social betterment, partly effected by savings on military provision made possible by improved Anglo-Russian relations that he himself had done much to bring about. But in 1912 a bomb thrown during his state entry into Delhi seriously wounded him and shattered the nerve of his wife. During the early days of the war he

played a pivotal role in the sanctioning of a 'forward policy' in Mesopotamia that led eventually to the humiliating surrender of General TOWNSHEND's army at Kut. Hardinge was severely censured by the committee of inquiry that reported in 1917. By this time Hardinge was Permanent Undersecretary of State at the Foreign Office, from which post he three times offered to resign in consequence. LLOYD GEORGE effectively marginalised him at the Paris Peace Conference, and he ended his diplomatic career as Ambassador to Paris (1920–22).

Harington, Charles 'Tim' (1872–1940) British staff officer. 'Tim' Harington was an outstanding soldier who spent the entire war in staff appointments, most notably as PLUMER's chief of staff at Second Army (5 June 1916–29 April 1918). Harington was celebrated for the care he took in preparing attacks and for the sublime clarity of his briefings, a characteristic not always present among his contemporaries and much appreciated by the press corps. He ended the war as Deputy Chief of the Imperial General Staff to Sir Henry WILSON. His brilliant post-war handling of the Chanak Crisis (1922) displayed his political judgement, tact and skill at their best and almost certainly prevented the outbreak of war between Britain and Turkey. In retirement Harington wrote a very reticent memoir, *Tim Harington Looks Back* (1940), and an equally reticent biography of his old chief, *Plumer of Messines* (1935). During the inter-war years he regularly visited the great British military cemetery at Tyne Cot, on the old Passchendaele battlefield. During these visits he would fall to his knees and pray that those buried there had not died in vain.

Harjes, Herman Henry (1872–1926) French-American banker and philanthropist. As senior partner in the Morgan-Harjes Bank, Harjes played a leading backstairs role in negotiating American loans for the Allies. As head of the American Relief Clearing House he controlled the flow of American charitable contributions to France. As chief representative of the American Red Cross in France from 1914 until July 1917 he founded the volunteer ambulance driver group, the Harjes Formation, which later merged with Richard NORTON's American Volunteer Motor Ambulance Corps. Harjes ended the war as liaison officer for the American Expeditionary Force at French GQG [GHQ].

Harmsworth, Alfred Charles William, Viscount Northcliffe (1865–1922) British newspaper proprietor and propagandist. Harmsworth was the eldest of the eleven children of an alcoholic barrister. He left school at 16 determined to become a journalist. Within six years he made his mark with the phenomenally successful magazine *Answers*, which catered to the contemporary popular passion for self-improvement. He later founded the *Daily Mail* (1896) and the *Daily Mirror* (1903). The *Daily Mail* was probably his greatest achievement. It transformed the staid world of Fleet Street, bringing a brash, populist style, sensational news presentation and photo-journalism to the nation's newsstands. Lord Salisbury memorably dismissed the *Mail* as a 'newspaper written for office boys by office boys', but it was hugely successful. Harmsworth became a rich man and a 'press baron', with a keen awareness of his social and political influence. Salisbury's successors in high political office, especially LLOYD GEORGE, learned to have a healthy respect for the opinion of office boys. In 1908 Harmsworth acquired *The Times*, a prestigious establishment newspaper with a greater influence than its circulation suggested, as a vehicle for his political ambition. During the war he used both newspapers to launch (often vitriolic) press campaigns demanding a ruthless prosecution of the war, including conscription, full mobilisation of a war econ-

omy and direction of labour. The *Daily Mail*, in particular, developed an unlovely reputation for jingoism and xenophobia, forcing Prince LOUIS of Battenberg and R.B. HALDANE from office for their supposed 'pro-German' views. Harmsworth was also one of ASQUITH's most vehement and irreconcilable critics. When Lloyd George came to power in December 1916, he tried to bring Harmsworth under control, never an easy thing to do. The *Mail's* campaign to improve Britain's air defences and its advocacy of retaliatory air attacks against German civilian targets led to his being offered the newly established Air Ministry, but he turned it down. Instead, he became head of the British War Mission to the United States and, in February 1918, director of propaganda against enemy countries. Harmsworth was one of the greatest pioneers of British mass circulation journalism. He financed new scientific and technological developments, especially in aviation, and raised huge sums of money for the benefit of sick and wounded soldiers. But he was increasingly overtaken by megalomania and a lust for power without responsibility that polluted British political life. 'I know of few men in this world who are responsible for more mischief, and deserve a longer punishment in the next,' Asquith declared, by way of farewell.

Harmsworth, Harold Sidney, Viscount Rothermere (1868–1940) British newspaper proprietor, who worked closely with his brother Alfred in the years before the war but broke with him in 1914 to concentrate on running the *Daily Mirror*, which he turned into a mass-circulation newspaper to rival the *Daily Mail*. He was Air Minister from 1917 to 1918 in the LLOYD GEORGE coalition government. He was very financially astute and a great benefactor of the arts and higher education. During the inter-war period he wrote admiring articles in the *Daily Mail* about Adolf Hitler.

Harper, (George) Montague (1865–1922) British military commander. 'Uncle' Harper made two unwise enemies who have ever since blighted his reputation. The first was Sir Basil LIDDELL HART, who blamed Harper for opposing machine-gun development before the war. The second was J.F.C. FULLER, who blamed the Cambrai reverse on Harper's supposed misunderstanding of tanks. Neither charge is fair. Harper proved himself an outstanding staff officer, handling the day-to-day deployment of the BEF in August 1914 with complete authority. He later turned the 51st (Highland) Division into one of the best divisions in the BEF, the only Territorial division to be granted elite status. Recent research has shown him to have been an outstanding commander of IV Corps in 1918. His *Notes on Infantry Tactics and Training* (1919) is an excellent piece of work.

Hašek, Jaroslav (1883–1923) Czech novelist, whose best-known book, *The Good Soldier Schweyk*, rivals *Catch-22* as the greatest satire ever written on military life. Hašek himself deserted from the Austrian army in 1915, showing a healthy respect for the principles of his drunken, lying, scrounging hero.

Haus, Anton von (1851–1917) Austro-Hungarian naval commander. Haus fulfilled the dual role of Commander-in-Chief of the Austro-Hungarian navy and Chief of the Navy Section in the Ministry of War from February 1913 until his death from pneumonia on 8 February 1917. He was the designated commander of the Triple Alliance fleets in the Mediterranean, but the defection of Italy to the Entente in May 1915 destroyed any hope of the Austro-Hungarian navy taking part in major offensive operations. Despite German pressure, Haus believed that the most effective strategy for his outnumbered capital ships was for them to remain 'a fleet in being', tying down considerable Allied naval resources without risking destruction themselves. Meanwhile, he waged war more aggressively with his light forces and submarines and was a powerful advocate of unrestricted submarine warfare.

Hausen, Max Klemens von (1846–1922) German military commander, who led the Third Army in the invasion of France and Belgium, advancing as far as the Marne. The withdrawal of BÜLOW's Second Army after the Allied counter-attack on 5 September exposed Hausen's right flank and compelled him to withdraw. Like other German army commanders in 1914, Hausen was, at 68, rather elderly. He found the tantalising advance and dramatic retreat of his army exhausting. Once the German line became stabilised on the heights above the river Aisne, he was relieved of his command and replaced by General Karl von EINEM.

Hawker, Lanoe George (1890–1916) British fighter ace. Hawker was the Royal Flying Corps' first 'ace' (with nine victories) and the first man to be awarded the Victoria Cross for air combat. He was shot down by Manfred von RICHTHOFEN on 23 November 1916.

Hay, Ian (1876–1952) Pen name of John Hay Beith, British soldier, writer and propagandist. Hay was the son of a Manchester cotton manufacturer. He gave up a career as a public schoolmaster to concentrate full time on writing in 1912. When the war broke out he immediately volunteered and was commissioned in the 10th Battalion Argyll and Sutherland Highlanders, later transferring to the Machine Gun Corps. In 1915 he published his best-known book, *The First Hundred Thousand*, an account of life in the KITCHENER armies that portrayed in an amusing way the determination, adaptability and humour of the 'citizen soldiers'. It was a tremendous popular success, not only in Britain but also in the United States. It was later followed by

Carrying on after the First Hundred Thousand (1917) and *The Last Million* (1918). In 1916 Hay was sent to the United States, where he served with the Information Bureau of the British War Mission, charged with propagandising the British cause.

Headlam, John Emerson Wharton (1864–1946) British artillery specialist. Headlam began the war as Chief Gunner of 5th Division in the original British Expeditionary Force. He became Chief Gunner at Second Army in February 1915 and at General Headquarters of the BEF in December 1915. He held this post until May 1916, when the Commander-in-Chief, Sir Douglas HAIG, replaced him with Noel BIRCH on the eve of the great Somme campaign. Headlam's career on the Western Front exemplifies the transitional nature of artillery tactics and command and control during the first part of the war. As BGRA 5th Division at the battle of Le Cateau (26 August 1914) his guns took part in one of the last great, traditional artillery duels fought by the Royal Artillery. His insistence on the closest possible artillery support for the infantry was very costly. Le Cateau marked a turning point in the history of the Royal Artillery that began its move towards 'scientific gunnery'. By the end of 1914, however, Headlam's artillery operation orders for an attack in trench warfare already reflected the experience of the early fighting and represented a significant advance in artillery command and control. Unlike Birch, Headlam did not favour artillerymen becoming 'commanders' of their guns rather than 'advisers', a change that was eventually enforced by the discipline of events. In one respect, however, Headlam was not only correct but also prescient. He provoked considerable laughter at a conference at the Royal Military Academy, Woolwich, in 1913 by suggesting that wind speed had an effect on the flight of shells. By 1916, however, each gun battery in the BEF was receiving telegrams containing meteorological information so that each gun could be adjusted to allow for wind speed and direction, temperature and humidity. In 1917 Headlam accompanied Lord Milner as artillery expert on the Inter-Allied Mission to Russia, and in 1918 he led the Artillery Mission to the United States. His last assignment, prior to his retirement in 1921, was to preside over the Battles Nomenclature Committee, which was responsible for the official naming of all British battles and engagements of the Great War.

Heinrich (1862–1929) Prince of Prussia, the younger brother of Kaiser WILHELM II, a serious-minded professional sailor who commanded the German High Seas Fleet from 1906 to 1909, when he was dismissed for opposing the policies of Admiral TIRPITZ. From July 1914 until February 1918 he commanded the German Baltic Fleet, securing German supplies of iron ore from Sweden and preventing Allied supplies reaching Russia. This did little, however, to satisfy his ambition to mount aggressive, offensive operations and his career was ultimately one of frustration and disappointment.

Helfferich, Karl (1872–1924) German politician and banker, an ambitious careerist from a manufacturing background, who served as Secretary of the Treasury and Deputy Chancellor 1915–17. His policy of financing the war through loans rather than taxation increased inflation. After the war he became leader of the German National People's Party, a vehicle for his unyieldingly conservative and pro-military views, and an enemy of the Weimar Republic.

Hemingway, Ernest Millar (1899–1961) US novelist and war correspondent, who left his job as a cub reporter on the *Kansas City Star* in April 1918 to join the American Red Cross as a volunteer ambulance driver on the Italian front. On

8 July 1918, after only a month at the front, he was badly wounded in the legs by an Austrian trench mortar while running a mobile canteen near the river Piave. He kept pieces of the offending shrapnel in a pot next to his hospital bed in Milan and gave them as presents to well-wishers and visitors. Those who kept the gift would have made a shrewd investment. Hemingway's experiences later formed the basis of his novel *A Farewell to Arms* (1929). The title is ironical. Far from saying farewell to war in 1918, Hemingway said hello to it. From Caporetto to Castro no conflict was really complete without his larger-than-life presence. Posterity may yet conclude that the purpose of war in the first half of the twentieth century was to give Hemingway something to do between safaris.

Hemming, (Henry) Harold (1893–1976) Canadian soldier, who played a leading part in the development of 'flash-spotting', an important technique for identifying enemy gun batteries. 'Flash-spotting' worked on the observation of the muzzle flash made by guns when they were firing. It required accurate maps.

Henderson, Arthur (1863–1935) British politician and Labour leader, Secretary of the Labour Party 1911–34, President of the Board of Education 1915–16, Paymaster-General 1916–17. Ramsay MACDONALD's resignation as Secretary of the Labour Party in August 1914 because of his opposition to war made Henderson de facto leader of the parliamentary Labour Party throughout the Great War. He was the first member of the Labour Party to sit in Cabinet, when he joined ASQUITH's coalition government in May 1915. He continued in government under LLOYD GEORGE but resigned in August 1917 when the War Cabinet voted against his proposal to send delegates to the international peace conference in Stockholm. During the war Henderson greatly strengthened the Labour Party's organisa-

tion and was the principal author of its 1918 'socialist' constitution. His appeals for a peace of reconciliation went unheard and he lost his seat in the general election of 1918.

Henderson, David (1862–1921) British military commander, an extremely able and underrated man, whose claim to be the father of the Royal Air Force has been largely ignored by historians and over-shadowed in RAF legend by the powerful personality of his successor as GOC Royal Flying Corps (RFC), Hugh TRENCHARD. Henderson learned to fly in 1911 at the age of 49, making him the world's oldest pilot. He became Director-General of Military Aeronautics in 1913 and on the outbreak of war took command of the RFC in the field. After briefly commanding a division, KITCHENER insisted on Henderson's return to the RFC. In 1917 he was seconded to General J.C. SMUTS to assist him with his report on aviation. Henderson's views on the formation of a Royal Air Force strongly influenced Smuts, and he largely wrote the influential 'Smuts' Report. Henderson can also claim to be the founding father of the Intelligence Corps. His *Field Intelligence: Its Principles and Practice* (1904) and *The Art of Reconnaissance* (1907) established his reputation as the pre-war army's leading authority on tactical intelligence, ensuring that the fledgling air service would play a key role in intelligence gathering and reconnaissance. Henderson was an unusual combination of far-sightedness, intelligence, practicality and modesty, as well as being extremely good looking.

Henderson, Reginald Guy Hannam (1881–1939) British naval staff officer, who achieved a pre-war reputation as a gunnery expert, something usually guaranteed to recommend young officers to Admiral JELLICOE. Henderson served on HMS *Erin* during the battle of Jutland and followed Jellicoe to the Admiralty in 1916, serving in the anti-submarine warfare division and later on the naval war staff as Assistant to Admiral DUFF. Henderson's organisation of a trial convoy of colliers to France played an important part in demonstrating the feasibility of the convoy system and its subsequent adoption.

Heneker, William Charles Giffard (1867–1939) British military commander. 'Billy' Heneker was born in Canada, then very much a pioneer society, where his father helped found the town of Sherbrooke, Ontario. Heneker passed the Royal Military College of Canada at Kingston, Ontario, and was commissioned into the Connaught Rangers in 1888. He was unusual among British divisional commanders on the Western Front in not having served in the South African War. But he made up for this with considerable combat experience in West Africa. In 1912 he received a 'fast track' promotion to command the 2nd Battalion North Staffordshire Regiment. To his considerable frustration, the outbreak of war found him commanding this unit in India. It was several months before he was ordered home, where he took command of 54th Brigade, a New Army formation, part of the 18th Division, commanded by the formidable Ivor MAXSE. Heneker helped train the brigade, but his field command was brutally terminated by a German machine-gun bullet that struck his thigh on 15 December 1915. The wound was severe and kept him out of action for ten months. On his return to the Western Front, his first act was to seek a briefing from Maxse about the latest developments. After a short period in command of 190th Brigade, Heneker was promoted to divisional command, as GOC 8th Division, on 10 December 1916. He commanded the division for the rest of the war. Heneker was initially unimpressed by 8th Division, which had performed badly on the Somme, and ruthlessly set about reconstructing it, mostly by replacing subordinate comman-

ders and staff officers who did not reach his exacting standards. 8th Division had an arduous war, especially in 1918, when it felt the full force of the German attacks on three occasions, suffering huge numbers of casualties, exceeded only by those of 50th (Northumbrian) Division. Heneker was the commanding officer in the vital recapture of Villers-Bretonneux in April 1918, though most credit is usually given to the Australians. Later, on the Aisne, he was one of the British commanders who protested fiercely to General DUCHÊNE about the potentially disastrous deployment of the French Sixth Army in the event of a German attack. When this came, it effectively destroyed 8th Division as a fighting force, leaving Heneker with the melancholy job of rebuilding it with fresh troops during the summer. The future Major-General Essame, who served in 8th Division and admired Heneker greatly, considered this rebuilding to be Heneker's finest achievement. During the summer Heneker wrote a long, bitter analysis of the spring fighting for his old patron Maxse, by then Inspector-General of Training for the British Expeditionary Force. This was severely critical of the British obsession with linear defence, which Heneker considered had sacrificed unnecessarily the lives of many brave men. He was a fine example of the best type of pre-war Regular officer, who demanded the highest professional standards, which he himself did the utmost to uphold.

Hentsch, (Friedrich Heinrich) Richard (1869–1918) German staff officer, who briefly emerged from obscurity in 1914 to play a key, and controversial, part in the events that led to the battle of the Marne. Lieutenant-Colonel Hentsch was a member of General Helmuth von MOLTKE's staff and seems to have enjoyed his complete confidence. On 9 September 1914, armed with full powers, Hentsch was dispatched by Moltke to assess the worrying situation that had developed on the Western Front, where a big gap had begun to appear between the German First and Second Armies. Hentsch's mission seems to have been that of co-ordinating the movements of the German right wing. That Moltke should send such a low-ranking officer to try and reimpose his control on the battlefield seems astonishing. Hentsch arrived at the headquarters of General Karl von BÜLOW's Second Army to find its commander in characteristically pessimistic mood, much shaken by the threat posed to his right wing by the Allied counter-attack. Hentsch took his lead from Bülow, ordering a reluctant General Alexander von KLUCK, commanding First Army, to comply with Bülow's retreat. The order was later confirmed by Moltke. This signalled the collapse of the SCHLIEFFEN Plan. Hentsch has been blamed by some for 'losing the war', but what fault there was clearly lay with his Commander-in-Chief, Moltke. Hentsch spent most of the rest of the war as a staff officer on the Eastern Front.

Herbert, A[lan] P[atrick] (1890–1971) British soldier and writer. Although a barrister by training, Herbert never practised law, for which he retained throughout his life an amused contempt. He began writing for *Punch* in 1910 and joined its staff in 1924, the prelude to a long career in the forefront of British satire. Like many other literary men, he joined the Royal Naval Division in 1914, serving on Gallipoli and the Western Front until he was wounded in 1917. In 1919 he published *Secret Battle*, an account of the execution of Sub-Lieutenant Edwin Dyett, a fellow officer of the Royal Naval Division, and one of only two officers to be executed during the war. The book did much to influence public and parliamentary opinion against capital punishment in the army.

Herrick, Myron Timothy (1854–1929) US diplomat. Herrick was a banker and former Governor of Ohio. He had been

appointed US Ambassador to France by President Taft in 1912, and President WILSON kept him on until a suitable replacement could be found. This took some time and the name of Herrick's successor, William Graves SHARP, was not announced until June 1914. By the time Sharp arrived in France, the war was three weeks old. The US State Department decided against changing ambassadors at such a sensitive moment, and Sharp did not succeed Herrick until 1 December 1914. Herrick remained in Paris when the French government fled and, despite being responsible for German interests in France, immediately became involved in organising US relief work in France, work that he continued in the United States after his recall.

Hertling, Georg von (1843–1919) German politician, leader of the conservative wing of the Catholic Centre Party in the Reichstag and Prime Minister of Bavaria from 1912 to 1917. He succeeded Georg MICHAELIS as Chancellor and Prussian Minister-President in November 1917. His attempts to mediate successfully between a Reichstag increasingly favourable to reform and peace and a military command determined upon a ruthless prosecution of the war inevitably foundered. As a Catholic and a Bavarian with no real power base of his own, he was dragged inexorably into the orbit of HINDENBURG and LUDENDORFF. He resigned on 2 October 1918, with Germany facing the certainty of defeat.

Hindenburg, Paul von Beneckendorf und von (1847–1934) German military commander, national hero and imperial icon. Hindenburg was 'dug out' of retirement in August 1914 at the age of 67 and sent to East Prussia to assume command of German forces, threatened with encirclement by two larger Russian armies. He arrived on 24 August, to be met for the first time by his new chief of staff, Erich LUDENDORFF. He was handed a plan for dealing with the Russian advance that had been drawn up by General HOFFMANN, a staff officer in Eighth Army, and approved by Ludendorff. The plan resulted in the annihilation of SAMSONOV's Russian Second Army at Tannenberg (25–31 August 1914) and the heavy defeat of RENNEN-KAMPF's Russian First Army at the Masurian Lakes (10–13 September 1914). These stunning victories were the foundation on which Hindenburg's extraordinary future career ultimately rested. German propaganda gave the credit to Hindenburg, who was portrayed as a Teutonic knight defending the German marches against barbarian invasion. He added to his legend in 1915 by conquering Poland. He attributed his inability to knock Russia out of the war to the defensive mentality of Erich von FALKENHAYN, the German chief of staff. Falkenhayn was not only unwilling to give Hindenburg the reinforcements he needed to win the war in the east but also actually removed troops from the Eastern Front for the ill-starred attack on Verdun. The rising casualties at Verdun, the Anglo-French offensive on the Somme and Romania's invasion of Hungary led to Falkenhayn's removal on 29 August 1916. Hindenburg and Ludendorff were sent west to assume the German supreme command. The fighting at Verdun was scaled down. Falkenhayn's costly policy of counter-attack on the Somme was gradually replaced by a more sophisticated system of 'elastic defence in depth', with which the German army successfully held the Western Front throughout 1917 despite a numerical inferiority of 3:2. Hindenburg and Ludendorff became virtual dictators of Germany, seeking to mobilise for total war through the Hindenburg Programme's subordination of German political, social and economic life to centralised military control. They insisted on the adoption of unrestricted submarine warfare in February 1917 and on the removal of Chancellor BETHMANN-HOLLWEG in July. They would accept no limitation on German territorial ambi-tions. The imposition of the punitive treaties of Brest-Litovsk and Bucharest on defeated Russia and Romania did much to stiffen Allied resolve in the face of the German offensive of 1918, which they were instrumental in launching. Ludendorff was undoubtedly the instigator of these disastrous policies. Hindenburg's role was essentially symbolic, but the symbolism was powerful and essential. He survived Ludendorff's resignation in October 1918. Under the influence of Ludendorff's blunt and clear-sighted successor, Wilhelm GROENER, Hindenburg acquiesced in the inevitability of German defeat (for which he never accepted any responsibility) and ushered the Kaiser into abdication and exile. Hindenburg was a stoical and imperturbable commander. On the Eastern Front, with mainly military responsibilities, the formidable ballast that he brought to Ludendorff's temperamental energy and Hoffmann's acerbic intellect made a formidable combination. His assumption of political control, however, exposed his limited understanding. His narrow-minded militarism must take its place among the factors that brought Germany to ruin and destroyed the monarchy to which he had dedicated his life.

Hintze, Paul von (1864–1941) German diplomat. Hintze joined the diplomatic service in 1911 after a career in the navy that saw him retire with the rank of rear-admiral. After successive diplomatic postings to Mexico, China and Norway, in July 1918 he was somewhat surprisingly chosen as German Foreign Minister in the mistaken belief that he would be more amenable to the military than his moderate predecessor, Richard von KÜHLMANN. In fact, Hintze continued Kühlmann's policies, even managing in the dying days of the Hohenzollern empire to persuade the Kaiser to accept a belated liberalisation of his regime.

Hipper, Franz von (1863–1932) German naval commander. Hipper led the High

Seas Fleet Scouting Forces from 1912 and played a leading part in the naval war in the North Sea. His bombardment of the British coast in 1914 came as an unpleasant shock to British public opinion and provoked uncomfortable questions about 'what the Royal Navy was doing'. It also heaped odium on Hipper, who was vilified in the British press as a 'baby killer'. At the Dogger Bank (24 January 1915) Hipper's forces came close to disaster, but he demonstrated the tactical skill, courage, ruthlessness and luck that was to mark his command. Hipper's battle cruisers opened the hostilities at Jutland (31 May–1 June 1916), where the technical superiority of his ships helped him inflict considerable damage on Admiral BEATTY's squadron. During the later fleet engagement, Hipper's 'death ride' towards Jellicoe's battleships, combined with torpedo attacks from his escorting destroyers, saved SCHEER's fleet. Hipper succeeded Scheer in command of the High Seas Fleet in August 1918. In October his plan for a Wagnerian final reckoning with the British in a war that was clearly lost provoked a naval mutiny at Kiel, which helped bring about the proclamation of a German republic on 9 November.

Hobbs, (Joseph John) Talbot (1864–1938) Australian military commander. The London-born son of a journeyman joiner, Hobbs also worked as a carpenter before qualifying as an architect. His prewar military service with the Australian field artillery included four periods of training in England (1897, 1902, 1906 and 1913), largely at his own expense. He was Commander Royal Artillery (CRA) of the 1st (Australian) Division on Gallipoli and CRA 1st (Australian) Division and Australian and New Zealand Army Corps on the Western Front, before being given command of 5th (Australian) Division in January 1917, a post he retained until the end of the war. He made his debut as a divisional commander in the horribly mismanaged battle of Bullecourt,

against which he made strong but ineffectual protests. 5th Division later performed well at Polygon Wood (September 1917) and played a leading part in the vital recapture of Villers-Bretonneux in April 1918. Hobbs was a small, frail-looking but energetic man with a strong Christian faith; he was often found in the front line. His common sense was exceeded only by his integrity. He sought harmony in his commands, a difficult task when one of his brigadiers was 'Pompey' ELLIOTT. He was not, however, a weak or pliant man, never fearing to criticise the actions of higher authority, whether they were Australian or British. After the war, he returned to architecture and designed the West Australian War Memorial in Perth.

Hodgson, William Noel (1893–1916) British soldier and poet, who is principally remembered for his fine and moving poem 'Before Action', which captures perfectly the anxiety of young, temporary officers preparing to 'go over the top' for the first time. Hodgson wrote the poem shortly before his death in action on 1 July 1916 at Mametz, while serving as a subaltern with the 9th Battalion Devonshire Regiment. He is buried in the mournful Devonshire Cemetery at Mametz, close to where he was killed.

Hoffmann, Carl Adolf Maximilian (1869–1927) German staff officer. Max Hoffmann spent the whole of the war as a staff officer on the Eastern Front. He has long enjoyed a reputation as the real brains behind the victories of HINDENBURG and LUDENDORFF, not least the first – at Tannenberg – the plan for which he formulated before the duo's arrival to take command. Clever, unconventional, supremely self-confident, decisive, witty and acerbic, he perhaps comes closer to the modern idea of a hero than any other senior military figure of the Great War. He is, in short, 'cool'. His military reputation, however, is largely self-created and dependent upon uncritical acceptance of his own post-war accounts. Disciples of his 'genius' should remember his leading role in the decision to return exiled socialists, including LENIN, to Russia. There is no evidence for his supposed description of the British army as 'lions led by donkeys'.

Hohenlohe-Schillingsfürst, Gottfried, Prince zu (1867–1932) Austro-Hungarian diplomat, who served in the somewhat thankless task of Ambassador to Berlin, a position to which he was appointed on 4 August 1914. He strove manfully to maintain Austria-Hungary's interests in the face of increasing German contempt for the Empire's military contribution to the Dual Alliance. He was not assisted by the willingness of the Austrian Commander-in-Chief, CONRAD, to launch independent military campaigns without informing his ally. There were constant disputes over the future of central Europe, especially Poland. An already difficult task became virtually impossible after the appointment of HINDENBURG and LUDENDORFF to the German military supreme command in late August 1916. Their insistence on German commanders and staff officers assuming ever greater control of the war on the Eastern Front, their self-interested annexationist ambitions without regard to Austrian aspirations in the Trentino and their dismissal of Austrian concerns about the resumption of unrestricted submarine warfare left Hohenlohe-Schillingsfürst with little more than a ceremonial function.

Holbrook, Norman Douglas (1888–1976) British submariner, whose old and obsolete submarine, B 11, sank the Turkish battleship *Messudiyeh* in the Dardanelles on 13 December 1914, winning him the Royal Navy's first Victoria Cross of the war and the first ever to be awarded to a submariner.

Holland, Arthur Edward Aveling (1862–1927) British artillery commander. Hol-

land was an intelligent, forward-looking officer. Even from the early days of the war, when he was artillery adviser in 8th Division, he showed his openness to new ideas and appreciation of the role of artillery on a modern battlefield. He was instrumental in taking 1st Ranging Section Royal Engineers to the Western Front with 8th Division when it was deployed in November 1914. Holland became one of the leading advocates of artillery survey. His encouragement and support played an important part in establishing the organisation on which rested the future development of 'scientific' gunnery, including sound ranging, flash-spotting and battery survey. Holland's progressive ideas were rewarded with promotion but ultimately proved his undoing. As MGRA Third Army (June 1916–February 1917) he was charged with artillery preparation for the battle of Arras. He proposed an innovative forty-eight-hour hurricane bombardment, rather than the normal five-day affair that gave forewarning of an attack and allowed the Germans to reinforce their defences and bring up reserves. The plan was accepted by the GOC Third Army, General Sir Edmund ALLENBY, but abandoned after protests by his subordinate commanders. Holland was 'kicked upstairs' as GOC I Corps, where he languished for the rest of the war.

Holmes, William (1862–1917) Australian military commander. Although never a Regular, Holmes had soldiering in his blood. In 1872 he joined the colonial forces of his native New South Wales as a bugler at the age of 10. He was commissioned in 1886. He fought in the South African War as part of the New South Wales First Contingent and won the DSO. At the outbreak of war he was given command of the Australian Expeditionary Force that conquered German New Guinea. He led the 5th (Australian) Infantry Brigade on Gallipoli from August 1915 until the evacuation of the peninsula. In 1916 he led the 5th Brigade in the

Australians' baptism of fire on the Western Front at Pozières. In January 1917 he was promoted to command the 4th (Australian) Division, which he led on the Ancre (January–March 1917), in the advance to the Hindenburg line (March–April 1917), at Bullecourt (April 1917) and at Messines (June 1917). He died of wounds received while showing a party of Australian politicians round the battlefield of Messines on 2 July 1917.

Holtzendorf, Henning von (1853–1919) German naval commander. Holtzendorf commanded the High Seas Fleet from 1909 to 1913, when he became one of several leading German naval officers to be forced into retirement after opposing the ambitious naval plans of Grand Admiral TIRPITZ. It may have been better for Germany had he remained in retirement, but in September 1915 he was brought back as head of the naval General Staff where he became one of the most important converts to the (ultimately disastrous) policy of unrestricted submarine warfare. His influence with the Kaiser and his wildly exaggerated claims for the effectiveness of U-boats were instrumental in the decision to resume unrestricted submarine warfare in February 1917, a decision that led directly to US intervention in April.

Hood, Horace Lambert Alexander (1870–1916) British naval commander. Hood was given command of the 3rd Battle Cruiser Squadron in 1915 at the early age of 45, earning a reputation among his peers as an intrepid and clever commander. His handling of 3rd Battle Cruiser Squadron during the 'Run to the North' and the battle fleet action at Jutland (31 May–1 June 1916) confirmed his promise, but this was tragically cut short by his death in the catastrophic explosion that destroyed his flagship, HMS *Invincible*.

Hoover, Herbert Clark (1874–1964) US aid worker, whose Herculean efforts in organising humanitarian relief in Belgium and later in Eastern Europe and the Soviet Union won him an immense reputation that helped propel him into the presidency in 1928. Hoover organised the Commission for Relief in Belgium (CRB) largely on his own initiative, taking control of a vast logistical enterprise responsible for feeding millions of civilians in German-occupied Belgium and northern France. The American Relief Administration (ARA) in Europe extended these activities, playing a considerable part in the post-war reconstruction of Eastern Europe. In between, Hoover was the United States' Food Administrator, charged with conserving and increasing US food production. In this role he was not only successful but also popular, not least with the American housewife, who rallied behind his campaigns for 'Meatless Mondays' and 'Wheatless Wednesdays'.

Horne, Henry Sinclair (1861–1929) British military commander. Horne's career during the Great War closely followed that of Douglas HAIG. He began the war as Haig's chief gunner at I Corps. He was promoted to the command of 2nd Division in January 1915 shortly after Haig became GOC First Army. In January 1916, shortly after Haig became Commander-in-Chief of the British Expeditionary Force, Horne was promoted GOC XV Corps. In September 1916 he was promoted again to Haig's old command, First Army, which he led for the rest of the war. XV Corps was heavily involved in the early Somme fighting, including the bungled and costly attacks on High Wood and the first use of tanks. In April 1917 First Army, spearheaded by the Canadian Corps, captured Vimy Ridge. During the German spring offensive in 1918 it inflicted a decided defeat on the Germans in front of Arras on 28 March and later resolutely defended the vital Lys position. Horne was an austere and dedicated professional soldier, with a high sense of duty, exceptional self-control and great integrity. His military judgement inclined to the conventional, but he clearly understood the importance of thorough preparation and efficient administration. His army often contained the crack Canadian Corps, a stroke of good fortune more than justified by his careful treatment of it. He was also blessed with an outstanding chief of staff, Hastings ANDERSON, and (in the last months of the war) an innovative chief gunner, Ernest ALEXANDER VC.

Horthy de Nagybánya, Miklós (1868–1957) Austro-Hungarian naval commander, who became the last Commander-in-Chief of the Austro-Hungarian navy in March 1918. He maintained the deterrent strategy of his predecessor by preserving his main battle fleet but responded aggressively to the activities of Italian light forces. His energetic leadership helped to preserve the loyalty and morale of the fleet until the collapse of the Habsburg Empire. After the war Horthy crushed the Hungarian Communist government of Béla KUN and established himself as the Regent of Hungary in 1920, a post he retained until 1944. He died in exile in Portugal.

Hotchkiss, Benjamin (1826–1885) US weapons designer. Hotchkiss was a Connecticut Yankee who gave his name to one of the most famous weapons in twentieth-century French military history, the Hotchkiss Modèle 1914 machine gun. The gun itself was the product of a fruitful collaboration between Hotchkiss's successor, Laurence Benet (another American), and a French engineer called Mercier. They purchased the patents of an automatic weapon designed in 1893 by an Austrian army officer, Captain Baron von Odkolek, and developed it into an effective gun that was first adopted by the French army in 1897. Unlike heavy machine guns in other armies, the Hotchkiss was air-cooled and its ammunition fed by metal strips rather than belts. It was,

however, a very effective and serviceable weapon in the conditions of trench warfare, produced in huge numbers after 1914. The American Expeditionary Force was also extensively equipped with the gun.

House, Edward Mandell (1858–1938) US politician. 'Colonel' House came from a leading Texan family. During the 1890s he established himself as a formidable backstairs operator in Texas gubernatorial politics. He also dreamed of exercising national influence, but it was not until he met Woodrow WILSON in November 1911 that he found a leading political figure with whom he could work. After Wilson's election in November 1912, House gradually became one of the President's inner circle and, eventually, his closest confidant. House's self-confidence with regard to international affairs was boundless, and he undertook the role of presidential emissary with enthusiasm, hoping to make his mark in history. During his first visit to Europe, from January to June 1915, he quickly realised that the Allies had no intention of seeking or accepting American mediation and became converted to the inevitability of American intervention. During his second visit, January to March 1916, he negotiated an agreement with the British Foreign Secretary, Sir Edward GREY (the House–Grey Memorandum), to call Germany to a peace conference on what amounted to the threat of American military intervention. This act took him far beyond his brief and would probably have resulted in a serious disagreement with Wilson had the British government not rejected the proposal. House played a leading part in the framing of Wilson's Fourteen Points and in modifying them to obtain Allied acceptance prior to the Armistice. House was a self-dramatist. His copious letters gave the President not only a false view of House's influence but also a false view of that of the United States. House proved much more amenable to Allied pressure at the Paris Peace Conference than Wilson and equally urged his President to seek compromises with the Congressional opponents of the League of Nations, proposals for which House had drafted. He broke with Wilson in June 1919, later trying (and failing) to repeat his role as presidential confidant with Franklin ROOSEVELT.

Howse, Neville Reginald (1863–1930) Australian medical officer, who was primarily responsible for the establishment of the Australian Army Medical Corps (AAMC) on a proper professional basis. Howse was a man of outstanding physical and moral courage who won the Victoria Cross for rescuing a man under heavy fire while serving with the Australian 2nd Contingent in the Boer War. As staff officer to the Director of Medical Services of the Australian Imperial Force (AIF) on Gallipoli, he was shocked by what he called the 'criminal negligence' of the British authorities to make effective medical arrangements, and he personally supervised the evacuation of wounded from the beaches. His singular abilities and courage, however, often made it difficult for him to delegate and sometimes saw him abandon his proper supervisory role in favour of a 'hands-on' approach. In November 1915 he was appointed Director of Medical Services with responsibility for AIF medical arrangements in the field in all theatres of war. He fiercely maintained the AAMC's independence and did much to improve medical provision.

Hughes, Sam (1853–1921) Canadian politician and soldier. Hughes had a lifelong interest in military affairs, especially shooting. He served in the South African War, initially with the Canadian Contingent, with whose leaders he characteristically fell out, and later with the British forces, with whom he established a reputation as a dashing leader of irregulars. Hughes became Canadian Minister of Militia and Defence in 1911. He was especially active in promoting military skills through the cadet corps. On the outbreak of war his driving energy did much to facilitate the raising, training and equipment of the 1st Canadian Contingent at Valcartier Camp. The Canadian Expeditionary Force was equipped with the accurate and powerful Ross rifle, a splendid weapon for target shooting (in which Hughes was keenly involved). In trench conditions its distinctive 'straight-pull' bolt was notoriously prone to jamming, making it not only defective but also dangerous. Hughes' support for it, despite evidence of its inadequacy, brought him into conflict with the GOC Canadian Corps, Lieutenant-General Sir Edwin ALDERSON. Hughes' energy was always manic. This, and his uninhibited support for the Ross, made him an increasingly unstable and unreliable colleague. His overdue dismissal in November 1916 was greeted with relief in Canadian political and military circles.

Hughes, William Morris (1862–1952) Australian politician. Billy Hughes was born in London of Welsh parents. He emigrated to Queensland in 1884 and lived in real poverty before succeeding in business in Sydney, where he became an important figure in the Labor Party. Unusually for a Labor leader, he took a great interest in defence matters and was a powerful advocate of compulsory military training. His support for a vigorous prosecution of the war made him the unanimous choice to succeed Andrew FISHER as Prime Minister in October 1915. Hughes' views on the war and in particular his support for conscription for overseas military service gained him acceptance in the highest councils of the British Empire, where his belligerence, extraordinary memory, grasp of detail and powers of concentration made him formidable. His performance at the Paris Peace Conference was equally impressive, and he emerged from the war with a considerable reputation as an international statesman. His reputation in Australia, however, is much more controversial. He was regarded by many as a political thug and demagogue. His insistence on the two conscription referendums (in October 1916 and November–December 1917), both of which he lost, split his own party (from which he was expelled) and poisoned Australian politics for much of the war. A small, deaf, wizened man with a rasping voice, Hughes owed his position in life entirely to his own merits. As a war leader he exhibited great courage and imagination. He was, by any standards, a remarkable man.

Huguet, Victor Jacques Marie (1858–1925) French liaison officer. As French military attaché in London before the war, Huguet was instrumental in bringing about the Anglo-French staff talks (beginning in 1906) that established the detailed practical arrangements of Anglo-French military co-operation in a future war. Many have since claimed that these conversations effectively committed Britain to go to war and removed the possibility of independent action in August 1914. This may be doubted. After hostilities broke out, Huguet was attached to British GHQ as liaison officer, where he maintained close links with Field-Marshal FRENCH's Francophile MGGS Major-General Henry WILSON. Their relationship effectively sidestepped the official liaison structure and was pregnant with mischief. Colonel Des Vallières replaced Huguet as liaison officer once HAIG succeeded French as Commander-in-Chief of the British Expeditionary Force in December 1915.

Hulme, Thomas Ernest (1883–1917) British soldier-poet. Hulme was a tall, powerfully built, argumentative man, who loved processions, fighting and philosophy. He was twice sent down from Cambridge and did not take his degree. He became a great friend of the sculptor Henri GAUDIER, who made the solid brass knuckleduster that Hulme notoriously carried

around with him. Before the war Hulme established a reputation as an authority on BERGSON. He also wrote poetry. Five of his poems were published in 1912 under the amusing title *The Complete Poetical Works of T.E. Hulme*. His poetry was marked by its disdain for romanticism. His belief that poetry should deal in clear, visual images rather than chaotic emotion exercised great influence on the 'Imagist' movement. Hulme volunteered for military service on the outbreak of war. He served on the Western Front as an infantryman until he was wounded in March 1916. He returned to the front as an officer in the Royal Marine Artillery and was killed by a shell burst near Nieuport, in Belgium, on 28 September 1917.

Humbert, Georges Louis (1862–1921) French military commander, who led the Moroccan Division at St Gond in 1914 and, later, Third Army on the Somme (1916) and the Oise (1918). When the British Commander-in-Chief, Field-Marshal HAIG, reluctantly yielded to French pressure to take over part of their line in the late winter of 1918, the British Fifth Army under General GOUGH relieved Humbert's Third Army. As part of the deal, it was agreed between Haig and PÉTAIN that in the event of an attack on Fifth Army the French Third Army would come to its aid. In the event, this aid was not immediately forthcoming. Some of Humbert's subordinate units had been taken away from him and deployed to cover Paris. When Humbert arrived at General GOUGH's headquarters at 1 p.m. on 21 March 1918, the first day of the great German spring offensive, he made it clear that the only aid he brought was the pennant on his staff car (*'Mais, je n'ai que mon fanion'*). It was not until 25 March, and then only after intense British pressure at a high level, that Humbert's army was brought together and inserted into the line on Fifth Army's right. The delay was not Humbert's fault but that of his

Commander-in-Chief Pétain; once in position he showed himself to be a very competent commander and his army did much to stabilise the position on Fifth Army's flank. The difficulties in getting Pétain to observe his side of the bargain were instrumental in Haig's conversion to the idea of a unified command, which he called for after a crisis meeting in the *Mairie* at Doullens on 26 March.

Hunter, Archibald (1856–1936) British military commander. Hunter's pre-war career was closely associated with that of KITCHENER, first in the Sudan, then in South Africa (where he was prominent in the defence of Ladysmith) and finally in India. In 1896, at the age of 40, he became the youngest British major-general since Wellington. But when the Great War broke out, he was 58 and considered too old for field command. Instead, he was offered the post of GOC-in-C, Aldershot, where he became responsible for training the New Armies.

Hunter-Weston, Aylmer Gould (1864–1940) British military commander. Hunter-Weston, a sapper, commanded an infantry brigade in the original British Expeditionary Force, then the 29th Division and VIII Corps on Gallipoli, and VIII Corps on the Western Front. His commands were dogged by controversy. During the Gallipoli landings (25 April 1915) he made the classic mistake of reinforcing failure on 'W' and 'V' beaches while leaving the units unopposed at 'S', 'X' and 'Y' beaches without orders. As GOC VIII Corps, on Gallipoli, his command was marked by over-ambition and apparent indifference to casualties. His performance did not improve in France. On 1 July 1916 VIII Corps suffered the heaviest casualties of any unit engaged and failed to take any of its objectives, a disaster that owed much to Hunter-Weston's decision to explode two mines two and ten minutes before the infantry attack, forewarning the Germans and allowing them

to man their defences. He was never trusted with another major attack until the very end of the war. 'Hunter-Bunter's' survival in command is a mystery but owed something, perhaps, to his reputation as a 'card' and more to his election as Unionist Member of Parliament for North Ayrshire in October 1916.

Hussarek von Heinlein, Max, Baron (1865–1935) Austro-Hungarian politician, who succeeded CLAM-MARTINIC as Prime Minister in July 1917. He struggled gallantly but ineffectually to find a peaceful means of reconciling the Habsburg Empire's separatist nationalities, who could see all too clearly that the empire's impending dissolution would give them what they wanted without the need for compromise. He resigned in October 1918 after the defeat of Emperor KARL I's October Manifesto, with its proposal for a federation of autonomous states.

Hussein, ibn Ali ibn Mohammed (1856[54? 52?]–1931) Sherif of Mecca and King of the Hejaz, who proclaimed the Arab Revolt against the Ottoman Empire in June 1916 after negotiations with the British High Commissioner in Egypt, Sir Henry MCMAHON, convinced him that the British would support his ambition to become king of a post-war Arab state embracing Syria, the Lebanon, Iraq and most of the Arabian peninsula. He was, however, to be disappointed by the outcome of the war, which saw him confirmed merely as king of the Hejaz, a position from which he was forced to abdicate in favour of his son Ali in 1924.

Hussein, Kamil (1853–1917) Sultan of Egypt 1914–17. Hussein was chosen by the British as Khedive of Egypt in November 1914 after the deposition of his nationalist predecessor and nephew, Abbas Il Hilmi. His elevation from puppet Khedive to puppet Sultan signalled the removal of Egypt from the Ottoman Empire.

Hutchison, Graham Seton (1890–1946) British soldier and writer. Hutchison was a pre-war Regular in the King's Own Scottish Borderers from 1909 to 1913. Bored by peacetime regimental soldiering, he retired to the army reserve and went to South Africa, where he joined the paramilitary British South Africa Police as a trooper before finding an outlet for his considerable military talents in the Rhodesian military forces. He rejoined the British army in 1914, serving with the 2nd Battalion Argyll and Sutherland Highlanders and the Machine Gun Corps. As CO of the 33rd Battalion Machine Gun Corps in April 1918, he played a leading part in stopping the German advance in front of Meteren. After the war he was heavily involved in veterans' organisations and flirted with fascism. A prolific writer and journalist, his publications include *Machine Guns* (1938), an unofficial history of the Machine Gun Corps, and *Warrior* (1932), a philosophical reflection on the meaning of combat which displayed concerns similar to those of Ernst JÜNGER.

Hutier, Oskar von (1857–1934) German military commander, principally remembered for his use of 'infiltration tactics' against the Russian army at Riga in September 1917. During LUDENDORFF's first offensive on the Western Front in March 1918, Hutier's Eighteenth Army inflicted the deepest penetration against General GOUGH's British Fifth Army, before being brought to a halt by stiffening British and French resistance and supply problems across the old Somme battlefields. A sophisticated and resolute French defence stopped Hutier's later offensive, on the Matz, in June and he was thrown on to the defensive for the rest of the war. The British, with their love of personalising tactical developments, dubbed infiltration 'Hutier tactics', though they were the product of the German staff system, which built on French and British ideas. Hutier was, however, among the first commanders to employ the tactics on a large scale.

Hymans, Paul (1865–1941) Belgian diplomat and politician. Hymans' diplomatic mission to the United States on behalf of the Belgian government-in-exile in 1914 enjoyed great success in raising humanitarian aid for Belgium and in propagandising the Belgian cause. He served as Ambassador to Great Britain from 1915 to 1917, favouring closer and more formal links with the Entente powers than King ALBERT I. From 1918 to 1920 he was Belgian Foreign Minister. At the Paris Peace Conference he championed – not entirely effectively – the claims of minor powers. He succeeded in removing Belgium's neutral status and in placing her in the forefront of those states to receive German reparations, but his (rather shocking) attempts at Belgian territorial aggrandisement at the expense of Holland and Luxemburg failed. He became first President of the League of Nations in 1919.

I

Ibn Saud, Abd al-Aziz (1880–1953) Founder of the Kingdom of Saudia Arabia, a charismatic leader, careful strategist and able tactician. By 1902 he had established himself as ruler of the Nejd, a position recognised by the British in 1915. He was equally opposed to British and Ottoman power but saw clearly the need to be on the winning side in the First World War. He did not join the Arab Revolt in 1916 but accepted British subsidies of £5,000 a month and harassed his enemies, the Rashidis, who made the mistake of siding with the Turks. By the end of the war he was well placed to become the dominant figure in Arabia.

Immelmann, Max (1883–1916) German air ace, mythologised by German propaganda as 'the Eagle of Lille'. He is best remembered for the development of the 'Immelmann turn', a sudden climb, a half-loop followed by a roll and a dive designed to put a pursued pilot on the tail of his pursuer. This became a standard manoeuvre of air combat. Immelmann recorded 17 victories before he was shot down in a dogfight with a British pilot, Lieutenant George McCubbin, on 18 June 1916. There was a reluctance to believe this in Germany and other theories were put forward to explain his death, including the failure of his interrupter gear and 'friendly fire'. His loss struck a blow against German morale and the Kaiser ordered Germany's other famous 'ace', Oswald BOELCKE, out of combat for a month, fearing the impact of the loss of two such famous pilots in quick succession, a decision which only delayed Boelcke's fate.

Ingalls, David Sinton (1899–1985) US Navy fighter ace. Ingalls was the only US Navy (USN) ace of the war, with the minimum six victories. He became the USN's 85th pilot in 1917 and was sent to France on coastal patrol duties. He found this rather tame and managed to arrange a posting to 13 Squadron Royal Naval Air Service, flying Sopwith Camels. He also flew DH4s with 217 Squadron for 6 weeks, before returning to what was now 213 Squadron, Royal Air Force. He spent most of his post-war career as a lawyer but was also President of Pan-Am. He was called up again in the Second World War and rose to Rear-Admiral, USN Reserve.

Ingenohl, Friedrich von (1857–1933) German naval commander, Chief of the High Seas Fleet 1913–15. Ingenohl was the first of the German navy's leaders to try to work out what the fleet was for. Frustrated by the Kaiser's unwillingness to risk his major ships in action against the numerically superior Royal Navy, he was reduced to organising coastal raids on British towns, laying minefields and submarine warfare. His reward was to be accused of incompetence and inaction. The crushing defeat of SPEE's squadron at the Falkland Islands (8 December 1914) and the reverses suffered by HIPPER at the Dogger Bank (24 January 1915) fatally compromised him with the Kaiser, and he was replaced by Admiral Hugo von POHL on 2 February 1915. The high state of training and combat-readiness that the High Seas Fleet later demonstrated at Jutland (31 May–1 June 1916) owed much to Ingenohl's leadership.

Inglis, Elsie Maud (1864–1917) British doctor, a pioneer of female medicine and campaigner for women's suffrage. Inglis was the driving force behind the foundation of the largest British women's volunteer organisation in the Great War, the Scottish Women's Hospitals, established by the Scottish Federation of the National Women's Suffrage Societies in 1914. Undeterred when her offer of a fully equipped hospital, staffed by women, was refused by the War Office, Inglis made the same offer to the French, who accepted. A hospital was established at the Abbaye de Royaumont as early as December 1914; a second hospital, at Villers Cotterets, followed in 1917. In 1915 further units were sent to Serbia, Salonika and Corsica, and in 1916 to Russia. Inglis herself served in Serbia until the withdrawal of the defeated Serb army to Corfu.

Ishii, Kikujiro (1866–1945) Japanese diplomat. As Special Ambassador to the United States, Ishii was co-signatory (with US Secretary of State Robert LANSING) of the Lansing–Ishii Agreement on 2 November 1917. Ishii was a Liberal. He shared the view, common among Japanese Liberals, that the interests of both the United States and Japan in China and the Pacific could be accommodated. His agreement with Lansing tried to square several circles. It recognised Japan's position of 'special influence' in China but reaffirmed

China's territorial integrity and the importance of maintaining international equality of opportunity in trade with China, the so-called 'Open Door' policy. A secret protocol, revealed only in 1938, committed both countries not to take advantage of wartime conditions to establish a privileged position that would 'abridge the rights of the subjects or citizens of other friendly states'. Both sides could thus claim advantages as a result of the agreement. Although there can be little doubt about the sincerity of the co-signatories, there was less willingness to find a true compromise among the wider Japanese and American governments. In Japan the agreement was seen as a sign of American weakness and an encouragement to Japanese expansion in China. In the United States the agreement was widely seen as a way of keeping the Japanese 'on-side' for the duration of the war. By the end of 1918, however, the reality of US–Japanese rivalry was already apparent in Siberia, and in 1923 the Agreement was abandoned in response to Japanese policy in China.

Ivanov, Nikolai Yudovich (1851–1919) Russian military commander, a rather elderly man who owed his position to the Tsar's gratitude for his suppression of the military mutiny at Kronstadt in 1906. As a field commander in Galicia (August–September 1914), the Carpathians (March–August 1915) and Galicia again (November 1915), he was a disaster, completely unable to respond to battlefield events, hopelessly ponderous in the advance, incapable of concentrating his (often superior) force or co-ordinating his artillery and infantry. In May 1915 his armies suffered a shattering defeat by a combined German–Austrian army at Gorlice-Tarnów, losing the whole of Poland. Even after his tardy replacement in March 1916, he was retained as military adviser to the Tsar. In March 1917 he failed to suppress the rebellion in St Petersburg that overthrew the monarchy to which he had dedicated his life.

Izzet Pasha, Ahmed (1864–1937) Ottoman military commander and Grand Vizier. An experienced military commander and political moderate who gave qualified support to the Young Turk movement, his military career was ended by the crushing defeat of his offensive on the Caucasian front in the summer of 1916. As Grand Vizier in the dying days of the Ottoman Empire, his government signed the Armistice with the Allies at Mudros on 30 October 1918.

J

Jack, Evan Maclean (1873–1951) British cartographer. Jack was commissioned in the Royal Engineers in 1893 and soon came to specialise in survey work. When the war broke out he joined the British Expeditionary Force headquarters as head of the Topographical Section, a post he retained throughout the war. This anodyne-sounding position was, in fact, central to the British war effort. The Topographical Section was responsible for producing the millions of accurate, up-to-date maps upon which the increasing tactical efficiency of the BEF, especially its artillery, came to depend. Thirty-two million trench and other maps were printed during the war. Jack was Director-General of the Ordnance Survey from 1922 until his retirement in 1930.

Jack, James Lochead (1880–1962) British military commander and diarist. Jack began the war as a 34-year-old captain in the 2nd Scottish Rifles (Cameronians) and ended it as a 38-year-old brigade commander, a speed and degree of promotion that amazed no one more than himself. An austere, professional soldier who believed in the pre-war standards of discipline and smartness, Jack's loathing of war was exceeded only by his sense of duty. His 'trench diary', edited by John Terraine and published in 1964, is a valuable account of the war, especially illuminating during Jack's period as a battalion commander (August 1916–September 1918). It also offers eloquent testimony to the professional competence, integrity and humanity of the best of the pre-war British officer corps.

Jacka, Albert (1893–1932) Australian war hero. Jacka was the first member of the Australian Imperial Force to win the Victoria Cross, after recapturing a line of trench on Gallipoli, single-handedly killing seven Turks. This immediately made him a national hero. Ironically, the event took place on 19 May 1915, the same day that John Simpson KIRKPATRICK, the man whose legend would eventually eclipse that of Jacka, was killed. In France, where he was commissioned, Jacka proved himself to be a great front-line soldier and leader of men. It was not unknown for him to instil discipline with his fists. His courage was inspirational and his men referred to themselves as 'Jacka's Mob'. He added the MC and bar to his medal tally, though this would surely have been greater but for the frequent clashes with authority that made him an uncomfortable subordinate. He was gassed at Villers-Bretonneux in May 1918 and took no further part in the fighting. After the war he became a tireless advocate of the unemployed and veterans, but like many other old warriors whose forte was violence he found it difficult to readjust to civilian life. Jacka was much admired by the Australian official historian C.E.W. BEAN, for whom he encapsulated those qualities of physical courage and moral independence that were the essence of Australia.

Jackson, Henry Bradwardine (1855–1929) British naval commander, whose appointment as First Sea Lord following the resignation of Admiral FISHER in May 1915 was something of a surprise. His partnership with the new First Lord, BALFOUR, seemed almost deliberately contrived as an antidote to the dynamic and controversial pairing of Fisher and CHURCHILL. Jackson was by temperament a scientist and administrator. He did innovative and important work before the war on ship-to-ship radio communications, in conjunction with Marconi, research that won him election as a Fellow of the Royal Society. As chief of the infant naval war staff in 1913, he was also responsible for training the Royal Navy's first staff officers. Jackson had sound judgement. He recognised the flaws in Churchill's original design for the Dardanelles, believing it unworkable without military support. But as First Sea Lord his inability to delegate and to extricate himself from administrative detail limited his effectiveness. He was succeeded by JELLICOE at the end of 1916.

Jacob, Claud William (1863–1948) British military commander, the only senior officer of the Indian army to remain with the British Expeditionary Force and be promoted after the Indian Corps' withdrawal from France in October 1915. After a period spent in the difficult task of repairing 21st Division following its disastrous baptism of fire at Loos in September 1915, Jacob became GOC II Corps in May 1916, commanding it for the rest of the war. A charming, thoughtful man, devoid of personal ambition, his command was characterised by thorough planning and preparation. Divisions welcomed being moved to II Corps because

they knew that its staff work was efficient and above all because they appreciated that too much would not be asked of them. Jacob became known for his willingness to stand up to higher authority, not least Hubert GOUGH, in order to protect the interests of his troops. Despite these qualities, Jacob's record as a commander was not one of unbroken success. His failure to capture the Gheluvelt plateau on 31 July 1917 seriously hindered Fifth Army's main attack. Subsequent attempts to clear the plateau by II Corps were equally barren.

Jagger, Charles Sargeant (1885–1934) British sculptor. Jagger began his working life as a silver engraver with the jewellers Mappin & Webb, before studying at the Sheffield School of Art and the Royal College of Art. He enlisted in the Artists' Rifles on the outbreak of war and was later commissioned in the Worcestershire Regiment, serving on Gallipoli and the Western Front and winning the Military Cross. He was wounded three times. After the war he was employed on some major commemorative commissions, of which the Royal Artillery memorial at Hyde Park Corner and the Great Western Railway memorial at Paddington station are perhaps the best known and most important.

Jagow, Gottlieb von (1863–1935) German politician and diplomat, Undersecretary of State 1913–16, a sort of Prussian Cassandra, whose pessimistic political, strategic and diplomatic judgements failed to sober the intoxicating dreams of his colleagues. Jagow was one of the few Wilhelmine statesmen who wished to improve Anglo-German relations. He therefore opposed TIRPITZ's plans for naval expansion and the SCHLIEFFEN Plan's casual violation of Belgian neutrality. He did not share the complacent view that the British would remain neutral in a European war and seems to have been almost alone in fearing the British as an enemy. He did, however, believe that a war with Russia was inevitable. He gave his support to Chancellor BETHMANN-HOLLWEG in July and August 1914, clinging to the hope that a general European war could be avoided. When this hope proved false, he deferred to Germany's military leaders. Nevertheless, he immediately recognised the battle of the Marne as a disaster for Germany and pressed Bethmann to seek a negotiated peace. Later, he was equally prescient in fearing American belligerency and strenuously opposed the policy of unrestricted submarine warfare, opposition that led to his dismissal. Amid the subsequent wreckage of Imperial Germany it is doubtful whether he found much comfort in saying 'I told you so'. Jagow's career is a painful reminder that in politics and war it is not enough simply to be right.

James, Baron Trevenen (1889–1915) British air war pioneer. 'Bron' James obtained his pilot's certificate in June 1912 after only three days' instruction. In April 1913 he transferred from the Royal Engineers to the Royal Flying Corps, later undertaking important wireless experiments together with Donald LEWIS. Still with Lewis, he continued work on wireless and developed the 'clock code' method of artillery observation. He undertook numerous artillery observation flights, flying by himself as the weight of early wireless sets precluded carriage of an observer. It was on one of these solo flights that he was hit by a shell and killed on 13 July 1915.

Jaurès, (Auguste Marie Joseph) Jean (1859–1914) French Socialist Party leader, a prolific writer, passionate orator, supporter of Dreyfus, founder of the newspaper *L'Humanité*, opponent of imperialism and patriot. Jaurès found his inspiration in the principles of the French Revolution, rather than those of Marxism. He remained throughout his life a very *French* socialist, who retained a hu-

man commitment to the rights of the individual. His fraternal acceptance of the Second International's ruling that socialists should not participate in bourgeois governments, however, kept the French left in permanent opposition and meant that he never held ministerial office. Although Jaurès was the most charismatic political leader of his generation in France, responsible for many converts to socialism, in the years before 1914 his opposition to militarism and advocacy of Franco-German reconciliation made him increasingly unpopular. At the height of the 'July Crisis' in 1914 he visited Brussels in an attempt to persuade German socialists to strike against war. On his return to Paris (31 July) he was murdered by a nationalist fanatic, the appropriately named Raoul Villain. Germany declared war on France three days later.

Jellicoe, John Rushworth (1859–1935) British naval commander, Commander-in-Chief of the Grand Fleet 1914–16. A technocrat in a navy that traditionally valued character more than technical ability, his calculating personality and modesty have rendered him unsatisfactory as a naval hero. CHURCHILL famously described Jellicoe as 'the only man who could lose the war in an afternoon'. He was, of course, not expected to do this. On the contrary, the expectation was that when the time came the fleet on which the British had lavished so much taxpayers' money would destroy the German navy. Jellicoe's failure to deliver a 'second Trafalgar' at Jutland (31 May–1 June 1916) left a permanent stain on his reputation and that of the Royal Navy. He was always dubious about his ability to annihilate the German fleet. In a perceptive memorandum, dispatched to the Admiralty in October 1914, he outlined the dangers he perceived in 'closing with the enemy' in a major fleet engagement, explaining the circumstances in which he was willing to accept battle. He would try a decision only in line of battle, through a long-range big gun duel in daylight in the northern waters of the North Sea. When the moment came, he followed this plan to the letter. Displaying extraordinary calm, superb seamanship and tactical acumen, he twice crossed the 'T' of the German fleet and manoeuvred his ships between the Germans and their line of retreat. Only the skill and luck of his opponent, SCHEER, the technical weakness of British armour and gunnery and the often shoddy performance of his subordinates prevented Jellicoe from winning a famous victory. At the end of the battle he remained master of the North Sea. The British government's official dispatch seemed to imply that the Grand Fleet had suffered a defeat. British opinion has often seemed to agree with this. At the end of 1916 Jellicoe became First Sea Lord, professional head of the Royal Navy. At the Admiralty, in the face of unrestricted German submarine warfare, which by April 1917 threatened Britain with starvation, his perennial pessimism hardened into defeatism. His apparent refusal to introduce the convoy system alienated his political superiors and led to his unceremonious dismissal on Christmas Eve 1917.

Jemal Pasha, Ahmed *see* DJEMAL PASHA, AHMED.

Jerram, (Thomas Henry) Martyn (1858–1933) British naval commander. Jerram commanded the 2nd Battle Squadron in the Grand Fleet 1915–16, and led the battle line at Jutland (31 May–1 June 1916) in his flagship, HMS *King George V*. Like so many of Jellicoe's subordinates he was a competent and reliable officer so long as nothing out of the ordinary was expected, such as the use of initiative or independent judgement.

Jeudwine, Hugh Sandham (1862–1942) British military commander. Jeudwine was not a man who courted popularity. As commander of a small mobile column

in the South African War he achieved an 'awe inspiring' reputation for his ruthless crushing of Boer opposition. He could be equally ruthless with his colleagues. As ALLENBY's chief of staff at V Corps in 1915 he made himself 'cordially disliked'. But he was also a man of parts, three times winning the Royal Artillery Institution's gold medal. From January 1916 until the end of the war he commanded 55th Division, a Territorial unit recruited mainly from the western part of Lancashire between Liverpool and Lancaster. He was the only man to command the division in action during the war. He had sufficient imagination to recognise that Territorial divisions needed subtle handling, something often lacking among his brigade commanders, notably Reginald KENTISH. After the opening of the 'Passchendaele' campaign, Jeudwine went to great lengths to obtain what would now be called 'feedback' from the men who actually carried out attacks, with a view to modifying and improving the division's tactics. This process eventually became institutionalised within the division and may have helped bring him to the attention of higher authority, for in December 1917 he was invited to join a committee charged with producing a pamphlet on defensive tactics. Although the pamphlet was never published, the ideas that the committee generated, particularly the concept of 'blob' rather than linear defence, contributed significantly to 55th Division's finest hour in the spring of 1918.

On 9 April 1918 55th Division found itself holding the line at Givenchy. The German Sixth Army's attack on the Ypres salient had targeted the two Portuguese divisions to 55th Division's left. The Portuguese units broke in disarray, leaving a three-and-a-half mile gap in the British line as far as the river Lys. HAIG's famous 'backs to the wall' order of the day, issued on 11 April, applied to Jeudwine's division more than any other unit in the British army. Perhaps stung by (unjustified) criticisms of the division's poor performance in the German counter-attack at Cambrai the previous November, Jeudwine was determined that no ground would be yielded. He had no truck with the concept of 'elastic defence in depth', which he believed merely encouraged retreat. Retreat at Givenchy would invite disaster. Where 55th Division occupied high ground the front line would be held at all costs; where the front was low-lying and boggy defence would be focused on a strongly fortified village further back. His tactics were triumphantly justified. The line held. Haig later singled out the actions of 55th Division in the successful defence of Ypres and the Channel ports.

Joffre, Joseph Jacques Césaire (1852–1931) French Commander-in-Chief 1914–16, the eldest of eleven children of a provincial cooper in the Pyrénées Orientales. Joffre made his way on merit in a technical branch of the army, the engineers, achieving a modest pre-war reputation as an efficient officer, largely in colonial campaigns. It was his lack of objectionable political or religious affiliations, however, which secured him promotion to Chief of the General Staff in 1911. This appointment carried with it de facto command of the French armies in time of war. In this capacity, in August 1914, he was responsible for implementing the near-disastrous Plan XVII for an all-out attack against Germany through Lorraine. Joffre's claim to greatness as a commander lies principally in the fact that he was able to recognise the plan's catastrophic failure, to redeploy his armies and to counter-attack the German right wing, the 'miracle of the Marne', one of the most important battles in twentieth-century history. To extricate himself from the ruin of his own plan in the face of fundamental miscalculations of German strength and of patchy intelligence of German movements was a triumph of character as well as intellect. Joffre was a man of immense calm and self-control.

Critics (and admirers) claimed that he 'thought with his stomach', like the peasant he was. But his corpulent, cherubic appearance hid immense reserves of courage and self-belief. Throughout the calamitous days of August and early September 1914 he remained in control of himself and his armies. The victory was truly his. The Marne preserved France from defeat. But in 1915 and 1916 Joffre proved unable to deliver victory. No one was more aware than he that the 1914 campaigns had left the Boches 'at Noyon', a mere forty miles from Paris. The French had no choice but to attack if they were to liberate their country. In the spring and autumn of 1915 Joffre launched large-scale assaults against the German defences in the Champagne and Artois. Casualties were enormous. The French armies captured a few square miles of shell-pocked wasteland, while in the east the German armies occupied the whole of Poland. When the German Commander-in-Chief, Erich von FALKENHAYN, turned his attention to the west in February 1916, the German offensive at Verdun took Joffre by surprise and found the historic defences denuded of guns on his orders. Once more, however, Joffre showed his powers of recovery. PÉTAIN was put in command of the defence of Verdun while Joffre mobilised the huge resources of men and material that this required. France was again saved from defeat.

Joffre was by temperament an autocrat. He exercised virtually dictatorial powers in the very broad 'Zone of the Armies' that he established. France's political leaders, especially VIVIANI, struggled ineffectually to exercise any real control of the war. Joffre was also a superb actor, who could summon rage, tears, humour, emotion and sentimentality at will, a skill that was often employed with telling effect on his British allies. In the end, however, he ran out of luck. The scale of French losses at Verdun, the failure of the Anglo-French attack on the Somme to achieve a breakthrough, and the fall of Bucharest to

Austro-German forces on 6 December 1916 encouraged the BRIAND government to reassert its political authority. Joffre was dismissed on 13 December, consoled with the title of Marshal of France. He had no further influence on the conduct of the war.

John, Augustus Edwin (1878–1961) British war artist. John's gifts were prodigious, and he was widely recognised as the greatest artist of his generation from an early age. This was, perhaps, unfortunate. Throughout his long life he too often demanded and received the tribute due to 'genius'. This was true even during the war. Max AITKEN, the future Lord Beaverbrook, ever susceptible to the appeal of talent, used his influence as Canada's 'Eye Witness' on the Western Front to obtain John a commission in the Canadian Expeditionary Force. No restrictions were placed on what he did or did not paint and, contrary to military regulations, he was even allowed to keep his flowing black beard. This indulgence did nothing to stimulate John's creativity. He completed only one war painting, *Fraternity*, and was sent home in disgrace after a few weeks, following his part in a drunken brawl. Characteristically, he escaped a court martial through Aitken's intervention.

Jones, David (1895–1974) British soldier, poet and painter. Jones served as a private in the 15th Battalion Royal Welsh Fusiliers (1st London Welsh). In 1929 he published *In Parenthesis*, in which he tells – in prose and verse – the story of John Ball, a volunteer soldier in a Welsh New Army battalion. It is one of the most remarkable books to have emerged from the war. Artistically the war is generally considered to have advanced the cause of modernism, to represent a sharp break with the past, a sundering. This is the theme of Professor Paul Fussell's influential book, *The Great War and Modern Memory* (1975). Jones's view of the war

was quite contrary, seeking always to find connections between the experience of First World War soldiers and those who preceded them, not least on the battlefields of Picardy. Fussell dismissed Jones's work as an 'honourable miscarriage' and Jones himself as a 'turgid allusionist'. Jones's real failure, however, was to have written a book which did not fit Professor Fussell's thesis. Jones's paintings of the war are also very fine, full of accurate and interesting detail. He never succeeded in putting his war experience 'in parenthesis' and was still referring to it in letters written towards the end of his long life.

Jones, Robert (1858–1933) British surgeon. Jones was Professor of Orthopaedic Surgery at Liverpool University, where he presided over the only specialist orthopaedic teaching unit in Britain. He was the best possible choice as Inspector of Military Orthopaedics during the war. His was the greatest influence on the medical procedures adopted not only in British orthopaedic surgery but also American. The training regime he established for military orthopaedic surgeons made a formidable contribution to the tremendous advances in orthopaedics achieved during the war.

Josef Augustin, Archduke (1872–1962) Austro-Hungarian military commander. Josef was a soldier for whom the word 'dashing' might have been coined. He had none of the aristocratic languor of the *fin de siècle* Habsburg Empire, bringing energy and a sense of professional purpose to his military career. He served as a divisional commander in Galicia, a corps commander in Italy and an army commander in Romania. He was the only senior officer to support the establishment of a separate Hungarian army at a meeting of the Royal Council in January 1918, an action that severely limited his influence. His pessimism about the future of the empire deepened in 1918 after the failure of the Piave offensive, and he advocated an immediate peace. In 1919 he led a royalist counter-revolution against Béla KUN's Communists, retiring to private life shortly afterwards.

Josef Ferdinand, Archduke (1872–1942) Austro-Hungarian military commander. The epitome of Habsburg aristocratic fecklessness and military incompetence, his Fourth Army was virtually annihilated at Lutsk in Galicia on 4 June 1916 (his birthday), during the opening of the BRUSILOV offensive, seriously threatening a complete Austrian defeat. Josef's faith in the impregnability of his defences induced a fatal complacency that allowed him to ignore Russian preparations in favour of hunting expeditions and other frivolous self-indulgence, the price for which was paid principally by his men, 130,000 of whom were killed or captured in two days of disastrous fighting.

Judson, William Voorhees (1865–1923) US military attaché and Chief of the United States Military Mission to Russia 1917–18. Judson's brief was to try to keep Russia in the war. He rapidly concluded that Russia would make no effective military contribution unless the Provisional Government succeeded in imposing military discipline on the army. This brought him into conflict with official US diplomatic opinion in Russia, which believed that Russian soldiers would be inspired to fight for a 'democratic' cause after the fall of Tsarism. Judson showed an equally pragmatic and far-sighted understanding following the Bolshevik seizure of power. He was convinced of the necessity of direct negotiations between the US government and the Bolsheviks to prevent Russia from concluding a separate peace. On 1 December 1917 he arranged a meeting with TROTSKY. Reluctant, but official, sanctioning of the meeting by US Ambassador David R. Francis failed to save Judson from the censure of the US government, which preferred a policy of 'wait and see', and he was

recalled. Judson's valuable letters, memoranda and reports of his time in Russia were published in 1998.

Jünger, Ernst (1895–1998) German soldier and writer. Jünger volunteered for military service as soon as war broke out and was eventually commissioned in the 73rd Infantry Regiment. He saw much action, was wounded fourteen times and received many decorations, including Germany's highest gallantry award, the *Pour le mérite* (Blue Max). He announced his arrival on the literary scene with his first and most famous book, *Storm of Steel*, in 1919. Jünger's upbringing by an eccentric, overbearing anarchist father was essentially scientific, and much of the shocking power of *Storm of Steel* comes from the detached and clinical quality of its descriptions of combat. His evocation of what it feels like to be under shell fire, having a giant repeatedly aim blows at your head with a hammer and just miss, has never been bettered. Jünger's portrait of war, greatly influenced by his role as a stormtrooper during the German spring offensive of 1918, is essentially apocalyptic. Those who survived the storm of steel were made anew, reborn to rule. These views, with their Nietzschean echoes, made uncomfortable reading in post-war Germany, and Jünger has sometimes been portrayed as one of the 'gravediggers' of the Weimar republic. But he never followed a party line. His work was always more complex and opaque than his partial admirers could appreciate. At times in his long life he was a hero of the German right, the French left and the Greens. The Nazis courted him in the 1920s and 1930s and banned his books in the 1940s. Much of Jünger's writing is deeply Teutonic and ultimately, perhaps, alien to the pragmatic and empirical cast of the Anglo-Saxon mind. But *Storm of Steel* and the later *Copse 125* are two of the most compelling studies of combat ever written, retaining an elemental power almost a century later.

Jusserand, Jean (Adrien Antoine) Jules (1855–1932) French diplomat, Ambassador to the USA 1902–25. With his French-born American wife, his evident love of the United States and his ability, as a literary scholar and historian, to move effortlessly in high cultural and intellectual circles, Jusserand proved a powerful and effective emissary in the world's most important neutral country. Some accounts of American entry to the war have attributed to him a sinister, manipulative role; he certainly did everything he could to prevent President WILSON from pursuing a negotiated peace. But it is more probable that his most enduring achievement was to represent to American opinion-makers through his own person the liberal and humane values the Allies believed they were at war to defend.

K

Kaledin, Alexei Maximovitch (1861–1918) Russian military commander, a cavalryman whose career was closely associated with that of General BRUSILOV. Kaledin commanded a corps under Brusilov in Galicia in 1915 and succeeded him in command of Eighth Army in 1916. Eighth Army played a leading part in the success of the Brusilov offensive of June 1916, making the initial attack from trenches dug as close as possible to the Austrian positions, taking Archduke JOSEF FERDINAND's Fourth Army by complete surprise and causing his entire front to collapse. In September 1917 Kaledin was appointed Hetman (leader) of the Cossacks. He committed suicide in 1918 when the Cossacks deserted him and went over to the Bolshevik government.

Kamio, Mitsuomi (1856–1927) Japanese military commander, who successfully led the Japanese 18th Division in the conquest of Tsingtao (Qingdao), the German fortified naval base in north-east China, making skilful use of his artillery resources and avoiding costly infantry frontal assaults.

Kapp, Wolfgang (1858–1922) American-born German journalist and politician, founder of the extreme right-wing German Fatherland Party, who led the putsch that threatened to overthrow the infant Weimar Republic in March 1920. The German army's refusal to fire on their former comrades in the *Freikorps* forced Chancellor EBERT's government to flee to Dresden. But the putsch collapsed on 17 March, after four days, owing to a strike of Berlin workers and the refusal of ordinary soldiers and civil servants to take orders from Kapp. Military supporters of the putsch, including LUDENDORFF, were not punished. Even though Ebert had failed to get the army to fight the extreme right, he still needed it to fight the extreme left, a task for which it showed no inhibition.

Karl I (1887–1922) The last Habsburg emperor. Karl was an intelligent, humane, sincere man who tried to find an honourable way out of the war from the moment he succeeded his aged great-uncle FRANZ JOSEF I on 21 November 1916, an aim in which he was encouraged by his pro-Allied wife, the Empress Zita. But the peace feelers that he put out to France through the good offices of his brother-in-law, Prince SIXTE of Bourbon-Parma, were typically clumsy. They were deeply resented by the Germans and lost Austria what small influence it had over German policy. Karl's good intentions as a domestic reformer, expressed in the October Manifesto, with its proposal for a federation of autonomous states, were equally barren. He came to the throne too late to influence events. He offered too little.

And he had neither the authority nor the will to overcome his terrible inheritance. No one recognised more clearly than him the fatal consequences of the war for the Habsburg regime, but he never abdicated and indulged in the fantasy of a return to power until his death in exile and penury in Madeira at the age of 35.

Károlyi von Nagykároly, Mikhály, Count (1875–1955) Austro-Hungarian politician. A liberal Hungarian aristocrat from a great noble family, Károlyi moved steadily to the left during the war, forming his own party in 1916 to advocate Hungarian independence, land reform and universal suffrage. In a typically belated attempt to prevent the inevitable, Emperor KARL I chose Károlyi as Prime Minister of Hungary on 31 October 1918. Far from stemming the tide of Hungarian nationalism, however, Károlyi's appointment brought it to the flood. Károlyi obtained release from his imperial oath the day after his appointment and proclaimed a Hungarian republic on 11 November. His hopes that this change would obtain his country favourable consideration from the victors proved vain. The demands for territorial concessions were unabated and Károlyi's support ebbed away. In March 1919 his government was overthrown in a coup led by the odious Communist Béla KUN. He spent most of the remainder of his long life in exile.

Katō, Takaaki (1860–1926) Japanese politician. Katō began his career as an executive with Mitsubishi. The company had close links with Britain and Katō spent some time there, becoming something of an Anglophile. He later joined the Japanese diplomatic service and was Ambassador in London 1895–1899, before returning to Japan to become Foreign Minister in 1900. He was one of the principal architects of the Anglo-Japanese Alliance of 1902. This was brought about by mutual British and Japanese fear of Russian designs in Manchuria. It was regarded as a triumph in Japan, seeming to put Japan on an equal footing with the other Great Powers. It boosted popular nationalism in Japan and increased the influence of the military. It also provided Japan with the diplomatic self-confidence to declare war on Russia in 1904, knowing that Japan's alliance with Britain would prevent France from supporting Russia. Katō was a leading advocate of Japanese belligerency in 1914. This suited the British, for whom Japan's entry into the war solved many short-term problems, especially naval ones. But the limited role that the British envisaged for the Japanese was more difficult to maintain. Britain had no objections to Japan's annexing of German possessions in the Pacific and the mainland of China, but the Twenty-One Demands made to the Chinese government on 18 January 1915, China's acceptance of which would have reduced her to an economic satellite of Japan, alarmed both British and American opinion. China's communication of the Demands, which were made secretly, to the United States government embarrassed the Japanese and Katō was forced from office in July 1915.

Kavanagh, Charles Toler McMurrough (1864–1942) British military commander, who was given the rather thankless task of leading the re-formed Cavalry Corps on the Western Front in September 1916. The appointment was welcomed by his fellow cavalryman Brigadier-General A.F. 'Sally' Home, who described Kavanagh as 'a real leader of men' who knew his job and had a mind of his own. By the time of Kavanagh's appointment the Cavalry Corps consisted of a mere five divisions, less than three per cent of the British Expeditionary Force's total strength. By the spring of 1918 the Corps was down to three divisions. Trench warfare offered few opportunities for the cavalry to fulfil its traditional roles as shock troops or as scouts. But it maintained a residual function as a mobile reserve, capable of plugging gaps and covering withdrawals. Haig's appreciation of Kavanagh's role is indicated by his presence, as the only corps commander, on the famous photograph of the Commander-in-Chief, his army commanders and their chiefs of staff taken on the steps of the *Mairie* at Cambrai on 11 November 1918.

Kazakov, Alexander (1891–1919) Russian fighter ace, whose seventeen confirmed victories on the Eastern Front, where aerial warfare was less intense, have won him general acceptance as the top-scoring Russian ace.

Keil, Franz von (1862–1945) Austro-Hungarian military commander. Keil began the war as commandant of the important Adriatic naval station at Pola, but in February 1917 he assumed command of the 2nd Battleship Division. In March 1918 Emperor KARL I divided the naval command, giving the fleet to Admiral HORTHY. Keil became the Emperor's senior naval adviser. This was not an arduous post: the Emperor took no advice and the navy never put to sea. Keil was left to preside symbolically over the end of Habsburg naval power.

Kelly, Frederick Septimus 'Cleg' (1891–1916) Australian musician, composer, sportsman and soldier. Kelly enjoyed the possibly unique distinction of being a great oarsman and an outstanding musician. His record on the water included three Diamond Skulls at Henley (1902, 1903, 1905), a record that lasted until 1938. He also won an Olympic gold medal in 1908. He managed to combine this athleticism with an emerging career as a concert pianist and composer. In September 1914 he joined the Hood Battalion of the Royal Naval Division, where he served with Arthur ASQUITH, Rupert BROOKE and Patrick Shaw-Stewart, who were collectively known as the 'Latin Club'. Kelly served with the

Royal Naval Division at Antwerp, on Gallipoli and on the Western Front. Kelly was among those present at Brooke's burial on Skyros and later composed an 'Elegy' in memory of his friend. Kelly was himself killed on 13 November 1916 in the attack at Beaucourt-sur-Ancre, during which Bernard FREYBERG won the Victoria Cross.

Kemal Pasha, Mustapha (1881–1938) Ottoman military commander, who emerged from the war as a Turkish national hero for his defence of the Gallipoli peninsula, where his generalship was marked by fanatical determination and a disregard for casualties. His unauthorised attack against Chunuk Bair on 25 April 1915 was perhaps decisive in maintaining Turkish control of the southern part of the Gallipoli peninsula. His subsequent commands in Anatolia and Palestine enjoyed less success against unfavourable odds. Although Kemal ended the war still a subordinate military commander, he was personally untouched by the fall of the Young Turks. The war also removed Kemal's political nemesis, ENVER PASHA, from his path. He rallied nationalist opposition to Turkish dismemberment and defeated Greek expansionist ambitions at Smyrna in 1922. He was President of the Turkish Republic from 1924 until 1938, presiding over a ruthless dictatorship that dragged Turkey into the modern world of Western dress, the Latin alphabet, female emancipation, secularism and industry. He was one of the greatest men to emerge during the First World War.

Kennington, Eric Henri (1888–1960) British soldier and war artist. Eric Kennington trained at the Lambeth School of Art and held his first exhibition at the Royal Academy in 1908. He joined the 13th Battalion London Regiment (The Kensingtons), a Territorial unit, on the outbreak of war and served with them on the Western Front until he was badly wounded in June 1915. The wound eventually resulted in his being invalided out of the army in August 1917. Kennington's famous painting of *The Kensingtons at Laventie*, with its exceptionally detailed and realistic portrayal of real soldiers in a state of exhaustion, appeared in 1916 and made his name as a 'war artist'. After his release from the army, Charles MASTERMAN, head of the War Propaganda Bureau, invited him to become an official war artist. His best pictures include *Gassed and Wounded* and *The Die-Hards*. After the war he designed many war memorials and illustrated T.E. LAWRENCE's *The Seven Pillars of Wisdom*.

Kentish, Reginald John (1876–1956) British military commander and staff officer. Reggie Kentish was an independent-minded, exuberant officer with a powerful social conscience, fearless of higher authority, which – in the words of his nephew – often regarded him as the Antichrist. Kentish more or less deserted his post as a staff officer with a London Territorial Division in August 1914 to join his regiment, the 1st Battalion Royal Irish Fusiliers, soon winning one of the first DSOs of the war. In two years he rose from captain to brigadier-general, commanding 76th Brigade in Aylmer HALDANE's 3rd Division on the Somme and, later, 166th Brigade in Hugh JEUDWINE's 55th Division, a Territorial unit on whose sensibilities his Regular Army methods sometimes jarred. He was in command of 166th Brigade during 55th Division's defence of the vital position on the Lys during the German spring offensive (1918). But perhaps his greatest contribution came as the first Commandant of the pioneering Third Army School at Flixécourt and then as first Commandant of the Senior Officers School at Aldershot, where he organised courses designed to equip officers to command battalions. He himself gave memorable lectures on 'leadership and morale'. Kentish had a life-long affection for the underdog. He played the leading part in establishing

sports facilities for soldiers before the war and, in 1925, founded the National Playing Fields Association to do the same for the urban poor.

Kerensky, Aleksandr Fedorovich (1881–1970) Russian politician, a socialist lawyer and leading member of the Petrogad Soviet, who emerged during the February Revolution of 1917 as Minister of Justice in the Provisional Government. In May he became Minister of War and in July Prime Minister, following demonstrations by workers, soldiers and sailors against the government in Petrograd. Kerensky's opposition to German militarism made him determined to keep Russia in the war. It was a fateful decision. The Kerensky offensive of July 1917 was the last made by the Russian army during the Great War and finally broke its cohesion. Russian soldiers 'voted with their feet' and went home, where they added to the mounting urban and rural unrest. Kerensky's failure to end the war made it impossible for him to deal with the pressing problems of political anarchy, economic collapse and impending military defeat. He became increasingly isolated between the counter-revolutionary forces of the right, apparently led by General KORNILOV, and those of the revolutionary left, led by LENIN. His attempt to arrest the Bolshevik leaders on 5 November 1917 failed and two days later they overthrew his government, driving him into a long exile mainly spent in the United States.

Kettle, Thomas Michael (1880–1916) Irish nationalist politician, British soldier and poet. Tom Kettle was killed on the Somme at Ginchy on 9 September 1916 while serving as a subaltern with the Royal Dublin Fusiliers. He had already recognised the tragedy of his situation. Four months earlier, in April 1916, a group of Irish revolutionaries had launched a rising against British rule in Ireland. They included Kettle's own brother-in-law, Frank Sheehy-Skeffington, who was summarily executed by the British. Kettle immediately understood that their actions had forever damned constitutional nationalists like himself who had chosen to identify Irish freedom with the Allied cause, especially the defence of Belgium. He correctly predicted that the men of the Easter Rising would become martyrs and heroes, while men like him would be either forgotten or condemned as stooges or fools. He wrote his own epitaph five days before his death, in the final lines of a poem dedicated 'To My Daughter Betty': 'Know that we fools, now with the foolish dead, Died not for the flag, nor King, nor Emperor, But for a dream, born in a herdsman's shed, And for the secret Scripture of the poor.'

Keyes, Roger John Brownlow (1872–1945) British naval commander. Keyes was a man destined to divide opinion in both life and death. To his admirers, who included Winston CHURCHILL, he embodied the spirit of Drake and Nelson, seemingly so lacking in the Royal Navy during the Great War. To his detractors, he was recklessly aggressive and dangerous. The latter judgement is harsh. Keyes was undoubtedly a difficult subordinate. His contempt for passivity and determination to come to grips with the enemy was never hidden. He repeatedly clashed with his superiors, including FISHER, CARDEN, DE ROBECK and BACON. His was the most powerful voice advocating aggressive naval action at the Dardanelles. He was dismayed by De Robeck's refusal to renew the naval attack after the failure of 18 March 1915, believing that a great opportunity to defeat Turkey and end the war more swiftly had been squandered. In 1917, while director of plans at the Admiralty, he came into conflict with Admiral Bacon, commander of the Dover Patrol, about the best way to prevent German submarines from passing through the Channel. Keyes was not merely belli-

gerent, however. His audacity was leavened with calculation. It was he who devised the plan that led to the successful battle of the Heligoland Bight (28 August 1914). And, as Bacon's successor in command of the Dover Patrol, his barrage stopped German submarine traffic through the Straits. His planning and leadership of the famous Zeebrugge raid, made on St George's Day 1918, was a tremendous propaganda success at a low point in the war on land and sea. Although the claims made for it at the time were unfounded, the raid and Keyes' constant, unremitting aggression against German naval forces in Belgium undoubtedly disrupted the U-boat campaign.

Keynes, John Maynard (1883–1946) British economist, who spent the war on secondment from Cambridge University to the Treasury, which he represented at the Paris Peace Conference. He resigned in June 1919 in protest against the imposition of financial reparations on Germany, which he believed would seriously hamper the economic recovery of Europe. His brilliant book *The Economic Consequences of the Peace* (1919), justifying his resignation, was not only an attack on the policy of reparations but also a vivid and arresting analysis of the conference's leading statesmen. It brought him international fame and did much to shape subsequent views of the peace settlement, which many people increasingly came to believe had treated Germany badly.

Kiggell, Launcelot Edward (1862–1954) British staff officer, who was HAIG's Chief of the General Staff 1916–17. Few British officers, except perhaps CHARTERIS, have received such a uniformly hostile press as 'Kigg'. He is commonly dismissed as a tidy-minded clerk, capable of keeping Haig's office in order but incapable of offering his Commander-in-Chief the imaginative challenge to conventional wisdom that many of Haig's critics believe he needed. Kiggell is also accused of being out of touch with battlefield realities and is principally remembered for breaking down in tears when finally confronted with them at Passchendaele, a story that is almost certainly apocryphal. Kiggell was an able and dedicated officer. Despite being hampered throughout the war by poor health, he provided a stream of sensible advice to his Chief and to the BEF as a whole through a series of important pamphlets and training manuals, including (in all but name) the important *SS 135 Training of Divisions for Offensive Action*. His opinions on the use of tanks were also sound. His career is in urgent need of reassessment.

Kipling, Rudyard (1865–1936) British novelist and poet. As a patriot and imperialist, Kipling was anxious to lend his pen to the cause, but he was never anyone's tame propagandist. He wrote a popular account of the raising and training of *The New Army* (1914) and he was always willing to help publicise the work of the Royal Navy. After the war he agreed to write a history of the Irish Guards, perhaps the finest regimental history ever written. Kipling's most enduring contribution, however, came through his influence on remembrance. In 1917 Sir Fabian WARE invited him to become a commissioner of the newly established Imperial War Graves Commission. Kipling approached his role with the utmost seriousness. He was responsible for choosing the standard inscription in British war cemeteries, 'Their Name Liveth for Evermore', and for many of the inscriptions on headstones, including 'A Soldier of the Great War. Known Unto God'. He played a leading part in establishing a Tomb of the Unknown Warrior at Westminster Abbey and originated the nightly ceremony of the Last Post at the Menin Gate Memorial at Ypres. Kipling's war was forever haunted by the death at the battle of Loos (September 1915) of his beloved son John, a 2nd Lieutenant in the Irish Guards. John, like his father, was myopic,

and it took Kipling's intervention with Lord Roberts to obtain him a commission. John Kipling was originally posted as 'missing', that dreadful harbinger of false hopes, and his body was never found. The war inspired some of Kipling's bitterest poems, including 'Gethsemane 1914–18', 'Gehazi 1915', 'Mesopotamia 1917' and 'Epitaphs of the War 1914–18', as well as one of his most patriotic, '"For All We Have and Are" 1914'.

Kirchner, Raphael (1876–1917) Austrian illustrator, whose celebrated 'pin ups' that appeared in the pages of *La vie Parisienne*, and on postcards, were much sought after by French and British soldiers as decorations for billets and dugouts. Kirchner's females were essentially idealised and represented for many men not only the erotic but also the abandoned world of softness, femininity and scent.

Kirkpatrick, John Simpson (1892–1915) Australian war hero. Since the mid-1960s, Simpson (the name under which he enlisted) has eclipsed Albert JACKA VC as the greatest Australian war hero. This has much to do with the fixing of Gallipoli as the defining Australian national experience. A visit to the beaches at Anzac Cove is now part of the ritual for all Australian backpackers on their tour of the world. Thousands regularly gather each year on 25 April, the anniversary of the landings. Jacka has been forgotten, along with much of the Australian experience on the Western Front. Simpson is a surprising candidate for an Australian war hero. He was a quick-tempered British merchant seaman who jumped ship at Newcastle, New South Wales, in 1910, spent only four years in Australia as an itinerant labourer of unmalleable radical opinions and only joined the Australian Imperial Force (AIF) because he thought it would take him back to England. Instead, he landed on the Gallipoli peninsula on 25 April 1915 as part of the 3rd Field Ambulance, Australian Army Medical Corps. He seems to have detached himself from any formal structure of command almost immediately but soon acquired a donkey (variously known as 'Abdul', 'Murphy' or 'Duffy') which he used to carry wounded soldiers to the dressing station seemingly oblivious to enemy fire. He was killed while carrying out this work on 19 May 1915. His legend as 'the man with the donk' soon spread throughout the AIF and beyond, and he became one of the best-known images of the Australian and New Zealand Army Corps.

Kitchener, Herbert Horatio, 1st Earl Kitchener of Khartoum and Broome (1850–1916) British statesman. Kitchener served as Secretary of State for War from August 1914 until his death in the sinking of HMS *Hampshire* on 5 June 1916. In this role he exercised an influence on British conduct of the war, at home and abroad and for good and ill, that was probably greater than that of any other single individual. Kitchener's traditional reputation is a poor one. His death at the height of the war, when most things had gone wrong and were about to get worse, meant that he was never able to write his memoirs. The field was left free to his detractors. There emerges from the pages of LLOYD GEORGE and CHURCHILL, and from lesser figures such as Charles Hobhouse, the portrait of an autocrat painfully sinking beneath the weight of his manifold burdens but too vain and too powerful to allow others to come to his relief, of a mystic seemingly incapable of rational thought, proceeding by leaps of inspiration into the abyss of total war, of a thoughtless wrecker carelessly undoing the work of pre-war reform which produced the General Staff and the Territorial Army. This was a portrait that his principal biographers, Sir George Arthur and Sir Philip Magnus, did little to dispel.

There are three principal charges against him: that through ignorance and prejudice he chose to ignore the mechanism of the Territorial Army in expanding Britain's military forces, resulting in unnecessary confusion, duplication of effort and delay; that he opposed conscription, fatally undermining manpower planning; and that he not only failed to galvanise the country's production of munitions but also prevented others from doing so. Recent research has generally found him not guilty of these charges.

Kitchener's reliance upon the Regular Army's organisation was not only the instinctive response of a lifelong professional soldier but also the result of calculation. The Territorial Force was intended solely for home defence. Very few of its members had signed the 'Imperial Service' obligation allowing them to be sent abroad. The departure of the British Expeditionary Force (BEF) to France left the country denuded of Regular troops. If Germany succeeded in landing an army on the east coast of England, the so-called 'bolt from the blue' – which many feared – the Territorials would be needed to repulse it. They could not do this and undertake a massive programme of recruitment and training at the same time. Equally, the Territorial Army's expansion would serve no purpose if it could not be used abroad. It seemed sensible to leave the Territorial Army alone and make a fresh start. Kitchener's method of expanding the army was essentially that used in the Second World War, with the vital addition of conscription.

British experience during the First World War demonstrated conclusively that it was impossible to fight a major modern war successfully without compulsory military service. Kitchener was not alone in opposing conscription. Even had he thrown his weight behind the idea in 1914 it is doubtful whether it could have been brought about without a dangerous polarisation of political and public opinion. Kitchener was among the few to realise that the war would be a long one and would require a mass mobilisation of national resources. That was why he wished to expand Britain's small military forces. But he did not enter the war with a coherent manpower plan. His initial call for men was modest – an extra 100,000 – and these he knew he could acquire without recourse to a politically dangerous and unpopular measure such as conscription. The fact that it proved possible to introduce conscription in 1916 owed much to the astonishing response to his call-to-arms, which by taking men for the army indiscriminately, regardless of their value to the industrial war effort, eventually demonstrated to all the necessity and equity of compulsion.

Kitchener's record on munitions is also more impressive than his detractors, especially LLOYD GEORGE, charged. Kitchener's administration was not without faults. His other responsibilities left him with insufficient time to devote to munitions. He was reluctant to delegate. This resulted in a certain amount of caution and delay. New ideas were not taken up as quickly as they might have been. Pressure on manufacturers to complete orders that might have been placed with them was not always maintained. Accusations of apathy or lethargy, however, are unfounded. Kitchener's War Office presided over a nineteen-fold increase in the supply of munitions during the first six months of the war. Orders placed by the Ordnance Department were primarily responsible for supplying the army in the field until well into 1916. Guns and ammunition ordered by the Ministry of Munitions did not become available at all until the end of October 1915 and not in quantity until the following spring. Many of these were substandard.

Kitchener's strategy has also been the subject of reappraisal and rehabilitation. Kitchener was an imperialist. He took a global view of British power and interests. He saw the war as a way of preserving the Empire's long-term security. This was threatened as much by Britain's allies, and by neutrals such as the United States, as by her enemies. It was vital for Britain not only to win the war but also to win the peace. To this end Kitchener favoured a strategy of 'defensive attrition' in which the Russian and French armies would prepare the German army for defeat. It would fall to Kitchener's New Armies, when fully trained and equipped, to strike the *coup de grâce*. This was expected to be in 1917. Meanwhile, it was imperative that Britain do everything she could to keep France and Russia in the war. Unfortunately, it was the French army that became ripe for defeat in 1916. Kitchener's armies were launched against the still-formidable German lines on 1 July 1916, a year before they were ready. By then Kitchener had been dead for a month. Perhaps it was as well.

Kluck, Alexander von (1846–1934) German military commander, whose First Army spearheaded the German invasion of Belgium and France on the extreme right of the German line. Displaying a driving energy that belied his 68 years, Kluck found himself in constant conflict with the equally elderly but far more cautious and pessimistic General BÜLOW, who commanded the German Second Army on his left. MOLTKE's plan to put Bülow in overall control of the movements of the German First, Second and Third Armies had to be abandoned as early as 17 August 1914 because of the constant friction between Bülow and Kluck, who preferred to outflank opposition even at the risk of allowing gaps to appear in the German line. It was, therefore, surprising that Kluck should acquiesce in Bülow's request to alter the axis of his advance to the south-east in order to close a gap that had opened between the two armies after the French attack on Second Army at Guise (29 August). This proved to be a fateful change of direction, opening the right flank of Kluck's army to attack from the garrison of Paris and creating the conditions for the Allied counter-attack on the Marne. The full force of this fell on Kluck's army. As he shifted more and more troops to meet the threat a substantial gap again opened between First and Second Armies. This dismayed Bülow and decided him to begin a precipitate retreat, leaving First Army's left flank in the air. Kluck's forces were threatened with encirclement, from which he extricated them brilliantly. He alone among the commanders of the German right wing in 1914 had the driving power to give the SCHLIEFFEN Plan any chance of success. But he was also undoubtedly rash and too ready to believe that the Franco-British armies had been defeated, badly underestimating their powers of recovery and the threat that they posed to his advance. He suffered a serious shrapnel wound to his leg while visiting the front trenches in March 1915 and was retired from active service in October 1916.

Knox, Alfred William Fortescue (1870–1964) British military attaché to St Petersburg 1914–18 and liaison officer with the Russian army 1914–17. Knox spoke fluent Russian and was given *carte blanche* to visit all parts of the front. After the war he published *With the Russian Army, 1914–1917* (1920), an illuminating account of the Russian army and its commanders.

Kolchak, Aleksandr Vasilevich (1874–1920) Russian naval commander. Kolchak's command of light forces in the Baltic between 1914 and 1916 was characterised by aggression and some success in interdicting the valuable German imports of iron ore from Sweden. In July 1916 he was promoted and given command of the Black Sea fleet, where he established superiority over the Turkish navy through large-scale mining, attacks on coastal shipping and bombardment of port facilities and defences. He remained in command of the Black Sea fleet until his deposition by a sailors' soviet in July 1917. In November 1917 he returned from a period as naval attaché in Washington DC to take command of White

forces in Siberia, where he showed a conspicuous lack of either political or military judgement. He was captured during the Red Army's counter attack in 1920 and executed near Irkutsk.

Körber, Ernst von (1850–1919) Austro-Hungarian politician, who succeeded the assassinated STÜRGKH as Prime Minister in October 1916. His opposition to Hungarian demands for a division of the army into national components brought him into conflict with Emperor KARL I, who succeeded to the throne in November, and he resigned less than a month later.

Korfanty, Wojciech (1873–1939) Polish politician. Polish nationalists were united in their belief that the outbreak of war offered a great opportunity to achieve the dream of independence. They were divided about how to achieve it. Korfanty believed that a German victory offered the best hope. As a leader of the Polish grouping in the German Reichstag, he argued for the independence of Poland and the unification of Polish territory, including that annexed by Prussia. In the event, it was not a German victory but a German defeat that helped bring this about. After the war Korfanty led Polish risings against continued German rule in Silesia.

Kornilov, Lavr Georgevich (1870–1918) Russian military commander. Kornilov began the war as a divisional commander. He was captured in 1915 while directing a rearguard but escaped from an Austrian prisoner of war camp the following year, achieving immediate national celebrity. He was subsequently given command of XXV Corps, whose morale and fighting capacity he did much to restore, before participating with some distinction in the BRUSILOV offensive of June 1916. After the February Revolution Kornilov's popularity recommended him to the Provisional Government. He was appointed commander of the Petrograd Military District with a brief to impose order. This proved impossible in the face of urban unrest and political radicalism and he resigned in April. In July 1917 he was made Commander-in-Chief of the Russian army. The task of reimposing discipline and order in the aftermath of the KERENSKY offensive was probably impossible. Kornilov had the political sensitivity of a drill sergeant. His determination to reintroduce the death penalty exposed his detachment from reality and makes it difficult to understand how he came to be seen by Kerensky as a threat to the Provisional Government. He was not even a Boulanger, much less a Bonaparte. Confusion, rather than conspiracy, led to Kornilov continuing his march on Petrograd in August 1917 against Kerensky's orders. His humiliating defeat by a Bolshevik-led workers' militia did much to restore Bolshevik fortunes after the disaster of the July Days. Kornilov was killed in April 1918 while fighting against the Red Army near the Black Sea. It has been said of him that he had 'the heart of a lion but the brain of a sheep'.

Kövess von Kövessháza, Hermann (1859–1937) Austro-Hungarian military commander, a competent, unspectacular general, the highlight of whose career was the capture of Belgrade on 9 October 1915. His Third Army was then sent to the Italian front, where its involvement in the Trentino offensive was brought to a premature halt by the advance of BRUSILOV in Galicia. Kövess spent the remainder of the war in Galicia and on the Balkan front, where he had no success in stopping the inexorable Allied advance that began in September 1918. On 3 November 1918 he became the final Commander-in-Chief of the Austro-Hungarian army, a military force that by then existed in little more than name only.

Krafft von Dellmensingen, Konrad (1862–1953) The German army's leading mountain warfare expert and commander of the elite *Alpenkorps*. This unit was originally formed for service on the Italian front, but Krafft also led it in Serbia and Romania and on the Western Front. In the autumn of 1917 he was appointed chief of staff to General Otto von BELOW's Fourteenth Army, formed to spearhead the Austro-German attack on the Italian front at Caporetto. The *Alpenkorps* was to distinguish itself in the battle and its former commander's knowledge of the terrain and mountain warfare experience were invaluable in designing the German tactics. These involved the infiltration of infantry and motorised artillery and machine guns down the roads and valleys where they would sever Italian communications. Troops holding the high ground would be outflanked and 'mopped up' later. Below's stunning success led to his being given a key role as commander of the Seventeenth Army in the German spring offensive of March 1918. Krafft was again appointed his chief of staff. Seventeenth Army and Second Army were deployed on the vital right flank of the German attack, where LUDENDORFF planned to break through and roll up the British line. This time, however, Below and Krafft failed to repeat their success at Caporetto. Their blow fell not on the extended and undermanned line of General GOUGH's British Fifth Army but on the unyielding resistance of General BYNG's Third Army in front of Arras. Krafft was later given a corps and spent the remainder of the war on the northern part of the Western Front.

Kramár, Karel (1860–1937) Czech nationalist, whose long and celebrated trial, on a charge of inciting Czech units in the Austro-Hungarian army to desert, predictably sent out a clarion call to Czech separatism. Kramár was released from a fifteen-year prison sentence in July 1917 and continued to agitate for Czech independence. He represented Czechoslovakia at the Paris Peace Conference.

Kressenstein, (Friedrich) Kress von (1870–1948) German military commander. Kressenstein accompanied LIMAN VON SANDERS' military mission to Turkey in January 1914 and spent most of the war in the Ottoman service. After the Ottoman Empire joined the Central Powers in October 1914, Kressenstein was attached as military adviser to DJEMAL PASHA's Fourth Army. He advocated and planned the attack on the Suez Canal in January 1915, the failure of which did grave damage to Djemal's reputation. It was success, however, rather than failure that proved Kressenstein's undoing. His defeat of the British in the confused first and second battles of Gaza (March–April 1917) led to the removal of the British Commander-in-Chief, General MURRAY, and his replacement by General Sir Edmund ALLENBY. Kressenstein was to find Allenby a more formidable adversary. Allenby's preparations for an attack on the Beersheba–Gaza line in October 1917 were made in great secrecy, largely made possible by British air superiority. Kressenstein failed to anticipate Allenby's deployment and was powerless to prevent a breakthrough that led to the capture of Jerusalem in December. By then, however, Kressenstein had been replaced by General Erich von FALKENHAYN. Kressenstein commanded the Turkish Eighth Army until the summer of 1918, when he was transferred to the Caucasus.

Krivoshein, Aleksandr Vasilevich (1858–1921) Russian Minister of Agriculture from 1908 to 1915, the first leading political moderate to be dismissed following his opposition to the Tsar's assumption of direct control of the army in September 1915.

Krobatin, Alexander von (1840–1933) Austro-Hungarian Minister of War from December 1912 until April 1917. After struggling ineffectually for two years to mobilise the economy for war, Krobatin was left politically isolated by the dismis-

sal of the Austrian chief of staff, Field-Marshal CONRAD, of whom he was a leading supporter. In April 1917 he was transferred to a field command. His Tenth Army played its part in the great Austro-German victory over the Italians at Caporetto in November 1917 but was routed a year later at Vittorio Veneto.

Krupp, Gustav (1870–1950) German industrialist. He was born Gustav von Bohlen but changed his name in 1906 after marrying Bertha Krupp. This allowed him to take control of the great Krupp armaments empire. Krupp's splendidly engineered, robust, accurate, powerful and flexible weapons were the foundation of the German army's formidable fighting strength in two world wars. During the Great War Krupp supplied most of the German army's artillery, including the awesome 42-cm howitzer, the famous long-range 'Paris gun' (named 'Big Bertha' after his wife) used for bombarding Paris in 1918 and several other large-calibre railway mounted guns.

Kucharzewski, Jan (1876–1952) Polish historian and politician, who spent the early years of the war campaigning for Polish independence from exile in Switzerland. He was seduced into returning to Poland in 1916 by the Central Powers' establishment of a Polish state, of which he eventually became Prime Minister. His hopes of enlarging the state's limited sovereignty and of establishing a Polish army were, however, to prove delusory. He resigned in March 1918 following the complete disregard for Polish national aspirations shown by the Germans in the punitive Treaty of Brest-Litovsk imposed on a defeated Russia.

Kühl, Hermann Joseph von (1856–1958) German staff officer and military historian. Kühl began the war as chief of staff of KLUCK's First Army, spearhead of the German invasion of France in 1914, and ended it as chief of staff of Crown Prince

RUPPRECHT's Army Group, playing a leading part in the operational planning of the 1918 German spring offensive. He was also a key advocate of the German 'retreat to the Hindenburg line', brilliantly executed in February–March 1917, which shortened the German line on the Western Front, permitting a far more effective German defence and seriously disrupting the French NIVELLE offensive. Despite his wartime eminence, however, Kühl is probably principally important for his postwar writings. These throw interesting and informed light on the 'miracle of the Marne' and on the planning of the spring offensive. His two-volume history of the war, *Der Weltkrieg* (1930), in which he attempted to explain Germany's defeat, advanced an exaggerated opinion of the power of the naval blockade of Germany, providing helpful ammunition to adherents of a British 'blue water' strategy such as LIDDELL HART.

Kühlmann, Richard von (1873–1948) German diplomat. As German Foreign Minister from July 1917 to July 1918, his disbelief in the possibility of total victory persuaded him that Germany's best interests lay in a negotiated settlement made from a position of military strength that was unlikely to be maintained. His position was undermined by the defeat of Russia, which greatly strengthened those in the German military, especially LUDENDORFF, who favoured a military solution and were disinclined to limit German annexationist ambitions in the west or the east. Kühlmann's attempts to give the punitive treaties of Brest-Litovsk and Bucharest a gloss of moderation failed hopelessly, undermining any possibility of achieving a diplomatic end to the war. Ludendorff forced him from office in July 1918, by which time his policies were already bankrupt.

Kun, Béla (1886–1937?) Hungarian revolutionary, who founded the Hungarian Communist Party and established the world's second Communist government. Kun was captured by the Russians in 1916 while serving in the Austro-Hungarian army. He joined the Bolsheviks after the November Revolution and returned to Hungary as a Communist agitator. He was extremely successful. By allying with the Social Democrats he was able to form a coalition government that the well-organised and ruthless Communists began to dominate. He immediately nationalised industry and agriculture, but this proved to be too much too soon and he was forced to resort to a Red Terror to maintain control. This aroused not only fear but also opposition. On 1 August 1919 the regime collapsed in the face of Czech and Romanian invasions and the advance of a French-sponsored counter-revolutionary army ably led by Admiral HORTHY. Kun fled to the Soviet Union, where he eventually became a party *apparatchik*. He is believed to have met a fitting end in one of the Stalinist purges of the late 1930s.

Kuropatkin, Aleksei Nikolaevich (1848–1925) Russian military commander, who was recalled from active service in 1915 at the age of 67 despite his record of defeat in the Russo-Japanese war (1904–05). His performance during the First World War destroyed what vestiges were left of his military reputation. By February 1916 he had risen to command of the Northern Army Group. The appointment was as astonishing as it was disastrous. Timid and pessimistic, Kuropatkin's only talent was that of hanging on to precious resources that abler commanders might have made use of. He failed to support the offensives of either EVERT or BRUSILOV and was finally dismissed in July 1916. Even the Bolsheviks realised that he was too incompetent to cause trouble. They allowed him to survive and to eke out a living as a clerk in his home village during his final years.

L

Lacaze, Marie-Jean-Lucien (1860–1955) French naval officer and politician. In October 1915 Lacaze succeeded Jean AUGAGNEUR as Minister of Marine in the newly formed government of Aristide BRIAND. French naval power was concentrated in the Mediterranean, but this did not give France the dominant role in Allied naval operations that many naval officers and politicians felt was her due. The war was characterised by incessant squabbling between the British, French and Italian navies at many levels. Much of this was petty and personal, but some involved disputes about strategy. And, above all, there was the intractable nature of the anti-submarine war against the German U-boats. The Allied navies were severely handicapped by a lack of escort vessels. Lacaze did something to rectify this by commissioning destroyers from Japan. His ministry did not lack energy, but nothing seemed to have any effect in stemming the loss of shipping to U-boats. The impatience of his political critics, especially the Socialists, began to mount and eventually forced his resignation in August 1917.

Laffargue, André Charles Victor (1891–1994) French soldier and tactical innovator. After an unhappy experience leading an infantry assault on 9 May 1915, Captain Laffargue began to consider better offensive methods. It was clear to him that weight of shell ('artillery conquers, infantry occupies') was not enough. Instead, he formulated tactics based on surprise, depth, firepower and rapid manoeuvre. He believed the keys to success were a surprise artillery bombardment in depth, particularly targeting the enemy's guns, followed by a rapid infantry assault that would by-pass centres of resistance, leaving them to be subdued by the forces following on, and penetrate deep into the enemy's position, disrupting his communications and throwing his commanders 'off balance'. Laffargue's ideas aroused sufficient interest in the French High Command to permit their publication in a pamphlet, *The Attack in Trench Warfare*. This turned out to be unfortunate. In the early summer of 1916 a copy fell into German hands. It was immediately translated and its ideas made a significant contribution to the evolution of the German army's offensive doctrine, on which its spectacular advances in 1918 were based. Laffargue was a prolific author on military subjects after the war.

Laidlaw, Daniel Logan (1875–1950) British soldier, 'the Piper of Loos'. Laidlaw was an ex-Regular who re-enlisted on 1 September 1914. He was posted to the 7th (Service) Battalion King's Own Scottish Borderers, with whom he served as a piper. On 25 September 1915, his battalion, part of the 15th (Scottish) Division, was on a section of the front where the light breeze had failed to blow the British chlorine gas cloud towards the German trenches. This disoriented his comrades, who hesitated to advance. Laidlaw obeyed the injunction of 2nd Lieutenant Martin Young ('For God's sake, Laidlaw, pipe 'em together'), climbed on to the parapet and marched up and down through the gas cloud and under heavy machine-gun fire playing 'Blue Bonnets over the Border' on his pipes. Inspired by his example, the battalion went over the top, followed by the two other attacking battalions of 46th Brigade, overrunning the first two lines of enemy trenches, though at great cost to themselves. Laidlaw also went forward, still piping, despite being hit in the left leg and ankle by shrapnel. He was subsequently awarded the Victoria Cross.

Lake, Percy Henry Noel (1855–1940) British military commander. Lake succeeded Sir John NIXON as Commander-in-Chief, Mesopotamia, in January 1916. His most urgent task was to secure the relief of General TOWNSHEND's army, besieged at Kut following the failure of Nixon's rash attempt to capture Baghdad. Lake had great difficulty in making his numerical superiority combat effective. Three costly attempts to relieve Kut failed and the garrison surrendered on 29 April 1916, the biggest and most humiliating British imperial defeat since Yorktown. Lake was recalled to testify to the Mesopotamia Commission of Inquiry and never held another field command. He ended the war in the Ministry of Munitions.

Lamb, Henry Taylor (1883–1960) British medical officer and painter. Lamb originally trained as a doctor but abandoned his medical studies in 1905 to attend the Chelsea School of Arts. By the outbreak of war he was established as a painter, moving in the same circles as Augustus JOHN and Stanley SPENCER. Lamb's medical skills were at a premium in 1914, and

he thought it his duty to use them. He and Spencer volunteered for the Royal Army Medical Corps (RAMC) and were sent to France. Lamb returned to England in 1915 to complete his medical training. He was given a commission in the RAMC in September 1916 and sent to Salonika. He later served in Palestine with the 5th Battalion Royal Inniskilling Fusiliers. They were commemorated in his painting *Irish Troops in the Judaean Hills* (1919), commissioned for the national Hall of Remembrance, which was never built.

Lambart, Frederick Rudolf, 10th Earl of Cavan (1865–1946) British military commander. 'Fatty' Cavan was arguably the most successful British 'dugout' of the war. Having retired from the army in 1913 at the age of 48 to cultivate his estate at Wheathamstead in Hertfordshire, he was recalled from the Reserve on the outbreak of war and given command of the Territorial 2nd London Infantry Brigade. In September 1914 he replaced Brigadier-General Robert Scott-Kerr (badly wounded at Villers Cotterets) as GOC 4th (Guards) Brigade and never looked back. In June 1915 he was promoted to command the 50th Division and in August 1915 became first permanent commander of the newly created Guards Division. In January 1916 he also became first commander of XIV Corps, which he led (with a short interval) until March 1918, achieving a reputation as the best corps commander on the Western Front. XIV Corps was sent to Italy in November 1917 in the aftermath of the Caporetto disaster. In March 1918 XIV Corps was designated GHQ British Forces in Italy and Cavan made Commander-in-Chief. In the autumn of 1918 he commanded the Italian Tenth Army, which spearheaded the victory of Vittorio Veneto. A clear-sighted rather than far-sighted commander, his military arrangements were characterised by thorough preparation, attention to detail and concern for the welfare of his troops.

Lambert, William Carpenter (1897–1982) US/British fighter ace. Lambert was an American, from Ohio, who joined the Royal Flying Corps in Canada. He recorded eighteen victories over the Western Front in 1918. After the war he wrote two memoirs, *Combat Report* (1973) and *Barnstorming and Girls* (1980).

Lammasch, Heinrich (1853–1920)Austro-Hungarian politician. Although a political conservative and a staunch monarchist, Lammasch was also a pacifist. This unusual combination of views naturally endeared him to the young Emperor KARL I, who succeeded to the throne in December 1916. Lammasch, however, was reluctant to accept office, believing that his room for manoeuvre would be slight. He resisted until 25 October 1918, when he finally accepted the post of Austrian Minister-President. He resigned seventeen days later, correctly recognising that it would take more than the presence in government of a sincere pacifist to appeal to the idealism of the Allies and spare Austria from the consequences of defeat.

Langevin, Paul (1872–1946) French physicist. Langevin was well known before the war for his work on the molecular structure of gases and magnetic theory. He worked with J.J. Thomson and Pierre Curie and became Professor of Physics at the Sorbonne in 1909. During the war he developed sonar detection of submarines.

Langle de Cary, Fernand Louis Armand Marie de (1849–1931) French military commander, who led the spearhead Fourth Army in the opening offensive of the war, suffering a severe defeat. Within days of the outbreak of hostilities, Langle de Cary's army, far from inflicting the anticipated annihilating blow against the SCHLIEFFEN Plan, was back behind the Meuse and itself threatened with annihilation. Like his Commander-in-Chief, General JOFFRE, however, Langle de Cary kept his nerve. In savage fighting against the German Fourth Army of Duke ALBRECHT VON WÜRTTEMBERG, his troops maintained the French right flank, making possible the 'Miracle of the Marne' on the left. In 1915 he commanded the costly and ineffective French Champagne offensive and was promoted to command the Army Group Centre. This was responsible for the defence of Verdun. In March 1916 he was among the most senior military figures to pay the price for the lack of preparedness revealed by the German attack. He was removed from command and retired permanently in 1917.

Lanrezac, Charles Louis Marie (1852–1925) French military commander, a military intellectual and former professor at the French War College, whose command of Fifth Army in August 1914 placed him by chance in the path of the main German thrust and to the right of the British Expeditionary Force (BEF) on the far left of the French armies. Lanrezac harboured grave reservations about the wisdom of French strategy, with its concentration of forces in Lorraine. The realisation that Fifth Army was confronted by thirty German divisions confirmed his judgement but destroyed his nerve. His response was merely to say 'I always knew this was stupid'. His reluctance on 24 August to counter-attack KLUCK's First Army in order to relieve pressure on the British convinced the French Commander-in-Chief that Lanrezac was a defeatist. On 5 September JOFFRE unceremoniously replaced him with the dashing FRANCHET D'ESPEREY. Lanrezac had the dangerous gift of sarcasm, which never commends itself to the Anglo-Saxon temperament, and his relations with the British, especially Field-Marshal FRENCH, were disastrous from the start. The unannounced withdrawal of Fifth Army after the battle of Charleroi left the BEF with both flanks in the air, sowing in French's mind seeds of doubt and suspicion about his ally that were never entirely removed.

Lansbury, George (1859–1940) British socialist and pacifist. Despite an early association with the Social Democratic Federation of H.M. Hyndman (the only county cricketer ever to lead a Marxist party), Lansbury's social and political inspiration was essentially Christian. An ardent campaigner for the poor, who worked tirelessly for reform of the hated Poor Laws, he was elected Labour MP for Bow and Bromley, in London's East End, in 1910. He characteristically lost his seat in a self-inflicted by-election in 1912 fought on the issue of female suffrage, which he supported. He was a founder of the Labour newspaper the *Daily Herald* in 1912, becoming its editor in 1919. Lansbury's pacifism was uncompromising throughout his life. He opposed British entry into the war and was a doughty supporter of conscientious objectors at a time when such views were very unpopular. Lansbury led the Labour Party from 1931 until 1935, maintaining his pacifist position even in the face of the rise of Fascism. A.J.P. Taylor described him as 'the most lovable figure in modern political history'.

Lansing, Robert (1864–1928) US Secretary of State. Lansing's wartime career has been overshadowed by the public diplomacy and international popularity of his President, Woodrow WILSON. Lansing was a distinguished international lawyer, one of the founders of the American Society of International Law, who brought a strong element of legalism to his role as Secretary of State in succession to the isolationist William Jennings BRYAN. He supported the neutralist position taken by Wilson, but his definition of neutrality tended to be as much legal as it was political. He regarded any act as being 'neutral', even arms sales to the Allies, that did not violate his own interpretation of international law. This increasingly favoured the Allies, especially in relation to the war at sea. His strong religious convictions also prejudiced him towards the Allied cause. He came to see a German victory as a threat not only to the United States but also to civilised values. He also slowly, and somewhat reluctantly, accepted that the United States could only exercise a beneficial influence on international affairs, especially on a future peace, if she became a belligerent. Lansing's views, however, were not the only thing that endeared him to WILSON and his confidant Edward M. HOUSE. They also believed that Lansing would be a weak Secretary of State, who would allow them to carry out a personal diplomacy free of State Department inhibition. Although Lansing enjoyed some success during 1915 and 1916 in persuading Wilson to permit measures of practical support for the Allies, especially bank loans, his influence became increasingly marginal after the United States entered the war. His reasonable criticisms of the Fourteen Points and the League of Nations, and his pragmatic approach to negotiations with the Allies, not only undermined his position with the President but also strengthened the President's critics in Congress. He was dismissed in February 1920.

Lauder, Harry (1870–1950) Scottish comedian, one of the greatest figures of British music hall, whose droll songs – such as 'Roamin' in the Gloamin'', 'Stop Your Tickling, Jock' and 'A Wee Jock and Doris' – enjoyed immense success throughout the English-speaking world, making him rich and famous. During the war Lauder worked indefatigably as a recruiter and organiser of entertainment for the troops, spurred on by the death of his son, Captain J.C. Lauder, 1/8th Battalion Argyll and Sutherland Highlanders, on the Somme just after Christmas 1916. Lauder's theme tune, 'Keep Right on to the End of the Road', with which he often ended his act, embodied a strong strain of wartime public sentiment.

Lavery, John (1856–1941) British war artist. Lavery, together with his fellow Irishman William ORPEN, was established as one of Britain's leading portrait painters by the outbreak of war. Like Orpen, he was invited by Charles MASTERMAN, head of the War Propaganda Bureau, to paint portraits of Britain's military leaders in France but was prevented from doing so by a serious car accident that occurred during a German air raid. Instead, he painted pictures of the Home Front.

Law, Andrew Bonar (1858–1923) British politician. Bonar Law was a Canadian-Scots businessman and leader of the Unionist [Conservative] Party. He inherited the party leadership in 1911, following three successive general election defeats, with the mandate to bring greater aggression to the opposition front benches, restless under the languid regime of Arthur BALFOUR. This he certainly did. His determination to reunite the Conservatives, badly split since 1903 over the issue of tariff reform, led him to champion the opposition to Irish Home Rule. His infamous public statement that he could 'imagine no length of resistance to which Ulster can go in which I should not be prepared to support them' seemed an irresponsible incitement to civil war. It provided no clue to the patriotism, statesmanship and cunning that he displayed once war broke out.

Although, as leader of the opposition until May 1915, then as Colonial Secretary in the ASQUITH coalition, then as Chancellor of the Exchequer and Leader of the House of Commons in the LLOYD GEORGE coalition, he held no office central to the prosecution of the war, he was in fact one of its most important figures, without whose support effective government was impossible. Bonar Law recognised that he was the leader of a parliamentary minority. This necessarily limited his political options. It was a situation that could only be changed by a wartime general election. The thought of

this appalled him. It was bound to be divisive. It would distract the war effort, demoralise Britain's allies and delight her enemies. He was not only appalled by the thought of holding a general election, however, but also by the thought of winning it. Victory would leave the Unionists to confront alone in government the potentially explosive issues of conscription, Irish Home Rule and state regulation that were steadily undermining Liberal unity and self-confidence, while the Liberals, freed from the inhibitions of office, would be able to exploit working-class and Irish grievances to their own advantage. Support for the formation of the Asquith coalition delivered him from these dilemmas and placated his right wing, increasingly hostile to what they saw as Asquith's inaction. In government, Bonar Law and the Unionists were able to regain a reputation for patriotism while avoiding direct criticism for the war's intractable nature and ever-increasing human costs. Bonar Law's eventual defection in December 1916 from Asquith, under pressure from his backbenches and the Tory press, was fundamental to the emergence of Lloyd George as Prime Minister. Bonar Law's support was also essential for the survival of the Lloyd George coalition both during and after the war; its removal in 1922 resulted in the coalition's immediate collapse.

That the Conservative Party was able to emerge from the Great War so politically strengthened owed much to Bonar Law's canny leadership. He must take his place, with Stanley Baldwin, as one of the principal founders of inter-war Conservative political domination. The two elder of his four sons were killed on active service in 1917.

Lawford, Sydney Turing Barlow (1865–1953) British military commander, a courageous, well-dressed man, known throughout the army as 'Swanky Syd'. Lawford began the war as GOC 22nd Brigade in 'Tommy' CAPPER's 7th Division and was in the thick of the savage fighting around Ypres in the autumn of 1914, during which he personally led attacks, sometimes on horseback, armed only with a cane. In September 1915 he was promoted Major-General and given command of the 41st Division. He was the only man to command this division and ended the war as the longest-serving divisional commander in the British Expeditionary Force. Lawford had few claims to outstanding talent: he passed out from Sandhurst 41st in the same year that Douglas HAIG passed out top. He brought to the role of divisional commander the instincts of a regimental officer, for whom the welfare of his men was paramount. He also knew how to look after his own welfare. He left the army in 1926 after a scandal involving the wife of a brother officer in India. He later married the lady involved. Their son became the child actor and Hollywood star Peter Lawford, principally remembered as President John F. Kennedy's pimp.

Lawrence, David Herbert (1885–1930) British novelist, poet and critic, who had the misfortune in time of war between Britain and Germany to be married not only to a German baroness but also to a cousin of the fighter ace Manfred von RICHTHOFEN. Unsurprisingly, Lawrence was not among the group of writers invited by Charles MASTERMAN, head of the secret War Propaganda Bureau, to lend their pens to the British cause. Instead, his movements were closely monitored by the police. He and his wife were exiled from their cottage in Cornwall, where suspicious locals believed they had been signalling to German submarines. Nor did the noticeable loosening of sexual restraints brought about by the war diminish official hostility to Lawrence's work. His major novel of the war period, *The Rainbow*, was prosecuted for obscenity in 1915.

Lawrence, Herbert Alexander (1861–1943) British chief of staff on the Western Front 1918. Lawrence's elevation on 24 January 1918 to Chief of the General Staff of the British Expeditionary Force, in succession to Sir Launcelot KIGGELL, represented the remarkable resurgence of a military career that appeared over in 1903. Even more remarkable was the fact that the cause of Lawrence's retirement from the army was his new superior, Douglas HAIG. In 1903 Haig was appointed CO of Lawrence's regiment, the 17th Lancers, over his head. Lawrence resigned in protest and embarked on a City banking career, during which he accumulated a great reputation and a considerable fortune, achievements that he was more than ready to advertise. They also provided him with the security of what in the British army is known as 'fuck off money'. His Great War career was characterised by a resolute independence and a willingness to disagree with orders that he found uncongenial. Trained British staff officers were at a premium in the autumn of 1914 and Lawrence was recalled in September. Clever and self-confident, with an irritatingly superior manner, his success was dramatic. Within less than a year, he rose from retired major to major-general, commanding a brigade and two divisions on Gallipoli, preventing the Mediterranean Expeditionary Force's chaotic logistical arrangements on Mudros from completely disintegrating and playing a significant role in the evacuation of Cape Helles, which he was one of the last to leave. In the summer of 1916 he achieved another conspicuous success by defeating a German-Turkish force at Romani, a victory which returned the Sinai desert to British control. He then resigned for a second time, disbelieving in the wisdom of invading Palestine. He did not receive another field command until February 1917, when he was given a second-line Territorial division, the 66th (2nd East Lancashire). His command of this division was short-lived and unsuccessful, but in 1918 he was chosen as Haig's new CGS, part of a far-reaching reform of GHQ. Lawrence was not Haig's choice; he wanted BUTLER. The two men had a difficult personal history and were never close, but the choice of Lawrence proved inspired. He intruded an urbane and virile personality into the somewhat monkish world of GHQ. Lawrence had an eye for talent and brought his own men on to the staff, something Kiggell never did. These included the brilliant intelligence officer Edgar COX, Ivor MAXSE, and the independent-minded Guy Dawnay and John Dill. John Terraine described Lawrence as Haig's 'right arm'. His cool judgement, analytical mind, courage in adversity and ability to work well with the French lessened the burdens on Haig, who paid tribute in his Final Dispatch of 21 March 1919 to Lawrence's 'unfailing insight, calm resolution and level judgement which neither ill-fortune nor good were able to disturb'. Lawrence returned to the City after the war, helping to rejuvenate the armaments and shipbuilding firm Vickers. Both his sons were killed on the Western Front.

Lawrence, T[homas] E[dward] (1888–1935) British soldier. T.E. Lawrence was one of the most famous individuals to emerge from the Great War, celebrated throughout the world as 'Lawrence of Arabia'. Lawrence's connection with the Middle East began before the war, when he took part in archaeological expeditions in Syria, where he learned to speak Arabic. Handicapped by his small stature, he was not commissioned in the British army until 1915, when he joined Military Intelligence in Cairo. In October 1916 Lawrence was sent on a mission to the leaders of the Arab Revolt (proclaimed in June). He identified the Emir FAISAL IBN HUSSEIN as the most effective leader and was sent to work with him as British liaison officer. Lawrence's subsequent career in the Arab Revolt has become the

stuff of legend, where history and myth are difficult to disentangle. Traditional (western) interpretations and Lawrence's own account give the leading part to him, but this has since been disputed by Arab scholars. There can be little doubt, however, that Arab forces, especially in 1918, made a valuable contribution to the British war effort in Palestine, tying down Ottoman troops, interdicting their supply lines on the Damascus–Medina railway and capturing the port of Aqaba. Lawrence became painfully aware that his post-war hopes for an independent Arabia, within the British Empire, were unlikely to be fulfilled in the face of British and French imperial interests. The Paris Peace Conference, at which he acted as adviser to Faisal, confirmed his fears. From 1921 to 1922, however, Lawrence's role as adviser on Arab affairs to the Colonial Secretary, Winston CHURCHILL, was significant in ensuring a large degree of self-government for the British mandated territories of Iraq and Jordan. The fame that Lawrence had consciously cultivated as a political weapon during the war, together with his ambivalent response to sexual abuse while in Turkish captivity, came to haunt him after it. He resigned from the Colonial Office in 1922, enlisting under assumed names first in the Royal Air Force and then in the army. This, of course, merely added to his legend. He wrote two accounts of his part in the desert war, *Revolt in the Desert* (1927) and the posthumously published (unreadable) 'literary masterpiece' *The Seven Pillars of Wisdom* (1935).

Ledward, Gilbert (1888–1960) British soldier and sculptor, who served as a subaltern in the Royal Artillery on the Western Front, later playing a leading part in the war's commemoration, including the memorial on Horse Guards Parade in London.

Ledwidge, Francis Edward (1887–1917) Irish nationalist, whose pre-war poetry had celebrated Irish pastoral life and the faeries, killed by a shell on the first day of the Third Battle of Ypres ('Passchendaele') while serving as a lance-corporal with the 1st Battalion Royal Inniskilling Fusiliers. Ledwidge was among the well-known Irish nationalists who joined the British army on the outbreak of war, serving on Gallipoli and at Salonika before being sent to the Western Front. His world was shattered not so much by the war, which figured little in his poetry, but by the Easter Rising of April 1916. He died fully aware that the Rising and the fate of the Sinn Feiners had rendered the war futile from an Irish nationalist perspective and that the sacrifices made for the cause by men like himself would be forgotten and demeaned.

Leefe-Robinson, William (1895–1918) British fighter pilot, who shot down a German Schutte Lanz airship over Cuffley, in Hertfordshire, on the night of 2/3 September 1916. This was the first airship to be shot down over Britain. Its destruction was greeted with wild scenes of jubilation and relief. Crowds of decent middle-class English people cheered as the airship's crew burned to death. Leefe-Robinson became a national hero and was awarded the Victoria Cross. He was later shot down himself while commanding one of the first squadrons of Bristol fighters and captured. Weakened by the privations of his imprisonment, he died on 31 December 1918 in the Spanish influenza pandemic.

Leete, Alfred (1882–1933) British illustrator and cartoonist, whose poster of a youthful Lord KITCHENER sternly pointing at the viewer under the injunction 'Britons. Your country needs you' became a twentieth century icon. Its actual effect on recruiting was, however, largely mythical. Leete's design first appeared on the cover of the magazine *London Opinion* on 5 September 1914. It became instantly popular and the magazine was inundated with requests for reproductions. Among these was one from the Parliamentary Recruiting Committee, which began to issue the design (amended at Kitchener's insistence to include the words 'God Save the King') as a poster only at the end of September. The peak of voluntary recruitment came in the middle of September as news of the British Expeditionary Force's retreat from Mons began to appear in the press. It owed nothing to Leete's poster, the appearance of which failed to arrest the decline in recruitment.

Leman, Gérard (1851–1920) Belgian military commander, who defended the fortress of Liège from the Germans in August 1914. Liège and its ring of satellite forts occupied a key strategic position across the axis of the German advance between the Ardennes and the Maastricht appendix. Well aware of this, the Germans put in place special measures to deal with these forts, including the creation of a special task force with an imposing arsenal of super-heavy artillery, including the awesome KRUPP 42-cm howitzer. The obsolete Belgian forts were no match for the German guns, but they managed to slow down the German advance sufficiently to establish a legend of Belgian heroism that had important political implications inside and outside Belgium. Leman was captured, wounded and unconscious, and spent the war in German captivity. He returned to Belgium after the Armistice to find himself a national hero.

Lenin, Vladimir Ilich (1870–1924) Russian revolutionary. Lenin's early training was in the law, at which he briefly practised, but for most of his adult life he was a professional revolutionary, dedicated to the overthrow not only of Tsardom but also of capitalism. Despite his contempt for the intelligentsia and his belief in the importance of will in human affairs, Lenin's principal contribution to the socialist cause before the First World

War was as a theorist, developing the ideas that eventually became known as Leninism or Marxism-Leninism, including a distinctive concept of the role of the Communist Party. Following the split in the Russian Social Democratic Labour Party in 1903, Lenin became the leading Bolshevik. At the time, and for many years afterwards, this amounted to very little. Lenin spent the first years of the war in exile. His views on the war were clear. He wished for a Russian defeat ('revolutionary defeatism'), out of which there would occur a revolutionary opportunity. With German help he returned to Russia from Switzerland in 1917 in the aftermath of the February Revolution. In his April Theses he demanded that Russia move to the second – socialist – stage of the revolution. His opposition to the Provisional Government and to the continued prosecution of the war was implacable. Even so, his success was limited and in July he had to make an undignified retreat to Finland. But the failure of the KERENSKY offensive of July 1917 finally shattered the Russian army, whose soldiers – in Lenin's words – 'voted with their feet', returning home to accelerate the pace of political disintegration and social turmoil. This soon gave the Bolsheviks their opportunity and in October they overthrew the Provisional Government. No one understood better than Lenin that what had been achieved was merely a coup d'état and that the revolution was still to be made. He was anxious to proceed as soon as possible and was desperate for peace at any price, a policy that brought him into conflict with TROTSKY. When peace with the Central Powers was finally achieved, at Brest-Litovsk in March 1918, the price was severe. It also left a civil war still to be won, the winning of which Lenin prosecuted with single-minded savagery.

Leopold, Prince of Bavaria (1846–1930) German military commander. No one could accuse the German army of ageism.

Leopold was one of several elderly commanders to be recalled from retirement in the first few months of the war, in his case at the age of 69 to command the Ninth Army on the Eastern Front. Age proved no bar to success, however. He played a leading part in the shattering German offensive of 1915, during which his army captured Warsaw on 4 August. His reward was to be given command of all Austro-German forces in the central sector of the Eastern Front (Army Group Leopold). The German Commander-in-Chief, Erich von FALKENHAYN, remained dubious about the prospect of winning victories of total annihilation in the east and was maturing his own very different plans for winning the war in the west. He had no wish to see these compromised by the ambition of HINDENBURG and LUDENDORFF, and Leopold's elevation was a conscious attempt to limit the duo's influence. After Hindenburg and Ludendorff themselves assumed the Supreme Command, at the end of August 1916, Leopold succeeded them in the east, where his generalship has been overshadowed by the reputation of his able and self-advertising chief of staff, Max HOFFMANN. Leopold retired again in March 1918 after the Treaty of Brest-Litovsk terminated the war on the Eastern Front. He was 72.

Lettow-Vorbeck, Paul Emil von (1870–1964) Commander of German military forces in East Africa. Although he never had more than 3,000 German and 11,000 African troops (Askaris) under his command, he tied down Allied armies almost ten times as large. He realised that his small force could be most effective by seizing and retaining the initiative. His army fought on its own terms, lived off the land, improvised weapons and equipment, and traded space for time in the vast expanses of British East Africa, Portuguese Mozambique and Rhodesia. The devotion of Lettow-Vorbeck's African troops is extraordinary given the brutal nature of the pre-war 'pacification' of German East and South West Africa. His forces remained undefeated in the field at the time of the Armistice and surrendered on 25 November 1918 only when news of this reached him. He was welcomed as a national hero ('the African HINDENBURG') on his return to Germany. He immediately joined the *Freikorps* and led them in crushing the Hamburg Spartacists. He was forced to resign from the army after his involvement in the KAPP putsch but later opposed Hitler.

Levetzow, Magnus von (1871–1939) German naval staff officer. Levetzow commanded the battle cruiser *Moltke* for the first two years of the war, taking part in the raids on Yarmouth and Hartlepool and the battle of the Dogger Bank (January 1915). In 1916 he became chief of the German navy's operations division, under SCHEER's chief of staff Admiral TROTHA, and took part in the battle of Jutland (31 May–1 June 1916). In August 1918 Levetzow became chief of staff of the new unified Naval Supreme Command that Scheer had worked long and hard to bring about. He planned the final 'suicide' mission of the German High Seas Fleet that provoked the Kiel mutiny and brought Imperial Germany to final ruin. He later became a Nazi.

Lewis, Cecil Arthur (1898–1997) British fighter pilot. Lewis's service in the Royal Flying Corps, which he joined in 1915, was the prelude to a long and extraordinary life as a commercial aviator, playwright, translator, broadcaster, sheep farmer, international civil servant and journalist. His *Sagittarius Rising*, first published in 1936 and many times reprinted, is perhaps the finest memoir of the air war. Lewis also served in the Royal Air Force during the Second World War.

Lewis, Donald Swain (1886–1916) British air war pioneer. Together with B.T. 'Bron' JAMES, he pioneered the use of wireless in

aircraft and developed the 'clock code' and squared maps that greatly improved the effectiveness of air/artillery co-operation. He was shot down and killed on 10 April 1916, while CO Second Wing, by the battery with whose guns he had been co-operating. As a result of his death, TRENCHARD ordered that squadron commanders and above should not fly on operations, a regulation that was not always obeyed.

Lewis, Isaac Newton (1858–1931) US soldier and inventor. In 1910 Colonel Lewis perfected the light machine gun originally designed by Samuel MacLean. Unable to interest the United States army in the weapon, he set up his own manufacturing company in Belgium in 1913. Many of the company's staff fled to Britain after the German invasion in August 1914. Production of the 'Lewis gun', a gas-operated, air-cooled, shoulder-fired weapon firing a .303″ bullet (the same as the standard British Lee-Enfield rifle) from a 47-round revolving drum, continued at the Birmingham Small Arms (BSA) factory. It was introduced into the British Army in 1915, helping to transform the firepower of infantry units. Lewis guns were at the heart of the more flexible, platoon-based tactics adopted in 1917. Some 32,168 were in service with the British Expeditionary Force in France at the end of the war. The Lewis gun was also widely used to arm aircraft.

Lewis, (Percy) Wyndham (1884–1957) Canadian-born British painter, writer, critic and soldier. Lewis founded the British art movement known as Vorticism and edited its short-lived but controversial and polemic magazine *Blast*. Vorticism was a response to Cubism and, more particularly perhaps, Futurism. It was severely critical of the 'sentimentality' of nineteenth-century art, especially Impressionism, embracing the violence, speed and energy of machinery. This found artistic expression in abstraction and angularity.

Lewis served on the Western Front from 1916 to 1918 in the Royal Artillery. This experience produced his most famous wartime painting, *A Battery Shelled* (1919), and a memoir, *Blasting and Bombardiering* (1937). Lewis's political views moved far to the right in the 1920s and he was sympathetic to developments in Italy and Germany. He turned increasingly to writing, both novels and criticism, in which he expressed a radical contempt for contemporary society.

Lichnowsky, Karl Max, Fürst (1860–1928) German diplomat, Ambassador to Great Britain 1912–14. Something of an Anglophile who feared the consequences of a deterioration in Anglo-German relations, Lichnowsky was naively and cynically brought out of retirement by the Kaiser to charm the British government into neutrality in the event of a European war. Lichnowsky had a more realistic view of his influence. He repeatedly warned the German government of Britain's determination to uphold the balance of power in Europe and, during the July Crisis of 1914, of the certain British response to violation of Belgian neutrality. He was vilified for being correct when he returned to Germany.

Liddell Hart, Basil Henry (1895–1970) British military historian. Liddell Hart served briefly in the Great War as a captain in the King's Own Yorkshire Light Infantry on the Western Front, from which he was invalided out after being gassed on the Somme. His removal from the fighting at a relatively early stage meant that he had no personal experience of the British 'all-arms, deep battle' that emerged in 1918. He spent the rest of the war at home in training units and in 1920 wrote the army's official manual on *Infantry Training*. After leaving the army through ill health in 1924, Liddell Hart became military correspondent of the *Daily Telegraph* and (from 1935) of *The Times*. He wrote extensively on strategy and tactics, establishing himself in the front rank of military historians. Although he was originally supportive of the British prosecution of the Great War and of Field-Marshal HAIG, he became more and more critical, influenced to a great extent by the work of J.F.C. FULLER. By the mid-1930s he was recognised as the most formidable critic of British generalship during the war. His book *A History of the First World War, 1914–1918*, published by Faber in 1934, is one of the most influential ever written on the conflict. He criticised the Western Front strategy, advocating the 'indirect approach', while on the battlefield he propagandised the superiority of German 'infiltration' tactics and lamented the British failure to make effective use of tanks. Liddell Hart's view of war was, however, in many ways extremely traditional. He envisaged war essentially as an intellectual activity, a sort of chess, played best by 'Great Captains', arguing that 'battles are won and lost in generals' minds'. His work shows little appreciation of logistics or of the remorseless materialism of modern war, whose appalling losses he attributed to bad play by commanders rather than to the fatal combination of industrial technology and nationalism. During the 1930s he constantly advocated a British defensive strategy, based on strong air defences, and was opposed to a repetition of the 'continental commitment' of the Great War. During the Second World War his reputation plummeted and he was stigmatised as an 'appeaser'. After the war, however, he reinvented himself as a 'lone voice in the wilderness' uttering prescient warnings against the threat of German militarism and as the prophet of *blitzkrieg*. He was an inveterate networker who succeeded in establishing a collection of books and papers that will never be rivalled. These now form the core of the Liddell Hart Centre for Military Archives at King's College, London, a major research tool for students of the First and Second World Wars.

Liebknecht, Karl (1871–1919) German socialist and revolutionary, who co-founded the Spartacus League. Liebknecht was a Social Democratic Party member of the Reichstag until April 1916, when he was expelled for voting against war credits (the first member of the Reichstag to do so) and soon afterwards sentenced to four and a half years in prison for sedition. He was amnestied along with other political prisoners in October 1918. At the end of December 1918 the Spartacists broke with the Social Democrats and formed the German Communist Party. The paramilitary *Freikorps* crushed a revolutionary uprising launched in Berlin on 6 January 1919 within a week. Liebknecht was murdered by his captors on 15 January.

Liggett, Hunter (1857–1935) US military commander. Liggett was appointed GOC US 41st Division on the outbreak of war and took it to France in October 1917. He was fat, arthritic and – at 60 – very elderly by the standards of Allied divisional commanders. It is hardly surprising that there were many who doubted his fitness for a field command. It is more surprising that their number did not include the American Commander-in-Chief. General PERSHING, never a sentimentalist, not only retained Liggett in France but also promoted him to command a corps. Liggett's I Corps played a leading part in the American victory at St Mihiel in September 1918 and later in the Meuse-Argonne battle. In October 1918 he was promoted again, to command US First Army, which he reorganised and refitted before resuming the offensive on 1 November. Liggett was a commander of great tactical acumen and moral courage. He immediately recognised the need for thorough preparation and the efficacy of the 'set-piece battle' on the Western Front and resisted pressure from his formidable superior to attack before he was ready or to pursue grandiose objectives that were tactically impossible to achieve.

Liman von Sanders, Otto (1855–1929) German/Ottoman Empire military commander. Liman succeeded Colmar von der GOLTZ as head of the German Military Mission to the Ottoman Empire in 1913. This was hardly a tribute to his talents. Liman was one of the most unpopular men in the German army and (at 58) one of its most elderly divisional commanders. Some, including the acerbic Hans von SEECKT, thought he was unworthy of promotion to command a German corps. Nevertheless, the appointment of this unremarkable German officer was enough to antagonise Russian diplomatic sensibilities and to heighten international tensions. Liman was extremely uncomfortable with his diplomatic role, and his all too visible commitment to German interests weakened his influence in Ottoman affairs. His inability to effect an immediate Ottoman declaration of war against the Entente in August 1914 dismayed him and he asked – unsuccessfully – to be recalled. He did make some headway, however, in restoring the Ottoman army, badly damaged during the Balkan War of 1913, to a reasonable level of fighting efficiency. Liman's reputation ultimately rests on his command of the Ottoman Fifth Army on the Gallipoli peninsula in 1915. His command was undoubtedly flawed, but he redeemed his strategic weaknesses with a display of ruthlessness, particularly with regard to subordinate commanders, that contrasted starkly with his British adversary, Sir Ian HAMILTON. Liman's part in defeating the British landing, however, did nothing to increase his influence in Ottoman politics. His elevation to the command of Ottoman forces in the Middle East in February 1918 brought him into opposition with a powerful British army under the command of General Sir Edmund ALLENBY. Outnumbered, outgunned and lacking air cover, Liman's forces were shattered in Allenby's September 1918 offensive (the battle of Megiddo), Liman himself almost suffering the indignity of being captured in bed at Nazareth. After the war Liman was briefly detained by the British as a suspected war criminal for his alleged part in the Ottoman massacre of the Armenians. That he had tried and failed to stop the deportation of Armenians to Smyrna is a fitting commentary on his real influence in Ottoman affairs.

Lindsay, George Mackintosh (1880–1956) British soldier and machine-gun pioneer. Lindsay was one of the principal pre-war advocates of the machine gun, whose advantages he had come to appreciate while considering the problems of firepower during his tour as musketry instructor at Hythe (1913–15). He was later a staff officer and then Chief Instructor at the Machine Gun Training School at Grantham. A former army and navy middleweight boxing champion, 'Boss' Lindsay was a formidable personality, the sort of teacher who turned out disciples. He was an able publicist and was not above exaggerating German superiority in machine guns in order to galvanise official opinion, a tactic which left a virtually permanent mark on British perceptions of the war. He was an early advocate of an independent Machine Gun Corps (which was established in October 1915) and campaigned relentlessly for the centralised control of machine guns at the tactical level (achieved on the eve of the German spring offensive of 1918). His ideas on the use of machine guns in the offensive, including the infiltration of machine-gun teams and the machine-gun barrage, and on the motorisation of machine guns were innovative though not unique. Quite often, however, his ideas outstripped the actual supply of weapons, which caused frustration and encouraged a tendency, long present, to overestimate the power of his favoured instrument and to denigrate the importance of infantry. Towards the end of the war, in August 1918, he persuaded the GOC First Army, General HORNE, a keen supporter of 'mechanical power', to give him command of a machine-gun brigade, one of only two in the British army, though neither was ever used in the breakthrough battle for which they were designed. After the war Lindsay rose to major-general and ended his career in the Royal Tank Corps.

Linke-Crawford, Frank (1893–1918) Austro-Hungarian fighter pilot, the fourth highest scoring ace in the Austrian air service with twenty-seven victories. He was shot down and killed by two Italian aircraft on 30 July 1918.

Linsingen, Alexander von (1850–1935) German military commander, a protégé of Erich von FALKENHAYN, and – like his mentor – an extremely competent field commander. Linsingen spent most of the war on the Eastern Front. After impressing in command of a mixed force of Austrian and German troops in the Carpathians, he replaced MACKENSEN as commander of the Bug offensive in July 1915. Further success saw him elevated to command of Army Group Linsingen, occupying a key position in southern Poland. His Group was violently assaulted and severely damaged in the BRUSILOV offensive (June 1916), but he retained his composure and did much to retrieve the situation. After the Treaty of Brest-Litovsk (March 1918) terminated the war on the Eastern Front, Linsingen returned to Germany, where he found himself in command of the Berlin region, into which he failed to stem the flow of revolutionary elements in November 1918, resigning in disgust two days before the Armistice.

Lippmann, Walter (1889–1974) US journalist. Lippmann's support for President WILSON's re-election in 1916 through the pages of the *New Republic*, which he edited, brought him close to Wilson's confidant Colonel Edward M. HOUSE. Although Lippmann made a significant contribution to the framing of Wilson's Fourteen Points and seemed to share their sweeping ambition, he later expressed grave reservations about the conduct of the peace negotiations and was appalled by the apparent severity of the Versailles settlement towards Germany. As editor of the *New Republic* again after the war, he led opposition to the Treaty of Versailles and to the League of Nations.

Lipsett, Louis James (1874–1918) British military commander. When the war broke out, Lipsett was on attachment to the Canadian military forces, in which capacity he had been instructor to the future commander of the Canadian Corps, Lieutenant-General Sir Arthur CURRIE. Lipsett remained with the Canadians for much of the war, first as CO 8th Canadian Battalion, then as GOC 2nd Canadian Brigade (in succession to Currie) and, finally, as GOC 3rd Canadian Division (June 1916–September 1918). Lipsett was a front-line general, renowned for his unflappability. While in front-line trenches he used to hand out signed photographs of himself to ordinary soldiers, an unusually imaginative piece of public relations for a British Regular officer. Lipsett was hit in the face and killed by a German machine-gun bullet on 14 October 1918, while reconnoitring the front line as GOC British 4th Division. He was the fifty-ninth, and last, British general to be killed on the Western Front.

Little, Robert Alexander (1895–1918) Australian fighter ace, who sailed to England in July 1915 and qualified as a pilot at his own expense. He secured a commission in the Royal Naval Air Service (RNAS) and in October 1916 was sent to the Western Front with 8 Squadron RNAS, flying Sopwith Pups. He is perhaps best remembered for being shot down by Richthofen's flying circus, whose planes then strafed him. He was rather upset by this and returned fire with his revolver before amazed British troops persuaded him to join them in their trench. But this should not detract from his forty-seven victories, which make him

the top-scoring Australian pilot of the war and rank him fourteenth overall. He was killed in action on 27 May 1918 while serving with 203 Squadron Royal Air Force. His exploits are almost totally unknown in his native country.

Livens, William Howard (1889–1964) British soldier. Livens was a civil engineer who worked with his father, a senior figure in the important Lincoln engineering firm Ruston & Proctor that was later to play an important role in the development of the tank. Livens volunteered for military service in the autumn of 1914 and was still training at Chatham when news of the German gas attack at Ypres on 22 April 1915 inspired him to begin experiments to find an effective method of retaliation. In August 1915 he joined the Royal Engineers' Special [Gas] Companies, one of the few members of that remarkable outfit who was not a chemist by training. In 1916 he was given command of what was later designated Z Company, where he was instrumental in developing the first British flame-throwers, a development that was subsequently abandoned after only ten firings. Livens, however, was undismayed. He returned the attention of Z Company, packed with enterprising and ingenious men like himself, to the problem that had earlier concerned him of developing an effective gas weapon. The weapon designed by Z Company was a simple (if inaccurate) weapon, resembling a large mortar, that became known as the Livens projector. It first saw action, under the patronage of General GOUGH, in support of 48th Division's attack at Pozières beginning on 23 July 1916. From a tactical perspective and – not least – from the perspective of the troops handling it, the release of gas from projectors had many advantages over cylinder release, which made difficult demands on transport and was vulnerable to wind conditions. The Livens projector became an integral part of the British arsenal in 1917 and 1918.

Lloyd George, David (1863–1945) British politician. As Chancellor of the Exchequer (1908–15), Minister of Munitions (1915–16), Secretary of State for War (July–December 1916) and Prime Minister (1916–22), Lloyd George was the only minister to serve in government without a break throughout the war, in the prosecution of which he was a central figure. Some historians, notably A.J.P. Taylor, have touted him as the 'man who won the war'. Others, notably ASQUITH's biographer Roy Jenkins, have attributed the destruction of British Liberalism to Lloyd George's careless and self-interested ambition.

There can be little doubt that Lloyd George's establishment of the Ministry of Munitions galvanised British war production and began the mobilisation of the economy for 'total war'. Although Lloyd George always showed a healthy respect for the power of organised labour and organised capital, he was willing to push state control of industry as far as it would go. That was much further than anyone would have believed possible before the war. Even so, the frequently heard claims of Lloyd George and his acolytes for the *immediate* impact of the ministry on British output of munitions are misleading and the condemnation of his 'supine' military predecessors, especially General von DONOP, unfair. The real impact of the ministry's efforts was not felt until 1917 and, especially, 1918 when the British army was able to prosecute a 'rich man's war', possibly for the only time in its history.

Lloyd George's advocacy of a Ministry of Munitions and his own accession to it are sometimes seen as the first step in a plan to replace Asquith as Prime Minister. This may be doubted. Lloyd George's becoming Minister of Munitions may have revealed his ambition but it was also an act of political courage, a motif throughout his political career. Success in

the post, the powers of which had to be defined and to which much opposition could be expected, was far from guaranteed and Lloyd George's success in it was just as likely to strengthen Asquith as to weaken him. Lloyd George's eventual accession to the prime ministership in December 1916 was primarily the result of 'insider' dissatisfaction with the lack of ruthlessness and purpose in Asquith's prosecution of the war. Lloyd George's willingness as Minister of Munitions to slaughter any number of domestic sacred cows in pursuit of victory undoubtedly endeared him – if only temporarily – even to his most vehement political enemies, who retained painful memories of his pre-war attacks on 'privilege'. But Lloyd George himself did little to prepare the parliamentary ground for his accession to power, in which the entirely independent actions of the Liberal MP Christopher ADDISON were crucial.

Lloyd George's entry to 10 Downing Street reflected the determination of the political elite to 'win the war'. Lloyd George's first speech as Prime Minister, with its reference to 'knock out blows' and a 'fight to the finish', was eloquent of this ambition. He immediately set about transforming British central government, including the much-demanded establishment of a small War Cabinet with full executive authority. He established new ministries of labour, shipping, food and national service and, with a view to the future, of reconstruction. He intruded businessmen, with 'push and go', to the centre of British government. Though the changes were in many ways cosmetic, representing less of a break with the Asquithian past than has often been contended, they sent a signal to the British public and to Britain's allies and enemies of the national will to win. Lloyd George successfully embodied this throughout his wartime prime ministership. This was never more true than at the height of the German spring offensive of 1918. Despite being handicapped by one of his periodically enervating throat infections, Lloyd George refused even to acknowledge the possibility of defeat, a stance that was instrumental in maintaining the Anglo-French alliance and in coordinating an effective response to the success of German arms, including the appointment of FOCH as de facto Allied Commander-in-Chief. Maurice HANKEY, Secretary to the War Cabinet, later declared that no one who had not witnessed Lloyd George's courage in the spring of 1918 had a right to criticise him.

There is, however, a certain irony in the choice of Lloyd George as the embodiment of victory at all costs. His determination that Britain should prosecute the war to the fullest extent of its considerable power had often brought him into conflict with soldiers, for whose apparent lack of imagination and fatalism he developed a considerable contempt. His elevation to the War Office, in succession to KITCHENER, and the British Expeditionary Force's costly failure to win an authentic victory on the Somme confirmed his view. He was appalled at the human costs of what Field-Marshal HAIG later called 'ceaseless attrition'. Throughout the war he advocated alternatives to what he later referred to as the policy of 'Western holocausts', believing there must be a better strategy than that offered by the 'Westerners'. He failed, however, to convince his closest War Cabinet colleagues or his senior military advisers (especially the Chief of the Imperial General Staff, Sir William ROBERTSON) or his allies that it was sensible to divert military resources away from the Western Front to 'sideshow' campaigns on Gallipoli or in Salonika, Palestine and Italy. His impact on British strategy was therefore nil. In the end the war was won on the Western Front by a general for whom Lloyd George had the profoundest contempt. His attempt to subordinate the British Expeditionary Force to French command, made at the notorious Calais Conference in February 1917, destroyed Haig and Robertson's trust in him. It took months

for Lloyd George to escape from what Professor David Woodward called the 'yoke of Calais'. In his *War Memoirs*, written at the height of appeasement, Lloyd George used his apparent political weakness in 1917 to distance himself from the military conduct of the war, especially 'Passchendaele'. He established an influential and corrosive legend that the military had escaped from political control, exploiting the Prime Minister's political isolation in a government and press dominated by Tories, to fight a stupid and futile campaign that he had 'always opposed'. In fact, the War Cabinet sanctioned all British military operations in 1917, recognising that standing on the defensive in the west, to wait (as PÉTAIN said) for 'the Americans and the tanks', was not an option.

Lloyd George's continuance of his coalition government into the peace undoubtedly exacerbated wartime political divisions, felt most acutely by the Liberal Party, which suffered a humiliating defeat at the general election of December 1918. The coalition's overwhelming victory owed much to its unrestrained support for popular demands to take revenge on Germany. This conflicted somewhat with Lloyd George's enunciation in January 1917 of British war aims, deliberately intended to associate Britain with the idealism of the Fourteen Points, announced by President WILSON a few days later. In the event, Lloyd George's role at the Paris Peace Conference was to pursue a pragmatic and realistic line between American idealism and French determination permanently to weaken Germany. At home he showed similar realism in bringing to an end the Anglo-Irish war, signing the peace treaty that established the Irish Free State before falling victim to the political frustrations of the Unionist backbenchers in 1922. He never held public office again.

Lodge, Henry Cabot (1850–1924) US politician. Lodge was a member of an old-established family of 'Boston Brahmins' not famous for their humility. As Senator for Massachusetts, he led the majority conservative wing of the Republican Party, which he mobilised to oppose the pre-war social reforms associated with 'Progressivism'. The election of the arch-Progressive Woodrow WILSON to the Presidency in 1912 accordingly dismayed him. His opposition to Wilson was certainly ideological: Lodge regarded him as one of the most dangerous men ever to occupy the White House. But it was also personal. His dislike of Wilson was almost pathological and was to render him Wilson's most determined opponent. The hatred was certainly reciprocated by Wilson. It clouded the judgement of both men, with important and possibly tragic consequences. Lodge's conservatism, however, did not extend to the international sphere. He was no isolationist. On the contrary, he favoured American economic expansion and believed that the United States should play a leading part in shaping the world. After the outbreak of war in Europe, he was among the leading advocates of US military 'preparedness'. US entry into the war in April 1917 provided Lodge not only with an opportunity to weaken the Progressive faction in the Republican Party but also to destroy Wilson. His hand was greatly strengthened by the return of a Republican Congress in the mid-term elections of November 1918, after which Lodge became Senate Majority Leader and Chairman of the Senate Committee on Foreign Relations, from which he led the successful campaign against ratification of the Treaty of Versailles. This led, ironically, to an intensification of the isolationist impulse, to which Lodge was opposed, fundamentally weakening US influence on international relations and contributing to the international power vacuum in which the European fascist dictators came to thrive.

Lody, Carl (18??–1914) German spy. Lody's espionage activities predated the out-break of war. His success in observing British naval establishments in the guise of a travel guide persuaded the German spymaster Karl BOY-ED to choose Lody as his agent in Britain once hostilities began. After travelling around Britain and Ireland with a forged US passport, Lody was arrested in Killarney in possession of incriminating documents. He was tried, found guilty, sentenced to death and executed in the Tower of London on 6 November 1914, the first person to be executed in the Tower of London for 150 years. His fate was typical of that of Germany's spies, whose amateurism and incompetence in both world wars were extraordinary.

Lossberg, Friedrich ('Fritz') Karl von (1868–1934) German staff officer, whose reputation as a defensive tactician earned him the nickname of 'the fireman of the Western Front'. Lossberg was a thoughtful officer in the Prussian staff tradition who had been principal of the *Kriegsacademie* from 1911 to 1913. As FALKEN-HAYN's chief of operations in 1915, he directed the German defence in the Champagne despite his relatively lowly rank of colonel. It was here that he developed the theories of 'elastic defence in depth' for which he is now remembered. These were designed to counter increasing Allied material superiority by reducing the number of men in the front line and placing the bulk of the German infantry out of range of Allied artillery. The German infantry would not fight to hold the front line, but the 'main line of resistance' sited to the rear, usually on a reverse slope, from which specially trained 'counter-attack' divisions would repel an enemy advance from under the covering fire of German artillery. This method was completely at odds with Falkenhayn's orders on the Somme and, although he summoned Lossberg to the front within hours of the Anglo-French attack on 1 July, his refusal to adopt Lossberg's tactics cost him his command. Falkenhayn's successors, HIN-

DENBURG and LUDENDORFF, proved more sympathetic and readily adopted 'defence in depth'. This became the official doctrine of the German army in December 1916. It was used against the British at Ypres in the autumn of 1917 in less favourable terrain than in the Champagne or on the Somme and at increasing cost against the British Second Army, under General PLUMER. Lossberg also organised the 'retreat to the Hindenburg Line', one of the most impressive German operational achievements of the war, which shortened their line in the west and did much to allow them to maintain a two-front war throughout 1917.

Louis Alexander, Prince of Battenberg (1854–1921) British naval commander. In 1912 Prince Louis became First Sea Lord, professional head of the Royal Navy. One experienced observer thought him 'the ablest officer the Navy possesses'. Admiral FISHER was also an admirer. Together with CHURCHILL as First Lord of the Admiralty, Battenberg made an excellent peacetime First Sea Lord. The war soon undid him, however. A war against Germany presented Battenberg with grave difficulties. He was German born. He retained his German estates. He did nothing to distance himself from his German relations. He spoke with a German accent. Admiral Lord Charles Beresford openly referred to him as 'the Hun'. A less proud, more resilient man might have ridden the storm, but the barrage of popular anti-German sentiment directed at him by the press broke his nerve. He resigned on 29 October 1914 and was replaced by the returning Fisher. In 1917, five years too late, he relinquished his German titles and changed his name to Mountbatten.

Ludendorff, Erich (1865–1937) German military commander. Ludendorff was a self-made meritocrat from a rural merchant family. His pre-war career was based on his mastery of military logistics,

honed during his time as head of the German General Staff Mobilisation Section (1908–13), a post reserved for able and energetic officers. He came to public prominence within days of the outbreak of war after the daring and decisive part he played in the capture of the Belgian fortress town of Liège, considered to be a major obstacle on the German army's axis of advance into France. Soon afterwards he was sent to the Eastern Front as chief of staff to Field-Marshal HINDENBURG. The situation that Hindenburg and Ludendorff had been sent to retrieve, in the aftermath of an apparent German defeat at Gumbinnen, had already largely righted itself by the time they arrived. The staff officer Max HOFFMANN presented Ludendorff with a plan that he was astute enough to approve and resulted in the humiliating Russian defeat at Tannenberg in August 1914. This victory established the legend of Hindenburg and Ludendorff that was ultimately to bring them to power in Germany. During 1915 Ludendorff's ability to move armies swiftly and concentrate them at the decisive point was instrumental in achieving further sweeping German victories, especially at Gorlice-Tarnów, which brought the whole of Poland under German control. Ludendorff's success encouraged his boundless ambition and brought him into conflict with the German Commander-in-Chief, Erich von FALKENHAYN. Falkenhayn's reluctance to concentrate decisive force on one front dismayed Ludendorff, who believed that it denied him the opportunity to knock Russia out of the war in 1915. The failure of the German attack at Verdun launched in February 1916, the subsequent Anglo-French attack on the Somme in July and Romania's entry into the war in August, encouraged by the success of the Russian BRUSILOV offensive, proved too much for Falkenhayn's enemies, including Hindenburg and Ludendorff, who were brought west to replace him. They immediately scaled down German attacks in the west and abandoned the costly policy of immediate counter-attacks on the Somme. Ludendorff's advocacy of the retreat to the 'Hindenburg Line' in March 1917 was a master stroke. It shortened the German line in the west and created a reserve that allowed the German army to survive against powerful and determined French and, more especially, British attacks in 1917.

Together Hindenburg and Ludendorff constituted the Third Supreme Command, committed to the complete mobilisation of the German economy for war. This was to be achieved through the militarisation of German society free from parliamentary constraints. Its purpose was to bring about total victory and a peace of annexations that would establish Germany as the hegemonic power of Europe and one of the leading powers in the world. Ludendorff brushed aside objections to the renewal of unrestricted submarine warfare by Chancellor BETHMANN-HOLLWEG, whose resignation in July 1917 left Ludendorff with almost dictatorial powers. After the defeat of Russia, he used these to impose a Carthaginian peace on Russia and Romania (in the treaties of Brest-Litovsk and Bucharest), which did much to stiffen Allied resolve in the testing months ahead.

Encouraged by German victory in the east, Ludendorff turned to plan victory in the west. On 21 March 1918 he launched a massive offensive against the British on the Somme, using sophisticated artillery and infantry tactics that achieved an astonishing success on the front of General GOUGH's British Fifth Army. But Ludendorff failed to turn his tactical success into a strategic victory. Despite the strains, the Anglo-French alliance survived and was eventually strengthened by the appointment of FOCH as de facto Allied Commander-in-Chief. Further violent attacks against the British in Flanders met with effective resistance. By the summer no victory was in sight. Losses suffered by the flower of German infantry in the stormtroop units were catastrophic.

American troops were arriving in France at the rate of 150,000 a month. Some of these played a leading part in stopping Ludendorff's surprise attack on the Aisne that seemed to threaten Paris at the end of May. In July the Allies counter-attacked. Ludendorff quickly recognised that the game was up, a recognition driven home by the great British victory at Amiens on 8 August. Ludendorff increasingly descended into pessimism and appeared to suffer a nervous breakdown in September, when he called for an end to the war. He handed over power to Prince MAX von Baden. Civilian politicians would suffer the ignominy of German surrender. Ludendorff and Hindenburg's failure to admit any responsibility for defeat or to take part in the Armistice negotiations immediately established the disastrous myth that the German army had not been defeated in the field but 'stabbed in the back' by politicians, socialists and Jews, a legend that Ludendorff's post-war memoirs did much to reinforce.

The war did not end Ludendorff's role in German life. He took part in the KAPP putsch (1920) and Hitler's Munich Beer Hall putsch (1923) and led the National Socialists in the Reichstag from 1924 to 1928. Ludendorff was a military technocrat of remarkable virtuosity, but he was a contemptible strategist devoid of political understanding or judgement whose policies brought Wilhelmine Germany to ruin. He was one of the most evil and disastrous figures in the most evil and disastrous century of German history. His beloved stepsons were both killed in the war.

Ludwig III (1845–1921) King of Bavaria. Ludwig succeeded his mad cousin, King Otto, in 1913. During the war, as economic conditions worsened, Bavarians increasingly blamed him for failing to defend their interests and regarded his own isolation from the privations of war with contempt. Only at the beginning of November 1918, however, did he make constitutional concessions to popular unrest. This was far too late and on 7 November Kurt EISNER seized power, proclaiming the Bavarian Soviet Republic. Ludwig fled to Austria. His son, Prince RUPPRECHT, was a leading German field commander during the war.

Lufbery, (Gervaise) Raoul (1885–1918) Franco-American fighter ace. The son of an American father and a French mother, he joined the United States army in 1906, serving in the Philippines before leaving to become mechanic to his friend the aviator Marc Pourpe. When the war broke out Lufbery enlisted in the French Foreign Legion but remained as Pourpe's mechanic until he became a pilot himself, flying with the famous *Escadrille Lafayette*. By the time the USA entered the war, Lufbery was already an ace. He was killed in action on 19 May 1918, falling (or possibly jumping) to his death from a burning aircraft, while serving with the United States air service.

Luke, Frank (1897–1918) US fighter ace, generally credited with twenty-one kills, achieved in the space of eighteen days. Luke specialised in the highly dangerous business of shooting down balloons and became known as 'the Arizona Balloon Buster'. His attacking methods frequently proved fatal for his wingmen, and he also became known as 'Bad-Luck Luke'. Off duty he practised his marksmanship by firing at targets while riding a motorbike, using two guns simultaneously. Apart from shooting down balloons, Luke's favourite activity was insubordination. Despite being grounded and threatened with court martial, he ignored orders and took to the skies, achieving three kills on the day of his death (28 or 29 September 1918). He was shot down attacking a balloon, survived, but was killed attempting to fight off a platoon of German troops with his pistol. He was posthumously awarded the Congressional Medal of Honor.

Lukin, Henry Timson (1860–1925) South African military commander. Lukin was born in England, the son of a barrister. After failing in 1879 to obtain entry into the Royal Military College, Sandhurst, he was enticed to South Africa on the prospect of war, working as a foreman on a road-building gang until a war obligingly arrived, when he received a commission in a local unit, Bengough's Horse. By the outbreak of the Great War, he was Inspector-General of the permanent military forces of South Africa, having accumulated impressive combat experience in the late Victorian colonial wars of southern Africa. He also became an expert on the Maxim machine gun, about which he wrote a book. In the early part of the Great War he fought in German South West Africa (Namibia) and Egypt, before being chosen to organise and train the South African Infantry Brigade for service on the Western Front. He commanded this splendid unit in its most famous battle, the capture of Delville Wood, on the Somme, in July 1916. In December 1916 he was promoted to command the South African Infantry Brigade's parent formation, the 9th (Scottish) Division, reckoned by many to be the best British division on the Western Front, commanding it at Arras and Third Ypres, before being replaced in March 1918. Lukin was a popular and respected commander with a concern for the welfare of his troops. He was often seen in the front line, where he disdained gas-mask protection, despite himself having being gassed.

Lutyens, Edwin Landseer (1869–1944) British architect, whose appointment to the Imperial War Graves Commission in 1917 allowed him to play a leading part in the physical commemoration of the Great War. He designed the Cenotaph in Whitehall (1919) and many other war memorials, most notably perhaps the 'Memorial to the Missing of the Somme', which dominates what Scott Fitzgerald called 'the melancholy hill' of Thiepval on the old Western Front.

Luxemburg, Rosa (1871–1919) German socialist and revolutionary, born Raya Dunayevskaya in Russian-occupied Poland. Luxemburg co-founded the Spartacus League in 1916, later breaking with the Social Democrats to form the German Communist Party. Luxemburg's faith in the revolutionary potential of the masses did not blind her to the difficulties of organising a successful revolution in the face of armed opposition and a lack of working-class support for the fledgling Communist Party. She reluctantly agreed to a revolution only after being promised armed support by the shop stewards' movement. Her instincts proved sound. The paramilitary *Freikorps* crushed the Berlin uprising within a week (6–13 January 1919). Luxemburg was detained and then murdered by the victors.

Lvov, Prince Georgy Evgenevich (1861–1925) Russian politician, who became the first Prime Minister of the Provisional Government in the aftermath of the February Revolution. A liberal-minded landowner, he had come to prominence in 1915 through his attempts to co-ordinate the mobilisation of the Russian economy, enjoying some success in improving the Russian army's medical and supply services. Between February 1917 and his resignation on 8 July, however, he never exercised real political authority, which soon came to be exercised by the Petrograd Soviet and by KERENSKY. He also recognised the rising power of LENIN. Lvov bowed to the inevitable after the October Revolution and emigrated to France.

Lyautey, Louis Hubert Gonzalve (1854–1934) French soldier and politician, who became Minister of War in BRIAND's government in December 1916 after a career spent principally in colonial pacification and administration. He arrived from Morocco, where he had been High Commissioner, to discover that a new commander-in-chief of the French armies, General NIVELLE, had been appointed without his approval. Lyautey was completely unconvinced by Nivelle's plans and resistant to his famous charm. But his uncomfortable questioning served only to alienate those who wished to believe that Nivelle could end the war successfully. Lyautey resigned on 14 March 1917, an act which brought about the fall of the government two days later. But not even this could halt Nivelle. Lyautey returned to Morocco, from where he watched the Nivelle offensive of April–May 1917 proceed to its disastrous conclusion.

Lynden-Bell, Arthur Lynden (1867–1943) British staff officer. Lynden-Bell was commissioned in The Buffs in 1885. He was present at the siege of Chitral (1895) and severely wounded in the South African War, after which his career took the staff route. Following appointments at the War Office and Southern Command, he spent three years with the Territorial Lowland Division (1911–14). By August 1914 he had been in the army for twenty-nine years and was still only a major. His wartime rise, however, was rapid. He was immediately promoted Lieutenant-Colonel and sent to the War Office, where he was GSO1 and then Assistant Quartermaster-General. In February 1915 he joined Lieutenant-General PULTENEY's III Corps on the Western Front as chief of staff (BGGS) with the rank of brigadier-general. Pulteney was the least cerebral of commanders. His GHQ was regularly supplied with an intellectual stiffening of talented staff officers: Lynden-Bell succeeded John Du Cane and George MILNE. He held the post only until July 1915, when he was promoted again, this time to chief of staff (MGGS) of the new Third Army, commanded by Sir Charles MONRO. Lynden-Bell had risen from major to major-general in less than a year. During their brief period together on the Western

Front, Monro and Lynden-Bell did much to influence the future training regime of the British Expeditionary Force by their creation of Army Schools, and – not least – by Lynden-Bell's appointment of Major J.F.C. FULLER to organise them. In October 1915 Lynden-Bell accompanied Monro to Gallipoli as chief of staff to the Mediterranean Expeditionary Force (MEF). He immediately established excellent relations with his corps commanders, especially Julian BYNG, but attracted some criticism for his failure ever to visit the peninsula, which his chief famously and expeditiously decided must be evacuated.

When this was accomplished, Lynden-Bell remained in the Middle East as chief of staff to Sir Archibald MURRAY. Murray's command of the Egyptian Expeditionary Force was notable for its administrative and logistical achievements and for its lack of battlefield success. This exasperated LLOYD GEORGE, who replaced Murray in June 1917 with Sir Edmund ALLENBY. Within three months Allenby replaced Lynden-Bell with the man who had succeeded him at Third Army, Louis BOLS. Lynden-Bell spent the remainder of the war as Director of Staff Duties at the War Office.

M

McAdoo, William Gibbs (1863–1941) US politician. Although the United States did not enter the war until April 1917, as Secretary of the Treasury McAdoo had to deal with the consequences of the war in Europe, especially the disruptions caused to international trade, from the outset. The encouragement of US shipping to continue trading with Europe was high on his agenda and with this in mind he was instrumental in guaranteeing marine insurance arrangements. He also supported low-interest loans to the Allies in the hope that US financial assistance would prevent the eventual need for US military assistance. When this proved vain and the US entered the war, McAdoo showed himself to be a determined, energetic and pragmatic economic manager. The US war effort was supported financially principally by the sale of 'Liberty Bonds' after proposals for increased taxes on high incomes and profit duties provoked considerable opposition. He also established the Inter-Allied Purchasing Commission, which identified Allied needs and acted as purchasing agent on their behalf. Like LLOYD GEORGE in Britain, McAdoo surrounded himself with 'men of push and go' from business. This not only made available necessary and valuable expertise but also helped calm business fears about government control and regulation. McAdoo added to his considerable responsibilities in December 1917 when he was appointed Director-General of the newly formed US Railroad Administration. The laissez-faire American railway system was in danger of imminent collapse, with serious consequences for the expansion and supply of the American Expeditionary Force. McAdoo brought order into the chaos and placated the railways' demoralised workforce. It is small wonder that he ended the war in a state of exhaustion. He handed in his resignation on 12 November 1918.

McCarthy, (Emma) Maud (1858–1949) British nursing administrator. Maud McCarthy was born in Sydney, Australia, but came to England to train as a nurse at the London Hospital (1891–93). Her association with military medicine began with the South African War (1899–1902), in which she served with distinction. In 1902 she was closely involved with the establishment of Queen Alexandra's Imperial Military Nursing Service, which brought about the reorganisation of the Army Nursing Service (formed in 1881) and the Nursing Reserve (formed in 1897). McCarthy was Matron of the new organisation until 1910, when she transferred to the War Office as Principal Matron, professional head of British military nursing. In this capacity she went to France in August 1914 in the first ship of the British Expeditionary Force to set sail. From her base at Abbeville, McCarthy remained in charge of British nursing in Belgium and the whole of France for the rest of the war. She presided over a tenfold increase in the number of nurses, recruited from all over the British Empire, but continued to struggle with the chronic lack of trained personnel. From 1917 onwards nursing sisters and specialist nurses, such as nurse anaesthetists, began to play an increasingly important part in medical treatment, taking on unprecedented levels of responsibility. Nurses also provided contact with the lost world of femininity for often grievously hurt and frightened men.

McCay, James Whiteside (1864–1930) Australian military commander. After beginning his working life as a school teacher, McCay later qualified and practised as a solicitor. He was also a member of the Victorian and Federal parliaments and was briefly Minister of Defence. He developed a close friendship with his fellow Victorian and fellow citizen soldier John MONASH. When the war broke out he was given command of the 2nd (Australian) Brigade after a brief period as Deputy Censor in Melbourne. He led the brigade on Gallipoli and was wounded in the attack on Krithia, an assault that cost the Australians heavy casualties and for which McCay received much unfavourable criticism from his men. Neither his wound nor the criticism prevented his appointment to command the 5th (Australian) Division in February 1916. This was the last Australian division to be formed but the first to see action on the Western Front, in the botched attack at Fromelles (July 1916). Although the British corps commander Richard HAKING bore much of the responsibility for the attack's costly failure, the planning and preparation of McCay and his staff were also at fault. After mounting discontent expressed by his subordinate commanders, he was replaced by Talbot HOBBS in January 1917, spending the rest of the war in England training reinforcements.

He took the transfer badly and was constantly scheming to be reinstated to field command, though without success. McCay was an able, intelligent man, but his sarcastic, quarrelsome personality alienated the troops whose support he needed most and there were few to mourn their general's lack of luck.

McCrae, John (1872–1918) Canadian soldier, physician and poet, whose most famous and enduring poem, 'In Flanders Fields', was first published in *Punch* on 29 December 1915, achieving an immediate popularity. McCrae was a dedicated doctor who worked at front-line dressing stations and, later, at No. 3 General Hospital, Boulogne. He drove himself relentlessly, despite chronic asthma, and overwork almost certainly contributed to his death from pneumonia in January 1918.

McCudden, James Thomas Byford (1895–1918) British fighter ace, who recorded fifty-four victories before his death in a careless flying accident on 9 July 1918, which resulted from his making a rudimentary error when his engine stalled. McCudden joined the Royal Flying Corps in 1913 as a mechanic and, by the time of his death, was one of its longest-serving members. During the last months of his life he wrote *Five Years in the RFC*, one of the most interesting and revealing memoirs written by an ace. He was awarded the VC, DSO and bar, MC and bar, and MM.

MacDonald, J(ames) Ramsay (1866–1937) British politician. MacDonald was the illegitimate son of a Scottish fisherwoman who rose by his own efforts and his wife's money to a position of influence and importance on the British left. He was Secretary of the Labour Representation Committee (later the Labour Party) from 1900 until 1912, treasurer from 1912 until 1924 and MP for Leicester from 1906 until 1918. Unlike many of his

Labour contemporaries, he was an accomplished parliamentarian as well as a renowned platform orator, a bookish theorist and a practical organiser. He spent much of the war in uncomfortable isolation, ridiculed (but also feared) by the right and abandoned by many in the Labour movement, especially among the trades unions. This isolation resulted from his decision to oppose British entry into the war. Like many 'pacifists' he went down to heavy defeat in the 'Khaki' election of 1918. His principled stand against British belligerency, however, worked in his favour in the longer term, after wartime passions had cooled. Within ten years of the outbreak of war MacDonald became the first Labour Prime Minister. From then until his retirement as leader of the National Government in 1935 he had many opportunities to demonstrate that the reputation for dangerous radicalism that his opposition to war had established was entirely misleading.

Macdonnell, Archibald Cameron (1864–1941) Canadian military commander. Macdonnell was the son of a barrister. He joined Canada's permanent military forces in 1888 after graduating from the Royal Military College of Canada, at Kingston, Ontario. Within a year he sought greater excitement by transferring to the Royal North West Mounted Police. When the South African War broke out, he volunteered to serve with the 2nd Canadian Mounted Rifles, winning the DSO. After another period with the Mounties, as CO 'C' Squadron, he joined Lord Strathcona's Horse. He was in command of this unit when the Great War broke out. From 1915 to 1917 Macdonnell commanded 7th (Canadian) Brigade on the Western Front. In June 1917 he succeeded Arthur CURRIE in command of 1st (Canadian) Division (the 'Old Redpatch'), leading the veteran unit to some of its greatest successes, including the battle of Amiens (8 August 1918) and the breaking of the Hindenburg line (September–

October 1918). His 21-year-old son Ian was killed in action on the Somme on 2 July 1916 while serving with the Royal Flying Corps. Macdonnell himself was wounded in the left arm and shoulder by a sniper on 17 February 1917, while GOC 7th (Canadian) Brigade.

Macdonogh, George Mark Watson (1865–1942) British intelligence officer. Macdonogh accompanied the British Expeditionary Force to France in August 1914 as Sir John FRENCH's Chief Intelligence Officer. His services, and those of his staff, survived the sweeping changes made to French's headquarters in January 1915 by the new chief of staff Sir William ROBERTSON. When Robertson went home in December 1915 as Chief of the Imperial General Staff, he took Macdonogh with him as Director of Military Intelligence, a post he retained until 1918. He proved a careful and perceptive analyst of enemy intentions and capabilities, but his conclusions were far more cautious than those of his successor in France, John CHARTERIS. Macdonogh undoubtedly had a brilliant intellect: he passed second into the Staff College (behind Sir James EDMONDS), even finding time to qualify as a barrister while at Camberley, but the cut and thrust of advocacy was not his forte. A shy and retiring man, he shrank from disputes with more aggressive personalities. Chief among these was Sir Douglas HAIG, who distrusted Macdonogh's Roman Catholicism and regarded him as a pessimist and defeatist, preferring Charteris's more encouraging and inaccurate assessments of the war's impact on German morale and fighting capacity.

McDowell, John Benjamin (18??–19??) British cinematographer, who – together with Geoffrey MALINS – shot the footage that became the celebrated film 'The Battle of the Somme', which opened up a new era in the history of film, of photojournalism, of the cinema and of war itself. McDowell was awarded the Military Cross for courage under fire.

MacGill, Patrick (1889–1963) Irish soldier-poet. Patrick MacGill was the eldest of eleven children of a poor Irish farming family. He began his working life at 12 as a bonded labourer. His experience of social injustice and the stoicism of ordinary people inspired him to write, and he achieved a degree of pre-war celebrity as the 'navvy poet'. His account of working-class life, *Children of the Dead End. The Autobiography of a Navvy*, was published in 1914. He was dismayed by the political conservatism of Catholic Irish nationalism, but his socialist and anti-clerical beliefs did not prevent him from enlisting in the 18th (County of London) Battalion The London Regiment (London Irish Rifles) after the outbreak of war. 3008 Rifleman P. MacGill served with the battalion as a stretcher-bearer during the battle of Loos in September 1915, where he was wounded and invalided home. He took no further part in the fighting. MacGill's literary output during the war, poetry and prose, was considerable. Reading it is a salutary experience. Modern focus on the poetry of SASSOON, ROSENBERG and OWEN has led many commentators to connect the truthful depiction of war with 'anti-war' sentiments. This was not the case with MacGill. Few have described the violence of modern war more starkly ('In the street men fell as a bullock drops/ Sniped from the fringe of Hulluch copse'), but MacGill remained supportive of the war and uplifted by its camaraderie ('We're comrades in the dug-out and fight a common foe'). His wartime prose and poetry, including *The Great Push* (1916), *The Red Horizon* (1916) and *Soldiers' Songs* (1917), were reprinted by the Brandon Press in 1983 and 1984. MacGill's post-war writing became increasingly sentimental and stereotypically 'Irish'. He published nothing after 1937. He died in

the United States, where he spent most of his post-war life.

McKenna, Reginald (1863–1943) British politician. McKenna was a Cambridge-educated barrister. As Liberal MP for Monmouthshire (from 1895) his mastery of financial technicalities brought him to the notice of the party's leaders and in 1905 he was appointed to the key post of Financial Secretary to the Treasury. In 1908 he was the somewhat unlikely choice as First Lord of the Admiralty. As a prudent economist in charge of one of the greatest spending departments of the British state, McKenna was a revelation. Fully convinced of the German threat to British sovereignty, he threw his political weight and financial acumen behind the reforms of Admiral FISHER, including the construction of the revolutionary *Dreadnought* class battleships. It was principally due to McKenna's efforts that eight of these ships were built when the 'economists' wanted only four and their 'militarist' opponents only six. He was one of the principal architects of British victory in the naval arms race with Germany and of the Royal Navy that retained mastery of the sea during the Great War. McKenna's 'navalist' views were his undoing, however. His refusal to acquiesce in the War Office view of strategy, after the famous worsting of Admiral Sir Arthur WILSON by Major-General Henry WILSON at the meeting of the Committee of Imperial Defence in August 1911, led to his transfer to the Home Office, exchanging posts with Winston CHURCHILL. As Home Secretary from 1911 until May 1915, McKenna had to deal with the worst of the suffragette violence. His 'Cat and Mouse Act' of 1913, which allowed the release and re-arrest of hunger-striking suffragettes, brought him much odium. He attracted a different sort of odium during the opening months of the war, when his calm and considered approach to internal security angered press and public opinion infected with 'spy fever'.

The establishment of ASQUITH's coalition government in May 1915, however, saw McKenna succeed LLOYD GEORGE as Chancellor of the Exchequer, a post for which he was eminently suited. As Chancellor, McKenna sought to balance the demands of military mobilisation against those of financial stability. He took the view that British financial strength was a strategic asset not only to Britain but also to the alliance. Maintaining it was essential. In his budgets of September 1915 and April 1916, McKenna made the first serious attempts to put Britain's war finances on a secure footing that would preserve the nation's international position and the solvency of the alliance, to which Britain was banker. He did this by increasing income tax and by imposing import and other taxes, the 'McKenna duties', on luxury items. Britain raised a higher proportion of its wartime income through direct taxation than any other belligerent. By 1918 income tax stood at eight shillings in the pound, an eight-fold increase since the outbreak of war. The reliance on direct taxation helped keep down the cost of living for working-class people and had a mildly redistributive effect on incomes that helped maintain national solidarity. McKenna was also instrumental in raising $40M in securities from the Prudential Assurance Company that provided necessary collateral for J.P. MORGAN to execute British munitions contracts in the United States. McKenna's conviction that Britain must follow a 'maritime strategy' was unshakeable. He was opposed to the profligate expenditure of British economic strength in an attempt to become a great military power. 'Our ultimate victory is assured if, in addition to our naval and military activities, we retain unimpaired our power to assist in financing, supplying and carrying for the Allies,' he argued, 'but the retention of that power is probably the most indispensable element of success.' The government's reluctant acceptance of conscription, beginning with single men

in January 1916, dismayed him and he offered his resignation to Asquith, who refused it. McKenna remained as Chancellor, stonily watching the decline of British economic power as the army and nation became increasingly sucked into *guerre à outrance*. Lloyd George's accession to the premiership in December 1916 marked the end of McKenna's hopes that Britain could successfully pursue a war of 'limited liability'. He refused to join the Lloyd George coalition and lost his seat in the general election of 1918. He was Chairman of the Midland Bank from 1919 until his death in 1943. McKenna is one of the most underestimated British political figures of the pre-war and war period.

Mackensen, August von (1849–1945) German military commander. Mackensen spent the whole of the war on the Eastern Front, first as commander of XVII Corps in PRITTWITZ's Eighth Army and, later, HINDENBURG's Ninth Army, and then as commander of Ninth Army, Eleventh Army and Army Group Mackensen. It was XVII Corps that was badly handled at the battle of Gumbinnen in August 1914, a reverse that had important consequences for the war in the east and the west, but Mackensen recovered to play an effective part in the great German victories at Tannenberg (August 1914) and the Masurian Lakes (September 1914). As GOC Ninth Army in November 1914 he won an important victory over the Russian First and Second Armies at Łódz in Poland. As GOC Eleventh Army, he was reinforced by the considerable talents of a new chief of staff, Hans von SEECKT, and together they orchestrated the stunning breakthrough at Gorlice-Tarnów in May 1915. This led to the expulsion of Russian forces from most of Galicia and the whole of Russian Poland. Mackensen's fame became second only to that of Hindenburg. He increased it by defeating Serbia in November 1915, driving the Serb army out of its homeland across the mountains of Albania to exile on Corfu. In August 1916 he added Romania to his list of conquests, smashing the Romanian army and occupying most of the country. He spent the rest of the war commanding the occupation forces in Romania and organising its economic exploitation. Romanian supplies of food and oil did much to keep Germany in the war during its final two years. This did nothing to endear Mackensen to the French, ever concerned about the fate of Romania, and they briefly interned him after the war. Mackensen was one of Germany's most successful commanders in the First World War. His operations were invariably characterised by speed and surprise, designed to inflict deep penetrations on narrow fronts. He remained an important public figure in Germany between the wars, often appearing with Hitler, though at heart he was always a monarchist. At the Kaiser's funeral in 1941 the 92-year-old Mackensen placed his field-marshal's cloak over WILHELM II's coffin.

Mackenzie, (Edward Montague) Compton (1883–1972) British novelist and soldier. Mackenzie abandoned the law for the pen in 1907 and by the outbreak of war was well established as a novelist. He served during the war with the Royal Naval Division as an officer in the Royal Marines. He was invalided in September 1915 after serving on Gallipoli. In 1917 he became Director of the Aegean Intelligence Service, based in Syria. His prolific post-war output included three volumes of war memoirs, *Gallipoli Memories* (1928), *Athenian Memories* (1931) and *Greek Memories* (1932).

MacLaren, Donald Roderick (1893–1989) Canadian fighter ace. Although he did not join the Royal Flying Corps until 1917, MacLaren ended the war as Canada's third highest scoring ace, behind BISHOP and COLLISHAW, with fifty-four victories, mostly achieved flying the demanding Sopwith Camel.

Maclay, Joseph Paton (1857–1951) British shipowner and Shipping Controller. Maclay began his working life as a clerk in Glasgow, but by the time the war broke out he was a major figure in the British shipping industry as co-owner of the Clyde-based trampship line Maclay & McIntyre. Although a Liberal he was little interested in politics and distrusted politicians. Maclay was brought to LLOYD GEORGE's attention by his fellow Glaswegian Andrew Bonar LAW, leader of the Conservative Party. By the end of 1916 the strategic importance of shipping was increasing. Great though British shipping resources were, they were insufficient to meet the growing demands on them from all quarters, military, civilian and Allied. This situation was to deteriorate in 1917 with the onset of German unrestricted submarine warfare. Maclay was brought into the Lloyd George coalition government in December 1916 as Shipping Controller in a new Ministry of Shipping. He brought immense knowledge of the shipping industry to his task. He refused to enter parliament and did most of his business through Bonar Law. As a shipowner himself, he was able, in effect, to requisition the whole of the British merchant fleet and get their owners to run it in the best interests of the war effort without the fear of 'nationalisation' that a more political figure might have engendered. In making effective and rational use of the available shipping resources, he played a major role in the defeat of the U-boats and in ensuring the supply of the nation and its armed forces.

McMahon, (Arthur) Henry (1862–1949) British soldier and political agent. McMahon's reputation as an adept diplomat, honed in difficult territorial demarcation disputes on the frontiers of India, recommended him as the man to succeed KITCHENER as British High Commissioner in Egypt, following Kitchener's appointment as Secretary of State for War in August 1914. McMahon retained the post until his abrupt recall in 1916. The policy inherited from his predecessor was pro-Arab. Kitchener feared that a German–Ottoman alliance would have an unsettling effect on the millions of British Muslim subjects in India. At the end of October 1914 he sent a secret message to ibn Ali ibn Mohammed HUSSEIN, Sherif of Mecca, promising British support for Arab independence if the Arabs entered the war on the British side. The cautious Hussein hesitated. During the next year the diplomatic bargaining continued, principally through correspondence between McMahon and Hussein's second son, ABDULLAH, who favoured a British alliance. Almost exactly a year after Kitchener's original letter, McMahon confirmed that the British would support Arab independence. British arming of the Arabs began in January 1916 and the Arab Revolt was proclaimed in June. The nature of the undertakings promised by McMahon became the subject of much post-war controversy.

McMahon, Norman Reginald (1866–1914) British soldier. The British Expeditionary Force's outstanding rifle skills owed much to the transformation in training achieved by McMahon during his period as Chief Instructor at the School of Musketry, Hythe, between 1905 and 1909. McMahon was a thinking soldier who recognised the importance of firepower superiority in a future war. His preferred solution was to increase the scale of machine-gun provision and to expedite the introduction of a new, lighter version of the MAXIM. But these views could make no headway against Treasury economy, so he was compelled to try to achieve firepower superiority through rapid rifle fire, utilising the excellent new short-magazine Lee Enfield. The British Expeditionary Force of 1914 had probably the best-trained riflemen in military history, capable of achieving unprecedented feats of sustained, accurate musketry. By then, McMahon was commanding officer of the 4th Royal Fusiliers, ironically a battalion whose machine-gun section won the first two Victoria Crosses to be awarded during the war. In November 1914 he was promoted Brigadier-General and given a staff appointment, but he agreed to remain in command of his battalion until a successor could be found. During this period, on 11 November 1914, he was killed by a German shell near Hooge. He has no known grave.

MacMunn, George Fletcher (1869–1952) British staff officer, whose appointment as Inspector-General of Communications, Mesopotamia, was instrumental in the transformation of the British force's administrative and supply arrangements in that unforgiving theatre of war, making possible the later victories of Sir Stanley MAUDE.

McNaughton, Andrew George Latta (1887–1960) Canadian soldier. Andy McNaughton was born in Saskatchewan, the son of a successful shopkeeper. He graduated from McGill University in 1910 with a BSc in engineering, taking his Masters in 1912. When war broke out he was lecturing in engineering at McGill and had risen to major in an artillery unit of the Canadian militia, which he joined in 1910. During the war he played a leading part in the emergence of the Canadian Corps as one of the finest military formations on the Western Front, principally as Corps Counter Battery Staff Officer (CBSO) and, finally, as commander of the Corps' heavy artillery (GO-CRA). Effective suppression of enemy guns was essential to infantry assaults at acceptable cost. Under McNaughton's leadership counter-battery work in the Canadian Corps became state of the art. This was effected not only by McNaughton's outstanding abilities as an administrator but also by his personal involvement in the emerging technologies of flash-spotting and sound-ranging, essential to the identification of enemy gun positions.

McNaughton's finale during the war was the devastating fire plan he designed for the capture of Mont Houy, near Valenciennes, on 1 November 1918. This was so successful that it may have led to a future Canadian fixation with firepower to the neglect of manoeuvre. Both McNaughton and his protégé, and successor as CBSO, H.D.G. Crerar, commanded the Canadian First Army during the Second World War.

Madden, Charles Edward (1862–1935) British naval staff officer, whose pre-war career owed much to the patronage of Admiral FISHER. He was a member of the 'Fishpond' of talented officers, the 'brains of the navy', upon whose talents would rest the fate of the nation when the inevitable showdown with Germany arrived. Fisher chose Madden to serve on the committees that produced design briefs for the revolutionary *Dreadnought* class battleships and Fisher's favourite (though flawed) *Invincible* class battle cruisers. JELLICOE was also an admirer. He requested Madden as his chief of staff when he assumed command of the Grand Fleet in August 1914. Madden remained in this post throughout Jellicoe's tenure of command, including the battle of Jutland (31 May–1 June 1916). Jellicoe nominated Madden as his successor in December 1916, but the post went to Sir David BEATTY and Madden became C-in-C 1st Battle Squadron and Second in Command of the Grand Fleet. Madden was a faithful lieutenant to Beatty, as he had been to Jellicoe, but was often severely critical of Jellicoe's successor as First Sea Lord, Sir Roslyn WEYMSS. Madden remained in the Royal Navy after the war, becoming First Sea Lord in 1927, in which august post he was forced to preside over a sad decline in British naval power.

Magill, Ivan Whiteside (1888–1986) British anaesthetist, one of the founding fathers of modern anaesthetics. As Senior Anaesthetist at St Mary's, Sidcup, the specialist hospital for facial injuries, Magill and his team made possible the reconstructive surgery of the great plastic surgeon Harold GILLIES.

Maistre, Paul André Marie (1858–1922) French military commander. Maistre began the war as a staff officer in the French Fourth Army but enjoyed rapid promotion following JOFFRE's ruthless dismissal of senior officers during the first weeks of the war. Maistre was given command of XXI Corps, with the rank of lieutenant-general, after the Marne and became a full general a month later. He commanded XXI Corps throughout 1915 and 1916 at Vimy, Verdun and the Somme. In 1917 his career again prospered in the adversity of others, when he was promoted to command Sixth Army, which had suffered badly in the NIVELLE offensive, with a brief to restore its discipline, morale and fighting efficiency. The success of his efforts was tested in the careful, limited offensive at Malmaison in October 1918, during which he made good use of overwhelming artillery superiority on a narrow front. This consolidated his reputation as an effective 'crisis commander', and he was sent to Italy in November 1917 as GOC French Tenth Army to help stabilise the front after the Italian defeat at Caporetto. The even greater crisis occasioned by the German spring offensive of 1918 saw him recalled to the Western Front, where – in June 1918 – he took command of the four armies of Army Group Centre, presiding over a slow, but certain, advance on the right flank of the Americans. Maistre was an unspectacular commander whose name was never associated in the public mind with a particular triumph, but he showed himself throughout the war to be a competent and reliable soldier.

Maklakov, Nikolai Alekseevich (1871–1918) Russian politician, an instinctive reactionary and ardent monarchist, who held the key post of Minister of the

Interior from 1913 until 1915. Maklakov was one of the strongest figures in GOR-EMYKIN's government, in which he exercised his influence to oppose all attempts at concession to the Duma, to establish Russia's war effort on a broader base of political consensus and to find an advantageous compromise with Polish nationalism. His position became untenable after the Russian debacle at Gorlice-Tarnów in May 1915, and he was sacrificed to appease parliamentary opinion. The Bolsheviks executed him in 1918.

Malcolm, Neill (1869–1953) British staff officer and military commander. Malcolm's close association with Hubert GOUGH began in April 1916, when he was appointed chief of staff to the Reserve Corps (later Reserve Army, then Fifth Army), a post he retained until December 1917, when his extraordinary unpopularity resulted in his removal. Malcolm was undoubtedly energetic and able (he had a very successful post-war career in business and public service), but he tended to reinforce Gough's weaknesses rather than his strengths. He acquired a reputation for driving units beyond their endurance, and his sarcastic manner alienated many fighting soldiers. Malcolm was rewarded for his efforts with command of a second-line Territorial division, the 66th (2nd East Lancashire). He was wounded while commanding this unit during the German spring offensive of March 1918, returning to command the skeleton 39th Division in September 1918. Malcolm was a military intellectual, editor of the *Science of War* and author of a standard account of the Austro-Prussian War of 1866. He also wrote the entry on 'Tactics' in the first post-war edition of the *Encyclopaedia Britannica*, which still repays reading.

Malinov, Alexander (1867–1938) Bulgarian politician. As Minister-President from 1908 to 1911, Malinov was a leading advocate of an alliance with Russia. He distrusted the motives of the Central Powers in the Balkans and regarded Bulgaria's increasing economic dependence on Germany as a weakness. He urged Tsar FERDINAND I to remain neutral in August 1914 and opposed the Tsar's declaration of war on the side of the Central Powers in September 1915. In the summer of 1918, with Bulgaria staring at defeat, Malinov was restored as Prime Minister. Peace overtures to the Allies met with no response. Nor did this signal of war weariness encourage Germany to increase economic and military aid to Bulgaria, whose support the Germans valued only to the extent that it provided resources for the German war effort. Ferdinand's determination to keep faith with the Central Powers to the end left Malinov with no room for manoeuvre, but the Allied offensive at Salonika in September proved a breaking point. Malinov asked for an armistice without consulting the Tsar, an act that also completed LUDENDORFF's decline into pessimism and defeatism. Malinov remained in office until 28 November 1918, when he resigned in protest against Romanian occupation of the Dobrudja.

Malins, Geoffrey H. (1886–1940) British cinematographer. Malins, together with J.B. MCDOWELL, shot the footage that became the film 'The Battle of the Somme', many of whose scenes have now entered the British public's visual landscape of the First World War. The film was made by the British Topical Committee for War Films under the aegis of the War Office and went on general release on 21 August 1916. It was seen by a huge audience, many of whom were shocked by the scenes of dead, dying and wounded soldiers, never before filmed. Although some of the better-known scenes of soldiers being killed going 'over the top' have been exposed as fake, the film contains much genuine material of great interest and historic value and was far from being a self-conscious propaganda exercise. In 1920 Malins published *How I Filmed the War*, a boastful, exaggerated and (in parts) frankly unbelievable account of his part in the filming, which entirely omits mention of McDowell.

Malvy, Louis-Jean (1875–1949) French politician. Malvy, a Radical Socialist, became Minister of the Interior in VIVIANI's first government and retained the post through successive administrations until the summer of 1917. The *union sacrée* necessitated giving some ministerial posts to the left, but Malvy's choice for the politically sensitive Ministry of the Interior, and his longevity there, are perhaps surprising given his pre-war association with Joseph CAILLAUX, widely regarded in right-wing circles as a Germanophile and pacifist. Malvy's conciliatory attitude to wartime dissent (in August 1914 he resisted demands for the mass arrest of 'subversives' and later refused to suppress pacifist agitators or their literature) brought him into increasing conflict with his eventual nemesis, Georges CLEMENCEAU. In 1917 it was discovered that one of the newspapers subsidised by Malvy, *Le Bonnet Rouge*, had received money from the Germans to spread pacifist propaganda. He was forced to resign on 31 August and later charged with treason. In 1918 he was tried by a special commission of the Senate and acquitted, but he was found guilty of culpable negligence and sentenced to five years' exile.

Mangin, Charles Marie Emmanuel (1866–1925) French military commander, a native of the 'lost province' of Lorraine, whose unquenchable aggression and willingness to spill blood earned him the nickname 'The Butcher'. Mangin began the war as a brigade commander, winning renown for leading a vital counter-attack at Charleroi in August 1914. It was at Verdun in 1916, however, that he achieved national prominence, commanding 5th Division in its recapture of Forts Vaux and Douaumont. He was promoted to command Sixth Army, which was to provide the cutting edge of the NIVELLE offensive, an offensive that Mangin wholeheartedly supported. Despite Mangin's self-confidence and ruthless leadership, Sixth Army failed to capture the Chemin des Dames in May 1917, suffering huge numbers of casualties that temporarily destroyed it as a fighting unit and provoked mutiny. Nivelle showed no gratitude and immediately replaced Mangin, whose career seemed in ruins. But in the summer of 1918 the new Allied Commander-in-Chief, General FOCH, with a counter-attack already in mind, restored Mangin to command the Tenth Army. Before Foch's counterstroke could be executed, however, the Germans attacked first on the Aisne at the end of May, achieving a stunning strategic surprise that put them once more on the banks of the Marne, less than forty miles from Paris. Just as he had in August 1914, Mangin executed a vital counter-attack. The second battle of the Marne stabilised the Allied line in the west for the final time, making possible the successful advance that began in July. Mangin's early career was spent in the colonial army, often among black troops. He admired them for their dash and courage, qualities he himself shared, and they often bore the brunt of his attacks. Despite his reputation as 'the eater of men', however, Mangin never asked more of his troops than he himself was willing to give. He remained, even as an army commander, a front-line general and was wounded several times. His famous comment, during the battle of Verdun, that 'whatever you do, you lose a lot of men' might stand as a summary of the war on the Western Front.

Mann, Thomas (1856–1941) British socialist trade union leader. Tom Mann was one of the most important figures in late Victorian and Edwardian trade unionism, achieving national prominence through his part in the London dock strike of

1889. He was President of the Dockers' Union from 1889 to 1893 and Secretary of the Independent Labour Party from 1894 to 1897. His involvement in the establishment of the Workers' Union (1898) provided an early glimpse of his belief in the political (as well as the industrial) potential of trade union power. He spent the period from 1902 to 1910 in Australia, which did nothing to lessen his radicalism but widened his international perspectives. He returned to Britain in 1910, becoming the leading advocate of syndicalism, urging direct action by workers – through the strike – to achieve power. This coincided with a period of unprecedented industrial unrest, with major strikes in the docks, on the railways and in the mines. Some, then and since, believed that Britain was on the verge of revolution. Mann was arrested for incitement to mutiny in 1912 and briefly imprisoned. He opposed British involvement in the war, during which the booming war economy and contemporary atmosphere of national determination to defeat Germany brought a temporary halt to industrial militancy. In 1916 Mann joined the British Socialist Party. He took great encouragement from the February Revolution of 1917 in Russia and advocated the establishment of workers' soviets in Britain. A rash of industrial unrest and war weariness in the spring and early summer of 1917 gave renewed hope of a British revolution. But firm action by the government, especially the Prime Minister, brought the situation under control. LLOYD GEORGE showed himself master of the carrot and the stick. He addressed many of the workers' specific grievances about the price of food and housing and the operation of the Military Service Acts, while exiling and imprisoning their left-wing leaders. A Commission of Inquiry, chaired by the Labour minister George BARNES, dismissed 'revolutionary' feelings as a cause of the unrest. Mann, however, was soon to take even greater inspiration from the Bolshevik Revolution in October

1917 and, in 1920, became one of the founders of the Communist Party of Great Britain.

Mannerheim, Carl Gustav Emil (1867–1951) Finnish soldier. Mannerheim was of Swedish descent but was born in Finland, then part of the Russian empire. He joined the cavalry of the Russian Imperial Army and fought throughout the Great War against the Austrians. By June 1917 he had reached the rank of lieutenant-general and was commanding the VI Cavalry Corps in Transylvania. After the Bolshevik coup Mannerheim returned home. In the spring of 1918 he recaptured Helsinki from Finnish Communists and then, with German help, drove the Red Armies out of Finland and secured recognition of Finnish independence from the Soviet government.

Manning, Frederick (1882–1935) British soldier and writer. Frederick Manning was a little-known Australian man of letters who served as a private soldier in the 7th Battalion King's Shropshire Light Infantry on the Western Front. In 1922 he published anonymously a two-volume limited edition of a closely observed and realistic war novel, *The Middle Parts of Fortune*. An expurgated edition, shorn of its explicit language, appeared in 1930 under the title *Her Privates We*. Manning was not revealed as the author until 1943. *The Middle Parts of Fortune* is one of the finest novels ever written about soldiering. It focuses on the comradeship between ordinary soldiers and perhaps comes closer than any contemporary work of fiction to capturing the true sensibilities of the 'British working man in uniform'.

Mannock, Edward (1887–1918) British fighter ace and air war pioneer. 'Mick' Mannock was the top-scoring British ace of the war, generally credited with seventy-three victories. He is unique. Virtually blind in his left eye, brought up in poverty after being deserted by his alcoholic father, barely educated and with a prostitute for a sister, he completed his credentials by espousing fiery socialist beliefs. His emergence as an officer much less as an ace is extraordinary. He was working as a telephone engineer when war broke out. Unfortunately, his job was in Turkey. It took him until April 1915 to get back to England, after much unpleasant treatment. His telecommunications background won him acceptance in the Royal Engineers, but after reading about the exploits of Albert BALL he volunteered for the Royal Flying Corps and – amazingly – was accepted. He proved to be a natural pilot. He arrived on the Western Front in March 1917. In combat he was ruthless and implacable. He hated the enemy. His comment on hearing of the death of RICHTHOFEN, 'I hope the bastard burned the whole way down', has attracted some notoriety. But he was also a great patrol leader, trainer of pilots and tactician, who first intoned the fighter pilot's mantra 'Always on top; seldom on the same level; never below'. His aggression was calculated, his aim to inflict maximum damage on the enemy at minimum cost. Mannock was never bested in the air, succumbing to ground fire on 26 July 1918. He was awarded the MC and bar, DSO and two bars and a posthumous VC. His father sold them for £5.

Marc, Franz (1880–1916) German Expressionist painter. Marc's work was much influenced by Delaunay's theories of colour contrast, and he came to attention through his paintings of animals in non-naturalistic colours, which he believed had an expressive quality and spiritual force of their own. He collaborated closely with Kandinsky, with whom he co-founded the Munich Blaue Reiter group in 1911. Marc made his first abstract painting in 1913 and as war broke out seemed to be moving inexorably towards Abstract Expressionism. Franz Marc was killed in action at Verdun

on 4 March 1916. He was probably the leading artist to be killed during the war. His work had a lasting influence on Kandinsky.

March, Peyton Conway (1864–1955) US artillery commander and staff officer. March established a brilliant pre-war reputation among his peers, particularly for the administrative abilities he demonstrated in the Philippines. He rose quickly during the war, from artillery brigade commander in April 1917 to commander of all the American Expeditionary Force's artillery in August 1917. In March 1918 Secretary of State for War Newton D. BAKER recalled March to Washington as Army Chief of Staff. He greatly increased the power and influence of this office, to the dismay of some, including General PERSHING. He used his new-found authority to increase rapidly the size of the army and to streamline its administrative arrangements. He created new technical branches: the Air Corps; Chemical Warfare Service; Motor Transport Corps; and Tank Corps. He also abolished the distinctions between the Regular Army, the National Guard and the National Army for the duration of the war, to the fury of many traditionalists. March played one of the leading parts in transforming the United States army from a colonial cavalry force into a modern army capable of conducting major operations against great military powers. He had a clear idea of where he wanted the army to go and took it there, impervious to opposition, but his contribution was largely overshadowed by that of Pershing, with whom he had many disagreements.

Marghiloman, Alexandru (1854–1925) Romanian politician. As leader of the Conservative Party, Marghiloman was a leading advocate of an alliance with Germany. This was unwelcome advice in a country whose political sentiments were strongly Francophile, and he urged neutrality in August 1914. He opposed Romania's fateful declaration of war on the Central Powers in August 1916, foreseeing the military calamity that soon followed. The collapse of Russia after the KERENSKY offensive in 1917 rendered the resistance of even the tiny independent rump of Romania impossible. In the circumstances of defeat, Marghiloman's well-known pro-German views rendered him useful to Romania's devious and cynical king, FERDINAND I, who made him Prime Minister in March 1918 in an attempt to soften the demands of a victorious Germany. Marghiloman succeeded only to the extent that Romania was allowed to annex Bessarabia, previously under Russian jurisdiction, but in every other respect the Treaty of Bucharest was punitive. The success of Allied arms on the Western Front and in the Balkans in the autumn of 1918 led to the withdrawal of German troops from Romania. On 6 November, five days before the Armistice, Ferdinand decided that Marghiloman had served his purpose. He was replaced by the Liberal and pro-Allied BRATIANU. On 10 November Romania re-entered the war on the Allied side.

Marshall, George Catlett (1880–1959) US staff officer. Marshall's outstanding administrative abilities were apparent even before the war, when he passed out first from Fort Leavenworth. As G-3 (chief of operations) to the hastily improvised US 1st Division ('The Big Red One') in 1917, Marshall was painfully aware of the US army's limitations of training, doctrine, organisation and equipment. These put the army's small corps of professional officers under great strain, and Marshall had to suffer a scathing attack by PERSHING on his own abilities. Marshall's resolute defence of his record, however, endeared him to the Commander-in-Chief and he was later moved to Pershing's HQ, where he was instrumental in the planning of the St Mihiel and Meuse-Argonne offensives, together with Hugh DRUM and Fox CONNER. Marshall's experience in the

First World War reinforced his belief in the absolute importance of proper training and preparation to battlefield success and made him realise the need for effective inter-allied co-operation in coalition war. These insights informed his actions as the US army's Chief of Staff in the Second World War.

Marshall, William Raine (1865–1939) British military commander, who succeeded MAUDE as GOC-in-C, Mesopotamia, in November 1917, successfully completing the campaign by employing the same careful strategy and thorough organisation. He took the surrender of Turkish forces at Mosul on 1 November 1918.

Marterer, Ferdinand von (1862–1919) Austro-Hungarian military administrator, deputy head of the Military Chancery until the autumn of 1916, when he succeeded the aged BOLFRAS as head and Adjutant-General of Habsburg military forces. Unlike his predecessor, he was successful in achieving the replacement of the ambitious but unsuccessful Austrian Commander-in-Chief, CONRAD, on 27 February 1917. He had few other achievements, though his ability to say 'yes' endeared him to the new emperor, KARL I, a man who preferred to receive advice with which he agreed.

Martin-Leake, Arthur (1874–1953) British medical officer. Martin-Leake's was an adventurous life, including service in the South African War (1899–1902), where he was awarded the Victoria Cross for attending men under fire, and with the Serbian army in the Balkan Wars (1912–14). He rejoined the Royal Army Medical Corps in September 1914. During the First Battle of Ypres (October–November 1914) he won his second Victoria Cross for rescuing wounded soldiers lying close to enemy trenches near Zonnebeke. He was the first man to win the VC twice, a feat subsequently matched by only two others.

Marwitz, Georg von der (1856–1929) German military commander. Marwitz was a cavalryman from an old Pomeranian family. He had a difficult war. The conditions of war on the Western Front led to the disbandment of the cavalry group he had commanded, with no particular distinction, in December 1914. He was sent to the Eastern Front, where he commanded XXXVIII Corps at the second battle of the Masurian Lakes (February 1915), winning the *Pour le Mérite*. After further commands in the Carpathians and the Western Front, interrupted by illness, he became GOC Second Army at the end of 1916. Second Army took the brunt of the innovative British attack at Cambrai in November 1917, though it eventually managed to recapture lost ground. During 1918 Second Army was heavily engaged. At the opening German spring offensive, on the Somme, Second Army was responsible for the centre attack against the vital rail junction of Amiens. Marwitz's failure to capture Amiens after bitter fighting forced LUDENDORFF to change the axis of advance of HUTIER's more successful Eighteenth Army to the south, with great disruption to German logistical arrangements that helped bring the offensive to a halt. On 8 August 1918 Second Army again suffered a major reverse at British hands in the opening of the battle of Amiens, which Ludendorff famously described as 'the black day of the German army'. Marwitz ended the war as GOC Fifth Army.

Masaryk, Tomáš Garrigue (1850–1937) Czech philosopher and nationalist. By the time war broke out Masaryk was already well established as an influential figure among Czech nationalists, but the war was to magnify his influence considerably. In December 1914 Masaryk fled to London, where he established the Czech National Committee. His academic connections and reputation gave him access to many leading British political and public figures, to whom he outlined his vision of a post-war Europe of nation states arising from the ruins of the 'anachronistic' Habsburg Empire. He found a wider audience for these views in the influential journal *The New Europe*, published monthly from October 1916 and edited by the British historian R.W. SETON-WATSON. In 1917 he and Eduard BENEŠ established the Czechoslovak National Council in Paris. Later the same year Masaryk went to Russia, where he raised a Czech Legion from among Austro-Hungarian prisoners of war. The existence of this formation, Masaryk's lobbying of President WILSON and the support he received from the large communities of Czechs and Slovaks in the United States secured him recognition as leader of an Allied country in September 1918. He returned to Europe in December 1918 as President-elect of the new state of Czechoslovakia, a position he retained until 1935.

Masefield, John (1878–1967) British poet and wartime propagandist. After running away to sea at the age of 16 and then jumping ship to explore the United States as a tramp, Masefield returned to England in 1897. He had no qualifications and so looked for employment in an occupation where qualifications were not required, journalism. He also began writing poetry. In 1902 he published *Salt Water Ballads*, a volume that included the popular and much anthologised 'I must go down to the sea again'. By 1914 he was a well-established poet and a respected journalist on the liberal *Manchester Guardian*. When the war broke out Masefield joined the Red Cross, serving in France and then on Gallipoli. After the humiliating withdrawal of British forces from the peninsula, Masefield returned to England, where Charles MASTERMAN recruited him to work for the secret War Propaganda Bureau (WPB). Masefield was sent to the United States, where he embarked on a lecture tour propagandising the British cause. He later contributed two well-known pamphlets for the WPB, *Gallipoli* (1916) and *The Old Front Line* (1917), which painted the Dardanelles and Somme campaigns in the most favourable light. The enduring popularity of Masefield's verse and his long tenure as Poet Laureate (1930–67) were ultimately fatal to his reputation, but he was a pioneer in the poetic use of colloquial language. His work greatly influenced the 'war poets' SORLEY and SASSOON and, through Sassoon, OWEN.

Massey, William Ferguson (1856–1925) New Zealand politician. Massey became Prime Minister of New Zealand in 1912, when he formed the first Conservative government since 1890, retaining the post until his death in 1925. Much of New Zealand's preparedness for war was due to Massey's Liberal predecessor as Prime Minister, Sir J.G. WARD, whose government introduced compulsory military training under the Defence Act of 1909 and instituted the rapid expansion of New Zealand military forces under a British officer, Major-General Alexander GODLEY. As an avowed imperialist, however, Massey had given full support to Ward's defence policy (Massey and Ward's continued close collaboration during the war led to their being known as the 'Siamese twins'). During the war Massey showed himself to be a man of great energy and determination. Although he wished New Zealand to do all in her power to assist the British cause, he was never subservient and expected New Zealand's views to be heard. He formed a National Government in August 1915. The introduction of conscription ensured that the magnificent New Zealand Division, which served on Gallipoli and the Western Front, was always kept up to full strength. Massey was greatly assisted by his able Minister of Defence, James ALLEN. Massey attended the Paris Peace Conference and signed the Treaty of Versailles, a significant moment in the history of his country.

Masterman, Charles Frederick Gurney (1874–1927) British politician and propagandist. Masterman was an able man. He took a Double First at Cambridge, where he was President of the Union and editor of *Granta*, and later elected a Fellow of Christ's College. He was converted to Christian Socialism and went to experience working-class life for himself by living in a Camberwell tenement. This provided material for several books, the best remembered of which is *The Condition of England* (1909). These helped establish him as an authority on social conditions. He became MP for North-West Ham in the Liberal landslide of 1906, and his parliamentary performances soon saw him promoted to junior ministerial office, through which he became close to LLOYD GEORGE. In 1914, at the age of 40, he found himself in the Cabinet as Chancellor of the Duchy of Lancaster. The war, however, had a dramatic and, perhaps, detrimental effect on his political career. He was made Director of the War Propaganda Bureau (WPB), based at Wellington House in London. This organisation was responsible for disseminating British propaganda (what Masterman called the 'propaganda of facts') in neutral countries, the most important of which was the United States. Masterman was extremely successful in mobilising British writing talent, including major literary figures such as John BUCHAN and Arthur Conan DOYLE, to support the cause. He also realised that pictures were as important as words. In the second half of the war he became one of the greatest art patrons in British history, commissioning some ninety painters as official war artists and establishing a precedent that has been followed in every subsequent British war. Masterman controlled the WPB throughout the war but, because it was a secret organisation whose activities were not revealed until the mid-1930s, his contribution to the British war effort was unknown to the public in his lifetime. His reward was to lose his seat at the general election of 1918. He returned to the Commons only briefly in 1923, before again being defeated at the polls in 1924. His post-war political career was a sad diminuendo, increasingly troubled by depression, drink and drugs.

Mata Hari (1876–1917) Stage name of Gertrud Margarete Zelle, Dutch exotic dancer and prostitute, shot by the French as a spy on 15 October 1917. Although Mata Hari's name has become synonymous with espionage, there is no certainty that she was a spy at all. If she was, she was almost certainly the dupe of both sides. The idea that thousands of Allied soldiers died because of information she supplied to the enemy is patently absurd. Her profession and plausible German connections made her a convenient scapegoat to throw to the French pro-war press in its increasingly hysterical search for the enemy within.

Matania, Fortunino (1881–1963) Italian illustrator, whose superb artwork decorated the pages of the popular British magazine *The Sphere* from 1904. Matania specialised in historical subjects and took easily to illustrating the war. He was extremely professional, visiting the Western Front several times under the auspices of the Ministry of Information and seeking the advice of wounded veterans. He even had a replica trench built at his home so that he could bring verisimilitude to his subjects. Much of his war work appeared in *The Illustrated London News*.

Maude, (Frederick) Stanley (1864–1917) British Commander-in-Chief in Mesopotamia 1916–17. Maude was hand-picked by the Chief of the Imperial General Staff (CIGS), Sir William ROBERTSON, to command British forces in Mesopotamia in August 1916. The humiliating surrender of General TOWNSHEND's army at Kut-al-Amara in April had confirmed Robertson in his opposition to a 'forward' policy in

Mesopotamia. In Maude he appointed a commander whom he thought could be relied upon to avoid further embarrassments, who would hold the line with what he had and not demand to be reinforced with troops from the Western Front. Few generals have been appointed with the injunction 'take it easy, do nothing'. The brief did not suit Maude, who was able and ambitious. He set about reconstructing his largely Indian army in the methodical fashion suggested by his nickname, 'Systematic Joe'. New training regimes were introduced. Food, living conditions and medical services were improved. Supply arrangements were transformed. Morale rose. Once Maude was ready, he decided to move against the Turks. Realising that he had no room for errors where Robertson was concerned, he made none. Battle was largely avoided. The Turks were manoeuvred out of their positions and not so much out-fought as out-administered. Kut was recaptured in February 1917. Baghdad, fabled city of the Caliphs, fell on 11 March, the first unambiguous British victory of the war. Maude's follow-up operations were equally successful, but later in the year he contracted cholera, dying on 18 November despite (or perhaps because of) being intravenously fed with neat brandy and morphine.

Maud'huy, Louis Ernest de (1857–1921) French military commander. Maud'huy had a fluctuating military career that saw him meteorically (though temporarily) promoted to command of the newly-formed Tenth Army in 1914, before being reduced to corps commander (XV Corps) in 1916. Maud'huy's corps was among those French units forced into a precipitate and dangerous retreat by the surprise German attack on the Aisne in May 1918 that allowed the Germans to reach the Marne and threaten Paris. The disaster was principally the fault of Maud'huy's superior, General DUCHÊNE, but he was shown no mercy in the purge of commanders by Prime Minister CLEMEN-CEAU that followed. Marshal FOCH, who remembered Maud'huy's staunch contribution to the French defence in 1914, showed greater generosity. He appointed Maud'huy as Military Governor of Metz (his birthplace) in November 1918, a few days after its liberation.

Maunoury, Michel Joseph (1847–1923) French military commander. Maunoury was recalled from retirement in August 1914, at the age of 67, to command the 'Army of Lorraine', whose seven reserve divisions were destined to play a vital part in history. On 26 August they were redeployed by rail from the right to the left of the French line, near Paris. This placed them in a position to attack General Alexander von KLUCK's German First Army in flank, a plan devised and urged by one of Maunoury's successors as Military Governor of Paris, Joseph GALLIÉNI, who rushed reinforcements to Maunoury's renamed Sixth Army in a fleet of Parisian taxi cabs. Maunoury's attack on Kluck's flank inaugurated the battle of the Marne, which marked the collapse of the SCHLIEFFEN Plan and saved France from military defeat. Maunoury was wounded and made partially blind while visiting the front trenches in March 1915. He never held field command again.

Maurice, Frederick Barton (1871–1951) British staff officer, whose authorship of the notorious 'Maurice Letter', published in *The Times* on 7 May 1918, provoked a heated, though short-lived, political crisis. Maurice was an intelligent, well-read soldier, most of whose post-war career was spent in higher and adult education and in writing, his output including a biography of Sir Henry RAWLINSON. From 1915–18 he was Director of Military Operations at the War Office under the CIGS Sir William ROBERTSON, to whom he was close: A.J.P. Taylor described Maurice as Robertson's 'satellite'. Robertson's dismissal in February 1918 made

Maurice fearful of further political coups against the high command so he decided to get his retaliation in first. His letter accused the Prime Minister, LLOYD GEORGE, of lying to parliament about the strength of the British army in France at the beginning of 1918, a matter of some importance given the defeats that the army suffered in March and April. Lloyd George, however, proved far too slippery. With a conjurer's dexterity, he seemed to prove that the questionable statistics had been provided by Maurice's own office, and the debate on the issue, held in the House of Commons on 9 May, turned into a rout of Lloyd George's opponents, notably Maurice himself and – more importantly – ASQUITH. Lloyd George was unforgiving. The index entries of his *War Memoirs* for 'Maurice, Sir Frederick' are a triumph of character assassination: 'supports Robertson against War Cabinet, 1671; as comfortably placed as any politician, 1675; subservient and unbalanced, 1685; ... his astonishing arithmetical calculations, 1763–4; the instrument by which the government was to be thrown out, 1778; ... his astounding *volte-face* of 22/4/18, 1871; ... intrigues against the Government, his mind apparently being unhinged, 1784; false allegations against Lloyd George and Bonar Law published by, 1784–6; the tool of astuter men, 1786; ... his double-dealing denounced by Lloyd George, 1787–8; responsible for the statistics he questioned, 1788–9; not present, as he alleged, at Versailles discussion, 1790; his grave breach of discipline condoned by Asquith, 1891; dismissed, 1791'.

Max, Prince von Baden (1867–1929) German politician. Prince Max became the last Chancellor of Imperial Germany on 3 October 1918. It was hoped that his credentials as a liberal who had long advocated a compromise peace and opposed unrestricted submarine warfare would recommend themselves to President Woodrow WILSON, towards whose good intentions the German government looked for fair treatment in the face of impending defeat. Max quickly realised that it would take more than a cosmetic change to the German leadership to save the country from the dire consequences of its military failure. LUDENDORFF's dismissal was essential, as was a curtailment of the Kaiser's powers. Max's position, in the face of the Kaiser's intransigence, became increasingly impossible. On 9 November he announced that the Emperor and his son had abdicated and then abdicated himself, handing over the chancellorship of the German republic to the Social Democrat Friedrich EBERT, a decision which earned him the undying hatred of the German right. Max was a decent and honourable man overwhelmed by the tide of history.

Maxim, Hiram Stevens (1840–1916) US/ British inventor, an outstanding example of self-taught Yankee genius and ingenuity whose fertile imagination turned, in the 1880s, to the problem of producing effective and reliable automatic weapons. The result, first developed in 1884, was the Maxim gun, the first true machine gun, tripod-mounted, recoil-operated, water-cooled and belt-fed, capable of sustained fire of 600 rounds per minute over long periods of time. The gun's performance was enhanced in 1891 by the adoption of the new, smokeless cordite cartridge and it soon became the standard machine gun of the European Great Powers. In 1912 the British army replaced the Maxim with the Vickers, a modification of Maxim's design, his Maxim Gun Company having been absorbed by Vickers, but the Maxim remained the principal machine gun of the German and Russian armies throughout the Great War. Maxim settled in England, took British citizenship in 1900 and was knighted in 1901.

Maxim, Hudson (1853–1927) US inventor, younger brother of Sir Hiram Maxim, who made an equally important contribution to the technology of the Great War through his development of smokeless, fast-burning cannon powder, widely used by all armies in the conflict. He also developed maximite, an explosive charge that greatly improved the destructive power and effectiveness of torpedoes. He served as ordnance adviser to the United States Navy during the war.

Maxse, (Frederick) Ivor (1862–1958) British military commander and staff officer. Maxse commanded the Guards Brigade in the original British Expeditionary Force, before being sent home to raise and train the 18th (Eastern) Division, a unit of Kitchener's 'New Army'. His innovative training methods, in which the inculcation of independence and initiative in junior officers and NCOs was paramount, made 18th Division an elite unit, one of the few to capture all its objectives on the disastrous 1 July 1916. His outstanding performance as a divisional commander was recognised in his promotion to command the new XVIII Corps in January 1917. He commanded XVIII Corps with distinction throughout Third Ypres but was dismissed in June 1918 in the aftermath of the German spring offensive. Despite its importance and its suitability for a man widely regarded as the best troop trainer of the war, he regarded his appointment as Inspector-General of Training, BEF, in July 1918, as a badge of failure. A small, dynamic, voluble, pugnacious man, with a weakness for alliteration ('let's biff the bally Boche with the bayonet'), he loved nothing more than an argument but was always prepared to listen to good ideas, however lowly their origin. It is, therefore, somewhat ironic that this outstanding officer was – apparently – the 'the cheery old card' of Siegfried SASSOON's famous poem 'The General'.

Maxton, James (1885–1946) British socialist. Maxton was a schoolteacher and the son of schoolteachers. Throughout his life he retained the didactic instinct, though his classroom was the nation and his mission socialism. He joined the Independent Labour Party in 1904 and by 1914 was known throughout his native Scotland as a powerful orator and evangelist for the socialist cause, capable of speaking to working people in witty and moving language they could understand. In 1916 he was arrested on a charge of sedition following a speech calling for a general strike against government interference in the rights of trades unionists. He spent a year in prison. On his release he went to work in a shipyard, though one that was not involved in war work. After the war, Maxton became a much-loved figure and something of a parliamentary celebrity, but his wartime views were so unpopular, even on Clydeside, that his pet dog was stoned to death by an angry crowd.

Maxwell, Francis Aylmer (1871–1917) British military commander. Frank Maxwell was an Indian cavalry officer who won the Victoria Cross in the South African War (1899–1902), where he was also ADC to KITCHENER, who called him 'the Brat'. As CO of the 12th Battalion Middlesex Regiment (January–October 1916) and GOC 27th Brigade, in the elite 9th (Scottish) Division (October 1916–September 1917), Maxwell emerged as one of the finest combat commanders on the Western Front. He was one of those rare men who loved war. To many of his fellow Regulars, he was the ideal of a soldier, smart, fearless, courteous and kind, but firm. His personality was also capable of inspiring the 'citizen' soldiers whom he commanded at both battalion and brigade level. This was because there was far more to him than a mere 'gung-ho' thug. He was an original thinker, with innovative ideas about training. He had very strong views but was always prepared to listen and learn. As CO of the 12th Middlesex he often did this by

gathering his men round him for a 'chat'. His abolition of the degrading Field Punishment No. 1 (which allowed defaulters to be lashed to a fixed object in the open for several hours a day) soon after he was appointed to battalion command shows not only his self-confidence but also his sensitivity to the kind of men he was commanding. Most of all, however, he was a warrior, who inculcated his commands with the spirit of the offensive without losing their trust. He himself was always at the front. He was shot and killed by a German sniper on 21 September 1917 while observing the consolidation of positions won during the battle of the Menin Road Ridge. Throughout the war he wrote letters to his wife, revealing a curious mixture of touching human insight and crypto-fascism. These were published in 1921 as *Frank Maxwell V.C.: A Memoir and Some Letters*. He is buried in the Ypres Reservoir Cemetery, Belgium.

Maxwell, John Grenfell (1859–1929) British military commander. Maxwell began the war as British liaison officer at French GHQ but left in September 1914 to command British troops in Egypt. During the next two years Egypt became a major training, staging and supply base for the three military campaigns of Gallipoli, Salonika and Palestine. This was the source of much frustration to Maxwell, who began to see himself as little more than a quartermaster, with little influence on the actual fighting. In the spring of 1916 he asked to be relieved and returned home. The timing of his return was fateful. Within a few weeks he found himself C-in-C Ireland in the wake of the Easter Rising against British rule. He was given extensive powers to restore order, which he did within a few days but at the cost of turning a failed rising into a revolution. His decision to impose martial law and to execute fifteen of the rebels after trial by court martial transformed them from fools into martyrs and greatly strengthened the position of Sinn Fein within

Ireland. Maxwell has received savage criticism for his actions and is often portrayed as an ogre in Irish nationalist propaganda. But the real fault lay with the British government, and especially with Prime Minister ASQUITH, for what amounted to an abandonment of political responsibility, not only during the vital two weeks after the Rising but also for many months afterwards.

Maxwell, Ronald Charles (1852–1924) British staff officer, who succeeded Sir William ROBERTSON as Quartermaster-General of the British Expeditionary Force in January 1915 and held the post until Christmas 1917, when he was replaced (against HAIG's wishes) on age grounds. He was an outstanding administrator who presided effectively over the massive expansion of the BEF.

Mayo, Henry Thomas (1856–1937) US naval commander. Mayo became commander of the US Atlantic Fleet in June 1916 and retained the position after US entry into the war, with responsibility for all US warships in Atlantic and European waters.

Maze, Paul (1887–1964) French artist and liaison officer. Maze was a minor Impressionist painter who served with the British Expeditionary Force throughout the war, first as an interpreter and then as a liaison officer. An intelligent, perceptive and sympathetic observer, his memoir, *A Frenchman in Khaki* (1934), provides interesting insights into the British army and its leading personalities.

Mehmed V, Sultan (1844–1918) Ottoman Empire politician. As Sultan of the Ottoman Empire Mehmed was a mere cipher of the Young Turks who placed him on the throne in 1909. As Caliph, spiritual leader of Islam, Mehmed's declaration of holy war (*jihad*) against the Entente powers on 14 November 1914 disappointed expectations (not least German

ones) that it would provoke revolution among the Muslim subjects of the British and French empires.

Mehmed VI, Sultan (1861–1926) Last Sultan of Turkey. He succeeded his brother on 3 July 1918, presiding over the unconditional surrender of Turkish forces in October 1918 and signing the Treaty of Sèvres (1920) that dismembered the Ottoman Empire. This brought him into direct conflict with the nationalist forces of Mustapha KEMAL PASHA, who forced Mehmed into exile in November 1922.

Mehmed Talat Pasha *see* TALÂT PASHA, MEHMED

Meinertzhagen, Richard (1878–1967) British intelligence officer. Meinertzhagen was the kind of unconventional officer who often flourished on the 'extra Regimental attachments' common in the late Victorian and Edwardian army. In Meinertzhagen's case this was in East Africa, where he served with the King's African Rifles (on secondment from his regiment, the Royal Fusiliers). He spent the war in East Africa and Palestine, mostly in intelligence. He was a master of deception, contributing much to ALLENBY's success in 1917 and 1918. He later served as a delegate to the Paris Peace Conference, where he came to the notice of LLOYD GEORGE, who described him as the cleverest officer he had ever met, a compliment ill-designed to further Meinertzhagen's career. Meinertzhagen is now principally remembered for the publication, in 1960, of his *Army Diary, 1899–1926*, which is full of uncomplimentary observations about senior commanders. He became a renowned ornithologist after the war.

Mercier, Désiré Joseph (1851–1926) Belgian churchman, Roman Catholic Primate of Belgium. In the absence of King ALBERT I and the Belgian government, Cardinal Mercier became the effective leader of

German-occupied Belgium. He protested vehemently, consistently, publicly and bravely against German mistreatment, eventually succeeding in stopping the forced deportation of Belgians for work in German factories, and opposed German attempts to destroy the Belgian state through their encouragement of Flemish separatism.

Metaxas, Joannis (1871–1941) Greek soldier. Although only deputy chief of staff of the Greek army, Metaxas' pro-German and royalist credentials made him the most influential military figure at the Greek court. He favoured a Greek alliance with the Central Powers but was persuaded by King CONSTANTINE I to support the policy of neutrality. After the fall of the pro-Entente Prime Minister Eleutherios VENIZELOS in September 1915, Metaxas attempted once more to steer Greece towards the Central Powers. He raised royalist forces in Macedonia that co-operated with the Bulgarians, and the resistance he organised to Allied landings in Athens, in December 1916, inflicted serious losses and resulted in the dismissal of the Allied naval commander in the Mediterranean, Admiral DARTIGE DU FOURNET. This proved the summit of Metaxas' success, however. The problem with his policy was Allied naval supremacy, which made Greece extremely vulnerable to attack. The threat of this compelled Constantine's abdication in June 1917. Metaxas was exiled to Corsica, where he remained – powerless – for the rest of the war.

Meux, Hedworth (1856–1929) British naval commander, for whom the war came a little too late. As Commander-in-Chief Portsmouth (1912–16), he was responsible for securing safe passage of the British Expeditionary Force to France, his greatest achievement of the war. The King was among those who favoured Meux's appointment as First Sea Lord in succession to Prince LOUIS ALEXANDER of Bat-

tenberg, but Churchill made it clear that he would resign if FISHER were not appointed. Fleet command was also to escape Meux and in 1916 he retired at the age of 60. He could console himself with the fortune that he inherited in 1911 (when he changed his name from Lambton to Meux) and with his promotion to Admiral of the Fleet in 1915. He was sharply critical of JELLICOE's handling of the Grand Fleet at Jutland (31 May–1 June 1916) and used what influence he had to prevent Jellicoe's own promotion to Admiral of the Fleet. Meux was Conservative MP for Portsmouth from 1916 until 1922.

Michael, Grand Duke (1878–1918) A member of the Russian royal family and military commander, who put love before duty (not something to endear him to his brother, the Tsar) by eloping with and later marrying a twice-divorced commoner. Michael was allowed to return to Russia from exile in Austria only after the outbreak of war. Tsar NICHOLAS II abdicated in Michael's favour after the February Revolution of 1917, but Michael renounced the throne unless it was offered to him by a popularly elected constituent assembly. When this was not forthcoming, he gave his support to the Provisional Government. He was murdered in June 1918.

Michaelis, Georg (1857–1936) German Chancellor. Michaelis was essentially a civil servant, who spent the first three years of the war involved in managing grain supplies, a role in which he was a far from conspicuous success. In July 1917 he was the surprise choice to succeed BETHMANN-HOLLWEG as Imperial Chancellor, a post for which his subservience to LUDENDORFF was his only qualification. Michaelis was the first commoner to become Chancellor and was so obscure that the Kaiser had barely heard of him. He destroyed what little authority he had in the Reichstag by blaming an outbreak of mutiny in the German fleet on the Social Democratic Party and was forced to resign in October 1917, after barely four months in office. He was succeeded by HERTLING.

Michel, Victor (1850–1937) French military commander. Michel was appointed Vice-President of the Supreme War Council and Commander-in-Chief designate in January 1911. His tenure lasted less than a year, before he fell victim to the poisonous political animosities that impeded rational strategic planning in France. Michel was, in fact, prescient. He dismissed the currently fashionable view that any German attack on France would come from the German-occupied French province of Lorraine. He argued that the Germans would instead attempt an enveloping movement round the left flank of the French armies through Belgium. This seemed improbable to many observers at the time because the first-line German field army was too small to make such a strategy work. Michel recognised the problem too but believed that the Germans would overcome it by using their second-line reserves in the initial deployment. He thus anticipated two of the main aspects of the SCHLIEFFEN Plan. His response was to urge a French deployment along the Franco-Belgian border that would also deploy France's second-line reserves. The forces so deployed would stand on the defensive, seeking the most propitious time and place to take the offensive only when events on the battlefield began to unravel. Michel's reward was to be ridiculed. The right feared that the use of second-line reserves risked turning the professional army into a republican militia and an agent of social revolution. The left, in turn, feared that the degree of training required to make effective soldiers of reservists risked militarising the population. Having succeeded, for once, in uniting French political opinion, Michel was replaced by General JOFFRE. More importantly, Michel's suggestions were abandoned in favour of Plan XVII,

an all-out offensive in Lorraine designed to seize the strategic initiative and bring the war to a short, victorious conclusion that would not require the militarisation of French society. The plan was adopted not because of its military merits but because it was the plan that divided Frenchmen least. Michel became Military Governor of Paris. His removal from this post in August 1914 probably had more to do with his being right about the German deployment than with his alleged neglect of the capital's defences. He never held another command.

Micheler, Joseph Alfred (1861–1931) French military commander. By 1917 Micheler had risen to command the Reserve Army Group. In this capacity he was drawn into the planning of the proposed NIVELLE offensive, about which he soon developed grave doubts. Fearing the outcome and personal consequences of a frontal assault on the French Commander-in-Chief, Micheler opted instead for the flank attack of political conspiracy. But neither Micheler's plotting nor the resignation in March of General LYAUTEY, the Minister of War, and the subsequent fall of the BRIAND government could stop Nivelle, whose threat of resignation caused any effective opposition to evaporate. Reserve Army Group was dissolved after Nivelle's attack proceeded to its tragic conclusion. Micheler was given command of Fifth Army. Contemptuous of the caution displayed by PÉTAIN, Nivelle's successor as Commander-in-Chief, Micheler refused to adopt the strategy of 'defence in depth'. During the surprise German attack on the Aisne in May 1918, he suffered a serious defeat when German artillery fire and infantry infiltration tactics overwhelmed his troops, which were concentrated in the front line. This time his disobedience received the appropriate response. Prime Minister CLEMENCEAU ignominiously dismissed him, along with the Sixth Army commander, General DUCHÊNE.

Millerand, Alexandre (1859–1943) French politician. Millerand was twice French Minister of War, from 1912 to 1913 and from 1914 to 1915. Before the war he was an advocate of French rearmament and a supporter of the three-year conscription law. During the war he played a leading part in the mobilisation of the French economy, though Albert THOMAS increasingly undertook the organisation of munitions production from the spring of 1915. Millerand was a key supporter of JOFFRE, considering it a major part of his role to shield the autocratic Commander-in-Chief from political interference. His acquiescence in Joffre's dismissal in July 1915 of the Republican Left's favourite general, Maurice SARRAIL, from command of the French Third Army, and his subsequent failure to persuade Joffre to reinforce Sarrail in his new command at Salonika, severely weakened Millerand's political authority, however, and he did not survive the fall of the VIVIANI government in October 1915.

Mills, William (1856–1932) British inventor. Mills was the son of a Sunderland shipbuilder. After an apprenticeship as a marine engineer, he went to sea and soon displayed a talent for invention and innovation, especially in the field of metallurgy. He established the first aluminium foundry in the United Kingdom (in his native Sunderland in 1885) and did pioneering work on alloys. The onset of trench warfare in the late autumn and winter of 1914–15 saw the British Expeditionary Force handicapped by its lack of hand grenades, a particularly effective weapon in trench warfare. Mills turned his fertile mind to the problem and, in February 1915, designed a reliable and effective grenade. This consisted of a cast iron body filled with explosive. A tube, containing a detonator, fuse and percussion cap, ran down the centre of the grenade. An external lever, attached to a spring, restrained the striker. A pin, in turn, held the external lever. The user held the grenade so as to depress the lever, withdrew the pin and threw the grenade. The release of pressure on the lever activated the striker and detonated the grenade four seconds after release. In the confined spaces of trench warfare the percussive and fragmentation effect was considerable. The grenade entered service as the No. 5 Mills bomb. A factory for its manufacture was established in Birmingham and some 75M were produced during the war. Later modifications enabled it to be used as a rifle grenade (No. 23 and No. 36), a weapon that had considerable influence on platoon-based British infantry tactics in the last year of the war. The No. 36 grenade remained in British service until the 1960s. Mills was knighted in 1922.

Milne, (Archibald) Berkeley (1855–1938) British naval commander. Milne's pre-war career proceeded smoothly, eased by royal connections made during ten years spent in the royal yachts, two as commander. In August 1914 he was C-in-C Mediterranean, a post he had held since 1912. Admiral FISHER was contemptuous of Milne's appointment, believing that the Admiralty, under CHURCHILL and Prince LOUIS ALEXANDER of Battenberg, had sacrificed the public interest to their fear of royal disapproval. Milne's performance, once war began, merely confirmed Fisher's opinion. Milne's first priority was to intercept the German battle cruiser *Goeben* and the cruiser *Breslau*. They were spotted by the battle cruisers *Indomitable* and *Indefatigable* on 4 August, one and a half hours before the expiration of the British ultimatum to Germany. Bound by Admiralty orders, which he never thought to disobey, he made no attempt at a pre-emptive strike. Politically this was probably a wise decision. His subsequent actions, however, were far from wise. Convincing himself that the German ships would head west, for the Atlantic, he sent only one ship, the light cruiser *Gloucester*, in pursuit. Despite compelling evidence from the *Gloucester*'s captain, Howard Kelly, that the German ships were heading for the Dardanelles, neither Milne nor his subordinate, Admiral TROUBRIDGE, took decisive action. The escape of the *Goeben* and *Breslau* into the Sea of Marmora greatly strengthened the pro-German and pro-war party in Turkey. The Admiralty, only too aware of its own ambiguous role in the debacle, exonerated Milne, but he was crucified by the press, which expected the Royal Navy to 'close with the enemy' in the best traditions of Drake and Nelson. Milne never exercised command again.

Milne, George Francis (1866–1948) British military commander. Milne was an able gunner and Staff College graduate who was destined for a frustrating war spent largely in Salonika, where he was GOC 27th Division, GOC XVI Corps and, finally, GOC-in-C British forces, surviving under the often difficult control of three French commanders-in-chief. Milne's forces were small and often riddled with disease (especially malaria). They also suffered from the deliberate official neglect of the British Chief of the Imperial General Staff, Sir William RO-BERTSON, who had no wish to encourage offensive activity in a theatre that he regarded as an irrelevance. When Milne did get permission to advance, in the spring of 1917, his troops met with a sharp reverse at Lake Doiran, incurring heavy losses. He did not return to the offensive until the autumn of 1918, when the collapse of the Bulgarian army turned the Allied advance into a rout. Milne's troops were the first to enter Bulgaria and later occupied Constantinople. The constant in-fighting between the Allies at Salonika doubtless provided Milne with useful experience for when he became Chief of the Imperial General Staff in 1926. He ended his career as a field-marshal.

Milner, Alfred (1854–1925) British colonial administrator, businessman and politician. A leading imperialist of far-right views and a believer in 'efficiency', Milner was co-opted into government in 1914 to organise coal and food production. LLOYD GEORGE brought him into the War Cabinet in December 1916 and he became Secretary of State for War in April 1918, playing a leading role in the establishment of the Allied Supreme War Council and in the appointment of FOCH as Allied Commander-in-Chief. His fear of Bolshevism inclined him to favour an early peace but also encouraged his support for intervention in the Russian civil war. Several members of his celebrated *kindergarten* of able young administrators, with whom he surrounded himself while High Commissioner in South Africa, joined Lloyd George's entourage of unofficial advisers, known as 'the Garden Suburb' from their location in temporary accommodation in the grounds of 10 Downing Street.

Milyukov, Pavel Nikolaevich (1859–1943) Russian politician, the leading liberal critic of the Tsarist regime and a founder member of the centre-left Party of Constitutional Democrats (Kadets). Milyukov fully supported the Russian declaration of war, not least because it associated his country with Great Britain and France, to which he looked as beacons of progressivism and reform. During the war he was a member of the Progressive Bloc, subjecting the conduct of the war to a withering condemnation in a famous speech to the Duma in December 1916. He became Minister of Foreign Affairs in the Provisional Government formed after the overthrow of tsardom in the February Revolution of 1917, but his determination to keep Russia in the war and his support for constitutional monarchy alienated the Petrograd Soviet and rendered his position untenable. He resigned in May 1918, later helping ALEK-SEEV to form the Volunteer Army (the

'Whites') before fleeing to exile in France in 1919.

Mišić, Živojin (1855–1921) Serbian military commander. Mišić, who had been chief of staff during the Balkan Wars (1912–13), was recalled from retirement to command the First Army in 1914, playing a leading part in the defeat of the Austrian invasion that included a resounding victory at Rudnik in December. By January 1915 the Austrian invasion of Serbia had been completely repulsed, an astonishing achievement. A pugnacious man and an aggressive commander, he opposed the demoralising retreat through the mountains of Albania in the winter of 1915–16 occasioned by the German, Austrian and (eventually) Bulgarian invasion of Serbia that began in August 1915. Mišić himself suffered badly during the retreat, but by September 1916 he was able to assume command of a re-equipped Serbian army at Salonika. In the autumn of 1918 his troops were in the forefront of the Allied offensive that knocked Bulgaria out of the war. Mišić led his army deep into the Habsburg Empire, helping not only to ensure its collapse but also making inevitable the post-war creation of the South Slav (Yugoslav) state to which he had long aspired.

Mitchell, William Lendrum (1879–1936) US air force commander and pioneer of strategic bombing. 'Billy' Mitchell abandoned his university course in 1898 to fight as a private soldier in the Spanish-American War. He never resumed his studies. The influence of his father, who was US Senator for Wisconsin, obtained him a commission in the US Army Signal Corps. Mitchell's career prospered and, by 1913, he was the youngest officer on the US Army General Staff. By organisational chance the infant US aviation section was attached to the Signal Corps and in 1916 Mitchell became its head. After the United States' entry into the war, he was sent to France to observe the air war, where he

was immediately impressed and influenced by the GOC British Royal Flying Corps, Hugh TRENCHARD. Despite Mitchell's lowly rank – he was still only a major – he eventually talked General PERSHING, Commander-in-Chief of the American Expeditionary Force (AEF), into giving him command of the AEF's front-line air squadrons. He commanded these, together with Allied units, in the offensive against the St Mihiel salient in September 1918, unleashing an unprecedented air–ground attack on the German army. Mitchell was completely persuaded of the importance of air power but was prevented from proving his emerging theories of strategic bombing by the ending of the war. He was a man of great energy, determination and ambition, but his style was confrontational and his career marked by bitter feuds. His uninhibited post-war criticism of military authority for its failure to develop military aviation resulted in a spectacular court martial in 1925 and his retirement from the service.

Moltke, Helmuth Johannes Ludwig von (1848–1916) German military commander. Moltke succeeded SCHLIEFFEN as Chief of the German General Staff in 1906. He immediately, and characteristically, recognised his own deficiencies for such a position. He was nervous and highly strung and in far from robust health, a worrier more than a warrior. He found personal confrontations particularly draining. Most of all, he lacked the great commander's true self-confidence, which conferred the ability to make swift decisions in conditions of stress and confusion and to make them alone. Moltke was a man of enervating contradictions. He often expressed pessimistic insights about the fate of Germany and the world to his devoted wife. He feared that a war between the Great Powers would almost certainly not be decided by a single great battle but would degenerate into a 'long, weary struggle' with countries that would not 'acknowledge defeat until the whole strength of [their] people is broken'. The outcome of this struggle would be as ruinous for the victors as for the vanquished. Despite this recognition, he believed that war was inevitable. The rising military and industrial strength of Russia convinced him that, for Germany, it was better if the war came sooner rather than later. And he remained wedded to his predecessor's plan to win the war by striking successive knock-out blows against the armies of France and Russia. When the Kaiser delayed signing the German mobilisation order on 1 August 1914, it was Moltke who intervened decisively, though at great personal cost from which he probably never recovered, to insist that mobilisation must go ahead and the army must deploy against France first and through neutral Belgium. His pre-war rejection of Schlieffen's deathbed advice 'only keep the right wing strong' and his refusal to violate Dutch as well as Belgian neutrality have, however, damaged Moltke's reputation severely, especially among armchair strategists. In 1911, in response to fears of a French offensive towards Lorraine, he added newly created German corps to his left, reducing the relative strength of the German right, charged with making the enveloping movement round the French armies. Moltke compounded his 'error', once the war began, by redeploying two corps and a division to the east to stem the Russian invasion of East Prussia. Many commentators since, led by Wilhelm GROENER, have blamed the failure of the Schlieffen Plan, and Germany's subsequent defeat, on Moltke's tinkering. His real failure, however, was in not abandoning the whole mad idea. Once the invasion of France began to unroll, Moltke almost immediately lost control of events, allowing fatal gaps to develop between the German First and Second Armies, devolving key decisions to a junior officer, Colonel Richard HENTSCH, and failing to inspire, drive or replace his subordinate commanders. The Allied counter-attack on the Marne, beginning on 5 September, destroyed his hopes of a quick victory. Exhausted and despondent at the outcome of events, Moltke had a nervous breakdown and was replaced by Erich von FALKENHAYN nine days later.

Monash, John (1865–1931) Australian military commander. Monash was a citizen soldier of Prussian Jewish origin, whose pre-war service with the Australian militia emphasised the importance of thorough training, reconnaissance and planning, lessons that his professional experience as a civil engineer reinforced. Monash's reputation in Britain has been distorted by LLOYD GEORGE's description of him as one of the war's few authentic military geniuses, whose light was hidden from the political leadership by an anti-Semitic British High Command jealous of the abilities of a colonial 'amateur'. Nothing could be further from the truth. Monash was undoubtedly an exceptional man, but he was no 'genius'. His operations as GOC 4th (Australian) Brigade on Gallipoli and as GOC 3rd (Australian) Division (1916–17) and GOC Australian Corps (from June 1918) on the Western Front were often flawed, but he showed a capacity to learn from his mistakes. He was rarely fazed and could make rapid decisions under pressure, while his training as a barrister afforded him the power of clear exposition, an ability often lacking in his contemporaries. He understood the importance of careful preparation and that successful preparation meant getting the detail right. LIDDELL HART, in particular, much overrated him as a tactical innovator, largely on the basis of the battle of Le Hamel (4 July 1918). Generally, Monash played things by the book, pursuing limited objectives in set-piece battles supported by massive artillery resources. British High Command, far from holding back his career, actively supported him. HAIG was an early admirer, not least because of Monash's un-Australian attitude to discipline.

Mond, Alfred Moritz (1868–1930) British industrialist and politician. Mond was the son of a German-Jewish immigrant, Ludwig Mond, co-founder (with Sir J.T. Brunner) of the great chemical manufacturers Brunner-Mond. Alfred Mond trained for the bar. He joined his father's firm with some reluctance but eventually became its managing director, developing distinctive ideas about the future of industry. He was an exponent of rationalisation and amalgamation and investment in research. God would be on the side of the big industrial battalions taking advantage of economies of scale. He also recognised the need for industrial peace, seeking to identify workers with the fate of their industry through profit-sharing schemes and co-operation with the trades unions. The chemical industry was central to the British war effort. LLOYD GEORGE co-opted Mond to his new government in December 1916 as First Commissioner of Public Works. He was one of the 'men of push and go' to whom Lloyd George looked to achieve the mobilisation of the British economy for 'total war'. Mond remained in government until the end of the Lloyd George coalition, latterly as Minister of Health. He played a leading part in the creation of the British industrial giant Imperial Chemical Industries (1926) and continued to espouse the cause of industrial conciliation. He was created Baron Melchett in 1928. Mond was also a leading Zionist.

Monro, Charles Carmichael (1860–1929) British Commander-in-Chief in India 1916–20. Monro's career testifies that the pen is truly mightier than the sword, especially when Winston Churchill wields the pen. Monro rose effortlessly through divisional and corps command on the Western Front to become C-in-C Third Army in July 1915 despite HAIG's early dismissal of him as 'rather fat'. During his short command of Third Army, he was instrumental in instituting Army Schools for the training of senior officers, an innovation with far-reaching consequences. When Monro emerged merely stunned from the destruction of the Hooge chateau by four German shells on 31 October 1914, an explosion which mortally wounded Major-General Lomax and killed six staff officers, he may have thought that he was a 'lucky general', but fate was to decree otherwise. In October 1915 he was handed the poisoned chalice of GOC-in-C Mediterranean Expeditionary Force in succession to Sir Ian HAMILTON. Almost as soon as he arrived on the Gallipoli peninsula, Monro recommended evacuation of all Allied forces, a decision eventually confirmed by KITCHENER. 'He came, he saw, he capitulated,' wrote Churchill. The words have haunted Monro's reputation. They have also disguised the fact that Monro's assessment was correct and his evacuation plan one of the most brilliantly executed of the war and the only real achievement of the whole Gallipoli disaster. Monro returned to the Western Front as GOC-in-C First Army in January 1916. His command of First Army was undistinguished, including two distinct reverses – IV Corps' loss of part of the Vimy Ridge in May and the hopelessly bungled diversionary attack by XI Corps at Fromelles in June – and in October he was sent to India as Commander-in-Chief. Paddy Griffith has memorably described India as 'the sin-bin of the First World War', but its military resources represented the principal strategic reserve of the British Empire, and Monro proved the man capable of organising them. He greatly increased the power of the Indian army and its military efficiency, making a major contribution to the later victories of MAUDE in Mesopotamia and ALLENBY in Palestine.

Montague, Charles Edward (1867–1928) British journalist, soldier and writer. An impeccable Liberal, Montague was leader writer on the impeccably Liberal *Manchester Guardian* when the war broke out. After some initial intellectual confusion, he resolved his doubts and volunteered in September 1914. He used his credentials as an 'Alpinist' to obtain a commission in the 24th Royal Fusiliers (2nd Sportsman's Battalion). He was 47. He saw only a brief period of front-line service before being invalided home after injuring himself while practising grenade throwing. His editor on the *Manchester Guardian*, C.P. Scott, pulled strings to get Montague back to the front, but this time only as a press censor and later as a conducting officer, responsible for taking high-ranking visitors and members of the press round the trenches. He also wrote 'eyewitness' accounts of the fighting. He accepted the necessity for what he called 'cooked news' because the cause was just and the moral necessity of victory paramount in what he believed was a war of national survival. His contemporary zeal in these roles, however, stood in marked contrast to his post-war views, neatly summarised in the title of his best known book, *Disenchantment* (1922). Montague's disenchantment was not so much with the 'Crusade' as with many of the 'Crusaders', whose pettiness, selfishness and incompetence appalled his romantic sensibility. This not only distorted his own view of the war but also that of many of his readers.

Montecuc Coli degli Erri, Rudolf von

(1843–1922) Austro-Hungarian naval commander. Montecuc Coli was the decisive influence in the creation of a modern Habsburg navy. He identified Italy, Austria-Hungary's theoretical ally, as the greatest potential naval threat in a future war. He not only advocated naval expansion, inaugurating an Adriatic naval race, but also succeeded in persuading the imperial parliament to pay for his plans. By the time the 'Iron Count' retired in 1913, Austria-Hungary was a considerable naval power, deploying sixteen *Dreadnought* type battleships. Although, as Montecuc Coli predicted, Italy did emerge as an enemy, the fleet he built played little part in the war. Austrian

strategy chose to maintain the fleet 'in being' as a permanent threat to Italy and the Allies while pursuing a naval guerrilla war based on tip-and-run raiding of the Italian coast and submarine attacks on merchant shipping.

Montgomery, Archibald Armar (1871–

1947) British staff officer. Archie Montgomery was a protégé of Henry RAWLINSON. Their close association began at 4th Division in September 1914, when Rawlinson inherited Montgomery as his GSO1 (chief of staff) in succession to James EDMONDS, who had collapsed with strain. (There is no doubt that Edmonds felt his supercession deeply and resented Montgomery's subsequent rise to fame. The official historian's *Dictionary of National Biography* entry on Montgomery is wonderfully snide.) Montgomery followed Rawlinson to IV Corps and finally, in February 1916, to Fourth Army, where he remained as chief of staff for the rest of the war. Montgomery's reputation, like that of his chief, is dominated by two dates, 1 July 1916, the disastrous first day on the Somme, and 8 August 1918, the superbly planned and executed attack that LUDENDORFF called the 'black day of the German army'. His book *The Story of the Fourth Army in the Battles of the Hundred Days* (1919) gives a very fair-minded account of Fourth Army's role and is of particular value and interest on Amiens. Montgomery published nothing about the Somme, during which he deliberately destroyed the Fourth Army war diary dealing with the first part of the campaign. He was Chief of the Imperial General Staff from 1933 to 1936 and ended his career as Field-Marshal Sir Archibald Montgomery-Massingberd.

Montgomery, Bernard Law (1887–1976)

British soldier. Montgomery began the war as a lieutenant in the 1st Battalion Royal Warwickshire Regiment, part of 10th Brigade, 4th Division, in the original

British Expeditionary Force. During the retreat from Mons in August 1914, Montgomery's battalion was involved in the notorious St Quentin Incident that resulted in the court martial and cashiering of its commanding officer, Lieutenant-Colonel J.F. Elkington, who was compelled to redeem his reputation in the French Foreign Legion. (Despite this, Montgomery remained friends with Elkington, unveiling a memorial to his old CO in 1946.) Montgomery was severely wounded and left for dead at Meteren in October 1914, winning the DSO. After his recovery he spent most of the war as a staff officer, including spells with PINNEY's 33rd Division and HAMILTON GORDON's IX Corps before joining GORRINGE's 47th Division as GSO1 (chief of staff) in July 1918. From the perspective of his later fame as Field-Marshal Viscount Montgomery of Alamein, 'Monty' was generally dismissive of his experience in the Great War. He complained that he had served under two commanders-in-chief, FRENCH and HAIG, and never 'seen either of them'. His own command style has often been portrayed as a conscious rejection of the 'bad practice' he witnessed on the Western Front. In fact, 'the chief of staff system' he used as GOC Eighth Army in the Second World War was taken directly from his experience with Gorringe at 47th Division. His tactics, both at Alamein and in Normandy, also owed much to those employed by the BEF in the final days of the war.

Morel, Edmund Dene (1873–1924) British journalist. Morel established a pre-war reputation as a campaigning journalist and radical critic of British foreign policy. He played a leading part in the exposure of European mistreatment and exploitation of African workers and founded the Congo Reform Association. He became convinced that secrecy and lack of parliamentary control had corrupted the conduct of British foreign policy, a theme developed in his book *Morocco in Diplo-*

macy (1912). He opposed British entry into the First World War and was one of the key figures in the establishment of the Union of Democratic Control (UDC). This was an organisation of leading political figures devoted to returning foreign policy to parliamentary control and establishing arbitration as a key element in post-war international relations. The UDC became the most important anti-war organisation in Britain. Morel became its secretary and treasurer and one of its most prolific pamphleteers. As one of the most public faces of the UDC, Morel was exposed to odium in the press, especially the *Daily Express* (which incited violence against UDC meetings), and several times suffered physical attack. In 1917 he was arrested for a minor violation of the Defence of the Realm Act and sentenced to six months imprisonment, during which his health deteriorated and from which he never really recovered. Like many other leading figures in the UDC he left the Liberal Party after the war and joined Labour, memorably defeating Winston CHURCHILL at Dundee in the general election of November 1922.

Morgan, John Pierpont (1867–1943) American investment banker. Jack Morgan was the son of the founder of the great American banking house J.P. Morgan & Co. He was resident partner for the firm in London from 1898 to 1906 and developed a great love of England and close connections with the British royal family. When Morgan Senior died in March 1913, Jack succeeded him. Having an Anglophile as head of one of the world's most important financial institutions proved to be an asset for the British and not one they were slow to exploit. In January 1915 J.P. Morgan & Co. were appointed purchasing agents for the British government in the United States, eventually purchasing half of all the goods sold to the Allies during the war. Morgan's personal devotion to the Allied cause was so great that he also collaborated fully with British intelligence operations in the USA. His prominence as an Allied supporter resulted in an unsuccessful assassination attempt by a German sympathiser in July 1915. Morgan's career is usually compared unfavourably with that of his aggressive, pioneering father. But Morgan Senior was concerned mainly to attract foreign investment into the cash-starved late Victorian American economy; it was his son's destiny to bankroll the Entente, an activity that marked the United States' emergence as the world's greatest economic power and leading creditor nation. Morgan was a shy, modest man, scarred by an unpleasant streak of anti-Semitism often directed against Morgan's competitor New York banks, with their German-Jewish origins.

Morrell, Ottoline Violet Anne (1873–1938) British political hostess and literary patron, the flamboyant and bohemian daughter of a British general and granddaughter of the Duke of Portland. In 1906 her husband, Philip Morrell, became a Liberal MP. Lady Ottoline immediately took to metropolitan political life, becoming the centre of a circle of 'progressive' intellectual and literary figures, including Augustus JOHN, Henry LAMB, D.H. LAWRENCE and Bertrand RUSSELL. From 1913 this circle gathered at the Morrells' country home, Garsington Manor, in Oxfordshire. She and her husband were both staunch pacifists and during the war their house became a refuge for conscientious objectors. It was there that, in 1917 while on leave recovering from a wound, Siegfried SASSOON met Russell and the editor of *The Nation*, Henry Massingham, who encouraged him to make his famous statement against the war.

Moseley, Henry Gwyn Jeffreys (1887–1915) British chemist, whose paper 'The High Frequency Spectra of the Elements', published in 1913, established him as one of the leading scientists of his generation.

By using X-rays to study atomic structure, Moseley was able to achieve a more accurate positioning of the Periodic Table, resolving problems that had existed since the Table was first drawn up by Mendelev nearly fifty years before. During the Second World War someone like Moseley would almost certainly have been recruited to the 'boffins' war', but before the institution of conscription in 1916 there was nothing to prevent talented scientists from volunteering. Moseley joined the Royal Engineers. He was killed in action on Gallipoli on 10 August 1915. He has no known grave.

Mottershead, Thomas (1892–1917) British fighter pilot. Mottershead volunteered within days of the outbreak of war, joining the Royal Flying Corps, where he thought that his skill as a motor mechanic would be of use. He served as a mechanic until June 1916, when he qualified as a pilot. He was posted first to No. 25 Squadron and then to No. 20 Squadron on the Western Front. On 7 January 1917 he was on patrol with his observer, Lieutenant W.E. Gower, when his aircraft was attacked and set on fire. Despite being severely burned, Mottershead flew the aircraft back to his own lines and landed safely, saving the life of his observer. Sergeant Tom Mottershead died four days later and was posthumously awarded the Victoria Cross on 12 February 1917. He was the only non-commissioned officer to win the VC in the air war. He was also awarded the Distinguished Conduct Medal. He is buried in the Bailleul Communal Extension Cemetery, France.

Mottram, Ralph Hale (1883–1971) British soldier and writer. Mottram was commissioned as an officer in the 9th Battalion Norfolk Regiment, a Territorial unit, but spent much of the war in liaison duties with the civilian population of the Franco-Belgian border. These provided material for his post-war *Spanish Farm*

Trilogy (1927), a great commercial and critical success, which celebrated the continuity of human experience amid the destruction wrought by war on British and French civilisation.

Moynihan, Berkeley George Andrew (1865–1936) British surgeon. Moynihan, the son of a VC winner, was Professor of Surgery at Leeds University, where he had established himself as the leading figure in contemporary British surgery, especially that of the abdomen. As Consulting Surgeon to the British armies in France, his expertise was invaluable. Like all great (and not-so-great) surgeons he was a man of awesome self-assurance. He once operated on his own wife. When challenged about the ethics of this, he replied: 'My wife deserves the best.' In him, the British army got the best.

Mücke, Hellmuth Karl von (1882–1957) German sailor and war hero. Mücke was First Officer on the German light cruiser SMS *Emden*. On 9 November 1914 he led a raiding party ashore on Direction Island (in the Indian Ocean) to destroy a powerful British radio transmitter. While he was ashore, the *Emden* was intercepted and destroyed by HMAS *Sydney*. Mücke then began an epic voyage in an appropriated yacht, the *Ayesha*, in which he and his men sailed 1,700 miles until they were picked up by a German freighter. This disembarked them at the tip of the Arabian peninsula, from where they made their way, with exiguous help from the Turkish authorities, to Constantinople. Mücke's insistence on making public his criticisms of the Turks and his publication of two books about his adventures endeared him neither to German diplomats in Turkey nor to his fellow naval officers, who regarded him as a vulgar self-publicist. He was demobilised with the rank of captain, having spent most of the war in torpedo boats.

Müller, Georg Alexander von (1854–1940) German naval staff officer. As Chief of the Naval Cabinet from 1906, Müller was the Kaiser's chief naval adviser throughout the war. Although Müller's elevation owed much to the patronage of TIRPITZ, his views on naval strategy were closer to those of his sovereign, whose fear of a full-scale fleet engagement with the British he shared. Müller was also sceptical about the claims made for the operational effectiveness of U-boats and conscious of the grave political risks posed by the adoption of unrestricted submarine warfare. This moderation gradually alienated leading naval figures, not least his old mentor, Tirpitz. When the Kaiser sanctioned a return to unrestricted submarine warfare in February 1917, Müller's abandonment of his objections and willingness to try to convert Chancellor BETHMANN-HOLLWEG destroyed his moral authority in decision-making circles. By the time of his replacement in August 1918, he had already become an ineffective and marginal figure.

Müller, Karl Friedrich Max von (1873–1923) German sailor, who achieved international renown for his command of the light cruiser *Emden*, which enjoyed great success during the first weeks of the war in destroying Allied naval and merchant shipping, principally in the Indian Ocean. Müller combined elusiveness with humanity by first ensuring the safety of the crews whose ships he sank. The *Emden* was finally cornered by HMAS *Sydney* in the Cocos Islands and destroyed on 9 November 1914 with the loss of 134 men. Müller was captured. He spent most of the war in captivity before being repatriated to Germany, suffering from ill health, in October 1918.

Munro, Hector Hugh 'Saki' (1870–1916) British writer and soldier. Like another very English but very different writer, George Orwell, Munro began his working life in the Burma police but was forced to return to Britain after contracting malaria, a recurrent problem. Following a period as correspondent for the *Morning Post* in Russia and the Balkans, in 1904 he settled down to writing satirical short stories under the pseudonym 'Saki'. A dapper homosexual of strong Tory convictions, most of the work for which he is now remembered appeared first in the Tory press. Despite his age and ill health he volunteered for military service on 25 August 1914. He was killed by a German sniper on 14 November 1916 during the successful attack on Beaumont Hamel that terminated the Somme campaign. His last words were said to have been 'Put that bloody cigarette out!' 225 Lance-Sergeant H.H. Munro, 'A' Company, 22nd Battalion Royal Fusiliers, has no known grave.

Murdoch, Keith Arthur (1885–1952) Australian journalist. After being narrowly defeated by C.E.W. BEAN in a ballot to become Australian Official War Historian, Murdoch succeeded in reaching the Gallipoli battlefield only in August 1915 and only then to investigate alleged problems in the distribution of mail to the Australian Imperial Force. He immediately fell into a conspiracy with the British war correspondent Ellis ASHMEAD-BARTLETT, for whose uncompromising criticisms of the conduct of the campaign he agreed to act as courier by taking a letter to London for Prime Minister AS-QUITH. The plot was revealed by another British war correspondent, H.W. NEVINSON. Murdoch was arrested in Marseilles and Ashmead-Bartlett's letter confiscated. Undeterred, Murdoch proceeded to London, where he presented the criticisms to the British government, warmly supported by the NORTHCLIFFE press. Murdoch's intervention gave ammunition to those already opposed to the continuance of the Gallipoli campaign, but its importance in the dismissal of the British Commander-in-Chief, Sir Ian HAMILTON, has probably been overestimated. Murdoch's later

attempt, this time in conjunction with Bean, to have Brudenell WHITE succeed BIRDWOOD in command of the Australian Corps instead of Sir John MONASH was completely unsuccessful

Murray, Archibald James (1860–1945) British staff officer and military commander. Murray was an unhappy choice as Sir John FRENCH's chief of staff in the original British Expeditionary Force. His appointment represented a last minute compromise necessitated by Sir Henry WILSON's political unacceptability in the aftermath of the 'Curragh Mutiny'. Unfortunately, Murray inherited a group of subordinates who had all worked closely with Wilson at the War Office's Directorate of Military Operations, as well as a commander-in-chief who was a close friend of Wilson and who made no secret of his preference for Wilson's company and advice. Wilson himself hung about GHQ as MGGS, making no attempt to disguise his contempt for Murray and seeking to undermine his authority at every turn. Murray's position was, perhaps, intolerable, but he showed neither the force of character nor the ability to overcome the situation. His performance attracted censure from all sides. He could neither inspire nor drive. His orders were often confused and contradictory. His own morale and health were often poor and on one occasion the receipt of worrying news caused him to faint. His replacement by Sir William ROBERTSON in January 1915 was greeted with general relief. After successive appointments as Deputy Chief of the Imperial General Staff and Chief of the Imperial General Staff, Murray was given command of the Egyptian Expeditionary Force in January 1916. He brought the defences of Egypt into a superb state of organisation, an achievement for which he has rarely received credit, and advanced impressively into Palestine. But during the first and second battles of Gaza, in March–April 1917, he and his subordinates, notably

General DOBELL, made serious mistakes. These proved too much for the Prime Minister, LLOYD GEORGE, who replaced Murray with ALLENBY in June. Murray returned home as GOC-in-C Aldershot, a post he retained until the end of the war.

Murray, James Wolfe (1853–1919) British staff officer. Murray was an able, hard-working officer with a good knowledge of administrative minutiae. His appointment as Chief of the Imperial General Staff (CIGS) in October 1914, following the death of General Sir Charles Douglas, was unfortunate. Murray was utterly unable to exercise any influence or control over the Secretary of State for War, Lord KITCHENER, who treated him like a clerk. The system for the higher direction of the war, carefully constructed in the previous decade, collapsed overnight. Murray's failure resulted in his replacement, in December 1915, by the formidable General Sir William ROBERTSON, armed with unprecedented and unique powers as CIGS.

Mussolini, Benito Amilcare Andrea (1883–1945) Italian journalist and political agitator, the son of a blacksmith, who resigned from the Socialist Party in 1915 because of its opposition to war. He joined the army but after being wounded spent most of the war editing *Il Popolo d'Italia*, which he founded as a vehicle for extreme nationalist views such as a policy of Italian territorial aggrandisement and the suppression of 'unpatriotic elements'.

His wartime influence and importance, however, were much more limited than was subsequently claimed after his rise to power as leader of the Fascist Party in 1922.

Myers, Charles Samuel (1873–1946) British psychologist, whose use of the expression 'shell shock' in the *Lancet* on 13 February 1915 did much to dramatise the problem of wartime psychiatric casualties. The phrase was rooted in Myers' early belief, which he later recognised as completely erroneous, that war neurosis had a physical cause (shell blast). Myers soon came to understand that early treatment of psychiatric casualties was essential, and he was among the first to take psychiatry into the front line. Much could be done to restore soldiers to mental health by simple rest. More traumatised cases would need longer treatment from the growing band of army psychiatrists who were pushing back the frontiers of medical knowledge. From 1916 to 1918 Myers was consulting psychiatrist to the British army, establishing – often against fierce resistance from the military and medical authorities – the principles by which military psychologists now work. He often found the struggle exhausting and his efforts were little short of heroic. He was one of the great men of the war. He published *Shell Shock in France 1914–1918* in 1940, as a warning and reminder to those charged with treatment of psychiatric casualties in the Second World War.

N

Nash, John (1893–1977) British soldier and painter. Nash volunteered for military service on the outbreak of war and served on the Western Front. Although his reputation as a painter has been overshadowed by that of his brother Paul, who was an official war artist, John Nash's *Over the Top* (1918), based on his own experience, has become one of the most famous images of the war.

Nash, Paul (1889–1946) British soldier and war artist. Nash volunteered for military service on the outbreak of war and served on the Western Front as a subaltern in the Hampshire Regiment until May 1917, when he was injured and sent home. Nash was a well-known artist before the war, moving in the same circles as Stanley SPENCER, Mark GERTLER, and C.R.W. NEVINSON. An exhibition of war paintings, based on sketches he had made at the front, brought him to the attention of Charles MASTERMAN, head of the War Propaganda Bureau, who invited Nash to become an official war artist. He returned to the Western Front in November 1917. His war paintings include *The Menin Road*, *The Ypres Salient at Night* and *A Howitzer Firing*.

Navarre, Jean Marie Dominique (1895–1919) French fighter ace, the first pilot to record a double-victory in air combat. Famed for wearing a red silk stocking instead of a flying helmet, he had an almost suicidal approach to making kills. The death of his brother in action greatly distressed him, and he suffered a total nervous breakdown. He returned to combat towards the end of the war but was, unsurprisingly, far less effective than he had been.

Nelson, David (1886–1918) British soldier. Sergeant Nelson, together with Captain BRADBURY and Battery Sergeant-Major DORRELL, played a leading part in the famous action of 'L' Battery, Royal Horse Artillery, at Néry on 1 September 1914, acting as range setter to Bradbury's gun layer. Despite being severely wounded and ordered to retire, he stayed at his post until all ammunition was expended. Only after escaping from German captivity did he succeed in obtaining medical attention. He was commissioned in November 1914. Major David Nelson was wounded again during the German spring offensive of 1918 while serving with 'D' Battery, 59 Brigade, Royal Field Artillery. He died at the 58th Casualty Clearing Station, Lillers, on 8 April 1918 and is buried in the Lillers Communal Cemetery, Pas-de-Calais, France.

Nernst, Walter Hermann (1864–1941) German chemist, who pioneered the use of gas as a military weapon. His favoured method was tear gas produced by adding the irritant dianisidine chlorosulphonate to shrapnel shells. This was first used against the British at Neuve Chapelle as early as 27 October 1914 but produced no noticeable effect, and the experiment was deemed a failure. Nernst returned to his laboratory in Berlin and played no further part in Germany's gas warfare programme, which was developed by others, especially Fritz HABER. Nernst was awarded the Nobel Prize for Chemistry in 1920 for his pre-war work on heat theory and photochemistry.

Nevill, Wilfred Percy (1894–1916) British soldier. Prior to the great British offensive on the Somme, which began on 1 July 1916, Captain Nevill, a company commander in the 8th Battalion East Surrey Regiment, bought four footballs, one for each of his platoons. At zero hour Nevill instructed his men to kick the balls forward. He offered a cash prize for whoever got a ball closest to the German line. One of the balls was inscribed with the words: 'The Great European Cup. The Final. East Surreys v Bavarians. Kick off at Zero'. Nevill was a somewhat unusual officer (he often stood on the firestep to shout insults at the German lines), but he was not the first to use footballs in this way. His act is remembered because the day on which it took place became the most disastrous in the history of British arms. It has come to symbolise the naive enthusiasm, amateurism and doomed public-school team spirit of the Kitchener armies. Nevill was also symbolically killed in the attack, and no one was able to claim his prize. He is buried in Carnoy Military Cemetery. Two of the balls did survive, however. One is in the National Army Museum, the other in the Museum of the Queen's Regiment.

Nevinson, Christopher Richard Wynne (1889–1946) British war painter, the son of H.W. NEVINSON, journalist and war correspondent, and his wife Margaret, a feminist and suffragist. Nevinson trans-

ferred his parents' political radicalism into the artistic arena. By the outbreak of war, he was a leading figure in the artistic avant garde, both in France and Britain, where he staged well-publicised 'events'. He was co-signatory with Marinetti of the Futurist manifesto and was closely associated with Wyndham LEWIS and the Vorticists. As a pacifist, he joined the Red Cross on the outbreak of war, later serving in the Royal Army Medical Corps, nursing wounded soldiers in London. He was invalided out of the army with rheumatic fever in January 1916. He exhibited a collection of his war paintings in September 1916, including the famous *Machine Gun*, with its obvious Cubist influences. The title is significant. The picture showed two French soldiers and might legitimately have been called 'Machine Gunners', but Nevinson chose to emphasise the instrument of war. The picture is dominated by a sense of the mechanical, industrial, metallic nature of modern war. The robot-like soldiers serve the gun, rather than the other way round. Nevinson's exhibition brought him to the attention of the Great War's most important artistic patron, Charles MASTERMAN, head of the War Propaganda Bureau, who invited him to go to France as an official war artist. Nevinson was not inhibited by his 'official' status. He loved the work and took pride in making unsanctioned trips to the trenches. He regarded himself as an emissary between the front-line soldier and the incomprehending civilians who needed to be told the 'bitter truth'. The realistic *Paths of Glory*, which showed dead British soldiers lying in front of a barbed wire entanglement, was not exhibited until after the war, though most of Nevinson's paintings were well received, not least by soldiers themselves.

Nevinson, Henry William (1856–1941) British journalist. Nevinson became foreign correspondent of the *Daily Chronicle* in 1897. He achieved an outstanding reputation as a war correspondent for his coverage of the South African War (1899–1902). He later exposed slavery in Portuguese Angola and became one of the leading male campaigners for female suffrage, a position of considerable moral courage in the social and political climate of the time. Nevinson's radical political credentials did not endear him to official opinion (even in a Liberal government) and he was not included in the first batch of accredited war correspondents. This did not prevent him from reporting the war both on the Western Front and Gallipoli, where he was wounded. He was among those journalists who refused the offered knighthood at the end of the war.

Newbolt, Henry John (1862–1938) British poet and official historian. Newbolt was the son of the Vicar of Bilston, in the industrial heartland of the English Black Country. He was a contemporary of Douglas HAIG at Clifton College and became a barrister after leaving Cambridge. He began publishing novels in the early 1890s but became best known for his 'sea songs', especially 'Admirals All' and 'Drake's Drum', which celebrated British imperial power and the daring individuals of 'The Island Race' who had acquired it. He also wrote the now much-mocked 'Vitaï Lampada', with its evocation of the public-school spirit, fair play, loyalty and faithfulness unto death. His poetry remained popular throughout the war, much of which he spent as Controller of Wireless and Cables. The titles of his wartime publications, *The Book of the Blue Sea* (1914), *The Book of the Thin Red Line* (1915), *The Book of the Happy Warrior* (1917), are redolent of his attempts to fit the Great War into a comforting English and Christian tradition that was to appear increasingly hollow. His *St George's Day* (1918) helped propagandise one of the Royal Navy's most famous actions, the raid on Zeebrugge, and was firmly in the tradition of 'Admirals All'. Sir Henry Newbolt wrote

volumes four and five of the official naval history of the war.

Nicholas II (1868–1918) Tsar of all the Russias. The last Tsar had many attractive qualities. He was a loving husband and father. He had a high sense of duty. He was personally modest and self-effacing, with a simple – though deep – religious faith. But he was also poorly educated, inexperienced and unimaginative. He seemed pathologically incapable of engaging in dialogue and found it difficult to distinguish between reasoned argument and treason. Although he was not irredeemably stupid, like his wife, he was often apathetic and fatalistic, temperamentally incapable of concentrating for any length of time on complex issues. Unfortunately, most of the issues that confronted him after his sudden elevation to the throne following the death of his father in 1894 were complex. Russia was a vast country undergoing rapid modernisation, including industrialisation, urbanisation, migration and population growth, all of which subjected tsarist autocracy to unprecedented strain. Amid these uncertainties Nicholas truly understood one thing: that he was an autocrat whose powers were granted by God. His overriding concern was to preserve his authority and to pass it on, untrammelled, to his successors. Even had he been more intelligent, the depth of this belief would have given him little room for manoeuvre. Nicholas only compromised his views under extreme pressure, as in the Revolution of 1905 that followed Russian defeat in the war with Japan. And when he did yield authority to the Duma he always regretted it. This gave his reign its characteristic rhythm of obstruction, concession and reaction. By 1914 reaction was once more in the ascendant. During the diplomatic crisis that followed the assassination of Archduke FRANZ FERDINAND at Sarajevo, Nicholas did not actively seek war, but he could see no alternative to supporting Serbia and was compelled to submit to the discipline of events. In the short term the Russian political establishment rallied to the crown, but national solidarity was rapidly compromised by economic mismanagement, inflation and, above all, military defeat. The loss of Poland, which followed the crushing reverse at Gorlice-Tarnów in May 1915, led to a temporary compromise with the forces of parliamentary liberalism. But ultimately, and fatally, it persuaded the Tsar against the advice of nearly all his ministers to leave St Petersburg and go to the front to take command of the army. This had the doubly damaging effect of associating the Tsar personally with further military defeats and of handing the government over to the Tsarina ALEKSANDRA and RASPUTIN, whose systematic removal of competent ministers brought Russia to the brink of revolt. By the end of 1916 it was openly stated, even on the floor of the Duma, that the Tsar must go. It was entirely characteristic of Nicholas that he should bring on the moment himself by his complete misunderstanding of events in St Petersburg in the spring of 1917; his attempt at repression provoked open mutiny. It soon became clear that the Tsar's position was untenable, and he abdicated in favour of his brother, Grand Duke MICHAEL. The Bolsheviks murdered Nicholas and his family in the Siberian town of Ekaterinburg on 16 July 1918. The conjunction of Nicholas's understanding of his office, his personality and the times in which he lived meant, in the end, that the only thing he could realistically do for his beliefs was to die for them. He was canonised by the Russian Orthodox Church in 2000.

Nikola Petrovic Njegos (1841–1921) King of Montenegro, a devious, manipulative Balkan monarch who attempted to aggrandise Montenegro through a policy of divide and rule. His failure owed much to the lack of trust that he inspired in friend and foe alike and more to his inability to offer anything tangible in return for his demands, especially effective military support. The collapse of Serbia in October 1915 put his ambitions into cruel perspective. The Austro-Hungarian army occupied Montenegro in 1916 and Nikola fled to Italy. He was deposed in November 1918. Montenegro emerged from the war not as a major player in Balkan politics but as a province of the new state of Yugoslavia.

Nikolai Nikolaevich, Grand Duke (1856–1929) Russian military commander, a professional soldier and uncle of the Tsar, who was Commander-in-Chief of the Russian army from July 1914 until August 1915. Russia's hopeless communications system meant that Nikolai exercised little control over his vast armies, spread over hundreds of miles of front. Initiative (or lack of it) necessarily rested with local commanders. They had mixed success. In East Prussia Russian armies, superior in number, suffered humiliating defeats by the Germans in 1914 at Tannenberg and the Masurian Lakes. But in Galicia considerable success was achieved against Austria-Hungary in August 1914. In 1915, however, disaster struck here too. The German breakthrough at Gorlice-Tarnów in May inflicted colossal casualties and led to the virtual Russian evacuation of Poland. The Tsarina blamed Nikolai and brought pressure to bear on her husband to dismiss him, which he did on 23 August, before taking command of the army himself, a decision pregnant with danger. Nikolai spent the rest of the war in the Caucasus, presiding over the military victories of General YUDENICH. In March 1917 he added his decisive voice to those advising the Tsar to abdicate. The Grand Duke died in exile in France.

Nitti, Francesco Saverio (1868–1953) Italian politician. Nitti split from his close political associate Giovanni GIOLITTI over the issue of Italian neutrality in 1914. Nitti was an economist. His analysis of

Italy's economic position, especially its lack of money and coal, convinced him that the country's long-term future lay in co-operation with the Allies. He was also keen to establish closer economic ties with the United States. He brought these perceptions to the post of Treasury Minister, when he joined the government of Vittorio ORLANDO in October 1917. He won the battle for control over the Italian war economy by securing the resignation of Alfredo DALLOLIO, the Minister of Munitions, who had become embroiled in a financial scandal. He also pursued British and American aid and was successful in obtaining financial credits and supplies of coal. Nitti's determination not to alienate the British and Americans was apparent when he became Prime Minister in 1919. He reduced military expenditure and opposed the drive to colonisation. Faced with D'ANNUNZIO's occupation of Fiume, an act that no rational economist would ever have perpetrated, he attempted to ignore the problem but his government succumbed within a year. The advent of MUSSOLINI completed his political eclipse and he was driven into exile in 1924.

Nivelle, Robert Georges (1856–1924) French military commander, whose dramatic rise from artillery regiment commander in 1914 to French Commander-in-Chief by December 1916 ended in mutiny and defeat. Nivelle was undoubtedly a skilful and imaginative gunner. He established his reputation as commander of III Corps at Verdun, especially through the recapture of Fort Vaux (7 June 1916) and Fort Douaumont (24 October 1916). These successes rested principally on the achievement of overwhelming local artillery superiority, though he also made excellent use of deception and specially trained infantry. By the end of 1916 France was desperate for an end to the war. Peace overtures were even considered, though eventually rejected. If a negotiated peace could not deliver France from her suffering, the only alternative

was victory. JOFFRE had repeatedly shown himself unable to achieve this and in December 1916 he was sacrificed. Joffre was like the old family doctor, solid, methodical, trustworthy, but his treatment was painful and offered no prospect of a cure. Nivelle was the charming, eloquent and self-confident quack, who told the patient what he most wanted to hear: 'Follow my advice and you will get well, and not only that but the medicine won't hurt.' Nivelle's plan for victory without tears was based on the operational method he had evolved at Verdun, but on a much larger scale. The German line would be breached using massed artillery. French infantry would pour through the gap and roll up the German line. All in forty-eight hours. If the plan failed, the battle would be called off. There would be 'no more Verduns'. Doubts increasingly began to set in. Much French military opinion was opposed. General LYAUTEY, the War Minister, resigned and the BRIAND government fell. But their successors failed to stop Nivelle, who was driven on by his charismatic (and dying) chief of staff D'Alenson. What little chance of success the plan had was fatally compromised by the German 're-treat to the Hindenburg Line'. Despite this, the Nivelle offensive went ahead on 16 April 1917. By 9 May it had cost 130,000 French casualties for minimal gains. Its failure struck a damaging blow against French military and national morale. The French army mutinied, refusing to take part in further attacks. Nivelle was dismissed on 15 May and replaced by Philippe PÉTAIN. After his replacement, Nivelle became the 'man who never was' in French history, his memory virtually expunged from popular consciousness by that of Joffre, FOCH and Pétain.

Nixon, John Eccles (1857–1921) British military commander, whose appointment as Commander-in-Chief, Mesopotamia, in April 1915 marked a turning point in the conduct of the war in the Middle East. In the early part of the war British strategy was hampered by a serious division of authority between the British government and the government of India. The British government favoured a cautious policy designed to protect the oil fields around Basra, but the government of India, with its traditional concern to maintain British hegemony in the region, a policy directed as much against Britain's ally Russia as against her enemy Turkey, favoured a 'forward' policy. Nixon was chosen as the instrument of this policy by the Indian government. The policy was entirely suited to Nixon's aggressive personality and gambler's instincts. He shared the common British contempt for the fighting capacity of the Turkish army. He also overestimated the power of his own forces and the difficulty of the terrain in which they would be operating. The initial successes of his field commander, Major-General C.V.F. TOWNSHEND, encouraged him in October 1915 to order an advance on Baghdad, despite Townshend's objections, a decision approved in London. Townshend's small, inadequate force was halted by the Turks at Ctesiphon in November and forced to retreat to Kut-al-Amara, where it was besieged from December 1915 until its surrender in April 1916, one of the worst defeats in British imperial history. The Mesopotamia Commission, which investigated the calamity between August 1916 and April 1917, placed most of the blame for the reverse on Nixon's reckless optimism, and his career was ruined. Only the end of the war in 1918 saved him from worse repercussions.

Njegovan, Maximilian (1898–1930) Austro-Hungarian naval commander. Njegovan commanded the First Battleship Squadron from the beginning of the war until February 1917, when he succeeded Admiral HAUS as Commander-in-Chief of the Austro-Hungarian navy. The navy's long periods of operational inactivity were a fertile breeding ground for nation-

alist tensions. In February 1918 a mutiny took place at Cattaro, led by Czech nationalist seamen. The mutiny was suppressed within forty-eight hours, but Njegovan was blamed for allowing it to occur in the first place. He was dismissed and replaced by the more energetic Admiral HORTHY.

Nordmann, Charles (1881–1940) French mathematician and astronomer. Nordmann's mobilisation in the French artillery in August 1914 gave him a personal insight into the importance of artillery in modern war. In particular, he realised the importance of being able to locate and destroy enemy guns at long range, beyond human vision. He turned his scientific mind to the problem and soon realised the possibility of locating enemy guns by calculating the time between the arrival of a shell at different points along a measured base. His first attempts to do this used men with stop watches to make the key measurements, but under the patronage of Lucien BULL, at the Institut Marey in Paris, he began to seek a more 'objective', instrumental solution that dispensed with the need for human observation. It was this work that attracted the attention of the British and convinced them to set up their own field experiments under the direction of the physicist Lawrence BRAGG. Bragg's team – especially William TUCKER and Joe GRAY – made significant changes to the Bull–Nordmann system that turned 'sound ranging' into an effective weapon in the artillery war.

Northcliffe, Viscount *see* HARMSWORTH, ALFRED CHARLES WILLIAM

Norton, Richard (1872–1918) American philanthropist, who founded the American Volunteer Motor-Ambulance Corps for service on the Western Front. This later merged with the similar group founded by the banker Herman HARJES. The group refused to accept militarisation in the autumn of 1917, a consequence of

US entry into the war the previous April, and disbanded.

Norton-Griffiths, John (1871–1930) British public works contractor, politician and adventurer, whose commitment to the imperial cause earned him the nickname 'Empire Jack'. He founded the firm of Griffiths & Co., engineers and contractors for the construction of tunnels in clay. On his own initiative he went to France to press the military high command to adopt a system of tunnelling using the rapid and silent technique of 'clay kicking'. He was quickly appointed Engineer-in-Chief's liaison officer for mining work. Together with the British Expeditionary Force's Inspector of Mines, Brigadier-General R.N. Harvey, he brought military mining on the Western Front to a peak of efficiency, culminating in the great mine explosions that preceded the Battle of Messines on 7 June 1917. In 1916 Norton-Griffiths was sent to Romania to destroy its oil wells before they fell into German hands.

Norwest, Henry 'Ducky' (1888–1918) Canadian soldier, a Metis-Cree Indian, whose 115 confirmed kills earned him a reputation as the British army's top sniper on the Western Front. His chosen weapon was the Ross rifle, useless and dangerous in the hands of ordinary infantry but accurate and powerful in the hands of a skilled marksman who could keep it clean. Norwest was killed in action on 18 August 1918 while serving with the 50th Battalion Canadian Infantry (Albert Regiment), simultaneously killing the German sniper who shot him.

Noske, Gustav (1868–1946) German politician. Noske was a Social Democrat with an unusual interest in colonial and military affairs. His support for the war effort was gradually undermined by the Third Supreme Command's inflexibility over war aims, and he voted for the Reichstag Peace Resolution in July 1917. His subduing of the naval mutiny at Kiel as a member of the last Imperial government recommended him to the Weimar Republic's first Chancellor, Noske's fellow Social Democrat Freidrich EBERT. Noske recruited the *Freikorps* and used them to suppress the left-wing Spartacist revolt. He was equally resolute in using the army to suppress a workers' rising in Berlin but resigned from the SCHEIDEMANN government in March 1920 when he failed to persuade the army to act decisively against the right-wing KAPP putsch.

Novello, Ivor (1893–1951) Stage name of David Ivor Davies, British actor, composer, songwriter and dramatist, who wrote one of the most famous songs of the war, 'Keep the Home Fires Burning', in 1914. It was a tremendous popular success that captured the contemporary mood of sentimental yearning and made him rich and famous. Novello served in the Royal Naval Air Service, mainly as a clerk in the Air Ministry. After the war he became one of the leading figures of British musical theatre.

Nungesser, Charles (1883–1927) French fighter ace, more responsible than most for the image of the fighter pilot as the 'cavalier of the clouds', often seeming to go straight from a fashionable Parisian nightclub into combat. But he was also a dedicated patriot who returned to the fray despite being wounded many times. It was his frequent grounding through wounds that limited his victories to forty-five. He disappeared in May 1927 trying to fly the Atlantic westwards.

O

Oliver, Henry Francis (1865–1965) British naval staff officer, an able man of few words, who suffered from the besetting Royal Navy sin, an inability to delegate. This had a seriously inhibiting effect on the efficiency of the naval war staff, whose inexplicable failure in 1916 to send Room 40's decrypted German wireless signals to the Grand Fleet was described by JELLICOE as 'absolutely fatal' to the chances of securing an overwhelming British victory at the battle of Jutland. It took Admiral HALL's persuasive powers, exerted over many months, to convince Oliver to convert Room 40 into a section of the Naval Intelligence Division so that this situation would not recur. Oliver's attitude to the introduction of the convoy system was as ambiguous and dilatory as that of Jellicoe. Oliver was, nevertheless, an able technician who did much to improve navigation training and the accuracy of mine laying.

Orlando, Vittorio Emmanuele (1860–1952) Italian politician, who became Prime Minister in 1917 in the crisis that followed the Italian army's shattering defeat at Caporetto (October–November). Orlando played a major part in rallying Italian morale and in re-establishing Italy in the eyes of her Allies. He presided over the Italian triumph at Vittorio Veneto a year later. As leader of the Italian delegation at the Paris Peace Conference, how-ever, he and his Foreign Minister, Sidney SONNINO, struggled to reap the rewards of victory, their territorial ambitions in the Adriatic falling foul of President Woodrow WILSON's principle of national self-determination. Orlando's failure to obtain the 'Italian' city of Fiume brought down his government in July 1919. The advent of MUSSOLINI completed his political eclipse.

Orpen, William (1878–1931) British war artist. By 1914 Orpen was a well-known portrait painter of social and public figures. From 1916 onwards he became a sort of court painter to the British High Command, completing portraits of CHURCHILL, DERBY, HAIG, PLUMER and TRENCHARD. This role was originally pursued under the semi-official patronage of Sir John COWANS (Quartermaster-General of the British army), but in 1917 he was invited by Charles MASTERMAN (head of the War Propaganda Bureau) to become an official war artist. His painting of the signing ceremony of the Treaty of Versailles (*The Signing of Peace*) in the Hall of Mirrors became one of his most famous. Although essentially an establishment painter, Orpen developed a deep respect and affection for the suffering and resilience of the ordinary British soldier, whom he revealingly described as 'the British working man in khaki'. He tried to capture these feelings in his most controversial painting, *To the Unknown British Soldier in France*, which showed two ghostly figures of soldiers guarding a flag-draped coffin. The painting provoked so much public hostility that he was compelled to paint the figures out.

Owen, Wilfred Edward Salter (1893–1918) British war poet, the son of a railway worker from Shropshire, generally accepted as the finest English language poet of the war. When the war broke out Owen was teaching English in France. He returned to England in 1915, enlisting in the Artists' Rifles in October. In January 1917 he was sent to France as a second lieutenant in the 2nd Battalion Manchester Regiment. On 1 May his commanding officer noticed that he was behaving strangely. He was diagnosed as suffering from shell shock and sent to the Craiglockhart Military Hospital in Edinburgh for treatment. There he met the poet Siegfried SASSOON, who took an interest in the poems Owen had started writing about the war. Under Sassoon's critical eye Owen's writing became less self-consciously poetic, more colloquial, more direct and more powerful. During the following months he produced some of his most famous poems, 'Anthem for Doomed Youth', 'Disabled', 'Dulce et Decorum Est' and 'Strange Meeting'. Owen was passed fit for active service in August 1918, rejoining his battalion on the Western Front in September. On 1–2 October 1918 he repelled a German counter-attack, killing a large number of Germans with one of their own machine guns, an event about which he wrote exultantly to his mother and for which he was later awarded the Military Cross. He was killed on 4 November while leading his men across the Sambre Canal. He was 25. The telegram bringing news of his death arrived at his parents' house in Shrewsbury as the Armistice bells were sounding across the town. Only five of

Owen's poems appeared in print during his short life. Sassoon's publication of Owen's *Collected Poems* in 1920 (of which only 730 copies were printed) and, more particularly perhaps, the new edition by Edmund BLUNDEN in 1931 began the establishment of Owen's position in the great canon of English poetry. But it is only since the 1960s that he has become established as an iconographic figure, perhaps *the* iconographic figure, in British perceptions of the war, something that owes much to the presence of his poetry on school literature syallabuses, where it provides many young people with their first (and often their only) awareness of the Great War. Owen's youth, idealism, courage and tragic death have come to symbolise the 'futility' of war in general and the Great War in particular. His poetry and his life, however, were more complex than this current judgement allows.

Oxenham, John (1852–1941) British poet, whose entry in this volume alphabetically adjacent to that of Wilfred OWEN is deliciously ironical. Owen, now firmly established as one of the most important cultural figures of the war, was completely unknown to the British public in his lifetime. Oxenham, now almost completely forgotten, was the most popular poet of his day, his slim collections of cheaply priced verse selling by the hundred thousand. It is a widely held, but mistaken, view that only 'anti-war' poets wrote truthfully about the nature of modern war. Oxenham does not disguise the brutal realities of high explosive but – unlike Owen – offers a consolatory explanation of the suffering, which he himself clearly felt, within the prevailing Christian vision of the war, dominated by Christ's 'sacrifice' on the Cross. Oxenham's verse has a palpable sincerity that, in its day, touched the lives of millions.

P

Paderewski, Ignacy Jan (1860–1941) Polish politician, who used his position as an internationally renowned concert pianist to propagandise the cause of Polish nationalism. In 1917 he became the Washington representative of the Polish National Committee (based in Paris), playing an important part in securing Woodrow WILSON's support for Polish independence, the Thirteenth of the US President's Fourteen Points.

Page, Frederick Handley (1885–1962) British aircraft designer and manufacturer, who opened the world's first aircraft factory in 1909. During the war Handley Page specialised in building bombers, culminating in the O400, the first British four-engined bomber, deliberately designed to undertake strategic bombing.

Page, Walter Hines (1855–1918) US journalist and diplomat. Page's pre-war career was largely spent in journalism and publishing. He edited *Forum* (1890–95) and *Atlantic Monthly* (1896–99) and was one of the founding partners of the great publishing house Doubleday, Page & Co. His involvement in the politics of the Progressive era and support for Woodrow WILSON brought him, somewhat unexpectedly, to London in 1913 as US Ambassador, a position he retained until near the end of the war. Page was an uninhibited Anglophile and a friend of the

British Foreign Secretary Sir Edward GREY. He believed that the future of civilised values depended on an Allied victory. He was an early convert to US belligerency, which he urged on his government from 1915 onwards. This lessened his influence in Washington, where his President was desperate to maintain US neutrality. Despite the unpalatable nature of Page's advice, however, Wilson did not replace him.

Painlevé, Paul (1863–1933) French politician, a celebrated mathematician, who entered parliament in 1910, soon establishing himself as leader of the Republican Socialists. He took a keen interest in military affairs, especially aviation. He was an early and persistent critic of JOFFRE and the most important supporter of General SARRAIL and the 'Eastern' strategy. After entering the Cabinet in October 1915 as Education Minister in BRIAND's government, Painlevé continued to monitor military events closely, coming to favour PÉTAIN's defensive strategy and lobbying for his appointment as Commander-in-Chief. In March 1917 he became War Minister in the RIBOT government. He was appalled by the prospect of the NIVELLE offensive but proved powerless to prevent it. The offensive's disastrous outcome did, however, allow him to promote Pétain to command of the French armies in May 1917. He was also active in repairing the damage inflicted by the French army mutinies. He served briefly and ineffectively as Prime Minister from September to November 1917.

Pakenham, William Christopher (1861–1933) British naval commander, an officer of high intelligence and professional ability, shrewd enough to make his talents more palatable to the Edwardian navy under a veneer of witty eccentricity and sartorial elegance. He commanded the 2nd Battle Cruiser Squadron at Jutland (31 May–1 June 1916), flying his flag in HMS *New Zealand*, which came through the thick of the fighting unscathed, confirming its reputation as a 'lucky ship'. Pakenham succeeded BEATTY as C-in-C Battle Cruiser Fleet in December 1916, remaining in command for the rest of the war.

Paléologue, Georges Maurice (1859–1944) French diplomat, who became Ambassador to Russia in January 1914. During the July Crisis of 1914, against the stated wishes of his own government expressed only a few days earlier by President POINCARÉ and Prime Minister VIVIANI during their state visit, Paléologue encouraged the Russian government to take a hard line against Germany, promising (on his own authority) full French diplomatic support. After the war broke out, he urged an immediate Russian offensive against East Prussia to relieve German pressure on France. The Russian Chief of the General Staff, Yakov ZHILINSKI, yielded to this pressure with disastrous consequences for the Russian armies. Paléologue was an ambitious intriguer. His role during the July Crisis was central and did much to encourage conspiracy theorists, some of whom see him (wrongly) as Poincaré's 'warmonger'.

Pankhurst, Christabel Harriette (1880–1958) British feminist. Christabel Pankhurst was born into a radical Manche-

ster professional family and was politically active from an early age. In 1901 she joined the National Union of Women's Suffrage Societies (NUWSS) but two years later, frustrated by its apparent lack of success, formed the Women's Social and Political Union (WSPU), together with her mother and sister. In 1905 she discovered the power of the politics of gesture by deliberately interrupting a Liberal Party meeting, getting arrested, refusing to pay the fine and going to prison. The resulting publicity galvanised the suffrage movement and resulted in a leap in WSPU membership. The Pankhursts' roots were in the Independent Labour Party and Christabel's original involvement in the suffrage cause was occasioned by her desire to ameliorate the lives of working-class women. But she increasingly became detached from these origins and began to favour a strategy based on mobilising educated, would-be professional women like herself ('Votes for Ladies' rather than 'Votes for Women'). She was also the driving force behind the increasingly militant campaign of civil disobedience organised by the WSPU from 1909. Unlike other leaders, including her mother, however, she had no stomach for martyrdom and fled to Paris, from where she continued to encourage others to suffer for the cause. She also became more and more stridently anti-male. During the war she fully supported her mother's rallying to the flag and, in 1917, formed with her the Women's Party, which represented a final break with their socialist past. After failing to enter parliament as a Women's Party candidate after the war, she went to live in the United States, where she became a leading Second Adventist, lecturing and writing on the Second Coming of Christ.

Pankhurst, Emmeline (1858–1928) British feminist. The outbreak of war brought about another extraordinary twist to the extraordinary life of Emmeline Pankurst. The first twist came in 1898, when the death of her husband Richard, a radical Manchester barrister, freed her to participate more fully in the campaign for female suffrage. The second came in 1903 when she helped found the Women's Social and Political Union (WSPU) and later began to organise a sensational campaign of militant civil disobedience, including attacks on property and the person, that was considered revolutionary by many at the time. Mrs Pankhurst was constantly arrested, released and re-arrested as the result of hunger-striking while in prison. On the eve of war she was one of the most reviled (and admired) women in Britain. But within two days of the British declaration of war, the WSPU threw its weight behind the war effort. Those 'suffragettes' still in prison were released. Mrs Pankhurst herself led the campaign for women 'to be allowed to serve'. In 1917 she and Christabel founded the Women's Party, which advocated a war of annihilation against the Central Powers and the full legal equality of women. The formation of the Women's Party marked Emmeline's final repudiation of socialism and in 1925 she joined the Conservative Party.

Pankhurst, (Estelle) Sylvia (1882–1960) British feminist, who – together with her mother and sister – formed the Women's Social and Political Union in 1903 to campaign for female suffrage. But, appalled by her mother and sister's increasing rejection of the socialist inspiration of the suffrage cause, Sylvia broke with them in 1912, combining suffrage agitation with social work in the East End of London. She remained true to her socialist and pacifist beliefs for the rest of her life. She died in Addis Ababa, under the protection of the Emperor Haile Selassie, whose resistance to Italian Fascist invasion she had championed in the 1930s.

Papen, Franz von (1879–1969) German soldier. Papen, as German military attaché in Mexico and the United States from 1913

to 1915, and the German naval attaché, Karl BOY-ED, were instrumental in organising spy rings and saboteurs designed to disrupt US economic aid to the Allies. This undermined the attempts of the German Ambassador Count BERNSTORFF to maintain German—US relations and led to their expulsion from the United States in December 1915. Papen returned to military duties as a battalion commander and staff officer on the Western Front and as a staff officer in Palestine.

Parker, (Horatio) Gilbert (George) (1862–1932) Canadian-born British novelist, politician and propagandist, who was the chief architect of the secret British propaganda campaign designed to bring about US entry into the war on the Allied side. This was directed against American elite opinion. A list of American 'movers and shakers' was compiled from *Who's Who in America*. The list eventually comprised 260,000 names. These were subjected to a sustained campaign of 'grey propaganda', based on reasoned discussion pursued through pamphlets, leaflets, newsletters and (most insidious of all) private correspondence. Parker's revelations of the scale and sophistication of the British campaign, in a magazine article in 1918, produced a sharp reaction in the United States, where many leading Americans felt that they had been used. It also provided ammunition for some of the wilder assertions made later by Arthur PONSONBY.

Parr, John (1894–1914) British soldier. On 21 August 1914, while on a cycle patrol with members of the 4th Battalion Middlesex Regiment, Private Parr became the first British soldier to be killed on the Western Front. He is buried in St Symphorien Military Cemetery.

Partridge, Sydney George (1881–1957) British staff officer, who rose during the war from clerk in the War Office to become head of the British Expeditionary Force's Army Printing and Stationery De-pot, presiding with exceptional efficiency and dispatch over the biggest printing operation in the world, responsible for the dissemination of key training pamphlets. He is one of Paddy Griffith's 'four men who won the war'.

Pašić, Nikola (1845–1926) Serb politician, a leading figure in the history of Serbia, Yugoslavia and the Balkans during the first two decades of the twentieth century. Pašić's emergence was associated with the establishment of the Karadjordjevic dynasty on the throne of Serbia, following the coup of 1903. Between 1904, when he became Prime Minister, and the outbreak of war in August 1914 his ministry was dominated by deteriorating relations with Austria-Hungary and tension with the Serb military, frustrated by his lack of support for an expansionist foreign policy designed to achieve a 'Greater Serbia'. He was, nevertheless, instrumental in Serbian involvement in the Balkan Wars (1912–13), during which Serbia doubled the size of its national territory. There is little evidence to implicate Pašić in the murder of the Archduke FRANZ FERDINAND. (He later suppressed the Black Hand secret society that had organised the murder and had its leader, Dragutin DIMITRIJEVIĆ, tried and executed.) Pašić's conciliatory reply to the Austro-Hungarian ultimatum that followed the murder was a masterstroke, locating responsibility for war firmly with Austria and establishing Serbian 'innocence'. After the military defeat of Serbia, in the autumn of 1915, Pašić retreated with the Serb army to Corfu, where he established a government in exile. He was eventually forced to respond to pressure from Ante TRUMBIĆ's 'Yugoslav Committee' by accepting the Corfu Declaration (20 July 1917) to form a federal Yugoslav state after the war that embraced Serbs, Croats and Slovenes. Pašić was essentially a Serb nationalist and never embraced the idea of equality between the different ethnic groups, an outlook pregnant with

much future mischief. He led the Yugoslav delegation at the Paris Peace Conference (1919) that established the Yugoslav state.

Patton, George Smith Jr. (1885–1945) US military commander. Patton began the war as a captain on General PERSHING's staff, from which he was seconded as the first US army officer to receive tank training. In November 1917 he was sent to the American Expeditionary Force schools at Langres with the brief to organise a light-tank training centre. He not only did this but also recruited and trained the first American tank crews and devised their tactics. On 12 September 1917 he led the US 1st Tank Brigade, equipped with French Renault tanks, at St Mihiel, where he was slightly wounded. This was the only US tank unit to see action during the war. Later in September, at the Meuse-Argonne, he was more seriously wounded by machine-gun fire, which brought his war to an end. Although Patton's involvement in combat during the war was relatively slight, he was able to demonstrate the restless, driving energy, contempt for military bureaucracy and willingness to lead from the front that distinguished his brilliant career in the Second World War.

Pau, Paul Marie César Gerald (1848–1932) French general, who was recalled from retirement in August 1914 to command the Army of Alsace, on the right flank of the French line. His initial advance met with success but soon suffered serious reverses at Morhange and Saarbourg. The French Commander-in-Chief, General JOFFRE, then took the momentous decision to dissolve Pau's army and transfer its troops north to the Sixth Army for the battle of the Marne. His period in command lasted barely six weeks.

Payer, Friedrich von (1847–1931) German Imperial Vice Chancellor, principally remembered for his speech on war aims made in Stuttgart in September 1918. Though the opinions he expressed appeared too 'pacifist' for his pan-German colleagues, they were ill-designed to evoke interest or sympathy from the Allies. In eastern Europe, according to Payer, Germany would retain the vast territorial annexations extorted from Russia in the Treaty of Brest-Litovsk. In western Europe, Germany might consider 'restoring Belgium' but only if certain economic guarantees were given and the 'Flemish question' satisfactorily resolved, but there was no question of surrendering Alsace-Lorraine. What is most striking about Payer's views is not so much their arrogance as their unreality. They show the extent to which even elite German political opinion was out of touch with Germany's desperate military plight, less than two months away from defeat.

Pearse, Padraic Henry (1879–1916) Irish nationalist, a leading figure in the Gaelic revival, who joined the Republican Brotherhood in 1915 and in 1916 was the somewhat unlikely Commander-in-Chief of the Easter Rising against British rule in Dublin. It was Pearse who read the proclamation of the Irish Republic from the General Post Office. His subsequent execution, with fourteen other leaders of the rising, transformed a military failure into a moral triumph that dramatically altered Irish opinion and led to Sinn Fein's electoral triumph in 1918.

Pearson, Weetman Dickinson, Viscount Cowdray (1856–1927) British public works contractor, politician and philanthropist. Cowdray was one of the 'men of push and go' so admired by LLOYD GEORGE, who appointed him President of the Air Board in January 1917, with a seat in the House of Lords. Cowdray's confident predictions about aircraft production were, however, soon rendered hollow by the 'Gotha summer' of 1917, when German air raids inflicted considerable civilian casualties in London and the

south-east, outraging public opinion. Cowdray bore the brunt of criticism for failing to stop the raids. He resigned in November. His 23-year-old son, Hon. Francis Geoffrey Pearson, was killed on the Western Front on 6 September 1914 while serving as a staff sergeant in the Army Service Corps.

Peel, Dorothy (1872–1934) British journalist, author and public servant, a protégée of Arnold BENNETT, who worked as a civil servant in the Ministry of Food during the last year of the war but is now best remembered for her valuable social history of the home front, *How We Lived Then* (1929) (written under the name Mrs C.S. Peel).

Péguy, Charles Pierre (1873–1914) French poet, philosopher and soldier, whose death in action at Villeroy on 5 September 1914, the first day of the battle of the Marne, brought him martyr status at home and abroad. He came to symbolise the 'soul of France' through his willingness to die for the justice of the French cause, rooted in a revolutionary nationalism whose destiny was to bring freedom to Europe. He still represents, especially for those outside France, the 'spirit of 1914' among French intellectuals. In France, however, he is a much more controversial and ambiguous figure, whose legacy later inspired both Vichy and the French Resistance.

Penn-Gaskell, Leslie Da Costa (1882–1916) British airman. Together with Louis Strange, Penn-Gaskell was among the first members of the Royal Flying Corps (RFC) to undertake a ground attack mission, dropping home-made petrol bombs on German transport on 28 August 1914. He was also among the first members of the RFC to mount a machine gun on aircraft during the war. He died of injuries received in February 1916 while CO 5th Reserve Squadron. He collided with an elm tree near Northolt airfield while assessing the flying conditions, which were marginal, prior to allowing his less experienced pilots to take off.

Percy, (John Samuel) Jocelyn (1871–1952) British staff officer. Percy began the war as a staff officer at the Royal Military College, Sandhurst, with the rank of major. His rise was rapid, culminating in promotion to chief of staff, Fifth Army, in December 1917, in succession to Neill MALCOLM. His career survived the defeat suffered by Fifth Army during the German spring offensive of March 1918, and he ended the war as chief of staff, Second Army. General Percy changed his name from 'Baumgartner' in 1917.

Pergaud, Louis (1882–1915) French novelist and soldier, who was killed by 'friendly fire' on 8 April 1915 after being wounded and taken prisoner by the Germans. An anti-militarist, he established a unique pre-war reputation as a writer of stories set in his native Franche-Comté, in which the protagonists were animals.

Pershing, John Joseph (1860–1948) US military commander. By the time the United States entered the war, 'Black Jack' Pershing had accumulated as much combat and administrative experience as the small United States army could offer, including the Indian wars, the Spanish-American war (1898), the Philippines counter-insurgency (1899–1903) and the expedition against Pancho Villa (1916–17). He also served as US military attaché in Japan and observed the Russo-Japanese war (1905). He was the clear choice to command the American Expeditionary Force in May 1917. Pershing was a cold, aloof disciplinarian. He was acutely aware of the United States' special position as an 'Associated Power'. He was determined to keep his distance from the French and British and to resist their attempts to turn the US army into a piecemeal source of emergency reinforcements. Like KITCHENER before him, Persh-

ing wanted his army to be the 'last million men' who would decide the war. He had no wish to see them wasted in 'wearing out battles' conducted by Franco-British generals, whose strategy and tactics he believed were bankrupt. He was a difficult 'ally'. The German onslaught in the spring of 1918 softened only somewhat his refusal to allow American troops to fight under foreign command. Pershing's responsibilities were enormous. He allowed considerable latitude to senior staff officers, especially Hugh DRUM, chief of staff of First Army, and Fox CONNER, chief of operations (G-3) at GHQ. But he kept a watchful eye on his subordinate field commanders through a series of liaison officers. He insisted that divisional and corps commanders move their headquarters close to the front, which he urged them to visit personally. Subordinate commanders who failed to achieve their carefully delineated objectives were ruthlessly replaced. Pershing himself led the US First Army into its first major battle at St Mihiel on 12 September 1918, an attack that drew some Allied applause and some carping criticism (not least from FOCH) but which dismayed the Germans as they realised the scale and intensity of the American commitment. Foch pushed Pershing hard to follow up the St Mihiel attack later in the month. The Meuse-Argonne battle saw the US army perform less well, hampered by difficult terrain, naive tactics and logistical disintegration. The war ended before the American Expeditionary Force (5M strong by 1919) could quite have the effect on the war that Pershing envisaged for it, but he fiercely defended its role in the war, arguing that it had been a decisive instrument of victory in 1918. Pershing owed his nickname to his close association with black troops. It was not necessarily a compliment in an army and society that was strongly racist. Racism is not a charge that can be laid at Pershing's door, however. He insisted on black troops being used in combat and refused to allow their relegation to the lines of communication and support duties. He was a formidable man with a capacity to learn from experience, his own and that of others.

Pétain, Henri-Philippe Benoni Omer Joseph (1856–1951) French military commander, the son of a peasant from the Pas-de-Calais, who emerged in 1916 as the 'hero of Verdun' and in 1917 as 'the saviour of France'. Pétain began the war as a somewhat elderly commander of the 33rd Infantry Regiment, with the rank of colonel. By October he had risen to corps command (XXXIII Corps). This unit came close to breaking the formidable German defences on Vimy Ridge during the French attack of May 1915, a near-success that brought him a further promotion the following month, to the command of Second Army. His attack in the Champagne (September–October) met with little success but confirmed his reputation for calmness, prudence and thorough preparation. In February 1916 JOFFRE's chief of staff, General CASTELNAU, recommended Pétain as the man to rescue the serious situation that had developed at Verdun following the great German offensive. This was the first time in the war that Pétain had been called upon to organise a defence. It was to prove a significant moment not only in Pétain's career but also in the history of France. The defensive battle at Verdun gave Pétain the opportunity to execute the firepower theories he had developed before the war. Although considerably handicapped by pneumonia, Pétain soon emerged as the soul of the defence. He made major improvements in supply to the battle front, improvising a constant convoy of motor lorries along the single road ('la Voie Sacrée'), recognised the importance of taking units out of the line before they became completely worn out and made maximum use of proliferating supplies of artillery. Once the front was stabilised, however, Joffre became frustrated with Pétain's defensive mentality and, in May, replaced him with the flamboyant NIVELLE, the personification of aggression. Pétain was 'promoted' to command Army Group Centre. Nivelle's success at Verdun brought him to the high command itself after the dismissal of Joffre in December 1916. But the disaster that befell the Nivelle offensive in May 1917 once more threatened France with defeat. Pétain was given command of the French armies on 15 May and was immediately faced with a mutiny. During the next few months he isolated and punished the leading mutineers, addressed the soldiers' grievances about leave and food and finally restored their self-confidence in attacks with limited objectives supported by massive artillery resources. His attitude during the early days of the German spring offensive in March 1918 dismayed the British Commander-in-Chief, Field-Marshal HAIG, who set aside his long-standing opposition to the appointment of an Allied generalissimo and lobbied for the appointment of FOCH 'or some other French general who would fight'. Pétain's insistence on meeting German attacks with 'elastic defence in depth' was often unpopular with his subordinates, some of whom subverted his orders, but the gradual imposition of the doctrine did much to save French lives and to blunt the German offensives. He played little part in the planning for the counter-attack, begun in July, which was dominated by Foch and Haig. He was promoted Marshal of France in December 1918. Pétain was a prudent, calculating and humane commander at his best, pusillanimous and defeatist at his worst. Defeatism, married to his contempt for politicians and parliamentary government, was to prove his nemesis in a long life that ended in surrender, collaboration and – to some Frenchmen at least – treason.

Peter I Karadjordjevic (1844–1921) King of Serbia, who came to the throne in 1903 as Serbia's first constitutional monarch after a military coup overthrew the authoritarian Obrenovic dynasty. In June 1914, on the eve of war and suffering with ill health, he ceded executive power to his second son, ALEXANDER KARAD-JORDJEVIC, who became Regent. After the defeat of Serbia in the autumn of 1915, he had to be carried through the freezing mountain passes of Albania to sanctuary on Corfu. He appeared in public only briefly, in December 1918, to accept the throne of the new state of Yugoslavia.

Petit, Gabrielle (1893–1916) Belgian war heroine, a saleswoman from Tournai executed by the Germans on 1 April 1916 for espionage. She had been spying on German troop movements and was in the pay of British intelligence. German treatment of resistance in occupied Belgium was not only severe but also intentionally exemplary. Gabrielle Petit was one of eleven women to suffer the death penalty. In Petit's case, however, her execution did not have the desired effect. Her death went virtually unnoticed during the war, but afterwards she emerged from obscurity to become a national heroine, the 'Belgian Joan of Arc', and her cell in Sint-Gilles/St Gilles prison in Brussels was converted into a shrine. During the German occupation of Belgium in the Second World War no executions were made public.

Pflanzer-Baltin, Karl von (1855–1925) Austro-Hungarian military commander, brought out of retirement in 1914 to command the Seventh Army. This newly created unit, composed largely of Hungarian and Croat troops, developed a reputation as one of the most reliable in the Austro-Hungarian army, free from the enervating problems of morale and discipline all too familiar elsewhere. During the first two years of the war at least, Pflanzer-Baltin proved himself worthy of the troops he led, enjoying considerable

success in the eastern Carpathians and the Bukovina. In June 1916, however, Seventh Army was overwhelmed during the BRU-SILOV offensive. Pflanzer-Baltin's deployment was almost certainly faulty, leaving too many troops in the front line, where they fell victim to the Russian artillery bombardment. Despite this disaster, he was kept in command of the reorganised remnants of the Austro-Hungarian armies, and their German reinforcements, though his room for independent action was severely compromised by the influence of his German chief of staff, Hans von SEECKT. Pflanzer-Baltin ended the war as commander of Austro-Hungarian forces in Albania.

Phillimore, Richard Fortescue (1864–1940) British naval commander, who captained the battle cruiser HMS *Inflexible* at the battle of the Falkland Islands (8 December 1914) and at the Dardanelles (spring 1915). He was the principal beach master during the Gallipoli landings (25 April 1915), after which he was promoted Rear-Admiral and sent to Russia as head of the British Naval Mission. In 1916 he succeeded Rear-Admiral BROCK as commander of the 1st Battle Cruiser Squadron, later becoming a pioneer of aircraft carriers.

Piłsudski, Jósef Klemens (1867–1935) Polish soldier and nationalist. The outbreak of a European war involving Austria-Hungary, Germany and Russia, the three powers that had divided Poland between them at the end of the eighteenth century, seemed to provide a great opportunity for Polish nationalists to resurrect their country. On this, at least, they were united. How to achieve their aims, however, was less clear. In the event, Poles fought individually and collectively on all sides during the war. The most important organised Polish military force was Jósef Piłsudski's Polish Legion. Piłsudski, born in Russian Poland, was fiercely anti-Russian. His highly motivated unit was loosely allied with Austria. He saw the best hopes for Polish independence in the defeat of Russia in the east and the victory of the Allies in the west. He was prescient. In November 1916 Austria-Hungary and Germany proclaimed the independence of Polish territory 'liberated' from Russia. Piłsudski was appointed Minister of War in 'Kingdom Poland' but soon became disillusioned with German intentions. He repudiated the appeal of the German Governor of Warsaw, General Hans von BESELER, to co-operate, concluding emphatically: 'If I were to go along with you, Germany would gain one man, whilst I would lose a nation.' This refusal led to his arrest in July 1917 and the internment of his men. He was not released until the Armistice, when he immediately formed a provisional government. He became head of state in January 1919 and defeated Soviet forces during the Russo-Polish war of 1920.

Pinney, Reginald John (1863–1943) British military commander. Pinney served throughout the war on the Western Front from October 1914, first as GOC 23rd Brigade, then as GOC 35th and 33rd Divisions. By the time of the Armistice he was the second longest-serving divisional commander in the British Expeditionary Force. He was a man who divided opinions. He emerges from the pages of J.C. DUNN's influential memoir *The War the Infantry Knew* as a crank, much given to 'romancing' the inefficient 'stunts' organised by his staff, and as a man who denied comforts to the troops without himself being noticeably 'ascetic'. He is often considered to be the model for SASSOON's 'cheery old card', whose plan of attack did for 'Harry and Jack' (though Sassoon's most recent and authoritative biographer rejects this). Frank RICHARDS considered Pinney to be a 'bun punching crank ... more fitted to be in command of a Church Mission hut at the Base than a division of troops'. Pinney was a de-

vout, non-smoking teetotaller. He banned the rum ration in his division, a decision unlikely to endear him to Private Richards. Field-Marshal HAIG, however, was an admirer. 'When the 33rd Division was there, I could always be sure,' he commented. This was never more true than at Hazebrouck and Meteren in April 1918, when the division played a leading part in stopping the German advance that was threatening Ypres and the Channel ports.

Plehve, Wenzel von (1850–1916) Russian military commander, who maintained – in less cosmopolitan times – the tradition of German officers in Romanov service. He was 64 when war broke out and in poor health (possibly already a dying man), though he remained mentally strong and decisive. As GOC Fifth Army he performed competently in extricating his army from the possibility of encirclement during the invasion of Galicia. Later in 1914 Fifth Army played a leading part in the defence of Łódz during the fighting in Poland. In 1915 Plehve was transferred to command of the Twelfth Army. After the defeat of the Russian Tenth Army during the second battle of the Masurian Lakes (February 1915), which caused consternation in St Petersburg, Plehve succeeded in doing enough to check the advance of the German Tenth Army and the danger dissipated. His health finally gave way in the winter of 1916 and he was invalided from the army in February.

Plumer, Herbert Charles Onslow (1857–1932) British military commander. As GOC Second Army from May 1915 until he was sent to command British forces in Italy at the end of 1917, Plumer was responsible for defence of the vital Ypres salient guarding the Channel ports and the British Expeditionary Force's line of retreat. 'Daddy' Plumer is everyone's favourite British general of the First World War, even A.J.P. Taylor's. He is one of the few senior commanders to be spared the odium heaped on his contemporaries. His reputation, based on his impressive victory at Messines (June 1917), is that of a careful planner, sparing with the lives of his men, whose method was the set-piece attack supported by intense artillery bombardments on narrow fronts. This reputation is in some ways surprising, perhaps, given his close association with the conduct of the Third Battle of Ypres ('Passchendaele', July–November 1917), most evil of all battles in the British collective memory. Responsibility for this battle was originally given to General GOUGH's Fifth Army, but at the end of August, frustrated by Gough's failure to capture the Gheluvelt plateau and by mounting casualties for little reward, Field-Marshal HAIG gave control of the offensive to Plumer. In a series of set-piece battles distinguished by crushing artillery fire-plans, beginning at the battle of the Menin Road Ridge (20 September) and followed by Polygon Wood (26 September) and Broodseinde (4 October), Plumer inflicted hammer blows on the German defenders. He was careful not to allow his infantry to outstrip the covering artillery. This disrupted the German method of defence, based on 'elastic defence in depth', and LUDENDORFF was compelled to return briefly to a more linear form of defence, with a reinforced front line. This proved equally vulnerable to Plumer's attacks. It should be noted, however, that Plumer's battles were never cheap and succeeded in capturing less ground than Gough's original assault of 31 July. They often pushed British forces into narrow salients where they could be enfiladed by German machine-gun and artillery fire. Plumer's attacks later in October (at Poelcappelle and Passchendaele), hampered by extremely wet weather, met with much less success and were extremely costly. British casualties in October 1917 were the third highest for any month of the war, exceeded only by July 1916 and April 1917. Plumer was recalled to the Western Front from Italy in time to organise Second Army's defence of the vital Lys position in April 1918. After the Armistice, he commanded British occupation forces at Cologne. Plumer's appearance was that of an old buffer, and he later became – ironically given his reputation – the model for the cartoonist David Low's satirical depiction of unreconstructed military incompetence, Colonel Blimp. Plumer was fortunate in being able to draw on the support of able subordinates, notably 'Tim' HARINGTON (chief of staff 1916–18), a talented soldier who understood the importance of good PR, a concept foreign to most British officers of the period.

Pohl, Hugo von (1855–1916) German naval commander, who succeeded INGENOHL as C-in-C High Seas Fleet after the near-catastrophe suffered by the German battle cruisers at the Dogger Bank in January 1915. His tenure, which was terminated by ill health, was marked by no significant surface activity in the North Sea, but he strongly favoured increasing the scale and intensity of the submarine war. Pohl was succeeded by Reinhard SCHEER a month before his death.

Poincaré, Raymond Nicolas Landry (1860–1934) French politician, a Republican lawyer from the 'lost province' of Lorraine, who was President of France from 1913 until 1920. At the time of Poincaré's election the French Presidency was regarded as essentially a ceremonial office, but he intended from the outset to treat it as an executive one and throughout his tenure he was uninhibitedly interventionist. An ardent nationalist and patriot, he favoured military expansion at home and the strengthening of France's alliances abroad. He was especially keen to reinforce French ties with Russia. The promises that he made to the Russian government during his visit to St Petersburg in July 1914 are seen by many as deliberate warmongering. Whether he had a long-term plan to engineer a war is doubtful. But it is clear that he was unwilling to acquiesce in an Austrian defeat of Serbia. Such an outcome would shift the balance of power decisively in favour of the Central Powers and leave France in danger of isolation against her powerful neighbour, a circumstance that a generation of French foreign policy makers had been determined to avoid. Once war began, Poincaré struggled to have any real influence on its conduct, which was dominated by the formidable JOFFRE. The fall of Joffre in December 1916, however, brought little respite. Poincaré gave full support to the Nivelle offensive, despite the reservations expressed by senior political figures who included two Prime Ministers, RIBOT and PAINLEVÉ, and the Minister of War, LYAUTEY. The disastrous outcome of the NIVELLE offensive, resulting in the French army mutinies, brought French politics to the brink. In November 1917 Poincaré was forced to abandon the politics of coalition that he had attempted to orchestrate since the outbreak of war. The path of peace, however, did not beguile. He chose, instead, the path of victory. But the personal political cost was high. Throughout 1918 he was firmly subordinated by the most powerful of France's wartime Prime Ministers, Georges CLEMENCEAU, who also succeeded in excluding Poincaré from the deliberations of the Paris Peace Conference.

Polivanov, Aleksei Andreevich (1855–1920) Russian soldier and Minister of War, who emerged after the Russian debacle in the war against Japan (1904–05) as a powerful advocate of military and political reform. His appointment as Minister of War in June 1915, in succession to the grotesquely incompetent SUKHOMLINOV, signalled one of the more hopeful interludes in Russia's disastrous war. Polivanov brought energy and enterprise to his office. He focused on the two issues that had bedevilled the Russian war effort, manpower and supplies. He built up a

trained reserve that eventually reached 2M men. He did his utmost to rationalise recruitment, establishing the concept of 'reserved occupations' for key industrial workers, and to stimulate domestic production of munitions, where he improved relations between the state and suppliers. He also looked abroad for supplies. This was too good to last. When the Tsar's intention to leave St Petersburg and command his armies personally in the field became known in August 1915, Polivanov was dismayed. He signed a letter to NICHOLAS II, pleading with him to reconsider. This act was not only unavailing but also brought Polivanov the enmity of the Tsarina ALEKSANDRA, who engineered his dismissal in November 1915. Polivanov's influence on the remainder of the war was negligible and he eventually joined the Red Army.

Pollard, Alfred Oliver (1893–1960) British soldier. When the war broke out Pollard was working as a clerk at the Alliance Insurance Company in London. He was encouraged to enlist by his employers' promise that they would keep his job open for him when peace returned. He joined the Honourable Artillery Company as a private soldier and was commissioned in January 1916. A tall, brash, arrogant and aggressive man, he loved the war, especially 'walking about No Man's Land at night'. He won the DCM MC and bar and VC. Like many warriors, his post-war career was mixed and at one time he was reduced to trying to pawn his Victoria Cross. In 1932 he published *Fire Eater*, a JÜNGEResque celebration of combat. He did not return to the Alliance Insurance Company.

Pollen, Arthur Joseph Hungerford (1866–1937) British inventor and pioneer of naval fire control. A barrister with an interest in big-game shooting, Pollen became fascinated by the problems of naval gunnery. He was concerned to make gunnery from moving ships, firing at moving targets, as accurate as that of stationary guns firing at fixed targets on land. He devised what was, in effect, a mechanical computer capable of predicting the deflection and range required for shooting accurately at moving targets. Pollen's civilian status, lack of tact and disastrous alienation of Admiral FISHER severely handicapped him in an acrimonious competition with the system designed by a naval officer, Captain F.C. DREYER, and it was the Dreyer system that was finally adopted.

Pomeroy, John (1873–1950) New Zealand engineer, who gave his name to the 'Pomeroy bullet', which he devleoped in 1902 and was used by the British air service to shoot down German airships. The bullet was filled with nitroglycerin, designed to ignite the hydrogen escaping from the airship's punctured gas bag. He received royalties of £25,000 for his invention.

Ponsonby, Arthur (1871–1946) British politician. Despite his impeccable establishment credentials as the son of Queen Victoria's Private Secretary, Ponsonby was one of the most radical backbench critics of the Liberal government's pre-war foreign policy. He was strongly opposed to Britain's entry into the war and was instrumental in the formation of the influential Union of Democratic Control (UDC). The UDC became the most important anti-war organisation in Britain, dedicated to establishing parliamentary control over foreign policy and a post-war system of international arbitration and to ensuring a fair and just peace settlement. Like many Liberal members of the UDC, Ponsonby defected to the Labour Party after the war. In 1928 he published an influential book, *Falsehood in War-Time: Containing an Assortment of Lies Circulated Throughout the Nations During the Great War*, which exhibited a fine upper-class disdain for the 'lower orders', whose malleability Ponsonby consistently exaggerated.

Potiorek, Oskar von (1853–1933) Austro-Hungarian military commander, who announced himself to the world by his incompetent organisation of the security arrangements for Archduke FRANZ FERDINAND's visit to Sarajevo in June 1914, incompetence that would have been comic except for its tragic outcome. His conduct of the invasion of Serbia in the ensuing war did nothing to retrieve his reputation. After a series of dispiriting defeats, he was replaced in December 1914 by Archduke EUGEN, whereupon he retired.

Pretorius, Philip Jacobus (18??–1945) South African scout, who left an interesting memoir of the guerrilla war in East Africa, *Jungle Man*, first published in 1947.

Prezan, Constantine (1861–1943) Romanian military commander, who led the Fourth Army in the invasion of Transylvania (August 1916). He achieved an orderly retreat to the Carpathians in October in the face of greatly superior Austrian forces. He became Romanian chief of staff in November and Commander-in-Chief a year later on the eve of Romania's armistice with the Central Powers. He was one of very few remotely capable Romanian commanders.

Price, George Lawrence (1893–1918) Canadian soldier. Private Price, a native of Nova Scotia, was killed in action on 11 November 1918 (according to some accounts just two minutes before the Armistice came into effect), while serving with the 28th Battalion Canadian Infantry (Saskatchewan Regiment). He was the last member of the British Expeditionary Force to be killed during the Great War, though – of course – in reality the war continued to claim its victims for years to come. Price is buried in the same cemetery, St Symphorien, east of Mons, as

Private John PARR, the first British soldier to be killed.

Prichard, (Hesketh Vernon) Hesketh (1876–1922) British soldier. Prichard's pre-war reputation was that of a sportsman, traveller, big-game shot and author. He played cricket for Hampshire from 1899 to 1913, where his prowess as a fast bowler was aided by his immense height, and published a series of books about his travels in Patagonia, Haiti and Labrador. He also wrote novels, the best known of which was *Don Q* (1904), written in collaboration with his mother. The outbreak of war gave him the opportunity to obtain the commission that he had been previously denied owing to a slightly defective heart. In 1915 he succeeded in obtaining the highly unofficial position of 'sniping expert' in Third Army, where he was supported by General MONRO, ever willing to encourage initiative among his subordinates, and Lieutenant-General HAKING. Prichard was aware of British inferiority in sniping and was determined to end it. He brought his considerable expertise as a big-game shot to the training of snipers. He also introduced the system of snipers' observers and was fertile in expedients for camouflage. His work gradually gained acceptance through its effectiveness, and his account of it, *Sniping in France*, was published in 1920. His death from blood poisoning at the age of 45 was directly attributable to his war service.

Princip, Gavrilo (1895–1918) Assassin, whose murder of Archduke FRANZ FERDINAND and his wife SOPHIE in Sarajevo on 28 June 1914 started the train of events that plunged Europe into war. The son of a Bosnian Serb peasant family, Princip was the ideal mixture of naivety, fanaticism and frustrated ambition for exploitation by the sinister henchmen of the Serb secret societies who armed and trained him. After a remarkable display of cowardice and incompetence by Princip's fellow conspirators, the attempt on the Archduke's life appeared to have failed. But Franz Ferdinand's car took a wrong turn, fortuitously stopping right in front of Princip in order to reverse. He mounted the running board and fired the shots 'heard around the world'. He was captured and tried but escaped death owing to his age, succumbing to tuberculosis in Austrian captivity on 28 April 1918.

Prittwitz und Gaffron, Maximilian von (1848–1929) German military commander, whose nickname, *Der Dicke* (the 'Thick One'), referred to his corpulence rather than to his lack of mental equipment. As commander of the Eighth Army in August 1914 he found himself having to defend East Prussia against two Russian armies, with a numerical inferiority of 1:4. Encouraged by one of his junior staff officers, Max HOFFMANN, Prittwitz decided to draw RENNENKAMPF's Russian First Army into East Prussia, defeat it and then turn south to confront SAMSONOV's Russian Second Army. This sensible plan was subverted by the actions of one of Prittwitz's subordinate commanders, Hermann von FRANÇOIS (GOC I Corps), who was unable to acquiesce in the thought of East Prussia being defiled by a Slav invasion and attacked Rennenkampf at Gumbinnen. This small battle had important consequences. Prittwitz's decision not to support François turned Gumbinnen into a defeat. News of a defeat in East Prussia caused consternation in Berlin. The German Commander-in-Chief, Helmuth von MOLTKE, was compelled to detach two corps from the invasion of France to reinforce the eastern frontier against barbarian invasion. The panic proved to be misplaced, for the regrouping necessitated by François' insubordination also fortuitously created the circumstances for the stunning German victory at Tannenberg in August 1914. Before then, however, Moltke replaced Prittwitz and his chief of staff General Waldersee. The laurels fell instead on the brows of their successors, HINDENBURG and LUDENDORFF.

Protopopov, Aleksandr Dmitrievich (1866–1918) Russian politician, whose surprise appointment as Minister of the Interior in September 1916 dismayed his erstwhile colleagues among the Octobrist deputies to the Duma. Protopopov's judgement may have been affected by the ravages of syphilis. His behaviour became increasingly unstable and his only apparent policy was to increase his own power and bully his subordinates. He had no effect on the accelerating disintegration of the government except to exacerbate the general disgust in which it was held. He was imprisoned by the Provisional Government and executed by the Bolsheviks on New Year's Day 1918.

Pulkowski, Erich (1877–19??) German soldier, who pioneered 'silent registration', a method for registering guns on their targets without having to fire them, greatly strengthening the element of surprise on the battlefield. Pulkowski's method depended on mathematically predicted correction factors derived from meteorological data and accurate recording of the individual firing errors of each gun. He worked closely with Georg BRUCHMÜLLER on the preparation of the artillery bombardments used in the German offensives of 1918 on the Western Front.

Pulteney, William Pulteney (1861–1941) British military commander. On the outbreak of war there were only three serving officers in the British army who had commanded a corps, and none of them had commanded a corps in war. One, Field-Marshal Sir John FRENCH, was already serving above that level. By the time III Corps was deployed, in September 1914, the British army had therefore already exhausted its supply of experienced corps commanders. The choice of Pulteney as commander of III Corps is indicative of the difficulties experienced by the British army in finding suitable officers at that level. Pulteney was a Scots Guardsman who entered the army via the militia. He had attended neither the Royal Military College, Sandhurst, nor the Staff College. It was said that the best officers were allotted to III Corps in order to compensate for its commander's deficiencies. These included John DuCane, George MILNE, Louis VAUGHAN, Walter CAMPBELL and Stanley MAUDE. His chief of staff in 1917, Charles Bonham-Carter, described Pulteney as 'the most completely ignorant general I served under during the war and that is saying a lot'. Pulteney was notably unmilitary in appearance. One observer compared him to 'a peaceful country squire'. His actions, however, were not always those of a gentleman. His scapegoating of Major-General Barter (GOC 47th Division), after the capture of High Wood in September 1916, is notorious. The difficulties faced by 47th Division and its heavy losses were almost entirely due to Pulteney's plan, which Barter had protested about before the attack. Pulteney's replacement on 16 February 1918, in the aftermath of the Cambrai debacle, was long overdue.

Putnam, David Endicott (1898–1918) US-French fighter ace. Putnam joined the French air service in April 1917. Much confusion exists over his final score. His first kill came in January 1918, and he began to score heavily in April. Many of these victories were scored over enemy lines and could not be verified. By the time he joined the United States Air Service, he had an unofficial score of thirteen. He later claimed four more officially and seven more unofficially. Some authorities believe that he may have had as many as thirty-four victories, which would put him well in front of the officially recognised top American ace, Eddie RICKENBACKER. Unlike Rickenbacker, however, Putnam was killed in action (on 12 September 1918) and is now virtually forgotten, not least in his own country.

Putnik, Radomir (1847–1917) Serbian military commander, an outstanding soldier with a long record of successful military service going back to the Turkish wars of the mid-1870s. As Minister of War from 1906, he presided over Serbia's victories in the Balkan Wars (1912–13), during which Serbia doubled the area of her national territory. In 1912 he became the first Serb to reach the rank of field-marshal. The outbreak of war in 1914 did not begin auspiciously for him, however. His health had broken down after the Second Balkan War, and in August 1914 he was interned by the Imperial authorities while recuperating at an Austrian spa. His release was personally authorised by Emperor FRANZ JOSEF I and the Austro-Hungarian chief of staff, General CON-RAD. If they believed that Putnik was too old and ill to matter, they were wrong and the next few months provided ample opportunity for them to reflect on their generosity. Putnik not only successfully defended Serbia against the hapless Austrian invasion commanded by POTIOREK but also expelled Austrian forces from Serbia, mostly conducting operations from a well-heated room. The second invasion of Serbia in November 1915, by a combined force of Austrian, Bulgarian and German troops commanded by MACKENSEN, overwhelmed the Serb army, however, and forced it into a dispiriting retreat across the freezing mountains of Albania in mid-winter to sanctuary on Corfu. Putnik had to be carried in a sedan chair the whole way. His reward was to be relieved of command.

Q

Quast, Ferdinand von (1850–1934) German military commander, best known for his role in Operation Georgette, the attack spearheaded by his Sixth Army on the Lys in April 1918. It was this attack which provoked Field-Marshal Sir Douglas HAIG's famous 'Backs to the Wall' order of the day on 11 April. Once again the German bombardment was orchestrated by Colonel Georg BRUCHMÜLLER, falling on a ten-mile front from Bethune to Armentières. At the focal point of the attack were the two Portuguese divisions of British First Army. Sixth Army smashed through the Portuguese defences, advancing three and a half miles to the river Lys and outflanking Armentières, which was abandoned. Quast was close to inflicting a catastrophic defeat on the British, but the day was saved by the magnificent resistance of Major-General JEUDWINE's 55th Division on the Portuguese flank. Further sanguinary fighting followed, but by the end of April the final German attempt to capture the Channel ports had been decisively repulsed.

R

Radoslavov, Vasil (1854–1929) Bulgarian politician, whose strongly pro-German views closely resembled those of Tsar FERDINAND I. Bulgaria's defeat in the Second Balkan War of 1913 both confirmed Radoslavov's Russophobia and brought him to power as Minister-President. The outbreak of the European war in August 1914 presented an opportunity for Bulgaria to regain its losses of the previous year, especially Macedonia. Radoslavov continued to believe that only an alliance with the Central Powers could achieve this, but he was reluctant to commit Bulgaria from the outset. Instead, he conducted diplomatic negotiations with both sides for more than a year, though he was never in earnest about an alliance with the Entente, despite the popularity of this with important sections of Bulgarian political opinion. Bulgaria finally joined the Central Powers in September 1915, an act that decided the fate of Serbia. Germany was, however, to prove a demanding ally. Bulgaria's enforced participation in the invasion of Romania in the autumn of 1916 dismayed many Bulgarians, while Germany's ruthless exploitation of Bulgaria's economic resources led to increasing levels of popular discontent. Radoslavov survived until the summer of 1918, when the failure of the German army's offensive on the Western Front led to his replacement by MALINOV. Radoslavov fled to Germany in October 1918 and died in exile.

Raemakers, Louis (1869–1956) Dutch cartoonist, whose savage satires on German 'kultur' brought him world fame and did irreparable damage to Germany's international reputation. Raemakers was horrified by German violation of Belgian neutrality and by the behaviour of the German army in Belgium. His cartoons portray German soldiers as monstrous figures towering over innocent women, children and peasants, intent on murder, rape and extortion. One cartoon, entitled 'Prussianism and Civilisation', shows a female figure, dress torn at the breast, tied to a cartwheel. The caption is a quotation from BERNHARDI: 'Might is the supreme right, and the dispute as to what is right is decided by the arbitrament of war.' Pre-war Germany had often been extolled, not least in sections of British opinion, as a model of what an 'advanced', 'modern' state should be. But, under Raemakers' influence, Germans became branded as barbaric 'Huns'. The propaganda value of Raemakers' work was quickly spotted by the British, who arranged for the publication of cheap, paperback collections of his cartoons.

Rasputin, Grigorii Efimovich (1872–1916) Russian holy man, confidant of Tsar

NICHOLAS II and the Tsarina ALEKSANDRA FEODOROVNA. Rasputin was a drunken lecher who underwent a religious conversion after a chance meeting with a Bible student, becoming a member of the Khlytsy sect. Happily for a man of his appetites, this sect believed in the regenerative power of sexual excess, through which ordinary men could attain Christlike powers, including the ability to perform miracles. Rasputin was introduced to the royal family in 1905. He owed his subsequent influence at court to his power, probably achieved through hypnosis, to stop the haemophiliac Tsarevich Aleksei from bleeding. The Tsar and Tsarina were so grateful that Rasputin's behaviour was constantly indulged. They referred to him as 'our friend'. Reports of his debauchery and embezzlement were attributed to the jealousy of his enemies and those of the Tsar. The war was Rasputin's undoing. For many Russians he came to symbolise the worst excesses of the tsarist regime. His 'evil counsel' provided a simple explanation for the war's military reverses. Many thought him a German spy and believed he had seduced the Tsarina. In September 1915 the Tsar left for the front to take command of his armies, leaving the government in the hands of his wife and Rasputin. The Tsarina proceeded to purge all ministers she thought were enemies of the Tsar. These included all the competent ones. A group of conspirators, led by Prince Felix Yusupov, decided that something must be done and, on 16 December 1916, they murdered Rasputin. If his assassination was an attempt to save the monarchy, it came much too late and signally failed.

Rathenau, Walther (1867–1922) German industrialist and wartime administrator. Rathenau was the son of the founder of the giant German electrical combine AEG. He did not share the 'short-war illusion' of many Germans and immediately recognised the importance of centralised control over strategic raw materials

once war broke out. He drew this to the attention of the Prussian Minister of War, Erich von FALKENHAYN, who immediately appointed Rathenau as the first head of the War Raw Materials Department (the KRA). This organisation owed much to the ideas of an AEG engineer, Wichard von Möllendorf. Under Rathenau's energetic direction it undoubtedly gave German economic mobilisation a short-term advantage over its enemies. Rathenau led the KRA only until April 1915, when he was compelled to resign under pressure from the owners of Germany's large industrial corporations, who resented interference in their affairs by a Jew. Rathenau became head of AEG in June 1915. Fearing the social and political consequences of a German defeat, he later supported HINDENBURG and LUDENDORFF's attempt to achieve a full-scale mobilisation of the German war economy, though often despairing at its over-centralisation, bureaucratic inertia and cavalier disregard for the maintenance of working-class living standards. He also opposed the Third Supreme Command's annexationist policies in Eastern Europe and their resumption of unrestricted submarine warfare. With defeat in sight, however, he could be found urging mass civilian resistance to an Allied invasion of Germany. After the war Rathenau served in the government of the Weimar Republic, ultimately as Foreign Minister. He was assassinated in June 1922 by two right-wing gunmen, shortly after signing the Treaty of Rapallo with Russia.

Rawling, Cecil Godfrey (1870–1917) British military commander. Rawling found pre-war fame as the explorer and surveyor of Western Tibet and Dutch New Guinea. In August 1914 he was given command of the 6th (Service) Battalion of his regiment, the Somerset Light Infantry. He was responsible for its training and took it to the Western Front in May 1915. In June 1916, shortly before the Somme offensive, he was promoted to command 62nd Brigade, 21st Division. His was one of the first command changes instituted by 21st Division's new commander, David CAMPBELL. Rawling announced his arrival with 62nd Brigade's brilliant capture of Shelter Wood on 3 July 1916. His fearless, front-line style of command was not conducive to longevity, and he was killed by a shell in Hooge Crater on 28 October 1917.

Rawlinson, Henry Seymour (1864–1925) British military commander. Sir Henry Rawlinson was the son of a distinguished Orientalist. He was an able, intelligent and energetic man, who took his profession seriously. His pre-war career was conspicuously successful and included an important period (1903–06) as Commandant of the Staff College, whose instruction he succeeded in making more practical and relevant. He was known to his friends as 'Rawly', but his personality evoked considerable distrust and many more referred to him as 'The Cad' or 'The Fox'. These included the British Commander-in-Chief on the Western Front, Sir John FRENCH. Rawlinson's awareness of French's animosity drew him into the orbit of French's eventual successor, Douglas HAIG. Rawlinson's sense of obligation to Haig made it difficult for him to raise effective objections to Haig's proposals. This had tragic consequences. By the spring of 1916 Rawlinson was one of the most experienced British generals on the Western Front, having commanded a division in 1914 and a corps in 1915, including the first British offensive battles of trench warfare at Neuve Chapelle (March 1915), Aubers Ridge and Festubert (May 1915) and Loos (September–October 1915). He seemed the best choice to command the new Fourth Army that would spearhead the British attack on the Somme. Rawlinson's original plan advocated a 'bite and hold' strategy, but this dismayed Haig, who thought it was too limited in scope. The ensuing discussions

between GHQ and Fourth Army resulted in an unsatisfactory compromise between Haig's strategic optimism and Rawlinson's tactical realism that undoubtedly played an important part in the disaster of 1 July 1916. Rawlinson's performance in the ensuing weeks was also unimpressive, as he presided over a series of costly, piecemeal attacks on narrow fronts that seemed to lack any coherent purpose. Rawlinson's star was somewhat eclipsed towards the end of the Somme campaign by the more successful attacks of General GOUGH's Fifth Army. Fourth Army took no significant part in the fighting of 1917 on the Western Front, other than its role in planning a proposed amphibious assault on the Flanders coast that never took place. By the beginning of 1918 Rawlinson found himself at Versailles as British representative on the Supreme War Council, an organisation widely derided in British military circles as a 'talking shop'. His career was resurrected by Gough's defeat during the German spring offensive of 1918. Rawlinson took over command of Fifth Army (soon to be renamed Fourth Army) at the end of March. He successfully defended the key rail centre of Amiens in savage fighting that incurred huge numbers of casualties, culminating in the world's first ever tank versus tank battle at Villers-Brettoneux, which was recaptured on 25 April and which marked the defeat of the German attack on the Somme. During the summer and autumn of 1918, again in savage fighting, the Fourth Army, including the Australian and Canadian Corps and two US divisions, inflicted an unbroken series of defeats on the German army. The brilliantly planned and executed move of the Canadian Corps south to the Somme front, which included an important role for signals' deception (perhaps for the first time in war), preceded the important victory of Amiens on 8 August (famously described by LUDENDORFF as 'the black day of the German army'), inaugurating the hundred days' advance to victory.

Rawlinson ended his career as Commander-in-Chief in India, where he died after an operation for appendicitis.

Read, George Windle (1860–1934) US military commander. Read was given responsibility in April 1917 for recruiting a mass US army; after the Armistice his career achieved a certain symmetry when he was charged with returning the American Expeditionary Force from France via its embarkation centre at Le Mans. In between, he commanded US 30th Division and US II Corps. As a corps commander, Read collaborated closely with the British and two of his divisions, the 27th and 30th, participated in British Fourth Army's successful assault on the Hindenburg Line on 29 September 1918.

Redmond, John Edward (1856–1918) Leader of the Irish National Party. After the general election of 1910 the Irish National Party held the balance of power in the House of Commons. Redmond's support for ASQUITH in passing the Parliament Act of 1911, which limited the power of the House of Lords, was purchased at the price of an Irish Home Rule Bill the following year. There were many who thought that the passage of the Home Rule Act, which occurred in September 1914, would provoke civil war in Ireland. But the issue never came to the test. The European war broke out first. Redmond agreed to the postponement of the Home Rule Act's implementation and threw his support behind the war effort. Thousands of Catholic, nationalist Irishmen followed Redmond's lead and volunteered. The war's seemingly positive effect on British–Irish relations, however, proved a chimera. Redmond was astonished and appalled by the Easter Rising of 1916, but its brutal repression by the British military fatally compromised his position. Irish nationalism fell increasingly under the control of Eamon DE VALERA and Sinn Fein.

Redmond, William Hoey Kearney (1861–1917) Irish nationalist, whose decision to fight in the Great War has relegated him, and other constitutional nationalists like him, to the margins of history, leaving the field to Sinn Fein and its followers. Redmond, brother of the Irish National Party leader, believed that 'the future freedom, welfare and happiness of the Irish people depend on the part Ireland plays in the war'. Despite his age, 53, he insisted on serving in the front line. On 7 June 1917 he died of wounds received while serving as a major with the 6th Battalion Royal Irish Regiment at Messines.

Reed, John Silas (1887–1920) US journalist and political activist. Reed was a sickly, bookish child, with an imagination fed on literature and history. After a brilliant career at Harvard he established a reputation as a radical journalist. In December 1912 he became an editor of *The Masses*, which he used as a platform to campaign for workers' rights. He was appalled by the outbreak of war in Europe and opposed US intervention. After his attempts to report the war on the Western Front at close quarters failed, he turned his attention to the Eastern Front, publishing an account of the fighting, *The War in Eastern Europe*, in April 1916. He denounced US entry into the war and later in 1917 went to Russia, meeting Kerensky (who failed to impress him), Trotsky and – eventually – Lenin. His increasing commitment to the Bolshevik cause was signalled by his involvement with the Bureau of International Revolutionary Propaganda, charged with spreading socialism among the German army's rank and file. Reed's communist sympathies had already attracted notice in his homeland and, on his return, he was arrested and charged with conspiracy to obstruct the draft and later with sedition. Both trials ended in hung juries. In March 1919, he published the book on which his fame now rests, *Ten Days that Shook the World*, a sympathetic, first-hand account of the Bolshevik uprising. Reed died of typhus in Moscow, after returning from Finland, where he had been detained in possession of more than $1M in gold and jewels, a gift from the Comintern designed to provide financial support for the American Communist Party.

Remarque, Erich Maria (1897–1970) German soldier and writer, whose celebrated novel *All Quiet on the Western Front*, published in 1929, is widely regarded as the finest novel of the war and perhaps even the finest 'war book' ever written. Its influence on shaping perceptions of war was very great and was reinforced by Lewis Milestone's remarkable film version, which appeared in 1930. Remarque wrote the book in six weeks. It was an instant success, selling 2.5M copies in the first eighteen months, and was translated into twenty-five languages. The book's description of the life of a group of ordinary German soldiers, told in simple, plain language, seemed to capture the nature of modern war. Many front-line infantry veterans have testified to its authenticity. The book was promoted as Remarque's own story, but the truth was rather different. Remarque was conscripted in November 1916 but never fought in the trenches. In July 1917 he was wounded by shrapnel. Although the wounds were not serious, he managed to malinger in hospital until twelve days before the Armistice. After the war he posed as an officer, appearing in a lieutenant's uniform with the insignia of the Iron Cross, first and second class, until his fantasies provoked official censure. This behaviour was later held against him by Nazi and other opponents of his work, which they regarded as Bolshevik defeatism. Remarque's book made him rich. He left Germany in 1933 to pursue a bohemian playboy existence, gathering a string of glamorous mistresses who included Marlene Dietrich, and a fabulous art collection. His third wife was the Hollywood star Paulette Goddard. The Nazis avenged themselves on him by executing his sister, Elfriede, by decapitation.

Renn, Ludwig (1899–1979) Pen name of Arnold Friedrich Vieth von Golsseneau, a German Regular officer who later became a communist and fought in the Spanish Civil War. In 1929 he published *War*, a realistic account of the war service of a German NCO. Renn's book has been perpetually overshadowed by REMARQUE's *All Quiet on the Western Front*, which appeared in the same year, but it remains a powerful and interesting study of the effects of 'attrition' on the morale of a small unit. (Even in this book, Renn is fated to be preceded by Remarque.)

Rennenkampf, Pavel Karlovich von (1854–1918) Russian military commander. In August 1914 Rennenkampf's First Army was ordered to invade East Prussia from the north-east and to tie down the German Eighth Army, while the Russian Second Army, commanded by SAMSONOV, would advance against Eighth Army's rear, from the south. Rennenkampf failed dismally. After being attacked by FRANÇOIS' Corps at Gumbinnen on 20 August, Rennenkampf halted. He allowed his own army to be pinned down by a light screen of German cavalry, while the main forces of Eighth Army were allowed to move against Samsonov, whose army was virtually surrounded and annihilated at Tannenberg. Rennenkampf himself only just avoided complete disaster a few weeks later at the first battle of the Masurian Lakes (9–14 September). This brought the Russian invasion of East Prussia to an ignominious conclusion. Rennenkampf's failure brought his Baltic-German origins under scrutiny and led to allegations of treason, but he survived to become Governor of St Petersburg in 1915. He was murdered by the Bolsheviks in 1918.

Repington, Charles à Court (1858–1925) British journalist, principally remembered for his role in the 'Shell Scandal' crisis of

May 1915. Repington took to journalism when his military career was ended in 1902 by involvement in a messy divorce case. He became military correspondent of *The Times* in 1903, a position he held until his resignation in January 1918. Repington provoked strong emotions in others, and many regarded him as a self-interested intriguer and irresponsible political manipulator, amusingly dismissed as 'the Gorgeous Wreckington' and 'the Playboy of the Western Front'. He was undoubtedly conceited and a gossip, but his assiduous networking was invariably designed to prosecute his view of defence policy. He was perfectly capable of sacrificing friendships in pursuit of his ideas, and he could be both outspoken and courageous. His resignation from *The Times* was on an issue of principle. There was also a consistency in his ideas. He believed in the need for a strong army and ridiculed the pretensions of the navalist lobby, especially Admiral FISHER, whom he held in considerable contempt. He feared and expected a war against Germany and advocated closer relations with France. He favoured conscription but realised the political impossibility of compulsion in peacetime. The support he gave to the pre-war army reforms of R.B. HALDANE, especially the establishment of the Territorial Force, was unwavering despite the opposition of many of his 'friends', especially Field-Marshal Roberts. Repington regarded Haldane as 'the greatest War Minister of modern times'. During the Great War he favoured the Western Front strategy and generally took the side of the 'brass hats' against the 'frocks', but this resulted from his perception of strategic realities rather than prejudice and he was never starry-eyed about either. His report in *The Times* on 14 May 1915, which included the fateful sentence 'The want of an unlimited supply of high explosive shells was a fatal bar to our success [at Aubers Ridge]', played a significant role in the fall of Britain's last Liberal government and the formation of the ASQUITH coalition.

Reuter, Ludwig von (1869–1943) German naval commander. Reuter spent the war mainly in cruisers, culminating in his appointment by HIPPER as commander of the High Seas Fleet's scouting forces in 1918. After the Armistice he was given the melancholy task of surrendering the German fleet to the British at Scapa Flow. There, on 21 June 1919, he scuttled his ships (sixty-six in all), an act that many considered to have saved the German navy's honour, and he was greeted as a hero on his return to Germany.

Rhodes-Moorhouse, William Bernard (1887–1915) British fighter ace, who won a posthumous Victoria Cross for the bombing of Courtrai station on 26 April 1915, during which he was severely wounded in the thigh by a barrage of small arms fire from the belfry of Courtrai church. His determination to regain his own lines and make his report probably cost him his life. Had he landed behind enemy lines and his wound been treated immediately, he would probably have survived. He died the following day. His last words are supposed to have been: 'If I must die, give me a drink'.

Ribot, Alexandre Felix Joseph (1842–1923) French politician. As French Foreign Minister from 1890 to 1893 Ribot negotiated the Franco-Russian military convention that was instrumental in ending France's diplomatic isolation and became the keystone in the arch of French pre-war foreign policy. From August 1914 Ribot served in the VIVIANI and BRIAND governments as Finance Minister. Unlike his British equivalent, Reginald MCKENNA, Ribot resisted increases in direct taxation and the imposition of war taxes, preferring to finance the war by borrowing, especially from Great Britain and the United States. Following Briand's resignation in March 1917, Ribot became Prime

Minister. Although he opposed the plans of the French Commander-in-Chief, General NIVELLE, for an offensive on the Aisne, he recoiled from the potential consequences of Nivelle's threatened resignation and let the offensive proceed to its conclusion in defeat and mutiny. During the summer of 1917 Ribot became progressively more isolated, alienating both right and left. The dismissal in August of the radical Interior Minister Louis MALVY in response to right-wing demands completed the collapse of Ribot's parliamentary support. He resigned on 7 September.

Rice, (Spring) Robert (1858–1929) Engineer-in-Chief of the British Expeditionary Force, an old friend of Douglas HAIG, whose Chief Engineer he was at I Corps, First Army and finally (from March 1916) at GHQ, where he succeeded George FOWKE. Rice was an able, hard-working, forward-looking man who left three-and-a-half miles of bridging in engineering parks, ready for a return to mobile warfare, when he was replaced on age grounds in November 1917.

Richards, Frank (1884–1961) British soldier, an old-sweat reservist who was recalled to the colours in August 1914, serving throughout the war on the Western Front in the 2nd Battalion Royal Welsh Fusiliers, never rising above the rank of private. Richards fought in every major campaign of the war and suffered nothing worse than piles. In 1933, with the help of his former company commander Robert GRAVES, he published a classic account of his war service, *Old Soldiers Never Die*. The book captures the spirit of the pre-war Regular, often very different from that of the familiar New Army memoirists. The book was a great success, and he followed it with *Old Soldier Sahib* (1936), an account of pre-war Regular Army life in India. Frank Richards was awarded the DCM and MM.

Richmond, Herbert William (1871–1946) British naval staff officer and historian. Richmond was destined to be a Young Turk throughout his life. Self-consciously brilliant and irreverent in a service with a strong sense of hierarchy, he was a natural member of the awkward squad. He was one of the original appointees to the Naval War Staff, established in 1912, but his talents were used for little more than clerical work. He was relieved when the war allowed him to escape in May 1915 to spend four months as liaison officer with the Italian navy. In September 1915 he was given command of the battleship HMS *Commonwealth*, later commanding HMS *Conqueror* and HMS *Erin*. He was severely critical of JELLICOE's handling of the Grand Fleet at Jutland (31May–1 June 1916), believing that he had twice fluffed opportunities to destroy the Germans. Later he accused Jellicoe of bringing the country to the verge of ruin by his apparent passivity in the face of German submarines. He greeted Jellicoe's dismissal with the words: 'one obstacle to a successful war is now out of the way'. The fall of Jellicoe, however, made Richmond's war no more successful. In April 1918 he was appointed Director of the Training and Staff Duties Division at the Admiralty, but his attempted revolution in naval training failed when all his proposals were rejected by higher authority. After his retirement in 1931 he became Vere HARMSWORTH Professor of Imperial History at Cambridge and, later, Master of Downing College. His masterpiece on naval strategy, *Statesmen and Sea Power*, was published in 1946.

Richthofen, Manfred Albrecht von (1888–1918) German fighter ace, one of the most famous individuals to emerge during the war, immortalised as the 'Red Baron'. He joined the German air service in September 1916, learning to fly in Oswald BOELCKE's *Jagdstaffel* 2. A crack shot, with a hunter's instincts, he preyed principally on slow-moving British reconnaissance aircraft, struggling to regain their own lines against the prevailing wind. His own brother, also an ace, described him as a 'butcher'. Image, however, is often greater than reality in war. Richthofen's promotion in January 1917 to command *Jagdstaffel* 11, the famous 'Flying Circus' of gaudily painted aircraft, seemed to confirm him as a latter-day Teutonic knight, a chivalrous enemy of supreme courage and skill. He was shot down behind British lines on 21 April 1918 in his red FOKKER tri-plane, shortly after recording his eightieth victory, and was buried with full military honours. His loss struck a severe blow to German morale at a crucial stage of the war. Richthofen is generally recognised as the top-scoring ace of the war.

Rickenbacker, Edward Vernon (1890–1973) US fighter ace. A well-known racing driver before the war, he went to France in 1917 as General John J. PERSHING's chauffeur. After qualifying as a pilot, he joined 94 Squadron in March 1918, later commanding it. He is generally credited as the leading American 'ace' with twenty-six victories. After the war Rickenbacker had a successful career in civil aviation and was one of the founders of American Airlines. *Fighting the Flying Circus*, an account of his wartime career, was published in 1973.

Ricketts, Thomas (1901–1967) Canadian soldier. Ricketts joined the Newfoundland Regiment in 1916, under age. He was sent to the Western Front in 1917 and was wounded at Cambrai. On 14 October 1918, near Ledeghem, he was part of a Lewis gun team attempting to outflank a German battery that was causing heavy casualties to his battalion. The team ran out of ammunition 300 yards from the battery. Ricketts volunteered to return for more supplies. This involved twice crossing 100 yards of open ground swept by intense machine gun fire. Once resupplied, the Lewis gunners drove off the

enemy gun teams, capturing four field guns, four machine guns and eight prisoners. For his part in these events, Ricketts was awarded the Victoria Cross in January 1919. He is the youngest person ever to have received the award. After the war he returned to Newfoundland, where he qualified and practised as a pharmacist.

Riddell, George Allardice (1865–1934) British newspaper proprietor. Riddell was the son of a photographer. After qualifying as a solicitor, he worked for a law firm that had close links with the newspaper industry. By 1903 he had become chairman of the *News of the World*, the world's largest circulation newspaper. As chairman of the Newspaper Proprietors' Association, he acted throughout the war as liaison officer between the British press and the government. Riddell was one of the many press cronies of his fellow adulterer LLOYD GEORGE, who put a high value on Riddell's political compliance. *Lord Riddell's War Diary 1914–1918* and *Lord Riddell's Intimate Diary of the Peace Conference and After* were published in 1933.

Rider-Rider, William (1889–1979) British/Canadian war photographer. Like other leading photographers of the First World War, Rider-Rider learned his trade on the pre-war *Daily Mirror*, the leading pictorial newspaper of the day. In 1917 he had the good fortune to succeed Ivor Castle (another ex-*Mirror* man) as Canadian official photographer on the Western Front. Rider-Rider, unlike his predecessor, was committed to authenticity, taking some of the most famous and compelling images of the 'campaign of the mud' at Passchendaele, captured by the Canadians in November 1917.

Rivers, William Halse Rivers (1864–1922) British social anthropologist, neurologist and psychologist, one of the brilliant team gathered by Richard ROWS at Maghull Hospital, near Liverpool, to work on the swelling number of psychiatric casualties produced by the war. Rivers soon transferred to Craiglockhart Military Hospital in Edinburgh, where he developed treatments for 'anxiety neurosis' founded on Freudian theory. His method, based on gentle, probing conversation, sometimes exasperated the military authorities, who wanted 'quick-fix' solutions, but he eventually began to gain a reputation for effecting miraculous recoveries. No one was more aware than Rivers himself that the consequence for those who underwent a 'miraculous recovery' could be a return to combat, wounds and death. Rivers' most famous patient at Craiglockhart was the poet Siegfried SASSOON, who called Rivers his 'father confessor'. Their relationship has been sympathetically portrayed in Pat Barker's novel *Regeneration* (1991). Rivers himself found Craiglockhart mentally and emotionally exhausting and left there after a year to become the first psychologist to the Royal Flying Corps, in which capacity he undertook pioneering work on the special stresses of aerial combat.

Roberts, William Patrick (1895–1980) British painter, a close friend and collaborator of Wyndham LEWIS. He also worked in the Cubist idiom as a painter of working-class life. He joined the army in 1916 as a gunner in the Royal Artillery but was recruited as a war artist in 1917, producing several well-known works, including *Burying the Dead*, *A Shell Dump* and *A Group of British Generals*.

Robertson, William Robert (1860–1933) British staff officer, the son of a Lincolnshire village tailor. In 1877, to his mother's shame and disgust, he enlisted as a private soldier, beginning his singular rise to field-marshal. It was eleven years before he was commissioned, at the age of 28. A man of formidable intellect and even more formidable determination, his facility with foreign languages won him an opening as an intelligence officer, from

which he broadened out into more general staff work, which his clarity of mind and organisational genius admirably suited him for. In 1896 he became the first officer promoted from the ranks to enter the Staff College. Fourteen years later he became its commandant, introducing realistic war training to its curriculum. During the First World War, he was successively Quartermaster-General of the British Expeditionary Force (BEF), Chief of the General Staff to Field-Marshal Sir John FRENCH and Chief of the Imperial General Staff, professional head of the British Army. As Quartermaster-General Robertson's foresight and energy in dumping supplies of food at strategic points during the retreat from Mons helped ensure the BEF's survival as a fighting force. As Chief of the General Staff (from January 1915) he carried out a ruthless reorganisation of French's chaotic GHQ. As Chief of the Imperial General Staff (from December 1915), he was a key figure in Britain's prosecution of the war. Armed with unique and unprecedented powers, deliberately given him to curb the influence of Lord KITCHENER, he was the 'sole' official channel of strategic advice to the British government. This advice was always clear and cogent, emanating from a ruthlessly logical appreciation of the realities of the war. British interests required a German defeat. Germany could only be defeated on the Western Front and with French help. Britain, therefore, had to do its utmost to keep France in the war. French military inferiority to Germany meant that the BEF would have to play a major role in wearing down the German army. This would inevitably result in high casualties. Robertson was resolutely opposed to 'sideshow' operations that deflected resources from the main battlefields in France and Belgium. He would have preferred to detach the Ottoman Empire from the Central Powers by diplomacy and saw much danger to British interests and to the long-term security of the

Middle East in the disintegration of Ottoman power. As the human costs of the western strategy inexorably rose, Robertson's advice became increasingly unacceptable to the new Prime Minister, LLOYD GEORGE. Lloyd George's covert attempt, at the notorious Calais Conference of February 1917, to place the BEF under French command alienated Robertson, who never trusted him again. Robertson increasingly devoted himself to protecting Douglas HAIG from the Prime Minister's mischievous conspiracies. Although a faithful defender of Haig, Robertson was not an uncritical admirer, often counselling against his strategic grandiosity and optimistic projections. Robertson finally succumbed to one of Lloyd George's intrigues in February 1918 and was replaced by Sir Henry WILSON. Robertson was one of the great men of the war, not at all the inarticulate, incompetent buffoon of Lloyd George's post-war caricature.

Rodzianko, Mikhail Vladimirovich (1859–1924) Russian politician, an Octobrist deputy who became President of the Duma in 1912. Rodzianko was the embodiment of moderate, patriotic opposition, whose reasoned attempts at reform the Tsar was congenitally incapable of understanding. During 1915 Rodzianko was a leading figure in the War Industry Committees that attempted to galvanise the Russian war economy, an endeavour in which he was fundamentally constrained by the Tsar's refusal to contemplate social or political reform. Rodzianko was among those who unsuccessfully counselled the Tsar against the decision to command his armies in person. The collapse of tsarism in 1917 and the overthrow of the Provincial Government by the Bolsheviks completed Rodzianko's political eclipse. He fled into exile in Yugoslavia in 1920.

Rohr, Wilhelm Martin (1877–19??) German stormtrooper. Willy Rohr was given command of the German army's Assault Detachment in August 1915. The Assault Detachment had been created in March 1915 to develop offensive tactics in trench warfare, but its initial deployment had been in a costly defensive role that terminated the career of its first commander, Major Calsow. Rohr had better fortune. The patronage of senior military figures, especially Colonel Max BAUER, allowed Rohr considerable freedom to develop his own tactics and to acquire the uniform and equipment essential to them, including Austrian mountain boots, mobile artillery, trench mortars, flamethrowers and machine guns. Successful assaults required surprise, speed and maximum violence. To this end, he replaced the traditional line of skirmishers with squads of stormtroops, operating as miniature all-arms units. Suppression of the enemy's firepower had to be conducted at the lowest possible level of command to be effective. When this was achieved, trenches could be cleared by 'bombers', troops armed with grenades. The successful execution of this tactical formula required highly trained, highly motivated, fit troops with initiative. After successfully testing his tactics in an attack against the French in the Vosges, Rohr's unit was used in the great attack at Verdun, where its reputation was enhanced. In April 1916, however, the Assault Detachment was renamed Assault Battalion 'Rohr' and given responsibility for converting the German army's *Jäger* battalions into Assault Battalions (stormtroops) from its base at Beauville, near Verdun.

Rommel, Erwin (1891–1944) German soldier. By the autumn of 1917 Lieutenant Rommel was a much-decorated and much-wounded officer. His exploits on the Western Front and in Romania showed him to be an exceptionally aggressive soldier, always seeking to penetrate the enemy's position using infiltration tactics, speed and daring. But, as yet, he remained unknown to fame.

This was changed by his part in the Italian disaster at Caporetto (October–November 1917). Rommel's Württemberg Mountain Battalion infiltrated the Italian flank, breaching not only the Italian first line but also the second. Typically, Rommel chose not to widen or consolidate the breach but to push on deep into the enemy position, forcing far stronger forces to surrender by attacking them from the flank or rear. When he finally met effective resistance from troops on the summit of Monte Matajur, Rommel personally scaled the rear of the peak and took the garrison in flank. Rommel's force was never stronger than 100 riflemen and six machine guns. In a little over two days they captured 150 Italian officers, 9,000 men and 81 guns for the loss of six dead and thirty wounded, making a major contribution to the ignominious Italian collapse. Rommel was awarded Germany's highest military honour, the *Pour le Mérite* (Blue Max).

Ronarc'h, Pierre Alexis (1865–1940) French naval commander, who served as Director of Anti-submarine Warfare from November 1915 until May 1916, when he was appointed to command French naval forces in the Channel, where he co-operated effectively with the British in maintaining the vital cross-Channel supplies of men, equipment, raw materials and food.

Roosevelt, Franklin Delano (1882–1945) US politician. As Assistant Secretary of the Navy from 1917 to 1920, Roosevelt played a leading part in the expansion of US naval power, a task to which he brought considerable energy, a love of the sea and of ships, fine political judgement (especially in his handling of organised labour) and a clear appreciation of the importance of naval power to US global political ambitions. After US entry into the war Roosevelt gave priority to the anti-submarine warfare campaign, authorising the building of destroyers and other escort vessels. He also lent his considerable support to the convoy system and the North Sea mine barrage.

Roosevelt, Theodore (1858–1919) US politician. The former President and hero of the Spanish-American war was one of the severest critics of Woodrow WILSON's foreign policy. Uninhibited by the restraints of office and contemptuous of public opinion, Roosevelt derided Wilson's policy of neutrality, demanding increases in defence spending and compulsory military training. Wilson's failure to respond effectively to the loss of American lives in the sinking of the *Lusitania* led to accusations of cowardice. After the United States entered the war in April 1917, Roosevelt's was one of the leading voices clamouring for a mass expansion of US military power and the waging of an aggressive war. His outspoken attacks on German and other 'hyphenated Americans' and on conscientious objectors were instrumental in releasing a wave of public hostility and paranoia that resulted in brutal attacks against the American left and restrictions on immigration after the war.

Roques, Pierre Auguste (1856–1920) French military commander and Minister of War. Roques was an undistinguished and ineffective soldier whose XII Corps suffered a severe defeat at Rossignol in August 1914 that was instrumental in the retreat of the French Fourth Army. Despite this, General JOFFRE's purge of senior French generals cleared a path for Roques' rise to command First Army in 1915. His performance as an army commander confirmed his mediocrity. It was this that seemed to recommend him most for the position of War Minister, in which he was expected to be the compliant servant of the high command. Such was his political naivety, however, that he failed even in this. In October 1916 Joffre sent Roques to Salonika, where it was expected that he would provide a hostile report on the leadership of the Allied expeditionary force under the command of the Republican left's favourite general, Maurice SARRAIL. Joffre wished for nothing more than to liquidate the Salonika campaign and get rid of its commander. Roques' report, however, was supportive of the expedition and of Sarrail. Roques' dismissal in December 1916 was inevitable, but it was swiftly followed by that of Joffre, for whose left-wing parliamentary enemies the Roques report was the final straw.

Rosenberg, Isaac (1890–1918) British soldier and poet, the son of a poor Russian Jewish immigrant family in the East End of London. He originally studied as a painter before turning to poetry, encouraged by Eddie Marsh, Gordon Bottomley, Lascelles Abercrombie and other leading figures among the 'Georgian' literary establishment. Rosenberg was in South Africa when the war broke out but returned to England in 1915. He enlisted at the end of the year. Rosenberg was an unlikely soldier. He hated the idea of killing. He was small and sickly. He was perennially disorganised and impractical. And the army soon proved anathema to him. Despite this, the war inspired his finest poetry, including 'Break of Day in the Trenches', 'Dead Man's Dump' and 'Returning, We Hear the Larks'. His current reputation among twentieth-century British poets and among war poets stands very high. 22311 Rosenberg, Private Isaac, was killed in action on 1 April 1918 while serving with the 1st Battalion King's Own (Royal Lancaster Regiment) on the Western Front.

Rosenthal, Charles (1875–1954) Australian military commander. 'Rosie' Rosenthal was a successful architect and part-time soldier before the war, which he began as CO of the 5th Field Brigade Australian Artillery. He was twice wounded on Gallipoli in 1915. During a period of convalescence in England he took the opportunity to make a thorough

study of artillery tactics. He served throughout the Somme campaign as artillery commander of the 4th (Australian) Division and was wounded again. In July 1917 he was given command of 9th (Australian) Brigade, where his fearless front-line style of command attracted criticism from some but made him immensely popular with his troops. In May 1918 he succeeded the British General Nevill SMYTH as GOC 2nd (Australian) Division. His promotion did nothing to curb his command style. After being wounded yet again, in a French advanced post, he attempted to command his division from a hospital bed in Abbeville until MONASH put a stop to it. Rosenthal returned to command in the August battles, when his division achieved the remarkable capture of Mont St Quentin.

Rows, Richard (1867?–1925) British psychiatrist, who pioneered the sympathetic treatment of war neurosis at Maghull Hospital near Liverpool, gathering round him a group of brilliant men that included W.H.R. RIVERS. Rows' team utilised Freudian theory, especially the interpretation of dreams, concluding that 'shell shock' was caused by the repression of trauma. Treatment included occupational therapy. This 'advanced' and humane method of treatment was fully supported by the military authorities. The War Office funded Maghull and sent RAMC officers there on training courses from 1917 onwards.

Rupprecht of Bavaria, Crown Prince (1869–1955) German military commander. Although Rupprecht's military prominence owed much to his position as heir to the kingdom of Bavaria, he was undoubtedly a competent professional, perhaps the most competent of all the royal commanders in the Great War. In 1914 he led the German Sixth Army in Lorraine. His allotted task, under the terms of the SCHLIEFFEN Plan, was to draw French forces into Lorraine, facilitating the

German envelopment of the French left. But after a few days of retreat he became dissatisfied with this role and obtained MOLTKE's permission to attack, pushing French forces back to their fortress line, though at great cost. Sixth Army was later deployed north, in the 'race to the sea', fighting on the Lys and in the First Battle of Ypres (October–November 1914). In 1916 Rupprecht was given command of his own Army Group, with responsibility for the whole of the northern part of the German line. This was mainly opposite the British, against whose remorseless attacks in Flanders he was called upon to defend throughout the second half of 1917. This he did with much skill and even greater resolution. In April 1918 Army Group Rupprecht's offensive against the Ypres salient met with striking initial success, but all hope of a break-through to the Channel ports was soon brought to a halt by fierce British resistance. From July onwards Rupprecht was pushed steadily backwards by the careful, though irresistible, Allied advance. The abdication on 8 November 1918 of his father, King LUDWIG III, and Germany's subsequent surrender denied him his inheritance, and he spent much of the rest of his life in exile.

Russell, Andrew Hamilton (1868–1960) New Zealand military commander. Russell was educated in England (at Harrow) and served in the Border Regiment from 1887 until 1892, when he resigned his commission to go sheep farming in New Zealand. But this did not terminate his military activities. In 1900 he formed and commanded the Hawke's Bay Mounted Rifles. Russell later came to the attention of Major-General Alexander GODLEY, the British officer commanding New Zealand forces. Godley failed to persuade Russell to join the New Zealand Staff Corps as a Regular, but when war broke out he had no hesitation in offering him command of the New Zealand Mounted Rifles Brigade, which Russell accepted. Russell

distinguished himself in the Gallipoli campaign of April 1915, and he was given command of the New Zealand Division on its formation in March 1916. Russell was the only commander of the division during the war. By the Armistice he was the third longest serving divisional commander in the British Expeditionary Force. In September 1916 the New Zealand Division launched its first major attack on the Somme, at Flers, the battle in which tanks were used for the first time in war. The division established a reputation as an elite unit that was strengthened at Messines (June 1917) and Third Ypres (July–November 1917). Russell initially brought to his command the instincts of a former British regimental officer. He was a strict disciplinarian who insisted on smartness and proper military etiquette and strongly supported the death penalty. He led from the front and demanded that his officers put the comfort and safety of their men first. But he also grew tactically with the war, and his division became efficient as well as 'smart'. He was an early convert to limited set-piece operations and trained his division to a high standard that emphasised the importance of initiative and leadership at junior levels. Russell was an intelligent, cultivated man with a tremendous sense of duty rooted in a strong Christian faith, as modest as he was brave.

Russell, Bertrand Arthur William (1872–1970) British mathematician, philosopher and pacifist. By the time war broke out Russell had already established his reputation in the field of mathematical logic with the publication of *The Principles of Mathematics* (1903) and *Principia Mathematica* (1910–13; co-written with A.N. Whitehead). But the war was to launch him on a lifelong career as a political and public controversialist. The defining issue was pacifism. Subsequent portrayal of the Great War as an incompetently managed exercise in tragic futility has obscured how popular it was at the time. It was probably the most popular of all British wars. Public pronouncements of pacifism took moral (and sometimes even physical) courage and came at a price. In Russell's case this was the loss of his Cambridge fellowship as a result of his involvement with the two most important British anti-war organisations, the Union of Democratic Control and the No-Conscription Fellowship, which he chaired after the imprisonment of Clifford ALLEN and Fenner BROCKWAY. Russell himself spent six months in Brixton Prison in 1918, though his incarceration (unlike that of some other pacifists) was not sufficiently severe to prevent his completing a book, *Political Ideals: Roads to Freedom*. But the wartime activity for which he is best remembered is, perhaps, the leading part he played in encouraging Siegfried SASSOON to publish his celebrated and iconic statement against the war. Russell was a civilian, the grandson of an earl and a former prime minister. Sassoon was a serving officer, subject to military law, who could have faced the death penalty for his actions. Sassoon was saved from the martyrdom that his aristocratic friends had laid down for him by the intervention of his friend Robert GRAVES. Graves' wonderfully histrionic performance before an Army Medical Board succeeded in having Sassoon referred to the Craiglockhart Military Hospital with 'shell shock', inadvertently opening a new chapter in the history of English poetry.

Ruzsky, Nikolai Vladimiravich (1855–1918) Russian military commander. Ruzsky was a cautious and indecisive commander whose principal military achievement was the defence of Łódz in November 1914. Caution and indecision distinguished his subsequent commands on several fronts, but in March 1917 he proved he could act decisively by pressuring the Tsar, who was fortuitously at Ruzsky's headquarters, into abdication. Characteristically, Ruzsky later regretted his action. He was captured and executed by the Bolsheviks in 1918.

Ryan, Eugene 'Micky' (1873–1951) British medical officer. Colonel Ryan was Chief Medical Officer at GHQ under Field-Marshal HAIG. Haig was an asthmatic. He is regarded by some of his many detractors as a valetudinarian if not a hypochondriac. His diary is full of references to his state of health. He had great faith in Ryan's medical judgement and would submit meekly to him when ordered to rest or take medication. Ryan's ability to do this was regarded with amazement by the rest of Haig's staff.

Ryrie, Granville de Laune (1865–1937) Australian military commander. Ryrie's military career was spent in the Australian Light Horse, which he originally joined as a trooper in 1898. He served in the South African War, where he was wounded. In September 1914 he was given command of the Australian Imperial Force's 2nd Light Horse Brigade. He was wounded twice on Gallipoli in 1915, where he was conspicuous by his presence in positions of danger. After the withdrawal from Gallipoli, the Light Horse were given a more suitable role, playing a leading part in the fighting in the Sinai and Palestine that culminated in the crossing of the Jordan in September 1918 and the capture of Amman.

S

Salandra, Antonio (1853–1931) Italian politician. As Prime Minister from March 1914 until June 1916 Salandra, together with his Foreign Minister Sidney SON-NINO, played a leading part in Italy's decision for war in May 1915. Many myths came to surround Italian 'intervention'. Salandra's motives, however, seem clear. He was a conservative statesman not a 'ranting nationalist demagogue'. He had come increasingly to believe that Italy's future as a world power depended upon entering the war on the Allied side. Italian belligerency was essentially a conventional diplomatic decision. Salandra expected to fight a 'Cabinet war' of limited duration and for limited aims of territorial expansion at Austrian expense. He was to be disappointed. After a year of fighting Italian arms had achieved nothing. The war had proved neither instrumental nor glorious. The authoritarian Commander-in-Chief of the army, Luigi CADORNA, increasingly dominated its conduct and Salandra struggled to have any influence. Italian defeat on the Trentino in May 1916 forced the government's resignation the following month. His was the first government to fall in a belligerent country. He held no further office during the war.

Salmond, John Maitland (1881–1968) British air force commander. Like many other pioneering figures in the history of British military aviation, Jack Salmond's reputation has been overshadowed by that of his predecessor as GOC Royal Flying Corps, Hugh TRENCHARD. Nevertheless, Salmond had a remarkable war. In August 1914 he took 3 Squadron to France as a 33-year-old captain. Three years later he was a major-general in command of training in England, then Director-General of Military Aeronautics at the War Office. On 18 January 1918, still only 36, he succeeded Trenchard in command of the RFC in France. Salmond subscribed fully to Trenchard's view that the RFC should be engaged principally in army co-operation, a policy that survived the creation of an independent Royal Air Force on 1 April 1918, despite the first experiments in 'strategic' bombing.

Samson, Charles Rumney (1883–1931) British naval aviation pioneer. Samson joined the Royal Navy in 1899 and qualified as a pilot in 1911. By the time war broke out he had already pioneered many of the techniques central to military aviation, including night flying, aerial reconnaissance and bombardment, and air–ground radio communication. In 1912 Samson became the first man to fly an aircraft from the deck of a ship. The outbreak of war gave him the opportunity to put his experience to effective use. In the early days of the war he achieved considerable celebrity for his attacks on

Zeppelin sheds at Cologne and Düsseldorf. He also undertook ground attack missions against German positions along the Belgian coast and, in 1915, on Gallipoli, where his aircraft also spotted for the navy's guns. From 1916 he became increasingly concerned with the application of air power to the vital campaign against German and Austrian submarines, first in the eastern Mediterranean and then, from 1917, in the North Sea.

Samsonov, Aleksandr Vasilevich (1859–1914) Russian military commander, whose Second Army suffered a humiliating defeat at Tannenberg in August 1914. Samsonov was inexperienced in command of large formations in the field. His army had been hastily assembled from poorly trained reservists and was badly short of transport animals, artillery ammunition and competent staff officers. Samsonov was intelligent enough to realise this and his realisation made him pessimistic. But the determination of the Russian High Command, itself under intense French pressure, to launch an offensive in East Prussia forced him to press on despite his doubts. The plan was for the Russian First Army, commanded by Samsonov's bitter rival Pavel von RENNENKAMPF, to advance from the north-east and tie down the German Eighth Army, while Second Army advanced from the south and took Eighth Army in the rear. First Army utterly failed to carry out its part of the plan. After being attacked by General FRANÇOIS' corps at the inconclusive battle of Gumbinnen (20 August), Rennenkampf became inert. The Russian army's woeful communications and intelligence systems meant that Samsonov knew nothing of Rennenkampf's halt or of the German forces that were manoeuvring against him, unhampered by pressure from First Army, until he came under attack. Two of Samsonov's five corps were encircled and destroyed and the rest of his army badly handled. Realising the magnitude of the disaster that had befallen his army, Samsonov apparently committed suicide on the night of 29–30 August. His body was never found.

Sandes, Flora (1876–1956) British nurse and Serbian soldier, the daughter of a Scottish clergyman, who volunteered for service in a Serbian ambulance unit on the outbreak of war. During the winter of 1915 she took part in the Serbian army's painful retreat across the freezing mountains of Albania to safety in Corfu. In 1916 she published *An English Woman-Sergeant in the Serbian Army* in order to raise funds for the Serb cause. She remained in the Serb army after the war, reaching the rank of major. She married a former Russian general in 1927.

San Giuliano, Antonio Paterno Castello, Marquis di (1852–1914) Italian politician. As Minister of Foreign Affairs from 1910 until his death in 1914, he manoeuvred skilfully within the Triple Alliance, cultivating German friendship and obstructing Austro-Hungarian ambitions in the Balkans. He favoured neutrality in the July Crisis of 1914, seeking to maintain good relations with all the belligerents until it became clearer which would be the winning side.

Sargent, John Singer (1856–1925) British war artist. Sargent was born in Italy of American parents but in 1885 settled in England, where he established a preeminent reputation as a portrait painter. In 1918 a commission to paint a large canvas symbolising British–US collaboration resulted, instead, in one of the most haunting images of the war, *Gassed*, in which an orderly leads a file of men blinded by mustard gas, each gripping the shoulders of the man in front.

Sarkotić von Lovčen, Stephan, Baron (1858–1939) Austro-Hungarian military commander. At the start of the war Sarkotić was named as 'Governor of Serbia', a title that Austria's defeat and expulsion from Serb territory rendered suitably empty. Instead, Sarkotić spent most of the war as commander of Imperial forces in Bosnia-Herzegovina and Dalmatia, proving himself both a competent general and a ruthless ruler. In January 1916 his forces overran Montenegro. The decisive event in the conquest was the storming of Lovćen, which Sarkotić subsequently added to his name. He favoured the union of his native Croatia with Bosnia-Herzegovina and Dalmatia but opposed the union's becoming part of a 'Triple' Monarchy. He also opposed the creation of separate Austrian and Hungarian armies in December 1917.

Sarrail, Maurice Paul Emmanuel (1856–1929) French and Allied military commander, whose republican and socialist views endeared him to established political authority in France and ensured that he be given a senior command. His criticism of the French Commander-in-Chief, General JOFFRE also ensured, however, that this would not be on the Western Front. Joffre dismissed Sarrail as GOC French Third Army in 1915 but was forced to compensate him with command of the grandiosely named French 'Army of the Orient'. This was deployed in October 1915 to the malarial backwater of Salonika. The need to keep Sarrail in a command commensurate with his political importance did much to ensure that the Salonika front was kept open despite the lack of military success and the steady drain of men from sickness and disease. Sarrail's command, which included all Allied forces from January 1916, was vitiated by intrigue and inter-Allied suspicion. His one attempt to break the military stalemate, at Monastir in the autumn of 1916, met with only limited success. The Germans regarded the Allied efforts with contempt and dismissed Salonika as 'the largest internment camp in Europe'. CLEMENCEAU was unimpressed with Sarrail's performance. He dismissed him un-

ceremoniously in December 1917 without political ill effects.

Sassoon, Siegfried Lorraine (1886–1967) British war poet. Sassoon's pre-war life was one of wealth and privilege, much of which was spent in the hunting field or on the golf course. But in 1906 he published privately his first collection of poems and began increasingly to move in literary circles, at the centre of which was the ubiquitous Eddie Marsh. Sassoon volunteered for military service as early as 1 August 1914 and greeted the war already in uniform. He served with the elite 2nd Royal Welsh Fusiliers, where one of his fellow officers was Robert GRAVES. Sassoon was an aggressive soldier known to his comrades as 'Mad Jack'. But in the spring of 1917, while on leave in England recovering from a wound and much encouraged by Bertrand RUSSELL, he turned against the war, castigating what he called 'the political errors and insincerities for which the fighting men are being sacrificed'. These words form part of his celebrated public statement of opposition to the war, made as a 'wilful act of defiance' against military authority in an open letter to his commanding officer. At the same time, he tore the ribbon of the Military Cross from his tunic and threw it into the River Mersey, an act that has since achieved iconic status in British perceptions of the war. Sassoon was saved from court martial largely through Graves' wonderfully theatrical testimony before the medical board that sent Sassoon to Craiglockhart military hospital in Edinburgh, suffering from 'shell shock'. Here he was treated by the psychologist W.H.R. RIVERS and gave great encouragement to the writing of fellow officer Wilfred OWEN, whose Keatsian sensibilities he exposed to the bracing influence of Thomas Hardy. Sassoon returned to active service in 1918 but was invalided from the army in July after being accidentally shot by one of his own men. Unlike his friend Graves, Sassoon was never really able to say 'good-bye to all that'. He constantly reworked his wartime experience in autobiographical and fictional form, including *Memoirs of an Infantry Officer* (1930), *Sherston's Progress* (1936) and *Siegfried's Journey* (1945). Although he continued to write poetry throughout his long life, none of it made the same impact as his war poetry, and he is condemned to be remembered as a war poet rather than a poet. Despite the impression sometimes given in anthologies of war poetry, few of Sassoon's poems were explicitly critical of the military conduct of the war. His real targets were politicians, profiteers, shirkers, all those who gloried in war but shared none of its sufferings, privations and dangers.

Sazonov, Sergei Dmitrievich (1860–1927) Russian politician, Foreign Minister from 1910 to 1916. Sazonov was an intelligent, cautious diplomat who sought to reduce the temperature of international relations, especially in the Balkans. In this he was often undermined by pan-Slav elements within the Russian political elite and army. During the July Crisis of 1914 that followed the assassination of FRANZ FER-DINAND, Austria-Hungary's ultimatum to Serbia made him almost resigned to the inevitability of war, but he counselled Serbia to accept as many as possible of Austria-Hungary's deliberately humiliating demands. Beyond this he had neither the political authority nor the force of character to influence events, which continued their downward spiral to war. Once hostilities began, his attempt to find an advantageous compromise with Polish nationalism that would serve Russia's interests and weaken Austria-Hungary was undermined by the reactionary Interior Minister MAKLAKOV. His calm and courteous manner, however, did much to maintain fruitful Allied relations. In March 1915 he succeeded in obtaining British and French acquiescence in future Russian control of the Dardanelles, and his diplomacy helped keep Romania out

of the Central Powers' camp. This degree of competence was, however, too much for the Tsarina ALEKSANDRA, who engineered his dismissal in July 1916.

Scheer, Reinhard (1863–1928) German naval commander. Scheer succeeded the ailing Admiral Hugo von POHL as Commander-in-Chief of the German High Seas Fleet in January 1916. The very existence of a powerful German fleet was an inescapable reality for the British. The High Seas Fleet did not even need to leave port in order to exercise an influence on the war. Maintaining a 'fleet in being', however, was not enough for a man of Scheer's aggressive instincts. His aggression was nevertheless tempered with caution. He did not relish taking on the untrammelled might of the British Grand Fleet, which enjoyed a superiority of thirty-seven to twenty-one in capital ships. Instead, he planned to defeat the Royal Navy in detail. His tactic would be the ambush. On 31 May 1916 he made his gambler's throw. By offering Admiral HIPPER's battle cruiser squadron as bait, he attempted to lure Admiral BEATTY's British battle cruisers into the jaws of the High Seas Fleet, while employing sixteen U-boats to interdict the British Grand Fleet as it raced to the rescue. The resulting losses to the British fleet would allow the German navy to resume the conflict at a later date on much more favourable terms. Scheer's plan was an initial success. Beatty only narrowly avoided disaster, but when he turned away from the German High Seas Fleet (in 'the run to the north'), he was not merely fleeing but also drawing Scheer on to the guns of the British Grand Fleet. Unknown to Scheer the British had broken the German naval code. The Grand Fleet was at sea long before the Germans expected it, and their U-boats signally failed to impede its passage. As a result, it was not Admiral JELLICOE who was surprised but Scheer. For a tantalising few hours Scheer seemed to be in a position to hunt Beatty's fleet to destruction, when he suddenly found himself faced with annihilation. Jellicoe responded magnificently to his opportunity, twice placing his battleships between Scheer and the High Seas Fleet's line of retreat. Twice, however, Scheer manouevred away, executing the 'battle turn-around' (*Gefechtskehrtwendung*) of his fleet, finally escaping back to base during the night. He had shown immense calm under pressure. The superiority of German engineering had resulted in fewer losses of men and ships for the High Seas Fleet than for the British, but he had been lucky and the British remained in command of the sea. Scheer was able to present the battle of Jutland as a German victory, but he was never again prepared to contest the supremacy of the British surface fleet. Instead, he became a leading advocate of unrestricted submarine warfare, to the extent even of refusing to commit his U-boats to long-range operations unless restrictions were lifted. His estimation of the operational effectiveness of the U-boat fleet, however, was grotesquely exaggerated and his willingness to risk the United States' entry into the war reckless. In August 1918, far too late, Scheer succeeded in imposing a unified command structure on the German navy. But the naval high command's attempt to effect a Wagnerian showdown with the Royal Navy was scuppered by the mutiny of the High Seas Fleet at Kiel on 30 October 1918. This also spelled the end of Imperial Germany. The English translation of Scheer's account of Jutland, *Germany's High Seas Fleet in the World War*, was published in 1920.

Scheidemann, Philipp (1865–1939) German politician. Scheidemann was a well-known socialist orator. He enthusiastically supported a 'defensive' war in 1914 but became increasingly alienated by the annexationist policies of HINDENBURG and LUDENDORFF. He opposed the punitive Treaty of Brest-Litovsk imposed on defeated Russia and joined Prince MAX

von Baden's government in October 1918. On 9 November he made his most important contribution to German history by proclaiming a republic from the balcony of the Reichstag. He did this without the knowledge or approval of the leader of the Provisional Government, Friedrich EBERT, in order to pre-empt the establishment of a more radical regime. Scheidemann's act also dashed Ebert's hopes of establishing a constitutional monarchy. Scheidemann became the first President of the republic he had proclaimed but resigned in June 1919, refusing to sign the Treaty of Versailles. His part in the establishment of the Weimar Republic brought him the undying enmity of the far right, and he was forced into Danish exile after Hitler came to power.

Schlieffen, Alfred von (1833–1913) German staff officer. As German chief of staff from 1891 until his retirement in 1905, Schlieffen devoted his life to designing a military strategy that would allow Germany to win a two-front war, the likely outcome of the disastrous Franco-Russian *rapprochement* of 1892, which had marked the end of Bismarckian diplomacy. Schlieffen's plans went through many versions, but most were characterised by a disregard for anything other than narrowly technical military considerations, a willingness to make a pre-emptive strike and a determination to win a battle of annihilation through rapid manoeuvre. The final version of his plan, accepted in 1906, was breathtaking in its ambition. The key decision was to deploy first against France. This was based upon the differential rates of mobilisation between the French and Russian forces. French mobilisation would be quicker. The French army would be into the field first. It would therefore have to be beaten first. To ensure its defeat, Schlieffen was prepared to deploy seven-eighths of the German army against France, leaving only a screening force to defend East Prussia against a Russian invasion. The German army would seek to envelop the French left, avoiding the difficult wooded country and fortified towns that lined the Franco-German border. This meant violating Belgian neutrality, which risked British intervention. (Schlieffen would have preferred to violate Dutch neutrality as well, allowing the German deployment to pass through Maastricht and avoid the difficult diversion round the 'Maastricht appendix'.) It also meant placing the bulk of Germany's attacking forces on the French left, leaving relatively weak forces to defend the Franco-German border in Lorraine. The German right would drive through Belgium, cross the Meuse and sweep south in a great outflanking movement that would take it west of Paris, trapping the French army between the two wings of the German army, the classic 'Cannae manoeuvre', the 'Holy Grail' of German strategy. In order to execute the plan, Schlieffen and his staff drafted an operational schedule that allowed precisely thirty-nine days for 'victory in the west' before the German armies redeployed to the Eastern Front to smash the Russian steamroller as it slowly rolled into position. To Schlieffen's admirers, notably Wilhelm GROENER, the plan was the product of a military genius that represented an infallible blueprint for victory. Germany's eventual defeat was attributable to the corruption of the plan by Schlieffen's inadequate successor, Helmuth von MOLTKE. The plan was, of course, perfectly mad. It put short-term military considerations before long-term political ones. It was absurdly prescriptive, allowing nothing to the friction of war or to the weather or to the independent initiative of the enemy. It underestimated the speed of Russian deployment and ignored the ability of Russian forces to attack in the east before full mobilisation was completed. It also implicitly risked the possibility of an Austrian defeat by the Russians. And, finally, for the whole of Schlieffen's life, even allowing for the immediate use of

reserve forces that he advocated, the German army was too small to carry the plan out. In the event, the plan was never executed. It is more proper to call the German deployment in August 1914 the 'Moltke plan'. Before 1914 Moltke made significant changes, strengthening the left flank of the German deployment and weakening the right (the chief charge made against him by Schlieffen's admirers). And, in August 1914, he was compelled to redeploy troops from the west to the east in order to counter the invasion of East Prussia by partially mobilised Russian armies that caused consternation in Berlin.

Schmidt von Knobelsdorf, Constantin (1860–1936) German staff officer. Schmidt was Crown Prince WILHELM's chief of staff at Fifth Army. In this capacity, Schmidt took part in the battle of Verdun, the sanguinary logic of which he and the Crown Prince only reluctantly accepted after a three-day debate with FALKENHAYN in December 1915. By the following summer, however, fearful of witnessing the destruction of Fifth Army, Schmidt's opposition became so flagrant that Falkenhayn sacked him on 21 August 1916.

Schönburg-Hartenstein, Aloys, Prince von (1858–1944) Austro-Hungarian military commander. Schönburg-Hartenstein commanded the 6th Division and the elite XX (Edelweiss) Corps, serving on the Russian and Italian fronts. In January 1918, however, he was charged with suppressing domestic unrest, effecting the arrest of strike leaders and rounding up 44,000 deserters. Although there were some who hoped that he would impose a military dictatorship on the Empire, neither he nor the Kaiser, KARL I, had the stomach for this. In the summer of 1918 Schönburg-Hartenstein returned to 'proper soldiering' as GOC Sixth Army in the disastrous Piave offensive, during which he was wounded in the leg.

Schröder, Ludwig von (1854–1933) German naval officer, who was called out of retirement in 1914 at the age of 60 to command German naval forces along the Belgian coast. He took part in the capture of Antwerp in October 1914 and then spent most of the rest of the war guarding Bruges, Ostend and Zeebrugge. The Royal Navy's raid on Zeebrugge, on 23 April 1918, was portrayed in Germany as a humiliating British defeat, for which Schröder was given the credit, earning the soubriquet 'The Lion of Flanders'.

Scott, Percy Moreton (1853–1924) British naval gunnery expert. Scott was one of the most dynamic, controversial and far-sighted officers in the Edwardian navy, responsible for many technical innovations in naval gunnery. As Inspector of Target Practice 1905–07, he helped transform gunnery training, pursuing a single-minded campaign to establish 'director firing' centralised gun control on board ships. His aggressive, charmless style, however, provoked much opposition and intensified the navy's already clique-ridden culture. Scott was also a great advocate of naval air power and submarines, forecasting the death of the capital ship even before the war began. He was recalled from retirement on the outbreak of war and placed in command of London's air defences, in which capacity he founded the Anti-Aircraft Corps.

Seeckt, Johannes Friedrich Leopold ('Hans') von (1866–1936) German staff officer. Seeckt's outstanding organisational ability was apparent from an early stage of his career, and he was seconded to the General Staff in 1899 while still only a lieutenant. From then until the outbreak of war he spent virtually all his time in staff appointments. In August 1914, by now a colonel, he was III Corps' chief of staff in KLUCK's First Army, spearhead of the German invasion of France, during which he added to his reputation. He was promoted Major-General and appointed chief of staff to MACKENSEN's Eleventh Army on the Eastern Front. In this capacity he is generally credited with designing the breakthrough tactics at Gorlice-Tarnów (May 1915), for which he was awarded the *Pour le Mérite*, and for planning the conquest of Serbia (October 1915). After the virtual collapse of the Austro-Hungarian army following the BRUSILOV offensive (June 1916), Seeckt became a sort of 'trouble-shooter' brought in to stiffen various Austrian armies, including PFLANZER-BALTIN's highly regarded Seventh and the Archduke KARL's Army Group. The reality of Seeckt's actual command was disguised by his appointment as chief of staff in order to assuage Austrian sensibilities, something that failed in the case of Pflanzer-Baltin. In December 1917 he was given a similar role in the Ottoman army, which seems rather a waste of his talents. After the war Seeckt became Commander-in-Chief of the German army (1921–26), focusing all his energy on establishing a 100,000-strong force (to which Germany was restricted under the terms of the Treaty of Versailles) as a highly trained cadre that could be expanded rapidly. It was this army that Hitler inherited in 1933 and which was the foundation of German military strength in the Second World War.

Seeger, Alan (1884–1916) US poet and French soldier, a Harvard contemporary of T.S. Eliot, Walter LIPPMANN and John REED, who joined the French Foreign Legion in August 1914. His fate was to belong to the small band of 'war poets' whose reputation is based on one poem, in his case the prophetic 'Rendezvous'. Seeger had no reservations about the justice of the Allied cause, for which he was quite willing – even anxious – to die. He made his own rendezvous with death on the Somme at Belloy-en-Santerre on 4 July 1916. He would have approved of the symbolism of dying on American Independence Day.

Service, Robert William (1874–1958) Canadian war correspondent, novelist and poet. Service was a travelling correspondent for the *Toronto Star*. His pre-war poems about Canadian frontier life enjoyed immense popularity despite the scorn of the London literary establishment. During the war he served for two years as an ambulance driver on the Western Front and knew something of the realities of war. His war poetry shows an unsentimental Kiplingesque respect for the ordinary soldier, who is portrayed as a determined, resilient individual exercising moral choice and not simply as a passive victim of great events. Service's novels, *Ploughman of the Moon* (1945) and *Harper of Heaven* (1948), are autobiographical.

Seton-Watson, R[obert] W[illiam] (1879–1951) British historian and propagandist, a romantic nationalist with a large, independent fortune and an enviable talent for languages who founded British Slavic studies. During the war Seton-Watson devoted himself to the destruction of the Austro-Hungarian empire, acting as Tomáš MASARYK's principal impressario in the pages of *The New Europe*, the journal he founded. In 1919 Seton-Watson's leading articles in the Paris edition of the *Daily Mail* landed first on the breakfast table of President Woodrow WILSON, whose opinion they were principally intended to sway.

Seymour, Ralph Frederick (1886–1922) British naval staff officer, who served on HMS *Lion* as Admiral BEATTY's Flag-Lieutenant, responsible for choosing the wording and the means (visual, wireless or morse) by which the Admiral's intentions in battle were communicated to his subordinate commanders and their ships. At Heligoland (August 1914) and the Dogger Bank (January 1915), the ambiguity of Seymour's signals caused confusion, undermining the prospects of achieving decisive success. During the

battle-cruiser action at Jutland (31 May–1 June 1916), they imperilled first Beatty's ships and then those of Admiral EVAN-THOMAS. Beatty later complained that Seymour had 'lost three battles for me', but he had only himself to blame. Seymour had no training as a signaller. His retention after Heligoland is surprising. His retention after the Dogger Bank is inexplicable.

Sharp, William Graves (1859–1922) US diplomat. Sharp's appointment as US Ambassador to France was announced in June 1914, but he did not arrive in Paris until three weeks after the outbreak of war and did not take up his post until 1 December 1914. Sharp was a lawyer who had made a fortune in manufacturing before being elected Congressman in his home state of Ohio in 1909. He had no diplomatic experience, though he had served on the House Committee on Foreign Affairs. In the event, this proved unimportant and was more than compensated for by his industrial credentials, which enabled him to provide shrewd and practical assessments of French military and economic needs. Once the United States entered the war, Sharp also established good and effective relations with the US Commander-in-Chief, General John J. PERSHING, not always the easiest thing to do.

Shcherbachev, Dmitry Grigorevich (1857–1932) Russian military commander. Shcherbachev was a gunner and his operations favoured attacks on narrow fronts with overwhelming artillery support. Although this method brought little success in the disastrous campaigns directed by General IVANOV in 1915, it fitted well into the tactics employed by General BRUSILOV. And it was under Brusilov's command that Shcherbachev's Seventh Army enjoyed its greatest success in the summer of 1916. After the February Revolution of 1917, Shcherbachev was given command of Russian forces in

Romania, and it was from this base that he took part in the Russian Civil War against the Bolsheviks. He was a leading figure in the creation of a White army among the Don Cossacks. This force carried on the struggle until 1921, though Shcherbachev himself fled into exile in France in 1919.

Shephard, Gordon Strachey (1885–1918) British air force commander. Strachey was an Etonian and the son of an Indian civil servant. He was commissioned in the Royal Fusiliers in 1905 but transferred to the Royal Flying Corps (RFC) in 1912, the year of its formation. He was also an excellent sailor. His friendship with the novelist Erskine CHILDERS, author of *The Riddle of the Sands*, so excited Strachey's own interest in intelligence work that he found himself under arrest by the German authorities in Emden in 1911 as a suspected 'spy', though he was soon released (he spoke fluent German). In July 1914 he used his skill as a yachtsman to assist Childers in landing a consignment of weapons for the (nationalist) Southern Irish Volunteers, an action that would almost certainly have terminated his military career had it become known. Once the war broke out, his rise was rapid. During the first part of the war he pioneered the Royal Flying Corps' artillery co-operation role, together with Donald LEWIS and 'Bron' JAMES. Popular fascination with the lives of fighter aces has disguised the importance of the RFC's role in artillery spotting and reconnaissance, much its most important work during the war. Sir Frederick SYKES considered Shephard to be the finest reconnaissance officer in the RFC. Shephard played an important part in the evolution of British fighter tactics and of air–infantry co-operation. He was also an excellent talent spotter. His promotion to command I Brigade Royal Flying Corps in 1917, with the rank of brigadier-general, gave him greater opportunity to further the careers of able pilots. Shephard was killed in a

flying accident on 19 January 1918. He was 32.

Sherriff, Robert Cedric (1896–1975) British playwright. Sherriff served during the war as a temporary officer (and gentleman) in the 9th Battalion East Surrey Regiment. Although he had been humiliatingly rejected for a commission in 1914 because he had not attended public school, Sherriff later wrote one of the most sympathetic depictions of the public-school officer at war. His play *Journey's End* focused on the relationship between two public-school officers, the younger Raleigh and Raleigh's school senior and hero, Stanhope. It was first produced in 1928 at the Savoy Theatre, where it ran for 594 performances. *Journey's End* and *Oh! What a Lovely War* are the most influential plays about the Great War to appear on the British stage.

Shute, Cameron Deane (1866–1936) British military commander. Shute's career has been overshadowed by his unhappy experience as GOC 63rd (Royal Naval) Division between October 1916 and February 1917. The members of the Royal Naval Division were very self-consciously 'sailors'. Shute was unimpressed by their peculiarities. He set about imposing army standards of discipline and, worst of all, uniform. His harsh and unsympathetic behaviour before and after the fighting on the Ancre in November 1916 was especially resented, provoking A.P. HERBERT's bitter poem 'After the Battle'. Herbert was also the author of a celebrated song that poured scorn on Shute's criticism of the division for the state of its trenches (which they had recently taken over from the Portuguese). The concluding verse went: 'For shit may be shot at odd corners /And paper supplied there to suit,/But a shit would be shot without mourners/If somebody shot that shit Shute'. From then on, he was always 'that shit Shute'. The song effectively finished him as commander of the Royal Naval

Division. In February 1917 he was transferred to the 32nd Division, which he commanded with great skill and imagination. On 28 April 1918 he was promoted to the command of V Corps. During the Hundred Days (August–November 1918) Shute emerged as an outstanding corps commander, spearheading the underrated advance of Third Army across the old Somme battlefields and the Canal du Nord.

Shuvaev, Dmitry Savelevich (1854–1937) Russian military commander and Minister of War. Shuvaev was one of the Russian army's leading staff officers, with particular expertise in logistics. From 1909 until December 1915 he was Quartermaster-General of the Russian army, whereupon he took up the same duties in the field. The main problem facing the Russian army was its chaotic supply system, which often left troops without sufficient food, clothing, equipment and ammunition, even when these items had been successfully manufactured. Shuvaev's promotion in March 1916 to Minister of War, in succession to POLIVANOV, therefore represented a rare interval of reason on the part of Tsar NICHOLAS II. Logic, however, was not enough. Shuvaev's technical expertise could not compensate for his lack of political authority at the reactionary court of the Tsarina, who opposed him from the start. Shuvaev was a rather didactic figure, much given to homilies on the importance of supply but lacking the executive ability to carry through his sensible policies. These included co-operation with moderate, patriotic forces in the Duma, without whose involvement he saw no effective way of mobilising Russia's economic resources. This was too much for the Tsarina, for whom the idea of sharing power with the Duma was anathema, and she engineered his dismissal in January 1917. Shuvaev's military abilities, allied to his lack of political ambition, allowed him to survive the Bolshevik Revolution and to contribute to the early military education of the fledgling Red Army.

Sikorsky, Igor (1899–1972) Russian aircraft designer, who built the world's first four-engined bomber in 1913, later effecting improvements which allowed it to carry more than 2,000 pounds of bombs. The limitations of the Russian war economy, however, meant that only about seventy-five were built, mostly for use in bombing East Prussia and Lithuania. Sikorsky fled Russia after the revolution, finally settling in the United States, where he founded a successful aircraft company and pioneered the development of the helicopter.

Sims, William Sowden (1858–1936) US naval commander. When the United States declared war on Germany on 6 April 1917, Sims was already at sea on his way to Britain to act as liaison officer with the Royal Navy. At his first meeting with Admiral JELLICOE, the First Sea Lord, Sims was left in no doubt of the severity of the situation with which the British were faced as a result of unrestricted German submarine warfare. The United States Navy was strong in battleships, but so was the Royal Navy. The need was for escort vessels, without which the introduction of a convoy system would be difficult. Sims immediately recognised this, and his report was influential in giving these unglamorous but vital ships top priority in the American shipbuilding programme. As early as 2 May 1917 it was agreed that Sims should command all anti-submarine warfare vessels in European waters, including those of the French navy. Sims' relations with the British, including Jellicoe, BEATTY and Admiral Sir Lewis BAYLY, C-in-C Western Approaches, were excellent. Ironically, the level of co-operation he received from Washington was more problematical. Sims did not really fit into the US Navy's command structure, descending from the Secretary of the Navy, Josephus DANIELS, through the Chief of Naval Operations, Admiral BENSON, to the C-in-C Atlantic, Admiral MAYO. Daniels and Benson were reluctant to 'hand over' the US Navy to the British, as Sims seemed to be suggesting. Sims regarded their tactics as obstructive and inefficient. In retrospect, there can be little doubt that Sims correctly diagnosed the fundamental problem of the naval war, German submarines, and the fundamental solution, the convoy system. His determination to mobilise as much American naval power as possible in the eastern Atlantic and the Mediterranean played an important part in the submarines' defeat and in keeping Britain fed through the winter of 1917–18.

Sinclair-MacLagan, Ewen George (1868–1948) Australian military commander. A school contemporary of Alick GODLEY, Lionel DUNSTERVILLE and Rudyard KIPLING, Sinclair-MacLagan spent the whole of the war with the Australian Imperial Force (AIF), commanding the 9th (Australian) Brigade (1914–17) and the 4th (Australian) Division (1917–19). This was largely fortuitous, the result of his being Director of Drill at the Royal Military College, Duntroon, when the war broke out. He was one of very few British officers to remain with the AIF throughout the war, surviving even the deliberate 'Australianisation' of senior posts in June 1918. This was due, in large part, to the support of Lieutenant-General Sir John MONASH, who was a great admirer of Sinclair-MacLagan, describing him as 'every inch a soldier'. Sinclair-MacLagan exhibited the considerable virtues of the best type of pre-war British Regular officer. He was not only courageous but also prudent. He put the welfare of his men first and had no hesitation in standing up to higher authority when he believed operations were ill conceived. He and his division played a leading part in the innovative attack at Le Hamel on 4 July 1918.

Sixte, Prince of Bourbon-Parma (1886–1934) French peace emissary. KARL I, who succeeded the aged FRANZ JOSEF I as Habsburg Emperor in December 1916, made no secret of his desire for a negotiated peace, which he believed was essential for the survival of his inheritance. In March 1917 he used Prince Sixte, the brother of his pro-Allied wife, the Empress Zita, to approach the Allies unofficially about the possibilities of a separate peace. Sixte's mission received some slight initial encouragement from the French but this soon faded. In April 1918, at the height of the fighting on the Western Front, the French Prime Minister, Georges CLEMENCEAU, broke his predecessor's undertaking to keep the mission secret by publishing the letters Sixte had delivered. This had the desired effect of disrupting Austro-German relations and led directly to the dismissal of the Austrian Foreign Minister, Count CZERNIN.

Skoropadsky, Pavlo Petrovych (1873–1945) Russian military commander and Ukrainian head of state. After a distinguished wartime career notable for physical courage, during which he reached the rank of lieutenant-general, Skoropadsky attempted to retrieve personal political opportunity from the wreckage of the tsarist regime. His ambition focused on the Ukraine. Although born in Germany and thoroughly Russian, Skoropadsky came from an old Ukrainian family. In March 1917 the Provisional Government appointed him to command the Ukrainian Corps; in October he was elected leader of the Ukrainian Free Cossacks, whereupon he offered the force under his command to the new radical Ukrainian government, which was suspicious of his intentions and refused it. These suspicions were soon proved to be justified. On 29 April 1918 Skoropadsky, with German help, organised a successful coup against the Ukrainian government, assuming power under the traditional title of Hetman. His conservative regime relied increasingly on German support and collapsed after the German surrender in the West. Skoropadsky fled into exile in Germany, where he was killed in an Allied air raid on 26 April 1945.

Sloggett, Arthur Thomas (1857–1929) Director-General of Medical Services (DGMS), British Expeditionary Force, 1915–18. Sloggett was responsible for the massive expansion of medical services in a war with unprecedented British casualties. He quickly recognised that effective medical provision was beyond the experience and abilities of the Royal Army Medical Corps alone. It would require civilian expertise, especially that of leading consultants. Civilian consultants were often a law unto themselves. They could be prickly, opinionated and vain. But Sloggett successfully integrated them into a medical organisation that responded impressively to the challenge of trench warfare. His mind was open to persuasion of the best practice from whatever source it came, and he did not allow military protocol to interfere with selecting the right men for the job. Medical arrangements on the Western Front were the best the British army had ever enjoyed and far superior to those on other fronts. Major improvements, some at the leading edge of medical science, were achieved in antisepsis, casualty evacuation, blood transfusion, sanitation and surgery. The achievements of Sloggett and his colleagues have rarely received the recognition they deserve; popular opinion in Britain persists in believing that the state of military medicine during the First World War had advanced little since the Crimea. Only 7.6 per cent of the 2,174,675 British and Dominion battle casualties on the Western Front died and only 0.78 per cent of the 3,342,780 non-battle casualties.

Śmigły-Rydz, Edward (1886–1941) Polish soldier and nationalist. Śmigły-Rydz served with Jósef PIŁSUDSKI's Polish Legion, distinguishing himself on numerous occasions in the war against Russia. When Piłsudski's disillusionment with German intentions towards Polish independence resulted in his internment in July 1917 and the disbandment of the Polish Legion, Śmigły-Rydz assumed command of the underground Polish Military Organisation, building up a force strong enough to bargain with established political authority in eastern Europe or – even better – to replace it in the event of a Central Powers' collapse. Marshal Śmigły-Rydz was Commander-in-Chief of the Polish Army in September 1939, when his catastrophic defeat resulted once again in Poland's occupation and partition.

Smith-Barry, Robert (1886–1949) British air-force officer, who transformed the Royal Flying Corps' appalling training regime, which killed more pilots than did combat. Even in a service woefully cavalier about its own history, the Royal Air Force's neglect of Smith-Barry is scandalous. The 'Smith-Barry system', worked out at the School of Special Flying at Gosport and adopted late in 1917, halved the death rate in training by teaching pilots to understand the limits of their machines but to fly to those limits. Smith-Barry was undoubtedly eccentric. His contempt for paperwork was so great that he once set fire to his office.

Smith-Cumming, Mansfield (1859–1923) British spymaster. Smith-Cumming (the original 'C') was appointed first head of the British secret (or special) intelligence service (SIS) in 1909. He enjoyed fast cars and his immunity from prosecution for speeding. In 1914, however, he lost a leg after a serious car crash. (He did nothing to discourage the legend that he escaped from the wreck only after amputating his leg with a penknife. He later disconcerted visitors by jabbing a pair of scissors into his artificial leg, made out of cork, and by whizzing down the corridors of power on a child's scooter.) During the war he presided over a rapid expansion of Britain's spy network. Despite frequent attempts by the Whitehall machine to subordinate him and his department, he not only succeeded in acquiring important information about the German order of battle (his original brief) but also diversified into escape, sabotage and black propaganda, prefiguring the Second World War work of the Special Operations Executive (SOE). One of his greatest achievements was to run a network of agents behind German lines in Belgium through a group with the code name La Dame Blanche, in which Walthere Dewé, eventually chief executive of the Belgian telephone service, was a key figure.

Smith-Dorrien, Horace Lockwood (1858–1930) British military commander. Smith-Dorrien was one of the most experienced and able commanders in the pre-war British army. His appointment to command II Corps of the British Expeditionary Force (BEF) in August 1914 after the sudden death of General GRIERSON, however, dismayed the BEF's Commander-in-Chief, Sir John FRENCH, whose relations with Smith-Dorrien were poisonous. French's feelings were certainly reciprocated by Smith-Dorrien and both were men of volcanic temper. In these circumstances, it was perhaps inevitable that the epic fighting of the war's opening days would fall principally on Smith-Dorrien's command. This included the battle of Mons, after which the BEF was forced to retreat in the face of the overwhelming numerical superiority of General Alexander von KLUCK's German First Army. The Duke of Wellington described a retreat in contact with the enemy as one of the most difficult operations in war. After three days, Smith-Dorrien judged that his corps was faced with annihilation unless it could find some relief from the pursuit. This could only be achieved by delivering a delaying blow to the German advance. On his own initiative Smith-Dorrien ordered his troops to make a stand at Le Cateau on 26 August 1914. II Corps fought the whole of Kluck's army for eleven hours, successfully avoiding a double envelopment. The battle allowed the BEF to regroup and made the German advance more cautious, but the cost was heavy. Many commentators believe that Smith-Dorrien's actions saved the BEF. Field-Marshal French at first seemed to agree with them, saluting II Corps' achievements in an official dispatch. On later reflection, however, he came to believe that Smith-Dorrien's costly and unsanctioned act had recklessly threatened the survival of the small British Regular Army, which French had been specifically ordered to preserve in his instructions from the Secretary of State for War, Lord KITCHENER. Smith-Dorrien's temporary difficulties during the first German gas attack at the Second Battle of Ypres in April 1915 gave French the chance for revenge. Smith-Dorrien was peremptorily and cursorily dismissed by telegram. This was later confirmed by French's chief of staff, Sir William ROBERTSON, in the famous phrase ''Orace yer fer 'ome'. The tactical withdrawal that Smith-Dorrien had advocated, and which French refused to sanction, was eventually carried out by Smith-Dorrien's successor, General PLUMER. Smith-Dorrien's dismissal removed a major obstacle in the path of Sir Douglas HAIG's subsequent rise to command of the BEF.

Smuts, Jan Christian (1870–1950) South African politician and military commander and British imperial statesman. Smuts was a British-educated lawyer of intellectual and philosophical disposition, a natural seeker of compromise and a believer in peace who fought in two wars and led his country in a third and was capable of the ruthless use of military force. Smuts' Afrikaner roots led him to take the Boer side during the South African War (1899–1902), during which he commanded forces in the field. His legal training and negotiating skills made him a valuable member of the Boer delegation at the peace conference that ended the war. In the years that followed Smuts cemented his position at the forefront of South African politics and became one of the leading advocates of an 'Imperial' future for South Africa within the British Empire. After the outbreak of the European war he founded the South African Defence Force and used it to suppress striking miners on the Rand. In 1915 he took part in the conquest of German South West Africa (modern Namibia) under the command of Louis BOTHA. This success led to Smut's appointment to command imperial forces in East Africa (1916–17), where he was led a merry dance by the German guerrilla leader Paul von LETTOW-VORBECK. His failure to destroy Lettow-Vorbeck's army, however, did not count against him. The capture of Dar-es-Salaam, capital of German East Africa, provided a headline-grabbing achievement in a war short of conspicuous British successes. Smuts' arrival in London in March 1917 to head the South African delegation to the Imperial War Conference brought him to the admiring attention of the British Prime Minister, David LLOYD GEORGE, who invited him to join the War Cabinet. Despite this, Smuts remained a firm supporter of the Western Front strategy and of its chief executor, Sir Douglas HAIG. But he also favoured a British advance into Palestine, one of Lloyd George's favourite projects, though himself rejecting the offer to command it. In 1918 Smuts was a pivotal figure in the creation of the world's first independent air force, the Royal Air Force. He was a member of the South African delegation to the Paris Peace Conference, where he became a leading advocate of a League of Nations, labouring unsuccessfully for a peace of reconciliation. The placing of captured German colonies and dismembered Ottoman provinces under League of Nations' 'mandates' was also his idea. As Prime Minister of South Africa from 1939 to 1948 he led his country during the Second World War and helped found the United Nations. His defeat in the general election of 1948 marked the beginning of South Africa's descent into apartheid.

Smyth, Nevil Maskelyne (1868–1941) British military commander. Smyth was the son of a distinguished scientist, an unusual background for a pre-war Regular officer. But Smyth was an unusual man. In a pre-war career packed with incident he commanded not only cavalry but also infantry and machine guns. He suppressed the Khalifa Sherif's rising on the Blue Nile and surveyed the Sudan. He charted the Nile cataracts preparatory to the annihilating victory at Omdurman, where he was severely wounded in winning the Victoria Cross for rescuing two war correspondents from a Dervish spearman. (Given the contempt that most Regular soldiers felt for journalists, this act must be considered genuinely above and beyond the call of duty.) In 1913 he obtained his aviator's certificate. His flying ability came in useful when, as GOC 2nd Australian Division, he achieved a certain degree of notoriety for 'borrowing' aircraft to do his own trench spotting. Smyth spent most of the war in command of Australians, first as GOC 1st (Australian) Brigade on Gallipoli (which he was one of the last officers to leave in December 1915) and the Western Front, and from December 1916 to May 1918 as GOC 2nd (Australian) Division. Smyth was a cautious commander who liked to look before his men were ordered to leap. His willingness to appear in the front line and his imperturbability under fire endeared him to his troops. As a commander he was always thorough and professional, with a careful regard for the importance of detail. John GELLIBRAND, one of his brigade commanders, held Smyth and his staff responsible for the Bullecourt debacle in May 1917, but other leading Australian commanders, including Smyth's successor as GOC 2nd (Australian) Division, Charles ROSENTHAL, continued to hold him in high esteem. This was certainly reciprocated by Smyth, who emigrated to Australia after his retirement in 1924.

Snow, Thomas D'Oyly (1858–1940) British military commander. Snow took the 4th Division to war in the original British Expeditionary Force. During the battle of the Marne (September 1914) his horse fell and rolled on him, breaking his pelvis. Snow was a big man (six feet four). The injury was serious and had lasting physical effects. After his return to health, he was given command of another Regular division, the 27th, and then – in July 1915 – promoted GOC VII Corps, where he remained in command until January 1918. Snow's army nickname was 'Slush'. His reputation was that of a fusspot, overly concerned with military trivia. Criticism of his performance was apparent from the beginning of the war, not least from one of his brigade commanders, Aylmer HALDANE. The inefficiency of VII Corps was an open secret. Its planning and execution of the diversionary attack at Gommecourt on 1 July 1916 ought to have done for Snow, but he succeeded in shuffling the blame on to Major-General Montagu-Stuart-Wortley, commander of the 46th Division. Snow's command of VII Corps at Arras (April 1917) also left much to be desired. At Cambrai in November 1917, pressed by one of his divisional commanders, Hugh JEUDWINE, and the repeated warnings of his chief of staff, 'Jock' Burnett-Stuart, Snow took more seriously than did other senior commanders evidence of German preparations for a counter-attack, but even then he failed to co-ordinate the defence of the key sector where III Corps and VII Corps joined. VII Corps bore the brunt of the German assault and was forced to retreat, losing Villers-Guislain. Much of the ground captured during the original British tank attack had to be abandoned. Snow's health deteriorated during the winter and he asked to be relieved of command. The future Field-Marshal MONTGOMERY declared that: 'Snow was of course quite useless; he was an old man [60] and ought to have been sent home long before.'

Solf, Wilhelm (1862–1936) German politician, who established a pre-war reputation as the leading advocate of a German colonial empire, becoming Colonial Secretary in 1911. The rapid annexation of Germany's colonial possessions in the Pacific and Africa by the forces of the British Empire and Japan left Solf in the galling position of a Colonial Secretary without any colonies. This did nothing to diminish his enthusiasm for them. He opposed Germany's adoption of unrestricted submarine warfare and advocated a negotiated peace at which Germany's conquests in the west, especially Belgium, would be exchanged for the restitution of her African colonial empire, which – with the addition of the Belgian Congo – would stretch from the Indian Ocean to the Atlantic. Solf became German Foreign Minister in the last days of Imperial Germany.

Solly-Flood, Arthur (1871–1940) British staff officer, whose important contribution as a tactical innovator has been overshadowed by the reputation of the British Expeditionary Force's eventual Inspector-General of Training, the flamboyant Sir Ivor MAXSE. Maxse was not appointed Inspector-General of Training until the summer of 1918. Solly-Flood's involvement went back to October 1916, when he was given responsibility for organising schools for senior officers. On 30 January 1917 he was sent to GHQ to establish a Training Directorate, with the brief to revise and standardise the British army's tactical doctrine and to rewrite its manuals. Within less than a month the directorate published *SS 143 Instructions for the Training of Platoons for Offensive Action*, the 'stormtrooper's bible', almost a year before the German equivalent. In its revised form, published in February 1918, *SS 143* laid the doctrinal foundations on which the British victories of 1918 were won. Paddy Griffith has described Solly-Flood as 'one of the four men who won the war'.

Solomon, Solomon Joseph (1860–1927) British artist and camouflage pioneer. When the war broke out Solomon immediately sought to interest the military in the importance of camouflage on a modern battlefield, something already recognised in the British army's adoption of khaki service dress. The British Commander-in-Chief, Sir John FRENCH, was predictably dismissive of Solomon's suggestions, but he found a more sympathetic reception from French's successor, Sir Douglas HAIG, a man perennially receptive to new ideas even when they came from civilians. Solomon was made technical adviser to the British camouflage service that Haig established. He was responsible for recruiting the diverse collection of artists, theatrical designers and sculptors who were eventually given proper military form in the Special Works Park R.E., commanded from March 1916 by Lieutenant-Colonel F.J.C. WYATT.

Sonnino, (Giorgio) Sidney (1847–1922) Italian politician, a Conservative veteran of Italian unification, he maintained (often unchallenged) control of Italian foreign policy from 1914 until 1919. Sonnino's vision of Italy as a major European and colonial power anticipated that of MUSSOLINI. He believed that a policy of neutrality in the war would serve only to undermine this ambition. At first he favoured joining the Central Powers, to which Italy was joined in the Triple Alliance of 1882, but the German setback on the Marne in September 1914 made him more cautious, and he determined to establish which side was going to win before joining it. The opportunities for the territorial expansion that he sought were also more likely to come at the expense of Austria-Hungary than France. In the Treaty of London (26 April 1915) he managed to persuade the French and British to give secret support to Italian territorial aggrandisement in the Balkans. He and Prime Minister SALANDRA were almost completely responsible for Italy's entry into the war. Territorial expansion remained Sonnino's war aim, but the later commitment of the Allies and the United States to the principle of national self-determination, laid down as one of President WILSON's Fourteen Points, destroyed his hopes of seeing Italy adequately 'rewarded' at the Paris Peace Conference. The Treaty of Versailles was regarded as a defeat in Italy. The fall of the Italian government in June 1919 signalled Sonnino's retirement.

Sophie, Duchess von Hohenberg (1868–1914) Murder victim. Countess Sophie Chotek von Chotková und Wognin came from a Czech family of the lesser nobility. Her marriage to Archduke FRANZ FERDINAND, heir apparent to the Austro-Hungarian throne, was very much a love match, one of only two remarkable events in that unremarkable man's life. The other remarkable event was, of course, his assassination in Sarajevo on 28 June 1914. His wife was shot alongside him. This is, perhaps, a little surprising. Emperor FRANZ JOSEF I agreed to allow the marriage only on condition that Franz Ferdinand swore a morganatic oath. This prevented Sophie from assuming her husband's royal titles and meant that her public life was one of systematic insult, including being prevented from travelling in the royal coach with her husband. Motor cars clearly did not count as royal coaches. In the end, with bitter irony, she may be accounted a victim of modernity.

Sopwith, Thomas Octave Murdoch (1888–1989) British aircraft designer, whose Sopwith Aviation Company, based in Surrey, produced some of the finest fighters of the war, including the One-

and-a-Half Strutter, Pup, Triplane, Snipe, Camel and Dolphin. Sopwith's designs were often innovative. The One-and-a-Half Strutter (1915) was the first British two-seater fighter and the first aircraft of any type to be designed with a synchronised forward-firing machine gun. The agile Pup (1916) was the first aircraft to land on an aircraft carrier and the Triplane (1916) the first of its type. Sopwith produced more than 16,000 planes for the British and Allied air forces; the effective, but notoriously difficult-to-fly, Camel alone accounting for 1,200 enemy aircraft.

Sorley, Charles Hamilton (1895–1915) British soldier-poet. When the war broke out Sorley was in Germany, where he was spending time before taking up a scholarship at University College, Oxford. He was briefly imprisoned but eventually allowed to leave. He enlisted soon after his return to Britain and was commissioned in the Suffolk Regiment. Sorley was self-mocking and ironical, and it is impossible to tell what his reasons for volunteering were or even if he understood them himself. He was sharply critical of the jingoism of Rupert BROOKE's poetry and had a great love of Germany. One of his most famous poems, the sonnet 'When you see millions of the mouthless dead', was found in his kit after his death. *Marlborough and Other Poems* was published by the Cambridge University Press in 1916 and ran into four editions. His work was greatly admired by SASSOON and GRAVES. Captain C.H. Sorley, 7th Battalion Suffolk Regiment, was killed in action on 13 October 1915 at the battle of Loos and has no known grave.

Souchon, Wilhelm (1864–1946) German naval commander. As commander of the German navy's Mediterranean squadron when the war broke out, Souchon fired the first shots of the Great War by bombarding two of France's Algerian

ports on 4 August 1914. He returned to Messina to re-coal, but Italy's declaration of neutrality threatened his squadron with internment. He sought to escape from this predicament by making a dash for Constantinople. This decision, combined with the ineptitude of the British 1st Cruiser Squadron under Admiral TROUBRIDGE, had historic consequences. The entry of Souchon's ships, the *Goeben* and *Breslau*, into the Sea of Marmora was instrumental in bringing about Turkish entry into the war on the side of the Central Powers. Not content with having started the war in the Mediterranean, on 29 October 1914 Souchon – by now head of the neutral Turkish fleet – conspired with pro-war members of the Ottoman government to bounce Turkey into war by attacking the Russian port of Odessa. He remained in command of the Turkish fleet until September 1917, but his experience was one of continual frustration. He was contemptuous of Turkish inefficiency. He received only exiguous support from home, and his pleas for more submarines with which to contest Russian control of the Black Sea fell on deaf ears. His return to Germany to command the High Seas Fleet's 4th Battleship Squadron was prestigious but equally frustrating. An unsatisfactory war was brought to an unhappy conclusion when, as Governor of the Kiel naval base in November 1918, he watched helplessly as the German navy succumbed to mutiny and revolution.

Spare, Austin Osman (1886–1958) British war artist. Spare was among the artists sent to France by Lord Beaverbrook (see AITKEN, WILLIAM MAXWELL) after his appointment as Minister of Information in March 1918. Beaverbrook had long since recognised the importance of keeping a visual record of the war, and he greatly expanded the number of official war artists. Spare's war paintings were mostly concerned with the work of the Royal Army Medical Corps.

Spears, Edward Louis (1886–1974) British liaison officer. The bilingual Spears was sent to France in August 1914, before Britain's formal declaration of war, to co-operate on a military cipher book for use between the two armies. This soon led to his appointment as British liaison officer with the French Fifth Army, led by the acerbic General LANREZAC. Spears' goodwill and linguistic fluency did nothing to arrest a disastrous decline in confidence between Lanrezac and the British Commander-in-Chief, Field-Marshal Sir John FRENCH. Later in the war, Spears was appointed head of the British Military Mission in Paris with the rank of brigadier-general. He was wounded four times during the war. Spears left two vivid and compelling accounts of his service. The first, *Liaison 1914* (1930), remains an indispensable account of Anglo-French relations during the first months of the war. The second, *Prelude to Victory* (1939), recounts the tragic and remorseless unfolding of the NIVELLE offensive. Both books are full of fascinating psychological insights into the leading personalities in both the British and French armies. In 1940 General Spears was instrumental in bringing the then largely unknown General de Gaulle to Britain.

Spee, Maximilian von (1861–1914) German naval commander. The outbreak of war found Spee in command of the German East Asia Squadron. He ordered light cruisers on individual commerce raids, causing panic among Allied merchant shipping, and the destruction of Spee's squadron became a priority for British naval forces. These were, however, far from strong. When Admiral CRADOCK's obsolete squadron succeeded in intercepting Spee, at Coronel off the coast of Chile on 1 November 1914, it suffered an annihilating defeat. After his success Spee entered the South Atlantic, with a view to attacking the routes between Argentina and Brazil and Europe, important links in the British food chain. But against the

advice of his subordinate commanders, he chose first to destroy the wireless station at Port Stanley in the Falkland Islands. There he ran into Admiral STURDEE's powerful force, sent to retrieve British naval honour in the aftermath of Coronel. This it duly did, sinking the *Gneisenau*, *Leipzig*, *Nürnberg* and *Scharnhorst*. Spee's fate was, in some ways, emblematic of the German navy during the war. He was undoubtedly a talented and aggressive officer, but his resources were too small to achieve anything other than limited propaganda successes. Spee was killed in the battle of the Falkland Islands, together with both his sons. The ship named after him in 1934 was also destined to find an inglorious end in South American waters in December 1939.

Spencer, Stanley (1891–1959) British painter. Spencer volunteered for the Royal Army Medical Corps at the outbreak of war, together with Henry LAMB. He worked at a hospital in Bristol until August 1916, when he was sent to Salonika. His only 'war picture', *Travoys Arriving with Wounded at Dressing Station at Smol, Macedonia, September 1916*, did not appear until after the Armistice. The war did, however, exercise a long-term effect on Spencer's singular and powerful artistic imagination. This found its fullest expression in the remarkable series of murals of army life painted for the Sandham Memorial Chapel at Burghclere in Hampshire, culminating in the stunning altarpiece, *The Resurrection of the Soldiers*, one of the most remarkable works of art to be inspired by the war.

Spring-Rice, Cecil Arthur (1859–1918) British diplomat, who served in the key post of Ambassador to the United States from 1913 until January 1918. Spring-Rice's role was an unenviable one. He was faced with an American president determined to maintain his country's neutrality, while British conduct of the naval war was bound to provide many opportunities for conflict with American interests. Spring-Rice took the view that only the discipline of events could bring the United States into the war and that his best policy was one of 'masterly inactivity'. This became so pronounced that it earned him the nickname 'the silent ambassador'. The policy came at a price. Important American political figures, notably President WILSON's confidant 'Colonel' HOUSE, came to regard Spring-Rice as a cipher and ignored him. Britain's friends in the USA were dismayed at his failure to offer public rebuke to attacks on British policy emanating from the German-American and Irish-American communities. The British press could be equally critical of his perceived failure to support British interests with sufficient aggression. American entry into the war, far from making Spring-Rice's life easier, made it more difficult. A series of heavyweight British politicians were sent to Washington over his head, undermining what small authority he retained in US political circles. He recognised the impossibility of his situation and agreed to resign. He died suddenly in Ottawa on his way home. He wrote the hymn 'I vow to thee my country', whose final lines ('her ways are ways of gentleness and all her paths are Peace') may serve as an epitaph to a decent and tactful man committed to the unfashionable principle of conciliation.

Stalin, Iosif Vissarionovich (1879–1953) Russian revolutionary. Stalin was a Georgian by birth (his family name was Dzhugashvili) and spoke no Russian until the age of 11, though he later wrote it with great clarity and cogency. After training as a priest while a young man, Stalin became a professional revolutionary, robbing banks and trains to fund revolutionary activity. He was exiled to northern Siberia in 1913 and remained there until freed by the February Revolution of 1917. He soon found himself the senior Bolshevik in Petrograd, where his early actions –

including general support for the Provisional Government – enraged LENIN. When Lenin returned from Switzerland, however, Stalin soon conformed to the strategy laid down in Lenin's April Theses. He worked closely with Lenin and was appointed Commissar of Nationalities by the Bolshevik government, with responsibility for non-Russians in the new Soviet Union. During the civil war he displayed enormous energy, often being sent to trouble spots with full authority to sort them out. His distrust of TROTSKY and competition with him for the succession to Lenin date from this period.

Stamboliski, Alexander (1879–1923) Bulgarian politician, the leading opponent of Tsar FERDINAND I. He was rewarded for his prescient prediction that Bulgaria's alliance with the Central Powers would end in disaster by being sentenced to life imprisonment in September 1915. He was released only in September 1918, with Bulgaria on the verge of defeat. Somewhat uncharacteristically, this essentially democratic, parliamentary figure allowed himself to be placed at the head of revolutionary forces, which suffered immediate defeat by German and Bulgarian troops. After the war Stamboliski became a radical prime minister of Bulgaria, committed to improving the lot of Bulgaria's peasantry. He was murdered by right-wing terrorists in 1923.

Stamfordham, Baron *see* BIGGE, ARTHUR JOHN

Stanley, Edward George Villiers, 17th Earl of Derby (1865–1948) British politician and diplomat. Before the war Derby's fame was based on his wealth, public generosity and ownership of successful race horses. But, on the outbreak of war, his involvement in the voluntary recruiting movement brought him to national political prominence. Derby originated the idea of 'Pals' battalions' in Liverpool in August 1914. As an encouragement to voluntary recruitment, men who lived and worked together and who joined the army together would be allowed to serve together. The concept captured the public imagination, but since 1916, when many pals died together on the Somme, their fate has haunted British perceptions of the war. Derby's credentials as an opponent of conscription recommended him to ASQUITH, who made him Director-General of Recruiting in 1915. The 'Derby Scheme' (October 1915) introduced all the elements of conscription except compulsion. Its failure to get sufficient men to 'assent' to serve if called upon, with married men being called upon last, made conscription almost inevitable. As Secretary of State for War 1916–18, Derby's influence was marginal, especially under LLOYD GEORGE, who was deeply suspicious of his close links with the military high command and support for the 'Western' strategy. He was replaced in the aftermath of the German spring offensive of 1918 and sent as Ambassador to Paris, where he remained until 1920.

Stein, Hermann von (1854–1927) German staff officer, military commander general and Prussian Minister of War. Stein began the war as MOLTKE's chief of staff, suffering the same fate as his master in September 1914. After two years as a corps commander on the Western Front, during which he received Germany's highest military honour, the *Pour le Mérite*, he was appointed Prussian Minister of War. Although he gave steady support to HINDENBURG and LUDENDORFF's attempts to mobilise the German war economy, he expressed doubts about the prudence of extending military conscription to all adult males aged 18 to 60. He acted swiftly in February 1918 to stem the wave of strikes affecting the home front and played a leading part in forcing Ludendorff to reconstruct his headquarters staff in September 1918. He retired shortly after the Armistice.

Stern, Albert (1878–1966) British tank pioneer. Stern began the war as a lieutenant in the Royal Naval Volunteer Reserve armoured car section. He rose swiftly, becoming Secretary of the Landships Committee (CHURCHILL's brainchild, charged with finding a mechanical means of breaking the deadlock of trench warfare) in 1915 and Chairman of the Tank Committee in 1916. Having played a role in designing the tank, Stern was then given the job of producing it, becoming Director of Tank Supply at the Ministry of Munitions in December 1916. He never succeeded in manufacturing the new weapon in the quantities that either he or Field-Marshal HAIG would have liked. His memoir, *Tanks 1914–1918, The Log-Book of a Pioneer*, was published in 1919.

Stevenson, Frances Louise (1888–1972) Secretary and mistress of the British Prime Minister, David LLOYD GEORGE. Frances Stevenson was a London University Classics graduate who spoke excellent French. She became Lloyd George's mistress in 1913. She was 25. Lloyd George was 50. He made it clear from the outset that he would not commit political suicide for her by divorcing his wife. Frances' position, for much of her adult life, was therefore one of ambiguity, embarrassment and deception. There can be little doubt that she did much to sustain Lloyd George emotionally throughout their life together, and especially during the war. She was also a very competent private secretary, to whom posterity owes much for her work in preserving Lloyd George's private papers. Margaret Lloyd George died in 1941. Two years later, to the horror of some members of the Lloyd George family, David Lloyd George married Frances Stevenson and she died a countess. Lloyd George's letters to her, *My Darling Pussy*, were published in 1975.

Stobart, Mabel St Clair (1862–1954) British nursing organiser. The daughter of a wealthy county family, Mabel St Clair Stobart was a striking and uncomfortable personality imbued with extraordinary will power and courage who paid little heed to the social conventions of the age. With a contempt for bureaucracy as chilling as it was often admirable, she was designed to be a pioneer. In 1912 she founded the Women's Sick and Wounded Convoy Corps, staffed entirely with female doctors and nurses. During the Balkan War of 1912–13, her organisation established a surgical hospital with the Bulgarian army, where it became the first all-female medical unit in history to serve under front-line conditions. This might be considered a sufficient achievement for a woman already well into middle age, but the outbreak of the European war was the prelude to even greater things. In August 1914 she set about organising hospitals in Belgium and France for the St John Ambulance, was captured by the Germans at Antwerp and threatened with execution as a spy before being released and repatriated. In March 1915 she responded to the well-publicised plight of the Serbs. Given her front-line war experience and knowledge of the Balkans, she was a natural choice to lead the Third Serbian Relief Fund unit, taking up its position at Kragujevac in April. In October 1915, with the Serbian army facing defeat, Major St Clair Stobart took command of a 'flying field hospital' that accompanied the arduous and demoralising retreat across the mountains of Albania to sanctuary in Italy and Corfu. In 1917 and 1918 she lectured in Canada, the United States and Ireland for the Ministry of Information, giving her fee to the Serbian Relief Fund. After the war she consolidated her reputation as a leading spiritualist.

Stöger-Steiner, Rudolf, Edler von Steinstätten (1861–1921) Austro-Hungarian military commander and politician. After periods as a divisional commander on the Eastern Front and as a corps commander in Italy, Stöger-Steiner was appointed Minister of War in April 1917. His task was an unenviable one. He had not only to secure the increasingly difficult supply of the empire's armed forces but also to maintain public order. The two were clearly connected. At the heart of his problem was the difficulty – felt by all belligerent powers at this stage of the war – of balancing the need for resources of the army and of the economy – especially manpower, in the face of huge human losses. Stöger-Steiner's assessments were always realistic, without descending into pessimism and despair. He concluded in a detailed memorandum sent to Emperor KARL I in August 1917 that Austria-Hungary could survive the winter, but by the turn of the year he had become convinced that military victory was impossible. Despite this, he strove to the end to do his duty and to maintain public order in the face of overwhelming events.

Stokes, (Frederick) Wilfrid Scott (1860–1927) British civil engineer and inventor, Chairman and Managing Director of Ransomes & Rapier, engineers, of Ipswich, best known for their manufacture of industrial cranes. Stokes began experimenting with the design of a 3-inch trench mortar in the autumn of 1914, as a counter to the German *Minenwerfer*, much touted in the British press as a 'terror' weapon. He obtained trials for his simple-to-use-and-manufacture weapon, but his invention was finally rejected in June 1915 on the grounds that it did not use existing forms of ammunition. It took the intervention of Lieutenant-Colonel J.C. Matheson, of the Trench Warfare Supply Department in the new Ministry of Munitions, and of LLOYD GEORGE, the Minister of Munitions, to rescue the project. General HAIG also approved the mortar's suitability as soon as he was shown one. 'Mr Stoke's drainpipe' became one of the most important weapons in the British arsenal and the template for all future mortars. By the summer of 1916 British infantry divisions had three trench mortar batteries. Eventually 11,241 3-inch and 1,123 4-inch Stokes mortars were supplied to the British army, firing more than 15M rounds of ammunition and greatly strengthening the firepower available to the infantry.

Stolypin, Petr Arkadievich (1862–1911) Russian politician. Stolypin's assassination at the Kiev Opera in 1911 terminated the career of one of pre-war Russia's most ruthless modernisers. By the time of his death, his attempts to remove the perennial economic restraint imposed by Russia's backward agriculture had met with comparatively little success. His encouragement of individual peasant ownership, however, was enough to dismay conservatives and the reactionaries at court, who granted him little credit for the way in which his changes to electoral law (in 1907) successfully undermined the constitutional concessions of the 1905 Revolution. This was an achievement, however, that was quite enough to dismay democrats. Stolypin's career, and fate, exemplify the profound difficulties of economic modernisation in an environment of political rigidity and obscurantism.

Stopford, Frederick William (1854–1929) British military commander. Stopford began the war as Lieutenant of the Tower of London, a ceremonial position entirely suited to a courteous man in the twilight of his career. But in June 1915 he was given command of IX Corps, which was to be responsible for the attack at Suvla Bay that was intended to break the deadlock into which the Gallipoli campaign had fallen by wresting control of the central heights of the peninsula from their Turkish defenders. The choice of Stopford seems extraordinary. His career had been spent mostly as a staff officer, and he had no experience of command in the field. He was 61 and in poor health. He lacked the energy and force of personality necessary to press an attack in which speed was

of the essence. His appointment was a sad comment on the contemporary fixation with hierarchy, for which Lord KITCHENER must take much of the blame. The Suvla attack began on the evening of 6 August 1915 and was reinforced the following day. Initial progress was good but Stopford fluffed the opportunity to make a rapid advance against weak Turkish opposition. The British Commander-in-Chief, Sir Ian HAMILTON, was slow to realise what was (not) happening. By the time he ordered Stopford to attack it was too late. Stopford was sent home on 15 August.

Stresemann, Gustav (1878–1929) German politician, best known for his post-war career as the Weimar Republic's Foreign Minister, culminating in 1926 with the award of the Nobel Prize for Peace, the only German to receive the honour. This was perhaps surprising and, in retrospect, astonishing. Streseman's policy was little different from that pursued by Hitler in the 1930s: to free Germany from the financial reparations forced on her by the victors at Versaillies; to remove foreign troops from German soil; to achieve union with Austria; and to restore Germany's eastern frontier. The policy itself, however, is unsurprising. Amid the poisonous divisions of the Weimar Republic the one thing that united Germans was hostility to the Versailles Settlement. Streseman's pursuit of it was clearly prefigured in his pre-war advocacy of German *Weltpolitik*, including naval and colonial expansion, and wartime support for the Third Supreme Command's annexationist policies and attempts to achieve the mass mobilisation of a German war economy.

Studdert-Kennedy, Geoffrey Anketell (1883–1929) British army chaplain. Studdert-Kennedy was a radical priest, whose impassioned preaching and calls for social justice alarmed many of his conservative superiors. His pre-war ministry brought him into close contact with the urban working class, for whose fundamental decency and humanity he had a high regard. During the war he served as an army chaplain, styling himself 'Chaplain to the Forces' and earning an enduring reputation as 'Woodbine Willie' through his habit of handing out cigarettes as well as benison to the troops. At his funeral in Liverpool a working man broke through the cordon to place a packet of Woodbines on his coffin.

Sturdee, (Frederick Charles) Doveton (1859–1925) British naval commander. During the Great War the Royal Navy was rarely blessed with lucky admirals. Sturdee was, however, the exception. When war broke out he was Chief of the Naval War Staff, a post for which he was singularly ill suited. But the return of Admiral FISHER as First Sea Lord in October 1914 ironically signalled a change in Sturdee's fortunes. Fisher had no time for the naval war staff and no time for Sturdee, who had opposed his pre-war reforms. The embarrassing defeat of Admiral CRADOCK's squadron at Coronel on 1 November ensured Sturdee's replacement. But, to his great good fortune, Fisher gave him command of a powerful task force, including two fast, modern battle cruisers (*Inflexible* and *Invincible*) and five cruisers, with orders to find and destroy SPEE's squadron of commerce raiders. Sturdee's pursuit was lethargic and ponderous. By 7 December he was undertaking repairs and re-coaling at Port Stanley in the Falkland Islands. Spee's squadron arrived on 8 December, intending to bombard the islands, but Spee misread the situation, fluffing his opportunity to attack the British fleet in port, and turned east. Sturdee's faster ships gave chase. Despite some skilful German manoeuvring and poor British gunnery, Sturdee eventually managed to bring his superior force to bear, sinking all but one of the German ships for the loss of five men killed and sixteen wounded. The victory was suitably annihilating for

British public taste. It had an important effect on British and German naval morale, seeming to confirm the superiority of British naval power. The Royal Navy was relieved of the threat of German surface ships everywhere except the North Sea. The weaknesses of British gunnery and the limitations of the battle cruisers' design remained hidden. Sturdee commanded the 4th Battle Squadron at Jutland (31 May–1 June 1916), later becoming a vehement critic of JELLICOE's handling of the Grand Fleet, but was passed over for promotion in favour of BEATTY when Jellicoe became First Sea Lord in December 1916.

Stürgkh, Karl, Count von (1859–1916) Austro-Hungarian politician. As Minister-President of Austria, a position to which he was appointed in 1911, Stürgkh supported the decision to deal with Serbia. He had also welcomed the proroguing of the Austrian parliament in March 1914, declaring later in the war that his greatest achievement had been to turn the parliament building into a hospital. An administrator rather than a politician, he preferred to govern by fiat rather than through the messy business of discussion, negotiation and compromise. Compromise was, admittedly, difficult to achieve amid the competing demands of the Habsburg Empire's restless minorities, but Stürgkh brought neither imagination nor energy to the issue. His conduct during the war was like that of an ostrich. He buried his head in the sand and hoped for the best. This inactivity proved far from masterly, engendering a political frustration that was to prove personally fatal. On 21 October 1916 Friedrich Adler, son of the leader of the Austrian Socialist Party, shot Stürgkh dead in a restaurant in Vienna.

Stürmer, Boris Vladimirovich (1848–1917) Russian politician, whose appointment as Chairman of the Council of Ministers in January 1916 marked the beginning of the end for tsarist Russia. A complete nonentity driven solely by personal vanity and ambition unleavened by political judgement or administrative ability, his one talent lay in being able to suck up to the Tsarina and her 'friend' RASPU-TIN. The Tsar's decision to remain at the front with his armies virtually rendered him *hors de combat* politically, handing the government over to the Tsarina and Rasputin. They used the ever-pliable Stürmer systematically to replace all the regime's most competent ministers. He was removed only in November 1916, with Russia staring at the prospect of total collapse. He died in prison in September 1917, following his arrest by the Provisional Government in February.

Sueter, Murray Fraser (1872–1960) British naval commander and naval aviation pioneer, an independent-minded, unorthodox officer who used his position as Director of the Admiralty Air Department (from 1912) to develop torpedo attack aircraft, anti-submarine dirigibles, armoured cars and the tank. His even more heretical advocacy of a separate air service proved too much for his superiors, and he was silenced by being sent to command Royal Naval Air Service units in southern Italy. This posting ended in January 1918 and he was offered no further employment. He retired in 1920, still only 48, a prophet without honour in his own land.

Sukhomlinov, Vladimir Aleksandrovich (1848–1926) Russian Minister of War 1909–15. Although Sukhomlinov's understanding of the demands of modern war was limited, he was not a reactionary. He secured major increases in Russian military spending from the Duma, though his attempts to spend well were hamstrung by conservative factions within the army. During the July Crisis of 1914 Sukhomlinov successfully argued for Russian mobilisation against both Germany and Austria-Hungary. His mobilisation plans put the Russian army into the field much more quickly than was believed possible by the Germans, whose plan for winning the war (the SCHLIEFFEN Plan) was based upon the supposed lethargy of Russian mobilisation. Russia's early defeats, however, dispelled Sukhomlinov's hopes of a short war, on which he had based many of his assumptions, and began the unravelling of his position. The Russian army's notorious supply difficulties were blamed on him, and his dissolute lifestyle gave his many enemies the opportunity to undo him. Sukhomlinov's need for money to finance his extravagance had led him into some unwise friendships, including two with members of his staff who were certainly spies. Russia's heavy defeats in the spring of 1915 led the Tsar to dismiss Sukhomlinov in June. His dismissal was followed by a sensational trial that exposed the corruption and incompetence at the heart of Russian military administration. Sukhomlinov was convicted for treason and imprisoned. Released and re-arrested after the February Revolution of 1917, he somehow managed to avoid being executed by the Bolsheviks and fled into exile.

Sulzbach, Herbert (1894–1985) German soldier. Sulzbach was a member of a wealthy Jewish banking family from Frankfurt-am-Main. He volunteered on 8 August 1914 and was accepted into the 63rd (Frankfurt) Field Artillery Regiment. He found himself on the Western Front within less than a month of joining the army and spent nearly the whole of the war there. He kept a diary, published in German as *Zwei lebende Mauern* in 1935. The book's evident patriotism and the author's high sense of duty and admiration for the courage of the German army recommended it to reviewers and guaranteed it a certain celebrity and success. Within two years, however, Sulzbach was forced to leave Germany. He moved to England and during the Second World War served in the British army, where he was involved in the de-Nazification of German prisoners. After the Second World War Sulzbach worked at the German Embassy in London, devoting the remainder of his long life to cementing Anglo-German relations, especially at the cultural level. His account of the war was published in English in 1973 as *With the German Guns. Four Years on the Western Front.*

Swinton, Ernest Dunlop (1868–1951) British soldier, historian and originator of the tank. Swinton began the war as 'Eyewitness', the British army's official war correspondent, charged with producing highly censored, bland accounts of frontline fighting at a time when journalists were strictly barred from the Western Front. Even though Swinton could not write freely about what he saw, what he saw appalled him. His fertile imagination began to contemplate means by which advances could be safely made against barbed wire and machine guns. During his leave at Christmas 1914 a chance sighting of a Holt tractor towing a gun gave him his inspiration. He wrote a paper proposing the construction of a 'power-driven, bullet-proof, armed engine capable of destroying machine guns, breaking through entanglements and climbing earthworks'. He ignored initial official lack of interest, sending his idea to the Secretary of the War Council, Maurice HANKEY, who passed it on to Winston CHURCHILL. Churchill established the Landships Committee in February 1915 and made resources available for development. The first prototype tank (Little Willie), designed by TRITTON and Walter WILSON at Foster's engineering works in Lincoln, was demonstrated in September 1915. A year later Swinton's brainchild made its debut on the battlefield at Flers.

Sykes, Frederick Hugh (1877–1954) British staff officer, an exceptionally able man who had an ability to make himself disliked that bordered on genius. He

obtained his pilot's certificate (No. 95) in 1910 and transferred to the Royal Flying Corps (RFC) in 1912. In 1914 he became GSO1 (chief of staff) to the RFC in France. His attempts to replace Sir David HENDERSON as GOC RFC proved one intrigue too many. He was packed off to the Dardanelles and then to the outer darkness of a Territorial Cyclist Division in East Anglia. He eventually managed to retrieve his career, via the Machine Gun Corps, the Tank Corps and the Supreme War Council at Versailles. In April 1918 he became part-time Chief of the Air Staff, following TRENCHARD's resignation. Sykes had a penchant for designing uniforms for new units and truly execrable handwriting.

Sykes, Mark (1879–1919) British diplomat, principally remembered for his part in negotiating the notorious Sykes–Picot agreement of May 1916. This was a secret agreement between Britain and France for the post-war partition of the Ottoman Empire. From a British perspective, it gave precedence to direct British control over the oil-rich region between Baghdad and Basra. The naked imperial ambition that the agreement represented seemed to conflict with undertakings given by Britain to the Arabs in the HUSSEIN–MCMAHON correspondence. The later acceptance of the agreement by Russia, in return for the annexation of Turkish Armenia, eventually brought the text of the agreement into the hands of the Bolshevik government, which released it, causing considerable embarrassment to Britain's relations with the Arabs. The agreement became the source of bitter recriminations between the British and French after the Armistice. LLOYD GEORGE believed that Britain's leading role in the defeat of the Ottoman Empire entitled her to a paramount position in the Middle East, and he was determined to deny France the territories she had been promised in the Levant under the agreement. Sykes' credentials for negotiating the agreement included not only his reputation as an Oriental expert but also an unusual ability to get on with the French. He later dictated General MAUDE's Declaration after the capture of Baghdad (March 1917) and exercised some influence on ALLENBY's Declaration after the capture of Jerusalem (December 1917). Sykes' Zionist sympathies also led to his involvement in the BALFOUR Declaration (November 1917), promising that the British government would 'view with favour the establishment in Palestine of a National Home for the Jewish people'. By the end of 1917 he had been party to a British policy that simultaneously embraced imperialism, support for Arab nationalism and Zionism. Sir Mark Sykes died in Paris during the great influenza pandemic. His memorial in the family church at Sledmere in Yorkshire shows him in the guise of a latter-day crusader.

Szurmay, Alexander, Baron (1860–1945) Austro-Hungarian military commander, whose defence of the Carpathian passes, especially the Uzsok Pass in March 1915, earned him the soubriquet 'Saviour of the Fatherland' in his native Hungary. As Hungarian Minister of War (from February 1917) he supported the division of the Austro-Hungarian army into separate national contingents.

T

Talât Pasha, Mehmed (1874–1921) Ottoman politician, who was Interior Minister throughout the war and Grand Vizier from February 1917. Talât was a leading figure in the Young Turk revolution of 1908. By 1914 he had established himself as one of the most powerful figures in the Ottoman Empire, together with ENVER PASHA. He favoured an alliance with Russia, but when this proved impossible – not least because of British and French opposition – he accepted the inevitability of a German alliance. Even so, he was reluctant to commit Turkey to the war immediately, delaying entry until the beginning of November 1914. Although Talât's role in Turkish entry to the war seems clear, he was much less optimistic about the war's outcome than his rival Enver, to whose ambitious military plans he nevertheless attempted to provide full domestic backing by subordinating Ottoman society to the needs of the army. As Interior Minister, however, responsible for public order and the distribution of food, he soon confronted the social and political dislocations inflicted on Ottoman society by the war. It was Talât who ordered the deportation of the Armenian population from eastern Anatolia after rebels captured the city of Van in April 1915. The deportation was exceptionally brutal, resulting in the first great genocide of the twentieth century. Talât's subsequent attempts to distance himself from the 'Armenian massacres' seem hollow. He remained at the heart of Ottoman government until 1918, presiding with increasing ineffectiveness in the face of continuing military defeats in the Caucasus, Mesopotamia and Palestine. He resigned in October 1918 and fled to Germany, where an Armenian assassinated him on 15 March 1921.

Tappen, Karl von (1879–1941) German chemist and gas warfare pioneer, who first had the idea of adding xylyl bromide to artillery shells. The effect of xylyl bromide, a powerful irritant, was lachrymatory. 'T[for "Tappen"]-Stoff' was first used on the Eastern Front at Bolimov on 31 January 1915 but had no noticeable effect in the intense cold. Xylyl bromide's lack of effectiveness at low temperatures was only one of its limitations; it was also extremely corrosive and tended to leak from its containers. After another failure of the shells, this time against the British on the Western Front at Nieuport in March 1915, Tappen seems to have played no further role in the German chemical warfare effort, in which his colleague at the Kaiser Wilhelm Institute in Berlin, Fritz HABER, became the leading figure. Nevertheless, the early German use of gas in shells was prescient; the tactical future of gas warfare lay with shell, rather than cylinder, release, something that the British, who suffered from the first German cylinder release of chlorine in April 1915, were reluctant to accept.

Tardieu, André Pierre Gabriel Amédée (1876–1945) French journalist, diplomat and politician, who established a virtually unrivalled pre-war reputation as a commentator on international relations through his foreign affairs editorship of *Le Temps* and *Le Petit Parisien*. Although initially favourable towards the idea of Franco-German reconciliation, the Second Moroccan Crisis of 1911 convinced him of the need for diplomatic 'firmness' and military preparedness. This brought him closer to POINCARÉ and CLEMENCEAU. During the first two years of the war Tardieu served on the staffs of both JOFFRE, whose replacement he later advocated, and FOCH before being wounded. As a leading advocate of Allied and American co-operation, he was sent to Washington as French High Commissioner by President Poincaré with a brief to mobilise US material support for France that he certainly fulfilled. During the war Tardieu identified ever more closely with Clemenceau's determination not only to defeat Germany but also to achieve a peace settlement that would guarantee French security. He was a leading member of the French delegation to the Paris Peace Conference. When it became clear to him that French plans to weaken Germany permanently through a set of draconian penalties would be unacceptable to the other allies, especially the United States, he persuaded Clemenceau that acceptance of an Anglo-American guarantee of French security was sufficient to meet French concerns. In this, he was to be disappointed.

Tennyson d'Eyncourt, Eustace (1868–1951) British armoured warfare pioneer. Tennyson d'Eyncourt is an unlikely sounding name for one of the principal pioneers of the tank. Although his father, a metropolitan magistrate, was a cousin of the poet, Eustace Tennyson d'Eyn-court's background was in engineering, particularly shipbuilding. He was apprenticed at the age of 18 to Armstrong-Whitworth's great shipyard at Elswick, near Newcastle-upon-Tyne. Armstrong's speciality was warships, and it was in this area that Tennyson d'Eyncourt specialised after successfully completing the naval architecture course at the Royal Naval College, Greenwich. His reputation as one of the leading naval architects of his day brought him to the notice of the First Lord of the Admiralty, Winston CHURCHILL, who appointed Tennyson d'Eyncourt Director of Naval Construction at the Admiralty in 1912, a post he held throughout the war. Churchill's desire to find a technical means of breaking the trench deadlock on the Western Front led him in February 1917 to establish a committee, the Landships Committee, to investigate the possibilities. Tennyson d'Eyncourt was a member of the committee. His pioneering spirit, assertiveness and self-confidence were the equal of his chief, and he played a leading part in forwarding tank development and later advocated the mass production and surprise tactical use of tanks.

Thaon di Revel, Paolo (1859–1948) Italian naval staff officer. As chief of the Italian navy's general staff from 1913 to October 1915 and from February 1917 until November 1919, Thaon di Revel was the leading advocate of the 'fleet in being' strategy. This brought him into conflict with the Italian navy's Commander-in-Chief, the Duke of the ABRUZZI, who wished to use Italian naval power more aggressively. Thaon di Revel was determined not to expose the fleet to the danger of Austrian submarines but to preserve it intact either until it faced a showdown with the Austrian battle-fleet or as a diplomatic bargaining counter in the post-war Mediterranean. This was one battle he did win. His equally formidable determination to uphold Italian interests and prestige made him an uncomfortable and disruptive ally who did much to prevent the achievement of a unified Allied command in the Mediterranean naval war, considerably weakening the fight against Austrian and German U-boats.

Thomas, Albert (1878–1932) French politician. Thomas's career had many similarities to that of LLOYD GEORGE, with whom he collaborated closely. Both came from humble backgrounds (Thomas was the son of a baker). Both made their way through their own talents, though in Thomas's case this was through the more traditional French meritocratic route of the École Normale Supérieur. Both were on the left of their countries' political spectrums. And both found themselves in charge of munitions production, to which each was appointed – at least in part – to curb the powers of a War Minister, in Thomas's case MILLERAND, in Lloyd George's KITCHENER. Unlike Lloyd George, however, Thomas did not obtain cabinet status until May 1915, nine months into the job, and only at the end of 1916 was his post given full ministerial status. This was a recognition not only of the vital importance of war production but also of Thomas's success. French industrial mobilisation during the Great War, severely hampered by the loss of industrial capacity in the German-occupied areas of the north, was nevertheless a triumph. Thomas's role was vital and entitles him to a leading place among his wartime contemporaries. In the first year of Thomas's administration French shell production rose from 9,000 a day to 300,000 a day. The daily production of artillery pieces rose twelve-fold during the war. France also produced some 50,000 aircraft, many of which flew with the British and American air services, and 4,800 tanks. Thomas recognised labour supply as the key to production, mobilising women, refugees, colonial workers and prisoners of war. He also took on the army, succeeding not only in establish-

ing the exemption of key skilled workers from military service but also in obtaining the release of half a million men already serving. As a Socialist he had no qualms about increasing state intervention to protect rates of pay, but he also recognised the importance of maintaining good relations with employers. The most important thing was to maintain production, even if this meant removing restrictions on working hours and safety measures. Thomas remained in office, through successive administrations, until September 1917, when his Socialist colleagues opposed his continuing in government.

Thomas, Bert (1883–1966) British cartoonist, who drew one of the most famous cartoons of the war, showing a Tommy lighting his pipe above the caption ''Arf a mo' Kaiser'. It helped raise nearly a quarter of a million pounds to supply tobacco and cigarettes as 'comforts' for the troops in the front line. The cartoon made a reappearance in the Second World War, with a few uniform detail changes, above the caption ''Arf a mo' 'itler'.

Thomas, David Alfred, Viscount Rhondda (1856–1918) British businessman and wartime administrator. Thomas was one of the great coal barons of the Rhondda Valley in South Wales. He endeared himself to LLOYD GEORGE not only as a Welshman and a Liberal but also as a businessman with 'push and go'. When Lloyd George became Minister of Munitions in May 1915, he sent Thomas to the United States to organise the supply of American munitions to the British army. In June 1917 Thomas replaced the incompetent Lord Devonport as Food Controller. It was a key appointment. Reports into the widespread outbreak of industrial unrest during the spring and early summer of 1917 emphasised the importance of popular dissatisfaction with the price and availability of food and huge resentment towards the rich, whose spending power allowed them to command all the food they needed. Military censorship also began to pick up the anger front-line troops felt about the deprivations that their families at home were being forced to undergo while the rich continued to tuck in. The spectacle of Russia's fate gave these concerns greater force. Thomas considerably expanded the scope of the Food Controller's operations, increasing the staff of his central office by 3,000 in less than six months (some 26,000 people were employed in food administration by the end of the war). Thomas's indifferent health led him to delegate much more than his predecessor, something that endeared him to his civil servants, especially his Permanent Secretary, Ulrick Wintour. Considerable research was undertaken into diet and useful statistics on working-class patterns of consumption collected. More and more of the country's food imports were purchased directly by the government. Despite this, the food situation remained intractable. Thomas's attempts at price control were no more successful than his predecessor's, often serving only to drive food from the market. Shortages of sugar, potatoes and coal were serious and led to demoralising queues. By the turn of the year Lloyd George was becoming increasingly concerned and was contemplating replacing Thomas. Thomas saved the situation and his reputation by the decision to institute compulsory rationing, first in London and then – from 8 July 1918 – nationally. Its adoption owed more to the grass-roots action of local Food Vigilance Committees and the establishment of municipal schemes than it did to initiative at the centre. Rationing became associated in the public mind with Thomas, nevertheless, and made him one of the most popular men in the country, the champion of the housewife and the poor and the restorer of social solidarity. At his death the Prime Minister who had come so close to sacking him lauded Lord Rhondda. Despite the political difficulties arising from inequalities of food distribution, Britain never experienced widespread deprivation on the home front, and Britain's armies were exceptionally well fed. Nutrition-based diseases showed a marked decline during the war. British access to global supplies of food and the ability of the Royal Navy to secure the sea lanes gave Britain and the Allies a tremendous advantage over the Central Powers. Food was one of Britain's principal war-winning weapons.

Thomas, Margaret Haig (1883–1958) British suffragist and public servant, who achieved notoriety before the war by her involvement, as an arsonist, in the campaign of militant civil disobedience organised by the Women's Social and Political Union (WSPU), and by her subsequent hunger strike in prison. After the outbreak of war, however, she supported the decision of the WSPU leadership to rally to the flag. In the early part of the war she worked closely with her father, the Welsh businessman David Alfred THOMAS, who was sent to the United States in 1915 by Lloyd George to organise the supply of munitions to the British army. It was during a return trip across the Atlantic that she survived the sinking of the *Lusitania*. In 1917 she became Director of the Women's Department in the new Ministry of National Service. In this capacity she was called upon in 1918 to investigate the state of the Women's Royal Air Force (WRAF). Her hostile report led to the dismissal of the WRAF's commander, Violet DOUGLAS-PENNANT, another leading Welsh female figure of the war. Margaret Haig Thomas inherited her father's title, by special remainder, after his death but failed in a characteristic attempt to take his seat in the House of Lords. In 1920 Lady Rhondda founded, and later edited, the magazine *Time and Tide*.

Thomas, (Philip) Edward (1878–1917) British soldier and poet. Thomas was not a 'war poet' in the sense of OWEN,

ROSENBERG or SASSOON. He did not write directly about 'battle', but war was an inescapable part of his poetry. There is a sense, perhaps, in which the war made him a poet. Until the autumn of 1914 his literary output was confined to prose and the hack work of reviewing on which his livelihood depended. But then, with the encouragement of Robert Frost, verse began to flow from his pen. By the time of his enlistment in July 1915 at the age of 37, he had written some of his most famous poems, including 'The Sign-Post', 'Tears', 'November' and 'Adlestrop'. Thomas was a life-long depressive, a proud man, often driven to anger by poverty and discouragement, a predicament movingly captured in the later memoirs of his devoted wife, Helen Noble. He found consolation in nature and the English countryside, which he portrayed with loving accuracy, though without sentimentality. His greatest theme is the effect of the war on the natural order of things, captured magnificently in one of his finest poems, 'As the team's head brass'. Edward Thomas was killed by a shell on Easter Monday 1917 while acting as a forward observation officer during the battle of Arras. His death was the greatest loss suffered by English literature during the war.

Thomas, William Beach (1868–1957) British journalist and war correspondent. The war catapulted Beach Thomas from his comfortable billet as a writer of countryside features for the *Daily Mail* to the equally comfortable billet of official war correspondent on the Western Front. His first visit to the front was, however, unofficial and led to his arrest on the orders of Lord KITCHENER, a man whose own career had benefited greatly from news management but who was hostile to the presence of journalists in the war zone. In January 1915, however, it was recognised that the war could not forever be excluded from the news and Beach Thomas was chosen as one of the original

five official correspondents, contributing heavily censored patriotic pap to the readers of the *Daily Mail* and *Daily Mirror*. He was knighted after the war.

Thompson, John Tagliaferro (1860–1940) US soldier and weapons designer. Thompson began his military career in the artillery, but from 1890 he worked at the US Ordnance Department, where he played a leading part in the development of the Springfield M1903 rifle and the Colt M1911 pistol, perhaps the most successful service pistol in military history. He retired from the US army in November 1914 and went to work for the Remington Arms Corporation, for which he established special factories to produce Enfield rifles for the British army and Mosin-Nagant rifles for the Russian army. When the United States entered the war in April 1917, Thompson was recalled to duty and eventually given responsibility for small arms and ammunition supply to the American Expeditionary Force. Thompson's work on an automatic rifle, or sub-machine gun, a weapon of great utility in trench warfare, did not find its fulfilment until after the war, when the 'Tommy' gun became the favoured weapon of Irish guerrillas and American gangsters.

Thuillier, Henry Fleetwood (1868–1953) British military commander. Thuillier was a sapper who became the British Expeditionary Force's first Director of Gas Services on 7 March 1916. His appointment coincided with a reorganisation of the BEF's gas warfare effort. Thuillier was given overall responsibility for all aspects of gas war and had two Assistant Directors, C.H. FOULKES, with operational responsibility for 'offensive' gas war, and S.L. Cummins, Royal Army Medical Corps, with responsibility for 'defensive' gas war. Foulkes proved a difficult, wilful subordinate with a tendency to act on his own initiative without reference to higher authority. By the time Thuillier was promoted to command 15th (Scottish) Division on 17 June 1917, Foulkes' persistent advocacy of gas release from cylinders and determined empire building had rendered their relationship particularly fraught. Foulkes' elevation to Director of Gas Services in succession to Thuillier allowed him to continue his perverse policy.

Tilley, Vesta (1864–1952) Stage name of Matilda Alice Powles, one of the great stars of the Victorian and Edwardian music hall, famous for her male impersonations. In August 1914 she was one of the best-known public figures to lend her support to the recruiting campaign, singing patriotic songs specially written by her husband, Walter de Frece. She became known as 'England's Greatest Recruiting Sergeant'. Her role in forcing impressionable young male members of her audience into the armed forces ('I'll make a man of any one of you') was satirised in the influential stage-play and film *Oh! What a Lovely War*. It is doubtful, however, whether her contribution to the raising of a volunteer army of 1M men by Christmas 1914 was anything other than cosmetic. Her war services were rewarded indirectly in 1919, when she became Lady de Frece.

Tirpitz, Alfred von (1849–1930) German naval officer. As Prussian Navy Minister from 1897 until 1916, Tirpitz was the principal architect of the German High Seas Fleet, which was to be the instrument of German global domination. Tirpitz's ability to obtain funding for a great navy was a testament to his promotional skills, akin to those of the company promoter or patent medicine man. He was fortunate in having a Kaiser who fancied himself as a student of naval strategy (having read and misunderstood the works of the American naval theorist Alfred Thayer Mahan) and who was jealous of the British fleet. He was also adept at selling the economic advantages of naval construction to Ger-

man business and organised labour. Tirpitz understood that building a great fleet was the 'work of a generation', earmarking 1920 as the date by which the German navy would be able to challenge the Royal Navy on terms of equality. He also realised that the Germans might not have a generation in which to build it, and he lived in fear of a British pre-emptive strike. So he invented his famous 'risk theory' to justify the expenditure of money on a fleet capable of producing a short-term reward. Even a fleet smaller than that of the British would be large enough to deter Britain through the risk that so many ships might be lost that British naval superiority over France and Russia would be compromised. He even persuaded himself that Britain might yield part of her colonial empire to Germany in return for an alliance with such a strong naval power. The risk theory certainly succeeded in persuading the Reichstag to provide money for Tirpitz's ships, but it was otherwise disastrous. The British understood from the start that Tirpitz's policy was directed against them. It was an important factor in driving Britain to seek a diplomatic understanding with France, an understanding ultimately fatal to German ambitions. Far from acquiescing in the rise of German naval power, the British rose to the challenge, comprehensively outspending the Germans in an unprecedented naval race that the Royal Navy had clearly won by 1912. The British victory would allow them to concentrate sufficient force in the North Sea to defeat the German High Seas Fleet and to maintain their other global commitments. No one understood this better than Tirpitz. Knowing that the German navy was not ready and fearing a British invasion, he advocated peace in 1914. Once the war broke out, however, he demanded unrestricted submarine warfare as the most effective way of attacking the British. He resigned when the Kaiser refused to remove operational restrictions on the

U-boats in March 1916. To his astonishment, his resignation was accepted.

Tisza de Boros-Jëno, István, Count (1861–1918) Austro-Hungarian politician. As Prime Minister of Hungary from June 1913 until May 1917, Tisza brought to his position the perceptions and instincts of a Magyar. During the July Crisis of 1914 these led him to advocate a diplomatic rather than a military offensive against Serbia. He regarded the possibility of a European war as a 'calamity'. Even victory might be dangerous. Tisza was acutely aware that Slavs already outnumbered the Magyars in their own country. He had no desire to see the Habsburg Empire acquire even more Slav subjects, and he demanded assurances that there would be no annexation of Serbia. Beyond this, his influence upon events was limited. He was increasingly marginalised by Imperial Foreign Minister BERCHTOLD's determination to have a final reckoning with Serbia, even at the risk of a European war, though Tisza's intervention succeeded in delaying an immediate attack on Serbia, perhaps to Austria-Hungary's military cost. Once the war began, however, Tisza became fully committed to the victory of the Central Powers, though this did not make him a pliable colleague. He halted the free passage of food from Hungary to Austria as early as the spring of 1915 and did not agree to join a Joint Food Committee with Austria until February 1917. He used the threat of withholding Hungarian food to influence Imperial policy, especially to prevent what he regarded as the disproportionate recruitment of Hungarians into the army. Although his domestic rule in Hungary became ever more dictatorial, Tisza skilfully kept the Magyar parliament in session in order to legitimise his actions in the eyes of Vienna and to minimise internal dissent. He also refused to challenge Magyar patriotism by increasing direct taxation or by instituting special war taxes, preferring the softer option of borrowing, with its attendant risk of inflation. This was another reason to pursue victory: the defeated enemy would pay for the war. Tisza was hostile to all attempts to turn the Dual Monarchy into a Triple Monarchy, either by the addition of Poland (which he believed should be absorbed into Austria) or – even worse – by the addition of some kind of South Slav state. The accession to the throne of Emperor KARL I in December 1916 further weakened Tisza's position, already compromised by military defeat, by his identification in the minds of his fellow Magyars as a supporter of all-out war and by his opposition to social and political reform. The Emperor forced him to resign in May 1917. Communists assassinated Tisza in Budapest on 31 October 1918.

Toller, Ernst (1893–1939) German soldier, who spent thirteen months on the Western Front before he became ill and was discharged unfit for military service. After the war he suffered political persecution as a revolutionary before establishing himself as one of Germany's leading playwrights. In 1933, not an auspicious year for Jewish socialists, he published an account of his wartime experiences, *I Was a German*. The past tense referred to Toller's discovery of a common humanity amid the searing violence of the trenches, the one redeeming feature of a war marked by brutality, violence, death and destruction. Toller served at Verdun in 1916. The battle played the same role in shaping his disillusionment as the Somme did for many British writers. It was at Verdun that Toller recognised modern war as mechanical and impartial, consuming its human cogs without regard to nationality or individuality. These views did not endear him to the Nazi government and he was forced to flee to the United States. Ernst Toller committed suicide in New York in 1939.

Tonks, Henry (1862–1937) British artist. Tonks gave up his career as a surgeon to teach at the Slade Art School, where his pupils included C.R.W. NEVINSON, Mark GERTLER, William ROBERTS and Stanley SPENCER. He volunteered for the Royal Army Medical Corps on the outbreak of war and served on the Western Front until chosen to join the team of plastic surgeons led by Harold GILLIES. Tonks worked principally as a medical artist, recording the process of facial reconstruction in individual patients in a series of extraordinary portraits. He became an official war artist in 1918, painting two well-known canvases with medical themes, *An Advanced Dressing Station in France* and *An Underground Casualty Clearing Station*. He was Slade Professor of Fine Art from 1917 until his retirement in 1930.

Townshend, Charles Vere Ferrers (1861–1924) British military commander, whose surrender to Turkish forces at Kut-al-Amara in April 1916 constituted one of the most humiliating defeats in British imperial history. Townshend's pre-war reputation was based on his part in the siege of Chitral (1895). He was an able soldier who found himself the unwilling tool of the reckless policy favoured by his superior, Sir John NIXON. Townshend's advance into Mesopotamia (modern Iraq) initially went well. LIDDELL HART described the capture of Amara on 3 June as a 'brilliant little victory'. But as Townshend's small, inadequately equipped force plunged deeper into the Iraqi interior it became less and less effective. The attempt to capture Baghdad, which Townshend opposed, was defeated by the Turks at Ctesiphon in November 1915. Townshend's army was forced to retreat, finally seeking shelter at Kut. All attempts to relieve him failed and on 29 April 1916 the starving garrison surrendered. Townshend's men attached no blame to their commander, whose skill in the retreat and resolve during the siege evoked their admiration. His behaviour in captivity, however, was less praiseworthy. He was treated with lavish hospitality by his captors and released within a year to plead their cause. But he obtained better terms for his dog than he did for his men, mostly Indian troops, who were subjected to barbaric treatment, including homosexual rape. Two-thirds of them died during their long march into captivity. Townshend's reputation never recovered and he died in some odium.

Toynbee, Arnold Joseph (1889–1975) British historian, who had already established himself as a leading authority on the Hellenic and Byzantine world by 1914. He was prevented by ill health from undertaking active service, an exclusion that haunted him all his life, and he served for most of the war in the Political Intelligence Department of the Foreign Office. In this capacity he compiled the first report into the Turkish genocide against the Armenians. This took the form of an official *British Blue Book*, published in November 1915. Although apologists of the Ottoman government have always dismissed the report as a work of black propaganda by an enemy power, it remains a powerful and compelling indictment of Ottoman atrocities, based on a wide range of eye-witness and survivor testimonies, not at all like the notorious BRYCE report.

Trakl, Georg (1887–1914) Austrian Expressionist poet, whose poems – though deeply personal – reflect, in their overwhelming concern with decay, the fate of the empire into which he was born. In August 1914 he was mobilised as a lieutenant in the Austrian Medical Corps. Trakl had trained as a pharmacist, an ideal profession for a confirmed drug addict. He was hospitalised in November 1914 after the battle of Grodek, in Poland, during which he was distressed by the fate of wounded men at his field hospital and diagnosed as a schizophrenic. He died of a drug overdose on 3 or 4

November, whether intentional or not is uncertain, though he had threatened suicide many times, even before the war.

Trenchard, Hugh Montague (1873–1956) British air force commander, commonly regarded as the 'Father of the Royal Air Force'. Trenchard gave few early signs of future distinction. He only entered the army after his third attempt at passing the Militia exam, having previously failed twice to pass into Woolwich and once into the Royal Naval College, Dartmouth. He was, however, a man of unusual spirit and determination. After suffering a severe wound to his lung in South Africa, he recuperated by tackling the Cresta Run and becoming a tobogganing champion. His decision to join the infant Royal Flying Corps in 1912, made at the suggestion of a friend, transformed his career. When war broke out, he was given command of the Royal Flying Corps Military Wing at Farnborough, which was charged with the air defence of Britain (at that time threatened only by German airships) and training new squadrons for front-line service in France. In December 1914 he went to France himself to command First Wing RFC. In August 1915 he succeeded Sir David HENDERSON as GOC Royal Flying Corps, remaining in command until January 1918. His policy was clearly established from the outset. First was the need to establish air supremacy. This could only be achieved by taking the fight to the Germans over enemy lines, even using, if necessary, obsolete aircraft, a strategy for which he received much contemporary and subsequent criticism. Second was the RFC's duty to support the army in the field, through reconnaissance, artillery co-operation and – eventually – tactical bombing. His postwar views on strategic bombing were very different from those he espoused during the war, when he saw the RFC very much as the servant of the ground forces. He opposed the establishment of the independent Royal Air Force on 1 April 1918 and

resigned as Chief of the Air Staff soon afterwards. He regarded his command of the Independent Air Force, charged in June 1918 with strategic bombing of German factories, as a complete waste of time, men and money. A commanding – even intimidating – personality, known as 'Boom' owing to his stentorian voice, Trenchard was much admired by HAIG, a faithful supporter of the RFC throughout the war.

Tritton, William Ashbee (1876–1946) British tank pioneer, whose firm Tritton, Foster & Co. of Lincoln played a leading part in the development and manufacture of the tank. Tritton's design partnership with Walter WILSON, an automobile engineer, was decisive in the emergence of a viable prototype capable of securing the funding necessary for further development. Tritton himself designed the new type of tracks that the tank needed to cross the shell-pocked and trench-scarred landscapes of the Western Front.

Trotha, Adolf von (1868–1940) German naval staff officer. Trotha was a protégé of TIRPITZ. He shared, unequivocally, his patron's belief that the German High Seas Fleet should seek a decisive naval engagement with the British. He also supported the policy of unrestricted submarine warfare and welcomed HINDENBURG and LUDENDORFF's authoritarian Third Supreme Command. As chief of staff to the High Seas Fleet from January 1916, he was, together with Admiral SCHEER, a leading proponent of a unified naval command structure, an achievement that took them until August 1918 to bring about. In October 1918 the desire of Trotha and HIPPER to launch the High Seas Fleet on a final suicide mission against the British provoked the Kiel mutiny and accelerated the collapse of Imperial Germany.

Trotsky, Lev Davidovich (1879–1940) Russian revolutionary. When the tsarist regime collapsed in February 1917, Trotsky was in New York. He had been abroad for ten years, after escaping from a second period of exile in Siberia imposed because of the part he played in establishing the St Petersburg Soviet during the Revolution of 1905. He instantly perceived the possibility of a wider revolution than the one achieved in February. He made his way back to Russia by May 1917, determined to assist in its birth. He joined the Bolshevik Party in July and played a role in the October Revolution second only to that of LENIN. As Commissar of Foreign Affairs in the Bolshevik government he looked to orchestrate world revolution. He stalled on signing a formal peace with the Central Powers, believing that revolution would shortly break out in Berlin. He was disappointed. He seriously underestimated the Germans' capacity and will to restart the war on the Eastern Front. The German resumption of war compelled the Bolsheviks to accept a humiliating peace treaty at Brest-Litovsk in March 1918, far more severe than the settlement they could have expected to negotiate in November 1917. Trotsky sought to distance himself from the debacle as soon as possible, refusing to attend the treaty signing. Instead, he became Commissar for War and President of the Supreme War Soviet. In the ensuing months he created the Red Army from nothing and, during the civil war, displayed skill as a military leader of which there were few hints in his previous career as polemicist and political theorist.

Troubridge, Ernest Charles Thomas (1862–1926) British naval commander, whose dismal failure to prevent the escape of the German ships *Goeben* and *Breslau* from Messina into the Sea of Marmora in August 1914 was instrumental in bringing about Turkish entry into the war on the German side. Troubridge allowed himself to be convinced by his Flag Captain, Fawcet Wray, that the interception of the German ships, which was well within the

capabilities of his squadron, would be a violation of his Admiralty orders to avoid combat with superior forces. Official opinion was immediately condemnatory. The First Sea Lord, Prince LOUIS ALEXANDER of Battenberg, denounced Troubridge's failure as 'shameful'. Troubridge's subsequent court martial acquitted him of blame, largely on account of characteristically ambiguous Admiralty orders, but his career was broken and he never received a sea command again. It is likely that the vilification of Troubridge was a factor in Admiral CRADOCK's fateful decision to attack a superior German force at Coronel in November 1914, a decision that he paid for not with his career but with his life and the lives of his men.

Trumbić, Ante (1864–1938) Croat politician, an established enemy of the Habsburg Empire, who fled to London in 1915, where he established the Yugoslav Committee to co-ordinate attempts to obtain Allied support for a South Slav state. He was equally determined that the new state would have a federal structure guaranteeing the rights of Croats, an endeavour in which he was considerably assisted by the collapse of Serbia's closest ally, Russia. Trumbić became the first Foreign Minister of Yugoslavia, which he skilfully represented at the Paris Peace Conference in 1919.

Tucker, William Sansome (18??–19??) British soldier. Tucker was a lecturer in physics at Imperial College, London, who joined Lawrence BRAGG's 'sound ranging' pioneers in 1916 as a corporal, Royal Engineers. In June 1916 Tucker provided the critical breakthrough in the development of an effective (and objective) instrumental system of 'sound ranging' enemy guns through his invention of a 'hot wire' microphone capable of identifying the shell wave and the following report of the gun that fired it. By September 1916 Tucker microphones had been supplied to all sound ranging sections, whose ability to locate enemy guns improved dramatically.

Tudor, (Henry) Hugh (1871–1966) British military commander. 'Owen' Tudor was one of the best artillery and divisional commanders to emerge in the British army during the war. A small, neat, restless, quick-witted, pugnacious man, as a junior officer he had been one of the best lightweight boxers in the army. He was fearless not only of personal safety but also of superior authority, which he was not above abusing both to its face and behind its back. From the autumn of 1916 his career was intimately associated with the 9th (Scottish) Division, the senior division of the New Army, first as its artillery commander and (from March 1918 until the Armistice) as its GOC. Tudor was tactically innovative. He was possibly the originator, and certainly the leading advocate, of smoke shells. Smoke could be extremely effective in screening movement and confusing the enemy about the real point of assault ('Chinese assaults'). He was also the inspiration behind the decision to dispense with a preliminary bombardment at the battle of Cambrai in October 1917. This met with much opposition, but with the uncompromising support of the Third Army commander, Sir Julian BYNG, Tudor's faith in the 'new gunnery' created by the survey and location units was triumphantly demonstrated. The attack came as a complete surprise to the Germans. The barrage and counter-battery fire was exceptionally accurate and some ninety per cent of German guns were effectively engaged. This, far more than the famous use of tanks, explains the impressive success of the battle's opening. It marked the way ahead for the BEF in 1918. As a divisional commander, Tudor retained his front-line instincts, regularly visiting his forward units and always endeavouring to see for himself. The staff work of the division was outstanding, and no trouble was too much in ensuring the safety and

comfort of the troops. That Tudor could also be ruthless was demonstrated by his period as Chief of Police in Ireland during the 'Troubles'.

Tull, Walter David (1888–1918) British army officer, the son of a Bajan joiner and the grandson of a slave, brought up in a Bethnal Green orphanage. A keen sportsman, his football skills brought him to the attention of Tottenham Hotspur, who signed him in 1908. He was only the second black man to play professional football in England. In 1910 he joined Northampton Town, for whom he remained a popular and successful player until the outbreak of war, when, like many footballers, he volunteered for the 17th Battalion Middlesex Regiment (1st Football). He was quickly promoted to the rank of sergeant and fought on the Somme in 1916. In 1917, after a period of convalescence at home, he was promoted Second Lieutenant and sent to join the 19th Battalion Middlesex Regiment on the Italian front, where he was mentioned in dispatches during fighting on the Piave. In 1918 his battalion was returned to the Western Front, and he was killed in action on 25 March 1918. Walter Tull was the first black officer in the history of the British army.

Tyrwhitt, Reginald Yorke (1870–1951) British naval commander. Tyrwhitt belonged to the 'Fishpond' of young, talented officers whose pre-war careers were advanced by the First Sea Lord, Admiral Sir John FISHER. In 1913 Tyrwhitt was given command of the destroyer flotillas based in the southern part of the North Sea at Harwich. He commanded the 'Harwich Force' throughout the war. It was the perfect instrument for a man of his outstanding initiative and aggression. His destroyers played major roles in the successful British actions at the Heligoland Bight (28 August 1914) and the Dogger Bank (24 January 1915), but to his disgust his ships were kept in port under Admiralty orders during the major fleet engagement at Jutland (31 May–1 June 1916). Despite this, he constantly took the war to the enemy, using tip-and-run tactics, and his ships spent more time at sea than any other part of the British fleet. He advocated seaplane attacks against German coastal positions and strongly supported the Zeebrugge raid of April 1918. Tyrwhitt accepted the surrender of the German submarine fleet at Harwich in November 1918. Arthur Marder described him as the 'outstanding British sea officer of the war'.

U

Udet, Ernst (1896–1941) German fighter ace, credited with sixty-two victories. At first he found it impossible to shoot down the enemy but steeled himself to become one of the most successful aces. He was one of the first pilots to escape from an aircraft by parachute and carried out arguably the only successful attack on a tank in the First World War. After the war he played a key role in the development of the *Luftwaffe*.

Uniacke, Herbert Crofton Campbell (1866–1934) British artilleryman. His ex-perience in the South African War (1899–1902) convinced him sooner than most of his contemporaries that the days of artil-lery standing in the open were over. In future wars gunners would not have visual contact with their targets. They would have to embrace the scientific methods essential to effective 'indirect' fire. An outspoken man, no respecter of rank, as chief artillery adviser to Fifth Army (1916–18) he played an important role in bringing together the dash of the pre-war Horse Artillery and the 'slide-rule' gunnery of the Garrison Artillery.

V

Van Deventer, Louis Jacob (1874–1922) South African general. Having fought against the British as a guerrilla in the South African War (1899–1902), 'Japie' Van Deventer found the tables turned when, during the First World War, he commanded British 2nd East African Division and then the East African Expeditionary Force in pursuit of General Paul von LETTOW-VORBECK's elusive Afro-German guerrilla army. He eventually chased Lettow-Vorbeck out of British East Africa but never succeeded in bringing him to a decisive engagement. The remnants of Lettow-Vorbeck's army were still in the field when the German armies surrendered on the Western Front.

Vasić, Peter (1862–1931) Serb military commander. He led a corps under MIŠIĆ at the defence of Monastir (September–November 1916) and played a leading part in the second battle of the Vardar (September–October 1918), the offensive that liberated Serbia and brought about the surrender of Bulgaria.

Vaughan, Louis Ridley (1875–1942) British staff officer. Vaughan joined the Indian army in 1896 as an officer in the 2nd Battalion 7th Goorkha Rifles. The choice of this warrior-formation was perhaps slightly surprising. Vaughan's appearance and manner were donnish. He spoke softly and was exceptionally even tempered, characteristics that earned him the nickname 'Father'. His personality seems ideally suited to staff work and this was the path that his career soon took. When the war broke out he was GSO2 at the War Office in London, with the rank of major. By 1917 he had risen to chief of staff Third Army, with the rank of major-general. He was only 41. His appointment slightly preceded that of Sir Julian BYNG as GOC Third Army, but Byng retained him and they formed an effective combination right through until the end of the war. Vaughan was one of the most successful Indian army officers on the Western Front, a theatre in which they did not generally shine.

Venizelos, Eleutherios (1864–1936) Greek politician, Prime Minister of Greece 1910–15, 1917. Although a Cretan by birth, Venizelos was a determined Greek nationalist whose dream was to unite all Greeks, including those under Ottoman rule, in one nation. He made a dramatic advance towards this end during the Balkan Wars (1912–13), when Greece succeeded in more than doubling her population and almost doubling her land mass. The outbreak of the First World War constituted both an opportunity and a danger to Venizelos's ambition. The Greeks of Macedonia, Smyrna and the Aegean islands might be prised away from the Ottoman Empire and brought into the

Greek state in the event of an Ottoman defeat. But there was also a danger that an Ottoman–Bulgarian rapprochement would threaten Greece's gains of 1912–13. Venizelos was clear that Greek interests lay with the Allies, but this brought him into conflict with his king, CONSTANTINE I, brother-in-law of Kaiser WILHELM II. In October 1915 Venizelos, without consultation, allowed a Franco-British army to land at Salonika, undermining Constantine's policy of neutrality. In October 1916 Venizelos established his own regime at Thessaloniki, and this was soon recognised by Britain as the legitimate government of Greece. After one of the last displays of British (and French) gunboat diplomacy, Constantine was forced to abdicate in June 1917 and Greece entered the war on the Allied side. The diplomatic results of the war were as favourable to Greece as Venizelos predicted. The Aegean islands and most of Thrace were ceded to Greece, though control of Smyrna was lost to Turkey after Greece's defeat in the war of 1922, by which time Venizelos was out of power. Although Venizelos's post-war career was marked by defeat, controversy and, ultimately, exile, he remains a pivotal figure in the history of modern Greece, his importance confirmed by the number of memorials to him in one of Europe's most statued countries.

Victorio Emanuele III (1869–1947) King of Italy 1900–46, a tiny, shy, secretive, devious man who succeeded to the throne at the age of 31 after the assassination of his father, Umberto. His wishes were instrumental in Italy's repudiation of the Triple Alliance with Germany and Austria and in Italy's entry into the war on the Allied side (May 1915), despite a parliamentary majority in favour of neutrality. Although nominal Commander-in-Chief of the Italian army, he left the war to the often incompetent management of his generals, occasionally intervening to adjudicate their quarrels. His public defiance

in the face of the crushing Italian defeat at Caporetto (October–November 1917), when he insisted that there would be no Italian retreat beyond the line of the Piave, reassured Allied opinion and guaranteed the dispatch of British and French reinforcements.

Vieille, Paul (1854–1934) French chemist. Working with a French army officer, Captain Desaleux, in the 1880s, Vieille developed a smokeless gunpowder (Poudre B), first used in cartridges for the French Modèle 1886 Lebel rifle. Vieille's invention transformed the conduct of war. For the first time the firer would not betray his position by a cloud of dense smoke and mass small arms fire would no longer obscure the battlefield. The new powder was also much more powerful. Rifles could fire accurately at ranges as great as a thousand yards (the short-magazine Lee Enfield rifle with which the British army went to war in 1914 was sighted to 2,000 yards), allowing fewer men to hold a greater length of front on a much deeper battlefield.

Viviani, René (1862–1925) French politician, a left-wing moderate, co-founder of the socialist newspaper *L'Humanité*, who became Prime Minister in June 1914. He was still in the process of forming his government when the Archduke FRANZ FERDINAND was assassinated at Sarajevo. In the middle of July Viviani and President POINCARÉ left aboard the battleship *France* for a state visit to Russia, Sweden and Denmark. As Europe began its dramatic descent into war, they were cruising the Baltic, out of touch with events. Viviani played almost no role in the French decisions for war, constantly deferring to Poincaré. This 'hands-off' style of government continued after the war began. Viviani dealt with day-to-day matters of administration. Matters of political substance were left to Poincaré and matters of military substance to the increasingly autocratic French Commander-in-Chief,

JOFFRE, who sought to exclude politicians completely from his widely defined 'zone of the armies'. Nevertheless, it was Viviani, rather than Poincaré or Joffre, who paid the price of French military failures in 1915. He resigned in October and was replaced by Aristide BRIAND.

Voisin, Gabriel (1880–1973) French aircraft manufacturer. Inspired by the success of the Wright brothers, Voisin was determined that France should regain the lead in aeronautical science first established by the Montgolfier brothers in the eighteenth century. His company built the first really practical aircraft and, by 1914, had helped establish France as the leading aircraft manufacturer in the world. The Voisin design was of the 'pusher' type, with the engine behind the pilot. The Voisin III, with which the French army was equipped at the outbreak of war, was the only aircraft in the world fitted with a machine gun. One of them was responsible for downing the first enemy aircraft on 5 October 1914. The Voisin design was soon superseded by more powerful 'tractor' types, especially when the introduction of the interrupter gear allowed them to carry a machine gun that could fire forward through the propellers, but Voisins remained useful as reconnaissance aircraft. Later types were used principally as bombers, taking part in some of the first 'strategic' bombing missions against German factories.

Voss, Werner (1897–1917) German fighter ace, a skilful and courageous pilot, whose forty-eight victories ranked him fourth among his fellow countrymen. He was RICHTHOFEN's closest rival until he met his death in combat with seven aircraft of 56 Squadron Royal Flying Corps, commanded by James MCCUDDEN, on 23 September 1917.

W

Waldstätten, Alfred, Baron von (1872–1952) Austro-Hungarian staff officer, a former instructor at the War Academy, who served successively as chief of staff Army Group DANKL, XX (Edelweiss) Corps, Seventh Army and, finally, as deputy chief of staff and head of operations under ARZ VON STRAUSSENBERG from March 1917. Although a mediocre military talent at best, Waldstätten exercised considerable influence over Emperor KARL I, persuading him to resist German High Command attempts to exercise direct control over the Austro-Hungarian army. His attempts to win German support for an Austrian offensive on the Italian front at the start of 1917 failed, however. HINDENBURG and LUDENDORFF had little faith left in the military capability of Habsburg forces, but in the surprising event of a significant Habsburg success they suspected that it would simply create a platform from which Karl would seek a separate peace. Instead, Waldstätten was forced to agree to an Austro-German offensive later in the year at Caporetto. This battle's dramatic success clearly demonstrated German military superiority, as Waldstätten feared.

Walker, Harold Bridgwood (1862–1934) British military commander. 'Hooky' Walker was a staff officer in India when the war broke out, but he soon found himself posted to the Australian and New Zealand Army Corps as General BIRD-WOOD's chief of staff. Walker had not passed Staff College, and he made no secret of his distaste for staff work, but he was clear sighted and unafraid to express his opinions. These were decidedly against the landing on the Gallipoli peninsula that took place on 25 April 1915, which he believed stood no chance of success. The following month he succeeded General BRIDGES as GOC 1st (Australian) Division. Walker's tenure of command lasted only until 13 October 1915, when he was severely wounded by Turkish machine-gun fire at Silt Spur. Walker always liked to see for himself. In sharing the dangers of the front line, he won the respect and affection of his troops. By the time Walker returned to command his division, in March 1916, it had been transferred to the Western Front. He remained in command until the summer of 1918 when the 'Australianisation' of the Australian Corps led to his replacement by Bill GLASGOW. Walker's generalship was marked by prudence and concern for the welfare of his men, even – on occasion – to the point of threatening resignation. He ended the war commanding the British Territorial 48th (South Midland) Division on the Italian front at Vittorio Veneto.

Ward, John (1866–1934) British politician and soldier. Ward's remarkable career began as a navvy, an experience that led to his political radicalisation. He joined the Marxist Social Democratic Federation (SDF) in 1886 and was arrested for his part in the Trafalgar Square riots by the unemployed on 9 November 1887. He founded the Navvies' Union two years later. He was also closely involved for many years (1901–29) with the General Federation of Trade Unions and in 1906 was elected Liberal MP for Stoke-on-Trent. His championing of the miners' cause led to his being dubbed the 'Miners' MP'. But there was another side to Ward's interests. He was also a soldier, having served in the Sudan campaign of 1885. When the Great War broke out, Ward was instrumental in raising several Pioneer battalions, a wartime expedient designed to relieve the infantry from non-combat duties and to provide a pool of labour for the Royal Engineers in the construction of roads and trenches. Ward raised three of the first twelve Pioneer battalions, the 18th, 19th and 26th Battalions Middlesex Regiment (1st, 2nd and 3rd Public Works). Although raised in London, they contained many Staffordshire miners, miners being ideally suited for the work. Ward was given the rank of lieutenant-colonel. He served on the Western Front and in the Far East, where he became involved in the anti-Bolshevik rising in Vladivostock, an unlikely consummation for a former member of the SDF.

Ward, Joseph George (1856–1930) New Zealand politician. As Prime Minister from 1906 to 1912, Sir Joseph Ward's Liberal government did much to improve New Zealand's military preparedness, including the formation of a part-time national militia, the Territorial Army, that became the nucleus of the volunteer units raised for overseas service on the outbreak of war. His government also paid for the building of an *Indefatigable* class battle cruiser, HMS *New Zealand*, which saw much action during the war. Ward

joined in a coalition with W.F. MASSEY's Conservative majority in August 1915 and accompanied him to meetings of the Imperial War Cabinet in London. Their collaboration was so close that they were nicknamed 'the Siamese twins'.

Ward, Mary Augusta (1851–1920) British writer and wartime propagandist. By 1914 Mrs Humphry Ward had long been established as one of Britain's leading popular novelists. This, and the popularity of her work in the United States, made her an attractive candidate for the campaign of 'white' propaganda organised by Charles MASTERMAN, head of the secret War Propaganda Bureau (WPB), and Sir Gilbert PARKER, who was principally responsible for British propaganda in the United States. Having first ensured that patriotic duty did not incur financial loss, she agreed to contribute, publishing two books, *England's Effort* (1916) and *England's Goal* (1917), written after the first visit to the Western Front by a woman journalist. Despite having a famous maiden name (she was the grand-daughter of Thomas Arnold), she chose to publish under her formal married name. It is not surprising, therefore, that she was a staunch opponent of female suffrage.

Ware, Fabian Arthur Goulstone (1869–1949) British originator of the Imperial War Graves Commission. Ware's pre-war career was spent in educational administration and newspapers. He was assistant director and director of education for the Transvaal from 1901 to 1905 and editor of the *Morning Post* from 1905 to 1911. His age denied him the opportunity of active service, but he went to France in September 1914 to command a mobile unit of the British Red Cross. Ware was surprised to discover that there was no official organisation responsible for the marking and recording of graves. He suffered the customary fate of persons bringing inadequacies to official attention: he was asked to repair the omission himself. In 1915, however, the War Office acknowledged the importance of Ware's work by establishing the Graves Registration Commission, under his command. This not only recorded graves but also dealt with the sensitive enquiries of the bereaved. Ware was not content with the present, however; he looked also to the future commemoration of the dead. The Imperial War Conference of May 1917 established an Imperial (later Commonwealth) War Graves Commission. The Prince of Wales was appointed President and Ware Vice-Chairman, a post he held until his retirement in 1948. Ware established the IWGC as the sole executive body concerned with the empire's war dead. He took charge of negotiations with foreign governments, which included not only Britain's wartime allies but also her enemies, notably Turkey, without which the work of the Commission could not have proceeded. He recruited the finest horticulturists and architects to design the cemeteries and commissioned Rudyard KIPLING to choose or compose the wording of their memorials. He is principally responsible for ensuring remembrance of Britain's war dead and for the haunting cemeteries in which many are buried.

Warneford, Reginald ('Rex') Alexander John (1891–1915) British fighter pilot. On 7 June 1915, while serving with No. 1 Squadron Royal Naval Air Service, Warneford destroyed the German airship LZ37 near Ghent, in Belgium, by dive-bombing it in mid-air. The destruction of Zeppelins had enormous propaganda value, and Warneford's Victoria Cross was gazetted a mere four days later. Ten days after that, on 17 June 1915, Warneford and his passenger, the American journalist Henry Beach Needham, were killed when the aircraft he was test-flying crashed after going into a spin. Warneford was a bumptious young man with a chip on his shoulder whose few days of fame seemed only to exacerbate his boastful and reckless nature.

Warwick Brooke, John (18??–19??) British war photographer. Warwick Brooke, a professional photographer employed by the Topical news agency, became the second official photographer appointed to the Western Front, joining the first, Ernest BROOKS, in July 1916. Warwick Brooke took over 4,000 photographs, including some of the most reproduced images of the war, notably that of stretcher bearers, thigh-deep in mud, carrying a wounded man to treatment on the second day of 'Passchendaele'.

Watson, David (1871–1922) Canadian military commander. Watson was a journalist by profession and owner of the *Quebec Chronicle*. He began the war as CO of the 2nd Canadian Battalion, rising to brigade command as GOC 5th (Canadian) Brigade in September 1915. In April 1916 he was promoted GOC 4th (Canadian) Division, remaining its sole commander throughout the war.

Weddigen, Otto (1882–1915) German U-boat commander, whose exploits as Captain of *U 9* in sinking three elderly British cruisers, *Aboukir*, *Hogue* and *Cressy*, on 22 September 1914 made him a national hero. The loss of the British ships confirmed Admiral JELLICOE's fear of underwater attack during a major fleet action and hardened his caution. Weddigen was killed six months later, on 18 March 1915, when his new boat, *U 29*, sank with all hands after being rammed by HMS *Dreadnought*.

Weizmann, Chaim (1874–1952) British chemist and Zionist. The British chemical industry began the war in a marked state of inferiority to that of Germany, a world leader. The British munitions industry found itself in the unhappy position of dependency on German supplies of acetone, a vital substance for the manufacture of cordite, the principal propellant used in British ammunition, from small arms to heavy artillery. Weizmann, Professor of

Chemistry at Manchester University, succeeded in producing acetone from maize
and (later) from horse chestnuts. This
important contribution brought Weizmann to the notice of LLOYD GEORGE
and gave him an entrée into the highest
British political circles, where he campaigned indefatigably for the Zionist
cause, influencing the BALFOUR declaration of 1917, with its commitment of
British support for the establishment of a
'national home' for the Jewish people in
Palestine. After the war Weizmann became President of the World Zionist
Organisation and, in 1949, first President
of an independent Israel.

Wekerle, Alexander (1848–1921) Austro-
Hungarian politician, who became
Minister-President of Hungary for the
third time on 20 August 1917 at the age
of 70. His appointment represented a
victory for conservative forces in Hungary
and struck a blow at Emperor KARL I's
hopes of liberalising the Hungarian political system. Although favouring the
Compromise of 1867 that established the
Dual Monarchy, Wekerle demanded from
the Emperor the separation of the Austrian and Hungarian armies after the war
as the price of his continuing support for
the Compromise. During 1918 Wekerle
moved steadily towards a Hungarian
nationalist position. On 16 October he
denounced the October Manifesto, the
Emperor's final and belated attempt to
accommodate the Empire's diverging nationalist aspirations, despite its guarantee
of Hungary's political arrangements, and
two days later he declared Hungary's
independence. The Emperor remained
King of Hungary, and he used his authority to dismiss Wekerle soon afterwards.
But it was all too late. The Empire was
disintegrating and Wekerle's successor,
Count KÁROLYI, declared the Hungarian
Republic on 11 November 1918.

Westarp, Kuno von (1864–1945) German
politician, for whom Prussia's hierarchical

three-class suffrage represented the zenith
of political achievement. By 1914 he was
the leading Conservative in German politics. He was in favour of a war of annexation, the more sweeping the better. He regarded Chancellor BETHMANN-HOLLWEG
as a dangerous liberal, siding with the
odious Colonel Max BAUER to help bring
about Bethmann-Hollweg's removal in
July 1917.

Wetzell, Georg (1869–1947) German staff
officer. Wetzell spent the first two years of
the war on the Eastern Front, eventually
becoming chief of staff of III Corps. His
record there brought him to the notice of
Erich LUDENDORFF. When Ludendorff
and HINDENBURG replaced FALKENHAYN
in command of the German armies at the
end of August 1916, Wetzell was appointed chief of operations at OHL,
despite his lowly rank of major. As chief
of operations he found himself in command of a small group of about a dozen
very talented officers with responsibility
for German tactical doctrine. It was apparent to Ludendorff that the central
reality of the war in the west was the
accumulating weight of Allied material
superiority. It was necessary to find a
more effective way of combating this than
Falkenhayn's wasteful policy of contesting
every foot of lost ground on the Somme,
which was speedily abandoned. Within
six months of Hindenburg and Ludendorff's appointment, Wetzell's operations
section at OHL had completely reshaped
German tactics, organisation and training.
*The Principles of Command in the Defen-
sive Battle in Position Warfare* was published on 1 December 1916. It established
the system of 'elastic defence in depth'
through which the German armies in the
west successfully maintained their position against an Allied numerical superiority of 3:2 throughout 1917. On 23
October 1917 Wetzell wrote the key
OHL appreciation paper on the strategic
situation likely to face Germany in 1918.
His conclusions, that the Western Front

was the decisive theatre and that the German army must strike an annihilating blow against the British before American aid could become effective or lose the war, were accepted by Ludendorff. OHL then turned its attention to the creation of an offensive operational doctrine capable of achieving this strategic aim on the battlefield, publishing *The Attack in Position Warfare* on 1 January 1918. This document provided the tactical foundations for the German offensives of 1918, based on depth, penetration and disruption. Ironically, Wetzell often disagreed with Ludendorff's strategic ideas while providing the tactical methods to implement them, an ultimately ruinous combination.

Weygand, Maxime (1867–1965) French staff officer. Weygand spent the entire war two steps behind Ferdinand FOCH, occasionally whispering advice into the great man's ear but mainly converting his chief's endless flow of ideas into clear, precise and practical orders. 'Weygand, c'est moi,' Foch famously declared. It was Weygand, sitting to Foch's left, who read the Armistice conditions to the German delegation in the forest of Compiègne. He appears in the famous photograph taken on the railway carriage steps, standing behind his chief. Compiègne was, however, to become Weygand's nemesis. In May 1940 he was recalled from retirement to save the French army from defeat only to recommend capitulation to the Germans, who took their revenge at the place of Foch's (and Weygand's) triumph.

Weymss, Roslyn Erskine (1864–1933) British naval commander. 'Rosy' Weymss successfully overcame his association with the British defeat at Gallipoli in 1915 to emerge, in December 1917, as First Sea Lord, professional head of the Royal Navy, in succession to JELLICOE. Weymss began the war in command of the 12th Cruiser Squadron, guarding the Western Approaches, but in February 1915 he was

sent to the Aegean island of Lemnos to prepare its primitive port, Mudros, as the base for the forthcoming naval (and, eventually, military) attack on the Dardanelles. He might have succeeded CARDEN in command of the naval assault but deferred to the appointment of DE ROBECK. This is usually portrayed as an act of generosity on Weymss's part but it also turned out to be shrewd, distancing him from the misfortunes that befell the renewal of the naval attack in March 1915. Weymss, nevertheless, supported Admiral KEYES' proposal for further attempts to force a naval passage of the Dardanelles and opposed the evacuation of the Gallipoli peninsula. Throughout 1916 and 1917 Weymss commanded the Egyptian Squadron, providing amphibious support for the campaigns of MURRAY and ALLENBY in the Sinai and Palestine and struggling, somewhat ineffectually, to find effective measures against German submarines. At the end of 1917, however, he found his most suitable position. Weymss was far more adept as an administrator and 'enabler' than he was as a commander. His courtly, charming personality was instrumental in galvanising the feud-riven naval war staff into a real team. He was, again, a great supporter of Keyes and did much to bring about the raid on Zeebrugge in April 1918. He worked closely and effectively with his political boss, Eric GEDDES, and with the American Admiral SIMS. He represented the Allied navies at the Armistice negotiations in the forest of Compiègne. He resigned in November 1919, following an unpleasant campaign to replace him with David BEATTY.

White, (Cyril) Brudenell (Bingham) (1876–1940) Australian staff officer. White was an Australian Regular, who became the first officer of the Australian Military Forces to attend and pass the British Staff College. Despite being an ardent believer in the imperial ideal, he was never subservient to narrowly British interests and was fearless in defending the Australian

Imperial Force from ignorant criticisms by higher authority. The ability of the Australian and New Zealand governments to raise and deploy an expeditionary force within three months of the outbreak of war owed much to secret contingency plans drawn up by White before the war. White served BRIDGES and his successor BIRDWOOD as chief of staff on Gallipoli in 1915, planning and supervising the successful evacuation of Australian forces. He accompanied Birdwood to France as chief of staff I Australian and New Zealand Army Corps. Birdwood devolved not only much of I Australian and New Zealand Army Corps' operational planning to White but also wider responsibility for Australian forces in France and Egypt. In July 1918 White turned down the offer to command the Australian Corps and accompanied Birdwood to Fifth Army as his chief of staff. White was an extremely able man of great integrity, much admired by the Australian war correspondent and official historian Charles BEAN, to whom he represented the military and masculine ideal. Bean described White as 'the greatest man I ever knew'.

Whitehead, Robert (1823–1905) British engineer, who designed the first self-propelled torpedo in 1866, providing a cheap and effective means of sinking very large, expensive ships and transforming the military potential of the submarine.

Wilhelm, Crown Prince of Prussia and Germany (1882–1951) German military commander, eldest son and heir of Kaiser WILHELM II. Wilhelm's reputation in British eyes has been indelibly stamped by the wartime ridicule of him as 'Little Willy'. With his cad's cigarette holder, lounge-lizard body and handsome face, hat permanently set at a rakish angle, he could easily pass for a gigolo. But for the accident of birth he might have earned a precarious living in pursuit of rich widows and young heiresses through the fashionable spas of Europe. This caricature has, ironically, saved him from more serious criticism. It portrays him as essentially lightweight, a trivial, harmless, silly little man with a liking for parties and cheap popularity. This ignores his close connections with the most aggressively militarist groups in pre-war Germany, his important role in the overthrow of Chancellor BETHMANN-HOLLWEG and his post-war dalliance with Nazism. It also ignores his role in the fighting on the Western Front, where he served as an army commander throughout the war, especially during the battle of Verdun in 1916. Wilhelm was sceptical about the attack, and it took three days of intense debate with FALKENHAYN before he consented to it. Falkenhayn gave Wilhelm the distinct impression that the purpose of the attack was to capture Verdun, and this is certainly the impression that Wilhelm gave his troops. This meant that Falkenhayn's strategic purpose of 'bleeding France white' would not be achieved through operational attrition but through an attempt to break through the French lines that would be as costly to Germany as it was to France. At first Wilhelm showed no reluctance to feed his infantry into the Verdun 'meat grinder'. He spent much of his time playing tennis and chasing girls at his headquarters thirty miles from the front line. Although Wilhelm surrendered to pessimism as early as March, it was five months later, faced with the loss of his army, before he rebelled. Outraged by Fifth Army's increasing subversion of his orders, in mid-August Falkenhayn sacked the Crown Prince's chief of staff, General SCHMIDT VON KNOBELSDORF. Wilhelm was promoted in September to command Army Group Crown Prince, in the centre of the German line, where he remained for the rest of the war, winning one of the German army's last and most stunning victories, on the Aisne, in May 1918. Wilhelm was far from stupid. He recognised before almost anyone else at his level in the German High Command that the war would be long. He was also among the first to see the coming end for Germany, urging HINDENBURG and LUDENDORFF to retreat to strong defensive positions from where they might be able to obtain reasonable terms. He followed his father into Dutch exile after the Armistice.

Wilhelm II (1859–1941) German Emperor. Wilhelm succeeded his father, Kaiser Friedrich III, as King of Prussia and Emperor of Germany in 1888. The auguries were not good. His grandmother, Queen Victoria, described Wilhelm with unerring accuracy as 'a hot-headed, conceited and wrong-headed young man'. He was also blustering and indecisive and prone to depression and anxiety. Although Wilhelm's dismissal of Bismarck in 1890 seemed to signal his determination to rule as well as reign, in fact the Kaiser's 'personal rule' was a sham. Throughout his reign he deferred to his ministers and military advisers on almost every important issue. This trait was apparent soon after Bismarck's dismissal when he acquiesced in Caprivi's abandonment of Bismarckian diplomacy by allowing the secret Reinsurance Treaty with Russia to lapse. France, which had been completely hamstrung by Bismarck, rapidly filled the gap in Russia's affections. Not content with this, Wilhelm then set about antagonising the British, not only through his bombastic and vainglorious pronouncements but also through his support for Admiral TIRPITZ's attempt to build a High Seas Fleet to challenge British maritime supremacy. This was doubly stupid. Germany lacked the resources to build a fleet capable of defeating the British, who responded in kind by initiating a naval arms race that they had clearly won by 1912. It also decided Britain to seek colonial accommodations with France and Russia, something it had achieved by 1907. Germany's aggressive behaviour during the first and second Moroccan Crises (1905–06 and 1911)

brought Britain and France even closer together and helped solidify anti-German opinion among the political elites of both countries. Far from breaking Germany's 'encirclement', the Kaiser had helped bring it about. Germany's sense of insecurity was self-inflicted. By 1914 Germany had only one reliable ally, Austria-Hungary, whose fears and ambitions were to bring Germany and Europe to ruin. Wilhelm's role during the July Crisis of 1914 was characteristically inconsistent. His initial recognition that Serbia must be punished inclined him to support a short, sharp punitive war, but Serbia's emollient response to Austria's ultimatum and the firm line taken by Britain gave him pause, to the despair of his generals, especially MOLTKE. Wilhelm's hesitation in declaring war on France, on 1 August, showed his apparent lack of understanding of Germany's war plan. He consented to execute it only after a bruising intervention by the German chief of staff that left Moltke emotionally exhausted, perhaps with important consequences for his subsequent conduct of military operations. The rest of the Kaiser's war was equally inconsistent. He had the temperament of an autocrat but not the will. He was lazy and self-indulgent. He preferred appearance to reality. His mood shifted with the ebb and flow of battle, veering between overweening ambition and fatalistic pessimism. He fell more and more under the influence of the military, especially HINDENBURG and LUDENDORFF. Under pressure from them he agreed, in February 1917, to the disastrous return to unrestricted submarine warfare that brought the United States into the war on the Allied side within two months. His acquiescence in the dismissal of Chancellor BETHMANN-HOLLWEG, in July 1917, marked the beginning of military dictatorship in Germany. The Kaiser's popularity, which reached record levels at the outbreak of war, declined dramatically in 1917 as inflation, food shortages and industrial unrest began to unravel the 'social peace' he had encouraged Germans to pursue in the heady days of August 1914. His association in the public mind with a war to the finish and a peace of annexations made it impossible for him to retain his position in the face of impending German defeat. In the end, the army high command that he had done so much to support abandoned him. General GROEN-ER, Ludendorff's plain-spoken successor, told Wilhelm that his continuation on the throne was an obstacle to the army's ability to maintain social order at home. But even then he hesitated, indecisive to the last. The Chancellor, Prince MAX von Baden, made the decision for him, announcing the Kaiser's abdication on 9 November 1918, without Wilhelm's agreement. On the same day, Philip SCHEIDEMANN declared Germany a Republic. The Kaiser fled to exile in Holland, where he remained on his estate at Doorn until his death. His life and reign were a disaster for Germany and for Europe.

Wilkinson, Norman (1882–1934) British stage designer, who was well known for his pre-war work with Sir Harley Granville-Barker. The war drew Wilkinson into the increasingly important and sophisticated business of camouflage. He suggested the concept of 'dazzle' camouflage for merchant and 'Q'-ships (armed decoys) designed to distort the shape of vessels in order to give them a greater degree of concealment against U-boat attack. Wilkinson also painted some fine pictures of the Dardanelles campaign, in which he took part as a naval officer.

Willcocks, James (1857–1926) British military commander. Willcocks was the son of an officer in the Honourable East India Company's Service. He was born and brought up in India and had a good command of the vernacular. Despite twice failing the Sandhurst entrance examination, he was eventually commissioned in the British army, soon transferring to the

Indian army, with which he spent the rest of his career. He made a fine reputation in frontier warfare, especially in command of the Mohmand Expedition (1908). His swift suppression of frontier unrest led to his campaigns being dubbed 'Willcocks' Weekend Wars'. In 1914–15 he commanded the Indian Corps on the Western Front. It was not an entirely happy experience. The Indian army was not trained or equipped for trench warfare against so formidable an opponent as the German army. Many of its British officers were old and unfit. Indian troops suffered appallingly in the winter of 1914–15. The localised nature of their recruitment in India meant that morale was badly affected by casualties. Willcocks was a vain man. He resented having to serve under Douglas HAIG, to whom he was senior. Differences between them were apparent as early as the battle of Neuve Chapelle (March 1915). They gradually intensified and caused Willcocks to resign at the end of 1915. He was later appointed Governor of Bermuda, where he ended the war.

Williamson, Henry (1895–1977) British soldier and writer. Williamson served in the ranks of the socially exclusive London Rifle Brigade on the Western Front before being granted a temporary commission in the 10th Battalion Bedfordshire Regiment. He found the war a searing experience, being haunted in particular by the hope of international comradeship reflected in the Christmas Truce of 1914 and its subsequent collapse into another four years of unprecedented violence. In his post-war novel sequence *A Chronicle of Ancient Sunlight* (1955–69), five volumes of which span the era of the Great War, Williamson provided a vivid and bitter portrayal of the 'war experience' of Philip Maddison, like Williamson a sensitive lower-middle class man from the London suburbs. Williamson's determination that the world should avoid at all costs another such blood letting persuaded him to embrace Fascism between the wars, displaying a naive belief in the goodwill of his fellow front-line veteran Adolf Hitler.

Wilson, Arthur Knyvet (1842–1921) British naval officer. As First Sea Lord, professional head of the Royal Navy, from 1910 to 1912, it was Wilson ('Old 'ard 'eart') who lost the strategic argument with his namesake Sir Henry WILSON, Director of Military Operations, at the 23 August 1911 meeting of the Committee of Imperial Defence. Wilson the Admiral was no match for the forensic and histrionic skills of Wilson the General, who exposed the bankruptcy of naval planning. This occasion was instrumental in the eventual adoption of a 'continental' strategy and of closer military and naval co-operation with France. CHURCHILL replaced Admiral Wilson with Prince LOUIS ALEXANDER of Battenberg soon afterwards and a naval staff was finally established in 1912.

Wilson, Henry Hughes (1864–1922) British staff officer. As Director of Military Operations before the war, Wilson played a key role in secret staff talks with the French army, of which he was an ardent admirer, though attempts to portray him as a significant figure in the eventual British decision for war are without foundation. He brilliantly planned the mobilisation of the British Expeditionary Force and executed its deployment in August 1914. His support for the Ulster cause and his involvement in the 'Curragh Mutiny' made him politically unacceptable to the Liberal government, and he was denied the coveted post of Sir John FRENCH's chief of staff. Instead, he loitered around French's GHQ, undermining the actual chief of staff, Archie MURRAY, at every turn. Murray's replacement by Sir William ROBERTSON in January 1915 terminated Wilson's capacity for mischief, and he was packed off as liaison officer at French GHQ, where his fluent French and open admiration of the French army made him a welcome appointment. After a year

indifferently commanding IV Corps, Wilson was again sent to French GHQ. In 1917 he returned home as GOC Eastern Command, acting as unofficial military adviser to the new Prime Minister, LLOYD GEORGE. His appointment as British Representative to the Supreme War Council at Versailles was instrumental in Lloyd George's successful intrigue against Robertson, whom Wilson replaced as Chief of the Imperial General Staff in February 1918. During the final year of the war Wilson proved himself an excellent CIGS, much assisted by his friendship with FOCH, whose appointment as Allied generalissimo he strongly supported. Wilson's unenviable reputation as a self-interested intriguer, reinforced by the posthumous publication of his indiscreet and intemperate diaries, has perhaps been overdrawn. A clever man, but often whimsical and indecisive, he was murdered by two Sinn Fein gunmen on the steps of his London house after returning from a formal dinner, valiantly but ineffectually trying to defend himself with his sword.

Wilson, (Thomas) Woodrow (1856–1924) President of the United States. Wilson was elected President in November 1912 on the Democratic ticket. He brought to the office a degree of high-mindedness, strongly reinforced by legalism, unusual in a politician. He also brought a determination to use the executive power of the presidency to its full. This determination expressed itself most forcibly in domestic affairs, where Wilson embarked on a reform programme that made important changes in the United States' fiscal system and in trade union and employment law. Tariffs were reduced, business trusts attacked, competition encouraged, the legal position of trade unions strengthened, child labour restricted and workmen's compensation introduced. Although Wilson publicly disapproved of Theodore ROOSEVELT's 'big stick' foreign policy, he showed no reluctance to wield it himself in defence of

US interests, especially in Central America and the Caribbean ('Uncle Sam's backyard'), sanctioning military intervention in Nicaragua, Haiti and the Dominican Republic. Intervention in a European war, however, held few attractions. Wilson declared US neutrality on 19 August 1914, a position strongly supported by his isolationist Secretary of State, William Jennings BRYAN. The activities of German U-boats made Wilson's attempts to maintain a policy of even-handed neutrality towards the belligerents increasingly difficult, however. Bryan resigned after the German sinking of the Cunard liner *Lusitania*, with the loss of 128 American lives, believing that it was only a matter of time before Wilson abandoned his policy of neutrality. Bryan was, perhaps, premature. It was nearly two years before the US declared war, following German resumption of unrestricted submarine warfare. During that period Wilson attempted to pursue a personal foreign policy through the diplomatic missions of his confidant Colonel Edward M. HOUSE, seeking to marginalise the influence of the Secretary of State, Robert LANSING. Despite Bryan's prescience, Wilson did not relish the prospect of intervention. He narrowly won the presidential election of November 1916 on the slogan 'he kept us out of the War'. But the failure of his attempts to mediate between the belligerents, in December 1916, slowly began to convince him that if the United States was to decide the peace it must first enter the war. US entry was marked by an unprecedented degree of Federal intervention in American life, including conscription, massive military and naval expansion programmes and increases in taxation. It is difficult to overstate the importance of US intervention on Allied, and especially French, morale. Wilson's enunciation of his famous Fourteen Points, on 8 January 1918, lifted the Allied war effort on to a new plane, legitimising the struggle and the sacrifices with the promise of a new world order based on national self-determination and international arbitration through a League of Nations. Wilson's visit to Europe, masterminded by his propagandist George CREEL, was a triumph. No American President had stood so high in world opinion or been greeted with such genuine rapture by ordinary people. It could not last. Wilson's belief that Allied dependency on American credit would allow the US to make the peace was to be sorely disappointed. The Versailles settlement was a compromise between American idealism, French fear and British pragmatism, in which Wilson's was not the decisive contribution. The disappointing performance of the Democrats in the mid-term elections of 1918 weakened his position at home. Wilson's inept handling of the Republican majority, ruthlessly organised by the implacably hostile Senator Henry Cabot LODGE, and his failure to respond to the reasonable compromises suggested by Lansing resulted in Congressional rejection of the Treaty of Versailles, including US membership of the League of Nations, Wilson's instrument of future international peace. Woodrow Wilson suffered a major stroke in October 1919. The last months of his presidency were spent in silence. The Republican Warren Harding won an overwhelming victory in the presidential election of 1920.

Wilson, Walter Gordon (1874–1957) British tank designer. Before the war Wilson was a successful automobile engineer. When the war broke out he joined the Royal Navy, soon becoming involved in building armoured cars for the Royal Naval Air Service. This made him a natural choice to join William TRITTON, general manager of Foster's of Lincoln, the engineering firm that had been given a contract for the design and production of a wheeled 'tank'. Wilson's partnership with Tritton was fruitful. Together they solved the main technical problems and produced a promising prototype, the Lincoln No. 1 'Quasi Rhomboidal', a tracked vehicle that formed the basis for all subsequent British tank design during the war, and which made its debut in September 1915.

Winnington-Ingram, Arthur Foley (1858–1946) British cleric. Winnington-Ingram was Bishop of London from 1901 to 1939, during which time he built upon the fine reputation as a mission preacher and pastor that he had established as head of Oxford House and Vicar of Bethnal Green, in London's East End. But he is now principally remembered for the controversial part he played in the First World War. Like many Christians, Winnington-Ingram regarded the outbreak of war as an expression of God's wrath for the sins of the modern world. But he had no doubt that the Germans were the greatest sinners. Accordingly, he saw the war as just. He threw his energy into the voluntary recruiting campaign, urging Christians to join the fight, which he portrayed as a crusade and the work of Christ. He made many visits to the front, earning the title 'bishop of the battlefields'. Winnington-Ingram expressed a strong strain of contemporary public sentiment, not least among the religious, many of whom were among the most passionate supporters of the war and of Germany's defeat. Later, however, he became the most prominent symbol of the blood lust and xenophobia against which the Church of England recoiled between the wars.

Winterbotham, Harold St John Loyd (1878–1946) British soldier. Winterbotham began the war as a major in the Royal Engineers, attached to the Ordnance Survey at Southampton. He went to France at the end of 1914 in command of a 'Ranging Section', formed with the object of fixing enemy guns. From this obscure beginning, he became a key figure in the history of survey, cartography, sound ranging and flash spotting. These were to prove vital techniques in the artillery war, especially counter-battery fire against enemy guns. Winterbotham gathered round him a talented team, including his trigonometry assistant, Lieutenant F.J. Salmon, his map supply officer, Lieutenant O.G.S. Crawford, Captain H.J.S. Gaine and Captain Norman MacLeod. He also provided invaluable patronage and support to the work of Lawrence BRAGG and Harold HEMMING. As CO of the 3rd [Army] Field Survey Company, he influenced Major-General HOLLAND in his abortive advocacy of a 'hurricane' preliminary bombardment before the battle of Arras (April 1917). Winterbotham was able to rely throughout the war on the support of Colonel Charles Close, Director General of the Ordnance Survey, a post that Winterbotham himself later filled.

Wiseman, William George Eden (1885–1962) British intelligence officer and diplomat. Wiseman's distinctive contribution to the war began in 1915 when he transferred to the Secret Intelligence Service (SIS), commonly known as MI6, after being badly gassed on the Western Front. Under cover of his appointment as a member of the Ministry of Munitions Purchasing Commission in New York, he took charge of all British espionage and counter-espionage activities in the United States. More importantly, perhaps, he also became the diplomatic confidant of President WILSON's close adviser Colonel HOUSE, who used Wiseman to maintain backstairs communication with the British government. The backstairs were House's spiritual home. His intrigues often gave him the false impression that he was in control of events. It is doubtful that he was in control of Wiseman, and it is often difficult to know where House ended and Wiseman began.

Witos, Wincenty (1874–1945) Polish politician, who led the Polish Peasant Party in the Austrian parliament from 1916. A convinced Polish nationalist, he was opposed to any solution of the 'Polish question' that did not result in the establishment of a unified Polish sovereign state. This brought him into direct conflict with the policy of the Central Powers, especially Germany, but his membership of the Austrian parliament protected him from German action. Witos played the leading part in bringing about the withdrawal of Polish nationalist support from the Austrian government in May 1917, shortly after the United States entered the war, increasing still further the strains on the rapidly disintegrating Habsburg Empire. Witos became Prime Minister of an independent Poland in 1920.

Witte, Sergei Yulevich (1849–1915) Russian politician. Witte was the most able minister to serve the last tsarist regime. He was the driving force behind Russian industrialisation, contributing much to the improvement in Russian finances and infrastructure, especially railways. His contempt for fools, of whom there were many at the heart of Russian government, his independent-mindedness and lack of reverence for hierarchy made him an uncomfortable figure at court. He was useful in a crisis, such as the Revolution of 1905 – when he did more than anyone to preserve the monarchy – but to be dispensed with as soon as order was restored. Without the economic changes that he initiated, it is difficult to see how Russia could have participated to the extent that it did, and with the effect that it did, in the Great War.

Wittgenstein, Ludwig Josef Johann (1889–1951) Austro-Hungarian soldier and philosopher. When the war broke out, Wittgenstein had only recently returned to his native Vienna from Cambridge, where he had been teaching at the university. Unlike his mentor in Cambridge, Bertrand RUSSELL, Wittgenstein did not follow the pacifist path. He volunteered immediately for the Austro-Hungarian army as a gunner, though his

medical history would have entitled him to an exemption. He took part in heavy fighting in Galicia and the Carpathians, winning the Silver Medal for Valour in 1917. In 1918 he found himself on the Italian front, where he was captured in the Trentino a week before the Armistice. Wittgenstein was a great patriot, though continually pessimistic about the outcome of the war for Austria. In 1916 he made a gift of 1M crowns to the Imperial government to enable it to purchase a 12-inch howitzer. His brother, Paul, a concert pianist, also fought on the Eastern Front, losing his right arm.

Wood, Edward Allan (1865–1930) British military commander. Wood was born in India, the son of a civil servant, who later became a judge. Theirs was a large family whose income did not stretch to providing for younger sons. Wood joined the 2nd Dragoon Guards in India as a private soldier, later transferring to the 17th Lancers, before obtaining a commission in the paramilitary British South Africa Police, with whom he served in the South African War (1899–1902). In August 1914 his official military status was Captain, Reserve of Officers, British South Africa Police. From this unlikely beginning he embarked on a remarkable wartime career that saw him win four DSOs, command 6th Battalion King's Shropshire Light Infantry and, from November 1917, 55th Brigade in the elite 18th (Eastern) Division. Small, rotund and red-faced, Wood was an unlikely looking warrior, but there was no doubting his presence. Robert Cude, a private soldier in 55th Brigade, declared that he would 'fight in Hell, so long as Brigadier-General Wood commanded the brigade'. Wood was never far from the front line. On 20 September 1918, single-handedly and unarmed, he captured more than twenty Germans by pelting them with lumps of chalk and old boots. Wood found the post-war adjustment difficult. He succeeded Frank CROZIER in command of a division of the Black and Tans in 1920, but the end of the Anglo-Irish war terminated his military career. He spent the rest of his life in fruitless pursuit of a British army pension, to which he was not entitled (never having held a Regular commission), gradually alienating his admirers, including King GEORGE V, by his behaviour. He died of cirrhosis of the liver.

Wood, F(rancis) Derwent (1871–1926) British sculptor, who volunteered for the Royal Army Medical Corps in March 1915 and was later commissioned. He ran the Masks for Facial Wounds Department, producing enamelled copper masks to hide the terrible disfiguring wounds suffered by many soldiers. After the war one of his most important commissions was the Machine Gun Corps Memorial at Hyde Park Corner.

Wood, Leonard (1860–1927) US staff officer. Wood was Chief of Staff of the United States Army from 1910 until 1914, when he was replaced by General John J. PERSHING. Wood's advocacy of American military preparedness brought him into frequent conflict with American politicians, many of whom were suspicious of the democratic credentials of the General Staff, a situation that deteriorated after Woodrow WILSON succeeded to the Presidency in 1912. In 1915 Wood founded the Preparedness Movement to campaign for universal military training, but the National Defense Act of 1916 opted for a system of 'selective service'. Pershing's hostility to Wood denied him a field command in Europe and ensured that he spent the rest of the war training troops in a Kansas backwater.

Woodville, Richard Caton (1856–1927) British artist, one of the most celebrated of Victorian 'battle painters', who produced a prolific number of illustrations in the early part of the war when visual images were difficult to come by. Caton

Woodville illustrated prose accounts using an artistic imagination steeped in ideas of individual heroism and hand-to-hand fighting that later war photography and war painting exposed for the sham they were.

Woyrsch, Remus von (1847–1925) German military commander, recalled from retirement in 1914 to command the Silesian *Landwehr* corps on the Eastern Front. He was soon in action and was principally responsible for saving the Austro-Hungarian First Army from complete annihilation at Rava Russka by covering the retreat of General DANKL at great cost to his own command. Woyrsch spent most of the war in Poland, latterly in command of Army Group Woyrsch, probably achieving his greatest success in inflicting a serious defeat on EVERT's Russian Fourth Army during the BRUSILOV offensive (June 1916). Army Group Woyrsch was disbanded after the collapse of Russia. Woyrsch returned to retirement, this time consoled by promotion to field-marshal.

Wrangel, Petr Nikolaevich (1878–1928) Russian military commander. Wrangel commanded the Russian cavalry corps during the Great War but is best remembered for his part in the Russian civil war that followed. He joined the White Russian forces in August 1918 and led his troops with some effect in the Caucasus, capturing Tsartisyn (modern Volgograd) in July 1919. Wrangel's relations with the Whites' Commander-in-Chief, DENIKIN, were not good, however, which eventually led to his dismissal. Nevertheless, he succeeded Denikin in April 1920. His command of White forces in the Crimea showed not only military but also political judgement, but by then there was little anyone could do to save the White cause. Wrangel's final contribution was to organise the successful evacuation of 150,000 Whites to Turkey after the Red victory of November 1920. In exile he set up an organisation of White veterans, the Russian Social Union.

Wright, Almroth Edward (1861–1947) British physician. Almroth Wright was one of the greatest figures in contemporary science, a polymath learned in literature and the law as well as medicine. He was Consulting Physician to the British Expeditionary Force throughout the war. As the world's leading authority on preventive medicine, including his pioneering work on inoculations against bacterial infections, he was instrumental in sustaining the rude health enjoyed by the British and Allied armies on the Western Front. In 1942 he published a standard work on the treatment of war wounds. His advanced scientific views, however, were not replicated in the social sphere, where he was a vehement opponent of female suffrage.

Württemberg, Duke Albrecht von *see* ALBRECHT VON WÜRTTEMBERG, DUKE.

Wyatt, Francis Joseph Caldwell (1882–19??) British soldier. Wyatt was a captain in the Royal Engineers when the war broke out, but in March 1916 – as a lieutenant-colonel – he was given command of the Special Works Park. This was a motley collection of artists, theatrical designers and sculptors charged with improving British camouflage, building on the pioneering efforts of the artist Solomon SOLOMON. Their work, especially that of the stage designer L.D. Symington, was so successful that a Camouflage School was later established in London. Symington devoted his fertile imagination, in particular, to camouflaging snipers and machine-gun positions. Camouflage also began to play an increasing role in deception by disguising the movement of guns and equipment and laying false trails.

Y

Yanushkevich, Nikolai Nikolaevich (1868–1918) Russian staff officer, who was appointed chief of staff to Grand Duke NIKOLAI NIKOLAEVICH in March 1914. Yanushkevich's promotion was the result of his political acceptability to the tsarist regime and the amiability that recommended him to the Tsar and the Grand Duke. Unfortunately, too often in tsarist Russia political correctness and amiability were not accompanied by military ability and experience. Yanushkevich's incompetence quickly became apparent, and he was reduced to spending his time persecuting Russian Jews, belittling the courage of his men and blaming others for his military failings. He was relieved in August 1915.

Yealland, Lewis Ralph (1884/5–19??) Canadian-born British psychiatrist, who emerges from the pages of Pat Barker's novel *Regeneration* (1991) as little more than a medieval torturer. Yealland worked at the National Hospital for the Paralysed and Epileptic in Queen Square, London, where he developed the electric-shock method of treatment for hysteria that he called 'faradization'. Yealland was a commanding personality who also used the technique of 'auto-suggestion'. He had a reputation for returning even the most intransigent cases to military service in the shortest space of time. He published his findings in *Hysterical Disorders of Warfare* (1918).

York, Alvin Cullum (1887–1964) US war hero, a devout Christian from rural Tennessee who abandoned his original conscientious objection to military service on being drafted. On 8 October 1918, cut off behind enemy lines in the Argonne, York almost single-handedly took on a German machine-gun battalion, killing twenty enemy soldiers and capturing 132, as well as thirty-five machine guns, an extraordinary achievement for which he was awarded the Congressional Medal of Honor. York's original reluctance to fight and subsequent ruthless determination to win seemed to mirror the feelings of his country, and he emerged from the war as one of its principal icons. His story became the subject of a memorable film, *Sergeant York* (1940), starring Gary Cooper.

Yudenich, Nikolai Nikolaevich (1862–1933) Russian military commander, who had the great good fortune of facing the Turks in the Caucasus, first as commander of II Turkestan Corps and then (until August 1915) as Commander-in-Chief, when he was subordinated to Grand Duke NIKOLAI NIKOLAEVICH. He inflicted a severe defeat on the Turkish Third Army in December 1914 and repulsed ENVER PASHA's invasion in 1915. Not even the advent of the Grand Duke could prevent him from capturing Erzerum and Trebizond and conquering Turkish Armenia in 1916. By the time he regained the overall command in March 1917, the state of Russia made further military operations in the Caucasus impossible. Yudenich was arguably the most successful Russian general of the Great War, a garland for which he has few rivals.

Z

Zaionchkovsky, Andrei Medardovich (1862–1926) Russian military commander, whose Russo-Romanian Dobrudja Detachment was charged with defence of the Romanian–Bulgarian border after Romania, encouraged by the success of the Russian BRUSILOV offensive, declared war on Austria-Hungary (27 August 1916). The resources at Zaionchkovsky's disposal were inferior. His first contact with the Romanian army was inauspicious; thinking Zaionchkovsky's troops were Bulgarian, the Romanians attempted to surrender to them! The Russian and Romanian elements were often more concerned to fight one another than the enemy. Zaionchkovsky proved unable to resist MACKENSEN's invasion of the Dobrudja and was forced to evacuate the strategically important port of Constanza in October. The invasion by a second, more powerful, German army, commanded by FALKENHAYN, completed Zaionchkovsky's fate. Failure, however, was rarely a bar to promotion in the Russian army and in 1917 Zaionchkovsky was given command of XVIII Corps. Like his mentor Brusilov, he avoided the revolutionary purge of army officers, ending his career as an instructor at the Red Army Military Academy, where he led the commission that investigated the military lessons of the war.

Zeppelin, Ferdinand von (1838–1917) German airship designer. Zeppelin built his first airship in 1900, and by 1906 he had developed a practical design. In 1915–16 the German navy and army used Zeppelins to launch air raids on Britain and France. They were hampered in this by their slow speed, poor bad-weather capabilities and the increasing efficiency of Allied air defence. But the Zeppelins' huge size and sinister, looming presence had an impact on morale out of all proportion to the physical damage they inflicted. No one who saw a Zeppelin ever forgot the experience. They also helped to puncture the centuries old British sense of invulnerability to enemy attack. Zeppelins, and other airships, were abandoned as bombers at the end of 1917. Zeppelin himself had by then already turned his attention to the development of large, multi-engine bomber aircraft, with which the future of strategic bombing lay, as the British were to discover in 1918.

Zhekov, Nikola (1864–1949) Bulgarian soldier and politician, Commander-in-Chief of the Bulgarian army 1915–18. Zhekov spent much of the war vainly trying to preserve some degree of strategic and operational independence from his German allies, notably MACKENSEN, who seemed to regard the Bulgarians as mere auxiliaries to be employed entirely according to German wishes. Zhekov was not helped by constant friction with his own government. Although he resisted attempts to involve him in overthrowing Prime Minister RADOSLAVOV in 1917, he finally threw his weight behind the opposition which removed Radoslavov in June 1918. Ever unable to escape from the orbit of his powerful ally, Zhekov fled into exile in Germany before Bulgaria's collapse and later became a Nazi.

Zhilinski, Yakov (1853–1918) Russian military commander, the first in a long line of dismal Russian generals whose ineptitude lit the funeral pyre of tsarist autocracy. An ambitious careerist, Zhilinski either performed what he ought not to have promised or promised what he could not perform. He belonged to the party that favoured attacking Russia's strongest enemy, Germany, first. As Chief of the Russian General Staff in 1911, he had made a rash undertaking to the French that Russia would attack Germany within fifteen days of mobilisation. The two Russian armies that invaded East Prussia in August 1914 therefore did so before full mobilisation was completed and were ill prepared and ill equipped. Zhilinski failed utterly to co-ordinate the actions of the armies' intended pincer movement and must bear a major share of the responsibility for their defeat in detail by numerically inferior German forces at Tannenberg (20–31 August) and the Masurian Lakes (9–14 September). Defeats of this magnitude could not be ignored even in Russia. Zhilinski was relieved of command and sent as liaison officer to French GHQ, where his performance was equally inept. After the outbreak of the Russian civil war, displaying his customary shrewd judgement, Zhilinski chose the Whites. He was killed fighting with them somewhere in south Russia at a date that has never been reliably determined.

Zimmerman, Arthur (1854–1940) German Foreign Secretary from November 1916 to August 1917. A hardworking nonentity, he rose to high office by siding with the military hardliners during the split between German civil government and the army high command at the end of 1916 over the issue of unrestricted submarine warfare. His name will be forever associated with the disastrous telegram that he sent to the German embassy in Mexico City in January 1917 offering German support for a Mexican invasion of the United States. The telegram was intercepted and decrypted by the British, who passed its contents to President Woodrow WILSON. Zimmerman's offer was so ludicrous that publication of the telegram was met by disbelief in many quarters and it was denounced as a fraud. Zimmerman was, however, a fatal combination of stupidity and honesty. He refused the opportunity to escape from his mistake and to embarrass the British by confirming the telegram's authenticity on 3 March. The United States entered the war on the Allied side just over a month later. Zimmerman's actions are indicative of the arrogance and naivety of much Wilhelmine foreign policy and of an extraordinary and foolish contempt for the economic power and military potential of the United States, a mistake the Hitler regime was later to repeat.

Zweig, Arnold (1887–1968) German soldier and writer. Zweig was a published writer of socialist outlook before the war began, but he volunteered for military service in 1914, serving at Verdun and at German headquarters on the Eastern Front. He returned to writing after the war. *The Case of Sergeant Grischa* (1928), based on the actual case of a Russian prisoner of war executed as a German army deserter even after his true identity became known, is one of the best novels to have emerged from the war. Zweig's Zionist views did not endear him to the Nazis and he fled into exile in 1934. He lived in East Germany for the last forty years of his life. He was a prolific letter writer and included Sigmund Freud among his correspondents.